26.95

LL

7-94

LOST RIGHTS

Also by James Bovard

The Farm Fiasco

The Fair Trade Fraud

LOST RIGHTS

★

The Destruction of American Liberty

JAMES BOVARD

ST. MARTIN'S PRESS
NEW YORK

Scholarly and Reference Division,
St. Martin's Press, Inc., 175 Fifth Avenue,
New York, N.Y. 10010

First published in the United States of America in 1994

Printed in the United States of America

ISBN 0-312-10351-4

Library of Congress Cataloging-in-Publication Data

Bovard, James.
Lost Rights : The Destruction of American Liberty / James Bovard.
p. cm.
Includes bibliographical references and index.
ISBN 0-312-10351-4
1. Civil rights—United States. 2. Liberty. I. Title.
JC599.U5B598 1994
323'.0973—dc20 93-31028
CIP

Interior design by Digital Type & Design

First Edition: April 1994
10 9 8 7 6 5 4 3 2 1

Contents

LOST RIGHTS

-1-

THE NEW LEVIATHAN

Government is not reason, it is not eloquence—it is force.

—GEORGE WASHINGTON[1]

The Restraint of Government is the True Liberty and Freedom of the People.

—EIGHTEENTH-CENTURY COMMON AMERICAN SAYING[2]

Americans' liberty is perishing beneath the constant growth of government power. Federal, state, and local governments are confiscating citizens' property, trampling their rights, and decimating their opportunities more than ever before.

Americans today must obey thirty times as many laws as their great-grandfathers had to obey at the turn of the century.[3] Federal agencies publish an average of over 200 pages of new rulings, regulations, and proposals in the *Federal Register* each business day. The growth of the federal statute book is one of the clearest measures of the increase of the government control of the citizenry. But the effort to improve society by the endless multiplication of penalties, prohibitions, and prison sentences is a dismal failure.

The attack on individual rights has reached the point where a citizen has no right to use his own land if a government inspector discovers a wet area on it, no right to the money in his bank account if an IRS agent decides he might have dodged taxes, and no right to the cash in his wallet if a DEA dog sniffs at his pants. A man's home is his castle, except if a politician covets the land the house is built on, or if his house is more than fifty years old, or if he has too many relatives living with him, or if he has old cars parked in his driveway, or if he wants to add a porch or deck. Nowadays, a citizen's use of his own property is presumed illegal until approved by multiple zoning and planning commissions. Government redevelopment officials confiscate large chunks of cities, evicting owners from their homes and giving the land to other private citizens to allow them to reap a windfall profit. Since 1985, federal, state, and local governments have seized the property of over 200,000 Americans under asset forfeiture laws, often with no more evidence of wrongdoing than an unsubstantiated assertion made by an anonymous government informant.

A. V. Dicey, the great English constitutional scholar, wrote in 1885, "Discretionary authority on the part of the government means insecurity for legal freedom on the part of subjects."[4] Government officials now exert vast arbitrary power over citizens' daily lives, from Equal Employment Opportunity Commission bureaucrats that can levy a $145,000 fine on a Chicago small businessman because he did not have 8.45 blacks on his payroll to federal agricultural bureaucrats that can prohibit Arizona farmers from selling 58 percent of their fresh lemons to other Americans. Customs Service inspectors can wantonly chainsaw import shipments without compensating the owner, Labor Department officials can nullify millions of employment contracts with a creative new interpretation of an old law, and federal bank regulators are officially empowered to seize the assets of any citizen for allegedly violating written or unwritten banking regulations. Federal regulations dictate what price milk must sell for, what size California nectarines can be sold, what crops a person may grow on his own land, what apparel items a woman may sew in her own home, and how old a person must be to deliver Domino's pizzas. The Internal Revenue Service is carrying out a massive campaign against the self-employed that seeks to force over half of America's independent contractors to abandon their own businesses. From Drug Enforcement Administration agents seizing indoor gardening stores in order to prevent people from cultivating the wrong types of plants to Food and Drug Administration agents with automatic weapons raiding medical-supply companies, government agencies are more out of control than ever before. And the Supreme Court—the supposed protector of the Bill of Rights—has imposed scant curbs on the capricious power of federal employees.

Privacy is vanishing beneath the rising floodtide of government power. Government officials have asserted a de facto right to search almost anybody, almost any time, on almost any pretext. The average American now has far less freedom from having government officials strip-search his children, rummage through his luggage, ransack his house, sift through his bank records, and trespass in his fields. Today, a citizen's constitutional right to privacy can be nullified by the sniff of a dog.[5] Florida police recently announced that they must be allowed to smash down people's front doors without knocking because modern plumbing makes it too easy for drug violators to flush away evidence. Army units, National Guard troops, and military helicopters conduct sweeps through northern California, Kentucky, New Mexico, and Arizona, trampling crops, killing dogs, and generally seeking to maximize intimidation in a search for politically incorrect plants. Federal officials have given rewards to hundreds of airline ticket clerks for reporting the names of individuals who paid for their tickets in cash, thereby allowing police to confiscate the rest of people's wallets on mere suspicion of illegal behavior. Local police are conducting programs in 200,000 classrooms that sometimes result in young children informing police on parents who violate drug laws. The number of federally authorized wiretaps has almost quadrupled since 1980,[6] and the Federal Bureau of Investigation is trying to prohibit the development of new types of phones that would be more difficult to wiretap.[7]

Freedom of speech and freedom of the press are increasingly under assault by ambitious bureaucrats and spiteful politicians. In many locales, politicians have filed multimillion-dollar libel suits against private citizens who criticized them. Even congressmen and senators have used massive libel suits to spike critical comments by leading newspapers. Federal bureaucrats have the power to revoke the licenses of private radio and television stations, thereby blunting the broadcast media's criticism of the government. A chain of twenty small newspapers in California was bankrupted as a result of a government-financed lawsuit over a classified housing ad that mentioned "adults preferred"—a violation of the Fair Housing Act's ban on advertisements that discriminate against families with children. The Food and Drug Administration is preventing cancer patients from learning about legally approved drugs that could save their lives solely because the drug makers have not spent the millions of dollars necessary to satisfy the FDA's certification process to advertise additional uses. The proliferation of vague federal regulations has had a severe chilling effect on the free speech of millions of businessmen who cannot criticize federal agencies without risking retaliation that could destroy them. As part of the war on pornography, parents have been jailed for taking pictures of their babies in bathtubs.[8] Thanks to a 1992 federal appeals court decision and a late 1993 congressional uproar, even pictures of clothed children can now be considered pornographic—thus greatly increasing the number of Americans who can be prosecuted for violating obscenity laws.[9]

The government is manufacturing more criminals now than ever before. The government is increasingly choosing the citizen-target, creating the crime, and then vigorously prosecuting the violator. During the past fifteen years, law enforcement officials have set up thousands of elaborate schemes to entrap people for "crimes" such as buying plant supplies, asking for a job, or shooting deer. Dozens of private accountants have become double agents, receiving government kickbacks for betraying their clients to the IRS.

Total federal spending has increased from under $100 billion in 1963 to over $1.5 trillion in 1994, and as spending has grown, so has bureaucratic control and political power. Since 1960, the federal government has created over a thousand new subsidy programs for everything from medical care to housing to culture to transportation.[10] Government controls have followed a short step behind the subsidies; as a result, more and more in our society and economy are now dependent upon government approval. Subsidies are the twentieth-century method of humane conquest: slow political coups d'état over one sector of the economy and society after another. Government subsidies have become a major factor in squeezing out unsubsidized developers, unsubsidized schools, unsubsidized theater producers, and unsubsidized farmers.

Beggaring the taxpayer has become the main achievement of the welfare state. The federal tax system is turning individuals into sharecroppers of their own lives. The government's crusade to, in Franklin D. Roosevelt's words, provide people with "freedom from want" has paved the way for unlimited taxation. In the 1930s, New Deal planners waxed eloquent about "potential plenty" and denounced businessmen for refusing to unleash a cornucopia of higher living standards. Now, in the 1990s, we have "potential plenty"—except for government policies that hollow out people's paychecks and preempt their efforts to build better lives for themselves.

Total government spending now amounts to roughly 43 percent of the national income.[11] On top of this, the Clinton administration's Task Force on Reinventing Government estimated in September 1993 that "the cost to the private sector of complying with [government] regulations is at least $430 billion annually—9 percent of our gross domestic product!"[12] Nobel Laureate economist Milton Friedman observes, "The private economy has become an agent of the federal government. . . . At least 50 percent of the total productive resources of our nation are now being organized through the political market. In that very important sense, we are more than half socialist."[13] The average American now works over half of each year simply to pay the cost of government taxes and regulations.

High taxes have created a moral inversion in the relationship between the citizen and the State. Before the income tax, the government existed to serve the people, at least in some vague nominal sense; now, the people exist to provide financial grist for the State's mill. Federal court decisions have often bent over backward to stress that citizen's rights are nearly null and void in conflicts with the IRS. Internal Revenue Service seizures of private property have increased by 400 percent since 1980 and now hit over two million Americans each year.

Not only do we have more laws and regulations than ever before, but the laws themselves are becoming less clear, consistent, and coherent. James Madison observed in *The Federalist Papers,* "It will be of little avail to the people that the laws are made by men of their own choice if the laws be . . . so incoherent that they cannot be understood; if they be repealed or revised before they are promulgated, or undergo such incessant changes that no man, who knows what the law is today, can guess what it will be tomorrow."[14] It is now practically impossible for citizens to keep track of government's latest edicts; as the Clinton administration's September 1993 report on reinventing government noted, "The full stack of personnel laws, regulations, directives, case law and departmental guidance that the Agriculture Department uses weighs 1,088 pounds."[15] Today the law has become a tool with which to force people to behave in ways politicians approve, rather than a clear line that citizens can respect in order to live their lives in privacy and peace. With the proliferation of retroactive regulations, government agencies now have the right to change the rules of the game at any time—even after the game is over. The Rule of Law—the classical concept endorsed by the Massachusetts Constitution of 1780 as a restraint on government power—has been replaced by the "Rule of Memo," whereby federal officials on a whim create new rules to bind and penalize private citizens.

Government now appears more concerned with dictating personal behavior than with protecting citizens from murderers, muggers, and rapists. In 1990, for the first time in history, the number of people sentenced to prison for drug violations exceeded the number of people sentenced for violent crimes.[16] The number of people incarcerated in federal and state prisons in 1992 was almost triple the number incarcerated in 1980, and America now has a higher percentage of its population in prison than any other country.[17] Unfortunately, the more government has tried to control people's behavior, the more out of control American society has become. Violence is at an all-time record high: over five million Americans were robbed, assaulted, raped, or murdered in 1992.[18]

Coercion has become more refined and more pervasive in recent decades. We rarely see scenes like the Los Angeles police beating Rodney King or IRS agents dragging Amish tax resisters out of their meager homes. But just because few people physically resist government agents does not mean that the State is violating fewer people's rights. The level of coercion imposed by government agencies is less evident today primarily because the vast majority of citizens surrender to government demands before the government resorts to force. Economist J. A. Schumpeter wrote: "Power wins, not by being used, but by being there."[19] The lack of an armed uprising is no proof of a lack of aggression.

The key to contemporary American political thinking is the *neutering of the State*—the idea that modern government has been defanged, domesticated, tamed. Many Americans apparently believe that modern politicians and policy experts have been wise enough to create a Leviathan that does not trample the people it was created to serve. The question of individual liberty is now often portrayed as a question of a ruler's intentions toward the citizenry. But lasting institutions are far more important than transient intentions. And the last seventy years have seen the sapping of most restraints on arbitrary government power. American political thinking suffers from a romantic tendency to appraise government by lofty ideals rather than by banal and often grim realities; a tendency to judge politicians by their rhetoric rather than by their day-to-day finagling and petty mendacity; and a tendency to view the expansion of government power by its promises rather than by its results.

The decline of liberty results not only from specific acts of government—but also from the cumulative impact of hundreds of thousands of government decrees, hundreds of taxes, and legions of government officials with discretionary power over other Americans. We have tried to improve the quality of life by vastly increasing the amount of coercion, by multiplying police powers, by giving one group of people the power to command others as to how they must live. The power that accumulates in a centralized government is not put in a display case at the Smithsonian Institution—it is used in everyday life. The larger government becomes, the more coercive it will be—almost regardless of the intentions of those who advocate a larger government.

Americans' comprehension of liberty and the threats to its survival has declined sharply since the nation's birth. The Massachusetts colonists rebelled after the British agents received "writs of assistance" that allowed them to search any colonist's property. Modern Americans submit passively to government sweep searches of buses, schools, and housing projects. Virginia revolted in part because King George imposed a two-pence tax on the sale of a pound of tea; Americans today are complacent while Congress imposes billions of dollars of retroactive taxes—even on people who have already died. Connecticut rebelled in part because the British were undermining the independence of judges; nowadays, federal agencies have the power to act as prosecutor, judge, and jury in suits against private citizens. Maine revolted in part because the British Parliament issued a decree confiscating every white pine tree in the colony; modern Americans are largely complacent when local governments impose almost unlimited restrictions on individuals' rights to use their own property. The initial battles of the Revolution occurred after British troops tried to seize the colonists' private weapons; today, residents in Chicago, Washington, D.C., and other cities submit to de facto prohibitions on handgun ownership imposed by the same governments that grossly fail to protect citizens from private violence.

The 1775 Revolution was largely a revolt against growing arbitrary power.[20] Nowadays, seemingly the only principle is to have no political principle: to judge each act of government in a vacuum, to assume that each expansion of government power and each nullification of individuals' rights will have no future impact. The Founding Fathers looked at the liberties they were losing, while modern Americans focus myopically on the freedoms they still retain.

America needs fewer laws, not more prisons. By trying to seize far more power than is necessary over American citizens, the federal government is destroying its own legitimacy. We face a choice not of anarchy or authoritarianism, but a choice of limited government or unlimited government. Because government is a necessary evil, it is necessary to vigilantly limit government's disruption of citizens' lives. John Locke, whose *Second Treatise of Government* had a profound influence on the Founding Fathers' thinking, wrote: "The end of Law is not to abolish or restrain, but to preserve and enlarge Freedom."[21] The Founding Fathers realized that some amount of government was necessary in order to prevent a "war of all against all." But coercion remains an evil that must be minimized in a free society. The ideal is not to abolish all government—but to structure government to achieve the greatest respect for citizens' rights and the least violation of their liberties.

Regrettably, the examples in this book do not divide themselves as neatly and cleanly as an author or reader might wish. Thus, there will be some overlap in analyses of specific government agencies among chapters. But I hope the book will help readers to navigate the maze of government policies and to better understand how much power government officials now hold over their daily lives.

The question is not whether Americans have lost all their liberties, but whether the average American is becoming less free with each passing year, with each session of Congress, with each new shelf row of *Federal Register* dictates. As a Revolutionary-era pamphleteer declared in 1768, "As the total subjection of a people arises generally from gradual encroachments, it will be our indispensable duty manfully to oppose every invasion of our rights in the beginning."[22] Although it is too late to start opposing invasions of our rights "in the beginning," American liberty can still be rescued from the encroachments of government. The first step to saving our liberty is to realize how much we have already lost, how we lost it, and how we will continue to lose unless fundamental political changes occur.

·2·

Seizure Fever: The War on Property Rights

The right of property is the guardian of every other right, and to deprive the people of this, is in fact to deprive them of their liberty.

—Arthur Lee of Virginia (1775)[1]

Every person enjoys property rights, including the right to own, use and dispose of property, both individually and jointly with other individuals. Ownership rights are guaranteed by law. The inalienable right to own property guarantees personal individual interests and freedoms.

—Russian Constitution (1991)[2]

In 1775 New England patriots marched against the British army under a flag depicting a pine tree—a symbol of British tyranny. Because pine was an excellent material for the masts of the British navy, the Parliament in the early 1700s banned citizens in several colonies from cutting down any white pine trees—claiming them all for the British crown. The king's agents also launched attacks on private mill owners, smashing their mills and arresting citizens accused of chopping down pine trees. In 1730, settlers near the Sheepscot River in Maine formally complained that the king's agents "came with an armed force, turned them from their lands, seized their timber, burned and destroyed their houses," and "even threatened to throw them into confinement" for violating the pine laws.[3] Historian Joseph Malone noted, "Strict enforcement of the Act of 1729 would have prevented the settler from clearing his land for the planting of crops. If he built his rude cabin out of white pine . . . the Surveyor General could bring him to trial."[4] Historian Robert Albion wrote in 1926: "The royal interpretation of 'private property' practically rendered that term nugatory, so that, in spite of appearances, the pines were virtually being commandeered for the Navy."[5] The British government consistently refused to compensate colonists for the seizure of pines on their land or for the damage that the king's agents did to their land in clearing space to harvest large pines. Though contemporary history books have largely forgotten these clashes, historian Rufus Sewall wrote in 1859: "The great issue [the American Revolution] began in the forests of Maine in the contests of her lumbermen with the King's surveyor, as to the right to cut, and the property in white pine trees."[6]

Now, more than two centuries later, mass confiscation has again become politically fashionable. Politicians and the courts have created an overwhelming presumption in favor of the government's right to seize control over private land; seize possession of private homes, boats, and cars; and even seize the cash in people's wallets. While the dispute over property rights is often portrayed as merely an economic contest, the power of government officials to seize private property directly subjugates citizens to the capricious will of those officials.

Private property marks the boundary between the citizen and the State. The degree of respect the State shows for property rights will largely determine how much privacy, autonomy, and independence the citizen has. Property is the exclusive right to use and dispose of an object or idea. The Supreme Court declared in 1917:

> Property is more than the mere thing which a person owns. It is elementary that it includes the right to acquire, use, and dispose of it. The Constitution protects these essential attributes of property. . . . There can be conception of property aside from its control and use, and upon its use depends its value.[7]

Private property delineates the domain over which the individual is sovereign. While property once symbolized "the individual's rights against the world," the concept of property has been so narrowed that currently government is often not considered to have violated a person's rights unless it physically ejects him from his house or his land.

Property is protected by the Fifth and Fourteenth Amendments to the Constitution, as well as by the common law traditions that Americans inherited from England. The Fifth Amendment declares that private property shall not "be taken for public use without just compensation," while the Fourteenth Amendment adds: "nor shall any State deprive any person of life, liberty, or property, without due process of law."

GOSSIP VS. DEEDS, TITLES, AND OTHER PROOF OF OWNERSHIP

Once upon a time, possession was nine-tenths of the law. Nowadays, gossip is sometimes nine-tenths of possession. Thousands of American citizens are being stripped of their property on the basis of rumors and unsubstantiated assertions made by government confidential informants. Beginning in 1970,

Congress enacted legislation to permit government to seize the property of Mafia organizations and big-time drug smugglers.[8] In succeeding decades, other forfeiture laws were enacted, and federal agents can now seize private property under over 200 different statutes.[9] From 1985 to 1991, the number of federal seizures of property under asset forfeiture laws increased by 1,500 percent—reaching a total of $644 million.[10] State and local governments have also seized hundreds of millions of dollars of property in recent years.[11] Steven Kessler, a New York lawyer who authored a three-volume 1993 study on federal and state forfeiture, writes, "The use of forfeiture has probably increased a hundred-fold in the last ten years."[12]

Unfortunately, the more forfeiture laws legislatures enact, the less attention police seem to pay to major criminals. Rep. Henry Hyde of Illinois noted in June 1993 that 80 percent of the people whose property is seized by the federal government under drug laws are never formally charged with any crime.[13] Rep. John Conyers declared at a June 1993 congressional hearing: "A law designed to give cops the right to confiscate and keep the luxury possessions of major drug dealers mostly ensnares the modest homes, cars and hard-earned cash of ordinary, law-abiding people."[14]

Willie Jones of Nashville was flying to Houston on February 27, 1991, to purchase plants for his landscaping business. Because Jones was black and paid cash for his plane ticket, the ticket clerk reported him to nearby Drug Enforcement Agency officers, who presumed Jones was a drug courier. DEA officers at the Nashville airport approached Jones, checked his identification, and asked permission to search him. Although Jones refused to grant permission, the officers searched him anyhow and found $9,000 in cash. The DEA agents then announced that they were "detaining" the money. Jones observed: "They said I was going to buy drugs with it, that their dog sniffed it and said it had drugs on it." (A 1989 study found that 70 percent of all the currency in the United States had cocaine residue on it.)[15] Jones never saw the dog. The officers didn't arrest Jones, but they kept the money. When Jones asked the officers for a receipt for his money, they handed him a receipt for an "undetermined amount of U.S. currency." Jones objected and asked the officers to count the money out, but the officers refused, claiming that such an action would violate DEA policy. Federal judge Thomas Wiseman, in an April 1993 decision, concluded that "the officers' behavior at this point was casual and sarcastic . . . they believed that the seizure of the currency was all but a *fait accompli* . . . they cared little for Mr. Jones's feelings of insecurity."[16] Judge Wiseman concluded that the DEA officials' testimony on the seizure was "misleading," "unconvincing," and "inconsistent" and ordered the money returned—after a two-year legal battle. Jones observed: "I didn't know it was against the law for a 42-year-old black man to have money in his pocket."[17]

Asset forfeiture increases the power of local policemen over people whom they do not like. In Washington, D.C., police routinely stop black citizens and "confiscate small amounts of cash and jewelry on the streets and in parks—even when no drugs are found or charges filed."[18] Ben Davis, a resident of Washington, complained, "I've got money in both pockets, but I don't know how much. The assumption is, if I can't tell you exactly how much I have, it must be from criminal enterprise."[19]

Increasingly, the mere suspicion of a government official is sufficient proof to nullify proof that a citizen legitimately owns his property. The Volusia County, Florida, sheriff's department set up a "forfeiture trap" to stop motorists traveling Interstate 95 and seized an average of over $5,000 a day from motorists between 1989 and 1992—over $8 million total. In three-quarters of the seizures, no criminal charges were filed. An investigation by the *Orlando Sentinel* revealed that 90 percent of those seizure victims were black or Hispanic.[20] When confronted with this statistic, Volusia County sheriff Bob Vogel said, "What this data tells me is that the majority of money being transported for drug activity involves blacks and Hispanics." People whose cash was seized by the deputies received scant due process of law; as the *Sentinel* noted, one deputy told two blacks from whom he had just confiscated $19,000: "You have the right to follow us back to the station and get a receipt." Even citizens who provided proof that their money was honestly acquired (including a lottery winner's proof of his lottery receipts) were treated like drug dealers. Volusia County officials routinely offered "settlements" to drivers whose cash they seized, offering to return a percentage of the seized cash if the drivers would sign a form promising not to sue.

Asset forfeiture laws are turning some federal agents into the modern-day equivalents of horse thieves. Ranchers are being victimized by seizures based on allegations of violations of environmental laws. On March 10, 1992, U.S. Fish and Wildlife Service and state agents trespassed fifteen miles onto Richard Smith's Texas ranch, accused him of poisoning eagles, and seized his pickup truck. The agents later tracked down Smith's seventy-five-year-old father, W. B. Smith, and seized his pickup truck—threatening to leave an old man who had had five heart bypass operations ten miles out of town with no transportation.[21] The agents produced no evidence to support their accusation and returned the trucks nine months later without filing charges.[22] W. B. Smith complained: "The Fish and Wildlife Service is out of control, and the Endangered Species Act has given them the tools to destroy the ranching industry."[23] Lawyer Nancy Hollander told the House Government Operations Committee in June 1993: "All too often, in my practice back in Albuquerque, I see cases where someone loses the family pickup truck at the time of arrest for a non-money-related, non-drug federal crime. These persons frequently give up the criminal case, even when the prosecution has little merit, to negotiate the release of a vehicle which provides their livelihood."[24]

Confiscation based on mere suspicion is the essence of contemporary asset forfeiture. In Adair County, Missouri, local police seized Sheri and Matthew Farrell's sixty-acre farm based on an unsubstantiated tip from a paid drug informant who claimed that Farrell had a vast field of marijuana and used tractors outfitted with special lights to harvest it at night. Police made no effort to investigate the allegations before seizing Farrell's farm. The case against Farrell and thirty-four other local defendants collapsed when the informant refused to testify in court—first because he claimed he had laryngitis and then because he claimed a total loss of memory.[25] Despite the collapse of the government's case, the police refused to return Farrell's farm. They had a change of heart after the *Pittsburgh Press* exposed the case, although they required that the Farrells sign an agreement promising not to sue before they gave back the farm. The case cost the Farrells over $5,600 in legal fees.

Asset forfeiture distorts law enforcement priorities; instead of chasing violent criminals, some police target wealthy citizens. Early in the morning of October 2, 1992, a small army of thirty-one people from eight law enforcement agencies smashed their way into sixty-one-year-old Donald Scott's home on his 200-acre Trail's End Ranch in Malibu, California. The raiders were equipped with automatic weapons, flak jackets, and a battering ram.[26] Scott's wife screamed when she saw the intruders, Scott came out of the bedroom with a pistol in his hands, and police gunned him down. After killing Scott, the agents thoroughly searched his house and ranch but failed to find any illicit drugs. Ventura County district attorney Michael Bradbury investigated the raid and issued a report in 1993 that concluded that a "primary purpose of the raid was a land grab by the [Los Angeles County] Sheriff's Department."[27] Bradbury revealed that at a briefing before the raid took place, government agents were informed that the ranch had been appraised at $1.1 million and that "80 acres sold for $800,000 in 1991 in the same area."[28] The law officers at the briefing were told that if they discovered as few as "14 marijuana plants" on the ranch, the entire property could be seized.[29] Bradbury also concluded that a Los Angeles sheriff's deputy had lied to obtain a search warrant and declared: "This search warrant became Donald Scott's death warrant. This guy should not be dead."[30] Los Angeles officials claimed that a confidential informant told them that marijuana was being grown on Scott's ranch, but the informant denied ever making such an statement.[31]

The Justice Department's 1992 annual report on asset seizures declared, "No property may be seized unless the government has probable cause to believe that it is subject to forfeiture."[32] In reality, government officials are seizing people's property based solely on "hearsay"—rumor and gossip—from anonymous informants.[33] (Hearsay evidence is held in such low esteem in the American judicial system that it cannot be introduced into court in criminal proceedings.) Police routinely refuse to reveal their source of a rumor about the forfeiture target; some policemen have likely invented anonymous informants to give them a pretext to take private property they covet. In Fort Lauderdale, Florida, police seized the $250,000 home of a dead man from his heirs who had cared for him while he was dying of cancer. The justification for the seizure? A "confidential informant told police that [two years earlier] the owner . . . took a $10,000 payment from drug dealers who used a dock at the house along a canal to unload cocaine. The informant can't recall the exact date, the boat's name or the dealers' names, and the government candidly says in its court brief it 'does not possess the facts necessary to be any more specific,'" as the *Pittsburgh Press* reported.[34] Although the police had no evidence that the deceased homeowner was involved in drug dealing, an informant's vague, uncorroborated assertion was sufficient to evict the owners and seize the property. While government agents can use hearsay evidence to justify a seizure, property owners are usually prohibited from offering hearsay evidence to support their claims.

Law enforcement officials are also seizing apartment buildings to punish the landlords for not eradicating drug dealing in the apartments. (If the same standard were applied to inner-city public housing projects, almost every public housing project in the country could be seized *from* the government; in 1993 Baltimore mayor Kurt Schmoke blamed maintenance problems at one public housing project on drug dealers who refused to let city workers enter the buildings.)[35] In Florida, the Dade County Commission revised county laws in 1989 to allow county officials "to demolish a nuisance building within 30 days after the police report drug activity at the property. Proof of drug activity is defined in the ordinance as one arrest."[36] The owner of a thirty-six-unit apartment building in Milwaukee sought to placate the police by evicting ten tenants suspected of drug use, giving a master key to local beat cops, forwarding tips to the police, and hiring two security firms to patrol the building. The city still seized the building because, as Milwaukee city attorney David Stanosz declared, "Once a property develops a reputation as a place to buy drugs, the only way to fix that is to leave it totally vacant for a number of months. This landlord doesn't want to do that." The owner had encouraged the police to send undercover agents into the building—but the police claimed they were too short of officers.[37] In July 1992, several Cleveland landlords informed the police of drug dealing in their buildings; the city responded by quickly seizing the buildings and evicting all tenants, even in a building where drug dealing occurred in a single apartment.[38] Apparently, the more the police fail to control crime, the more power police acquire to seize law-abiding citizens' property.

Asset forfeiture is spreading like wildfire through the statute books. Some Islamic countries impose draconian penalties on men who approach and talk to women in public. In Washington, D.C., Portland, Oregon, and Hartford, Connecticut, police confiscate the cars of men who drive up and suggest a "capitalist act between consenting adults" to streetwalkers. Customs Service officials in Texas seized a $138,000 Lear jet after discovering that the owner had made a typographical error on paperwork he submitted to the Federal Aviation Administration.[39] (The FAA's usual response to such a mistake is to require the owner to correct the form.) The Immigration and

Naturalization Service has seized over 30,000 cars and trucks since 1990 from people helping illegal immigrants enter the United States or construction companies transporting illegal immigrants to job sites.[40] Customs agents confiscated the $113,000 that a Vietnamese mother had collected from twenty families in the Seattle area to take back to Vietnam for humanitarian relief for their relatives.[41] (Customs officials pronounced the woman guilty of violating the Trading with the Enemy Act.) The FBI seized three Mercedes-Benzes from a businesswoman in Augusta, Georgia, after alleging that her husband had used the car phones to place a few illegal bets on sporting events.[42] Monmouth County, New Jersey, officials confiscated "office furniture, desks, stationery, telephones, a copy machine and other furnishings from a home in which a man was charged with practicing psychiatry without a license."[43] A New Jersey mother's Oldsmobile was confiscated by police after they alleged that her son had used it to drive to a store where he shoplifted a pair of pants.[44] One New York businessman was forced to forfeit all of his gas stations because of a failure to pay New York sales tax.[45] A New Jersey construction company had all its equipment seized after state officials decided that the company was technically ineligible to bid on three municipal projects that it had already completed.[46] Suffolk County, New York, legislators considered a law in May 1993 to allow local officials to confiscate the "cars, boats and planes used in connection with any misdemeanor."[47] In 1993, Massachusetts attorney general Scott Harshbarger promoted an environmental forfeiture act that would allow confiscation of the assets of corporations that violate environmental laws.[48]

Asset confiscation programs are creating thousands of new police informants. The Justice Department routinely gives monetary rewards to individuals who report information or make accusations that lead to a seizure. The forfeiture program thus turns many airline ticket agents into conspirators with the government, since anyone who pays cash for an airline ticket stands a chance of being reported as a suspected drug dealer or an accomplice to drug dealing.

Forfeiture is the biggest growth area in law enforcement partly because federal and local police agencies usually keep a large amount of the booty they seize. Federal judge Richard Arnold noted in 1992 that some observers were questioning "whether we are seeing fair and effective law enforcement or an insatiable appetite for a source for increased agency revenue."[49] In Nueces County, Texas, Sheriff James Hickey used assets from a federal drug forfeiture fund to grant himself a retroactive $48,000 salary increase just before retirement ($400 a month for the previous ten years). The sheriff was indicted for embezzlement by a federal grand jury in August 1993.[50] Even internal government documents concede that federal agents have gone overboard: a September 1992 Justice Department newsletter noted, "Like children in a candy shop, the law enforcement community chose all manner and method of seizing and forfeiting property, gorging ourselves in an effort which soon came to resemble one designed to raise revenues."[51]

Prosecutors and legislators stack the deck against property rights. A 1990 Justice Department directive declared, "It is the Department's position that no advance notice or opportunity for an adversary hearing is statutorily or constitutionally required prior to the seizure of property, including real property."[52] Professor Claudio Riedi noted in 1992 in the *University of Miami Law Review*, "Frequently, the government can meet its burden of proof by simply qualifying one of its detectives as an expert, who then testifies that a particular way of bundling money is typical for drug dealers. Standing alone, such testimony may be enough for a showing of probable cause, and may therefore entitle the government to forfeiture. In contrast, an innocent owner must adduce massive evidence to prove her case."[53] The *Orlando Sentinel* noted, "Deputies routinely said bills in denominations of $1, $5, $10, $20, $50 and $100 were suspicious because they are typical of what dealers carry. But that leaves few alternatives for others."[54] In most forfeiture court proceedings, it is up to the owner to prove that his house, his car, or the cash in his wallet was legally obtained. The fact that a government official makes an unsubstantiated assertion that a piece of property was somehow involved in illicit activity effectively automatically transfers the ownership of that property to the government.

Asset forfeiture is proliferating in part because of a technicality in the law that allows the government to claim that it is suing only the item of property, not the property's owner. This is why forfeiture cases often have peculiar titles such as *U.S. v. 1960 Bags of Coffee*, *U.S. v. 9.6 Acres of Land and Lake*, or *U.S. v. 667 Bottles of Wine*. And since the Bill of Rights recognizes the rights only of citizens and state governments, not the rights of chunks of land or bottles of wine, there are almost no due process restrictions on government's attacks on property. A federal appeals court recognized this when it announced in August 1992: "We continue to be enormously troubled by the government's increasing and virtually unchecked use of the civil forfeiture statutes and the disregard for due process that is buried in those statutes."[55] The citizen must show vastly more evidence to reclaim his property than the government did to seize it in the first place.

Government officials routinely refuse to return seized property even after an accused person has been tried and found innocent. The costs of suing the government to recover property are extremely high, routinely exceeding $10,000, and citizens must post a bond of up to $5,000 before filing suit. (The bond is required to cover the government's legal costs in having to defend against a property owner's efforts to reclaim his property.) The legal battles required to recover wrongfully seized property often take two, three, or more years. If the property seized is only worth a few hundred dollars, the person cannot possibly break even by suing the government. Most forfeiture statutes deny a private citizen any compensation for his attorney's fees when he successfully reclaims forfeited property.

Although the number of asset forfeiture actions has skyrocketed in recent years, Justice Department officials apparently believe that the seizure bull market has only just begun. Cary Copeland, director of the Department of Justice's Executive Office for Asset Forfeiture, declared at a June 1993 congressional hearing: "Asset forfeiture is still in its relative infancy as a law enforcement program."[56] The Federal Bureau of Investigation announced in 1992 that it anticipated that its total seizures of private property would increase 25 percent each year for the following three years.[57] The Supreme Court marginally limited government forfeiture powers in several 1993 decisions, but Justice Department spokesman Mark Sakaley indicated that the decisions were not expected to have a major impact on forfeiture programs.[58]

Cary Copeland declared that asset forfeiture "is to the drug war what smart bombs and air power are to modern warfare."[59] Asset forfeiture basically allows government agencies to carpet bomb the rights of the American people. The Federal Eighth Circuit Court of Appeals complained in 1992 that it was "troubled by the government's view that any property, whether it be a hobo's hovel or the Empire State Building, can be seized by the government because the owner, regardless of his or her past criminal record, engages in a single drug transaction."[60]

Law enforcement in the United States is reverting back toward the conditions existing in England before the Magna Carta, when rulers almost automatically seized all the property of any person convicted of a felony. Such seizures spurred English barons to force King John to limit his powers in 1215.[61] Unfortunately, some federal officials appear to cherish a pre-thirteenth-century philosophy of government power. (A 1992 U.S. Solicitor General's brief quoted the Old Testament and praised forfeiture as an "ancient punishment.")[62] Asset forfeiture provisions presume that government officials should have the power to inflict economic capital punishment on private citizens for the breaking of scores of laws.

The asset seizure controversy redefines the relation between the State and the citizen: What pretext does the State need to claim that a citizen's property actually belongs to the State? Do people have a right to their property only until some "secret informant" tells police something bad about the citizen's use of his property? If Congress proposed to forcibly alter all private deeds and titles in the United States by adding a clause stating that the government acquires automatic ownership rights if any law enforcement official hears a rumor about a property's possible illicit use, the public backlash would raze Capitol Hill. But, increasingly, that is the law of the land.

ZONING OUT LIBERTY

Modern zoning laws presume that no citizen has a right to control his own land—and that every citizen has a right to control his neighbor's land. In zoning disputes, property rights, like some type of mysterious vapor, reside any place except with the actual property owner. Government power over land use has vastly increased in the last seventy years. As Clint Bolick of the Institute for Justice, a Washington nonprofit organization, observes, "A welfare recipient has a greater property interest in her welfare check than a homeowner has in protection of her real property."[63]

The use of zoning laws began in the first years of the twentieth century and spread rapidly. Many of the first zoning codes were instituted to forcibly quarantine blacks. Civil rights lawyer Yale Rabin, in *Zoning and the American Dream*, wrote that blacks and other minorities have suffered from "expulsive zoning . . . frequently employed in ways that have undermined the character, quality, and stability of black residential areas; zoning not only has been used to erect barriers to escape from the concentrated confinement of the inner city, it has been used to permit—even promote—the intrusion into black neighborhoods of disruptive incompatible uses that have diminished the quality and undermined the stability of those neighborhoods."[64] St. Louis, Missouri, adopted a zoning plan designed to expel a large portion of its black residents; a St. Louis commission complained in 1936 that "by such zoning we are deliberately planning to reduce our total population from 822,000 to 517,000 . . . Zoning of this sort is totally unsound and accomplishes nothing other than the deliberate creation of slums."[65] Early zoning laws helped create some of the ghettos that would later provide a pretext for urban renewal programs and the bulldozing of American cities. Since the 1950s, the federal government has heavily subsidized local zoning activities and has even required extensive land-use restrictions as a condition for receiving lavish federal housing and development subsidies.

Zoning laws have become far more invasive and restrictive in recent years. Floosmoor, Illinois, in an act of legislative snobbery, banned pickup trucks from its streets—and even from private driveways.[66] San Francisco zoners banned architecture offices from certain areas of the city where government planners believed rents were already too high.[67] Wellesley, Massachusetts, passed a zoning law limiting homeowners to only two live-in servants.[68] (The law sought to restrict the proliferation of group houses.) Phoenix, Arizona, requires that new homes use Spanish tile roofs—an ornate touch that adds up to $6,000 to new home prices.[69] Coral Gables, Florida, requires Spanish tile roofs on any children's playhouses in families' backyards.[70] Local governments have invoked zoning codes to require builders of apartment buildings to install whirlpool tubs and special electric ranges (in one case identified by brand name).[71]

Zoners apparently feel entitled to transform humanity's habitat. Malibu, California, enacted a new zoning code in 1993 that made up to 80 percent of the homes in the city nonconforming—and required that nonconforming homes be torn down after twenty years.[72] A zoning plan proposed in Houston in 1993 could result in the forced shutdown of 128 businesses.[73] In April 1993, Fairfax County, Virginia, threatened to close down thirty large furniture and appliance stores because they disturbed the peace by violating an obscure zoning provision that prohibited stores located in warehouse districts from having more than 40 percent of their floor space devoted to retail sales.[74]

Zoning boards often ban individuals from working in their own homes. In Glencoe, Illinois, the city government forced a financial planner to shut down his home-based business.[75] The city of Chicago issued a cease-and-desist order in 1984 to a couple using two personal computers in their home to write software and magazine articles.[76] In Highland Park, New Jersey, a rabbi was fined for having a photocopying machine, a filing cabinet, a typewriter, and miscellaneous business documents in his home, which violated a local ban on home offices.[77] *Nation's Business* noted, "Los Angeles prohibits home-based businesses in residential neighborhoods; the prohibition extends even to those such as free-lance writers, artists, dentists, and others who often work from home."[78] Some towns, such as Plano, Texas, dictate that not more than 20 percent of the floor space of a residence can be used for business purposes, thereby discriminating against people with smaller homes.[79] Other locales dictate the amount of business-related material that may be stored on premises: Mount Prospect, Illinois, "allows a home business owner to store up to 100 cubic feet of inventory indoors, about enough to fill a closet."[80] The Bureau of Alcohol, Tobacco and Firearms sought to drive scores of federally licensed gun dealers in Colorado and elsewhere out of business in 1993 by informing local governments that the individuals were selling guns out of their own homes—in locales that prohibited any home-based business in residential areas. (The individuals were not violating any federal or state firearms laws.)[81] A publication of the American Planning Association, an association consisting primarily of government officials, asserted: "Under its zoning power, a local government has the authority to entirely prohibit all business enterprises from operating in residential districts."[82]

Some local governments use zoning to exercise dictatorial control over every square foot of land under their domain. Laguna Beach, California, prohibited a family from moving into their new home because city inspectors decreed that the owner had painted his house the wrong shade of white.[83] In 1991, the city prosecuted a woman because the picket fence she built in front of her house was six inches too high. The city zoning board targeted the woman even though twenty of her neighbors signed a letter stating they had no objection to her fence and even though there were forty other houses in her neighborhood that also had fences higher than the four-foot limit. (The zoning rule had been put into effect ten years before, dictating that new fences had to be significantly lower than existing fences.)[84] A 1991 zoning ordinance allows the city of Camarillo, California, "to abate any problem that diminishes property values," as the *Los Angeles Times* reported. Camarillo city manager William Little explained: "It's broad enough to cover virtually anything. But we are very judicious in what we go up against."[85] Little's remark exemplifies how zoning to protect property values gives government officials almost unlimited power to restrict the use of property—thereby defeating the whole notion of property rights.

Governments can even decide the type, number, and arrangement of plants and shrubs that new homes or office buildings must have. Herndon, Virginia, for example, requires developers to post a bond with a government planning agency to be forfeited if the shrubs or trees a developer plants die within two years.[86] Pasadena, California, proposed banning residents from having weeds in their yards, a policy sometimes referred to as "crabgrass fascism."[87] The Alhambra, California, city council decreed that 50 percent of each front yard in the city must consist of live vegetation. Many California homeowners have been caught in the cross fire of government regulations: water authorities prohibited them from watering their front yards, and zoning authorities fined them if their grass died.[88]

The essence of zoning is the shotgun behind the door—the pending call on police to drag someone away in handcuffs and bulldoze their home. Zoning is not simply a question of bureaucrats and local politicians coming up with byzantine ordinances but of the full force of government waiting to fall on the head of anyone who violates one of the constantly changing local land-use decrees. In Laguna Beach, California, Al Maier, a retired Marine pilot, was jailed for six months largely because he had some old cars parked in the driveway of his house. Maier was also jailed for allowing a homeless family to live with him in a spare room free of charge. Frank Battaile, deputy city attorney for Laguna Beach, explained: "Mr. Maier is known for supposedly doing charitable things and being the Laguna Beach Santa Claus. But his neighbors complained about property values."[89] In Skaneateles, New York, the local government responded to one couple's zoning violations by sending in sheriff's deputies to drag out and jail the owner's wife and raze their $350,000 lakefront home.[90] The Office of Code Enforcement in Alexandria, Virginia, sent certified letters to twenty-two homeowners in June 1993 threatening to condemn their properties unless they fixed chipping paint on their windowsills or door frames.[91]

Zoning über alles appears to be the motto of many local governments. In 1985 the city of New York gave a developer permission to build a thirty-one-story apartment building. After the building was up, the city announced that its officials had misread their own zoning maps—and demanded that twelve stories be slashed off the building. As a result of the city's ruling, the developer was forced to spend $1 million to pay for a 7,000-pound robot to smash down the illegal floors of the building, floor by floor.[92] In August 1993, Seal Beach, California, ordered a homeowner to remove a six-foot dome atop his house—even though the city's planning department explicitly approved the house and dome design three years earlier. (The homeowner had built the dome so that his children could learn about astronomy.) The city council ordered the destruction of the dome in part because it did not comply with zoning rules enacted *after* the dome's construction.[93] The owner estimated that removing the dome would cost him $13,000.[94] Huntington Beach, California, forced one homeowner to raze the top floor of his luxury home after it announced that city officials had mistakenly approved (after a lengthy study) his house plans in 1985. The *Los Angeles Times* reported on the city council members' rationale on the vote: "In rejecting [the owner's] request to allow his home to stand, council members noted that to grant a code variance, they must first determine that special circumstances justify waiving city zoning regulations. The fact that [the] home is already built does not constitute such a circumstance, they said."[95] In 1987, Laguna Beach annexed an area known as South Laguna, imposed new zoning rules, and proceeded to force hundreds of homeowners in the annexed area to tear down the extra rooms, garages, and porches they had legally added to their homes. The California Fourth District Court of Appeals in May 1992 struck down the city's action, noting that "California municipalities are not fiefdoms unto their own. . . . Laguna Beach spent considerable tax dollars in an effort to deprive some of its own citizens of the benefits clearly accorded them by a state law."[96]

Zoning forces average citizens to beg politicians and bureaucrats for permission to use their own property. Local governments in New York may be abject failures at preventing violent crime, but they have a good record in fighting garage conversions. *Newsday* printed the docket of an upcoming meeting of the Babylon, New York, Zoning Board of Appeals for January 23, 1992. Among the items slated for public hearing: a person seeking permission to maintain an awning, a person seeking permission to maintain a front porch, a person seeking to "legalize an open porch on the rear of a house at 416 S. Eighth St.," a person seeking permission to install sliding glass doors, a person seeking "to legalize the conversion of a detached garage to a playroom and storage room at 212 S. Sixth St.," and a person seeking permission "to maintain a second kitchen for personal use at 132 Houston St."[97]

And getting zoning changes in New York can be a torturous process. *Newsday* columnist William Murphy observed:

> It is a fact of New York City life that the average citizen who wants to add a backyard porch or make other alterations to the family home that might require city approval gets little or no help when he asks the Buildings Department for advice on how to proceed. So, over the years, a shadowy species called "expediters" emerged to help out the helpless. For a fee ranging from hundreds of dollars to thousands of dollars, these expediters shepherd the average citizen through the Buildings Department. A deputy buildings commissioner, Stewart O'Brien, told members of a City Council committee last week that he has frequently heard stories of expediters charging clients $2,500, with $500 going for department fees, $1,000 for the expediter's fee and $1,000 for bribes to department employees. If you want to add a backyard porch to your house, put $2,500 in cash in your pocket, go to the Buildings Department office in your borough, and ask someone in the lobby where you can find an expediter.[98]

Corruption is the natural result of arbitrary zoning power. The *Chicago Tribune* observed,

> Chicago aldermen use their power over city zoning laws to reward friends and backers with multimillion-dollar opportunities, to amass thousands of dollars in campaign contributions and to determine who can live, do business and prosper in their wards. And since the [city] council has the ability to transform land values virtually at will, property owners are forced to seek the indulgence of their alderman, creating opportunities for favoritism and corruption. Chicago aldermen have almost complete authority to reject or approve any project in their wards, no matter the size, merit or impact of the proposed development.[99]

Citizens often bitterly resent zoning officials' intrusions. The American Planning Association offers helpful tips to government officials on how to intimidate average citizens:

> Ideally, inspectors should carry cameras at all times and make immediate photographic records of all alleged violations. Virtually all courts will admit properly documented photographic evidence. The other benefit of using a camera in inspection efforts is its intimidation effect—some citizens are more impressed by the formality of having their violations photographed than by the initial warning letter.[100]

Some local zoning officials act as if they should automatically have a right to compel obedience and subservience from anyone within the range of their imaginations. The city of Galena, Illinois, sought to prohibit a dairy farmer from building a home on his farm, which was a mile and a half outside city limits, simply because a clause in the city's comprehensive zoning ordinance decreed that the city had the right to control development in areas outside the city limits. (An Illinois appeals court blocked the city's power grab.)[101] Newtown Borough, Pennsylvania, requires citizens to pay a $10,000 nonrefundable fee in order to challenge the constitutionality of the local zoning ordinance.[102]

Zoning routinely sacrifices some people's freedom to inflate other people's property values. In Takoma Park, Maryland (a suburb of Washington, D.C.), up to a thousand renters (8 percent of the city's population) were evicted in 1988 primarily to boost the property values of a minority of homeowners. Takoma Park is full of large Victorian homes that can easily be divided into apartments. But in 1978, some property owners sued the Montgomery County government to get it to enforce a 1923 county zoning code that prohibited the subletting of apartments in single-residence homes. The county government announced that existing houses must comply with the regulations within ten years.

Ten years later, in 1988, the Washington area had a large number of homeless people. In January 1988, Montgomery County chief executive Sidney Kramer complained to the *Washington Post*: "We do not have adequate low- and moderate-income housing in this county."[103] Yet two months later, Kramer—by enforcing the restrictive regulations—effectively abolished up to 400 dwelling units, displacing up to 1,000 people. Local resident Reuben McCornack observed, "Most of the tenants . . . are in low-paying jobs such as service industry, clerical and construction work, child care and mechanical or technical service work. . . . The force behind the evictions is a small group of people, most of whom live in the historic section of Takoma Park, where houses sell for $300,000 or more. They see the removal of tenants from other, more modest neighborhoods as a method to help property values appreciate."[104] McCornack denounced the government's action as "a scheme of social engineering for removal of lower income tenants." One of the displaced tenants moved from his apartment into his ten-year-old car.[105]

Zoning codes sometimes openly discriminate against certain groups of Americans. Stratford, Connecticut, imposed a zoning regulation that allowed much higher densities per house for families than for groups of unrelated individuals. The Connecticut Supreme Court ruled in the 1991 case of *Dinan v. Board of Zoning Appeals* that zoners could discriminate against nontraditional households: "Neighbors are not so likely to call upon them to borrow a cup of sugar, provide a ride to the store, mind the family pets, water the plants or perform any of the countless services that families . . . provide to each other as a result of longtime acquaintance and mutual self-interest. . . . [The] police power may be used to promote 'family values' and 'youth values' that contribute to creating 'a sanctuary for people.'"[106] In cases like this, the police power is used to create a "sanctuary" for some people by prohibiting other people from living where they choose. In Connecticut, people's freedom to use their own property is not as important as promoting the possibility that someone may ask to borrow a cup of sugar.

Some government officials use almost any pretext to increase their power over landowners. In May 1992, rioters burnt down or severely damaged over 540 buildings in South-Central Los Angeles and surrounding areas. Some of the same Los Angeles politicians who verbally coddled looters favored harsh, unforgiving treatment of store owners. City zoning officials seized this opportunity—caused largely by the failure of the Los Angeles police to protect store owners and homeowners—to impose new rules for the reconstruction of liquor stores, gun shops, secondhand stores, and auto-repair shops. City officials decided that because these were "sensitive use" businesses, they were effectively entitled to prevent the owners from rebuilding. Los Angeles lawyer Craig Collins observed, "Many of the destroyed businesses in South-Central LA were created prior to the 1980s, when the city really got aggressive in applying its zoning power. Now the city council has an opportunity to kill the businesses it doesn't like."[107] The *Los Angeles Times* reported that the rules "have a far wider impact—affecting even grocery stores and gas stations that sell alcohol. For instance, seven gas stations owned and operated by the Atlantic Richfield Co.—the area's biggest gas retailer—remain closed."[108] The city government had no good rationale for the de facto banning of the rebuilding of auto-repair shops; perhaps they thought that making it more difficult for South-Central Los Angeles residents to get old cars repaired would spur the sales of new Mercedes to ghetto residents.

Eleven states currently allow zoning restrictions—i.e., denials of permission to build on one's property—based on aesthetic criteria alone.[109] As Kenneth Regan noted in the *Fordham Law Review:*

> There are several variations of architectural design regulations. Some ordinances contain anti-similarity provisions permitting an architectural board to disapprove a permit for excessive similarity to any other standing or approved structure within a specified distance. These provisions are designed to avoid block after block of homogeneous housing. In contrast, other communities have established regulations prohibiting excessive differences between structures. These provisions seek to encourage some amount of homogeneity. Another type of ordinance prohibits building of structures that are "inappropriate" in design. Finally, some communities enact statutes which, oddly enough, simultaneously prohibit excessive similarity, dissimilarity, and inappropriateness to the area. All of these architectural review ordinances generally give the board of review power to approve or deny an owner's building permit application based on these aesthetic standards.[110]

On June 27, 1991, a New Jersey appellate court ruled that a town could deny permission to build a subdivision even though a developer's application met all the town's standards, largely because the planning board felt that the development's layout was not the most attractive possible.[111] Zoning officials are sometimes extremely blunt about their need for more power over other people's housing designs. Christina Griffin, a member of the Board of Architectural Review for Hastings-on-Hudson, New York, complained to the *New York Times:* "Clearly we need more clout. Sometimes people are aesthetically blind, and they need guidance. The way things are now there is no fear of this board. People ask our advice, but they don't have to listen to us."[112]

Several states have created master plans to restrict development. In 1973, the Oregon legislature enacted a land-use program to preserve the state's prime farmland. Subsequently, the Oregon Land Conservation and Development Commission proceeded to vastly expand the definition of "prime farmland"—originally estimated at three million acres statewide—and eventually banned development on almost all of the state's twenty-five million rural acres. Bill Moshofsky, vice president of Oregonians in Action, a landowners' organization, complained, "The present policy of Oregon is being interpreted to outlaw a rural lifestyle."[113] Oregonian Gary Eisler complained that if he was denied a building permit for his forest land, the value of his property could fall by over 90 percent.[114] Not only is land being held in farmland use, but farmers have been prohibited from building homes on their own farms or even from parking mobile homes on their farms, so that they can watch their cattle, for more than thirty days out of every six months.[115] State officials banned a farmer from building a house on his eight-acre strawberry farm because they claimed that he could not gross at least

$10,000 a year from his strawberries and thus was not a real farmer by their definition.[116] (The U.S. Department of Agriculture, on the other hand, defines a farmer as anyone who produces over $1,000 in agricultural commodities.)[117] In another case, the state Land Use Board of Appeals ruled that a woman's plan to plant seven acres of Christmas trees and to have two dairy cows on her thirteen acres was not a sufficient agricultural operation in order to allow the woman to build a house on her rural land.[118] In Oregon, property rights depend on counts of cows and Christmas trees. Walter Betschart, who lives thirty miles west of Portland, Oregon, was jailed in 1986 for violating the state plan by leaving 300 autos stored on his land—land that the state decreed must be used only for farming.[119] The end result, Moshofsky complained, is that state government "is mandating higher densities in urban areas, making it more and more difficult to expand urban growth boundaries that have become Berlin walls around all cities in the state. So while rural living is being outlawed, more and more people are being crammed into cities, thereby increasing traffic congestion, using up green space, driving up the cost of land and destroying the quality of life for many urban dwellers."[120]

Farmers in many other areas have been hog-tied by government restrictions on the conversion of farmland to other uses. In the late 1970s, Baltimore County, Maryland, "effectively zoned its agricultural area to allow only one dwelling per every 50 acres."[121] McHenry County, Illinois, imposed a minimum lot size of 160 acres to protect farmland. *Planning* magazine noted, "More than 500 jurisdictions now have zoning controls to restrict development on prime farmland," affecting tens of millions of acres of farmland.[122] Many older farmers count on being able to sell their farms to give themselves a financial nest egg for retirement or to leave to their children. But because of zoning restrictions, their land value is decimated. While the restrictions are often couched in language glorifying farms and farmers, the officials often have other motivations. A 1992 article in the *APA Journal* (published by the American Planning Association) noted that "because farmland provides nearby urban and exurban land with scenery, privacy and other benefits, there is an amenity value increment to urban and exurban land. . . . Indeed it is easy to conclude that the primary motivation behind farmland preservation is open-space preservation."[123]

In 1979, the New Jersey legislature adopted the Pinelands Protection Act, which decreed that on 400,000 acres of private farm/forest land, only one house would be allowed on each forty acres and "only if the residences are clustered on one-acre lots and the remaining 39 acres allocated to each residence are permanently dedicated to agricultural use by a recorded deed restriction."[124] As a 1985 study noted, under these restraints, "practically no new use was permitted except for blueberry and cranberry farmers."[125] This amounted to a huge loss for Hobart Gardner, who previously would have been allowed to build one house per acre on his 200 acres.[126] Gardner sued the state, and in August 1991, the New Jersey Supreme Court ruled that the law (which sharply devalued his land) did not amount to an unconstitutional taking; the controls were justified because "land itself is a diminishing resource."[127] The court did not mention that land in New Jersey is somehow mysteriously vanishing or being sucked into a black hole, thereby creating an emergency. Instead, the court simply asserted that land "is a diminishing resource," thereby justifying practically any restrictions. In other words, since land is limited, politicians' power must be unlimited.

With zoning, governments now impose restrictions on citizens almost solely for the government's own convenience. In February 1992, Montgomery County, Maryland, chief executive Neal Potter urged a revision of the county's master zoning plan "to concentrate employment and residences near existing public transportation."[128] Thus, the fact that the county government provided (often unreliable) public transportation somehow gave it a trump card to prevent individuals from building homes in areas that government transit planners chose not to serve. In June 1992, the county announced that it might ban the construction of new homes in the eastern part of the county because of possible overcrowding in county schools.[129] Because school officials failed to prepare for future school enrollments, the local government sought to commandeer the use of almost all vacant land in an area where hundreds of thousands of people could live. This is a classic case of the incompetence of the government becoming a pretext to destroy the liberty of the governed. Montgomery County, Maryland, has some of the highest tax rates in the nation—yet it claims to be too poor to afford to allow its citizens to use their property as they wish.

In many places, zoning laws are a tool to fill a city's coffers via legalized extortion. In Washington, D.C., the city zoning board auctions off exemptions to the zoning rules like a medieval church selling dispensations to breakers of the Ten Commandments. The city zoning board's official plan for development was designed in 1958 and is comically out of date and totally fails to reflect the development of the city in the subsequent third of a century.[130] Thus, almost every proposed new building requires some sort of variance from the zoning board. As the *Washington Post* reported, "For six years, the D.C. Zoning Commission has granted zoning variances worth millions of dollars to downtown developers who agreed in return to pump money into low-cost housing and social services in other parts of town."[131] The *National Law Journal* noted, "Other localities have gone further, seeking to link development permits with a new roof on city hall, a fleet of fire trucks or a staff of urban planners."[132]

If there is a housing shortage in the United States, it is largely the result of zoning restrictions. A 1991 report by the federal Department of Housing and Urban Development estimated that the repeal of local zoning bans on subletting rooms in private homes could add up to 3.8 million accessory apartments to the nation's housing supply[133]—more than twenty times the number of apartments built nationwide in 1992.[134] The *Los Angeles Times* noted:

> Roughly one out of every three single-family homes, or about 15 million homes, have enough surplus space to accommodate a new rental unit within their walls. Accessory units do not require development of new land. Accessory apartments don't even require much construction, and cost about one-third as much as to build conventional rental units. Accessory units provide older homeowners with added income, security, companionship. . . .[135]

But most cities restrict or prohibit the creation of accessory apartments in existing housing. Fairfax County, Virginia, announced that it would allow accessory apartments (sometimes called "granny flats") in 1983—but imposed so many restrictions on the permit process that only thirty units were legally sanctioned in ten years.[136] The Prince William County, Virginia, Board of Supervisors formally rejected a proposal to permit accessory apartments for the elderly and handicapped; county planning director Roger Snyder explained, "If a house with an accessory unit were to come on the market, I think the buyer would have the idea to live for free by renting out the other half." County zoning enforcement officer Sager Williams observed, "It does penalize those who want to do things right, but the enforcement problems would be overwhelming."[137] The convenience of the regulators is now more important than the rights of the property owner.

Some of the same politicians who bewail the shortage of affordable housing routinely severely restrict the construction of apartments in their own domain. In Prince George's County, Maryland, "less than 1 percent of the developable land is zoned for apartments, while in neighboring Montgomery County, only 2 percent of the developable land" is zoned for apartments.[138] The federal Advisory Commission on Regulatory Barriers to Affordable Housing (known as the Kemp Commission) reported in 1991 that zoning and other restrictions add up to 35 percent to the price of a new home.[139] The National Association of Home Builders estimates that government regulations knock over one million home buyers out of the market in the nation's twenty-five largest metropolitan areas.[140] The state of California tried to counter the inflationary effects of zoning restrictions by imposing quotas for low-income housing for every community in California. The affluent communities of San Marino and Bradbury met the law's requirements by classifying maid's quarters and servant's cottages as low-income housing.[141]

Zoning advocates sometimes seem to glorify zoning's arbitrariness. Sylvia Lewis, editor of *Planning* magazine, observed in a 1991 article, "You can think of planning as a giant Monopoly game—with the board representing all the land in town and the moves representing the rules of land-use law. But in real life, as opposed to the games, the rules are always changing."[142] Zoning rules are binding only on citizens, not on governments, who can make hundreds of thousands of exemptions, variances, or revisions to their master plans each year. And because zoning officials in most states effectively have absolute immunity against lawsuits from property owners, there is little to restrain their creativity.

The reigning principle of legislation in the former Soviet Union was, "Everything is prohibited which is not specifically permitted."[143] The American Planning Association recommends a similar rule to subjugate American citizens:

> As a matter of legislative drafting, it is good practice to include a general 'violations' section in zoning regulations that, in part, says, "It shall be a violation of this ordinance to make any use of property not expressly permitted by this ordinance or a permit or other approval granted hereunder."[144]

This is the situation already existing in many areas in the United States. As zoning expert Dick Cowden observed, "Anyone who buys property and hopes to alter its use is considered, almost by definition, to be in violation of a land-use plan."[145]

Government abuses of zoning laws were clearly foreseen back in 1926 by Supreme Court justice Willis Van Devanter. That year, the Court upheld a Euclid, Indiana, zoning code that imposed stringent land-use controls primarily to boost the value of favored areas of the town. In his dissent, Justice Van Devanter wrote, "The plain truth is that the true object of the ordinance in question is to place all property in a strait-jacket. The purpose to be accomplished is really to regulate the mode of living of persons who may hereafter inhabit [the community]. In the last analysis, the result to be accomplished is to classify the population and segregate them according to their income or situation in life."[146] The Supreme Court's 1926 seal of approval on zoning became an invitation for politicians to assert almost unlimited control over private citizens' use of their land.

Some restrictions on private land use are both necessary and beneficial. Zoning controls for public safety are rational and defensible; there is no need to allow the building of an ammunition plant next to an apartment building. Long before the advent of government zoning, American cities restricted development through the imposition of codes for fire prevention, building safety, and the abatement of public nuisances.[147] As University of Chicago professor Richard Epstein wrote, "Zoning should be confined to the prevention of ordinary nuisances, or on limited occasion to overcoming certain collective-action problems, as with the placement of signs over public streets and sidewalks."[148] But the current level of control has gone far beyond any reasonable concept of public safety.

CONFISCATION BY THE CALENDAR

Across America, the older a house becomes, the less right homeowners have to control their own property. The power to pronounce the magic word *historic* gives thousands of government officials the power to instantly strip any property owner of the right to control his residence. Property owners are being turned into indentured serfs of historic preservation commissions.

There are now over 1,800 state and local historic preservation ordinances.[149] A California historical commission designated a 1949 Bob's Big Boy restaurant as a historical landmark over the fierce objections of the owner.[150] The Montgomery County, Maryland, historic commission proposed in 1993 to designate a pet cemetery as a historic landmark.[151] A 1950s motel in New Jersey was designated as a historic landmark.[152]

Preservationists have "progressed" from targeting specific buildings to targeting neighborhoods to targeting entire cities for strict, government-enforced controls. The Escondido, California, city government designated all buildings more than fifty years old as historic structures and prohibited owners from demolishing them without paying a large demolition fee to the city government. The owner of one rickety, boarded-up old shack was stopped from selling it, even though he offered three times to donate the shack to the city as long as the city would pay to move the shack away.[153] (The city government rejected his offers.)

In the 1950s, intellectuals denounced prevailing suburban architecture styles (uniform, box-type houses) as proof of the soullessness of American culture. In the 1990s, activists on historic preservation boards are decreeing that 1950s neighborhoods are so special that local police must prohibit homeowners from improving their homes' exteriors. In Hanover, Virginia, the local government imposed strict preservation controls over a forty-three-acre tract surrounding an old courthouse. One outraged woman retaliated by placing tacky pink flamingoes on her front lawn. Elmyra Taylor complained, "I cannot paint my house, I cannot paint the fence, I cannot remove trees or tree limbs without permission from an architectural review board and county supervisors, who have been most unreasonable."[154]

In January 1991, the Washington, D.C., Historic Preservation Review Board imposed historic landmark status on a boarded-up, deteriorating, four-story apartment building on a stretch of Massachusetts Avenue long since gone to urban hell. The board hailed the apartment building as an "excellent example of the popular transference of many of the forms . . . of the traditional Washington rowhouse to early apartment house design."[155] The building is now a crumbling flophouse that has long been used by vagrants, junkies, and prostitutes; nine fires occurred there over a two-year period. (Ironically, the building sits across from a boarded-up fire station.) The building's owner wants to tear it down and replace it with commercial office space but is tied up in court battles stemming from the building's historic status.[156]

Historic preservation has become a tool for racial discrimination—a strategy to drive up housing prices and drive out poor people. A Department of Housing and Urban Development investigation in 1988 concluded that a decision by Alexandria, Virginia, to designate a fifty-block black neighborhood as a historic district "was specifically intended to displace low- and moderate-income blacks" from their homes "in order to upgrade properties

[and] . . . to promote the rise of property values and attraction of new residents."[157] In Arlington County, Virginia, blacks living in the "historic" Maywood neighborhood bitterly protested in 1991 about being required to submit formal applications and ten copies of forms to get permission to install air-conditioning in their old homes.[158]

Historic preservation restrictions are also increasingly undermining freedom of religion. In 1991, Washington, D.C., imposed a preliminary injunction against a Christian Science church to prevent modification of the church and an office building while the structures were being considered for historic landmark designation. Unfortunately, the Washington Christian Science church exemplifies the worst of modern architecture; as one cynic noted, "This is a building of which Saddam Hussein would be proud. It could take a direct hit with a missile and nothing would happen—it is a solid block of concrete."[159] The church has already spent tens of thousands of dollars in legal fees fighting this case.

St. Bartholomew's Church on New York's Park Avenue sought permission to sell its community house next to the church and replace it with an office high-rise in order to raise $100 million to finance repairs to the church itself and to fund the church's charitable activities. The New York City Landmarks Preservation Commission denied the church's request because of the historic designation of the church. The church sued, and a federal appeals court ruled in 1991: "The church has failed to prove that it cannot continue its religious practice in its existing facilities. . . . So long as the church can continue to use its property in the way that it has been using it—to house its charitable and religious activity—there is no unconstitutional taking."[160] The court's decision redefined property rights to exclude every possible use of property except its current use—effectively giving local governments unlimited power to put private property in a political deep freeze.

Some preservation commissions have acted as if they are entitled to interpret Holy Writ. In 1987, the Boston Landmarks Commission prohibited the Immaculate Conception Church of Boston from altering the lighting, windows, paint scheme, doors, finishes, and a painting of the Assumption of Mary inside the church. The commission justified its sweeping control over the interior of the church on the grounds that the interior "has major aesthetic importance independent of its religious symbolism."[161] The Society of Jesuits, who owned the church, had proposed to renovate the interior in order to reflect architecturally the changes made to the Roman Catholic liturgy during the Second Vatican Council. The Jesuits sued the Boston Landmarks Commission, and the historic designation was eventually overturned by the Massachusetts Supreme Court. As Professor Angela Carmella wrote in the *Villanova Law Review:*

> By determining which religious beliefs are worthy of architectural expression, the state compels affirmation of particular religious beliefs. . . . Design control involves

> fundamental threats to religious liberty . . . because they result from the state's conviction that it can codesign religious architecture, consequently reserving for itself a role as co-author of doctrine and worship and of religious expression. For the state to require the maintenance of the painting of the Virgin Mary and to deny permission to replace it with another image of Mary, an image of another figure, or no image at all, is not the preservation of aesthetic or historical values. The state is passing judgment on a tenet of faith, determining the appropriate image for the visual environment of the sanctuary.[162]

Chicago, on the other hand, passed a landmarks ordinance that allowed religious properties to exempt themselves from historic designation. The National Trust for Historic Preservation was outraged and warned that such an ordinance was unconstitutional because it "has the purpose and effect of endorsing religion, in violation of the First Amendment establishment clause."[163] In other words, if the government is effectively persecuting property owners in general, it is unconstitutional if the government does not also persecute churches.

In 1991 Texas passed a statute requiring any owner who intended to damage a designated historic landmark in any way to get permission from the local government or from the Texas Historical Commission before acting. Anice Read of the Texas Historical Commission warned, "Those not securing the required permits would be required to reconstruct the structure or to make just compensation to the city or to the Texas Historical Commission of an amount equal to the value of the structure."[164] The Texas statute vivifies the real meaning of historic preservation controls: once controls are imposed, the government becomes the de facto owner—and the property owner must compensate the government for any damage he does to the government's property.

Many preservationists appear to hold a Manifest Destiny attitude toward other people's property. In 1990, Pamela Plumb, a Portland, Maine, city council member, asserted: "An historic district ordinance acknowledges the community's interest in the history of the city and therefore the community's right to have some control over that."[165] According to Councilwoman Plumb's logic, the community automatically has a right to control anything in which community members are interested. Jackson Walter, president of the National Trust for Historic Preservation, commenting on cases in which a homeowner in a large historic district makes unapproved modifications, complained, "When someone bolts and says all of this is fine but I want vinyl windows or a third floor or skylights, that attacks the authenticity of the whole community. That threatens the future of historic districts."[166] The notion that installing new windows is an attack on the entire community is peculiar—and an example of how the preservation movement is maximizing intolerance among neighbors.

Power lust sometimes appears to be the driving force of the preservation movement. Laurie Beckelman, chairwoman of the New York City Landmarks Commission, hailed the St. Bartholomew's court ruling as affirming the commission's "absolute power . . . to designate and regulate religious properties as landmarks."[167] Chuck Geitner, chairman of the Naperville, Illinois, Historic District Commission, with jurisdiction over a sixty-block area, announced in 1991, "We listen to people, and, when we think it's appropriate, we grant them the power to do what they wish."[168] David Caney, chief of the District of Columbia Building and Land Regulation Administration, complained in March 1992 that activists demanded harsh penalties for people who modified their homes in violation of historic restrictions: "The preservationists want punishment and retaliation."[169]

Preservationists often sound as if they wish to summon the local police to enforce their own sentimentality. *Washington Post* architectural critic Benjamin Forgey wrote in 1991: "There's a simple test one can apply [to determine whether government should impose preservation controls]: Stand in front of such a building, close your eyes and picture it gone. If the result is that you would really, really miss it, then it may need help."[170] This is a wonderful guide to decide whether to effectively expropriate property owners—simply whether people would "really, really miss" seeing a certain building. Forgey's statement exemplifies the self-indulgent nature of preservationists, who try to seize control of other people's land solely because of their emotional preferences. As Mel Garbow, a Washington land-use lawyer, observed, historic preservationists "are like butterfly collectors: they don't have any appreciation for butterflies, they just want to have another one for their collection trophy case. You have a small group of politically adroit people who create a kind of city museum by requiring individual owners to make their buildings exhibitions in this museum."[171]

Preservationists have advocated that buildings almost automatically be classified as historic when they become fifty years old. Yet according to the U.S. Census Bureau, there are over eighteen million housing units in the United States that were built before 1940—almost 20 percent of the nation's housing stock.[172] Does an individual's right to control his own property automatically decline by 2 percent a year?

The National Trust for Historic Preservation saves its greatest hostility for those who advocate respect for private property rights. (The National Trust for Historic Preservation receives $7 million from the federal government each year.)[173] Arnold Berke, editor of the Trust's *Historic Preservation News*, declared, "Many of those who mouth this claim [about property rights] are opportunists and extremists" and declaimed, "The public interest in the use of private land must be defended."[174] Preservationists sometimes recognize that preservation controls can heavily burden an individual property owner. Their solution: allowing the homeowner to apply for a "certificate of economic hardship" from the local preservation board. In other words, a person must plead poverty in order to be permitted to modify his own home. This is the perfect inversion of property rights: the government has no obligation to justify taking control of the individual's property, but the individual must grovel to government officials to be allowed to modify his own property.

Some courts are beginning to rein in the power of historic commissions. In July 1991, the Pennsylvania Supreme Court struck down a historic designation imposed on a movie theater by the Philadelphia Historical Commission. The court concluded that by imposing the historic designation, the commission "obtained almost absolute control over the property, including the physical details and the uses to which it could be put" and that the theater owner would be "legally obligated to obtain permission from the Commission to move a mirror from one wall to another."[175] The court derided the process for historic designation in Philadelphia and most other locales, noting that it was "troubled by a procedure where the commission . . . recommends properties for historical designation, provides the testimony and evidence in support of its recommendation, argues the case for historical designation . . . and then decides whether the property it recommended should be so designated. There is an obvious lack of due process in such a procedure." In a similar case, on December 4, 1991, Ohio judge Lee Bixler struck down the historic preservation ordinance of Dayton, Ohio, as "a confiscatory measure which violates the Fifth Amendment . . . The ordinance takes the [warehouse] and deprives the owners of any real use for the structure."[176]

LOST IN THE SWAMPS

In 1900 the Supreme Court characterized wetlands as "the cause of malarial and malignant fevers" and proclaimed that "the police power is never more legitimately exercised than in removing such nuisances."[177] Later in the century, politicians changed their minds about wetlands. Currently, federal officials often act as if "the police power is never more legitimately exercised" than in punishing and imprisoning private citizens who want to modify property they own that federal agents allege to be wet.

On November 25, 1991, William Reilly, chief administrator of the Environmental Protection Agency, held a press conference to brag that the EPA had "once again had a record year for enforcement . . . Environmental crime is no less a crime than theft or blackmail or assault. And more and more assuredly, if you do the crime you'll do the time."[178] The federal government's war on violators of wetland regulations was part of Reilly's achievements—and an example of racking up a political body count of violators of unclear, contradictory, and constantly changing federal rulings.

Wetlands serve valuable environmental functions: providing a habitat for many species of fish and wildlife, storing floodwaters, and acting as a natural filter to improve water quality and help moderate local temperature and precipitation. Wetlands are also an important breeding ground for waterfowl. Unfortunately, U.S. Army Corps of Engineers projects have destroyed much of the nation's wetlands over the last ninety years, and lavish agricultural subsidies have encouraged farmers to plow under millions of additional acres of wetlands. Although the nation has lost much of its wetlands, there is no evidence that the nation faces an imminent shortage of swampland. In fact, a 1991 survey by the Fish and Wildlife Service estimated that "from the late 1970s until the mid-1980s . . . the U.S. actually gained 500,000 acres of wetlands a year."[179] (Other studies dispute this finding.)

From the early days of the republic, the U.S. government claimed jurisdiction over all navigable waters in the nation. In 1972, Congress passed the Clean Water Act to, among other things, restrict the pollution of navigable waters. The Army Corps of Engineers received the power to approve or deny permits to discharge dirt or other materials into navigable waters, and Congress gave the EPA the power to veto Army Corps' permits. In 1975, a federal judge revealed that the Clean Water Act also applied to wetlands that were adjacent to navigable waters.

In 1988 presidential candidate George Bush declared that "all existing wetlands, no matter how small, should be preserved" and promised "no net loss" of wetlands if elected president.[180] Bush's promise was a go-ahead signal for federal regulators to greatly expand the definition of wetlands. A few days after Bush was sworn in, EPA and the Army Corps of Engineers publicly released the Federal Manual for Identifying and Delineating Jurisdictional Wetlands, which contained a new definition of wetlands that repudiated the numerous preceding definitions of wetlands promulgated by federal agencies. The new manual was written in secret; officials of several federal agencies met behind closed doors and effectively decided between themselves to claim jurisdiction over the property of hundreds of thousands of American landowners. This was a stark violation of the federal Administrative Procedures Act, which requires public notice and comment before a major federal regulation acquires the force of law.

Under the 1989 definition, land that was dry 350 days a year could be classified as a wetland. Even land that had no water on the surface could be classified as a "federal jurisdictional wetland."[181] Fairness to Land Owners, a Maryland advocacy group, estimated that the new definition magically increased the amount of wetlands in the United States from roughly 100 million acres to up to 200 million acres. The vast majority of these new "paper wetlands" were owned by private citizens.[182] Robert J. Pierce, an Army Corps of Engineers official who helped to write the 1989 manual, later observed, "Ecologically speaking, the term 'wetland' has no meaning: natural systems exist on a hydrologic gradient from ocean to desert. Somewhere in the middle are what society calls wetlands. For regulatory purposes, a wetland is whatever we decide it is. The type of natural systems that have been defined as wetlands has changed virtually every year for the last decade."[183]

Federal bureaucrats enforced the new definition with a vengeance:

- Ronald Angelocci dumped several truckloads of dirt in the backyard of his Michigan home largely because a family member had acute asthma and allergies that were severely aggravated by the plants growing in the backyard. The Army Corps of Engineers decided to make an example out of Angelocci, launched a full-court offensive, and had him jailed for violating the Clean Water Act.[184]
- Ocie Mills, a Florida builder, and his son were sent to prison for two years for placing clean sand on a quarter-acre lot he owned.[185]
- Rep. James Hayes observed, "In Nevada, [housing] developments in the midst of cactus and parched earth are now being classified as 'wetlands' because standing water can occur for 7 days in a hole dug for a foundation. The fact that such a rain occurs very rarely no longer seems relevant in what was once considered a desert state, but which is now 'The Great Wetlands State.'"[186]
- A small Oregon school district was hit by a federal lawsuit for dumping clean fill to build a baseball-soccer field for its students and had to spend thousands of dollars to remove the fill.[187]

Congress specified in the Clean Water Act that normal farming practices and operations should be exempt from federal controls. But the Army Corps of Engineers evaded this limit on its power by issuing a "clarification" of federal law that announced that, from the Corps' perspective, cranberries, apples, blueberries, hay, and alfalfa were not agricultural commodities—and thus that those farmers were subject to the Corps' control.[188] A Louisiana family wanted to use eighty acres of land to build a crawfish pond and spent $35,000 to get the federal permits. But at the last minute, the EPA denied permission because: "High quality habitats such as these provide food, shelter, nesting and spawning areas to a wide variety of game and non-game fish and wildlife species including the red swamp crawfish." Rep. Billy Tauzin of Louisiana denounced the EPA for "denying a permit to raise crawfish in an area they say should be used to raise crawfish. That is Alice in Wonderland reasoning there."[189] (EPA officials may have been so accustomed to denying permits that they did not even read the application.) Federal officials in Arkansas prohibited farmers from constructing levees for rice production—even though this would increase the amount of wetlands.[190] Rep. Bill Brewster of Oklahoma complained of receiving a deluge of protests from Oklahoma residents over "the Army Corps of Engineers' and the EPA's intimidation of farmers and ranchers. Many private property owners who make their living off the land, and have for generations, are being told that they can no longer engage in normal ranching or farming activities. They have lost the ability to use their land to support their families."[191] Former Justice Department attorney William Laffer observed, "Any time the Army Corp or EPA think a parcel of land is beneficial to wildlife, they arbitrarily apply the wetlands definition to prohibit the owner from using the land."[192]

The U.S. government sent Bill Ellen, a Vietnam veteran and marine engineer, to prison for building duck ponds as part of a wildlife sanctuary on Maryland's Eastern Shore. Ellen began the construction of the wildlife sanctuary in 1988 after getting thirty-eight government permits and having been advised by Army Corps of Engineers officials that the land was not classified as wetlands. In February 1989, armed with a new definition of wetlands, an Army Corps official reversed his position and arrived on the scene with a cease-and-desist order. Although Ellen ceased construction within forty-eight hours, the Army Corps still prosecuted him. Though environmental regulators tend to deify ducks, the Army Corps in this case claimed that Ellen was a polluter in part because the ponds he constructed attracted ducks, which generated waterfowl fecal matter.[193] Ellen had created at least four times as many wetlands as he may have impaired, yet the U.S. government fought tooth-and-nail to send Ellen to prison; a federal prosecutor demanded that "those who commit criminal environmental insults [should] come to learn and appreciate the inside of a federal correctional facility."[194] After the Army Corps had Ellen arrested, they dynamited his duck ponds to create a 400-yard channel connecting the land to a body of salt water—thereby destroying many of the environmental benefits from his project.[195]

The EPA and the Army Corps claim that their wetlands authority extends to almost every moist patch of land of more than a few square feet in the country. In April 1992, federal judge Daniel Manion struck down part of EPA's expansive definition of wetlands. EPA had imposed a $50,000 penalty on Hoffman Homes Inc. for placing excavated dirt on "navigable waters"—eight-tenths of an acre in an isolated corner of its development near Chicago. Judge Manion noted, "The EPA claims jurisdiction over the intrastate wetland solely on the ground that migratory birds could, potentially, use the wetland as a place to feed, or nest or as a stopover on the way to the Gulf States for the winter months."[196] (This became known as "the glancing geese" test. If passing geese might glance down and consider stopping at a water hole, and the geese were on a flight that crossed state lines, then that water hole and the surrounding land became involved in interstate commerce and thus fell under federal jurisdiction.) Even an area as small as one-hundredth of an acre (twenty feet by twenty feet) can fall under federal control as the result of passing birds.[197] EPA has argued that isolated wetlands are indirectly involved in interstate commerce in part because duck hunters often cross state lines in their pursuit of ducks.[198] Manion noted, "In fact, there is not even any evidence that migratory birds, or any other wildlife, actually used [the area] for any purpose."[199] The government appealed the decision, and the case was remanded to the same panel of Seventh Circuit judges. In the second decision, the judges narrowed the scope of their ruling, finding for Hoffman Homes but allowing EPA to retain its "glancing geese" test. The court once again admonished the government: "After April showers not every temporary wet spot necessarily becomes subject to government control."[200]

Unfortunately, the court's pretty words will have no effect as force of law, so EPA officials can continue claiming jurisdiction over areas based on passing ducks. Lawyer Virginia Albrecht noted that the EPA invented its "glancing geese" test (referred to by the agency as the "reasonable bird" rule) in 1985.[201] Although the rule was never officially announced as federal law, EPA officials have applied the bird rule in thousands of cases. Because the EPA never formally announced the rule, a federal court in the Fourth Circuit struck it down in 1989. EPA has repeatedly promised to formally promulgate the regulation, but has never done so. The EPA is still using the "glancing geese" test to claim jurisdiction over private land in most regions of the United States.

The 1989 wetlands regulations devastated the construction industry in many areas. In the New England and Seattle regions, the Army Corps of Engineers approved only 8 percent of applications for construction in late 1990 and early 1991 because of concerns of possible wetlands violations.[202] In Chatham County, Georgia, near Savannah, the Army Corps did not issue a single construction permit between early 1989 and early 1991, and EPA officials ordered developers to tear down new houses after the agency decided that the Army Corps had mistakenly classified land as non-wetlands several years earlier.[203] Hampton, Virginia, mayor James Eason said, of the corps' sweeping findings of wetlands in his area, "It's conceivable it could halt *all* development in the city of Hampton."[204] Bernard Goode, former chief regulatory official of the Army Corps, publicly complained that as a result of the 1989 manual, "the regulated sector was on the verge of anarchy."[205]

Wetland classification routinely amounts to a near-total nullification of the value of property. A New Jersey judge ruled that the classification of a 240-acre tract of land near East Rutherford as wetlands officially lowered its assessed value from $20 million to only $1 million.[206] The Southeast Planning District of Virginia estimated that the revised definition of wetland could potentially cut property values by up to $50 billion in its area.[207] Former White House environmental analyst Jonathan Tolman estimated, based on one study of the effect of wetlands designations on property values, that wetlands rulings may cost local governments nationwide over $6 billion in lost property taxes a year.[208] The U.S. Claims court has awarded landowners over $10 million in just compensation, interest, and legal fees in cases involving takings claims over wetlands designations.[209]

The Clinton White House released an official position paper on wetland policy in August 1993, proclaiming a national goal of no net loss of wetlands. The White House conceded that the definition of wetlands used by EPA and the Army Corps of Engineers extends federal control over far more private land than is authorized by legislation enacted by Congress. The White House proposed a simple solution to the problem: "Congress should amend the Clean Water Act to make it consistent with the agencies' rulemaking."[210] With this single sentence, the Clinton administration effectively sought to codify the nature of modern government: Congress as a tail being wagged by the federal bureaucracy. In earlier eras, the statement that federal agencies were imposing burdens and restrictions on private landowners that were not justified by federal law would be a confession that the government was violating people's rights. But nowadays, it is simply a technicality requiring a few words from Congress to retroactively sanctify the actions of lawless bureaucrats.

Kathleen McGinty, director of the White House Office on Environmental Policy, declared of the new policy: "This plan is balanced and *fair*."[211] The White House paper asserted, "In rare instances the public interest in conserving wetlands may substantially interfere with the rights of landowners."[212] But 75 percent of the wetlands in the lower forty-eight states are privately owned—and most of the EPA's and Army Corps' actions banning development on wetlands and alleged wetlands substantially interfere with landowners rights. (In 1992, fewer than half of the applications nationwide for development on so-called wetlands were approved by the Army Corps of Engineers.)[213] The White House asserted, "Where a property owner believes that government action amounts to a taking, the courts are available to review such claims and to determine whether compensation is due. Due to the unique nature of each situation, these issues must be considered on a case-by-case basis."[214] But property owners routinely have to spend hundreds of thousands of dollars contesting federal actions on wetlands in court. In the case of Loveladies Harbor, a New Jersey development partially blocked by a wetlands designation, the dispute has been going on for over fifteen years, despite repeated findings that the federal government violated the property owners' rights; both of the original owners of the land have since died.

While EPA and the Army Corps have heavily fined many farmers for wetlands violations, the U.S. Department of Agriculture followed a different wetlands policy. Keith Bjerke, a high-ranking USDA official, gave North Dakota farmers explicit permission in 1989 to drain 6,500 acres of swampland in order to expand their crop acreage.[215] While the EPA was sending people to prison for filling a quarter-acre of wetlands, USDA—by promising farmers lavish subsidies for future crops—effectively underwrote the destruction of thousands of acres of wetlands. Federal farm price subsidies far above market prices provide a strong incentive for farmers to produce more crops than they otherwise would, thereby encouraging them to bring more land into production than would otherwise be planted. Federal price supports and strict import quotas are the main reasons why sugar is still produced in Florida—and sugar production is the main reason why the Everglades are being poisoned, with the loss of thousands of acres of wetland each year. But it is easier for politicians to send federal agencies on vendettas against landowners than to end the gravy train for selected campaign contributors.

OTHER ENVIRONMENT-RELATED TAKINGS

In 1958 the federal government began offering bonus payments to states that agreed to ban or restrict billboards along federal highways; most states rejected the federal program. In 1965 President Lyndon Johnson commanded states to "beautify or else!" with the Highway Beautification Act.[216] State governments that did not ban billboards along federally financed highways (except in business or industrial areas) faced reductions in their federal highway trust fund allocations—even though the trust fund consisted of gasoline taxes paid by motorists in all states.

With the Highway Beautification Act, Congress effectively ruled that one person's property rights should be constrained by other people's field of vision. Rep. Richard Hanna complained in 1965: "Each person using an automobile is forced to view unsightly sections of the road."[217] Politicians spoke as if driving through an area should automatically convey a right of ownership and control over everything the driver sees. The more freedom of movement private automobiles gave some people, the more intolerant they became of how other people used their private property. The *Rocky Mountain News* warned: "If it is a proper function of State government to determine what is aesthetically pleasing, what is 'nice' or 'not nice,' then every business and personal activity in which we engage is subject to the dictates of elected or appointed officials."[218]

The 1965 act banned billboards within 660 feet of rural federally funded highways. Naturally, businesses began putting up larger signs just outside the 660-foot limit. In 1974, Congress vastly extended controls by banning billboards within the "limit of vision" from roadways—imposing government controls over the use of land for as far as the eye could see.

Some highway officials invoked the beautification act to harass roadside residents. The American Farm Bureau complained in 1979 that highway officials told "farmers that they cannot have their own farm machinery and equipment parked in sight of a highway and that it must be stored in sheds or barns."[219] Other farmers were commanded to move their fuel storage tanks away from the highway side of their farmhouses "so as not to be unsightly to highway users."[220] Federal billboard restrictions had a harsh impact on tourist industries in sparsely populated western states that depended on drawing in passing tourists. South Dakota governor William Janklow declared in 1979, "No federal law in my experience has caused more unnecessary controversy and divisiveness than the federal billboard control laws. . . . Under the existing circumstances in my state the federal beautification sanctions are nothing more than blackmail."[221]

The ban on rural billboards greatly increases the amount of property that government effectively commandeers when it puts in a road—and thus compounds the damage to rural landowners. Much of the roadside land used for billboards has little value for other uses. People living next to an interstate are obliged to listen to eighteen-wheelers thundering by twenty-four hours a day yet are routinely prohibited from profiting from the nuisance.

River scenery has become politically popular in recent years, so, naturally, politicians are commandeering the use of thousands of miles of land along rivers. Since 1968, 119 rivers have been declared by Congress to be "wild, scenic or recreational," three categories that allow the U.S. Department of the Interior to restrict owners of riverside land from developing their property.[222] Once Congress blesses a river with a "wild" or "scenic" label, the National Park Service becomes very aggressive against landowners; in 1991, the Park Service announced it would begin condemnation proceedings against any landowner along the St. Croix River in Wisconsin and Minnesota whose activity resulted in "any residential or commercial development which is within sight of the river" or "any use which would require a variance of any zoning regulations."[223] As of mid-1991, there were over 3,000 federal condemnation cases pending against private landowners as the result of the Wild and Scenic Rivers Act.[224]

In 1986, Congress declared that the Columbia River Gorge was a wild and scenic river, thereby imposing controls on citizens who owned land near the river. It was ironic that Congress was so concerned about any private development along the riverbanks, since the U.S. Army Corps of Engineers, along with other congressionally authorized projects, had already severely disrupted the river with over thirty major dams and reservoirs. Environmentalist Zach Willey notes of the dams and reservoirs: "Operated by more than a dozen federal agencies . . . they have been major destroyers of salmon and steelhead habitats."[225] The U.S. Forest Service announced that, in order to minimize development, forty acres of land would subsequently be required for the construction of any new home. Skamania County, Washington, residents voted ten to one against the proposed scenic river restrictions but were still dragooned under federal controls.[226] Government officials dictate what colors families can paint their homes and even decreed that local homes cannot function as bed-and-breakfasts except for those listed on a historic register—and even those houses cannot serve breakfast to hunters or fishermen before 5:00 A.M.[227] In the original act, Congress promised to provide $35 million in aid to the six counties that would be most heavily impacted by the restrictions, but later reneged.[228]

In 1985 the New York Department of Environmental Conservation banned all development and nullified all previously granted building permits for sites within half a mile of a sixteen-mile stretch of the Peconic River on Long Island. The decision by the state administrators halted hundreds of planned projects and basically took control of the lands of 4000 people. Hundreds of homeowners were prohibited from making any alterations or repairs to the outsides of their homes without written permission from the state agency. The ruling imposed strict controls on the side of Main Street in Riverhead, New York, that fell within the half-mile, destroying local officials' efforts to revitalize Riverhead's downtown.[229] The value of the land that was placed under the restrictions plummeted to half its previous value.[230] All existing businesses in the restricted zone were prohibited from altering the current use of their premises unless it was in some way related to the river (such as selling bait to fishermen).[231]

EMINENT DOMAIN FOR FUN AND PROFIT

For the first 175 years of the American republic, it was clearly recognized that government should not casually seize people's property and give it to other people for their private use. The Supreme Court ruled in 1937 that "one person's property may not be taken for the benefit of another private person without a justifying public purpose, even though compensation be paid."[232] But recent decades have witnessed a collapse of judicial restraint on legislatures' and city councils' proclamations of public purposes. Nowadays, anything that benefits some politician or some political interest group is practically considered a bona fide "public purpose."

Martin Anderson, author of the classic 1964 study *The Federal Bulldozer*, observed, "The federal urban renewal program has drastically altered the traditional concept of eminent domain."[233] Urban renewal was launched in 1949 to, among other goals, achieve "the realization as soon as feasible of the goal of a decent home and a suitable living environment for every American family." Between 1949 and 1971, however, urban renewal razed five times as many low-income housing units as it created[234] and evicted over one million people from their homes.[235]

In one of the first major challenges to the federal urban renewal program, a federal district court struck down a Washington, D.C., land seizure program in 1953:

> There is no more subtle means of transforming the basic concepts of our government, or shifting from the preeminence of individual rights, to the preeminence of government wishes, than is afforded by redefinition of "general welfare," as that term is used to define the Government's power of seizures. . . . In essence the claim is that if slums exist the Government may seize, redevelop and sell all the property in any area it may select as appropriate, so long as the area includes the slum area. This amounts to a claim on the part of the authorities for unreviewable power to seize and sell whole sections of the city.[236]

But in November 1954, the Supreme Court overturned the federal district court and effectively gave government officials unlimited power to confiscate and redistribute land. Justice William Douglas, writing for the court, declared, "The concept of the public welfare is broad and inclusive. The values it represents are spiritual as well as physical, aesthetic as well as monetary. It is within the power of the legislature to determine that the community should be beautiful as well as healthy, spacious as well as clean, well-balanced as well as carefully patrolled."[237] Douglas concluded, "Once the object is within the authority of Congress, the right to realize it through the exercise of eminent domain is clear. . . . The rights of these property owners are satisfied when they receive that just compensation which the Fifth Amendment exacts as the price of the taking."

The Supreme Court's decision opened the floodgates to confiscation in the name of renewal. While the Supreme Court effectively showed unlimited faith in the motives and competence of local government officials, the projects themselves rarely succeeded. As Martin Anderson observed, "Buying, moving, and destroying has proved much easier to accomplish than building."[238] The Washington, D.C., project that the Supreme Court approved was a near total flop. The city government, in its brief to the Supreme Court, promised that one-third of the new homes built would be low-rent housing to accommodate poor people displaced by the project. But as a *Pacific Law Journal* article noted, "No low-cost housing was built in the project area"; instead, "the redevelopers constructed a shopping mall and a complex of high-rent apartments and townhouses."[239] Gideon Kanner, a professor at Loyola of Los Angeles Law School, observed, "Urban redevelopment is essentially a wealth transfer program—it now has nothing to do with slum clearance. All kinds of people are getting thrown out of their homes and businesses and they are undercompensated and the land is turned over to a redeveloper who typically puts up a shopping center and makes a fortune."[240]

Urban renewal is based on blind confidence in government planners to coercively reshape American cities. Like Marx, who assumed that utopia would almost automatically occur after the destruction of capitalism, urban planners often act as if the destruction of low-income housing will automatically beget urban utopias. Urban renewal has often been called "Negro removal," because in its first thirteen years, over two-thirds of the people evicted from their dwellings were black or Puerto Rican. By sharply reducing the supply of low-income housing without reducing the number of low-income people, urban renewal drove up the rent for the lowest quality apartments and dwellings in many areas. The General Accounting Office concluded in 1963 that urban renewal "contributed to a shortage of housing for low and moderate income families," thus harming the people the program was allegedly intended to help.

Federal community development funds are still bankrolling the razing of large areas of American cities. Tom Gogan, a New York City housing activist, reported that since 1979 federal funds have helped pay for the destruction of up to 30,000 apartments in New York City.[241] In Asheville, North Carolina, federal funds helped pay for the destruction of 190 low-income housing units between 1979 and 1987.[242] Almost half of the low-cost housing units in downtown Cincinnati have been destroyed as a result of redevelopment activities since 1970.[243]

The history of urban renewal is largely the history of politicians' broken promises. The Boston Redevelopment Agency proudly announced in 1990 that it would begin building housing for families displaced by the urban renewal demolitions of the 1950s.[244] In 1965, the city of New York evicted 1,300 families on the Lower East Side for an urban renewal project, promising the evictees that they would have first dibs on housing to be built to replace the demolished units. But in 1988, the city government announced plans to permit the building of luxury apartments on the site instead.[245]

While the pace of urban renewal has slackened, local governments continue to forcibly redistribute land from the politically weak to the politically strong. In Brooklyn, New York, one business owner affected by a $770 million urban renewal project was Kam Chin, who, with her husband, lost her art supply store, which she had spent fifteen years building up. Chin had fled China in 1969 after the Communist government seized her father's art supply store. The *New York Times* noted, "The couple see little difference between the tactics of the Chinese Communists and the city. 'They're doing the same thing,' Mrs. Chin said of the city. 'They condemn my property. They take it away like in a Communist country. Not only that but they give it to the rich. The whole thing is really sick.'"[246] John Weicher, assistant secretary of Housing and Urban Development during the Bush administration, observed, "The typical urban renewal project harms the poor and helps the rich by raising housing prices for the former and lowering them for the latter."[247] In a 1993 decision, a California appeals court ruled that Santa Ana, California, had violated the law by neglecting its legal obligation to provide replacement housing for the evictees. The judges noted, "At oral argument before the trial court, the city asserted identification of replacement housing would constitute an 'impossible' burden. . . . The city reiterated its position that it is 'enough' simply to promise adequate replacement housing rather than actually identify it."[248]

Single-room occupancy hotels (SROs) were vigorously eradicated in many cities until the mid-1980s, in part because city planners felt that SROs were inherently blighted. George McDonald, executive director of the Doe Fund, a nonprofit housing group, observed: "In the city of New York, there were laws passed to push the private sector out of the SRO business on the theory that SROs were inhumane. Consequently, people sleep on grates outside."[249] New York City, after decades of condemning and razing SROs, reversed itself in 1985 and banned all privately owned SROs from being destroyed or converted to other uses; owners were required to pay the city government $45,000 for each SRO unit that they destroyed as well as build a replacement unit.[250] This is a case of city officials using eminent domain on both sides of the same issue—first invoking it to destroy private property and then invoking it to prevent owners from modifying their own property. The only consistency in the politicians' position was the notion that they themselves should have absolute power over housing markets. The New York Supreme Court struck down New York City's SRO preservation law in 1991, ruling: "We believe it is evident . . . that the moratorium and antiwarehousing provisions inevitably force property owners alone to bear public burdens which, in all fairness and justice, should be borne by the public as a whole" and that the law violates the takings clause of the state and federal constitutions.[251]

In 1979, San Francisco, after bulldozing thousands of low-income housing units in previous decades, forced owners of low-priced hotels to set aside a certain number of their rooms for use by local low- and moderate-income families. Adam Sparks, a San Francisco hotel owner, refused to comply, claiming that the ordinance would bankrupt him. City officials retorted that the planning code gave the government a right to dictate how each room would be used and ordered Sparks to rent sixty-nine of his eighty-nine rooms to local residents. Tourists paid $65 a night for Sparks's rooms, but he could charge the locals only $100 to $150 a week. Sparks still refused to comply and was fined $100,000 and sentenced to six months in jail. He complained:

> In any other community in this entire nation a hotel owner who rents rooms to tourists would be considered an upstanding citizen and entrepreneur. . . . In San Francisco they are hunted and jailed. It's insane. Can you imagine the government conducting a survey that identifies all the vacant guest bedrooms in the city's single-family homes, and subsequently passing a law commanding those homeowners to rent those rooms to low-income persons? And furthermore enforcing this Draconian mandate under penalty of imprisonment?[252]

U.S. District Judge John Vukasin, Jr., denounced the San Francisco law as a "heinous and egregiously horrid solution . . . To say the ordinance is unfair and unjust is a gross understatement. It is an unconscionable and flagrantly unreasonable attempt to solve a social problem."[253] Vukasin could not rule on the law's validity but declared that he believed it unconstitutional.[254] Sparks was driven into bankruptcy by the heavy fine and the legal fees from his fight with the city government.[255]

Local and state governments routinely abuse their power to label land as "blighted" in order to avoid paying people fair value for land they intend to seize. The *Los Angeles Times* reported in 1991, "In the tiny but wealthy desert city of Indian Wells, the council sought to resolve a budget crisis by declaring almost the entire city blighted. It planned to use redevelopment funds to build a championship golf course and other incentives to attract luxury resort hotels."[256] The city government of Marion, Illinois, announced that the entire city—including farmland inside the city limits—was blighted.[257] The city council of Mission Viejo, California, sought to declare the entire city "blighted by traffic"—and thus vastly increase their own power over the city's residents.[258] Columnist Dan Walters noted, "Vallejo, California used redevelopment powers to declare a golf course to be blighted so it could be folded into the Marineworld-Africa USA tourist development."[259] The city of Wheaton, Illinois, enacted an ordinance that allowed the city government to declare as blighted (and eligible for eminent domain) any parcel of land that had "vacancies in all or part of any building."[260] Thus, almost any commercial building with vacant space became a candidate for seizure. (An Illinois court overturned the ordinance as excessively vague.) In Columbus, Ohio, a landowner's property was condemned and confiscated because it was being used as a parking lot—and the local Community Urban Redevelopment Corporation declared that the land could be better utilized as a parking garage.[261] Gideon Kanner observed, "Maryland and New York courts have said that the definition of blight includes the possibility that the property would become blighted in the future. You read the definition of blight and it includes most of the city."[262] Pennsylvania Supreme Court judge Genevieve Blatt observed in a 1980 dissenting opinion criticizing the sweep of Pennsylvania's urban renewal law: "The entire scheme for the certification of an area as blighted is weighted against the landowners [and business owners] in favor of the condemnor, leaving the Redevelopment Authority with unbounded, unfettered and limitless discretionary power to appropriate and condemn as dilapidated . . . as large an area as they believe can be made more prosperous."[263]

Politicians now have a blank check to evict almost anyone (in actuality, only the politically unorganized or weak). In 1980, the cities of Detroit and Hamtramck, Michigan, evicted 3,400 people from an area known as Poletown, bulldozed their homes, and gave the razed area to General Motors to build a Cadillac plant.[264] One hundred and fifty businesses, sixteen churches, and one hospital were driven off their land by the cities' action.[265] Most of the evicted businesses received only minimal compensation for their losses. The Michigan Supreme Court upheld the action because the city governments claimed that the destruction of private homes was necessary in order to save jobs. (General Motors had threatened to move its Cadillac plant to some other state if Detroit did not clear space for it.) But a 1989 General Accounting Office investigation found that the new factory hired only fifty-nine workers from the Poletown area.[266] In 1986, Detroit again sought to bulldoze its way to economic salvation, condemning another thousand homes and businesses in order to pave the way for a new Chrysler plant.[267] Despite these valiant efforts, Detroit continued in an economic free fall. In 1993 Detroit's official city ombudsman, Marie Farrell-Donaldson, publicly suggested that the government move residents out of dying neighborhoods and turn the land into an urban pasture.[268]

Hawaiian politicians have used eminent domain to establish their right to seize control of much of the state. In the mid-1960s, local, state, and federal governments owned almost half of the land of Hawaii, with most of the remaining land concentrated in the hands of less than a hundred landowners and large plantation owners. Instead of selling off some of the government's landholdings, Hawaii politicians enacted a law in 1969 allowing them to seize land from private owners for redistribution. In 1975, the Hawaii legislature amended the authorizing legislation to declare that eminent domain must be exercised in part to combat the "inflationary trend" of land prices and announced that the "happiness of the people of the State" would be promoted through the land seizure program.[269] As part of the confiscation program, the Hawaiian government effectively acquired the power to determine who was allowed to buy land for homes, how many lots a buyer could hold, and the price for which they could sell their land. One Hawaiian landowner took the Hawaii Housing Authority to court; the federal Ninth Circuit Court of Appeals denounced the Hawaiian program in 1983 as a "form of majoritarian tyranny . . . We see a naked attempt on the part of Hawaii to take the private property of A and transfer it to B solely for B's private use and benefit."[270] The Supreme Court, however, overturned the Ninth Circuit decision in 1984; writing for the majority, Justice Sandra Day O'Connor observed, "Regulating oligopoly and the evils associated with it is a classic exercise of a state's police powers. . . . We cannot disapprove of Hawaii's exercise of this power."[271] Yet the state government was by far the biggest oligopolist in Hawaii. O'Connor stated that the Hawaiian government's seizure program was a justified response to a "market failure." But the pretext for the land confiscation—the shortage of land for housing—was largely the result of the state government's own policies. Much of the private land in Hawaii is restricted to agricultural uses by state zoning decrees. David Ramsour, chief economist for the Bank of Hawaii, observed: "The real problem here is that the vast majority of the land is tied up in agricultural production that is no longer competitive. Residential land will not become available until the state's plantation economy is restructured."[272] While politicians proclaim that the housing crisis is so severe that it can no longer respect private property rights, the state government leases about 15,000 acres of land a year to the Kekaha Sugar Company for $3.79 an acre.[273] Hawaiian sugar farmers have survived largely because of the federal sugar program. So that Americans can retain the privilege of paying two or three times the world price for their sugar,[274] Hawaiians are denied the opportunity to buy land for a house.

CONCLUSION: HOLDING TITLE AT THE PLEASURE OF THE STATE

If a group of neighbors voted to seize someone's front yard to make a picnic ground for themselves, that would be seen as rank thievery. But if the same neighbors incorporate into a local government, do the same thing, and offer the yard owner only 10 cents compensation on the dollar for his losses, this is supposedly fair play. It is important to have a sounder distinction between democracy and thievery than simply counting votes. The mere decree of a general zoning plan, complete with restrictions on the use of every square foot within city limits, does not make those restrictions legitimate. Simply because the local police have the firepower to prevent a person from using his land as he chooses does not entitle the local government to put every property owner in a legal straitjacket. The essence of modern zoning is the pervasive sacrifice of permanent property rights to transient property values —as if the sole right of property owners is to have the highest immediate market value for their property.

In the Middle Ages, governments bound peasants to their land for the benefit of their lords. Today, governments bind landowners to the current use of their land, indenturing the owners to the whim of local government officials. If government officials decreed that no one was permitted to change their profession, people would widely recognize that as tyranny. Yet there is little protest when governments make a similar declaration prohibiting residents from changing the use of their property. We are increasingly turning landowners into the serfs of the zoning and planning commissioners.

Federal officials have asserted that the government is entitled to effectively nullify almost all of the value of a person's property without compensating them. The federal Ninth Circuit Court of Appeals declared in 1987, "In order to succeed with a regulatory taking claim, a property owner must demonstrate that *all or substantially all economically viable use* of the property has been denied."[275] Sen. John Chaffee of Rhode Island asserted in 1991 that only "where Government action denies a property owner *ALL* economically viable use of his property, that property owner is owed just compensation."[276] The "all or substantially all" test is an engraved invitation for the abuse of power. A New Jersey Meadowlands commission banned the owner of a 12.5-acre plot of prime real estate from developing his land, thereby reducing the value of the land to almost nothing. Yet government officials claimed that since the landowner was receiving $13 a year in rent from one billboard, the land was still "economically productive" and thus the government had not violated the owner's rights.[277]

Increasingly, only the rich have semi-inviolable property rights in America. Sen. Steve Symms observed, "Those who cannot afford to sue currently have no protection of their property rights if they come in conflict with a regulation."[278] The decline of property rights in the United States has had perhaps the sharpest impact on poor people and minorities since they are far more likely to have their land taken for urban renewal projects, to be excluded from buying a home by zoning restrictions, and to be financially overwhelmed by the burden of historic preservation ordinances. A person is only entitled to own his property if he has the resources and the will to sue government officials who try to wrongfully seize it.

Martin Anderson concluded from his discussions on urban renewal with dozens of politicians and community leaders: "They were not seriously concerned with the poor people living in the areas they had tentatively marked for renewal; they were not concerned with any personal gain; they were not even very concerned with getting a substantial amount of cash from the rest of the taxpayers via Washington. But they were concerned with *power*."[279] In a 1991 case, the U.S. Court of Appeals ruled that a Sterling Heights, Michigan, city councilman was guilty of "autocratic exercise of elective office for the achievement of a personal objective" after he engineered the city government's denial of a company's development plan that had previously been approved by the city.[280] Nowadays—in some states and locales—election onto a city council confers the right and the power to attempt to destroy any part of the city that the council member personally dislikes. The decline of the sanctity of private property has meant a vast increase in the discretionary power of government employees over private citizens.

Congressmen warned that asset forfeiture powers were necessary to break the power of the Mafia—and then authorized federal agents to seize the cash of any suspicious person passing through a major airport. Urban planners warned of disease and pestilence from overcrowding unless comprehensive zoning ordinances were enacted—and ended up jailing people for having old cars in their driveways. Historic preservation advocates began talking about the majesty of great American buildings—and ended up threatening to jail people for installing the wrong type of window in their 1950s homes. Federal regulators warned about the importance of wetlands in preventing an environmental debacle—and ended up prosecuting corporations and individuals based on the possibility that passing geese would glance at their land. The decline of property rights has been driven by the endless proclamations of bogus emergencies, by constant demands for more government power in order to protect people against crises that existed largely in the minds of ambitious politicians. In each case, the emergency turned out to be a pretext to vastly expand government power to deal with things unrelated to the emergency.

Currently accepted legal doctrines will allow further extensions of government power over property in the future. The 1992 Report of the American Bar Association's Committee on Land Use, Planning, and Zoning Law proclaimed: "The inevitable march toward a comprehensive plan as the legal equivalent of a constitution for future growth is gaining momentum."[281] The notion that a plan by a zoning commission would become a "constitution"—thereby trumping the original Bill of Rights—is a sad sign of the tattered condition of the Fifth Amendment. The question of whether politicians will respect the rights of property owners is largely a question of whether a nation will have limited or unlimited government. Government cannot control property without controlling people. Every extension of control over property means a decrease in citizens' ability to rely on themselves and plan their own lives. Every decrease in the sanctity of private property will mean an increase in insecurity for some citizens. To allow the government practically unlimited control and jurisdiction over private property is to give politicians and bureaucrats almost unlimited power to intervene in private lives. We face a choice of private property or political subjugation.

-3-

The Proliferation of Petty Dictatorships

When we consider the nature and the theory of our institutions of government . . . we are constrained to conclude that they do not mean to leave room for the play and action of purely personal and arbitrary power. . . . The very idea that one man may be compelled to hold his life, or the means of living, or any material right essential to the enjoyment of life, at the mere will of another, seems intolerable in any country where freedom prevails, as being the essence of slavery itself.

—U.S. Supreme Court (1886)[1]

The liberty of the individual, which is rightfully one of the proudest possessions of the American people, is largely a freedom from arbitrary action by those possessed of the power of government.

—Minnesota Supreme Court (1960)[2]

The Fifth Amendment of the U.S. Constitution states: "No person shall be . . . deprived of life, liberty, or property, without due process of law." Thomas Jefferson wrote in 1787, "A bill of rights is what the people are entitled to against every government on earth."[3] Unfortunately, the Bill of Rights—the most important treaty between the government and the citizenry—has often been shown as little respect by federal courts as the early treaties between the federal government and Indian tribes. The federal government is obliged to respect its promises to the citizens—unless it is convenient to renege on those promises.

In its day-to-day operation, the federal government is increasingly a pseudo-benevolent dictatorship. The Supreme Court declared in 1971 in the case of *California v. Byers*, "The sweep of modern governmental regulation . . . could of course be thought to present a significant threat to the values considered to underpin the Fifth Amendment. . . . As uncertain as the constitutional mandate derived from this portion of the Bill of Rights may be, it is the task of this Court continually to seek that line of accomodation which will render this provision relevant to contemporary conditions." Thus, the Supreme Court almost explicitly defined its job as accomodating the growth of government, rather than upholding the rights of the citizens. In recent decades, the due process clause has been largely swept aside in citizens' dealings with federal regulators, inspectors, enforcers, and tax collectors. While courts have created new due process rights for welfare recipients, disruptive school children, and criminal defendants, the rights of farmers, homeowners, parents, and businessmen have been shredded. We have seen marginal development in due process mechanisms and a vast proliferation of government agencies with the power to trample due process. The modern idea of due process appears to be to permit citizens to exhaust their life savings fighting court battles against heavy-handed government agencies.

The trademark of modern political thinking is an implicit faith in discretionary power wielded by benevolent politicians and administrators—in letting government employees treat private citizens as they think best. While in previous eras the citizen worried only about the sheriff and the tax collector, he must now often face the power and authority of the zoners, the wage regulators, the compulsory preservationists, the import price controllers, the occupational licensers, et al. We have far more federal agencies, and the agencies are under less restraint than they used to be. The federal judiciary has created an overwhelming presumption in the legality of the actions of federal agencies, thus approving more and more acts by government officials that once would have been considered outrageous, illegal, or unconstitutional. The sheer volume of federal action—of laws, regulations, consent decrees, and memos-with-the-force-of-law—makes effective judicial and congressional oversight of federal agencies a near impossibility. The larger government has grown, the less controlled it has become.

We have had extensive government in the past, but never has it been so unconstrained by guiding principles, the Constitution, or any concept of the Rule of Law. Not only have government agencies gotten bigger, but they have also slipped their constitutional leashes. We have never before had so many government agencies—or so little concern with arbitrary power. As Kenneth Davis, the nation's preeminent authority on administrative law, wrote, "Perhaps the most significant twentieth century change in the fundamentals of the legal system has been the tremendous growth of discretionary power. And the prospect is, for better or for worse, that discretionary power will continue to grow."[4]

To a degree, most of the examples discussed in this book could be categorized as abuses of arbitrary power. However, there are some areas where arbitrary power has become the essence of the problem. In order to fully understand the proliferation of unrestrained government power, we need to examine more closely the policies of some of the more creative federal agencies.

A FEW PRELIMINARY WORDS ON AN ANCIENT SUPERSTITION...

Early Americans venerated the law and saw it as the key to safeguarding their freedom. Thomas Paine wrote in 1776 that "in America THE LAW IS KING. For as in absolute governments the King is law, so in free countries the law *ought* to be King; and there ought to be no other."[5] In 1780, the Massachusetts Bill of Rights stated as its goal the establishment of a "government of laws and not of men." Americans of the Revolutionary Era glorified the law because it was seen as a means to restrain government and to secure the rights of the citizens. Nobel Laureate Friedrich Hayek defined the Rule of Law in 1944: "Government in all its actions is bound by rules fixed and announced beforehand—rules which make it possible to foresee with fair certainty how the authority will use its coercive powers."[6] Hayek later observed, "Because the rule of law means that government must never coerce an individual except in the enforcement of a known rule, it constitutes a limitation on the powers of all government."[7] The Rule of Law aims to minimize discretionary power.

The Rule of Law is a recognition of the government's obligation to the citizenry. Joseph Towers wrote in 1775, "In arbitrary governments, all are equally slaves. . . . A vague and indefinite obedience, to the fluctuating and arbitrary will of any superior, is the most abject and complete slavery."[8] Arbitrary power means subjugation to bureaucratic and political rulers who can exercise their personal will over their subjects.

Unfortunately, the modern interpretation of the term "law" is an invitation to the abuse of power. The English jurist Sir William Blackstone declared in 1765 that "law is not a transient order from a superior to or concerning a particular person or thing, but something permanent, uniform, and universal." The U.S. Supreme Court declared in 1908, "'Law' is a statement of the circumstances in which the public force will be brought to bear upon men through the courts."[9] But nowadays laws increasingly exist to bind citizens, not government. Laws are carved in passing political expediency. A law is simply a reflection of the momentary perception of self-interest by a majority of a legislative body. A law is binding only until enough congressmen find it in their self-interest to repeal or revise it. Law is increasingly something that government does to private citizens—until further notice.

The flood of laws and revisions of laws amounts to perpetually changing the rules of society to the point at which the United States degenerates into a Third World condition. Laws are always on the eve of the next sweeping revision, creating an atmosphere of legal instability. Neither the legislators nor the bureaucrats now have any sense of the *sanctity* of law—of the idea that law should not be changed simply for momentary political convenience. The more often the law is revised, the more that law becomes simply a series of arbitrary political commands that must be obeyed, a grant of unlimited power to government officials. The more often government officials change the rules by which individuals will be judged, the more those individuals will be left to the government's mercy, since most citizens do not know and cannot understand the laws and regulations they must obey.

In recent decades, support for the classical concept of the Rule of Law has evaporated; instead, competing bands of intellectuals champion the executive branch or Congress or judicial activism or some other fad. Rather than focus on the actual operations of government agencies, political thinking is often characterized by a "Do It Now!" philosophy. Discretionary power has been granted to bureaucrats by many laws because congressmen don't have the courage to say openly what they want the bureaucracy to do, leading to government by stealth.

DICTATORSHIP ON THE FARM

The *New York Times* reported on March 12, 1933, that Secretary of Agriculture Henry Wallace and a group of farm lobbyists urged President Roosevelt to ask for "farm dictator powers" to solve the farm crisis.[10] Today, over sixty years later, the Secretary of Agriculture is still effectively the czar of agriculture. He can, with a sweep of his pen, drive grain prices up or down, spend $50 million to buy up almost any farm commodity he chooses, change the regulations governing the profitability of a thousand businesses, shower benefits on favored states and congressional districts, cancel a farmer's right to sell his tobacco or peanuts, or give away $29 million in government commodities to a personal acquaintance.[11] Federal farm programs for over half a century have given federal officials the power to coerce farmers—primarily for the goal of driving up food prices.

Under the Agricultural Marketing Agreement Act of 1937, USDA appoints farmers to government marketing boards that impose "marketing orders." These boards restrict the sale of specific fruits and vegetables and can severely punish farmers who sell more of their crop than the boards permit. USDA has granted vast discretionary power to these marketing boards.

Since 1941, USDA's Navel Orange Administrative Committee has restricted the amount of navel oranges that California and Arizona farmers can sell to other Americans. The committee dictates the percentage of harvest that navel orange farmers will be permitted to sell. USDA officials fear that without government restrictions, orange growers would all sell their crop at the same time, glut the market, and destroy themselves. (This has never happened in the brief periods in recent years when government marketing restrictions were suspended.) But USDA's solution is the equivalent of killing someone to prevent them from committing suicide. The Justice Department noted that "a significant portion of [the 1989] navel crop . . . was fed to cattle."[12] Selling oranges for cattle feed is a guaranteed loss for orange growers. USDA dictated these restrictions on crop sales in disregard of the

Administrative Procedures Act, the federal law that is supposed to govern how agencies issue new regulations. Farmers who opposed the controls had almost no opportunity to influence USDA policymakers until the early 1990s. Orange grower Carl Pescosolido and his lawyer, Jim Moody, wrote hundreds of letters to the USDA criticizing the policies and asking for explanations of the department's rationales, but never received a substantive reply.

In September 1990, for the first time and under federal court order, USDA officially solicited comments from orange farmers on its plans to restrict their sales. By a 10 to 1 margin, farmers vehemently opposed USDA's plan to prohibit them from selling much of their harvest.[13] Farmer Oleah Wilson of Lemon Cove, California, complained, "I find it absurd that the government has a policy to protect the lazy and inefficient at the expense of individuals willing to do a better job." Kent Burke of Exeter, California, begged, "For God Sakes, give the farmer the benefit of the doubt and let him market his fruit as he sees fit." Despite the farmers' opposition, USDA prohibited California and Arizona farmers from selling 32 percent of their fresh navel oranges to other Americans in the 1990-91 season.[14] During the 1991-92 season, farmers were prohibited from selling 31 percent of their fresh navel oranges on the U.S. market.[15]

Restrictions on orange sales have been imposed largely at the behest of Sunkist, which dominates the California-Arizona citrus market. Federal marketing orders freeze existing market shares and thus minimize the competition against the dominant market power. The Justice Department complained in October 1990 that USDA's Navel Orange Administrative Committee acts "as a legalized cartel to set output and hike prices for navel oranges."[16] A lawsuit brought by a group of four orange growers in 1991 estimated that each of them had lost $10 million in sales during the 1980s as a result of the federal orange marketing order.[17]

Similar restrictions are imposed on the sale of lemons. USDA effectively requires California and Arizona growers to grow up to three lemons to receive government permission to sell one fresh lemon to their fellow citizens. In 1929, over 90 percent of the lemons grown in the country were sold fresh to the public. But by 1990, thanks to USDA restrictions, only 42 percent of the lemons were sold fresh.[18] A Justice Department study concluded that federal restrictions on lemon sales "reduced consumption of fresh lemons, misallocated resources due to chronic overproduction, reduced firm growth, reduced price competition . . . and wasted $72 million a year."[19] USDA restrictions also helped drive thousands of lemon farmers out of business.

Each year, USDA's Almond Board confiscates part of almond growers' crops and pays no compensation. The Almond Board dictates the percentage of each year's California almond harvest that is placed in reserve—i.e., cannot be sold without the government's board permission, even in export markets.[20] Upon the Almond Board's proclamation of the annual reserve portion of the harvest, the title to those almonds (over 100 million pounds of almonds in 1992) automatically, instantly, and fully vests with the Almond Board. The board requires individual farmers to pay to store the board's reserve almonds until such time that the board may consider it proper to return ownership of part of the restricted almonds back to the farmers. The Secretary of Agriculture can fine farmers $1,000 a day for each day they do not have the reserve almonds stored on their premises.[21] An Italian company that invested in a California almond farm was fined $216,000 for shipping its reserve almonds back to Italy.[22] The government Almond Board routinely forces farmers to sell the reserve almonds for a big loss as cattle feed or for other noneconomic uses. Almonds for humans sell for about $1.50 a pound, while almonds destined for cattle feed sell for less than 20 cents a pound.[23] The almond confiscation has cost Cal-Almond and Saulsbury Orchards and Almond Processing over $2 million each in recent years. (Cal-Almond spent almost half a million dollars storing its reserve almonds for the board in 1988-89.) Even though the restrictions cost almond producers millions of dollars in storage costs and lost profits, a 1991 court brief by USDA conceded that "it is virtually impossible to ascertain what effect the [restrictions on almond sales] have had upon the open market for almonds."[24]

USDA's Raisin Administrative Committee exercises intricate control over California raisin farmers' operations. The Raisin Administrative Committee prohibited California raisin farmers from selling 147 million pounds of natural seedless raisins (21 percent of their harvest) from the 1991-92 crop year.[25] The restrictions on the sales of California raisins have encouraged the growing of raisins in Arizona, where farmers are exempt from federal raisin controls. A smattering of Arizona raisins (less than 1 percent of the California harvest) is transported to California before being exported or shipped domestically. These token shipments threaten to disrupt USDA's master plan for California raisins. USDA warned in a solemn notice in the *Federal Register* on November 6, 1992, that "all non-California raisins received by [California raisin] handlers . . . [must] be identified, stored separately . . . and *kept under surveillance* until such raisins [are] disposed of by the handlers."[26] In an era when the Federal Bureau of Investigation fails to prevent terrorists from bombing New York's World Trade Center, USDA is demanding intensive surveillance of out-of-state raisins.

Federal marketing controls also restrict the size of fruit that American consumers are permitted to buy. In 1992, USDA effectively passed an economic death sentence on up to 500 million California peaches and nectarines. The California fruits' crime? A debilitating diameter deficiency. USDA made it a federal crime during the 1992 season for California farmers to sell nectarines less than 2⁵⁄₁₆ inches in diameter and peaches less than 2⅜ inches in diameter. Legions of nectarines one-sixteenth of an inch too small were banned from the marketplace. USDA issued a decree explaining its nectarine policy in the *Federal Register:* "The minimum size requirements established for California nectarines recognize that larger sized nectarines provide greater consumer satisfaction than those of smaller sizes."[27] Since many people prefer larger nectarines, USDA made it a federal crime to sell smaller nectarines—and sent in the nectarine police to enforce its dictates.

Federal and state agricultural bureaucrats can be extremely condescending toward farmers, claiming to need dictatorial power over some of the nation's farmers to protect those farmers against themselves. The only catch is that the bureaucrats usually know less than the farmers. California agricultural official John Field, who supervised the USDA program, when asked whether the government had any studies to justify restrictions on small nectarine sales, replied: "We don't have any empirical studies . . . but if you look at price quotes for plums, that would kind of indicate intuitively that there is not a great demand for" small nectarines and peaches.[28] Government officials effectively imposed millions of dollars of penalties on growers based on bureaucrats' guesses about consumer preference on fruit. Dan Gerawan, California's largest nectarine and peach farmer and the leading opponent of the controls, observes, "Through the years, the government has continuously raised the minimum size regulations. While a certain small size may have been a quality, edible fruit one year, the following year it would be deemed—by way of minimum size regulations—to be no longer of edible quality."[29] Also, while the federal government threatens heavy fines and jail sentences for the sale of small California peaches, it imposes no penalties on the sale of small Georgia peaches.

USDA officials claim that the marketing orders are democratic because large majorities of farmers vote for the controls. But USDA may have rigged 1991 referendums on peaches and nectarines to perpetuate marketing orders—and jobs for a handful of federal and state bureaucrats. USDA regulations require that marketing orders be supported by two-thirds of growers; fewer than two-thirds of peach and nectarine growers supported marketing orders, but USDA claimed that the growers who did support the orders accounted for just over two thirds of the *volume* of peach and nectarine production.

The peach marketing order was reapproved by only one vote out of the more than 700 votes cast. The referendum itself would have made Chicago blush: USDA announced after the vote that 140 ballots (out of roughly 2,000 ballots) had been "challenged," but refused to disclose who had challenged them, whose ballots were disqualified, or why they were nixed. The process was completely secret, and the electoral "judges" were government farm bureaucrats with a vested interest in perpetuating their controls over farmers. As Dan Gerawan notes, "It is almost as if they are rubbing it in our face and saying that they can rig the vote any way they want to."[30] Since marketing orders are a Soviet-style command-and-control system, perhaps it is appropriate that USDA also allows the farmers only Soviet-style elections.

Though government agricultural boards are empowered to coercively impose "orderly marketing," USDA has never defined what the term means.

When asked what orderly marketing was, USDA Assistant Secretary for Marketing C. W. McMillan admitted, "I have no idea what that is. I have never heard anyone define orderly marketing."[31] In practice, "orderly markets" has come to mean simply markets controlled by government officials and government boards.

In 1992, several nectarine, peach, and plum growers sued the federal marketing boards and the individuals on the boards, claiming that they had imposed much more restrictive standards on fruit sales than federal law authorized. The board members defended themselves by claiming that the Secretary of Agriculture had approved of their actions and thus that they were personally absolved of legal responsibility. The marketing boards sent copies of the minutes of their meetings to USDA officials in Washington—and thereby invoked the Doctrine of the Omniscient Filing Cabinet. Ronald L. Cioffi, chief of USDA's Marketing Order Administration branch, testified: "The action of the [USDA] marketing specialist in reviewing and approving the committee proposal and filing the communication from the [marketing board] committee in official USDA files constitutes approval of the Secretary."[32] This assumes that the Secretary of Agriculture automatically becomes fully cognizant of anything that is placed in any of the tens of thousands of filing cabinets in USDA headquarters. Since the Secretary of Agriculture did not go storming over to Room S-3742 of USDA headquarters and yank the memos of the board meetings out of the filing cabinet, the Secretary is presumed to know and approve of the board's decisions.

Marketing orders are an example of the quasi-covert nature of much of contemporary government coercion. If the USDA sent armed agents into every grocery store in the country and arrested shoppers who bought small California nectarines, USDA would be universally denounced as God's prize idiots. Instead, the government imposes its controls directly on California farms and fruit handlers—and most citizens never know how their government is thwarting the bounty of the nation's farmers.

Federal agricultural laws provide ample opportunity for congressmen to reward their friends or smite their enemies—or at least the enemies of their friends. In July 1985 the House Agriculture Committee voted to outlaw an egg-breaking machine—perhaps the first time in history that a congressional committee targeted a machine for prohibition. A California businessman had invented the Egg King, a machine that broke up to 700 eggs a minute and was being used by the Pentagon, Disneyworld, and major hotels. The Egg King allowed its users to rely on fresh eggs instead of on powdered or frozen eggs; this meant better taste and huge savings, since powdered or frozen eggs cost 50 percent more than fresh eggs. Richard C. Gohla, vice president of the Retail Bakers Association, noted, "The higher percentage of eggs in a product, the more the quality suffers by using frozen eggs."[33] But the Egg King was hurting the business of the United Egg Producers, whose members supplied most of the powdered or frozen eggs used in the United States.

So the Agriculture Committee came to the rescue: congressmen justified banning the Egg King based on concerns over its safety, even though there were no reported incidents of health problems connected with it. The California Department of Health concluded that the Egg King "appears to be superior to the present hand method of cracking and straining eggs."[34] The Food and Drug Administration had received no complaints of health problems involving the Egg King. The only people who complained about the new technology were the Egg King's competitors. The Agriculture Committee —with almost no discussion of the issue—thus voted to torpedo a successful businessman. (The full House refused to go along with the Agriculture Committee's vote, and the Egg King's execution was postponed.)[35] In 1986, the maker of the Egg King filed a suit against the United Egg Producers, claiming that he had lost over $1 million worth of sales because of the political counterattacks against his new product.[36] Shortly thereafter, the Egg King maker went bankrupt.[37]

IMPALING IMPORTERS AND OTHER NATIONAL ENEMIES

Trade policy has become much more arbitrary in the last twenty years. New laws and regulations have proliferated that give politicians and bureaucrats far more power to decree which foreign products Americans may buy. Most of the new discretionary authority is a result of so-called fair trade policies. But when politicians call for fair trade with foreigners, they routinely use a concept of fairness that is diametrically opposed to the word's normal usage. In exchanges between individuals—in contract law—the test of fairness is the voluntary consent of each party to the bargain: "the free will which constitutes fair exchanges," as Sen. John Taylor wrote in 1822.[38] When politicians speak of unfair trade, they do not mean that buyers and sellers did not voluntarily agree, but that U.S. government officials disapprove of the bargains American citizens chose to make. Fair trade, as the term is now used, usually means government intervention to direct, control, or restrict trade. Fair trade has become a political license for arbitrary power over $500 billion in imports each year—a license for government officials to seize, prohibitively tax, or embargo products that American citizens and companies paid for and often need for their survival. According to the Institute for International Economics, tariff-taxes and restrictions on imports cost American consumers $80 billion a year—equal to over $1,200 per family.[39]

Fair trade often consists of some politician or bureaucrat picking a number out of thin air and imposing it on foreign businesses and American consumers. Fair trade means that Mexico was allowed to sell Americans only 35,292 bras in 1989,[40] that Poland was allowed to export only 51,752 pounds of barbed wire to the United States in 1990,[41] and that Haiti is allowed to sell the United States only 7,258 tons of sugar a year. Fair trade means permitting each

American citizen to consume the equivalent of only one teaspoon of foreign ice cream per year,[42] two foreign peanuts per year, and one pound of imported cheese per year.[43]

The United States has over 8,000 different tariff categories, and the Customs Service is continually revising its definition of products, thus changing the tariffs that an importer must pay. Tariff classification rulings can result in massive, retroactive increases in tariff rates or in embargoes. The impact of these rulings is compounded by the fact that the United States imposes import quotas on over 3,000 different products, including tampons, typing ribbons, tarps, twine, ties, and table linen.[44]

Customs Service officials worked overtime in late 1989 to protect America against foreign shoestrings. Customs prohibited the import of a shipment of 30,000 tennis shoes from Indonesia because the shoe boxes contained an extra pair of shoelaces. One Customs official decided that the extra laces were a clothing product that required a separate quota license for importing, and his decision set a precedent for the entire Customs Service.[45] None of the tennis shoe importers were thinking of the extra laces as anything but part of the tennis shoe and thus they were caught in their tracks without textile import quotas for shoestrings.[46] (Some new tennis shoes have eyelets for more than one set of laces.) Customs proceeded to establish intricate rules for shoelace imports. In a judicious ruling, the U.S. government announced that an extra pair of shoelaces would be permitted in a box of tennis shoes as long as the extra shoelaces were laced into the shoes and were color-coordinated with the shoes. But Customs warned importers, "We note that where multiple pairs of laces of *like* colors and/or designs are imported . . . a presumption is raised" that the shoelaces are not actually part of the shoe.[47] Customs acted in the nick of time to prevent 250 million Americans from acquiring too many shoelaces of the same color.

Customs claims the right to reverse its tariff classification decisions even after a product has been imported and used. Proctor and Gamble imported topping packets for its Duncan Hines muffin mixes after the Customs Service advised the company that the toppings would not be subject to the sugar import quota. After the toppings were imported and the mixes bought by consumers, the Customs Service reversed its decision and informed Proctor and Gamble that it had violated the U.S. sugar quota and thus owed a $750,000 penalty for importing muffin toppings—whose sugar content was worth only $30,000.[48] (Customs later waived the penalty.)

Political pressure from American producers sometimes leads the Customs Service to make farcical classification decisions in order to suppress foreign competition. In 1992, the Customs Service ruled that Honda violated the U.S.-Canada Free Trade Agreement (FTA) because less than 50 percent of the value of Honda Civics imported into the United States in 1989 from Canada was added to the vehicles in the United States or Canada. (Under the FTA, autos shipped between the United States and Canada are tariff-free if over half of the auto's cost of production is attributable to U.S. and/or Canadian materials and labor.) Customs decreed that the automobile engine blocks, which were cast, shaped, machined, and finished at a Honda plant in Ohio, exported to Canada, installed in autos, and reexported to the United States, were *not made* in the United States. Customs issued the official regulations with this revolutionary definition of cost of production in February 1992, only a few days before its final ruling on Honda's imports, and made the regulations retroactive to 1989. Honda officials complained in a letter, "Honda will be judged in the audit on the basis of acts submitted before there were any rules, and without any opportunity once the rules were made known to submit additional data to show its compliance with the rules."[49] Honda was forced to pay a $17 million fine. By effectively penalizing Honda for the operations of its Ohio factory, Customs' ruling threatened the jobs of thousands of autoworkers in Honda's U.S. factories.

The U.S. Customs Service conducts a bureaucratic reign of terror against businessmen, pilots, and boaters. Some Customs inspectors appear to have been influenced by the 1970s cult film classic *The Texas Chainsaw Massacre.* In Seattle, Washington, Customs inspectors chainsawed an imported cigar store wooden Indian to prove beyond a shadow of a doubt that the Indian did not contain any narcotics.[50] Customs agents also used chain saws to "inspect" a large container tightly packed with paper products, rubber products, and an antique teakwood elephant.[51] Chain saws are an attractive, efficient means of inspecting imports in part because Customs never compensates anyone for damage it does during inspections. A 1990 House Ways and Means Committee investigation concluded, "The U.S. Customs Service has little or no incentive to avoid damaging cargo during examinations."[52]

Customs officials have invoked the war on drugs to assume unlimited power over any ship or plane crossing the U.S. border. On April 9, 1989, Customs officials "inspected" a sailboat owned by Craig Klein of Jacksonville, Florida, with axes, power drills, and crow bars. By the time the search was completed, the gas tank was ruptured, the engine was ruined, and fifteen large holes had been drilled below the waterline, rendering the sailboat worthless. Though no narcotics were found, Customs denied any compensation to the boat owner. A Customs agent later phoned Klein at home and threatened his life to try to dissuade him from complaining to his congressman about the incident.[53]

Rep. Barney Frank of Massachusetts proposed a bill to permit private citizens to sue to recover damages from Customs officials' actions. Deputy Assistant Attorney General Stephen Bransdorfer, testifying before the House Judiciary Committee late in 1991, opposed holding the Customs Service liable for "negligent destruction" of commercial cargo because "standard marine cargo insurance . . . is available at readily affordable rates."[54] If Bransdorfer's doctrine is adopted throughout the government, federal agents will have a blank check to destroy any private property for which insurance can be bought. Perhaps it would save paperwork if the federal government directly confiscated the assets of insurance companies, rather than going through the formality of destroying property that the insurance companies covered.

Thirteenth-century theologians debated the doctrine of the "just price." Nowadays, U.S. Commerce Department officials have engaged in multimillion-dollar scholastic disputes over the "fair value" of imports under provisions of the U.S. dumping law. Dumping supposedly refers to the act of selling foreign goods for less than their cost of production, or selling goods for less in the United States than in the foreign home market. The United States imposes dumping penalties for foreign goods that are imported at "less than fair value." Unfortunately, the U.S. Commerce Department has been very creative in its definition of "fair value."[55]

In a 1992 case, the Commerce Department compared the price of new Mazda minivans sold in Japan with the price of used Mazda minivans sold in the United States. Naturally, the used minivans sold in the United States for less than the new minivans sold for in Japan—which the Commerce Department claimed proved illegal dumping.[56] Commerce convicted Japanese forklift producers for dumping—after Commerce compared the price of new forklifts in Japan with the price of three-year-old forklifts in the United States.[57] In a 1987 flower dumping case, the Commerce Department effectively compared the price of wilted imported flowers sold in the United States with the price of fresh flowers in Amsterdam. Since the wilted flowers sold for less than the fresh flowers, that officially proved the Dutch were competing unfairly.[58] Commerce convicted a Hong Kong sweater maker of unfair trade because it made only a 2 percent profit on its exports to the United States.[59] (The U.S. dumping law says that foreigners are effectively cheating unless they earn an 8 percent profit on exports—the acid test of fair trade that, unfortunately, most American companies cannot pass.)[60] Commerce convicted a Taiwanese company of dumping because the company's factory had burnt down and the company could not answer all the questions in the one-hundred-page questionnaire that Commerce sent it.[61] Commerce increased the dumping margins (the penalty tariffs imposed on foreign companies) on Japanese television manufacturers after it ruled that Japanese donations of televisions to American charities were the same as selling the televisions for nothing—the ultimate proof of dumping.[62]

Dumping penalties routinely eject foreign companies from the U.S. market. This can have a devastating impact on U.S. companies that must rely on imported products. In July 1992, Commerce found a 62.67 percent dumping margin on Japanese advanced computer flat panel imports.[63] (The 62.67 percent margin was deduced largely by using a cost-of-production analysis that vastly overestimated research costs, thereby "proving" that a profitable Japanese company was actually incurring huge losses on its exports.) After Commerce announced the dumping penalty, the Customs Service imposed a

62.67 percent penalty tariff on flat panel imports. Computer flat panels are a key component of laptop and notebook computers, and there were no viable U.S. manufacturers.

The dumping duty added up to $1,100 to the cost of producing laptop computers in the United States and thereby made U.S.-made laptop computers uncompetitive with foreign-made laptops.[64] An IBM spokesman described the dumping penalty as "an eviction notice from the U.S. government to the fastest growing part of the U.S. computer industry."[65] After the dumping penalty was imposed, Apple Computer shifted its production of its hot new laptops from Colorado to Ireland, Compaq shifted its laptop operations from Houston to Scotland, Toshiba shifted computer-assembly operations from Irvine, California, to Japan, and Dolch Computer Company shifted production from Milpitas, California, to Germany.[66] The dumping penalty was estimated to have destroyed up to 3,000 American jobs, sacrificing a $42 billion personal-computer industry to a tiny segment of the business with less than $100 million in revenues.[67]

The dumping law forces foreign companies to run a nearly endless gauntlet of American bureaucrats. A federal judge concluded that the dumping law allowed American companies to conduct an "economic war" against their foreign competitors.[68] Between 1984 and 1990, the Commerce Department convicted 97 percent of all foreign companies that it investigated for dumping.[69] In 1989 and 1990, the average dumping margin and penalty tariff was 56 percent.[70] Over 2,000 foreign companies and American importers are now being forced to pay antidumping penalties—penalties that are effectively passed on to U.S. consumers. Before these dumping duties can be imposed, the U.S. International Trade Commission must conclude that the dumped imports have injured competing U.S. companies. The ITC finds injury in most cases, and even in cases where injury is not found, foreign companies must spend hundreds of thousands of dollars on legal fees, and imports are disrupted for a year while the allegations of U.S. companies are investigated.

In dumping cases, the Commerce Department is prosecuting attorney, judge, jury, and executioner, as Washington trade lawyer David Palmeter notes.[71] Though the U.S. government is supposed to be fair and objective in its judgments on foreign companies' prices, Commerce officials sometimes make their biases blatant. In a 1991 speech, Marjorie Chorlins, deputy assistant secretary of commerce for import administration, thanked the American Wire Producers Association (AWPA) for their frequent use of the antidumping law against wire imports, declaring, "The partnership which the AWPA and Import Administration have enjoyed over the past ten years has been active and rewarding."[72] If a judge in a criminal case publicly announced his "partnership" with the prosecutors, a public uproar would result. But in U.S. government administrative proceedings, the definition of fairness is whatever a federal judge will let an agency get away with.

ELIMINATING PREDICTABILITY FOR FOOD AND DRUGS

The Food and Drug Administration has jurisdiction over almost $1 trillion in product sales each year.[73] The FDA has vast discretion over the food and drugs that Americans can consume—and often life-or-death power over Americans with serious illnesses. The FDA must approve all new drugs and has the de facto power to financially destroy companies that displease FDA officials.

FDA officials seek to maximize fear among regulated companies. A 1991 laudatory *Washington Post* article on FDA commissioner David Kessler concluded, "What he cannot accomplish with ordinary regulation, Kessler hopes to accomplish with fear." (The article also noted that the chairman was called "King Kessler in reference to the almost imperial manner with which he swept into the FDA's top job.")[74] Kenneth R. Feather, head of the FDA's Drug Advertising Surveillance Branch, boasted in early 1991: "We want to say to these companies that you don't know when or how we'll strike. We want to eliminate predictability."[75] This may be an excellent rule of thumb for a Third World junta, but it is a peculiar goal for a high-ranking federal regulator. In advanced societies, clear distinctions are usually made between regulating and terrorizing. The purpose of laws and regulations is, first and foremost, to advise people on how to comply with federal law. But the FDA apparently prefers to maximize the number of newspaper headlines its crackdowns generate.

Prior to 1962, the FDA tested proposed new drugs solely to insure their safety. But since then, the FDA, on its own authority, has also demanded that drug manufactures prove the efficacy of their products. This efficacy requirement and the manner of its enforcement has made it far more difficult for companies to get permission to provide new drugs to ailing Americans.

Lawyer Sam Kazman of the Competitive Enterprise Institute noted, "The 1962 law fundamentally changed the new drug approval process. Rather than simply evaluate data submitted by drug companies, FDA now became involved in drug development itself, bringing with it a bureaucratic concern for avoiding politically embarrassing risks even if this meant undermining public health."[76] Largely because of this shift, it now takes the FDA three times longer to review new drugs,[77] and the number of new drugs approved each year has fallen by over 60 percent. Dr. William Von Valtier observed, "The effectiveness of a drug is far more complicated and expensive to determine than is its safety. Whereas safety evaluations can use animal studies heavily, can be completed in a relatively short time, and have relatively clear and objective end points, effectiveness studies must be done with human volunteer patients [and] require extraordinary amounts of data collection and clinical participation by teams of health professionals over many months if not years."[78] Charles Strother, a University of Wisconsin neuroradiologist, complained, "Scientists and engineers are now using state-of-the-art techniques to create products to address previously incurable diseases and save lives, only to deliver them to an FDA still mired in the horse-and-buggy days of 10-year, double-blind trials."[79] The FDA has an extremely timid, risk-averse approach to approving new drugs; National Cancer Institute officials have accused the FDA of being "mired in a 1960s philosophy of drug development, viewing all new agents as . . . poisons."[80]

The FDA sometimes manipulates test results, or forces drug companies to use weaker doses of a drug in tests, and then pronounces the drugs to be ineffective. In a 1991 test of medication for Alzheimer's disease, the FDA slashed the dosage—and then scorned the treatment as ineffective because only 41 percent of Alzheimer's sufferers tested responded positively to the lower dosage.[81] The FDA has almost unlimited power to manipulate the testing standards or the type of tests used and can squelch drugs that they oppose or punish drug companies they dislike. The *Washington Post* noted, "For each month that the approval of a drug with the potential of $200 million a year in sales is delayed, for example, the company loses about $10 million in profits."[82] David Matheson, a Boston pharmaceutical expert and consultant, estimated that every day a drug is held back from the market costs the drug company $1 million.[83]

Capricious FDA delays are destroying the American medical device manufacturing industry. In 1990, the FDA approved forty-seven new medical devices; in 1992, it approved only twelve new devices—a decrease in annual approvals of over 70 percent. A June 1993 congressional report noted that forty-nine American-made medical devices bogged down in FDA review have already been approved for sale in Europe, Japan, and other countries. The report concluded, "Many of the small companies that populate the industry may be driven out of business altogether by regulatory delays. The process also means that Americans are denied health-care options that could be safer, more effective or less costly than those on the market today. . . . Doctors and patients in the U.S. face the daunting prospect of either having to travel to a foreign land to have access to the latest medical technology or having to accept a less effective and/or a higher-risk treatment for their illness in the U.S."[84] Eleven thousand American companies produce almost half the world's medical instruments but are being driven out of their own market by federal bureaucrats.

The FDA's power to approve or deny permission to use medical devices routinely gives its officials the power of life and death—a power that is often exercised with bureaucratic negligence. In recent years, FDA restrictions have made it almost impossible for physicians to use certain new medical devices without specific permission from an FDA official in Washington. A *Wall Street Journal* editorial entitled "The FDA Meets a Patient" reported:

> To the elites of Washington, medical regulation is an abstract "social good." To a 75-year-old woman from Portland, Maine, the not-so-abstract FDA is the regulator that this week nearly caused her to go blind.

> The woman was diagnosed some weeks ago to have an aneurysm the size of a golf ball in her cavernous carotid artery. Pressure built against her third cranial nerve until she could barely open her eyes. She risked blindness or a rupture that could cause a stroke, yet the aneurysm's location made traditional brain surgery close to impossible.
>
> Dr. Eddie Kwan of Tufts University . . . proposed to use a device called a detachable silicone balloon. . . . Tufts University, it turns out, isn't one of the 25 U.S. sites approved under newly restrictive FDA rules for use of the balloon (which is widely available outside the U.S.). Neither is a site anywhere else in New England. But 75-year-olds with golf-ball sized aneurysms in danger of rupture aren't good candidates for travel. So Dr. Kwan proceeded to see if he could get permission through the bureaucratic politics at Commissioner David Kessler's FDA.
>
> "The first time I talked to someone at the FDA, he just brushed me off," says Dr. Kwan of his phone call last Wednesday. "I talked to so many people I can't remember their names."[85]

Kwan recruited other Tufts administrators to call the FDA to try to get permission; the callers were bounced around until they were instructed to file a formal request by fax. Tufts officials sent a fax explaining their case and pleading for immediate emergency approval—and heard nothing for four days. Finally, after another day of playing telephone tag and providing additional information, an FDA engineer with the illustrious title of "branch chief for neurological devices" gave permission to Kwan to use the silicone balloon in an operation the following day. The operation saved the woman's eyesight and perhaps also her life. The *Wall Street Journal* observed:

> One lesson . . . is that even the FDA can't face itself in the morning if forced to decide that a patient can't be treated. But what about all the other patients? What about patients who don't have a doctor or hospital willing to risk retribution by pestering the FDA? . . . How is it that an obscure bureaucrat without a medical degree can become in effect the Chief of American Neuroradiology, with life-or-death decisions in his hands?[86]

The FDA has sometimes acted as if it sought to destroy some companies in order to make other companies more fearful and submissive to the agency. In 1976, the Environmental Protection Agency approved Sporicidin, a product manufactured by a Maryland company, as a disinfectant. By 1990, Sporicidin had a 25 percent share of the market for medical-instrument disinfectants. The FDA then began to extend its own power by asserting that the disinfectants were actually "medical devices" and thus fell under FDA jurisdiction. Although the FDA sought to require new tests for disinfectants previously approved by the EPA, it never officially promulgated the rules for the new tests. On December 12, 1991, the EPA formally notified Sporicidin that its products performed according to the claims on its label.[87] The next day, however, FDA and EPA agents conducted a highly publicized raid on the firm's Rockville, Maryland, headquarters and seized a million dollars worth of its products. FDA Commissioner Kessler called a news conference and announced: "These products do not work. Doctors, dentists and other health care professionals should stop using them."[88] FDA officials publicly declared that there was a "reasonable probability" that death could result from using medical instruments sterilized with Sporicidin.[89] The company was forced to recall all its products and to send warning letters to medical professionals informing them that their products were unsafe. The Federal Trade Commission also piled on, imposing a $420,000 fine on the company for false advertising.

At the time of the seizure, the federal Centers for Disease Control had not received any reports over the previous fourteen years of illnesses stemming from Sporicidin,[90] nor had any complaints been lodged with the FDA or the EPA from doctors, dentists, or hospitals regarding Sporicidin. When Sporicidin's lawyers tried to get copies of the documents that justified the federal crackdown, the EPA and FDA fought their requests in court, first insisting that the documents were confidential and later claiming that the documents could not be located.[91] The federal government based its seizure of all of Sporicidin's products on an allegation that one of its products had failed a laboratory test. The federal government later admitted that Sporicidin samples had passed laboratory tests in 239 out of 240 trials. But the tests that the government used were widely perceived by professionals as unreliable—so even the single failure may have been due to the government's methods rather than the product's deficiencies.[92]

On May 15, 1992, Sporicidin settled most of the charges with the government, agreeing to forfeit the products the government seized in December and to keep its disinfectants off the market until the FDA approved new formulas. Assistant Attorney General Stuart Gerson hailed the settlement: "Once Sporicidin recognized the strength of the government's case, it cooperated fully in the resolution of all of the FDA's concerns."[93] But the company president, Robert Schattner, insisted that his company signed the consent decree simply to minimize legal costs: "We're out of business now because we had to suspend operations. If we went into court, we still wouldn't have a business and we'd be in court for five years." As part of its consent decree, as journalist Peter Samuel noted, "the FDA has insisted the company destroy reprints of scientific-journal articles that touch on its products. FDA officers have demanded to supervise the dumping of boxes full of articles on glutaraldehyde-based disinfectants published in *The Journal of Operating Room Research, The Journal of Clinical Microbiology*."[94] The FDA eventually announced that it would permit the company to once again sell some of its products; the only change required by the consent agreement was the insertion of a special product information sheet into each package.

In a final settlement with the Federal Trade Commission in February 1993, Sporicidin did not admit guilt on any charges but did promise not to violate federal advertising rules in the future.[95] Sporicidin's Schattner observed, "It's incredible what they've done to us. They've been trying to kill us."[96] He summarized his company's agreement with the FTC: "We promised never to say in the future what we never said in the past."[97] Samuel noted, "Sporicidin estimates its losses to the end of July [1992] at more than $10 million: $5 million in lost sales, $2 million in customer reimbursements, $1 million in legal fees, and $2 million in lost inventory. Thirty people in the manufacturing plant lost their jobs, and a dozen administrative and sales people have gone."[98]

The FDA's policy on new drugs is reminiscent of the saying about the old German doctor who would rather see a patient die than a medical axiom to be proven wrong. The FDA's arbitrary power over drug approval is especially unfortunate because FDA delays can be killers. Sam Kazman estimates that 8,000 to 15,000 people died during the FDA's review of misoprostol (a drug that reduces gastric ulcers among arthritis sufferers who rely on aspirin) and that 22,000 people may have died while the FDA dallied before approving streptokinase (a drug that dissolves clots in heart attack victims). Kazman concludes, "If a drug that has just been approved by FDA will start saving lives tomorrow, how many people died yesterday waiting for the agency to act?"[99]

MAULING THE MAIL WITH A MONOPOLY

The Postal Service, with a monopoly and almost $50 billion in annual revenue, is far more powerful than most Americans realize. The Postal Service has a monopoly over letter delivery (with a limited exemption for urgent, courier-delivered letters costing almost $3). Congress granted the U.S. Post Office a monopoly over letter delivery in the 1840s largely because the government agency was hopelessly uncompetitive with private carriers.[100] Over the decades, the Post Office (renamed the Postal Service in 1970) has striven to expand its monopoly to cover as much material as possible. In 1974, for example, the Postal Service extended its definition of a letter—the legal basis of the monopoly—to include intracorporate communications, blueprints, computer tapes, credit cards, and fishing licenses. The Postal Service began looking into electronic mail in 1977, and by 1979 it was considering banning all private electronic mail by stretching the definition of its monopoly. Luckily, the FCC and the Postal Rate Commission blocked the extension of the monopoly.[101] Federal judge Malcolm Wilkey observed in a 1979 decision that "the Postal Service has always latched onto whatever interpretation of the word 'letter' which would give it the most extensive monopoly power which Congress at that time seemed disposed to allow."[102] In 1985, the Postal Service sought unsuccessfully to extend its monopoly to control mail sent by U.S. corporations via private delivery services to Europe.[103]

The postal monopoly effectively prohibits businesses and citizens who need to mail information to a large number of people from having a cost-

effective private means of distributing their messages. The monopoly also gives the U.S. government power over every citizen or business that needs to use the mail services.

Unfortunately, the Postal Service has been far quicker in defending its monopoly than in delivering the mail. In 1980, a pack of Cub Scouts in New York City tried to raise money by carrying Christmas cards among neighbors. Postal Service lawyers responded by threatening the ten-year-olds with a $76,500 fine.[104] In June 1991, postal officials threatened to fine an eleven-year-old boy in Palm Beach, Florida, $300 for putting fliers advertising his lawn-mowing service in neighbors' mailboxes.[105] Federal Express complained at a public hearing in 1993 that Postal Service inspectors were visiting Federal Express customers and threatening to fine them in order to force them to shift their business to the Postal Service. Postal inspectors reportedly even threatened to punish companies for not paying U.S. postage on their interoffice shipments.[106] The Postal Service investigated seventeen companies for possible violations of its monopoly in 1993[107] and have imposed more than $500,000 in fines since 1990.

The Postal Service is curtailing the amount of mail service Americans can receive. Mail delivery to residence doorsteps was abolished in 1978 for new homes and is gradually being phased out for older homes. Instead, the Postal Service delivers mail to "cluster boxes," which requires people to travel up to a half mile or more to pick it up. The Postal Service is carrying out this service cutback solely because it is cheaper not to deliver mail all the way to people's homes. The *Miami Herald* reported in 1988 that "only 29 percent of South Florida residents get their letters delivered to their doors."[108] According to Meg Harris, a Postal Service spokeswoman, "Communities are growing so large and the volume of mail increasing so rapidly that new delivery methods are essential. Over time, door delivery is going to be phased out."[109] In Maryville, Tennessee, residents in one neighborhood who refused to surrender home delivery and sign up for cluster boxes were told that their mail would be temporarily held at the post office, where they could go and collect it.[110] This cluster-box program imposes a severe burden on elderly and disabled people who must struggle to the box locations each day. Though the Postal Service claims it can no longer afford to deliver to people's front doors (despite first-class postage rates rising over 800 percent since 1958), Postal Service lawyers will seek to punish any private carrier who delivers letters all the way to people's doorsteps. The Postal Service chooses to save costs by sacrificing its captive customers rather than stressing its work force; an audit by the Postal Inspection Service concluded that the typical letter carrier wastes an hour and a half a day.[111]

American citizens are hostages to a government monopoly that chooses to provide less and less service each year. In 1764, colonial Postmaster General Benjamin Franklin proclaimed a goal of two-day mail delivery between New York and Philadelphia.[112] Currently, the Postal Service considers it a success to deliver first-class mail from New York City to next-door Westchester County in two days. In 1990, the Postal Service launched a nationwide plan to intentionally slow down mail delivery, officially lowering its goals for overnight mail delivery. Rep. Frank McCloskey, chairman of the House Subcommittee on Postal Operations, complained, "Postmasters from locations across the country have informed this subcommittee that first-class mail is being delayed for no apparent reason."[113] Postmaster General Anthony Frank claimed that the new delivery standards will "improve our ability to deliver local mail on time."[114] But this is almost entirely a result of the Postal Service's lowering the definition of "on time." Sen. David Pryor observed, "This is like trying to fool the public by cutting the top off the flagpole when the flag is stuck halfway up."[115] The Postal Inspection Service issued a blistering report in 1991 that concluded that post offices "generally have a negative attitude towards service improvement, even when the capability is there at no additional cost." First-class mail is delivered almost 20 percent slower now than in 1969.[116] A 1993 Postal Inspection Service report concluded that Postal Service advertisements for its Priority Mail mistakenly implied that two-day national delivery was guaranteed—even though postal officials knew that actual delivery routinely takes three or more days.[117]

With its monopoly, the Postal Service effectively has a right to lose or destroy as much mail as its employees choose. A Postal Inspection Service audit found properly addressed mail dumped in the trash at 76 percent of the post offices it visited.[118] *Federal Times* reported that an investigation of Philadelphia post offices "found deliverable first-class mail strewn on the workroom floor and being walked on by employees . . . and the destruction of mail that could have been returned to senders."[119] Between October 1989 and March 1990, the Postal Inspection Service arrested almost a thousand postal workers for stealing, delaying, or destroying mail.[120] One Arlington, Virginia, postal clerk told a customer, "We don't have room for the junk mail—so we've been throwing it out."[121] A survey by Doubleday found that up to 14 percent of properly addressed third-class mail vanishes in the postal labyrinth.[122] The Postal Service is likely losing or throwing out over a billion letters a year.[123] Government officials insist that the Postal Service has a right to a monopoly—even when postal employees choose to throw away the letters instead of delivering them.

Local post offices have the power to ban mail delivery to some people's houses. In the old days, postal officials bragged that "neither snow, nor rain, nor heat, nor gloom of night stays these couriers from the swift completion of their appointed rounds." But in the 1990s the only thing necessary to stop mail delivery is a few leaves. The Altadena, California, post office informed one disabled woman that it would not deliver her mail until she picked up the leaves on the road in front of her house because postal officials feared that the leaves made the dirt road "slippery when wet," and therefore too dangerous for a postal carrier.[124] In Lynn, Massachusetts, postal officials ended mail delivery to dozens of residents on Vine Street after someone reportedly verbally harassed a female postal carrier. The residents were told that they could come to the post office to pick up their mail between 10:00 A.M. and 4:00 P.M. on weekdays. (A local police sergeant disagreed with the Postal Service's declaration that the neighborhood was dangerous for a female carrier.)[125] A private company facing the same problem would simply have assigned a male carrier to the area, but the Postal Service chose to punish an entire neighborhood for the alleged misbehavior of one person.

Far greater restrictions on mail delivery could be imposed in the future. Postmaster General Marvin Runyon announced in 1992 that he was considering abolishing home mail delivery on Tuesdays and Thursdays as a budget measure.[126] Postmaster General Al Casey suggested in 1986 that the Postal Service might abolish Monday mail deliveries.[127] Congressional committees during the 1980s repeatedly debated abolishing Saturday mail delivery as a cost-saving measure.

A 1976 *New Yorker* cartoon expressed the modern Postal Service's motto: "Neither lethargy, indifference, nor the general collapse of standards will prevent these couriers from eventually delivering some of your mail."[128] In 1843, Postmaster General Charles Wickliffe admitted that many people thought the government's mail monopoly was "odious," but insisted that it must be preserved for the good of the country.[129] Now, over 150 years later, the monopoly is still odious and less justified than ever. There is no need to give a government behemoth exclusive control over the transport of small envelopes. It should not be a federal crime to deliver the mail faster than the Postal Service.

"HAZARDOUS," THE TYRANT'S PLEA

Federal officials routinely show their dedication to the environment by bragging about the number of jail sentences imposed on private citizens and corporate officials. A May 1992 Justice Department press release proclaimed: "The department obtained the highest level of fines ever, a 10 percent increase in environmental criminal convictions from FY 90 and the second highest number of such convictions in history."[130] An October 29, 1992, Justice Department press release hailed a "series of record successes in enforcing the nation's environmental laws," bragging of "a record 191 criminal indictments" and "a record $163,064,344 in criminal penalties."[131] But while government enforcers are racking up record scores, private citizens are increasingly being wronged and oppressed.

One of the most disruptive and least effective environmental laws is Superfund. Congress enacted the Superfund program (its actual title is the Comprehensive Environmental Response, Compensation and Liability Act of 1980) to deal with the problem of abandoned hazardous-waste sites. Since

1980, EPA has cast the Superfund net far wider to exert federal control over more types of sites than Congress originally intended. The federal government has spent almost $10 billion for Superfund and forced private parties to spend up to another $80 billion.[132] Yet the program has cleaned up only 160 of the 1,202 most dangerous landfills and chemical dumps identified by EPA.

EPA has expansively interpreted the 1980 legislation to allow it to impose practically unlimited liability on tens of thousands of companies and private organizations. To impose responsibility for the cost of the entire cleanup of a polluted area, EPA need only allege that a company contributed a single item of waste to a site. As lawyer Kent Holland observed, Superfund liability is like

> imposing a new liability for sending a car to a junkyard. Any person whose car was found in a junkyard could be required to pay the total costs of cleaning up the junkyard regardless of whether that person's individual car caused any injury or damage to anyone. And just as with Superfund, the new junkyard law would apply not only to cars disposed of in junkyards after the law was enacted, it would also apply to cars put in junkyards at any time in the past. The company that made the car many years ago could be found liable if one of its cars was ever put into a junkyard. Likewise, if records show that 30 years ago one of your cars ended its life in a junkyard, you could be liable today for all cleanup costs associated with that junkyard under the new law.[133]

EPA has intentionally disregarded equity and fairness in its prosecution of companies that allegedly contributed hazardous materials to Superfund sites. EPA routinely seeks to force corporations to pay far more for waste site cleanups than the corporations are responsible for contributing to the site. EPA Administrator Lee Thomas declared in 1985, "The fair share concept is one we have not found viable in trying to settle sites."[134] But the agency does show some moderation in its demands. In a 1985 *Federal Register* announcement, EPA revealed, "In cost recovery actions it will be difficult to negotiate a settlement for more than a party's assets. . . . An excessive amount [of claims] could force a party into bankruptcy, which will of course make collection very difficult."[135] One federal judge observed in 1989 that Superfund "is not a legislative scheme which places a high priority on fairness to generators of hazardous waste."[136]

Superfund has given the EPA a license to shake down private companies. In 1991, the EPA sent letters to hundreds of automotive dealers in Oklahoma and northern Texas demanding payment for the cost of cleanup of the Double Eagle oil refinery site in Oklahoma City. As *Automotive News* reported:

> The letters not only ask whether the dealership sent used oil to Double Eagle for recycling in the past, but also request five years of tax records to determine a dealership's ability to pay the costs of cleanup. Dealers who sent their used oil to the recycling facility, some of it as far back as the 1950s, fear they may be stuck with bills of five or six figures at a time when many are struggling to survive a recession.

> "We see dealers who are not economically able to sustain a severe penalty for something they could not control," said W. L. McCulloh, an Oldsmobile-Cadillac-Honda dealer in Ardmore, Okla., and a regional vice president of the National Automobile Dealers Association. Most of the dealers have had to write checks for $10,000 to $20,000, but settlements of $100,000 or more per dealership are not unlikely. . . .[137]

None of the dealers who sent the used oil to the Double Eagle refinery site violated any law and actually behaved much more responsibly than auto dealers and gas stations that simply dump used oil on the ground. Oklahoma auto dealers were forced to make large payments for cleanup even in cases where there were no records showing that the company sent used oil to the site.[138]

A *Washington Post* editorial noted that Superfund "is generating intolerable injustices."[139] Superfund in some cases is degenerating into "robbery with an environmental badge." EPA requires almost no evidence in order to impose potentially bankrupting liabilities on private firms. Bruce Diamond, EPA's Director of Waste Programs Enforcement, conceded that, at some sites, "All you have is an aging truck driver who says, 'I took yellow liquid and I think it was from them.'"[140] At the Rosen Brothers Scrap Yard site in New York, EPA selected the potentially responsible parties largely based on memories of the scrapyard employees about what had happened twenty years before.[141] EPA notified Formal Ware Rental Services of Tulsa, Oklahoma, that it would be held responsible for the cleanup of a local Superfund site; the only evidence linking the clothing rental company to the site was the fact that it had paid someone $14 in 1972 to haul trash to the Superfund site.[142] EPA fingered a Boy Scout troop as a potentially responsible party to finance the cleanup of a Superfund designated scrapyard in Minneapolis.[143] At New York's Ludlow Sanitary Landfill, a court ruled that a butcher shop owner was liable because the *glue* on the boxes he threw in his dumpster (and which were later taken to the landfill) contained hazardous materials.[144] Several churches and local schools were identified as potentially responsible parties to finance the cleanup of a Superfund site in Gray, Maine.[145]

EPA is also financially punishing many private corporations for the negligent environmental practices of government agencies. EPA sued Shell Oil Company for the total cleanup costs at Rocky Mountain Arsenal in Colorado—even though the contaminated ground was used for years by the U.S. Army for chemical warfare tests.[146] Since 1964, the city and county of Denver, Colorado, has owned and operated a waste disposal site known as the Lowry Landfill. In 1983, EPA designated one sector of the landfill as a Superfund site. Even though the local government had complete control of the waste site's operation for the entire time when hazardous wastes were deposited there, it proceeded to sue the companies that sent their waste to the site—as if they, instead of the government, were responsible. In 1987, a list of 187 potentially responsible parties was made public.[147] As of August

1992, only $5 million had been spent to clean up Lowry—but $80 million had been spent on attorneys and other costs of the legal dispute.[148]

The more EPA exaggerates the health risks at potential Superfund sites, the more power EPA officials have over landowners, businesses, and others. The agency is increasingly getting rapped by federal courts for its capriciousness in placing private property on the National Priority List (NPL), the official list of Superfund sites. The *New York Law Journal* noted, "Presence on the NPL is often the economic death knell for a property because it renders the land essentially unmarketable and foreshadows years of costly work. The average NPL site takes 10 years to clean up, at an average cost of $30 million."[149] In 1991, a federal appeals court overturned an EPA Superfund designation of a Texas waste site. The EPA had justified putting the site on the Superfund list because it claimed that piles of slag there posed a threat of airborne arsenic contamination. But arsenic can only be released into the air at temperatures above 1,000 degrees Fahrenheit. (If the temperature in the general area of the slag reaches 1,000 degrees, then a little arsenic in the air will be the least of the problems of nearby residents.)[150] In Anne Arundel County, Maryland, EPA added a landfill to the NPL after it discovered contamination in a nearby drinking well, but it failed to notify the family using the well of the contamination.[151] The Federal Fourth Circuit Court of Appeals declared:

> We are rather dismayed that, in order to ensure a sufficiently high [Superfund hazard] score, the EPA would permit a citizen to continue using a well located within one mile of a landfill which it believed sufficiently dangerous to the public health and environment to justify considering it "a national priority." The EPA neither notified the petitioner nor the well user that the well had been identified for purposes of calculating the Landfill's [Superfund hazard] score.[152]

EPA apparently felt it was more important to have a bureaucratic triumph—adding another site to its Superfund list—than to actually protect an American family's health.

EPA is abusing Superfund to goldplate slightly contaminated areas that often pose little threat to human health. The cleanup of a Superfund abandoned quarry site in Oklahoma was delayed in 1988 after EPA and the Oklahoma State Department of Health clashed on the proper cleanup remedy; EPA demanded a $12 million cleanup, while the state health department concluded that a $1 million cleanup was all that was necessary.[153] (EPA won.) Peter Passell of the *New York Times* noted, "Virtually all of the risk to human health [from Superfund sites], most analysts agree, could be eliminated for a tiny fraction of these sums [$300 billion to $700 billion] spent to restore waste sites to pristine conditions." EPA estimated that Holden, Missouri's water supply could be fully protected from contamination from an abandoned factory site for only $71,000. But, as Passell notes, "State and Federal laws require a cleanup that would cost $13.6 million to $41.5 million."[154] EPA refused to accept the lower-cost cleanup. A study by the Congressional Office of Technology Assessment concluded that half of all superfund cleanups "address hypothetical risks rather than actual ones."[155] The stricter the cleanup standards the EPA imposes, the more power agency officials will have over private companies—since companies will have to spend far more to meet EPA's standards.

EPA has also made a mockery of due process in its implementation of the Resource Conservation and Recovery Act (RCRA). RCRA, first enacted in 1976, regulates the treatment, storage, transport, and disposal of hazardous waste. EPA has issued over 17,000 pages of regulations and proposed regulations on RCRA in the *Federal Register*, and EPA estimates that complying with RCRA costs businesses and governments an estimated $30 billion a year.[156] But the more regulations the agency issues, the more incomprehensible the program becomes. Though corporate officials face fines of up to $50,000 a day and imprisonment for up to five years for each RCRA violation,[157] EPA has done a pitiful job of informing them of how to comply with the agency's *interpretation du jour*. As lawyer Richard Stoll noted in an American Bar Association publication entitled *RCRA Policy Documents:*

> Most who have suffered even moderate exposure to RCRA and EPA's regulations would agree that they are astounding and confounding. It is challenging enough to try to discern what one paragraph in a regulatory section means. To then attempt to relate that paragraph to another inscrutable provision 100 pages earlier, then another provision 100 pages later, then a footnote in a 9-year-old Federal Register preamble . . . can be downright exhilarating. But that's just the beginning. . . . The real fun begins when you get to EPA's unpublished internal interpretations or "guidance." . . . What has emerged in its place is a truly non-systematic, ad hoc, and unpredictable approach. For years now, EPA RCRA personnel have articulated important RCRA interpretations in whatever format seems to strike their fancy at a particular moment. . . . Frequently, someone at EPA headquarters will send a memorandum to an EPA region in response to a request for an interpretation or clarification. Sometimes (but not always) the author at headquarters will decide to send copies of the memo to all ten regions. Sometimes EPA headquarters personnel decide, based on numerous inquiries, that a general headquarters guidance memo needs to be sent out to all regions. Sometimes EPA calls such a memo a "Directive" and assigns an internal number to it, other times . . . EPA does not. Sometimes new and important interpretations appear in letters from headquarters or regional officials in response to private inquiries. . . . EPA has made no effort to categorize or publicize these interpretations.[158]

RCRA requires that companies clean up their factory grounds to "background levels"—i.e., levels at which chemicals occur naturally in the surrounding environment. But background levels usually have no relation to safeguarding human health. If someone poured a glass of chlorinated tap water onto the ground at a RCRA cleanup site, he could be fined for polluting the environment, according to former EPA General Counsel Frank

Blake.[159] Yet under the Safe Water Drinking Act, the same person could have a federal permit to discharge heavily polluted waste water directly into a river. RCRA prohibits the disposal of some chemicals in double-lined landfills, yet EPA allows the same chemicals to be applied directly to the land as fertilizers. In 1989, EPA announced that extracted baby's teeth were a hazardous waste and prohibited dentists from giving the teeth back to children.[160] Under RCRA, EPA presumes that every citizen near a site would suffer maximum exposure to every toxin. In 1986, Office of Management and Budget official Wendy Gramm criticized proposed RCRA regulations for presuming "that the individual receives the maximum exposure to the substance—in effect that he would sink a straw into groundwater within the disposal facility property boundary and drank half a gallon of this [maximum-contaminated] water each day for 70 years."[161] EPA officials promulgated a rule declaring that any substance that was mixed with a RCRA-listed hazardous waste automatically became hazardous itself; federal prosecutors argued in a court case in Texas that if a company "put the contents of one eyedropper of hazardous waste into the ocean, the entire ocean then becomes hazardous waste under the law."[162]

Corporations that can afford a costly court battle over alleged RCRA violations have sometimes defeated EPA. In November 1992, an Arkansas federal court jury took less than an hour to acquit four corporate officials of Aviation Inc. of charges that they "conspired to knowingly transport hazardous waste without a manifest and knowingly discharged pollutants from a point source into waters of the United States without a permit." The company operated an aircraft refinishing and maintenance business that used solvents to strip paint from aircraft. The federal government prosecuted the firm because the waste water it poured on the ground contained 0.0003 percent of the solvent methylene chloride, which RCRA labeled as hazardous. Decaffeinated coffee contains a higher percentage of methylene chloride, yet EPA has yet to prosecute any housewives or househusbands who spill coffee grounds. As a press release on the court decision noted, "In this case, the government did not bother to run any laboratory tests on the aircraft process water or the paint gun residue to determine if these wastes exhibited any of the RCRA hazardous waste characteristics."[163]

Penalties for environmental regulations have become far more punitive. As Leslie Spencer of *Forbes* observed, "In the past few years Congress has made virtually any infraction of environmental statutes a criminal offense. In the process, it has blurred the traditional distinction between civil and criminal law."[164] Keith Onsdorff, the former director of EPA's Office of Criminal Enforcement, observed in 1992, "A fundamental tenet of this nation's criminal law requires that before an act can constitute a crime, the perpetrator must act with criminal intent. The origins of this principle can be traced back to ancient Greek and Roman law, and the requirement of criminal, or 'evil,' intent was carried forward into eighteenth-century English common law. The concept is also firmly rooted in our legal system."[165] Yet as Onsdorff noted, the EPA increasingly disregards this requirement in its criminal prosecutions. Corporate officials now face possible jail sentences—even for failure to file routine paperwork or pay permit fees on time. Prosecutors often have vast discretion as to whether to prosecute routine environmental violations as either felonies or misdemeanors. Los Angeles deputy district attorney Robert Brodney explained how he decides how to prosecute businessmen for environmental violations: "When the little hairs on the back of your neck stand up, it's a felony. When it just makes you tingle, it's a misdemeanor. If it does nothing to you at all, it's a civil problem."[166] Considering the extreme specificity and complexity of environmental regulations, assessing criminal penalties for violating some regulations is the equivalent of imprisoning someone for exceeding the speed limit by one-tenth of a mile per hour.

The Justice Department stretched the meaning of criminal behavior in its prosecution of Exxon after an Exxon tanker dumped ten million gallons of crude oil into Prince William Sound off the Alaska coast. Although Exxon had spent $2 billion to clean up the damage from the spill, the Justice Department pressured the company to sign a plea bargain admitting criminal violations of the Migratory Bird Treaty Act because many birds died in the oil slick resulting from the unintentional spill. As the Competitive Enterprise Institute's Kent Jeffreys observed, "Under the identical legal reasoning imposed on Exxon's inadvertent destruction of a few migratory birds, flying a jet could require a bird hunting permit. The only reason offered by the Justice Department for applying criminal laws to inadvertent pollution violations is to 'send a message' to polluters. This message seems to be that the politically unpopular will be denied fair treatment by the government."[167] Federal judge Russell Holland complained, "I have some difficulty with the concept that we criminalize unintentional environmental accidents—in effect, criminalizing the killing of birds and sea otters and so forth, yet we do not criminalize airline crashes, which result from negligence, and which kill people."[168]

The EPA scored a public relations coup in 1993 when it banned the sale of BearGuard spray in Alaska. Alaska has roughly one bear for every six residents, and in 1992 two people (including a six-year-old girl) were mauled to death by bears. Alaskan residents learned to defend themselves against the 700-pound bears by using a hot pepper spray known as BearGuard, which would stop a bear and force him to retreat when sprayed on the bear's face. Many Alaskans consider BearGuard highly reliable, and it was widely used during the months that crews cleaned up the mess from the 1989 Exxon *Valdez* oil spill. But in May 1993, the EPA ruled that the pepper spray is actually a pesticide (animal repellant) under the terms of the Federal Insecticide, Fungicide and Rodenticide Act—and then banned the sale of

BearGuard because it had not been properly tested to prove its effectiveness. Senator Frank Murkowski of Alaska went ballistic, declaring on the Senate floor: "This leaves Alaskans somewhat in the woods because the bears are now awake and they are hungry after a winter nap with only one choice: To carry guns and blast bullets rather than pepper at any bear that they may encounter that is looking for a tasty meal."[169] Murkowski declaimed, "What we have here is an interpretation made from the EPA by some mindless edict from the safety of a Virginia office. The ruling is terrible for hiker safety. It is probably terrible for the bears because it removes the only nonlethal means of protecting oneself from bear attack."[170] Murkowski complained to the *Washington Post:* "The EPA admits that the spray is probably safe to eat. It seems like you can use it on a dead bear, you can use it on bear stew, but you cannot use it on a live bear if the bear is after you."[171] Murkowski suggested that bureaucrats in Washington might be trying to force Alaskans to have to "throw a pot of spicy chili" on advancing bears.

"Hazardous" has become the contemporary equivalent of what ancient Romans termed "the tyrant's plea, emergency." "Hazardous" has become a blank check for unlimited power over regulated producers and individuals. Lawyers Bryan Tabler and Mark Shere observed in 1992, "Today, in the environmental area, we increasingly have a government of memoranda and not of laws. Regulation by memo is unlawful, undemocratic, and in many cases all but unstoppable. . . . A lone [EPA] administrator imposes binding requirements by typing a memorandum."[172] There will certainly be cases where environmental crimes justify severe criminal penalties, such as cases of midnight dumping of dangerous waste. But instead of writing good laws, Congress instead grants federal agencies power to punish almost any behavior that displeases agency officials or gains favorable headlines.

RESOLVING BANKING PROBLEMS WITH AN IRON FIST

In the 1930s, the federal government responded to a wave of bank failures by creating savings and loan institutions and federal deposit insurance for banks. Deposit insurance effectively guaranteed depositors that the federal government would reimburse them if their financial institution went bankrupt. From the beginning, the structure of deposit insurance created perverse incentives, allowing bank and savings and loan owners to keep the profits from their operations and obliging taxpayers to pick up the losses.

The savings and loan (S & L) industry went down in flames in the late 1970s and 1980s. An audit by the Federal Home Loan Bank Board concluded that the savings and loan industry had a negative net worth of $120 billion in 1980 before the Reagan administration took office.[173] In 1980 Congress partially deregulated the industry, allowing S & L operators to make much riskier investments, among other changes. At the same time, Congress increased the amount of federal insurance of individual account deposits from $40,000 to $100,000. Thus, while Congress decreased government controls on one side of the bank operations, it increased taxpayer exposure to savings and loan losses. Brookings Institution analyst Robert Litan noted that federal regulatory policy encouraged savings and loans to issue "phony financial statements" that misled the public as to the financial condition of the institutions.[174]

Savings and loan losses worsened as the 1980s progressed, thanks in part to the Reagan administration's negligent oversight as well as to congressional interference with auditors seeking to shut down bankrupt thrifts. But as long as Congress could deny that a problem existed, congressmen could avoid appropriating money to fix the problem and thereby avoid boosting the politically unpopular federal budget deficit. The cost of shutting down bankrupt savings and loans and banks eventually ballooned to up to $500 billion. Few media commentators recognized the debacle as another proof of the incompetence and irresponsibility of political management, instead blaming the problem on the free market. But as Reagan administration economic adviser William Niskanen noted, "The cost of this failure to the taxpayers is entirely attributable to the flawed system of federal deposit insurance."[175]

When Congress was finally forced to face the problems of S & Ls, congressmen sought to divert attention from their own mismanagement (and the millions of dollars of campaign contributions congressmen received from S & L operators) by portraying the crisis as largely the result of conniving bankers, dishonest lawyers, and other villains. Instead of fixing the underlying problem by phasing out federal guarantees of deposits, Congress instead maintained the guarantees and greatly increased the power of government officials to punish anyone vaguely associated with financial institutions. In 1989, Congress enacted the Financial Institutions Reform, Recovery and Enforcement Act (FIRREA), which created the federal Office of Thrift Supervision (OTS).

Many savings and loan institutions held so-called junk bonds as part of their investment portfolio. (Junk bonds are high-risk, high-yield securities issued by corporations without a blue-chip credit rating.) FIRREA required S & Ls to mark their so-called junk bonds to market value and to rapidly sell them off. This resulted in panic selling; in the six months after the law's enactment, the average value of a junk bond plummeted. Professor Glenn Yago observed, "Overnight, profitable S & Ls were turned into government-owned basket cases."[176] Yago further noted:

> A concrete example of this destructive process is Columbia Savings and Loan of California. Under FIRREA, Columbia was forced to sell off its junk-bond debt in early 1990 at the market's trough. It then became insolvent. A review of Columbia's $1.8 billion portfolio shows that if Columbia hadn't been forced to sell off its junk-bond debt, it would have had a profit of $200 million by September 1991, or a return of 9.8% in the two year period since the enactment of FIRREA.[177]

Though Congress severely penalized savings and loans for investing in junk bonds, the General Accounting Office (GAO) concluded that junk bonds were one of the more profitable investments that thrifts had made during the 1980s[178] and actually had a slightly higher return than investments in U.S. Treasury bonds.[179] A few years after Congress torpedoed the junk bond market, the demand for such bonds revived, and they once again became a highly profitable investment. This made stark the fact that Congress's order to sell in 1989 was a catastrophic mistake. Yet despite the revival of junk bonds' value, federal agencies still prosecuted numerous savings and loan officials for their previous investments in junk bonds, claiming that such investments had been a criminal abuse of their position. As economist Paul Craig Roberts noted, "Why should a thrift president, and the local doctor, lawyer and businessmen who sat on his board, be personally liable for losses suffered when the federal government drove down junk-bond prices and forced the thrift to sell at the bottom of the market?"[180]

Instead of closing down failing thrifts, the government preferred to arrange to have them taken over by creditworthy, solvent thrifts, thereby minimizing the cost to the government. Federal banking agencies signed written agreements promising specific benefits to institutions in return for their assistance in taking over failing thrifts. But in 1989 Congress, as a cost-saving measure, nullified many of these contracts, causing several profitable savings and loans to be forced into liquidation. Many savings and loans sued the government for breach of contract in the U.S. Claims Court, but lawyers for the U.S. government denied that any binding agreement existed because Congress had specifically declared that the agreements were not in the public interest. U.S. Claims Court chief judge Loren Smith observed, "On the government's reasoning, any statute breaching a contract would be immune . . . merely because its purpose was to breach the contract." Smith derided the government's position:

> [I]t would make all dealings with the government a very elaborate and expensive form of gambling to hold that the government may repudiate a contract whenever subsequent policy considerations dictate that it was not a good or prudent bargain. . . . The assertion that, in order to freely regulate, the government must have the power to disregard the rights and interests of its citizens is a novel proposition. . . . Sovereign power is always restricted, in one sense, by the rights of individuals. However, in our Nation that has never been seen as an improper restriction on regulatory power. Rather, it is the foundation upon which all law and regulation are built.[181]

The Office of Thrift Supervision has been extremely heavy-handed in its dealings. As *Legal Times* reported:

> Arthur Leibold, a banking lawyer . . . says the agency is imposing multiple punishments—often through multimillion-dollar fines—before allegations are proved in state or federal courts, or even before holding its own administrative hearings. Critics of the OTS say the agency is abusing due process, usurping the federal courts' role, imposing what amount to criminal sanctions for alleged administrative

> violations, and using test cases to expand its powers. Rarely has an agency enjoyed such prosecutorial powers; never, lawyers say, has an agency tried so hard to use them. The OTS also seems to be taking the lead in setting up sweeping settlements involving itself, other banking agencies, and the Justice Department. Some of those deals seek to confiscate the defendant's wages for the next 15 or 20 years, extend the statute of limitations for finding wrongdoing, and prevent defendants, their spouses, and their children from ever filing for bankruptcy protection.[182]

Congress further expanded the power of banking regulators by amending the Crime Control Act of 1990 to give "bank regulators authority to attach all the assets of any person without the showing of immediate and irreparable harm that is normally required for an attachment to issue."[183] Bank regulators were also empowered to fine any citizen $1 million a day. Congress's intent was that OTS would only fine people who had been involved in wrongdoing connected with financial institutions, but the law as written permits the OTS to fine any citizen.

The Office of Thrift Supervision also has de facto power to destroy individuals or organizations on purely circumstantial grounds. Lincoln Savings and Loan was shut down in 1989, but the OTS sought to penalize Kaye, Scholer, one of the nation's largest law firms, for its role in representing the failed savings and loan in its disputes with the government. OTS officials accused the firm of "loophole lawyering" and ordered the firm not to make significant omissions of facts to regulators "when Kaye, Scholer knows that the agency may have a different view of the law and regulations."[184] The OTS alleged that Kaye, Scholer lawyer Peter Fishbein had failed to disclose possible violations by his client to federal regulators and demanded that Fishbein be banned for life from representing banks or thrifts. (Yale Law School professor Geoffrey Hazard examined the government's charges and concluded that "disclosures and representations that the Office of Thrift Supervision alleges should have been made to the Bank Board by Kaye, Scholer . . . would have violated the standards of ethical conduct and professional responsibility generally recognized as applicable to Kaye, Scholer in its role as litigation counsel.")[185] Kaye, Scholer rejected the OTS's demands as a violation of the traditional right of lawyers to vigorously represent their clients. On March 2, 1992, the OTS effectively steamrolled the firm, freezing its assets and imposing a $275 million penalty. The OTS froze the law firm's assets on its own authority, without even consulting its own administrative law judges, much less any outside federal tribunal. OTS claimed a need to freeze the firm's assets to prevent the firm from escaping the government's wrath, but there was little danger that a leading law firm would pack up overnight and flee to Brazil. The freeze order, by destroying the firm's credit rating, paralyzed the law firm, which required a credit line of $1 million to $2 million a week for its operating expenses. Kaye, Scholer eventually agreed to pay a $41 million fine and to ban Fishbein from any further financial regulatory practice. The Association of the Bar of the City of New York later complained, "Because of the coercive freeze order, lawyers and the public have been deprived of any precedential effect from the Kaye, Scholer matter. The only thing that lawyers have learned is that if they represent the client vigorously, they risk financial ruin before an action against them is even brought before a judge."[186]

Federal financial institution policy vivifies how the worse a government policy fails, the more powerful government officials become. The OTS has bent over backward to impose liability on lawyers, accountants, and others, yet no federal official has proposed to hold members of Congress liable for their irresponsible laws and actions. In effect, because the federal government chose to guarantee bank deposits, federal regulators must have vast arbitrary power over the entire banking and thrift industry, and practically unlimited financial power over tens of thousands of individuals serving as banking or savings and loan officers, directors, consultants, or advisors.

EXHAUSTING LIBERTIES, OR MODERN STAR CHAMBERS

The liberty of today's Americans often rests on the thoroughness and vigor of judicial review of administrative rulings and decrees. If the courts are not vigorous in their analysis of bureaucracy's rulings, then the citizens are, for all practical purposes, at the mercy of the bureaucracy. Deference to bureaucracy increasingly means deference to arbitrary treatment of private citizens. Supreme Court Justice Hugo Black wrote in 1955: "Every procedure which would offer a possible temptation to the judge . . . not to hold the balance nice, clear and true between the [parties] denies . . . due process of law."[187]

Most citizens' disputes with government agencies are resolved within the agencies themselves, not by local, state, or federal courts. Kenneth Davis, author of the highly respected five-volume *Administrative Law Treatise*, estimates that federal administrative "trials" outnumber federal court trials by a ratio of more than 6 to 1 and that up to 93 percent of all disputes are resolved in federal agency settings rather than in federal court settings.[188] Thus, the sanctity of a citizen's rights rests largely on the justice of administrative procedures. Unfortunately, "administrative justice" is often an oxymoron.

The creation of over a thousand administrative law judges by the federal government in the 1930s and afterward was a radical departure from American common law. As Martin Shapiro observed, "In the early 1930s, the New Deal created a government based on concentrating power in the hands of technically expert administrative agencies. By the early 1940s administrative law had been well shaped to express this theory. . . . The central doctrines of the administrative law of the 1940s were the twin presumptions that agencies had correctly found the facts and had correctly interpreted the law. . . . Voila technocracy—rule by expert agencies."[189]

Unfortunately, expertise and objectivity are not necessarily the same. An American Bar Association task force found that administrative law judges at the Securities and Exchange Commission upheld the agency's position in fifty-eight out of sixty-two cases over a five-year period.[190] The General Accounting Office reported in 1992 that administrative law judges in six federal agencies believed that the agency had attempted to "compromise their independence."[191] One administrative law judge at the Interior Department told the *ABA Journal:* "We do operate in a wholly vindicative and retaliatory environment."[192] Edward Slavin of the Government Accountability Project in Washington, D.C., observed that administrative law judges "are employed by the agencies whose cases they decide. Rather than having the independence of a district court judge, they are essentially on the payroll and subjected to the pressure of the agencies."[193] Rep. Barney Frank observed in 1990: "We have gotten allegations from administrative law judges of coercion, threatened transfers and other kinds of pressures."[194] Yet, citizens are forced to spend months or years slogging through these systems as if they were real judicial systems.

The Social Security Administration (SSA) has an elaborate system of over 800 administrative law judges devoted largely to judging disability claims. When disability claims soared in the late 1970s and early 1980s, the SSA management responded by strong-arming the administrative law judges into rejecting more disability claims. The Senate Governmental Affairs Committee concluded in a 1983 report that "the Social Security Administration is pressuring its Administrative Law Judges to reduce the rate at which they allow disabled persons to participate in or continue to participate in the Social Security Disability Program."[195] In 1992 a federal judge ruled "that the Federal Government improperly denied disability benefits to 20,000 mentally and physically impaired New Yorkers in the late 1970s and early 1980s by systematically and restrictively misapplying its own eligibility regulations."[196] Politicians first compelled workers to pay for disability insurance—and then political appointees intervened to strong-arm administrative law judges to deny the same workers disability benefits. (Many of the cases did lack merit.)

Federal laws often require that a citizen "exhaust administrative remedies" within a federal agency before a federal judge will deign to hear the citizen's complaint against the government. But this creates an incentive for federal agencies to endlessly prolong the administrative appeals process, postponing as long as possible the citizen's chance to get a meaningful, semi-objective chance at relief. Some agencies have innovative definitions of "exhaustion of administrative remedies"; the Internal Revenue Service requires citizens to agree to waive the statute of limitations on the IRS's investigation of their tax returns as part of the citizen's "administrative remedies"—as if waiving one's legal rights were a necessary part of seeking legal remedies.[197]

The USDA's administrative law judge system has been slammed in federal courts for its politicization. In the case of *Utica Packing Company v.*

John R. Block, a USDA judicial officer made a decision with which USDA officials "violently disagreed," according to USDA's own testimony. A top USDA official removed the judge who made the "wrong" decision from the case, announced that the case would be reopened, and then appointed a deputy assistant USDA secretary who had no legal experience to preside over the retrial. Not surprisingly, the defendant was found guilty the second time around. A federal appeals court overturned USDA's conviction and condemned the agency's process: "There is no guarantee of fairness when the one who appoints a judge has the power to remove the judge before the end of a proceedings for rendering a decision which displeases the appointer. Yet this is exactly what happened in this case." The court concluded, "All notions of judicial impartiality would be abandoned if such a procedure were permitted."[198]

The administrative law judge system at the Agriculture Department is a good example of how "exhaustion of administrative remedies" results in exhaustion of individual rights. Cal-Almond Inc. filed suit in 1985 requesting relief from a requirement that forced it to pay for advertisements. (Cal-Almond was forced to pay hundreds of thousands of dollars a year yet received no benefit from the consumer-oriented advertisements because it sold all of its almonds to processors.) A year later, the company finally got a hearing from Administrative Law Judge Victor Weber, who dismissed the case. The company appealed to Donald Campbell, USDA's chief judicial officer. Campbell scornfully rejected the appeal, declaring that "whatever legal or factual merits may exist in Petitioner's views, they are submerged in sweeping opposition to the Marketing Order."[199] This is administrative justice at its best—implying that anyone who harshly criticizes a government agency forfeits his right to relief from that agency's arbitrary actions.

Carl Pescosolido, a California orange grower, filed suit in the administrative law judge system in 1980, protesting federal marketing order requirements that prohibited him from selling much of his orange harvest. Pescosolido's suit required six years to get a ruling from a USDA judge. When one administrative law judge vindicated Pescosolido, ruling that USDA restrictions on orange sales from 1979 to 1984 violated federal law, Chief Judicial Officer Campbell overturned that decision in 1988. Campbell's ruling was a tribute to the "judicial temperament," as exemplified in administrative law. The 284-page decision was replete with exclamation marks and warnings of a "bloodbath" if USDA ended its restrictions on orange sales.[200] Campbell proudly described himself "as a careerist who has been involved with USDA's regulatory programs since 1949." Pescosolido had to seek relief from a man who has spent his whole life working in and building the existing system; he had little chance of getting an objective hearing. Campbell overturned the earlier decision partly because:

> It is well settled that the lawfulness of a marketing order must be judged by the facts contained in the promulgation hearing record rather than the facts petitioners would

> seek to introduce at [this] proceeding. The Order must stand or fall upon the basis of the evidence before the Secretary adduced during the promulgation proceedings, and additional evidence is not relevant or admissible in the [this] proceeding.[201]

Campbell further noted, "All interested persons had the opportunity to testify at that [promulgation] hearing, file briefs, and file exceptions to the recommended decision."[202] But the hearing Campbell refers to was held in 1953. Because the USDA decided to effectively expropriate part of farmers' harvests thirty-six years before, the sons and grandsons of farmers have no right to raise legal challenges to the loss of their property decades later. (Pescosolido's lawyer, Jim Moody, apologized that he was not yet born in 1953 and thus missed the hearings.)[203]

Some states have administrative law judge systems that are even more overtly biased than the federal system. New Yorkers file hundreds of thousands of cases before state administrative law judges each year. Nathan Mark, a retired New York State administrative law judge, testified in 1987 that he was removed from his position as a judge at the Department of Motor Vehicles because he was "accused of being too far on the side of the motorist"; he observed that the agency "is 100 percent a revenue producing agency . . . not concerned with honesty or justice."[204] The president of the New York State Bar Association, Maryann Freedman, stated in 1988 that administrative law judges have complained to her of at least twenty instances in which they have been disciplined by state agencies for ruling too frequently against the state government's position.[205] New York administrative law judges serve at the pleasure of the agency director and thus can be fired far more easily than most civil servants. Agency directors also can reverse a judge's decision without providing any written explanation.[206] This is equivalent to allowing the president of the United States to overturn Supreme Court decisions on a personal whim. The bias of the administrative law judges became such an embarrassment that the New York state legislature has repeatedly passed bills to create an independent Office of Administration, but Governor Mario Cuomo vetoed the bills.[207]

CONCLUSION

Faith in discretionary power means faith in giving government officials the power to punish whomever they please—and assuming that this will make America a better society. The proliferation of discretionary power is turning government employees into a ruling class with the power to directly subjugate other Americans. The Paternalist State adapts arbitrary policies to vigilantly defend the citizen's safety. But the more arbitrary government policies become, the less secure the citizen will be. We have sought to achieve security for the average citizen by vesting government officials with sweeping discretion over how that citizen is treated, employed, promoted, paid, and housed. Faith in discretionary power is simply faith in the superiority of government employees over private citizens—faith in letting some people coerce other people to force them to follow government officials' will.

The issue of arbitrary power goes to the heart of the modern debate over the nature of liberty—whether people's liberty is the result of limits on government coercion or the result of unlimited government power—whether a citizen will be freer when the government is restrained or when government officials are given carte blanche to do what they please.

-4-

Politics vs. Contracts

Freedom is not constituted solely of having a government of our own. Under this idea most nations would be free. We fought in the revolutionary war against exclusive privileges and oppressive monopolies.

—Sen. John Taylor (1822)[1]

Freedom of contract was the great desire of many immigrants who came to America's shores from the 1600s onward. A group of New Orleans butchers petitioned the Supreme Court in 1873, "Free competition in business, free enterprise, the absence of all exactions by petty tyranny, of all spoliation of private right by public authority—the suppression of sinecures, monopolies, titles of nobility, and exemption from legal duties—were exactly what the colonists sought for and obtained by their settlement here."[2] In 1915, Supreme Court Justice Mahlon Pitney declared:

> Included in the right of personal liberty and the right of private property . . . is the right to make contracts for the acquisition of property. Chief among such contracts is that of personal employment, by which labor and other services are exchanged for money or other forms of property. If this right be struck down or arbitrarily interfered with, there is a substantial impairment of liberty in the long-established constitutional sense. The right is as essential to the laborer as to the capitalist, to the poor as to the rich; for the vast majority of persons have no other honest way to begin to acquire property, save by working for money.[3]

The early American principle of almost unlimited freedom of contract has now been replaced by the principle of "government knows best"—even when government officials don't know what they are doing. As the twentieth century has progressed, governments are increasingly preempting individuals' opportunities to build their own lives through their own agreements. In area after area, government officials have asserted a prerogative to make decisions for individuals, to forcibly impose those decisions on people, and to punish people who made agreements outside of government control—outside of the narrow channels in which government officials permit private citizens to contract. Politicians and bureaucrats are increasingly prohibiting individuals from making their own best bargains.

Supreme Court Justice John Marshall declared in 1820 that "the Constitution stood for the principle that contracts should be inviolable." Today, there is a general presumption of the right of politicians and bureaucrats to strike down, prohibit, and nullify private contracts. And as long as the politicians and bureaucrats can think of a plausible pretext, the courts will likely uphold their dictates. Federal bureaucrats have struck down private citizens' right to make contracts based on such things as the supposed inequalities of bargaining power, the presumed stupidity of low-wage workers, and the need to protect government monopolies. As a result, individuals are left with little or no choice in more and more areas of their own lives—subject to government fiat in the jobs they are allowed to do, the dues they must pay, the work arrangements they may accept, and the transportation they may take. Congress, state legislatures, and judges now have an overwhelming bias against respecting freedom and sanctity of contract.

Of course, freedom of contract is not an absolute. No one has a right to contract for something that they do not own or control. Thus, a "contract" to murder someone is no contract, because the contractor has no right to snuff the life of the person targeted for assassination. Likewise, a contract to defraud someone is an oxymoron, since fraud is inherently a violation of the right of the person defrauded—no one voluntarily signs a contract to be cheated. One person's freedom of contract is naturally limited by other people's equal right to freedom of contract. Government efforts to enforce prohibitions on fraud are not a violation of freedom of contract, and government efforts to punish companies that fail to pay workers as promised are a proper use of sovereign power.

THE CARTELIZING OF THE AMERICAN WORKFORCE

A worker's right to choose his own profession was recognized as one of the hallmarks of American liberty. A New York judge declared in 1912, "'Liberty,' as guaranteed by the Constitution, is the right of a citizen to use his faculties in all lawful ways, to live and work where he will, to earn his livelihood in any lawful calling, and to pursue any lawful trade or avocation."[4] The Supreme Court declared in 1959, "The right to hold specific private employment and to follow a chosen profession free from unreasonable governmental interference comes within the 'liberty' and 'property' concepts of provisions of the Fifth Amendment."[5]

But freedom to work has increasingly been taken hostage by government licensing boards. The American economy is degenerating into a guild system as government doles out privileges to one group of self-proclaimed professionals after another. Government licensing restrictions prohibit millions of Americans from practicing the occupation of their choice. Over 800 professions now require a government license to practice, from barbers to masseuses, to interior designers, to phrenologists, to tattoo artists, to talent agents.[6] An entire economy is becoming increasingly oriented toward whether people have pieces of paper signed by government officials. The licensing boards are almost always dominated by private individuals already established in the profession who have an incentive to use the law to minimize competition.

Licensing laws are almost always engineered by professional associations who want to protect the public from competitors who might charge lower prices. While the public is suffering from an epidemic of violent crime, state governments are increasingly devoting their limited resources to protecting people against unlicensed interior designers. The Texas legislature passed a law in 1991 requiring a person to have a combination of six years of education and experience in interior design as well as pass a two-day state exam to get a license as an interior designer. (The new law grandfathered most currently practicing designers, exempting those who had been practicing or teaching in the interior design field for six or more years.) The *Austin Business Journal* reported, "The adoption of the bill is a victory for the Texas Association for Interior Design (TAID), which for the past seven years has been lobbying for regulations to license interior designers." Lazin Mathews, vice president of the TAID, declared, "I think it's a very positive step for the public because they will now have a guideline [to locate] someone with a lot of education and experience versus someone who got into the business because somebody told them they had good taste."[7] Interior design advice tends to be highly subjective, but Texas police are objective and will throw anyone in jail for up to one year who calls himself an interior designer without the state government's permission.[8] The police power is thus invoked to prevent people from formally advising their neighbors on what color rug goes with which color curtain. Several other states have also recently made interior design a licensed profession.

Teacher licensing requirements shaft the American public and millions of would-be teachers. Most states require teachers to be graduates of education colleges, which is usually the equivalent of requiring a person to run a four-year mental gauntlet of dreary, often pointless courses. It takes little intellectual effort or ability to slosh through the average teachers college, which have been derided as "the intellectual slums" on campuses.[9] While teachers are frequently derided for their faltering literacy (such as misspelled words on picket signs during teacher strikes),[10] potentially good teachers are banned from teaching because they don't have an education college diploma. Rita Kramer, author of *Ed School Follies: The Miseducation of America's Teachers*, concludes "Everything [would-be teachers] need to know about how to teach could be learned by intelligent people in a single summer of well-planned instruction."[11] Teacher licensing restrictions create an artificial shortage of good teachers, resulting in higher salaries for less motivated and often less capable teachers. Emily Feistritzer of the National Center for Education Information observed: "The bottom line is that education is a very closed system. One of the things that would improve education is if we could open up the teaching ranks to people who are not inbred."[12]

Dentists have perennially used licensing laws to drill consumers. Economist Lawrence Shepard of the University of California at Davis estimates that unjustified state government restrictions on dental licensing add between 12 and 15 percent to the cost of dental care.[13] The Federal Trade Commission estimated that unjustified restrictions on dental service cost consumers $700 million a year.[14] Many state dental associations seem more devoted to wiring the law than to fixing teeth; in 1986, the Supreme Court condemned the Indiana Federation of Dentists for policies that amount to "nothing less than a frontal assault on the basic policy of the Sherman [Antitrust] Act."[15] The FTC brought suit against the California Dental Association in 1991 for prohibiting its members from advertising discount offers to senior citizens, free initial consultations, promises to refund money to dissatisfied customers, or claims that an office offers "gentle dental care," thereby restricting price and quality competition among dentists.[16] Two years earlier, the California Dental Association vigorously opposed a program to allow dental hygienists to provide tooth and gum care without being employed and directly supervised by dentists.[17] Yet one 1987 study concluded that "for the dental procedures studied, the quality of services provided by auxiliaries is equal to that provided by dentists."[18] Foreign dentists are especially discriminated against by dental licensing regulations. In most states, it is easier for a foreign doctor to get a license to perform bypasses on Americans' hearts than for a foreign dentist to get a license to fill cavities in Americans' teeth.[19] The FTC concluded that the restrictive state laws—and the resulting higher prices of dental care—were a major reason why 20 million Americans have never visited a dentist.[20]

In most states, citizens must pay lawyers to transact routine legal business that could easily be handled by legal secretaries or by the individuals themselves. As lawyer/journalist Doug Bandow observed, "Lawyers have enormous influence in our increasingly litigious and regulated society. . . . For more than a century it has been illegal for anyone except a licensed attorney to 'practice' law. It has always been lawyers, not consumers, who set professional entrance provisions, graded bar exams, and regulated treatment of clients."[21]

In Nashville, Tennessee, two paralegals set up the Tennessee Paralegal Help Center in 1991 to help people fill out and file routine legal matters such as uncontested divorces, simple bankruptcies, name changes, and wills. Paralegal Perry Belcher observed, "We are basically just glorified typists. It takes an hour to prepare a no-frills, uncontested divorce. We charge less than $100 for that. That's not the case with an attorney. They charge about $750 for that same hour's worth of work. It's ridiculous to charge $750 for something that's not even handled by the attorney anyway; it's handled by the attorney's paralegals.[22] Davidson County, Tennessee, District Attorney Torry Johnson announced that his office was investigating the center and observed, "We received a number of complaints from local attorneys in addition to the one from the Bar, but we haven't received any complaints from clients."

In 1990, California paralegal Mershan Shaddy was sentenced to forty-nine days in jail for the unauthorized practice of law. As the *Los Angeles Times* noted, "There is no definition for the 'unauthorized practice of law.' Paralegals charge that . . . terms are kept deliberately vague so that lawyers and judges can mold the law to fit a particular case."[23] As soon as Shaddy was convicted, the San Diego city attorney's office warned San Diego newspapers to "put a stop to [advertisements for] this unnecessary and highly irregular practice," declaring, "Non-lawyer advertising of legal services is 'criminal conduct' because paralegals don't have a law license." Newspapers were warned that they "did not have a First Amendment right to publish ads for illegal commercial activity" and that they could face "substantial liability."[24]

Most state bar associations effectively have monopolies over public criticism of individual lawyers. In February 1987, David Reed of West Palm Beach, Florida, filed an ethics grievance with the Florida Bar Association alleging that his lawyer had coerced him into signing a retainer agreement. The Florida Bar Association investigated, found the lawyer guilty, and issued a private reprimand. As *News Media and the Law* reported, "During the proceedings, bar officials warned Reed at least six times that Florida Supreme Court rules required him to keep his complaint secret from everyone but his new attorney. Under the rule, all attorney discipline matters were secret—even the existence of a complaint—until the bar issued a formal charge against a lawyer in state court. No charge was filed in Reed's case."[25] Reed sued the Florida Supreme Court and Florida Bar Association in federal court, alleging that his First Amendment rights were violated by the gag rule that prevented him from publicly criticizing his ex-lawyer or the bar association's handling of his complaint. A federal judge concluded that the ban on criticizing lawyers violated the First Amendment.[26] A 1990 study by Help Abolish Legal Tyranny (HALT), a reform organization, "found that every state but Florida and Oregon has such confidential proceedings that no one can find out how many complaints have been filed against a lawyer or if he's under investigation or has been privately reprimanded."[27]

Licensing restrictions are often draconian on occupations that have a dubious reputation. Lake County, Illinois, requires a $1,000 licensing fee from masseuses and also prohibits a masseuse or masseur from kneading a member of the opposite sex.[28] The Duluth, Georgia, City Council announced in 1993 that it would legalize opposite-sex massages but decreed that "doors to the massage area must remain unlocked, massages cannot be performed on anything other than a table, and affidavits affirming the good moral characters of the owner and masseur/masseuse must be provided to obtain a business license."[29] The Nevada Supreme Court ruled in 1989 that it was an unconstitutional invasion of privacy for North Las Vegas to require windows in massage parlor doors to allow government officials to easily look in and make sure that no one was getting rubbed in the wrong place.[30] A controversy broke out in 1992 in Mount Prospect, Illinois, after an undercover Cook County deputy sheriff alleged that a masseuse at the Sports Health Spa had massaged his genitals. The spa's massage license was temporarily revoked; the spa owner insisted that the masseuse had only momentarily touched the officer in an illegal place while trying to remove massage oils.[31] (At that time, Cook County had hundreds of unsolved murders—but the police had other priorities.)

Licensing restrictions are routinely justified by appeals to the government's duty to defend the public. But while state governments insist they must restrict entry to the medical profession, they also insist that people should not be allowed to know the records—the killed-and-maimed batting averages—of medical professionals. When the Public Citizen Health Research Group, a Washington activist organization, sought to compile a nationwide list of doctors who had been sanctioned by state medical boards, eighteen states refused to reveal the names of any doctors who had been disciplined.[32] Andrew Stein, president of the New York City Council, noted in 1986, "A New Yorker can routinely pick up a newspaper to learn whether his choice of restaurant has been cited by the Health Department for dirty kitchens. The same New Yorker, however, has no access to the malpractice records of the doctors into whose hands he may have to place his life."[33]

Though licensing boards routinely make it extremely difficult for people to enter a profession, they are paragons of tolerance once a person is government-approved. Even when state medical boards have proof that doctors have committed violent crimes, they routinely do not revoke the convicted felons' medical licenses. A 1988 *Washington Post* investigation revealed that the state of Maryland allowed over thirty-five doctors to retain their licenses despite criminal convictions for sex crimes, drug violations, theft, and fraud.[34] One Baltimore physician "was convicted of raping a gynecological patient in his office but allowed by the commission to continue practicing medicine."[35] The Maryland commission even allowed two dozen physicians whom it explicitly ruled incompetent to continue practicing medicine.[36] The New York Bureau of Professional Misconduct allowed a New Jersey anesthesiologist to continue practicing medicine in New York after he had been convicted by a jury in 1992 of raping a patient in New Jersey; the anesthesiologist returned the board's favor by getting arrested in May 1993 for allegedly sexually abusing a female patient in New York. After the controversy splashed across the New York newspapers, William Fagel, a spokesman for the State Health Department, explained that there were not sufficient grounds to suspend the doctor's license: "You can't go back to something that happened in '91, and you need evidence, you need witnesses."[37] (The New York officials apparently required a much higher degree of proof than did the New Jersey jury.)

Licensing restrictions are one of the most pervasive and least recognized triumphs of paternalism in the average American's everyday life. No matter how many hacks the boards unleash upon the public, or how often the boards resist punishing the incompetent, licensing boards have somehow maintained their sheen of respectability. Almost every licensing barrier is erected on the doctrine of consumer incompetence and government omniscience. The Federal Trade Commission recognized this in a 1990 report on the effects of occupational licensing: "To the extent that the disciplinary process is ineffective in weeding out incompetent professionals, licensing may provide consumers with an inaccurate signal of quality and a false sense of security."[38] The FTC also noted, "The bulk of the studies that measure the impact of certain licensing restrictions on quality find little, if any, quality enhancement."[39] There is no reason to presume that bureaucrats can judge the qualifications of many professionals better than consumers can. As economist Milton Friedman wrote, "There are many different routes to knowledge and learning and the effect of restricting the practice of what is called medicine and confining it . . . to a particular group, who in the main have to conform to the prevailing orthodoxy, is certain to reduce the amount of experimentation that goes on and hence to reduce the rate of growth and knowledge in the area."[40] The Federal Trade Commission recommends that instead of licensing, states rely as much as possible on voluntary certification programs. Individuals who wished to qualify for a state certificate could do so and use the state certificate as proof of meeting specific standards. This is currently the situation for accountants: almost anyone can be an accountant, but only those who pass government tests can advertise themselves as Certified Public Accountants. The FTC notes that "certification provides consumers with the option of choosing a certified, higher price professional or a lower price, noncertified professional."[41]

DESTROYING JOBS IN ORDER TO ACHIEVE FAIR LABOR

In 1930, a man owned his hands, body, and labor, and could sell them to whomever he pleased, on almost any terms mutually acceptable. Now a person can no longer profit from the use of his hands or mind as he chooses but must conform to hundreds of government decrees on "fair" labor. Once politicians claimed the power to define fair labor standards, they constantly expanded their control, continually creating new absurdities and new disruptions of millions of voluntary private contracts.

President Roosevelt declared in 1937, "All but the hopeless reactionary will agree that to conserve our primary resources of manpower, government must have some control over maximum hours, minimum wages, the evil of child labor, and the exploitation of unorganized labor."[42] The 1938 Fair Labor Standards Act (FLSA) sought to "conserve our primary resources of manpower" by driving hundreds of thousands of people out of the work force in order to rig higher wages for other workers. Though the national unemployment rate was 18 percent, the federal government tried to forcibly drive up wages by political command—as if employers were more likely to hire people at higher wages than at lower wages. The FLSA mandated a 25-cent-an-hour minimum wage and time-and-a-half pay for any work done over forty hours a week. The original minimum wage law was enacted in part to decrease the advantage that low-wage Southern factories had over Northern factories; Rep. John Dent of Pennsylvania later explained, "We had to do something; we were losing all of our jobs to the south."[43] The new wage law devastated Puerto Rico; as economist Benjamin Anderson noted, "Immense unemployment resulted there through the sheer inability of important industries to pay the 25 cents an hour."[44] Congress raised the minimum wage in nominal terms by 46 percent between 1977 and 1981; a federal commission estimated that the minimum wage hikes resulted in the loss of 644,000 jobs, including jobs that were not created.[45] A 1983 General Accounting Office report "found virtually total agreement [among economists] that employment is lower than it would have been if no minimum wage existed. . . . Teenage workers have greater job losses, relative to their share of the population or the employed work force, than adults."[46]

The current minimum wage effectively prohibits people from working unless their labor is worth at least $4.25 an hour. Government schools routinely fail to prepare people for work—and then government regulations ban them from the job market because their labor is not as valuable as politicians claim it should be. To decree a minimum wage without guaranteeing everyone a job is simply to knock those on the bottom rung off the ladder. President Carter's Minimum Wage Study Commission noted that "an explicit purpose of the minimum wage was, and is, to protect adult workers from low wage competition from youth."[47] One person's freedom to work is destroyed so that someone else can get an extra quarter or half-dollar an hour. The minimum wage has been described as "a tax from the poor to the poor" whereby some low wage earners increase their income while others lose all their income.[48] The *New York Times* editorialized in 1977, "Organized labor favors a high minimum wage because that reduces management's resistance to union recruiting. Where cheap alternative sources of labor are eliminated, high-priced union labor no longer looks so bad to company managers."[49]

Congress last raised the minimum wage in 1989—from $3.35 to $4.25 an hour. A 1991 National Restaurant Association survey found that as a result, 44 percent of restaurants were forced to reduce the number of employee hours worked, and 42 percent reduced the number of people employed.[50] Texas A & M University professor Finis Welch estimated that the 1989 increase in minimum wages reduced teenage employment by roughly 240,000 teenagers.[51]

The Clinton administration is on the verge of proposing another increase in the minimum wage. Secretary of Labor Robert Reich, arguing for a minimum wage hike in a July 20, 1993, confidential memo to President Clinton, declared that one reason for boosting minimum wages is "public perception"—though Reich did concede that "the potential effects of a minimum wage increase on employment should of course be weighed."[52]

The Fair Labor Standards Act originally applied mainly to factories and manufacturing work, but since then the law has been extended. The Labor Department's Office of Wages and Hours determines whether employers are in compliance with the FLSA. Some organizations have been dragged through bureaucratic hell trying to understand and comply with federal wage and hour proclamations.

Members of the National Association of Private Residential Resources—primarily group homes serving the mentally retarded—have struggled since 1987 to comply with conflicting federal rulings on whether group homes must pay residential employees for the time they spend sleeping.[53] The Department of Labor tentatively ruled in 1988 that group homes would not have to pay workers for the time they spent sleeping as long as the employees were sleeping in "private quarters in a home-like environment." Naturally, this spawned numerous disputes over the definition of a homelike environment. The DOL warned group homes: "The amenities and quarters must be suitable for long-term residence by individuals and must be similar to those found in a typical private residence or apartment, rather than those found in . . . short-term facilities for travelers."[54] According to Hyman Richman, a former DOL wage and hour investigator who now serves as a consultant, "One inspector in Maryland insisted that 'living facilities' meant a separate bedroom, kitchen, living room, and bathroom—and that was the minimum."[55] The DOL also decreed that "employees must get at least five hours of sleep each night."[56] If a group home worker is up for more than three hours during the night dealing with an emergency, the employer cannot simply allow the worker to sleep in the next morning; instead, the employee must be paid both for the hours spent sleeping and working. A Nebraska regional mental retardation services board was ordered to pay $300,000 in retroactive pay for sleep time to workers in 1990. (The amount of retroactive pay was sharply reduced by an appeals court.)[57] Lawsuits against group homes for violations of the vague and continually changing DOL rulings on sleep time have disrupted nonprofit organizations struggling to provide better care to the mentally retarded. There is no reason why federal labor department officials should be dictating when a worker in Idaho gets his sleep.

An expansive interpretation of the minimum wage law almost shut down one of the nation's most efficient and successful rehabilitation programs. In 1990, the Labor Department announced that the Salvation Army, a religious organization, would be required to pay minimum wages to alcoholics, drug addicts, and others engaged in the Salvation Army's rehabilitation program. (The program involved refurbishing furniture and other work-therapy activities.) Instead of a salary, the Salvation Army provides its 50,000 clients a year with food, shelter, spiritual counseling, and pocket change in return for their efforts. Labor Department officials decided that since some of the Salvation Army's refurbished furniture crosses state lines before being sold, its clients were engaged in interstate commerce and thus must receive minimum wages and overtime pay.[58] Salvation Army officials warned that they would be forced to close down most of their assistance programs if forced to pay the minimum wage.[59] Many Salvation Army clients have extremely low productivity, and the program could not afford to pay minimum wages for subminimal work. (Naturally, Labor Department officials had neither jobs nor rehabilitation programs to offer the thousands of people who would have been ejected from Salvation Army programs.) Labor Department officials backed down after a public and political uproar in defense of the Salvation Army.

Some local governments make it stark that their control over minimum wages is a know-nothing economic dictatorship. In 1991, the District of Columbia government whipsawed the local labor market. The three members of the D.C. Wage-Hour Board held a hearing at which only twelve people spoke, conferred among themselves, and then proclaimed a 70 percent increase in the minimum wage for thousands of clerical, health, and day care workers—from $4.25 an hour to $7.25 an hour—by far the highest minimum wage in the nation. The *Washington Post* denounced the decision as a "formula for economic suicide."[60] The board did not analyze the possible impact of the wage hike; instead, it relied solely on testimony from groups of workers who insisted that they needed higher wages to meet the rising cost of living. The *Post* reported that after the wage hike was announced, some workers were "terrified that the increase [would] lead to layoffs, transforming a poverty-level wage into no wage at all."[61] Chairman Lawrence Landry defended the board's command to raise wages, declaring, "The issue before us is a moral issue, a moral obligation and a moral imperative, not just an economic or political consideration or even a pragmatic or managerial concern."[62] Landry apparently perceived the dispute as moral theatrics, rather than a threat to the jobs of thousands of real people. The D.C. case vivifies the danger of allowing bureaucrats or politicians to have arbitrary power over wage rates—giving them what they think is a magic wand to raise wages but in reality is actually a scythe to cut down thousands of private jobs.

Federal regulations dictate that if a person is paid by the hour, he must be paid time-and-a-half for overtime (any work over forty hours a week). But if a person is a professional, administrative, or managerial employee paid by salary, he is permitted to reach a mutually agreeable contract with his employer for compensation for hours worked. (Federal regulations implicitly presume that the higher a person's income becomes, the more freedom of contract he should be permitted.) In August 1944, shortly after the Labor Department began issuing interpretations of the Fair Labor Standards Act, a bulletin declared that managerial employees "are normally allowed some latitude with respect to time spent at work."[63] A 1990 federal court decision sharply narrowed the definition of professional—and federal labor regulators seized upon the new definition with gusto. According to the Labor Department's new interpretation, if a company allows professional employees to take time off without pay during a work day, the professionals magically automatically become hourly employees. If a company allows a single professional to take a partial day leave without pay, then the company could potentially be forced to pay retroactive overtime pay for all professional employees for the previous three years. This effectively invalidated millions of contracts that private companies had voluntarily agreed upon with architects, accountants, and other professionals. DOL's ruling effectively prohibited companies from allowing millions of individuals to take part-day leaves without pay. The Employment Policy Foundation estimated that the total back pay liabilities of employers could reach $40 billion.[64]

DOL's policy is wreaking havoc on corporate personnel policies. Business owner Linda Froehlich noted in the *Wall Street Journal:*

> An Ohio company was taken to court by the DOL over a policy designed to accommodate semi-retired employees. Pierce Processing Inc. is a professional engineering consulting firm with 20 employees. It is open 12 hours a day. Engineers used to be able to work any hours they wanted as long as they worked 80 hours in a two-week pay period. If they worked more than 80 hours, they were paid straight overtime for each hour over 80. If they worked fewer than 80 hours, they either would take paid leave or have their pay reduced for each hour under 80.
>
> But when the Labor Department got wind of the practice, it forced Pierce Processing to stop it. The Department found Pierce in violation because, out of 58,000 total employees hours over a two-year period, 150 hours had been docked. The department claimed that this docking of $3450 should result in $47,000 in overtime expenses. Fortunately, a federal judge allowed Pierce simply to reimburse the employees for the 150 hours (after four years of legal wrangling). The end result is that Pierce now has a policy that requires everyone to either work a full day or take the entire day off.[65]

Froehlich complained that the DOL's interpretation made it much more difficult for her to hire female professionals who routinely need more time off for child-care responsibilities. Allowing professional employees the option to take unpaid time off during the day is extremely popular with employees—giving them a chance to take better care of their private affairs and their lives.

Malcolm Pirnie Inc., a New York engineering firm with 400 professional employees, was sued by the DOL to pay overtime to its entire work force because it permitted some employees to take unpaid partial day leaves; a federal court forced the company to shell out $875,000 in back pay.[66] John Foster, chairman of Malcolm Pirnie, condemned DOL for its "shock" prosecution and said the agency "wanted blood." Foster declared that this is "not a pay-docking issue as some have reported; it is a flexibility issue."[67] Among the practices that proved Malcolm Pirnie's "guilt" was permitting employees time off to attend parent-teacher conferences, to work on dissertations, or to attend medical appointments.[68] Former DOL solicitor William J. Kilberg condemned the courts and DOL: "The end result of these judicial interpretations is the civil law equivalent of capital punishment for spitting on the sidewalk."[69]

The Labor Policy Association reported that "some Labor Department regional offices are literally going through the phone book, randomly selecting unsuspecting small companies that perform hourly work (such as accounting and engineering consulting firms), and assessing fines or threatening costly legal action."[70] (The more fines the DOL imposes for fair labor violations, the more the agency appears to be protecting the public.) Many small businesses warned that the DOL's ruling could bankrupt them. Dan Yager, an attorney for the Labor Policy Association, declared, "A lot of people now are sitting on a powder keg of liability. A large company could be liable for $200 million, $300 million" in back overtime pay.[71]

Federal wage laws have spawned frequent court battles and much economic uncertainty. A federal Court of Appeals ruled in May 1993 that Chicago police officers are entitled to sue for overtime pay for time they spend eating lunch,[72] while a federal district court in Kansas ruled that paramedics were not entitled to overtime pay for meal periods.[73] Federal courts have also ruled that some convicts must be paid the minimum wage for work they perform in prison.[74] Despite the pretensions of modern journalism, reporters have sued their newspapers, denying that they are professionals and thus claiming a right to overtime compensation. The Labor Department is cracking down on accountants to force major accounting firms to treat accountants as if they were wage slaves, when they are actually slaving away on salary to become partners.[75] A 1993 proposal to impose minimum wage and overtime requirements on foreign employees who worked on cruise ships that visited U.S. ports threatened to disrupt the cruise industry and destroy up to 4,000 U.S. jobs providing on-shore support for cruise ships.[76]

TEENAGE LABOR POLITICAL RACKETEERING

The Fair Labor Standards Act also restricts teenagers' right to work. While newspaper headlines proclaim "Child Labor Violations Widespread," little attention is paid to the actual alleged crimes. In the Washington, D.C., area, one pizza operator was found guilty because he allowed seventeen-year-olds to deliver pizza, which the Labor Department considers a "hazardous job" for young people.[77] The Labor Department launched a highly publicized investigation of the Food Lion grocery chain in 1992 for child labor violations; Food Lion representatives claimed that Labor Department officials had told them that "90% of the violations relating to hazardous conditions involved workers under the age of 18 'putting cardboard into nonoperating bailers.'"[78] The *Washington Post* reported: "Inspectors sometimes find dozens of violations in a single community. A crackdown in the Ocean City-Rehobeth Beach area in August [1991] turned up 182 minors illegally employed in more than 30 businesses, including gas stations, hotels, and T-shirt and novelty shops."[79] But what is the danger in allowing teenagers to sell T-shirts in an ocean resort area during the summertime?

Child labor laws provide an opportunity for ambitious politicians to get their faces on the evening news. In March 1990, Secretary of Labor Elizabeth Dole received widespread acclaim for her suit alleging that Burger King had thousands of violations of child labor laws at its 755 franchises in the United States. Dole piously declared, "This action serves as a notice to employers that we will not hesitate to use available legal processes, in addition to investigative efforts, to protect America's children."[80] One of Burger King's major violations was to allow fourteen- and fifteen-year-olds to work after 7:00 P.M. But the primary impact of such restrictions may be to boost the Nielsen ratings for prime-time television; a 1992 Carnegie Corporation report concluded that teenagers watch 21 hours of television a week and spend only 5.6 hours a week on homework.[81] Tim Ferguson, a *Wall Street Journal* columnist, observes, "According to a 1988 Census data, 90,000 youths age 15 and under have dropped out of school. This is the cohort of youngsters subject to the tightest child-labor restrictions. Among 16- and 17-year-olds . . . the dropout total is about half a million."[82] Many companies, including Burger King and Hardee's, responded to the Labor Department's national crackdown by ceasing to employ anyone under the age of sixteen. Nationwide, the crackdown contributed to a decrease of over one million teenagers holding jobs between 1990 and early 1992.[83] Government officials treat working teenagers as if their paychecks were simply a luxury—as if government officials should have unlimited discretion to determine whether teenagers will be allowed to help feed their families. In 1993, Rep. Tom Lantos of California proposed an act called The Young American Workers' Bill of Rights; Lantos's bill would slash the number of hours sixteen- and seventeen-year-olds are allowed to work.[84]

The restrictions on child labor do contain exemptions for politically connected industries. Federal law allows fourteen- and fifteen-year-olds to work only between 7:00 A.M. and 7:00 P.M.[85]—except if the child gets up at 4:30 A.M. to deliver newspapers. (According to the International Association of Circulation Managers, 362,470 people under the age of eighteen worked as newspaper carriers in 1990.)[86] Florida in 1991 prohibited the employment of minors aged thirteen or younger—except in the entertainment industry or as a page in the state legislature (a redundant exemption?). In Washington State, "a 14-year minimum age is established for employment, except that 12- and 13-year-olds may be employed in the hand harvest of berries, bulbs, and cucumbers and in the hand cultivation of spinach during weeks when school is not in session."[87] The South Dakota legislature resolved in 1992 that children under the age of sixteen would face no limitations on their work hours on nonschool days when they were employed in roguing or detasselling hybrid seedcorn.[88]

Child labor laws received a black eye in 1993 when a DOL enforcer warned the Savannah Cardinals baseball team that it must fire fourteen-year-old batboy Tommy McCoy because he could not work after 7:00 P.M. while school was in session, or after 9:00 P.M. during the summer. The team's fans were outraged and announced plans for a "Save Tommy's Job" night. After the Labor Department was sufficiently embarrassed, Labor Secretary Robert Reich announced that the policy was "silly" and decreed that batboys would be exempt from the federal restrictions. Reich announced, "It is not the intent of the law to deny young teenagers employment opportunities, so long as their health and well-being are not impaired."[89] Reich did not explain how federal enforcement of restrictions on most other industries and occupations did not "deny young teenagers employment opportunities."

NOT IN YOUR HOUSE

In order to guarantee textile workers a "fair" wage, government officials prohibit all other Americans from doing certain types of work in their own homes. It is a federal crime for a woman to sew buttons on a dress for pay in her own home. In the early 1940s, the federal government banned people from earning money by making knitted outerwear, jewelry, buttons and buckles, gloves and mittens, handkerchiefs, embroideries, and women's garments at home for pay. The restriction was a bone tossed to the textile unions, who sought to force all knitters, sewers, and stitchers into factories and to get a chunk of their wages under compulsory collective bargaining. The union claimed to be concerned about the low wages paid to people who worked at home; in reality, unions sought to destroy their low-priced labor competition.

The federal government has vigorously enforced the antihomework regulations. In 1979, the government filed an injunction against several Vermont companies that purchased sweaters knitted at home; the jobs of over 1,000 people, including many retirees working to supplement their Social Security checks, were destroyed.[90] In 1986, Labor Department agents swooped down on North Carolina's Tom Thumb Glove Company and eliminated the jobs of twenty-seven women who had been sewing gloves at home for the company.[91] In 1991, the city of New York fined two companies $70,000 for employing Vietnamese immigrants in the Bronx.[92] The Labor Department launched a crackdown in the Dallas-Fort Worth area in 1992 on thousands of Vietnamese immigrants struggling to make a living by sewing at home. Tom Ha, vice chairman of the Vietnamese Community of Fort Worth and Vicinity, reported that almost 70 percent of the Asian American homes in the Dallas-Fort Worth area have at least one family member doing contract sewing and that the loss of this work would devastate the families since many had already spent $1,500 to $4,500 to buy their own sewing machines. Mr. Ha noted that a home sewer's average yearly earnings of $20,000 could account for more than 70 percent of a family's income.[93] Mr. Ha complained: "A lot of people think this [crackdown by] the Labor Department will be the kiss of death. They don't want to apply for food stamps or welfare. They want to work."[94]

Several states impose even more restrictive bans on homework. A Pennsylvania company, Overly-Raker, Inc., was forced by that state's Department of Labor and Industry to stop using home workers to sew together "soft sculptures of geese, cows, cats." The state government's order destroyed the jobs of a hundred women, but Helen R. Friedman, director of the labor standards bureau, justified the action: "We work to protect people's rights."[95] In 1991 New Jersey officially prohibited the sewing of any women's or men's apparel at home.[96] New Jersey had previously banned the sewing of women's apparel at home but judiciously expanded the ban to include men's apparel because some garments, such as sweat-suits, can be worn by both sexes.[97]

Government officials claim exemplary motives for prohibiting people from working at home. Lillian Roberts, New York State Commissioner of Labor, observed, "It is wrong to effectively deny women the right to union wages and union protection if they desire them, and it is wrong to keep women in a situation where home duties and work requirements are in conflict."[98] In contrast, conditions in factories are idyllic; some New York garment factory workers are so desperate for child care that they keep their young children in cardboard boxes next to them on the factory floor.[99] New York City has forty investigators snooping for homework violators. According to Robert Armer, director of enforcement of labor standards for New York:

> What we do is send out our investigators on surveillance. . . . If our investigators identify someone they feel is a likely homeworker, then they merely follow that person to where they may go. . . . If it is in a manufacturing area and you see a person carrying a well-worn shopping bag, and particularly if there are several people doing that, going in, the chances are quite good that it is going to be homework when you get in there.[100]

Though New York cannot protect its citizens against murderers and muggers, the city can afford a battalion of investigators to prowl for women carrying used shopping bags. Armer told the House Education and Labor Committee, "I am very concerned that we are going to increase the lack of payment for unemployment insurance, worker's compensation, Social Security, city, State and Federal Tax. . . . These people are not only engaged in exploiting workers but exploiting everybody else connected to [them] by means of these various programs that they escape." Yet at the same time that the New York city government is cracking down on honest workers, the government is paying welfare to hundreds of thousands of able-bodied adults who are not working. At a 1989 hearing in Los Angeles, government welfare fraud investigator Donald H. Andres opposed ending the homework ban because it would make it easier for welfare recipients to avoid reporting their income. Thus, because some welfare recipients might cheat on their income, all people should be banned from working at home—everyone's lives must be forcibly structured for the convenience of government regulators.[101]

Federal and state government restrictions on working at home are becoming more important as new technology vastly increases the number of people who could do some or all of their work at home. In 1985, the AFL-CIO called for an expansion of the ban on homework to include telecommuting, thereby destroying millions of potential jobs and insuring more crowded rush hours for tens of millions of Americans. A survey of Fortune 500 company managers found that telecommuting boosts productivity and decreases worker turnover.[102] Yet Communications Workers of America president Mort Bahr warned against telecommuting in early 1992: "How do we monitor whether the contract is being enforced? . . . It lends itself to corporate abuse, with the worker being somewhat intimidated—particularly if that worker wants to work at home."[103] According to Bahr, allowing people to work at home who want to work at home somehow exploits them. Bahr may have revealed the true source of his discomfort when he complained in 1984 that allowing telecommuting for telephone operations "certainly would make it virtually impossible for a union to maintain contact with its members."[104] Similarly, the Coalition of Labor Union Women issued a booklet on the dangers of homework in late 1991. The book (as summarized by *Telecommuting Report*) warned:

> Homework makes it hard to develop the kind of solidarity among employees which naturally occurs in a workplace. . . . Many home-based computer workers are treated as independent contractors. Independent contractors cannot be organized into unions. . . .[105]

CRIMINALIZING THE PURSUIT OF WORK

Politicians sometimes throw people into jail simply for asking for a job. In September 1989, the Costa Mesa, California, city council banned soliciting for work or hiring a day laborer from a vehicle and also decreed that anyone within 300 feet of certain areas who looked guilty of an intent to solicit employment would be arrested. The *Los Angeles Times* reported, "This addition to the city's existing anti-solicitation ordinance also empowered police to arrest people based on 'circumstantial evidence.' The measure did not define circumstantial evidence, but in practice police have arrested people in the targeted areas because they were known to have solicited work in the past. Previously, police had to catch a dayworker in the act of solicitation."[106] Ninety-six men were subsequently arrested for the crime of intent to solicit work.[107] As one critic complained, "It's about as fair and legal as drafting an ordinance that states it is illegal to be a Hispanic in the [city] park. That is the unwritten ordinance."[108] Costa Mesa police spent $40,812 on "observing day-worker activity, conducting undercover raids, purchasing video equipment and tapes, and writing reports," in addition to $48,000 to hire a private law firm to defend the constitutionality of the ordinance in court.[109] The police also relied on entrapment: An undercover officer drove a pickup truck to a park and shouted "I need ten"; several nearby men would respond by running and hopping in the back of the truck, after which the police would drive up and arrest all the lawbreakers.[110] An *Orange County Register* editorial observed, "Both ordinances cut to the heart of the most fundamental of human rights, the right to try to sustain your life. If declaring that certain phrases, like 'Need some work?' or 'How about a job?' are grounds for imprisonment isn't an unconstitutional infringement on free speech, it's difficult to image what is."[111] The California restrictions were put in place partly at the behest of the Immigration and Naturalization Service, which complained that "the sites pose a challenge to the INS."[112]

Other cities also punish job seekers. Agoura Hills, California, banned day laborers from soliciting work; a lawsuit filed against the city alleged that "Latinos, or those who appear to be Latino, have been arrested, criminally prosecuted, harassed, assaulted, humiliated, or ordered to leave the city . . . while waiting for buses, eating at a local fast-food restaurant or patronizing other businesses. The atmosphere is such that any Latino-appearing person who walks or stands in the city of Agoura Hills now faces the very real danger of arrest or worse."[113] Marietta, Georgia, banned soliciting employment on city streets in 1988. Marietta police sergeant Kirk Hollan declared, "We are a very visible presence in the morning. It costs us man-hours and time. We usually assign three beat officers out there every morning."[114] It is unfortunate that police in some locales treat people who are seeking jobs much more harshly than they treat people who are begging for handouts.

GIVING UNIONS THE RIGHT TO RAMPAGE

Federal labor relations law has nullified the rights of millions of workers to make their own contracts. Prior to the 1930s, courts and legislatures generally refused to recognize that individual workers' rights to make their own contracts could be nullified by the demands of groups of other workers. A Massachusetts court declared in 1912, "To enforce a collective contract would be to deny the individual's liberty to make his own contract."[115] Judges at that time recognized and respected voluntary collective bargaining contracts but did not uphold collective bargaining contracts that prohibited other workers from making their own contracts. Since the essence of a contract is voluntary consent by each party to the agreement, a collective bargaining agreement could not forcibly impose contract terms on workers who did not support the agreement.

But thanks to lobbying by unions and occasional savage actions by employers suppressing protesting workers, the U.S. Congress chipped away at the individual worker's right of contract. Congress exempted unions from the Sherman Antitrust Act in 1914, thus making it extremely difficult to sue or fine unions for restraint of trade. In 1932, the Norris-Laguardia Act prevented federal courts from issuing injunctions to end strike-related violence. In 1935, Congress enacted the National Labor Relations Act (also known as the Wagner Act) to force employers to bargain with unions and to make it far easier for unions to force workers to join or pay dues to the union. The essence of federal labor law is to give some people veto power over the contracts that other people are allowed to make. The Supreme Court declared in 1944 that "individual contracts, no matter what the circumstances that justify their execution or what their terms, may not be availed of to defeat or delay" collective bargaining or "to limit or condition the terms of the collective agreement."[116] Supreme Court Justice Wiley Rutledge, in a dissent in another labor case in 1944, observed that federal labor law gave unions "a thraldom over the men who designate them" by "creating rights in the unions overriding those of the employees they represent."[117]

Federal labor legislation currently implicitly permits some workers to use violence against other workers. Nowadays, a man's right to sell his labor is often totally at the mercy of whether other men feel that such a sale might damage their own bargaining positions. This is the equivalent of giving every business the right to firebomb any competitor that tries to undercut its prices. The preamble to the National Labor Relations Act of 1935 declared, "Experience has proven that protection by law of the right of employees to organize and bargain collectively . . . promotes the flow of commerce by removing certain recognized sources of industrial strife and unrest."[118] But, in reality, empowering unions has had the opposite effect.

On Long Island in 1991, in the middle of a bitter Teamsters strike, over a hundred customers' gas equipment was damaged, and in seven cases gas was left turned on, creating the potential for explosions. "Robert Armentano, president of Suburban Paraco, claimed yesterday that striking members of Teamsters Local 282 are behind the vandalism, which also has included damage to vehicles and homes of non-striking employees. He said the union is 'well aware of what's happening, and we consider it acts of extortion and terrorism.'"[119]

In Mansfield, Ohio, in 1990, "striking steelworkers paraded with baseball bats and wooden boards with nails, overturned several cars and set one on fire, and vowed to stop any replacement workers from entering a local steel plant. A firebomb thrown near the idled plant knocked out electricity in the surrounding area."[120]

In 1990, the New York *Daily News* was dying financially largely because of the huge inefficiencies built into its union contracts. Delivery truck drivers routinely earned $100,000—even though union restrictions on the number of newspaper bundles on each truck often mean that the trucks went out half empty. Once the *News* announced plans for job cutbacks, the union struck. Michael O'Neill, the former editor of the *News*, complained shortly after the strike began: "Even without adding any new automation, the *News* today has 50% more workers than it needs."[121] The *Boston Globe* noted, "Newsstands that have tried to sell the paper have been burned down. Men wielding baseball bats have attacked delivery trucks driven by replacements brought in by management. A vendor said that two men who visited his Manhattan stall last week said they would 'put my eyes out' if he sold the *News* again."[122] Hundreds of incidents of strike-related violence occurred, including the firebombing of a store selling the *News*, an arson attack that destroyed thirteen tractor trailers in the Bronx, the stabbing of a replacement truck driver, and the destruction of several delivery trucks. The *New York Times* noted, "In one of the more serious incidents, an employee was beaten by two carloads of strikers who descended upon him with baseball bats as he walked to the subway station near the Brooklyn plant. . . . Executives at Save Mart Electronic and Hillside Bedding, two of the remaining major advertisers at the *News*, said that most of their stores have been vandalized repeatedly since early January [for not bowing to a union demand to cease advertising in the *News*]."[123] After widespread violence had already occurred, New York governor Mario Cuomo addressed a rally of thousands of striking union members and their supporters and hailed "the courage and sacrifice of the union movement" and told the crowd: "Stay strong—You're fighting for all of us."[124] James Hoge, publisher of the *News*, complained, "I can't conceive of this. . . . We've seen no expression from the mayor, the governor or any other public official that this kind of criminal campaign against a business is unacceptable."[125] Michael Gartner, the president of NBC News, complained, "This is a campaign of violence not only against the *Daily News* but also against freedom. The campaign of terrorism is depriving us of buying—and thus reading—a newspaper we want to buy to read. . . . For the first time in my memory, this nation is just standing by and watching thugs firebomb freedom."[126]

Federal labor laws allow unions to take hostage not only non-union members and employers but entire cities. The Pittsburgh Press Co., which manages Pittsburgh's two main newspapers (the *Press* and the *Post Gazette*) announced plans in 1992 to abolish 450 of 627 delivery jobs. The paper's delivery system was archaic, slow, and inefficient. Randall P. Notter, spokesman for Pittsburgh Press Co., complained that the Teamsters' pay, overtime, and benefits averaged $58,000 a year for "about 4½ hours' work a day."[127] The Teamsters responded to the plan by striking and shutting down both newspapers for six months. The strike against the newspapers hurt the entire Pittsburgh economy. A local opera company reported that ticket sales were down $5,000 a day for the first weeks of the summer season. Game-day sales of baseball tickets for the Pittsburgh Pirates fell 40 percent. The strike made it much more difficult for people seeking jobs to find out which businesses had openings. When the company tried to deliver the paper with replacement drivers, strikers linked arms and blocked the trucks, hurled chunks of asphalt and bricks, broke the windows and headlights on delivery trucks, and slashed their radiator hoses. A Press Co. spokesman reported that a security guard and delivery driver were hurt when strikers attacked their vehicles with baseball bats.[128] And the strike version of the paper carried few advertisements because businesses had been warned of union retaliation; one local merchant explained his refusal to advertise in the papers: "I didn't want to get a brick through my window."[129] As a result of the strike, the *Pittsburgh Press* was permanently shut down and hundreds of jobs were lost.[130]

When it comes to unrestrained violence, it is difficult to surpass the United Mineworkers of America. In Fayette County, West Virginia, federal agents arrested nine people in 1989 in connection with a five-year series of bombing incidents at a UMW-targeted coal mine, including one bombing that caused up to half a million dollars worth of damage.[131] Federal investigators reported a total of fifty bombings and acts of arson in coal mines in southern West Virginia between early 1988 and mid-1989. In late 1989, New Beckley Mining Corp. closed its mine in Glen Daniels, West Virginia, because of strike violence and filed a RICO (Racketeering Influence and Corrupt Organization) lawsuit against the UMW alleging thirty-four counts of attempted murder, twenty-three counts of arson, and seventy-nine counts of extortion at Glen Daniels during 1989.[132] (The lawsuit was thrown out of court by a federal judge who declared that since the UMW and its members are one entity, it could not conspire with itself.)[133] During the 1989-90 Pittston Coal strike, there were over 3,000 related cases of assaults, explosions, burned vehicles, and broken windows in Virginia.[134]

In a 1991 report, the New York State Organized Crime Task Force concluded that the problem of labor racketeering in the New York City construction industry is "all the more serious because it is so pervasive, has so many victims, and is the catalyst for the commission of so many other kinds of crimes. It victimizes employers and employees, loots pension and welfare plans, mocks the federally guaranteed right to union democracy, stifles economic competition, and subverts the collective bargaining process. It is the wedge by which the Cosa Nostra has pried its way into the industry."[135] The Task Force noted that honest union reformers may be "laid off, blacklisted, intimidated, beaten, or even killed," and that the NLRB and other federal agencies "offer such victims little support."[136]

Unions routinely use their power to extort payment for make-work jobs. Through 1987, Burlington Northern railroad crews received hazardous-duty pay bonuses for working trains traveling through Montana because, according to the union contract, Montana was still classified as Indian territory.[137] Companies exhibiting at conventions at the Javits Center in New York City have long been subject to extortion by union work rules. One company official related to the *New York Times* how he "was forced to pay carpenters $200 to install a prefabricated booth that he could quickly assemble by himself without a tool. An electrician charged him $70 to plug in a lamp."[138] In February 1992, more than two dozen arrests were made of union officials and others as a result of "complaints by Javits Center exhibitors alleging shakedowns and thefts."[139] Management expert Peter Drucker observed,

> All available evidence indicates that [union-imposed] work rules and job restrictions are the main cause of the "productivity gap" of American (and European) manufacturing industry. The much-publicized higher productivity of the Japanese-owned auto plants in the U.S. is largely, perhaps entirely, the result of their having only three to five job classifications. GM, Ford and Chrysler are each burdened with about 60.[140]

Relations between employers and unions are governed by a byzantine web of federal regulations and rulings by the National Labor Relations Board. The NLRB has sweeping discretion to penalize companies, unions, or individuals for "unfair labor practices." In reality, an "unfair labor practice" is whatever displeases a majority of the five political appointees to the National Labor Relations Board.

The NLRB supervises union-management relations in part to insure that companies do not coerce unions. NLRB officials have a very expansive concept of coercion when it comes to management behavior; companies have been found guilty of "unfair labor practices" for merely criticizing unions or for offering raises to their workers before the workers vote on whether to join a union. (By the same standard, congressmen could almost always be found guilty of trying to bribe voters at election time.) Yet the NLRB ruled in July 1993 that a Teamsters union local affiliate's filing of a $20 million class-action lawsuit against an employer just before an election was not objectionable conduct or an unfair labor practice. NLRB Chairman Devaney dissented from the ruling: "I would find that the Petitioner's filing of a $20 million class action RICO lawsuit against the Employer on behalf of the employers, without cost to them, announcing the suit to the employees the evening before the election, and holding out the prospect of their recovering $35,000 each, while at the same time 'reminding' them that the Petitioner needed their votes the next day, would have a reasonable tendency to influence the outcome of the election and therefore interfere with the employees' exercise of their free choice."[141]

The NLRB has a practically nonexistent concept of coercion regarding unions' treatment of workers. Labor law expert Steve Antosh observed, "In the *Georgia Kraft* case, the Board found no violation where union members cursed a nonstriker in his home in the presence of his family, and stated they 'would take care of him' when they returned to the plant. The Board characterized these statements as 'ambiguous.' In the *A. Duie Pyle* case, a union threat to burn down a worker's home was ruled by the Board to be noncoercive because it was not a threat of personal violence and was not accompanied by positive action to implement the threat."[142] In a 1991 case involving Precision Window Manufacturing Inc. of St. Louis, the NLRB ordered a company to rehire and award back pay to an employee who was fired after he threatened to kill his supervisor. The fired employee promised to come back at quitting time and kill his boss; the worker actually returned at quitting time, and remained outside the plant until police arrived. NLRB chairman James Stephens and member Dennis Devaney ruled that the employee's "rambling, semicoherent mix of insult and threat"[143] were not so flagrant as to forfeit his right to favored treatment under federal labor law. A federal appeals court, overturning the decision in 1992, criticized the NLRB for ruling in the discharged employee's favor, especially since the ex-employee admitted to lying at the NLRB hearing on the case.[144]

One type of unfair labor practice NLRB punishes is pay raises and wage hikes. Though one of the implicit goals of the National Labor Relations Act was to achieve higher pay for laborers, the NLRB will punish corporations—or even impose injunctions—if the NLRB suspects that a pay raise for workers is not in the union's best interest. A New York company gave its employees a 5 percent wage increase shortly after a union lost a vote to represent the workers—and the company was found guilty of an unfair labor practice because NLRB officials believed the wage hike would interfere with a reelection for union representation.[145] The NLRB pronounced Behring International, Inc., guilty of an unfair labor practice because it granted a pay raise two months after a union lost an election to represent its workers simply because an objection could still have been made by the union to challenge the election results.[146] In the 1981 case of Soule Glass and Glazing Co., the NLRB ruled that a wage increase granted on the first day of a strike was an unfair labor practice.[147] The NLRB has issued cease-and-desist orders to nullify companies' premium pay plans[148] and investigated one company for giving Christmas bonuses to employees without the union's permission.[149]

According to the NLRB, violence by strikers is not an unfair labor practice unless the violence becomes excessive. In 1979, the NLRB announced, "Although an employee may have engaged in misconduct [during a strike], he or she may not be deprived of reinstatement rights absent a showing that the conduct was so violent . . . as to render an employee unfit for future service."[150] Most individuals who are attacked by an angry mob consider any amount of violence excessive, but NLRB officials—with their tenure and their comfortable offices—make judicious distinctions on just how much violence people should be required to suffer before the government recognizes it as an "unfair labor practice."

The NLRB's Office of General Counsel issued a ruling in 1990 concerning International Tank Service, Inc. (ITS), a company engaged in the repair and construction of petroleum and chemical storage tanks.[151] The company received a contract to repair a tank at the BP Refinery in Lima, Ohio. Shortly after the company began work, company manager John Evans received a call from Fernando Hinojosa of the Boilermakers Local Union No. 85, AFL-CIO. Hinojosa asked whether the company would sign with the union, and when Evans refused, Hinojosa later informed him that the company would begin picketing the site. (ITS employees had apparently expressed no interest in being represented by a union.) On August 30, 1989, the union began picketing the company workers' entrance gates at the BP Refinery demanding that the employer sign an agreement with the union—even though the union had made little or no effort to persuade the companies' workers to join the union voluntarily. Up to forty union members picketed the site. An NLRB investigation revealed that

> on each day of activity, the pickets prevented [ITS's] trucks from entering the site; they used rocks and lead pipes to damage vehicles owned by ITS . . . on August 30 and 31; and the pickets refused to move even when the local police were called to the site; on August 30 and/or 31 the pickets physically assaulted Evans and spit on him in the presence of his employees.[152]

An NLRB advisory decision noted judiciously: "It does not appear that this property damage was extensive" and "Evans was not seriously injured on either of these two days." The issue, according to NLRB's arcane regulations, was

> whether violence or picket line misconduct attributable to a Union shortens the "reasonable period of time" not to exceed 30 days during which picketing for recognition is allowed under Section 8(b)(7)(C) without a representation petition having been filed, when the Union's picketing is conducted to obtain an 8(f) contract; and (2) whether four days of picket line misconduct accompanying Union picketing for an 8(f) contract was more than a "reasonable period of time" without a representation petition being filed so that the picketing as to constituted a violation of Section 8(b)(7)(C).[153]

This case highlights the NLRB's calculus of violence—how much violence is permitted in the efforts of unionization. The opinion noted, "The contemporaneous use of violence and other misconduct by a construction union picketing for an 8(f) agreement will not, per se, render such picketing unlawful under Section 8(b)(7)(C). However . . . the reasonable time limitations set forth in that section may be shortened if the union also engages in violence or picket line misconduct." The NLRB explicitly stated that picket-line violence does not automatically make the picketing unfair—as if picketers were entitled to a certain quantum of violence.

The NLRB Office of General Counsel noted:

> In the instant case, we concluded that the Union's picket line misconduct was not so violent or coercive as to warrant shortening the time limitations prescribed [for

> picketing]. . . . For instance, the misconduct alleged herein was of limited duration, as it only occurred for 4 days. . . . In addition, in this case there was no serious physical injury and only minor damage to property. . . . In light of the foregoing analysis, the Region should dismiss the instant 8(b)(7)(C) charge, absent withdrawal.[154]

Picketing routinely degenerates into a simple economic blockade—an effort to cut off entrances and exits of the picketed site. Thus, it is surprising that the NLRB finds excuses or pretexts to discount the reality of picket-line violence. Apparently, union violence is not bad in itself—but only when it becomes an embarrassment to the NLRB. The NLRB's attitude toward picket-line violence is akin to the attitude of some old-time Southern white sheriffs' toward violence against black people: a little violence is okay, as long as there is no lynching. (A private lynching could embarrass public officials and make people think they were not earning their salary.) The assault by the mob would likely be almost terrorizing to a black person, since the black person would not know whether the mob was going to lynch him or just rough him up. Similarly, the business owner assaulted by a mob of union members trying to expropriate the jobs of his employees would not know whether they intend to only bloody his nose or to break his neck.

Hounding the Dogs: The NLRB and the Bankrupting of Greyhound

The NLRB's patronizing attitude toward violence had devastating impacts in its rulings on the 1990 Greyhound bus strike. After management and the Amalgamated Council of Greyhound Local, the sole union for the bus drivers, negotiated for four months, the union called a strike. At midnight on March 1, 1990, drivers walked off their jobs. Bus drivers who were on a scheduled run abandoned their buses at the next stop, stranding many passengers. The following day, Greyhound began hiring replacement workers and implemented the terms of its final contract offer to the union.

Strikers began a campaign of violence to bring Greyhound to its knees. On March 11, seven passengers were wounded as a result of shots fired at a Greyhound bus in Jacksonville, Florida.[155] In the early months of the strike, sniper attacks occurred fifty-two times on buses carrying passengers.[156] Bus ridership fell by two-thirds, and the company was unable to provide buses and drivers for almost half its scheduled runs.[157]

Despite the stark violence, the NLRB early on explicitly took the union's side. In May 1990, NLRB General Counsel Jerry Hunter sought to force the company to provide "immediate and full reinstatement" to the strikers and to fire "if necessary, any and all replacements in order to provide work for such strikers"—as well as provide the strikers with $143 million in back pay.[158] On May 30, 1990, NLRB Milwaukee Regional Director Joseph Szabo filed a complaint declaring that the strike "is and has been, at all times . . . an unfair labor practices strike"—thus effectively whitewashing the strikers from their violent actions. The NLRB claimed that Greyhound had committed an unfair labor practice by implementing its final contract offer without union consent—even after union members walked off the job and began a campaign of violence against Greyhound buses, stations, and employees.

NLRB dallied long before taking any action against union violence. In mid-June, NLRB issued a nationwide injunction against the strikers from continuing to throw Molotov cocktails, rocks, concrete, bricks, and bottles at buses or replacement drivers; engaging in industrial sabotage, such as breaking bus doors, mirrors, or windshield wipers; playing "cat and mouse" games with buses by shining lights at the vehicles or pulling in front of buses and braking unexpectedly in front of them; or committing other acts of violence and harassment. The union, while denying any responsibility for the violence, agreed to the NLRB cease-and-desist order and signed a court order-consent decree ratifying the agreement.[159] The union did not have to pay a single cent of damages or compensation to Greyhound under the terms of the NLRB agreement. When the violent attacks persisted on buses and striker replacements throughout the summer, the NLRB refused to enforce the terms of the consent decree.[160] Later, in the agency trial, NLRB lawyers argued that striker violence was essentially irrelevant to any settlement because the violence had been "remedied" by the consent decree.

Three months after the strike began, Greyhound filed for bankruptcy. Greyhound chief executive officer Fred Currey declared that it was the violence of the strikers—including the bombings, the shootings, and the beatings—that directly drove the company into bankruptcy. Currey declared: "I've dealt with supply-demand risks all my life, but I've never lost money as a result of criminal activity, and I deeply resent it. It's been open warfare."[161]

In July 1990, the NLRB issued a ruling as to whether the bus drivers union "violated Section 8(b)(3) of the [National Labor Relations] Act by planning and engaging in a campaign of violent strike-related misconduct while engaged in collective bargaining with the Employer for a new labor agreement." The NLRB General Counsel's office ruled: "We conclude that the Union did not violate Section 8(b)(3) as alleged. The instant charge should therefore be dismissed, absent withdrawal." Despite scores of violent incidents, the NLRB rationalized that "although the Union's conduct in the instant case was substantial and widespread, this case does not involve a situation where the Union brought its misconduct directly into the negotiations, by engaging in violence, threats or other restraint and coercion aimed directly at employer bargaining representatives." Apparently, since the strikers only shot up Greyhound buses, and did not shoot the company's chief executive officer and vice presidents, the strikers' crimes were irrelevant to federal labor law. The NLRB also ruled: "[T]he Union's misconduct appears to have been designed to coerce nonstriking employees and replacements in the exercise of their Section 7 rights to refrain from supporting the Union's strike, and to exert pressure on the Employer in order to extract bargaining concessions. The former objective is proscribed by Section 8(b)(1)(A) of the Act. The latter objective is present whenever a party uses economic weapons in a labor dispute. As discussed above, the Supreme Court has concluded that such use is not inconsistent with good faith collective bargaining." Greyhound management terminated negotiations with the union after the first wave of striker violence against Greyhound buses and employees; the NLRB ruled, "Concededly, the Union's misconduct did lead to a suspension of negotiations. However, this suspension resulted from the Employer's independent decision to terminate bargaining in response to the Union's misconduct."[162] The NLRB's definition of "bargaining in good faith" apparently carries an unlimited obligation for company officials to continue bargaining with representatives of a group that are violently trying to destroy the company.

The NLRB tried its case against Greyhound before one of its own administrative law judges. The government's complaint alleged Greyhound bargained unfairly with the drivers and forced the strike in an attempt to break the union.[163] The NLRB claimed that no bargaining impasse had existed at the time that the union went on strike, and thus that management had no right to unilaterally implement its contract offer after the union members left their jobs. This same issue had been tried earlier before U.S. bankruptcy judge Richard Schmidt as part of the determination of Greyhound's liabilities in bankruptcy proceedings. Judge Schmidt concluded that there was not "any serious doubt" that an impasse had existed. Schmidt, who approved the bus company's reorganization plan, reduced the government's claim against Greyhound for back wages and damages to workers from $143 million to $31.5 million.[164] (As a bankruptcy judge, Schmidt did not have the power to totally erase the claims.)

A key point in the government prosecution of Greyhound during a 1991 administrative law trial was that the company illegally fired workers after the workers abandoned their buses and walked off their jobs. Specifically, NLRB lawyers argued at length that Greyhound had committed an illegal "unfair labor practice" by firing two strikers who were convicted and sentenced to jail for shooting at a Greyhound bus carrying passengers. The NLRB argued that the workers had been engaged in union activities during the strike and shooting and thus that their activities were protected under federal labor law and that Greyhound owed them back pay—including for the time they were in jail.[165]

Under severe pressure from the Clinton administration and the NLRB, Greyhound settled with the striking union in April 1993, agreeing to provide over $30 million in back pay and to rehire many of the strikers who had been engaged in violence against the company. The union was not required to make any compensation to the shooting victims or others injured during the strike.[166]

The NLRB often is creative in finding pretexts to force companies to provide back pay to strikers for time the strikers did not work. But as a University of Pennsylvania–Wharton School of Business study noted in

1983, "The board has consistently refused to order unions to compensate employees who have incurred hospital or medical expenses as a result of union violence. It has likewise refused to order monetary awards covering union damage to company property and equipment."[167] The NLRB has also refused to force unions to compensate individuals for keeping them from earning a paycheck by imposing picket-line blockades around a business site.

Banning Free Speech on the Job

Federal labor law defines a labor organization as "any organization of any kind . . . in which employees participate, and which exists for the purpose . . . of dealing with employers concerning . . . conditions of work."[168] The National Labor Relations Act prohibits employers from creating company-dominated unions. In December 1992, the NLRB convicted Electromation, an Elkhart, Indiana, electronics manufacturer, of unfair labor practices for meeting with committees of employees in 1989 to discuss employee grievances. The NLRB ruled that Electromation's Action Committees were illegal in large part because the employees were paid for the time they spent meeting with management representatives to try to work out a more satisfactory benefit package. The NLRB's ruling condemned Electromation because the committees discussed "conditions of employment" and "other statutory subjects."[169] The National Labor Relations Act makes it a federal crime for employers and groups of employees to meet to discuss job issues outside of the pro-union framework mandated by Congress and the NLRB. NLRB chairman Dennis Devaney complained that Electromation, "by creating the illusion of a bargaining representative without the reality, denied employees wishing representation the service of a loyal and effective agent."[170]

The NLRB's decision in the Electromation case sent shock waves through the Fortune 500, since most large companies now have joint employer-employee "work-quality circles" that attempt to raise efficiency and productivity. Work-quality circles have been hailed as the great hope for the revival of American competitiveness. But because the circles are usually run by management instead of by a joint management-union committee, the NLRB decision implied that such circles are illegal under federal law. While American industry is in a struggle to survive in world competition, the NLRB cares only that companies' efforts to involve workers in improving product quality might undercut union organizing drives.

The Occupational Safety and Health Administration requires manufacturing companies to have joint committees of management and employees to deal with safety issues. But the NLRB warned in an April 15, 1993, memo that such committees may be illegal under federal labor law.[171] Though workplace safety and health programs are widely perceived as crucial to improving factory safety, the NLRB in June 1993 officially ruled that joint worker-management workplace safety committees were unfair labor practices and effectively banned them.[172] Apparently, only unionized companies should be allowed maximum opportunities to improve job safety. A *Wall Street Journal* editorial noted, "The NLRB rulings set up a legal squeeze in which even nonunion companies can't consult their workers without a by-your-leave from a union boss" and denounced the ruling as contributing to "Big Labor's . . . dream of elbowing their way back with an NLRB-enforced monopoly on conversation between the factory floor and the front office."[173]

If 51 percent of the citizens in a state voted to require all citizens in that state to pay $20 a month in tribute to either the Republican or the Democratic party, almost everybody would recognize this as a case of majority tyranny and oppression. Yet, the same practice is effectively tolerated by the NLRB—permitting unions to force millions of workers to pay tribute to unions that use the dues to finance political causes with which the workers disagree. (Six million workers nationwide are employed under "union shop provisions" that require them to pay union dues regardless of whether they choose to join the union.) In 1988, the Supreme Court made a landmark decision on the nature of federal labor law. Harry Beck and nineteen coworkers sued the Communications Workers of America in 1976, claiming their forced dues were being spent for purposes unrelated to collective bargaining and to support political causes they opposed. Court investigators concluded that 79 percent of the nonunion members' dues were being spent for activities not related to the cost of negotiating and administering the collective bargaining agreement, and that the nonunion members were being forced to subsidize the union's political activity. The Supreme Court ruled, "It simply does not follow from [the legislative history of federal labor law] that Congress left unions free to exact dues equivalents from nonmembers in any amount they please, no matter how unrelated those fees may be to collective bargaining activities."[174] The decision effectively meant that millions of nonunion members were being abused by requirements to bankroll unions as a condition of retaining their jobs. But the staff of the National Labor Relations Board has generally refused to enforce the Supreme Court verdict—even going so far as to routinely misrepresent it to individuals asking for NLRB assistance in gaining relief from paying forced dues.

The NLRB itself is hardly an impartial judge for labor-management clashes; the majority of its employees are union members, with separate unions representing the staff professionals and the clerical staff. As *Legal Times* newspaper noted, the NLRB has "a long tradition of unionism."[175] In 1992 the NLRB Professional Association (the union for NLRB attorneys) filed an unfair labor practice complaint against NLRB board member John Raudabaugh. Alan Ricca, an NLRB staff attorney and vice president of the NLRB Professional Association, stated that Raudabaugh's misbehavior started on his first day on the board: "During his welcoming speech, [Raudabaugh] said, 'If you have any problems, come directly to me.' We had to remind him that there is a professional association here. You can't have that kind of direct dealing."[176] According to the union, after a union officer told Raudabaugh to shut up, Raudabaugh declared that if anyone ever did that again he would "kill that person."[177] In October 1993 Raudabaugh and the union settled the case after Raudabaugh signed a one-page statement pledging that "he would not tell unionized employees to bypass the union and deal directly with him, that he would not threaten employees, and that he would not improperly question union officials regarding union matters," as *Legal Times* reported. (Raudabaugh did not admit that he had violated any federal labor laws.)[178]

When unions seek to forcibly shut down a business during a strike, union members sometimes act as if they own the jobs that they left. But does the fact that a businessman hired a worker automatically give that worker a perpetual right to employment on terms that the worker demands? A man has a right to walk off his job (unless the worker has voluntarily signed a no-strike contract) if he is not satisfied. But the right to walk off a job does not include the right to fracture the skull of someone else who walks into the job.

Federal labor law is largely based on a blind faith in the benefits of forcing people into herds—on a presumption of the total incompetence or inability of the individual worker to achieve justice for himself. Harley Shaiken, a labor analyst at MIT, condemned apparel homework in 1984: "It's bad because you must deal with the employer as an individual, rather than collectively."[179] But if unions were so superior to individuals, then unions would not be representing only 12 percent of private-sector workers. *Telecommuting Report* summarized union criticisms of possible telecommuting agreements from a 1992 meeting: "One union representative suggested that there was no conflict between having a collective agreement and allowing workers to choose work options, as long as there were no 'entirely individual agreements.'"[180] But the large majority of American workers do just fine in making their own terms with their employers. And the federal pro-union bias is especially unjustified considering the pervasive corruption of some of the nation's larger unions.

Unions can be an excellent means of handling grievances, making the will of the workers known to employers, and providing a medium for communication on key issues. The issue is not whether groups of workers should be able to form unions and bargain with employers. The right of freedom of association is guaranteed by the First Amendment. New York University law professor Sylvester Petro wrote, "The right to strike for higher wages and better working conditions is a fundamental right of working men in a free society, and it must be preserved largely intact if the society is to remain free."[181] The issue is whether contracts that some workers negotiate with employers should be allowed to nullify the right of other workers to make their own contracts.

"BLATANT HIGHWAY ROBBERY"

Government transportation policy routinely acts as if restricting competition is equivalent to serving the public. In many areas, prohibitions on private transportation are expressly designed to force people to patronize government-subsidized services that are widely perceived as unreliable and insufficient. Politicians have turned transportation into a political patronage system: masses of people are forced to wait away part of their lives so that politicians can continue collecting large contributions from transit workers' unions.

Local bus monopolies often seem devoted to seeing how little service they can provide. In 1991, service was cut back on 40 percent of the Metrobus routes in the Washington, D.C., area.[182] On seven representative Brooklyn bus routes studied in 1986, only 78 percent of scheduled bus trips were actually run. Dick Netzer reported in *City Journal*, "For the close-in segments of the routes, buses actually travel at speeds only a little faster than walking speeds."[183] *USA Today* reported in 1992, "New Yorkers rely on public transit more than any other major city—a factor that actually adds time to their daily commute."[184] "Fast enough for government work" is the standard that millions of urban Americans are often forced to rely on for their daily transportation.

Naturally, private entrepreneurs are trying to fill the void caused by shabby government service. In Queens, New York, *Newsday* reported, "'Gypsy' service has flourished . . . because riders' clamor for increased bus service in Rosedale, the Rockaways, Cambria Heights, Laurelton and environs, has largely gone unsatisfied during the decade after a 1980 city transit strike. Many loyal van riders have said that in the years following the strike, private buses [licensed, subsidized, and granted monopolies by the government] simply stopped dependable service altogether."[185] In 1992, the Transit Authority cut the fares on selected bus lines in Queens to underprice private vans but few riders returned to the government buses. The *New York Times* noted, "Many riders say they do not mind paying an extra quarter or two for the speed, comfort and convenience of the vans, which use side streets to avoid traffic, play music and often deliver passengers to their front doors."[186] Commuter Marjorie Lawla declared: "I like having a choice. Why not let me choose?"[187]

In 1991, New York City launched a crackdown on illegal vans serving investment bankers and other workers traveling from Manhattan's Upper East Side to Wall Street. New York City Transit Authority senior vice president Ronald Contino denounced private competition as "blatant highway robbery" and said that private vans cost public transit $30 million a year in lost revenue.[188] City transit officials, like medieval despots, sound as if they feel entitled to exact tribute from any person who seeks to travel through their domain. The fact that people voluntarily use private illegal services proves the private buses provide better service. When private van owners sought to secure a license to provide service legally, Jeffrey Shernoff, a lawyer representing fourteen van owners, observed, "Every one of these owners was strenuously opposed by the Transit Authority and all of the public transportation authorities on whose territory they thought the van drivers impinged."[189] New York transit police were so enthusiastic in their pursuit of private competitors that they would sometimes stop private vans and give them a *parking ticket.*[190] (One legitimate private van company received a $1 million court settlement in 1992 after city transit officials were convicted of illegally harassing his vans.)[191] While transit police were cracking down on private vans, there were 3,656 robberies, 2,737 cases of grand larceny, 580 assaults, 9 murders, 13 rapes, 102 burglaries, and 649 other felonies on the New York City subway in the first half of 1992.[192]

Many local governments have worked overtime to create a shortage of taxi service. The U.S. Department of Transportation estimated in 1974 that "regulations restricting entry of new cabs and preventing discounting of fares cost consumers nearly $800 million annually. Moreover, removal of these restrictions would create 38,000 new jobs in the taxi industry."[193] Boston refused to increase the number of taxi medallions required to own and operate a taxi for forty-five years. As a result, the cost of a taxi medallion was $90,000—more than five times the cost of a taxi. (A lawsuit by the New England Legal Foundation modified the policy and resulted in a slight increase in the number of medallions.) Cleveland, Dallas, and Philadelphia awarded a monopoly to provide taxi service to a single company. As Allen Randolph wrote, "Aspiring Philadelphia cab drivers must show the 'need' for cab service in an area they wish to serve. Licenses there transfer for $20,000."[194] While there are only 0.3 taxis per thousand people servicing Philadelphia, in Washington, no expensive licenses are required—and Washington averages 12 cabs per thousand people. New York froze the number of taxi medallions at 11,787—back in 1937.[195] New York City taxi medallions cost $140,000; 85 percent of the drivers rent or lease cabs from medallion owners, thus making a mockery of a system originally created to boost the income of cab drivers. (New York complements its strict cab licensing with rigorous taxi inspections; in July 1992, the city announced that over half of the city's fifty taxi inspectors had been arrested for extorting bribes to overlook safety and emissions violations.)[196] There is a severe shortage of cab service in many parts of New York; naturally, private entrepreneurs—"gypsy cabs"—provide service to meet public demand. The city government responded by proposing that officials of the Taxi and Limousine Commission receive authority to "confiscate the cars of anyone caught offering illegal car service."[197]

Restrictions on transit services are often essentially a political decree that citizens' time and convenience are disposable goods to be auctioned off to the highest political bidder. The key factor in determining what transit services will be offered or tolerated is not what people demand but what government officials feel they can afford to provide. For politicians and transportation officials, "need" is the basis of right—and since they need more revenue, citizens in many cities must be prohibited from using private transit services, regardless of how poor the government service is.

Americans have minimal opportunities to travel domestically on passenger ships largely because of restrictive shipping legislation enacted in 1886. In a free market, foreign cruise ships would offer pleasure trips from New York to Baltimore, Savannah to Miami, and from San Diego to San Francisco. But cruise ships are prohibitively expensive because of the buy-American and crew-American mandates enacted over a century ago. Rep. Walter Jones, chairman of the House Merchant Marine Committee, conceded in 1991, "We have no American-flag cruise industry to speak of."[198] Seattle is especially victimized by federal passenger cruise restrictions. Each year, hundreds of thousands of tourists fly to Seattle for cruises to Alaska but cross over to Vancouver, Canada, in order to catch the cruise ships. Without federal restrictions, Alaska cruises would originate in Seattle, not Vancouver. Mark Sullivan of the Port of Seattle estimates that this costs Seattle over $30 million a year in lost tourist business.[199] The ban on foreign cruise ships is largely the result of the $2 million a year in campaign contributions from the maritime unions.

ADMINISTRATIVE JUSTICE VS. PRIVATE CONTRACTS

In order to fairly judge freedom of contract it is necessary to examine what politicians and bureaucrats impose in lieu of contracts. The presumption of the wisdom and higher fairness of government regulation lies at the base of much of the vast expansion of government control over private behavior over the last century. In 1887, responding to a clamor by the farm lobby for cheaper grain shipping rates, Congress passed the Interstate Commerce Act, which created the Interstate Commerce Commission (ICC). The ICC became the arbiter of the fairness of rail shipment prices. In the early years of the twentieth century, federal courts raised the principle of ICC jurisdiction over prices into a quasi-religious doctrine; Supreme Court Justice Louis Brandeis proclaimed in 1915: "The rate of a carrier duly filed [with the ICC] is the only lawful charge. Deviation from it is not permitted upon any pretext. . . . Ignorance or misquotation of rates is not an excuse for paying or charging either less or more than the rate filed."[200] Thus, the "filed rate" doctrine: a shipping agreement between two private citizens is presumably unfair and patently illegal unless it has been sent to Washington and placed into a government filing cabinet. The ICC "filed rate" doctrine was premised on politicians' and bureaucrats' need to control the transport business in order to prevent "unjust discrimination," in Justice Brandeis's words.

ICC regulations (which were extended to trucking in 1935) cartelized the nation's transport industry. Trucking companies capitalized on the regulations to minimize competition. Trucking companies were required to get ICC permission before providing any new or modified service. Trucking companies exploited federal regulations to automatically challenge any proposal to provide new service. As Steve Chapman reported in the *New Republic*, "The classic case is the time a frustrated company filed a rate to carry yak fat, an imaginary product, from Omaha to Chicago. Though no one had ever heard of yak fat, no fewer than 13 carriers protested the rate."[201] ICC regulations specified exactly what product a truck could carry and which route it must take. Truckers were often forced to travel far out of the way because they lacked ICC approval for a direct route and to return home with an empty truck because the ICC prohibited them from carrying loads on a round trip. Secretary of Transportation Elizabeth Dole estimated in 1985 that the ICC had 30 trillion rates on file.[202] ICC regulations affect $75 billion in trucking each year.[203]

In 1980, Congress passed the Motor Carrier Act, ending the ICC's power to restrict entry into the hauling business. Trucking deregulation was one of the greatest successes of the 1980s. The number of trucking firms more than doubled; shipping costs fell by roughly $10 billion a year; and the greater efficiency of service was a key factor in allowing American companies to shift to just-in-time manufacturing.[204]

But a glitch in the 1980 act is allowing lawyers to ravage scores of thousands of American companies. Congress did not formally repeal the requirement that trucking companies must file their shipping rates with the ICC. Since the ICC took no action on the rate filings it received, many trucking companies ceased filing their rates. As of 1987, prevailing trucking rates were approximately 40 percent below the rates on file with the ICC.

Many trucking firms went bankrupt during the 1980s. Lawyers for bankruptcy trustees dusted off the filed rate doctrine, checked the ICC files, and began suing the trucking companies' former customers. The lawyers demanded retroactive payments at a higher rate than what the truckers had negotiated solely because the truckers had failed to file the lower rate with the ICC. Lawrence Fineran of the National Association of Manufacturers complained: "It's a complete disavowal of contract. It's exactly as if bankrupt Eastern Air Lines were going back to customers and saying, 'You know that supersaver fare we gave you to Florida back in 1987? Well, you now owe us another $800 for the full fare.'"[205] The ICC formally ruled that such retroactive undercharges were an "unreasonable practice,"[206] but the Supreme Court ruled in 1990 that the retroactive charges were legal.[207] The Supreme Court, worshiping its ancient decisions on the "filed rate" doctrine, basically gave some companies a legal right to rob other companies.

After the Supreme Court decision, "rate sharks"—lawyers trying to collect retroactive charges—went into a feeding frenzy. By early 1993, businesses had been hit with over 500,000 retroactive bills.[208] Because of the undercharge bonanzas, some trucking firms became worth more dead than alive and filed for bankruptcy in order to sue their former customers for retroactive surcharges.[209]

IBM was hit with a demand for $60 million from the bankruptcy of a single trucking company (Transcon Lines).[210] After P-I-E, one of the nation's largest trucking companies, went bankrupt, a P-I-E trustee was filing up to 300 undercharge suits a day against shippers.[211] Small businesses without in-house lawyers to defend them were especially hit hard. Tony Freese, a Houston entrepreneur hit by a large undercharge bill, bewailed: "I sell skateboards. I am not up on the legalities of interstate commerce."[212] One Kansas City carpet distributor was hit with a back shipping bill that raised his shipping rate from 16 cents per square yard to $32.06 per square yard.[213] A charity organization that collected products donated to the United Way was hit in 1993 with a demand for $100,000 in back charges.[214] Bankruptcy trustees even demanded back payments from a group of Massachusetts nuns.[215] Michael J. Curry, a Kansas City, Missouri, businessman, observed: "There is no way to physically jump a plane every time you want to fly to Washington, D.C., to go to the ICC and check a tariff. There are tariff-watching services up here, but it gets pretty prohibitively expensive. You are making $50 on a load to spend $30 to check and see if a rate has been filed or not."[216] The ICC estimated that up to 80 percent of all money shaken out of shippers goes to lawyers and collection agents, with only a small sliver going to the employees of the bankrupt trucking firms.[217]

Trucking companies and their trustees are collecting a mega-reward for breaking federal law. Since truckers had a legal obligation to file their rates with the ICC, it is solely through their own negligence or dishonesty that their former customers are getting bilked for retroactive charges. In many cases, trucking companies used "bait and switch" tactics: contracting with a company to ship their goods at a price they filed with the ICC and then canceling the rate with the ICC without informing the shipper.[218] The president of one defunct trucking company, Robert Tannenbaum, went to the ICC and tore out pages of filed rates, replaced them with phony rates, and then sued shippers for $17 million because the rates they had paid were not on file. On September 28, 1993, Tannenbaum was sentenced to prison for racketeering and ordered to forfeit $2 million to the federal government.[219] (The federal government will keep most of the $2 million for itself; little will be refunded to the companies that were shaken down by Tannenbaum.) William J. Augello of the Transportation Claims and Prevention Council observed, "Although it may be difficult to comprehend, even fraud is not a defense to the filed rate doctrine."[220]

The ICC estimates that the total demands for retroactive payments could reach $32 billion.[221] The $32 billion in losses due to the defects of federal legislation and regulation is more than four times the total amount stolen by thieves and burglars each year, according to the U.S. Census Bureau.[222] Yet while Americans' anxiety over private crime is at a fever pitch, little attention is paid to de facto robberies spawned by mangled regulatory regimes. Some small companies have been driven out of business by the retroactive undercharge demands. The *Journal of Commerce* characterized most undercharge claims as "thinly veiled attempts at extortion."

The undercharge crisis epitomizes the economic incompetence and moral irresponsibility of the U.S. Congress. Because Congress refused to formally relinquish the federal government's authority to approve shipping rates, thousands of shippers have been devastated by unjust lawsuits. Businesses skewered by the retroactive "undercharges" appealed to Congress to clarify the law and end the lawyers' rampage. But Congress has not deigned to clean up the law. The Teamsters union donated $2,442,552 to candidates in the last congressional elections,[223] and they apparently bought veto power over any sense of decency and fair play that congressmen might have.

Government's efforts to coercively impose "fair" prices for shipping services have led to more unfairness than any conceivable private arrangement short of open piracy. This fiasco is also an example of how the accumulation of power by federal agencies and by Congress over a regulated industry leads to the equivalent of dust explosions in grain elevators. Legal authority piles up over the years and few people notice until some lawyer or special interest group finds a way to invoke the federal power for their own advantage.

CONCLUSION

Almost all restrictive labor regulations rest, in the final analysis, on the empowering of government officials to evict some citizens from the labor market—to prohibit some people from working for a living. The state of Oregon, in a brief to the U.S. Supreme Court defending its 1914 minimum wage law, asserted: "If Simpson [a woman thrown out of work by the Oregon law] cannot be trained to yield output that does pay the cost of her labor, then she can . . . accept the status of a defective to be segregated for special treatment as a dependent of the state."[224] This statement vivifies how government stacks the deck to benefit some by throwing other people out of the game. Minimum wage laws presume that politicians are morally justified in reducing some people's freedom in order to increase other people's wages. Though politicians are rarely so honest about their intent these days, this is still frequently the essence of government labor law—dictating that some people have no right to be self-reliant and must become wards of the state.

The name of the Fair Labor Standards Act is typical of the dishonesty of the Paternalist State. "Fair labor" restrictions are almost inevitably fairer to politicians than to workers. The Fair Labor Standards Act contains no definition of "fair labor"; instead, the act permits politicians to endlessly manipulate and rig labor markets for their own advantage. The Fair Labor Standards Act is basically a blank check to allow political manipulation of the labor markets to reward some people by throwing other people out of the labor market. Once politicians achieved the power to define "fair" labor, they also claimed the power to ban people from laboring. "Fair labor standards" are simply what politicians claim they are—this week. There was no reason in

1938 to declare that 40 hours was the "fair" work week. "Fair labor" policies divide the labor force into political victors and political victims. It would be more accurate to rename the FLSA the Political Standards for Labor Act.

The right to contract is simply the right to decide what type of work one will do and what level of pay one will accept. Freedom of contract means freedom to structure one's working arrangements as one chooses. Restricting freedom of contract means restricting a person's freedom to use his labor as he chooses. Government cannot restrict freedom of contract without reducing some people's ability to improve their lives. To destroy a man's freedom of choice is to effectively take control of his life. Alexander Hamilton observed in *The Federalist Papers*: "A power over a man's subsistence amounts to a power over his will."[225] Government officials in dozens of ways have seized power over an individual's ability to earn his subsistence—thereby taking control over the individual's will.

We face a choice between government dictates or private voluntary agreements. Almost every restriction of freedom of contract means an extension of political and bureaucratic power over American citizens. For politicians and bureaucrats, the questions of whether to restrict freedom of contract is often simply a question of whether they should extend their own power and control. For many congressmen, the question of whether government should restrict freedom of contract is simply whether they can personally benefit from further shackling and trammeling the citizenry. Individuals face a choice of making their own terms or having those terms dictated to them by politicians, bureaucrats, or unions.

People almost never petition Congress to restrict their own freedom of contract; rather, one group petitions politicians to restrict everyone else's freedom for their own benefit. There are almost no "innocent" restrictions of freedom of contract. Almost every restriction of freedom of contract necessarily gives someone or some group an advantage over other people or other groups. The decision to restrict freedom of contract rarely occurs in a vacuum: there are competing interest groups—or at least one interest group striving to gain dominance over others. The government almost never restricts freedom of contract to achieve a level playing field between the contracting parties. Rather, most restrictions are an attempt to subjugate one of the contracting parties to the other party—to forcibly sacrifice one group's interest to other groups—to use the police power to forcibly transfer income. Almost every restriction on freedom of contract effectively forces some people to accept contracts that they would otherwise not have accepted.

There has been a vast increase in political exploitation in the name of curtailing economic exploitation. Politicians almost always profit from their restrictions on other people's freedom. The degrees of restriction of freedom of contract thus are one of the clearest measures of political imperialism. For almost every reduction and destruction of freedom of contract, members of Congress or the bureaucracy had an ulterior motive. In public, they proclaimed that the new restrictions would help some group that could not help themselves; in private, they bragged to their campaign contributors that they had once again earned their keep. When politicians dictate contract terms, it is almost inevitable that some people will be exploited for political benefit.

Restrictions on freedom of contract amount to a political expropriation of opportunity—a constant whittling away of a person's chances in life. A man's freedom to make his own contracts is a measure of his sovereignty over himself, his life, and his property. As no man is entitled to a share of his neighbor's income, no man is entitled to have his neighbor's freedom restricted so as to get more of his neighbor's income.

-5-

Subsidies and Subjugation

It is hardly lack of due process for the government to regulate that which it subsidizes.

—U.S. Supreme Court (1942)[1]

The history of government grants of a continuing cash subsidy indicates that such programs have almost always been accompanied by varying measures of control and surveillance.

—U.S. Supreme Court (1971)[2]

Since the early twentieth century, federal subsidy programs have proliferated for everything from medical care to housing, to tobacco farming, to bilingual education. The federal government now operates over 1,200 domestic assistance programs.[3] Government controls have followed a short step behind the subsidies; as a result, scores of activities in our society and economy are increasingly dependent upon government approval. Unfortunately, government subsidies are increasingly squeezing out unsubsidized activities and individuals. From unsubsidized farmers, to unsubsidized artists, to unsubsidized schools, government subsidies to some individuals and organizations allow politicians and bureaucrats to indirectly control other individuals and organizations. We will examine some of the larger areas of subsidies to see their impact on individual freedom and self-reliance.

THE HIGH COST OF "FREE SCHOOLS"

Public education is the most expensive "gift" that most Americans will ever receive. Government school systems are increasingly coercive and abusive both of parents and students. Government schools in most areas have been taken over by unions, judges, and grandstanding politicians.

Federal, state, and local governments impose over $270 billion in taxes to pay for public schools for forty million students. A 1992 study by the Center for Government Services at Rutgers University found that nationwide, the equivalent of almost 5 percent of Americans' per capita income is spent to pay for government elementary and secondary schools.[4] Most parents pay more in federal, state, and local taxes than the government spends to educate their children. Discussions about public education often almost implicitly assume that public education is a gift from benevolent politicians and wise administrators for which people must be grateful. But talking of "free schools" makes as much sense as talking of "free taxes." The reason that government schools appear to be "free" is that politicians force parents to pay for their children's schooling via taxes. But paying for schools with taxes, rather than by voluntarily writing a check out directly to the schools, radically changes parents' relation to the school. Forcing parents and others to pay for children's education via taxes has greatly increased government power over American families.

Government schools have a de facto monopoly on elementary and secondary education in the United States. Government schools enroll almost 90 percent of all children of school age because few parents can afford to pay twice for their children's education. Supreme Court Justice Lewis Powell observed in 1974, "Most parents cannot afford the luxury of a private education for their children and the dual obligation of private tuitions and public taxes."[5]

Government spending on public schools has soared over the last two generations. Since 1950, public school spending has increased from $259 per pupil to almost $6,000 per pupil—a quadrupling in spending after inflation.[6] Since 1973, in response to repeated proclamations of educational crises, spending in constant dollars per pupil has jumped over 50 percent.[7] Yet despite soaring expenditures, government schools are intellectually debilitating young Americans. Benno Schmidt, former president of Yale University, noted, "Nearly half of all high school graduates have not mastered seventh-grade arithmetic."[8] According to the National Assessment of Educational Progress, two-thirds of seventeen-year-olds were unable to read well enough to do high school work in 1989.[9] David Kearns, chief executive officer of Xerox, observes, "The typical Japanese worker enters the work force with a high school diploma equivalent to a four-year American college degree";[10] Kearns denounced public schools as suppliers with a "50% defect rate." The Department of Education announced in September 1993 that the literacy of the American public was sharply deficient; as the *New York Times* summarized the report, "Nearly half of the nation's 191 million adult citizens are not proficient enough in English to write a letter about a billing error or to calculate the length of a bus trip from a published schedule."[11] The 1993 survey found a sharp decrease in the literacy of Americans between the ages of fifteen and twenty-one, as compared to the results of a similar survey in 1985.[12]

Government schools have reacted to their failures by misrepresenting their performance. The worse schools perform, the higher students score. New York City introduced a new mathematics test in 1993 that involved subjective grading by teachers—such as awarding near-perfect scores for wrong answers.[13] School test data have been manipulated to allow "all 50 state education agencies to report above-average scores for their elementary schools, with most claiming such scores in every subject area and every grade level," as former Education Department official Larry Uzzell reported.[14] Public schools in Washington, D.C., announced a new policy of automatic promotion for all children in kindergarten and first and second grades, regardless of whether the pupils had learned their lessons[15]—even though "social promotion" policies have been widely ridiculed for minimizing students' incentives to learn. A 1993 Department of Education study concluded, "In nearly every subject, textbooks tackle too many topics and cover them superficially. Moreover, many textbooks have decreased in difficulty by two grade levels in the last 20 years."[16] Cornell professor Donald Hayes concluded in a 1993 study that contemporary "honors high school texts are no more difficult than an 8th-grade reader was before World War II."[17]

"Education" in government schools is increasingly the result of the dictates of political interest groups. Michael Meyers, executive director of the New York Civil Rights Coalition, complained in 1991 that "African-American immersion" public schools are attempting to "foster a mystical ethnic purity and tribalism; they desire to teach students to define themselves and their communities in racial terms."[18] In Illinois, a book with a story about cats was rejected by a school system because the cat popped a balloon; cat lovers protested that the story would turn children against cats. Lobbies that address a range of issues, from anti–junk food, to antiviolence, to anti–secular humanism, to antireligion, are dictating what reading materials schools may use. And the more politically accommodating school texts are, the less readable they usually become, thus making reading less enjoyable for beginning readers.

School officials often appear more interested in reforming children's values than in developing their minds. Connecticut parent Dana Mack complained of that state's Comprehensive Health Education Curriculum: "In the war on drugs . . . parents—not pushers are the enemy. Parents are purported to transmit 'positive attitudes' toward drug use and to 'involve' their children in it. How? According to the teacher's guide, when they request children 'to bring a beer from the refrigerator.'. . . One exercise in the second-grade lesson plan fairly extracts family confessions. It invites children to send 'secret messages' to their teacher about 'problems at home.'"[19] The *New York Times* reported that "the architects of [New Jersey schools'] family life curriculum say that . . . more specific information on such matters as . . . masturbation should be given to students, and at an earlier age."[20] One is puzzled by the concerns of the New Jersey educators: Do they fear that children will not learn how to masturbate, or that they will discover it on their own but fail to use progressive techniques?

In November 1992, New York City Schools Chancellor Joseph A. Fernandez fired the school board in District 24 in Queens because it refused to implement

Fernandez's 443-page "Children of the Rainbow" curriculum. Mary Cummins, president of the board in Queens, denounced the curriculum: "It was brainwashing. It said to the children, 'School is your family.' Next I expected it to say, 'The state is your family.'"[21] The curriculum portrayed gay lifestyles in an extremely positive manner; *Daddy's Roommate,* a book intended for first graders, showed a picture of two adult males together in bed. Fernandez declared that New York schools must teach the "Fourth R—Respect" for homosexuals and other groups.[22] Yet at the time, up to 70 percent of children in some New York city elementary schools were unable to read at or above their grade level. School officials were more concerned about indoctrinating politically correct values than in maximizing literacy. Fernandez's action sparked fierce public protests by parents. As journalist William Tucker noted, "In Park Slope, Brooklyn, an armed police guard had to be called to protect the white-liberal-dominated board against enraged Hispanic parents who argued the schools were attempting to pervert their children."[23] Three school board members who opposed using the Rainbow curriculum had their cars firebombed.[24] A *Wall Street Journal* editorial observed, "What the parents are protesting is the schools' attempt to hijack what belongs to them—the spiritual, sexual and social education of their children."[25]

School condom giveaway programs exemplify parents' loss of control over their children's schooling. Condom giveaways are often justified to prevent the spread of sexually transmitted diseases; but, as one editorial quipped, that is like trying to prevent the misuse of drugs by giving schoolchildren free drug paraphernalia.[26] In fact, public health experts disagree on whether condom giveaway programs actually reduce the net number of people newly infected with AIDS, since condoms are only reliable roughly 85 percent of the time.[27] Many parents fiercely oppose the giveaway programs because they feel that the schools thereby sanction teenage or preteen copulation. The New Haven, Connecticut, Board of Education voted in 1993 to begin passing out free condoms to fifth graders.[28] The New York City school board vetoed proposals to allow parents to exempt their children from the schools' condom giveaway programs. The *New York Times* noted, "In recent months, supporters of the condom plan have let it be firmly known that [vetoing] the parental permission provision was the litmus test of the loyalty to the condom plan itself."[29] Karen Norlander, a lawyer with the New York City Department of Education, declared, "The entire future of public education would be hard pressed if we came to a point where a parent could dictate what the child can learn and the child can't learn."[30] It is novel to label condom giveaways part of the learning process. (While New York schools are giving out free condoms, parents are still responsible for paying for any bulletproof vests children choose to wear to school.) The Washington, D.C., school system began giving away condoms in 1992. The condoms were distributed by school nurses employed by the Public Health Department; D.C. Public Health Commissioner Mohammad Ahkter announced that he would totally disregard parents' requests not to issue condoms to their children, declaring, "These are my clinics."[31] Condom giveaway programs presume that teenagers who buy $120 tennis shoes cannot afford 50-cent condoms.

Another example of schools' disregard for parents' preferences is bilingual education programs, which routinely sacrifice children to guarantee jobs to bilingual teachers. Stephanie Gutmann reported in *City Journal* in 1992, "When Hispanic parents with children in public schools were asked in a recent Gallup poll which language they prefer their children to be taught, only 3% favored mostly Spanish instruction."[32] The parents recognize that English is the language of the American workplace and that their children's future depends on their English fluency. But New York City schools routinely disregard parents' preferences. One school district in New York City "has a waiting list with 600 to 700 names of parents who have requested their children's placement in an English-only school."[33] Children who speak no foreign language are routinely dragooned into foreign-language bilingual classes largely because of school officials' snap judgments based on the children's foreign-sounding last names.[34] (Bilingual education has been derided as "often nothing more than teachers who can't speak English teaching students who can.")[35] Thomas Sowell, author of *Inside American Education*, observed, "In San Francisco, thousands of English-speaking children with educational deficiencies were assigned to bilingual classes, blacks being twice as likely to be so assigned as whites. Hundreds of other youngsters, who in fact had a foreign language as their mother tongue, were assigned to bilingual classes in a *different* foreign language. . . . A civil rights attorney representing minority children characterized the whole approach as a 'mindless' practice of 'assigning kids to wherever there is space.'"[36]

Government school systems provide ample opportunities to subjugate, coerce, and humiliate young citizens. In Nacogdoches, Texas, elementary school students who forgot their pencils were forced to wear bricks around their necks as a reminder.[37] In Bartow, Florida, students are required to chew gum ten minutes a day ever since some school official read that chewing sugarless gum helps prevent tooth decay.[38] In Colorado City, Arizona, a teenager was expelled from school for wearing a T-shirt with a penguin on it; the school principal suspected that the penguin image promoted devil worship.[39] School officials have received increased power in the last decade to strip-search children and to force them to submit themselves to the nation's leading experts on constitutional rights—drug-sniffing dogs. (For details of abusive searches, see Chapter 7.) On the other hand, government schools, increasingly paralyzed by lawsuits, routinely fail to do enough to restrain and punish students who commit violent acts against teachers and others.

Government schools are becoming more like a prison and less like a voluntary association of pupils and teachers for the advancement of learning. A 1976 federal report concluded that high schools "have become social 'aging vats' that have isolated adolescents and delayed their opportunity to learn adult rules, work habits, and skills"[40] and recommended reducing classroom time to between two and four hours a day. John Burkett of the U.S. Department of Education observed in 1991, "It is only in the last 25 years or so that we have had this prolonged adolescence by forced schooling."[41] A 1983 research brief by the Justice Department's National Institute of Justice recommended lowering the compulsory attendance age to fifteen "to eliminate those students who view school as a prison or as a compulsory recreation center, and thus provide a safe environment for those who want to attend."[42]

But the worse schools have failed, the more years of students' lives they are commandeering. Eleven states have extended the age of compulsory school attendance since 1978, and several states now make kindergarten mandatory.[43] Colorado governor Roy Romer proposed a law in 1992 that would make schooling mandatory for all "at-risk" four-year-olds.[44]

School systems are increasingly imposing heavy punishments on young citizens for missing a few classes—regardless of whether they have mastered their lessons. In 1991, the Washington, D.C., public school system instituted a new system of penalties, fining parents $100 and jailing them for up to five days if their child had two unexcused absences from school in a single month.[45] Fairfax County, Virginia, schools began in 1992 to fail any student who missed five days during a three-month quarter—regardless of the student's sickness or academic performance.[46] Fairfax parent Nancy Flynn complained: "The family sanctity has been threatened. This policy has interfered with my relationship with my kids. I am the one who decides whether they are sick enough to stay home."[47] School board member Anthony T. Lane responded: "Whether a parent has the right to take a child out of school, that's their prerogative. It's also the school's prerogative to fail them."[48] School officials thus create new prerogatives for subjugating students regardless of students' academic performance. Fairfax's punitive attendance policy did not improve student performance, but it did result in larger subsidies to local schools because of slightly higher "average daily attendance," which determines budget allocations. John Taylor Gatto, New York's Teacher of the Year of 1991 (according to the New York State Education Department), observed, "Government schooling . . . kills the family by monopolizing the best times of childhood and by teaching disrespect for home and parents."[49]

Some states now revoke the driver's licenses of youths who drop out of school before the age of eighteen. Especially in rural areas, this effectively takes young people hostage, putting an economic gun to their head in order to help education bureaucrats boost school enrollment. Arkansas even revokes the driver's licenses for teenagers who do not maintain at least a C average. While governments feel entitled to severely penalize any citizen who does not stay in the government schools, schools and teachers themselves are rarely penalized for their own poor performances. As the governor of Arkansas, Bill Clinton declared, "What we have to do is say . . . here is what government owes you. But, also say, here is the personal responsibility agenda: here is what you owe to yourself, your government, your country."[50] The government forces parents to pay for schooling—which the government then claims it is giving "free" to their children—and then a governor announces that the children "owe . . . your government" something for a service paid for by their parents.

Governments are increasingly portraying high school diplomas as a privilege that politicians and bureaucrats can award as they please, not as the right of students who have satisfied academic requirements. School districts in Atlanta, Pennsylvania, and the District of Columbia force students to labor in approved social activities before they can receive a diploma.[51] In 1992, Maryland became the first state to impose a statewide requirement of seventy-five hours of work in politically approved social activities as a condition to receive a diploma. The Maryland service requirement (known euphemistically as "mandatory volunteerism") was opposed by almost all the elected school boards in the state, but the governor's appointees on the state education board scorned local objections. Maryland State School Superintendent Nancy S. Grasmick hailed the new requirement: "I can't think of a better example of character development than the lesson that what we take from the community we give back to the community."[52] But it is difficult to understand how the students are "taking from the community" when, in most cases, their parents pay taxes to finance their schooling. The new requirement increases the power of school officials over students, since all student volunteer work will need to be approved by Superintendent Grasmick. Kathleen Kennedy Townsend, a politically connected Marylander who spearheaded the effort to impose mandatory service, declared that the service-work requirement would allow young people to become "resources to their communities."[53] Public education has thus gone from a system designed to teach young people to read to a system designed to provide cannon fodder for social work schemes and turn the supposed beneficiaries into "community resources." Admittedly, volunteer work can be very beneficial to youths, but the boards of education have no right to control the nonschool hours of state residents. If the Maryland board has a right to dictate 75 hours of service, then does it also have a right to dictate 750 or 7,500 hours? Opponents claimed the service requirement violated the Thirteenth Amendment's prohibition on involuntary servitude. But supporters of the mandate ridiculed the criticism since students were forced to serve "only" seventy-five hours. If the U.S. Justice Department prohibited major newspapers from publishing for "only" a single day, almost everyone would agree that the First Amendment had been violated.

Many states impose severe restrictions on parents who want to teach their children at home. Peggy Williams, a Hale, Michigan, mother of four, was arrested and jailed in 1993 for violating truancy laws by home schooling.[54]

Though home-schooled pupils on average perform far better than public school children on national standardized tests,[55] the public education establishment has fought tenaciously to suppress home schooling. Annette Cootes of the Texas State Teachers Association declared that "home schooling is a form of child abuse."[56] The National Education Association annually passes resolutions calling for a de facto ban on home schooling. According to the Home School Legal Defense Association, the number of children being taught at home by parents has increased over 1,000 percent since 1975 and now exceeds 750,000 children.[57]

Some states have required parents to be licensed teachers in order to be permitted to teach their children in their own homes. But requiring parents to obtain state teaching certificates effectively requires most parents to sacrifice several years of their lives (going to education college) to get government permission to direct their children's mental development. In 1987 the Michigan Court of Appeals upheld Michigan's prohibition against home schooling by parents who lacked a teaching license. The Michigan Court declared that it was not enough for the state government to dictate the curriculum guidelines and attendance requirements for home schooling because such requirements "do nothing to ensure that the material is imparted to the child in such a way as to be understandable. Alone, they are unlikely to stimulate intellectual curiosity and inquiry or to cause that fascinating conjunction of superficially incompatible facts that is creative thought."[58] Though the judges enjoyed proclaiming their support for stimulating intellectual curiosity, such declarations are almost comical considering the abysmal quality of Detroit inner-city schools.

Many school systems impede parents from teaching their children at home largely because they do not want to lose state and federal subsidies. The *New York Times* reported, "Some parents contend, and some school officials admit, that money is a major issue. School districts around the country receive an average of $4,000 to $7,000 in state and federal aid [per student] . . . When a student leaves public school, the system loses some or all of that amount, according to state education officials."[59] Hostility to home schooling is often a question of bureaucratic greed. The school system's burdens decrease with each child educated at home; thus, home schooling actually provides a budgetary windfall to government school systems. But many school officials and politicians care only about maximizing the money they have to control and dispense.

In the eyes of many politicians, judges, and administrators, schoolchildren are cannon fodder for social engineers. The clearest example of this is forced busing—"the compulsory transportation of school children out of their neighborhoods to increase school racial mixing or 'balance.'"[60] The forced segregation that existed in many Southern states prior to the 1960s was unjust and despicable; but forced busing is a totally inappropriate response that sacrifices young children who had no responsibility for the injustices committed by individuals in earlier generations. Public opinion polls in the early 1970s showed an overwhelming opposition to the idea of forced busing—but public opinion was not allowed to impede a moral crusade. Over one million children are now being bused away from their own neighborhoods as part of politically imposed or judicially imposed integration plans.[61] (Though the Justice Department is a party in 450 current school desegregation busing cases, Nathaniel Douglas, the head of the education sector of the Justice Department's civil rights division, was unable to provide any estimate of how many students are being bused under desegregation orders.) Supreme Court Justice Lewis Powell wrote in 1973, "Any child, white or black, who is compelled to leave his neighborhood and spend significant time each day being transported to a distant school suffers an impairment of his liberty and privacy."[62]

In some cases, forced busing has been the equivalent of a judge throwing a bomb into a classroom. Boston, Massachusetts, was the scene of the most exciting forced busing experiment. On May 21, 1974, Boston residents voted 15 to 1 against busing schoolchildren to achieve racial integration. On June 26, federal judge Arthur Garrity ordered Boston schools to integrate immediately anyhow. Under the imposed plan, schools in Roxbury, a poor black area, and South Boston, a poor white Irish area, were merged. The *New Republic* noted in 1983 that "the early years of busing [in Boston] furnished to the student passengers an educational experience of value only to those aspiring to careers in urban guerilla warfare."[63] The National Guard was called out to restore order in Boston after violent public protests and racial clashes in the areas around the schools; even the 82nd Airborne Division was put on alert for Boston duty. Members of the Boston School Committee denounced the busing program for causing "bloodshed and racial hatred." Boston mayor Kevin White banned all public meetings or gatherings of more than three people in South Boston to try to limit the opposition to busing. White student enrollment in Boston public schools fell from 59,000 in the early 1970s (61 percent of total enrollment) to 12,400 (20.7 percent of enrollment in 1992.[64]

Forced busing was imposed on students supposedly to improve the quality of education received by minorities, but in Los Angeles in the early 1980s, some children were bused ninety minutes *each way*, and school days were shortened to accommodate the need for the cattle drives before and after classes. Forced busing, by sending children to schools far away from their home neighborhoods, makes it much more difficult for parents to visit the schools, to know the teachers, or even to come and pick up their sick children. Forced busing helps to exclude parents from the governance—or even pseudogovernance—of local schools.

Forced busing is justified largely by the assumption that black schoolchildren cannot learn sufficiently except in classrooms with white schoolchildren. This is a naive and condescending assumption, especially since some all-black schools (such as Washington, D.C.'s Dunbar High School from the 1870s to the mid-1950s) have been paragons of excellence.[65] Academic studies have found little or no academic benefit to blacks from forced busing. Professor David Armor observes that in the last twenty years "blacks in predominantly minority schools show gains in reading and math that match or exceed those of blacks in majority white schools."[66] Professor Lino A. Graglia noted, "The National Black Convention held in Gary, Indiana, in March 1972 and attended by over ten thousand blacks overwhelmingly adopted a resolution condemning compulsory integration as a 'bankrupt, suicidal method of desegregating schools based on the false notion that Black children are unable to learn unless they are in the same setting with white children.'"[67]

Forced busing epitomizes the philosophy of children's minds as a public utility that government officials are entitled to divvy up as they please. But as desegregation expert Willis D. Hawley of Vanderbilt University observed in 1980, "There are simply not enough white children to go around."[68] Forced busing has failed to integrate big city public school systems; schools in most major cities are more segregated now than they were before busing began. Yet many judges, politicians, and school administrators have stuck to forced busing as a remedy—simply because of the moral aesthetics—because it makes them feel virtuous to impose racial quotas on other people's children. Educators have seized on the doctrines and practice of forced busing with so much enthusiasm because it ratifies their power to forcibly equalize children's minds.

Iowa legislators created a statewide "open enrollment" program, which allowed parents to request which public schools their children attended. In 1992, however, the Des Moines school board rejected the requests of 121 schoolchildren to transfer to neighboring school districts solely because the students were white. Even though Des Moines city schools have a far higher white enrollment than most big city school systems (roughly 80 percent), the school board was opposed in principle to allowing any white students to transfer to neighboring communities that had fewer minority students. (The school board did approve the requests of six minority children to transfer out.) Thomas Jeschke, director of student services for the Des Moines schools, warned the school board that allowing white student transfers would decrease the city schools' revenue (roughly half of schools' funding comes from the state government, based on schools' enrollments).[69] Jonathan Wilson, a Des Moines lawyer and ten-year school board member said, "In the name of choice, people are trying one way or another to get tax dollars out of the central cities"[70] and accused suburban school districts of "raping and pillaging" the Des Moines district's coffers.[71] Wilson denounced the parents' transfer requests for their children as "state-subsidized white flight"—as if parents should have absolutely no voice in how their education tax dollars are spent.[72]

Some school systems are invoking new pretexts to redistribute children as bureaucrats think best. In La Crosse, Wisconsin, the school board imposed a forced busing scheme in 1992 based on family income, dispersing "poor pupils currently concentrated in two of the district's nine elementary schools and busing affluent pupils to the low-income neighborhoods."[73] The plan aimed to achieve a "socioeconomic balance" with no school consisting of more than 41 percent or less than 27 percent poor students.[74] David L. Johnston, assistant superintendent of the La Crosse School District declared, "We are broadening the definition of diversity . . . along economic lines. I think socioeconomic status plays an important role in what happens to children and adults."[75] Much of the opposition from parents stemmed from cases in which their young children, instead of walking four or five blocks to a neighborhood school, would be bused six miles to schools on the other side of the city. School Superintendent Richard Swantz denounced opponents of his plan as "the silk stocking crowd."[76] Swantz declared that "it would be healthier for all of the children if there was a better mix in our classrooms . . . from the standpoint of the kinds of educational deficits kids bring to school."[77] Government schools' highest goal now is not to educate each child but to redistribute preexisting education deficits—as if the raison d'être of public schools was to produce equally illiterate graduates. Sociologist Christopher Jencks explained, "The main argument for what La Crosse is doing, to put it crassly, is that advantaged kids are a resource for any kid in a school. Kids who read books, who have values we want others to acquire . . . are a scarce commodity, and it's not easy to argue that because some families have money they should have a monopoly on all those nice kids."[78] Thus, the fact that a parent teaches a child to enjoy reading automatically turns the child into a widget for the public education system to insert where bureaucrats think he will benefit other children. The La Crosse plan sparked fierce opposition from parents, a special recall election, and the defeat of most of the school board officials who had voted for the plan.[79]

Scholar Sheldon Richman observed, "The organized bureaucratic classroom is a stifling environment. No child is permitted to get too far ahead of any other; if he tries, the reins are pulled sharply."[80] The issue of tracking—placing children in slower or faster classes depending on their individual ability—is becoming a frequent educational battlefield. Though schools have had separate classes for faster and slower learners for generations, the practice is now being curtailed by attacks from politically motivated school board members and egalitarian professors of education. Unelected school board members and school officials in Alexandria, Virginia, announced plans in 1992 to abolish a ninth-grade "honors" course in world civilization and instead to mix kids with reading abilities ranging from the second-grade level to the twelfth-grade level in the same classroom.[81] After fierce protests, the school board announced that they would hold a public meeting to explain the policy but made it clear that parents' comments would not result in a fundamental policy change. The school system flew in Paul George, an education professor and a guru of the antitracking movement, to enlighten the ignorant parents.

Professor George declared a few days before the meeting that "even if putting high-ability kids in their own groups led to higher achievement, if the other side effects of that were racial and ethnic isolation . . . we couldn't do it." *Washington Post* journalist Peter Y. Hong then asked George: "Is there any evidence that lower-achieving students . . . will improve their performance after being placed in heterogenous groups?" George replied: "I don't think so. That doesn't mean it doesn't happen. It just means that those situations are so rare that we don't have good research on those subjects."[82] Thus, the Alexandria school system was imposing a policy even though there was no evidence that it would benefit the least capable students.

The public meeting on the new policy was a fiasco; the *Washington Post* reported, "Alexandria school administrators and teachers engaged in shouting matches with parents at a community forum . . . underscoring deep concerns about the school system's policy of placing fast- and slow-learning students in the same classrooms. . . . A few of the parents walked out of the workshop after being interrupted repeatedly by teachers, administrators and a paid facilitator who were trying to develop consensus on the policy."[83] One Alexandria parent insisted: "My kid is not a laboratory mouse."[84] An Alexandria teacher noted, "There are not enough good students to go around. We have too many leftovers who are not ready to learn and will pull everyone down."[85] Alexandria PTA president Patricia Moran complained: "Nothing the community says affects what school board members do."[86] Alexandria high school teacher Patrick Welsh wrote of the controversy:

> We see an overwhelming number of low-income minority kids who cannot or will not do the work required to succeed in school—and a smaller number who are so disruptive that they poison classes and make it impossible for other kids to learn. . . . Grouping together large numbers of kids with weak skills or bad attitudes with high-achieving kids can be a disaster for both groups. . . . Black leaders seem to look on ability grouping as a vestige of segregation. One black board member recently called Alexandria's honors courses racist. . . . Several of the community leaders who are pushing to eliminate ability grouping have sent their own children to private or parochial schools.[87]

Because of their inability to control the quality of local schools their taxes pay for, parents increasingly resort to stealth to get their children into better public schools in other districts. The Sewanhanka school district of Nassau, New York, spends over $100,000 a year investigating students' residency claims. The school district's tactics include posting detectives with two-way radios to report all cars with school-age kids crossing the Queens-Nassau border; posting inspectors in trees with binoculars to see whether a child spends a night at a house before going to school; following children home from school; hiding investigators beneath cars to make videotapes of students leaving their homes; and having a van with a covert camera operator prowling for violators. School officials conduct three surprise visits on each student's home each year to verify that the student is actually living in the school district. If local police did the same thing, they could be sued for violating the Fourth Amendment's prohibition of unreasonable searches, but school officials have apparently exempted themselves from the U.S. Constitution. One school attendance officer complained that such tactics had turned the schools into a "police state."[88]

In 1993 the New Jersey state legislature considered a bill to allow communities to stiffen penalties for school enrollment fraud and to prohibit parents from putting their children under the guardianship of others "solely for the purpose of receiving a free public education within [that school] district."[89] Dr. Harvey Garner, superintendent of Brooklyn's School District 18, stated that some families have surrendered custody of their children to relatives near a desirable school.[90] Naturally, school officials and legislators see the solution not as improving the schools or ending the public school monopoly but as increasing penalties on parents. It is sad to see parents so desperate for a decent education for their children that they sacrifice the integrity of a family in order that a child may have a decent chance in life—somewhat like Irish parents putting their children on a ship to American during the potato famine.

Advocates of public education often insist that government schools are symbols and triumphs of democracy. But this dogma is a relic of the nineteenth century. Ninety years ago, local school boards controlled local education, in part because the majority of funding came from local sources. As educator Dwight Roper noted, "Small local districts were one of the last vestiges of direct parent control over the formal child-rearing process. Parents elected, knew and often used effective friendly persuasion on local board members. . . . The local board members' accountability was first to the parent, not to some administrative ideal of a standardized system."[91] Over the years, the federal and state share of education funding rose; states are now often paying more of local schools' costs than the towns themselves. Moreover, school districts have become centralized: the number of school districts nationwide has fallen from over 125,000 in 1900 to under 16,000. The power of most school boards has been vastly diluted, and school board elections are frequently shams—simply a chance for the local teacher unions and their allies to flaunt their electoral power. (Less than 10 percent of eligible New York city voters vote in school board elections.)[92] In other cases, school boards are mere puppets. Washington, D.C.'s elected school board is totally incapable of controlling the school system; in 1989, school administrators lied to school board members—exaggerating student enrollment by almost 10 percent—in order to get a larger budget.[93] D.C. mayor Sharon Pratt Kelly complained in 1992 that "there is no accountability, really none" regarding the school budget because school administrators could not or would not disclose how they planned to spend the tax dollars they received.[94] A 1993 confidential government audit of the D.C. schools concluded, "The District has no reliable operating information on how education funds are actually being spent."[95]

Government schools are increasingly run by the unions and for the unions. Former U.S. Secretary of Education Lamar Alexander observed, "After the post office, schools are the most unionized activity in America. [Teacher unions] collect a lot of money in dues, they are often the largest lobby in the state, they are very, very powerful."[96] Teacher monopoly bargaining laws (laws that permit unions to claim to represent and speak for all teachers, and to force school boards to deal with unions) in thirty-four states cover 67 percent of the nation's teachers.[97] Teacher unions have worked to destroy local control of education, subvert standards, prevent teacher accountability, and deny parents a significant voice in their children's education. Teacher unions are especially powerful in inner cities, where teacher performance is often the worst.[98] Unions have launched strikes to prevent and restrict "parental interference" in public education. Thanks to a strong union, New York school custodians are paid an average of $57,000 a year yet are required to mop the schools' floors only three times a year.[99] As a result, New York City public schools are sometimes filthier than New York City streets.

Teacher unions are increasingly dictating policy to the schools. The National Education Association denounced back-to-basics programs as "irrelevant and reactionary."[100] The NEA is the leading advocate of "no-fault" teaching—whatever happens, don't blame the teacher. The *Chicago Tribune* concluded in 1988 that the Chicago Teachers Association has "as much control over operations of the public schools as the Chicago Board of Education" and "more control than is available to principals, parents, taxpayers, and voters."[101] The *Tribune* noted that "even curriculum matters, such as the program for teaching children to read, are written into the [union] contract, requiring the board to bring any proposed changes to the bargaining table."[102]

Teacher unions blatantly exploit their power over schoolchildren. In Montgomery County, Maryland, union teachers refused to write letters of recommendations to colleges for students unless the students first wrote to the County Council urging an increase in government spending for education (and, naturally, higher salaries for teachers). One high school senior told the *Washington Post*, "The consensus among students seems to be it may be blackmail, but students are going to go along with it anyway."[103] In California in 1991, teachers required students to write to state legislators demanding more money for education; the tactic backfired because numerous letters contained threats of physical violence against the legislators.[104] At Wilson High School in Washington, D.C., teachers gave parents a formal notice that they would not write letters of recommendation for students unless parents wrote three letters demanding higher pay for teachers: "Please submit to each teacher from whom your child is requesting a college recommendation your letters to your city council member, the superintendent and your school board member along with three addressed and stamped envelopes."[105] Parents thus had to grovel in front of a teacher—to surrender their right to their own opinion on public education policy—in order for their children to receive consideration from the teachers.

Teachers have stronger legal rights to taxpayers' dollars than the taxpayers have to a quality education for their children. School systems face vastly more repercussions from firing an incompetent teacher than from totally neglecting schoolchildren. The *Chicago Tribune* reported:

> All 22 students in Grace Currin's 4th grade class must attend summer school this year because, their principal says, Currin did not teach the children enough to pass to the next grade. Dyanne Dandridge-Alexander, principal at [Chicago's] Spencer Elementary School: "Those children have suffered because they have a totally inept teacher that no one has been able to fire."[106]

A 1992 *Detroit Free Press* investigation entitled "Shielding Bad Teachers" concluded that it takes a school district seven years and costs an average of $100,000 to fire a single incompetent public school teacher. Seven years is over half of the schooling time of the average pupil. The *Detroit Free Press* concluded, "No protections are built in for the state's 1.5 million public school students, who can suffer physical, sexual or educational abuse."[107] The American Association of School Administrators conducted an audit of District of Columbia public schools and concluded that it is "nearly impossible" to fire bad teachers.[108]

Public education in many cities is a trap for the underclass. As the Cato Institute's David Boaz noted, "In New York City, as of 1988, no member of the Board of Education and no citywide elected official had children in the government schools."[109] The *Chicago Tribune* observed, "City leaders, school officials, and a long succession of mayors have long bypassed the deteriorating school system in favor of sending their children to private or parochial schools. City Alderman Edward Burke declared, 'Nobody in his right mind would send kids to public schools.'"[110] (The average student score on the ACT college admission test scores at over half of Chicago high schools is in the bottom 1 percent in the nation.)[111] Members of the National Education Association are twice as likely as other parents to send their own children to private schools.[112] University of California professor John Coons observed, "We are conscripting the poor for government schools. . . . The rich can *buy out of this social and ideological draft* and thereby maintain family sovereignty, but most parents are stuck."[113] When President Bill Clinton announced in early 1993 that his daughter would be attending an elite private school rather than a D.C. public school, spokesman George Stephanopoulos justified Clinton's decision: "You can't put politics into a personal family decision."[114] But for most American families, it is no decision at all: they cannot afford the luxury of paying private tuition to avoid having their children politicized and subjugated in public schools.

Government schools do a worse job for a much higher price than do private schools. Almost every study comparing the achievements of private or parochial school students and public school students show that private students read better than public school students from comparable backgrounds.[115] The high school dropout rate for inner-city public schools is, in many areas, ten times higher than the dropout rate for inner-city private schools.[116] Private schools in inner cities, charging tuition that is less than a third of the cost of educating a student in the public schools, routinely provide a far better education than the public schools. The question then becomes: Is there a good reason for having the government do badly and expensively what the private sector can do well and cheaply?

Government-provided education is based on the idea that the government can develop children's minds better than the parents—that government is a better judge of education than the parent and thus is justified in forcing citizens to pay for the type of education of which government officials approve. But if parents are such poor judges, then why do low-cost private schools outperform high-cost government schools?[117]

One measure of the coerciveness of the government school monopoly is the percentage of parents who would remove their kids from government schools if they could. If Americans could choose—if they had not already paid for public education through taxes—there would likely be a wholesale exodus from government schools in many cities. A 1992 poll of Milwaukee blacks revealed that 83 percent favored a voucher system that would allow parents to choose their children's school.[118] A 1991 Gallup poll found that 71 percent of people aged eighteen to twenty-nine and 62 percent of people aged thirty to thirty-nine favored vouchers. The Gallup survey found that "by a 10-to-1 margin, respondents said private schools do a better job of . . . giving students individual attention and maintaining discipline."[119]

The U.S. Department of Education has been rightfully aggressive in prosecuting vocational schools that take students' money (primarily federal grants) and then provide little or no training. Yet the main difference between shady vocational schools and floundering public schools is sovereign immunity. It is far worse to promise to teach a person how to read and spend twelve years not doing it than to promise to teach a person to be a hairdresser and spend three months not doing it.

Public high schools graduate an estimated 700,000 functionally illiterate teenagers each year.[120] In 1977, a functionally illiterate high school graduate in San Francisco sued the public schools alleging "misrepresentation—[the] defendants falsely and fraudulently represented to plaintiff's mother and natural guardian that plaintiff was performing at or near grade level in basic academic skills such as reading and writing and was not in need of any special or remedial assistance in such basic skills."[121] The California Court of Appeals dismissed the case, opining that to hold public schools "to an actionable 'duty of care,' in the discharge of their academic functions, would expose them to the tort claims—real or imagined—of disaffected students and parents in countless numbers."[122] But just because the schools could be accused of defrauding "countless numbers" of students and parents is no reason to absolve them of all responsibility for their misdeeds. In a similar case in 1979, the Court of Appeals of New York ruled: "Recognition in the courts of this cause of action would constitute blatant interference with the responsibility for the administration of the public school system lodged by Constitution and statute in administrative agencies."[123] Regardless of how badly school administrators have deceived and failed to serve students, parents are left no recourse but to file complaints with the same unresponsive bureaucracy. In 1981, the Maryland Court of Special Appeals rejected a suit by an ex-student: "The field of education is simply too fraught with unanswered questions for the courts to constitute themselves as a proper forum for resolution of those questions."[124] The educational system has enough "answered questions" to force Americans to pay $270 billion a year in taxes for public schools yet is too vague for state judges to consider any claims against the schools. In 1985 a suit was filed on behalf of an Ohio student alleging that as a result of the "negligent acts and omissions by the [public schools], plaintiff obtained the twelfth grade level and left Steubenville High School with a reading ability of only the first grade," and that the schools passed the plaintiff from grade to grade "so as to keep plaintiff in sports activities for the benefit of the athletic system in the schools."[125] An Ohio appeals court scorned the complaint: "The primary duty of education lies with the parent to vigilantly pursue the education of his or her children. The duty of the State is to provide the means of education. Thus, a child who attends school for 12 years and receives no education must look not to the State but rather to his or her parents for their failure to perform a duty imposed by nature and by law."[126] The state levied taxes on the parents so that it could perform the duty of education—and then deceived the parents and exploited the child by promoting him through his senior year of high school.

Parents have an unlimited liability to pay for public schools, but the public schools have no liability to the parents. Law professor Judith H. Berliner Cohen observed: "No plaintiff to date has been able to convince a court that a school owes him or her any more than 'a chair in a classroom.'. . . Insofar as they have been 'deluded' into believing that it is not necessary to find alternate means of education, the students are arguably worse off than they otherwise would have been."[127] Forcing parents to pay thousands of dollars a year in taxes solely for "a chair in a classroom" is especially unfair since a good child's chair costs less than $200. At current spending levels, parents and other taxpayers nationwide pay an average of almost $70,000 for twelve years of public schooling for each child. In Connecticut, New Jersey, and New York, which spend over $8,700 per public school student per year,[128] taxpayers are forced to pay over $100,000 for each child's schooling. And what are parents and other taxpayers entitled to for that payout? Less respect, poorer service, and fewer contract rights than a person who buys a $2.50 Big Mac hamburger. The fact that public schools have no liability even for the grossest negligence means that the individual parent is subjugated to whatever the schools choose to offer or inflict on his children.

A 1983 federal report entitled *A Nation at Risk: The Imperative for Educational Reform* observed, "If an unfriendly foreign power had attempted to impose on America the mediocre educational performance that exists today, we might well have viewed it as an act of war."[129] But many parents probably have as much of a chance of influencing a foreign dictator as they have of influencing a big city school board. (Actually, it may be safer to criticize foreign governments than American school officials: Two parents on a school advisory board in South-Central Los Angeles wrote letters to state officials criticizing the school principal; the principal responded with a $1 million defamation suit.)[130] Once the citizen loses control of his paycheck regarding his children's education, it is futile in most cities to try to regain that control. The citizen's rights end as soon as his tax dollar reaches the public treasury. He is treated as a supplicant rather than as an owner of the educational enterprise. Paying for schooling indirectly effectively turns parents from buyers into beggars. (Lawyer Adelle Cohen told the *New York Times* that if New York City's District 21 school board "considers you an enemy, they take your kid and put him in the slow class.")[131] Public schools vivify how control over financing for a service leads to political controls over people's lives.

In 1979 the Appellate Division of the New York State Court dismissed an educational malpractice suit, ruling, "It is our opinion that [the State constitution and state laws] merely require the creation of a system of free common schools. Their purpose is to confer the benefits of free education upon what would otherwise be an uneducated public."[132] This is the false dichotomy upon which the public school monopoly is based—public education or an "uneducated public." This view stands history on its head, since it was private schools and private learning that created the mass literacy for which America was renowned 200 years ago. John Adams wrote in 1765, "A native of America who cannot read or write is as rare an appearance as . . . a comet or an earthquake."[133] Alexis de Tocqueville, visiting America in the 1830s—at a time when many locales had no public schools—observed that "primary education is within reach of all."[134]

Author Ivan Illich observed in 1969, "The public school has become the established church of secular society."[135] The only effective way to reform the public schools is to end their monopoly. New York teacher John Taylor Gatto observed, "By preventing a free market in education, a handful of social engineers . . . has ensured that most of our children will not have an education, even though they may be thoroughly schooled."[136]

Government schools are constantly justified by their ideals, regardless of the violence and incompetence of public schools themselves. But judging public schools solely by the rhetoric of politicians and educators is like discussing monarchies and talking only of the ideal of an omnibenevolent king.

The mythology of public schools has endowed the school system with superior rights over both parents and children.

MAKING HIGHER EDUCATION POLITICALLY CORRECT

Federal and state governments are also massively subsidizing colleges and universities. Yet, as a 1985 Association for American Colleges report noted, "Evidence of decline and devaluation in college curriculums is everywhere.... We have become a people unable to comprehend the technology that we invent."[137] A 1986 report by the Carnegie Institution concluded that many colleges are "more successful in credentialing than in providing a quality education."[138] New York University dean Herbert L. London wrote, "Many colleges already have standards that are roughly the equivalent of what a high school had 30 years ago." The Carnegie Foundation for the Advancement of Teaching reported in 1989 that 67 percent of professors surveyed believed that there "has been a widespread lowering of standards in American higher education."[139]

Federal spending on financial aid to college students has increased from under $1 billion in 1965 to over $15 billion in 1993.[140] Roughly half of all students now receive some form of federal student aid. The more subsidies government has provided to higher education, the more dependent students have become on government aid to afford college.

Most colleges now depend heavily on students' ability to acquire federal loans or grants to pay their college tuition. A college must be approved by a federally recognized accreditation association in order for its students to qualify for federal loans and grants. This requirement was originally imposed to ensure that the federal government did not subsidize "diploma mills" that took students' federal grants while providing them no education. In recent years, however, accreditation organizations have demanded control over colleges' curriculum, faculty hiring, board of directors, and other areas in return for certifying students eligible for federal aid. Federal accreditation has become an instrument to inflict political correctness on colleges.

The Middle States Association of Colleges and Universities, with the power of accreditation over 500 higher education institutions, sought in 1989 to punish New York's Baruch College (the nation's largest undergraduate business school) because it did not graduate enough blacks. Baruch had an open admissions policy, accepting almost any high school graduate in the city of New York. As a result, it had high attrition rates because many of its black students (coming from low-quality inner-city schools) were more poorly prepared for college work than were its white students.[141] Baruch was also denied reaccreditation because blacks were underrepresented on the faculty, even though Baruch had far more minority faculty members than most American colleges.[142]

Some of the Middle States Association's demands violated both academic and religious freedom. The association ordered Westminster Theological Seminary in Pennsylvania to place a woman on its board of directors. But the seminary, run by the Presbyterian church, requires that only church elders can be on the board—and women were not allowed to be ordained as elders.[143] Howard Simmons, the executive director of Middle States, declared, "From my perspective, the commission rightly views equity and diversity as essential to academic quality."[144]

After extensive media controversy, Secretary of Education Lamar Alexander began investigating whether Middle States was coercing colleges and universities. At a hearing of the House Human Resources Subcommittee, Alexander asked, "Why does the gatekeeper to student loans then have the right also to be policeman for civil rights on campuses?" Committee chairman Rep. Ted Weiss told Alexander to "keep your hands off" the federally certified accrediting organizations.[145] But Weiss's demand would translate into giving near-absolute power to the accrediting bodies over thousands of private colleges. Alexander eventually renewed the association's authority to accredit universities but with some restrictions. Courts Oulahan, the counsel for Middle States, claimed that Alexander's intervention "has a potentially chilling effect. Middle States sustained financial damage over this . . . months of paying attorneys and public relations counsel and communicating with members."[146] This is the worst type of "chilling effect"—requiring an arrogant agency to defend itself against charges that it was coercing universities.

Political financing of colleges leads to political demands to control the distribution of diplomas.[147] New Mexico governor Garrey Carrutthers, chairman of the National Task Force for Minority Achievement in Higher Education, issued a report in 1991 demanding that blacks and Hispanics be graduated from public colleges in the same proportion as their population in each state.[148] In 1988, 1989, and 1990, the California state assembly voted by large margins to require California colleges and universities to graduate black and Hispanic students in the same proportion as the number of blacks and Hispanics in the state's population. Willie Brown, assembly speaker of California, announced that California's college and university systems are "prisoners of racism, and their hostile, wholly intolerant environment is contributing to a higher dropout rate among people of color." But, as Stanford University professor John Bunzel observed, "When 94% of Asians and whites have gotten better test scores than the average black freshman, is it any wonder that black graduation rates are only about half that of whites?"[149]

AFFORDABLE HOUSING AUTHORITARIANISM

In the last sixty years, federal, state, and local governments have devastated housing markets, manipulated housing values, and priced millions of

Americans out of the home-buying market. More than ever before, the average American's housing situation is a factor of his political connections—of his ability to qualify for federal handouts, state subsidies, or local preferences.

Public housing projects are the starkest example of government housing paternalism. There are now 1.4 million public housing units, providing a sometimes leaky roof to over three million people. The federal government is spending over $5 billion per year in direct subsidies for faltering public housing systems. Secretary of the Interior Harold Ickes promised in 1934 that as a result of public housing, "Our children will become healthier men and women. There will be a reduction in crime."[150] The 1937 Housing Act proclaimed a need to "remedy the unsafe and insanity housing conditions . . . that are injurious to the health, safety, and morals of the citizens of the Nation."[151] Department of Housing and Urban Development (HUD) analyst Irving Welfeld noted, "When the urban riots of the late sixties occurred, it was more than coincidental that in many cities the centers of the disturbances were in public housing projects."[152] George Sternlieb, director of the Center for Urban Policy Research at Rutgers University, observed that public housing creates "a moral and psychological bankruptcy" in "the people who live in it."[153]

Conditions were so dangerous in the Rockwell Gardens project in Chicago in 1991 that parents forced children to sleep in bathtubs—the only place safe from stray gunfire.[154] According to a HUD report, *Crime in Public Housing,* "crime rates in public housing complexes are in some cases . . . ten times higher than the national average."[155] The robbery rate at one large Baltimore public housing project was almost twenty times the national average.[156] In the Robert Taylor Homes project in Chicago, the violent crime rate is thirteen times the national average and more than twenty times the rate of safer neighborhoods in Chicago.[157] A survey of four public housing complexes in Boston found that 40 percent of the residents considered it "very dangerous" to be alone in their apartments at night.[158] In Washington, D.C., the nation's murder capital, 80 percent of all violent crime reportedly occurs in public housing projects.[159] One researcher concluded that the area in and around public housing often becomes "the territory of those who do not have to be afraid—the criminals, whose safety *is guaranteed* by a high level of fear in the potential victims around them."[160] The high crime rate in public housing can decimate the value of nearby private housing.

Many public housing residents feel treated like serfs on government land. As one Atlanta apartment manager observed, "In private housing you get what you pay for; in public housing, you get what they give you."[161] Since the government owns public housing, it sometimes shows little or no respect for the constitutional rights of public housing residents. Lenwood Johnson, a Chicago public housing tenant leader, complained, "The authority treated the tenants here like they were in a total dictatorship."[162] In 1988, the Chicago Housing Authority (CHA) and the Chicago police began "Operation

Clean Sweep," making warrantless searches of hundreds of apartments for drugs, guns, or other violations that could be used as a pretext to evict residents. The ACLU complained:

> These "inspections" have included searches of the dresser drawers, bedding and personal effects of tenants—unlikely places in which to find the squatters, gang members and drug dealers who are the alleged targets. Residents who were away from their homes at the time of the surprise raids have been subjected to pat-down searches, and their belongings, including Christmas gifts, were searched. Children returning from school have been kept in the cold and out of their family apartments for many hours because they did not have identification cards that were issued while they were in school. The CHA also imposed a new policy that, among other things, prohibited tenants from having guests in their homes between the hours of midnight and 9 A.M. This meant that CHA residents were unable to have out-of-town relatives for the holidays or babysitters arrive in time for parents to get to work.[163]

In April 1992, 300 Chicago police and federal agents swept through one high-rise public housing apartment building. The *Chicago Tribune* reported, "Some 450 apartments were 'inspected,' as officials looked for unauthorized residents. Everyone inside and their belongings were thoroughly searched. Within minutes, every black person—man, woman and child—who walked through the area was stopped and searched."[164] The head of a tenants' council at a Chicago public housing project, in response to sweeps conducted in 1993, complained: "Every time they come, I cry, because they couldn't do this to people with money."[165] The 1993 searches showed a pseudo-punctilious respect for residents' rights: residents were asked to sign a consent document agreeing to permit a search of their home—but if they didn't sign, their apartments were searched anyhow.[166] The director of the Chicago Housing Authority has almost unlimited authority to order an emergency sweep of a housing project.[167]

Though public housing is routinely a social disaster, it is often a political success. In Chicago, city aldermen resist efforts to raze high-rise housing hells and replace them with smaller housing units. The large public housing blocks are simply too convenient for politicians to control—even if the police may have long since stopped entering them because of sniper fire. As the *Chicago Tribune* noted, tenants in Chicago Housing Authority high-rises "were beholden to the [local political] machine for the very roofs over their heads."[168] William Tucker, author of *The Excluded Americans,* declared that public housing's "popularity among politicians, to a large degree, has been based on its usefulness in concentrating large blocs of voters in readily identifiable precincts. Often a large housing complex will form a single voting district. Elections booths are often located right in the lobby, making it extremely easy to monitor and deliver votes."[169]

Public housing offers other political dividends. A 1982 report for HUD on the Chicago Housing Authority found atrocious conditions in the housing projects and concluded, "CHA's purpose may not primarily be the provision and maintenance of good quality assisted housing for low-income families, but rather the acquisition of as many Federal government dollars as possible for the creation of patronage jobs and financial opportunities."[170] The report concluded, "Loyalty is a more important criterion in hiring and promotion than either competence or experience." In Philadelphia, almost all of the housing authority's 1,700 workers are political appointees.[171] Housing agencies routinely treat federal and state tax dollars as political slush funds; controls over the District of Columbia Housing Finance Agency are so lax that the agency contributed $4,000 to the mayor's reelection committee in 1992.[172]

The federal government guarantees to cover the losses of local housing authorities regardless of their inefficiency or incompetence. HUD deputy secretary Al Dellibovi observed in 1991 that for public housing authorities, "The more they lose, they more they get."[173] In recent years, as concern about homeless Americans has increased, the number of vacancies in public housing projects has skyrocketed, in part because the authorities collect federal subsidies on vacant units without the nuisance of having to place tenants in them. A 1991 report by the National Center for Neighborhood Enterprise noted that "with massive federal subsidies, the Public Housing Authorities (PHAs) became less dependent on rent as a source of revenue. Residents lost their bargaining power, since PHAs could assume that their income was guaranteed from other sources."[174]

Federal public housing subsidies can reward local housing officials for scorning the vitality of private homes. The city government of Washington, D.C., proposed to sell twenty-five rundown, vacant, city-owned homes in a borderline neighborhood. District of Columbia Council member Frank Smith, Jr., complained that "drug dealers and drug users" were using some of the units, increasing crime in the neighborhoods. But D.C. public housing officials staunchly opposed the sale, warning that the city would lose thousands of dollars in federal subsidies for the vacant homes. Public housing spokesman Lucy Murray explained, "One of our concerns is what the effect of selling them would be on the operating subsidy we get from HUD."[175] City housing officials apparently had no concern about how crime-ridden, city-owned homes were dragging down their neighborhoods—just as long as the federal subsidies kept rolling into the city housing department's coffers.

Federal housing programs have helped raze and depopulate large parts of major cities. In 1968, Congress passed the National Housing Act, which provided for federally insured mortgages to poor people in inner cities, among others. The 1968 act created a new program (Section 235) to provide heavily subsidized loan mortgages for low-income families and individuals in order to allow them to purchase homes. Section 235, which President Johnson described as a "Magna Carta to liberate our cities,"[176] devastated hundreds of neighborhoods across the country.

The *National Journal* reported in 1971, "The Federal Housing Administration . . . is financing the collapse of large residential areas of the center cities."[177] The most serious problem with the program was housing abandonment—scores of thousands of homes had been emptied and left to rot in previously stable neighborhoods. Abandonment was routine: since most families had almost no equity in their homes, it was often cheaper for them to abandon their homes than to repair them.[178] Detroit mayor Roman Gribbs declared that a single abandoned house on a block "becomes a magnet for vandalism, crime, fire, blight, drug addiction, and other kinds of socially pathological forces."[179] The *Detroit News* declared that the program was turning Detroit neighborhoods into "'ghost towns' where a handful of families exist amid vandalized and fire-gutted homes." Between 1970 and 1976, the federal Department of Housing and Urban Development took over 25,000 homes in Detroit alone after owners abandoned the houses or defaulted on federal loans. June Ridgway of the Detroit Board of Assessors declared in 1976, "HUD has cost every citizen in Detroit 20% on his house," due to a general decline in residential property values.[180] By decimating housing values, government housing policies effectively destroyed much of the life savings of the average Detroit family.

The *Chicago Tribune* denounced Section 235 for causing "the decay of hundreds of good neighborhoods" in Chicago. The *Tribune* concluded, "No natural disaster on record has caused destruction on the scale of the government's housing programs. . . . It took only four years of the federally insured mortgage program to reduce a neat, middle-class neighborhood into a shattered, decaying slum."[181] Southern Chicago Commission chairman Julian H. Levi called HUD "the greatest enemy of community stability within the city of Chicago."[182] President Richard M. Nixon bemoaned on September 19, 1973: "All across America the federal government has become the biggest slumlord in history."[183] Nationwide, Section 235 cost the federal government over $4 billion in direct losses from defaulted mortgage and demolition costs and did billions of dollars of damage to the value of non-HUD houses as well.[184]

In 1974, Congress shifted gears on housing policy and created the Section 8 program to provide direct rent subsidies to low- and moderate-income families and allow them to choose private housing. Section 8 currently gives $7 billion a year in rental subsidies to two million families. HUD establishes the Section 8 subsidy level with an arcane process known as the Fair Market Rents, which is based on a comparison of rents in each geographical area. But HUD's methodology has a strong upward bias, resulting in the government's offering to subsidize much higher rents than are prevailing in many local markets. (Many HUD administrators favor enabling low-income families to live in upper-middle class neighborhoods.) Any family whose income is slightly below the median income for their area (roughly 40 percent of the nation's families) are eligible for Section 8 subsidies,[185] though Congress does not appropriate money for all potential beneficiaries.

HUD explicitly permits families to use Section 8 to pay rents as high as $1,657 for a four-bedroom apartment—a higher rent than over 90 percent of American renters are now paying.[186] At the Manhattan Plaza building in New York City, Section 8 pays for apartments with wood kitchen cabinets, parquet floors, and on-premise swimming, racquet, and tennis facilities.[187] At New York's Taino Towers, HUD paid for a gymnasium, a greenhouse, and an indoor swimming pool for the subsidized residents.[188] At the Morningside apartments in Chicago, subsidized residents enjoy a billiard room, a library, and an arts and crafts room.[189] The Elm Street Plaza project in Chicago advertised that their Section 8 apartments included all the "luxury amenities" one would expect.[190] In 1993, Section 8 certificates were used to permit low-income families to move into an apartment complex in Silver Spring, Maryland, that includes a heated pool with water jets, microwave ovens, "deluxe modern kitchens with convenient breakfast bar," and a complete exercise and fitness room.[191] The GAO concluded, "The high rents and quality of this housing invite resentment on the part of the taxpaying public who see their subsidized neighbors living in better accommodations than they themselves can afford."[192]

Although Section 8 is hailed by many liberals and conservatives for giving lower-income people "freedom of choice" in housing, much of the analysis of the program has consisted of whether the subsidy recipients are pleased with the subsidy. However, Section 8 is having harsh impacts on some unsubsidized renters. Chicago has distributed thousands of Section 8 vouchers to public housing residents, who have used them primarily to move to a handful of communities on the city's southern edge.[193] The flood of former public housing residents has turned parts of some towns into a "Section 8 corridor." Officials in Pacesetter, Illinois, claimed that "a sudden influx into the neighborhood of subsidized families about six years ago turned a borderline neighborhood into a slum."[194] Delores Irving of Chicago's Leadership Council for Metropolitan Open Communities observed, "We are building ghettos in the suburbs."[195] Michael Roache, executive director of the Fair Housing Coalition of the South Suburbs, observed: "The intent of the Section 8 program is not to create Section 8 neighborhoods, but that's exactly what's happening."[196] A *Chicago Tribune* editorial noted, "Sixty-five percent of all the families in the Section 8 program run by the Housing Authority of Cook County are clustered in 14 south suburbs. Officials and residents in some of those towns believe they have become a dumping ground for a lazy bureaucracy that is contributing to resegregation in the south suburbs."[197]

Section 8 rental subsidies harm unsubsidized renters in other ways. A 1991 HUD report revealed that the Section 8 program could be inflating rents for unsubsidized Americans.[198] As the *Washington Post* noted on a 1991 HUD report on the effect of Section 8: "The increases in fair market rent levels could also prove a bonanza for local landlords who will be able to receive higher rents from low-income subsidized renters than they would be able to get from moderate-income people relying only on their own earnings to pay their housing bills."[199] The more subsidies the government gives, the more difficult it becomes for unsubsidized individuals to thrive. HUD analyst Irving Welfeld notes that

> the [Section 8] voucher program hurts those that it does not help. Most poor rely on the low end of the rental market for their housing. This is the sector that is in deep trouble because of the inability of unsubsidized poor tenants to pay the rents. . . . The voucher by drawing people out of these units and into the middle of the market is also pushing buildings off the market. The result of a weak market is the abandonment of buildings rather than lower rents. For those remaining it leaves the prospect of a smaller number of low rent units.[200]

The *Hartford Courant* noted that the provision of Section 8 subsidies to Hartford residents, allowing them to leave the city, "has begun to cripple city landlords, who are watching their buildings empty out and who are having more and more trouble paying their taxes. A significant movement of the poor out of the city would accelerate abandonment of residential buildings and threaten to undo recent gains of the 1980s in housing rehabilitation in the city."[201]

Subsidies increasingly allow politicians and bureaucrats to choose who can own a house. In 1981, the District of Columbia government gave away ten houses free to public housing residents; City Housing Director Robert Moore said, "People should not get something for nothing," and specified that the new owners (mostly welfare mothers) would be required to cut the grass on the lawns of their new homes.[202] Many states and localities have special subsidized mortgage funds with eligibility guidelines high enough to include most of the middle class. In 1987, the District of Columbia government launched a program to insure mortgage loans for people with bad credit ratings (people who had previously defaulted on loans). The city government also doles out heavily subsidized mortgage loans to families with "moderate incomes" of up to $75,000—a higher income than most American families earn. Some low-income buyers are not even required to repay government housing loans; instead, they are required to pay only if and when they sell their house. In February 1993, the Washington, D.C., Department of Housing and Community had a giveaway of certificates for $20,000 for home down payments. First-time home buyers with incomes of up to $69,200 were eligible; the *Washington Times* noted, "Housing Department Director Merrick Malone said yesterday's lottery made him feel like another kind of celebrity. 'I feel like Santa Claus,' he said, beaming after passing out certificates with the help of his daughter Piper."[203] There is usually far more demand for subsidized mortgages and down-payment giveaways than the governments have available—so the administrators must make discretionary decisions about who will get the subsidized mortgages.

In at least one town, the combination of housing subsidies and the powers of eminent domain led to the expulsion of almost all black residents. Nicholas

Goldberg of *Newsday* reported, "Island Park, N.Y., officials systematically drove poor, mostly black, residents from the village over a 25-year period, and repeatedly used HUD funds to provide new housing for politically connected villagers on the sites where the blacks had been evicted."[204] Goldberg later wrote in the *New Republic:*

> Harry Scully, who had served as Island Park's village clerk for thirty-one years, told investigators that [U.S. Sen. Alfonse] D'Amato had walked into his office in late 1979 or early 1980, looked at the list of applicants for the HUD houses, pointed to the names of his two cousins, and insisted that they both be given houses. Although the law required special outreach efforts to poor and non-white applicants, Scully told prosecutors that in some cases friends and relatives were told to slip their applications under the door before 9 A.M. on the very day the program was announced to the public. . . . D'Amato, who was then one of the top elected officials in Nassau County, checked the list of applicants carefully during the early phases of the program, approving some people and blackballing others. According to Scully, D'Amato would phone in with instructions for local officials, identifying himself, on occasion, only as "God."[205]

The New York City Department of Housing Preservation and Development (NYHPD) is especially covetous of private housing. Thanks to housing abandonments and confiscations for failure to pay taxes, the NYHPD has commandeered over 3,000 private apartment buildings since 1978, thereby becoming the city's largest slumlord. Seventy percent of the apartment buildings in central Harlem have been seized by the government.[206] Tenants in city buildings are often in a precarious state because the city government has openly renounced its duty to obey the law. *Newsday* reported,

> City-owned housing scores nearly three times as badly as private housing on all measures of poor quality. Rats and mice are a problem in 73 percent of the buildings, compared with only 23 percent of the private ones. Forty-six percent of the city-owned buildings have heat breakdowns; only 17 percent of the private ones do. Water leaks from broken plumbing in 57 percent of the city buildings, compared with 20 percent of the private. The city repeatedly has ignored a court ruling that it must provide decent housing.
>
> Tenants shivered through the winters for nearly eight years at 1244 Grant Ave. in the Bronx because it took HPD that long to install a new boiler. Julia Alamo's baby and several other tenants died because of the cold.
>
> HPD takes the position that it has to adhere to the housing code only under certain circumstances. "We acknowledge our obligation to follow the housing maintenance code in some respects, particularly in regard to maintaining essential services, but not in all regards," said William Spiller, deputy commissioner for property management. . . . HPD argued in court papers: "The City has no duty to repair the buildings if it finds, in its discretion, that such repair cannot be economically justified."
>
> There is a saying among city tenants: "When the city takes over, the drug dealers move in." According to a report last year by David Muchnick for the Bronx 2000 Research Project, drug activity was worst in city-owned buildings, based on Bronx district attorney records.[207]

NYHPD analyst Kaphil Bhati explained the agency's policy: "We could sell these units and make a lot of money, sure, but we would lose control. We want to be able to specify what building management can and can't do. We want control."[208] But as journalist Mark Riebling noted, "By effectively warehousing vacant buildings, the city pulls down stable neighborhoods, retards renewal efforts in others, and increases the supply of crackhouses."[209]

"Affordable housing" is the latest rallying cry for expanding political control over housing. Many politicians have invoked the need for "affordable housing" to justify increased government intervention in housing markets, since housing can presumedly only be affordable when government intervenes to provide special benefits to favored buyers or renters. But commission after commission since the 1950s has shown that government policies are the single largest factor in the inflation of housing prices. Most affordable housing programs presume that problems caused by government intervention can be solved only by more government intervention.

Montgomery County, Maryland, exemplifies the imperialistic tendencies of some local governments' housing policies. On December 3, 1991, the County Council imposed a tax of $6,000 on the typical new house and a tax of $795,200 on new office buildings. The local construction industry was already in a depression at that time; Thomas A. Natelli, president of the Montgomery Chamber of Commerce observed, "Developers are closing up shop, filing for bankruptcy. It just amazes me that [council members] don't have an understanding of what the economic reality is."[210] Two months later, Montgomery County Executive Neal Potter proposed "to 'jump-start' the local housing construction industry by pooling public and private money to help real estate developers who are strapped for cash."[211] Potter proposed to combine the money from the new construction tax and higher taxes on mortgages into funds to underwrite special housing revenue bonds and create a $100-million venture fund to subsidize local developers. Potter orated: "We can be creative and use the strength and special abilities of government to lend a hand in such difficult economic times."[212] The net result of the tax and the development fund would be to sharply increase the County Council's control over local development—giving some developers (those who kowtow to the Council) a big advantage over other developers.

Government-subsidized housing competes against private housing in many areas; the more generous public housing is, the more difficult it becomes for private low-rent apartments to survive and compete. Peter Salins, chairman of the department of urban affairs at Hunter College, noted, "By attracting many of that borough's most stable households, the Mitchell-Lama developments [a special housing program for middle-income renters] built in the Bronx in the 1960s helped to precipitate the collapse of the Bronx housing market and the wholesale abandonment that followed."[213] Public housing provides unfair competition for low-rent private housing because public housing administrators sometimes permit residents to go for ten years or longer without paying the rent. In Washington, D.C., over half of public housing residents are behind on their rent, with over a hundred families owing more than $10,000.[214]

A confidential 1993 audit revealed that HUD could lose up to $12 billion on its apartment building mortgage guarantee program. HUD, which already owns 29,000 apartments through mortgage defaults, could end up taking ownership of over 600,000 more. HUD is already doing a poor job of maintaining apartment buildings that it has taken over through this program.[215] HUD Secretary Henry Cisneros publicly admitted in June 1993: "HUD's management of its inventory has been abysmal. The physical condition of many buildings are deteriorating; others have been overrun by drug trafficking and crime. The truth is stark: HUD has in many cases exacerbated the declining quality of life in America."[216]

Rather than increase the total amount of housing available, federal housing subsidies have primarily transferred control of housing from private citizens to government officials. A 1992 Congressional Budget Office analysis concluded:

> Subsidized housing largely replaces other housing that would have been available through the private unsubsidized housing market. . . . A study of the effect of the supply subsidies that HUD administered in the 1960s and 1970s estimated that for every three units of subsidized housing constructed, starts of unsubsidized housing declined by at least two units. For subsidies aimed at middle-income households, this crowding out approached 100 percent.[217]

An analysis by the congressional Joint Committee on Taxation of the impact of the federal Low Income Housing Tax Credit (a tax break for developers and builders) concluded, "Subsidies to new construction could make it no longer economic to convert some . . . older properties to low-income use, thereby displacing potential low-income units."[218] Despite the flood of federal aid for housing, low-income rental housing is now in shorter supply than at any time in the last fifteen years.[219] Federal policies have played a key role in undermining the supply of low-income housing.

TAKING OVER RURAL AMERICA

Farmers are the classic dependent class in today's economy. The livelihood of hundreds of thousands of farmers depends on administrative decisions concocted in the ten miles of hallways of the headquarters of the U.S. Department of Agriculture. Federal bureaucrats manipulate markets in dozens of ways to pressure farmers to submit to Washington's latest five-year farm plan—dictating how much of their land they are allowed to grow on, what price they may sell their milk for, what interest rate they may pay for their loans, and even where they may turn their tractors around in their fields.[220] GAO compared USDA to a "20th century dinosaur" and noted in a 1992 report, "Today's USDA is an agglomeration of programs and structures that have remained virtually unaltered since the 1930s, despite evolutions in issues and advances in technology."[221]

Federal farm subsidies exceeded $30 billion in 1993, and consumers were forced to pay $12 billion in higher food prices as a result of government farm policy. This is the equivalent of over $100,000 for every full-time subsidized farmer.[222] But many farmers receive few federal handouts. Many crops and food items produced in the United States receive no subsidy. Uncle Sam's generosity to politically favored farmers has created economic tidal waves that devastated self-reliant farmers, farm-supply businesses, and farm laborers. Though many people are aware of the benefits farmers receive from the government, few people realize the costs farmers have paid.

Current farm programs originated largely as the result of the federal disruption of the grain markets in the early twentieth century. The federal government guaranteed farmers lavish prices for wheat during and shortly after World War I, which helped spark a boom and then a bust in crop prices and farmland values.[223] Farmers responded to the post–World War I crop price collapse by demanding government guarantees of high crop prices. Congress created the Federal Farm Board in 1929; President Herbert Hoover instructed the board: "I invest you with responsibilities and resources such as have never before been conferred by our government in assistance to any industry."[224] The Farm Board's $500 million budget was larger than any ever authorized for a nondefense expenditure. The Farm Board promptly wrecked the export markets for America's two most important crops (wheat and cotton), destabilized the grain trade, and created a massive price-depressing surplus.

In 1930, the *New York Times*, surveying the wreckage of agricultural markets after the federal intervention to drive up wheat prices, concluded, "It is perhaps fortunate for the country that its fingers were so badly burned at the very first trial of the scheme."[225] Unfortunately, President Franklin D. Roosevelt saw the farm crisis as the result of the failure of private markets, rather than the fiasco of government intervention. Roosevelt declared an economic emergency, rammed the Agricultural Adjustment Act through Congress, and imposed pervasive controls on American farmers. The Agricultural Adjustment Act clearly specified that federal controls over farmers would cease once the president issued a proclamation that the agricultural emergency was over. In the subsequent sixty years, no American president has had the courage to admit that the 1933 "emergency" is over.

The Agriculture Adjustment Act of 1933 set American crop prices far above prevailing world market prices. As a result, agricultural exports further declined. Economist Theodore W. Schultz (who later won the Nobel Prize) denounced New Deal farm programs for "putting a 'Chinese Wall' around our export farmers."[226] Roosevelt bragged in 1935 about his administration's destruction of farm exports: "Now, with export surpluses no longer pressing down on the farmers' welfare, with fairer prices, farmers really have a chance for the first time in this generation to benefit from improved methods."[227]

The political destruction of agricultural exports is the key to understanding how American farmers became government dependents. Federal agricultural policies have decreased farmers' efficiency, greatly increased their costs of production, and routinely priced American farmers' harvests out of the world market. Politicians then cite the lack of exports as proof of the need for political control over farming.

Farm programs imposed severe penalties on farmers who refused to obey the Roosevelt administration's demands to curtail their production. In a landmark 1936 case striking down farm programs as unconstitutional, the Supreme Court observed:

> The regulation is not in fact voluntary. The farmer, of course, may refuse to comply, but the price of such refusal is the loss of benefits. The amount offered is intended to be sufficient to exert pressure on him to agree to the proposed regulation. . . . This is coercion by economic pressure. The asserted power of choice is illusory.[228]

The Supreme Court's characterization of farm subsidies is as appropriate today as it was then. The only thing that has changed is the Supreme Court's interpretation of the Constitution's protection of individual rights. A few weeks after the Supreme Court struck down the Agricultural Adjustment Act, Congress reauthorized farm programs with minor changes intended to circumvent the specific grounds of the Supreme Court's nullification of federal farm programs.

In 1942, in the case of *Wickard v. Filburn,* a more progovernment Supreme Court ruled that farm programs could legally penalize an Ohio farmer for eating flour made from the wheat that he sowed. The federal wheat program dictated how many bushels of wheat each farmer could produce; government administrators were so concerned about maintaining a stranglehold on the wheat supply that they would seize the title to a farmer's entire wheat harvest if he planted a single acre more wheat than local farm bureaucrats permitted. The court observed:

> The wheat industry has been a problem industry for some years. Largely as a result of increased foreign production and import restrictions, annual exports of wheat and flour from the United States during the ten-year period ending in 1940 averaged less than 10 per cent of total production, while during the 1920's they averaged more than 25 per cent. The decline in the export trade has left a large surplus in production which, in connection with an abnormally large supply of wheat and other grains in recent years, caused congestion in a number of markets. . . .

Thus, because the federal government had intentionally undermined wheat exports, it automatically acquired the right to exercise unlimited power over every bushel of wheat produced in the United States. The court further noted,

> It is of the essence of regulation that it lays a restraining hand on the self-interest of the regulated and that advantages from the regulation commonly fall to others. . . . It is hardly lack of due process for the government to regulate that which it subsidizes.[229]

The court concluded that the government was justified even in restricting "the amount of wheat . . . to which one may forestall resort to the market by producing for his own needs."[230] The government's intent to benefit some wheat farmers gave government officials a right to absolutely control all wheat farmers—even those who were not selling their wheat.

In 1954, Congress set the U.S. price support for wheat at roughly double the world price and imposed new mandatory production controls on wheat and corn farmers. In 1955 and 1956, USDA arrested or sued more than 1,500 farmers for growing more wheat than was permitted. Stanley Yankus, a Michigan farmer arrested for illegally growing wheat to feed his chickens, told the House Agriculture Committee in 1959, "I am not fighting for the right to grow wheat. I am fighting for the right to own property. If I am forbidden the use of my land, then I do not own it. How can you congressmen justify the laws which have destroyed my means of making a living?"[231]

By 1960, the United States was spending over a billion dollars a year just to store surplus commodities. In 1961, Agriculture Secretary Orville Freeman decided to end the problem of surplus production by bringing independent corn growers to their knees—even though the surpluses were generated almost solely in response to high federal price supports. Freeman told a congressional committee in 1965 that the USDA "purposely [dumped government-held surplus corn on the markets] in order to move our prices down far enough so that they would be way below the support level, the loan level, so that we would thereby get compliance. That was the whole intent and purpose and thrust of the program."[232] Getting "compliance" simply meant driving down prices to force farmers to follow government orders and leave some of their fields unplanted. (Only farmers who had previously enrolled in government programs and submitted to demands to idle some of their fields were protected against price decreases.)

In 1981, Congress enacted a four-year farm program with extremely generous subsidies for most subsidized crops. By late 1982, the United States had huge grain surpluses, and exports were plummeting because federal price supports (which artificially drove up U.S. crop prices) made American crops uncompetitive on world markets. Yet Congress responded by raising price supports still higher, thereby signaling farmers to further boost production and create even more surpluses. The Reagan administration responded in early 1983 with the Payment in Kind program (PIK) to reward farmers for planting less. USDA paid farmers to shut down seventy-eight million acres—the equivalent of leaving idle all the cropland in California, Montana, Colorado, Kentucky, Louisiana, and Wisconsin. Across the Midwest, hundreds of fertilizer, farm-equipment, and seed dealers had to close shop because PIK cut their sales by up to 50 percent.[233] In Pennsylvania, Indiana, and elsewhere, PIK and an unexpected drought—which further reduced harvests and further boosted grain prices—helped drive hundreds of egg producers out of business. PIK cost poultry, egg, pork, and cattle producers up to $7 billion due to higher feed-grain costs. At a time when unemployment was at a post–World War II high, PIK slashed farm-related employment by up to 250,000 jobs.[234]

Federal farm programs still rely heavily on rewarding farmers to idle or "set aside" their acreage. In 1993, USDA required producers of extralong staple cotton enrolled in federal farm programs to leave 20 percent of their acreage idle,[235] corn farmers in federal programs to leave 10 percent of their acreage idle,[236] and rice farmers to leave 5 percent of their acreage idle.[237] Farmers who do not idle acreage and avoid involvement with federal farm programs risk being financially destroyed by political manipulations of commodity markets. Set-asides impose a heavy penalty on farm aid recipients. Dennis Avery of the Hudson Institute observes, "Our farmers could use the set-aside land they already own instead of diverting it—and cut out of pocket costs 15-20 percent. A 15% cost cut would be worth about $22 billion per year."[238] USDA rewarded farmers for idling a total of over fifty million acres in 1993.

The Conservation Reserve Program, under which the government pays farmers to idle their land for ten years, is the largest single set-aside program. While the CRP was created purportedly for environmental purposes, the program is far more effective at shutting down farms than in protecting the environment.[239] A *New York Times* report on the loss of rural population in North Dakota noted that one cause of the decreased economic activity was the Conservation Reserve Program.[240] Sen. Kent Conrad of North Dakota complained that the CRP has "absolutely wiped out small town after small town as we took land out of production."[241] Partly as a result of the government's shutting down the farms, over half of the nation's rural counties lost population between 1980 and 1990. A 1992 USDA study concluded that idling farm acreage in northern Missouri had reduced total economic activity in that region by almost 6 percent.[242] Federal farmland shutdowns, by decreasing U.S. harvests, undermine U.S. exports; between 1981 and 1992, the U.S. share of the world wheat market fell from 47 percent to 35 percent.[243]

Set-asides are a political response to "excess capacity"—too many acres producing a given crop. Congress rewards farmers to cut production in order to boost crop prices to politically preferred levels. Yet a 1988 USDA study concluded, "Excess capacity is a much more serious problem for the seven major [subsidized] crops than for the rest of U.S. agriculture."[244] USDA economist Dan Dvoskin concluded, "Excess capacity in agriculture is caused primarily by agricultural prices that are higher than market equilibrium prices."[245] Government first artificially raises the price and then artificially restricts production. The federal government annually shuts down a large part of rural America to "compensate" for this political mismanagement of farm prices. The higher Congress drives up prices, the greater the need for government controls on farmers.

Farm subsidies sometimes devastate unsubsidized farmers. In 1985, Congress declared that farmers who were paid by the government not to plant corn, wheat, and other subsidized crops on their land could plant unsubsidized crops on that land. Farmers effectively were promised up to $200 an acre in federal bonuses to grow any crop they chose. The new provision, by boosting production of unsubsidized crops, bushwhacked unsubsidized farmers. Rep. Byron Dorgan of North Dakota observed in March 1986, "The markets for edible beans have virtually shut down nationwide as processors wait to see how the provision is handled."[246] Harold Wilson of the Western Bean Dealers Association warned: "In Idaho, the pricing trend now is headed for destruction for the [unsubsidized] farmers."[247] Contract price offers for the fall popcorn crop fell more than 50 percent. Many of the independent growers who were victimized had long fought to avoid any federal "assistance" for their crops.

The federal government imposes feudal controls on some crops. The federal tobacco price support program guarantees American tobacco farmers roughly 50 percent more than the world price. But to grow tobacco, a farmer must have a federal license that specifies to the exact hundredth of an acre of tobacco how much the farmer is permitted to grow. Federal "tobacco police" crisscross the fields of North Carolina, measuring farmers' crops to see if they are growing a few square feet too many of tobacco. The tobacco acreage allotments were distributed back in the 1930s; most current tobacco farmers must rent the allotments from dentists, doctors, lawyers, or other city folk. The cost of renting the allotment from nonfarmers is almost as great as the total benefits farmers receive under the federal price-support program.[248] The arbitrary allocation of tobacco-growing licenses helped drive black farmers off the land, since blacks were far less likely to be awarded tobacco licenses by local USDA committees controlled by white farmers. The tobacco program also imposes controls on cigarette producers, requiring them to forecast in advance how much American tobacco they will buy; manufacturers who buy less than 90 percent of the amount predicted are penalized.[249]

Peanut farmers must have a federal allotment for each pound of peanuts they produce for domestic consumption. Since the USDA imposed peanut licensing restrictions in 1949, the number of peanut farmers has decreased by over 75 percent. Six thousand peanut farmers control the vast majority of the government's peanut licenses. For the lucky farmers who own licenses, GAO estimated in 1993 that USDA provided "an average minimum net return after costs of 51 percent"[250]—over eight times the average corporate profit in the United States.[251] The peanut program guarantees American farmers prices far above world market levels for their harvests; GAO estimates that federal peanut restrictions cost consumers up to $513 million a year. The federal government maintains draconian controls over peanut sales in order to prevent any illicit peanuts from entering Americans' stomachs. The *Washington Post* noted, "USDA employees study aerial photographs to help identify farmers who are planting more than their allotted amount of peanuts. Violators are heavily fined. USDA also issues each farmer a card imbedded with a computer chip that lists his quota. The farmer must present that card before he can sell his peanuts at a buying point."[252]

The sugar price-support program guarantees farmers who grow sugar beets and sugar cane lucrative prices between two and five times the world sugar price. GAO reported in 1993 that the federal sugar programs provide benefits of over $1 million each to the thirty-three largest sugar producers in the United States.[253] In the Red River Valley of Minnesota, heavily subsidized sugar growers have bid up the rents on farmland by over 50 percent. As a result, unsubsidized farmers can no longer find sufficient land to grow soybeans, America's premier export crop.[254] The high price of sugar in the United States has hurt U.S. food manufacturers; the U.S. Commerce Department estimated in 1988 that the sugar program has resulted in the loss of over 8,000 jobs in food manufacturing and 7,000 jobs at sugar refineries since 1980[255]—more than the total number of sugar farmers (13,000).

Congress has long been extremely generous to dairy farmers—and dairy organizations have been extremely generous to congressmen, providing $2 million in campaign contributions a year.[256] In the early 1980s, the federal government accumulated a mountain of over a billion and a half pounds of surplus dairy products—enough to supply the entire country's consumption of butter for three months, of cheese for two and a half months, and of dried milk for two years.[257] Dairy surpluses accumulated because federal price supports encouraged farmers to produce far more milk than consumers would buy. But instead of ending the surplus by lowering dairy price supports, Congress attempted to solve the dairy problem in 1986-87 by paying dairymen to kill their cows.[258] On March 29, 1986, USDA announced that it would soon send 1.6 million dairy cows to slaughter. This severely disrupted beef markets, driving prices down 20 percent in some areas.[259] (Most beef cattle producers receive no federal subsidies.) At the time of USDA's announcement, many cattlemen had already sent their herds to market and had no choice but to accept the decimated prices. Pat Casper, an agricultural banker with First National Bank in Billings, Montana, declared two weeks after USDA's surprise announcement that "from where I'm standing it looks like an absolute disaster. This has been the greatest injustice ever done to the cattle industry."[260] The National Cattlemen's Association estimated that cattlemen who were forced to sell their cattle during the period after the USDA announcement lost $260 million.[261] GAO estimated that USDA's cow massacre resulted in dairy prices being $7 billion higher than they otherwise would have been.[262]

Federal farm credit policies have bankrupted many farmers. Federal farm credit subsidies began early in the twentieth century, in response to an alleged shortage of credit for farmers. During the 1970s and early 1980s, despite ample private credit available for agriculture, federal farm credit programs exploded. By injecting huge quantities of cheap credit, the government helped cause a boom and, eventually, a crash in the market for farmland. Jonathan L. Fiechter of the Office of the Comptroller of the Currency observed, "From 1976 to 1981, farm debt doubled. The bulk of this lending came from the Federal Government and the [federal] farm credit system."[263] At the Farmers Home Administration (FmHA), USDA's loan agency for uncreditworthy farmers, employees were given lending goals to reach; their careers thus depended on how many subsidized loans they could foist on farmers. As Vance Clark, FmHA's administrator in the late 1980s, recalled, FmHA officials would call up farmers and say, "Hey, do me a favor. Take $75,000."[264]

The Farmers Home Administration exists as a lender of last resort to provide credit to farmers who are unable to obtain private credit. FmHA encourages struggling farmers to continue farming until they financially destroy themselves. According to the FmHA's own records, many farmers have gone bankrupt because they received too many subsidized loans.[265] GAO estimated that as of late 1990, almost three-quarters of FmHA's $20 billion in outstanding farm loans could default.[266]

Federal agricultural credit programs have been one of competent farmers' worst enemies. H. Allan Nation, editor of *Stockman* magazine, declared:

> These government [credit] programs have been the very thing that has killed the family farmer by raising the price of land, equipment and inputs to levels insupportable by honest farming. The influx of the millions of dollars of FmHA money had the same effect on honest farmers that the millions of dollars of "dope money" had upon small businessmen in south Florida. There is no way to compete with a guy playing by another set of rules.[267]

FmHA administrator Vance Clark told the Senate Agriculture Committee in 1988: "Land is bid up because the landlords know there's cash rent available through our program, and we find our borrowers bidding against other borrowers, and up goes the rent, which really works to [our borrowers'] detriment."[268] Good farmers had to pay inflated prices to acquire more land because the government bombarded inept farmers with cheap money to bid up the price of farmland. Some farmers have been technically bankrupt for more than eight years, but the FmHA keeps giving them new loans each year to "keep them in business," and thus keeps them producing surpluses and driving down prices for other farmers.

LIBERATING THE ARTS WITH GOVERNMENT HANDOUTS

Restrictions imposed on subsidy recipients receive little attention when the targets are farmers or public housing residents. But when government attempts to impose similar restrictions on artists or intellectuals, cries of "censorship" fill the air.

John Frohnmayer was chairman of the National Endowment for the Arts from 1989 until 1992. Under Frohnmayer's reign, the Arts Endowment funded displays of "Piss Christ" (a crucifix submerged in an artist's urine),

"Piss Pope" (a picture of Pope John Paul II also in urine), an art exhibit featuring an avant-garde photo of a bullwhip-in-a-bunghole, a woman stripping naked on stage and smearing herself with chocolate and bean sprouts, and another female artist inserting various vegetables into her vagina. (The *Washington Post* wrote of one subsidized artist: "John Fleck is noteworthy because he urinated onstage during a performance about homelessness.")[269] Many congressmen were outraged and voted to restrict what types of activities the Endowment could bankroll with tax dollars. Frohnmayer and others denounced the restrictions. Frohnmayer gravely warned in a speech to the National Press Club in 1992, "If the National Endowment for the Arts gets picked off . . . there will be no end to it. It's the Sudetenland now, Czechoslovakia next week, and after that, Poland"[270]—implying that a refusal to provide handouts for naked artists to play with chocolate was the moral equivalent of a Nazi conspiracy to take over the world. Frohnmayer continued: "When the government does support free expression it must do so with a level playing field, no blacklists, and no ideological preconceptions. . . . You and I don't have to like everything that the Endowment supports, because your government is not the sponsor of those ideas. The government is merely an enabler." When asked about the future of the NEA, Frohnmayer declared, "The American people will opt for both freedom of expression and the right of its citizens to create." Rep. Peter Kostmayer of Pennsylvania denounced criticism of the Endowment as "book burning in America, 1990."[271] Robert Brustein, whose theater received numerous NEA subsidies, declared, "The distinction between censorship and determining the distribution of taxpayers' dollars . . . derives from the pernicious American tradition of letting the marketplace rather than a Commissar of Culture or a Minister of Propaganda function as the censor of the arts. Every artist has a First Amendment right to subsidy."[272]

But as long as the government cannot finance all artists, political decisions must be made on who will receive subsidies. Former NEA deputy chairman Michael Straight observed in 1991 that "when 900,000 people call themselves artists in the census, it's preposterous for the federal government to pick out 500 of them and say, 'These are the ones who deserve support.'" Straight suggested that Endowment grant award panelists enjoyed "playing God" by selecting which artists would receive a windfall of tax dollars.[273] The government cannot provide grants to all Americans who want to exercise their "right to create"; instead, government officials must decide which Americans will receive slices of other Americans' paychecks to subsidize their artistic efforts.

The controversy over the Arts Endowment content restrictions epitomizes the *modern concept of freedom*—something that happens when dollars are transmogrified from private citizens' paychecks into government benefit programs and distributed by politicians. This vivifies the confusion about the nature of political power, leading to a concept of freedom that is absolutely dependent on bureaucratic and political preferences. This is the epitome of a paternalist freedom—where government takes everyone's money and uses it to "buy" freedom for a favored group. The more "freedom" the NEA gives government-preferred artists, the less income all other citizens will have to support artists of their own choice.

The NEA is using its subsidies to pressure literary reviews to adapt correct opinions. The *Hudson Review*, one of the nation's leading literary quarterlies, was denied a grant in 1993 (after receiving several previous grants) because, according to a May 27, 1993, letter from the NEA, "writers of color were significantly under-represented in the *Hudson Review*."[274] The *Hudson Review* grant application was also rejected because it had published an article in its summer 1992 issue about the black novelist Richard Wright that NEA panelists judged to be "isolating and condescending . . . This concern was exacerbated . . . when this essay was compared with the fulsome essay on [Emile] Zola in the same issue." Roger Kimball, managing editor of *The New Criterion*, observed, "The message from the NEA's panel is clear: Only institutions waving the banner of political correctness need apply. . . . Even if you have published articles about, say, black authors, were the articles sufficiently—that is, unequivocally and unreservedly—enthusiastic?"[275]

NEA subsidies also squeeze out unsubsidized artists. Playwright John Chodes observed in 1992:

> In 1991 the Arts Endowment lavished $174 million on many forms of creativity. This sum was greatly inflated by city, state and corporate matching grants. The funds have, paradoxically, undermined serious theater. . . . Because of subsidies, the price of renting theaters has increased dramatically: one typical New York City theater that rented for $400 a week a decade ago now costs more than $2,000. Government-financed groups have made permanent homes in what were formerly stages rented by the show. These favored companies monopolize theater access. The endowment has a penchant for financing "social issues" plays, and the lure of subsidies coerces these theater companies—often composed of blacks, gays, women and Hispanics—into creating them. The product may be relevant, but hewing to N.E.A. priorities is the antithesis of a personal artistic perspective. And the essence of theater is the individual viewpoint.[276]

The difficulty of combining government funding and freedom of speech was made stark in a 1990 controversy over a National Park Service magazine. In February 1990, a column in the magazine included a joking reference to Congress: "Having assured themselves a significant pay increase while retaining many of the 'perks' attendant to being a member of Congress, they made the nation safe again by recessing for the Christmas holidays in late December." A few months later, the House and Senate Appropriations Committee destroyed the magazine by specifically slashing its $75,000 annual publishing cost from the National Park Service's budget.[277]

RUST v. SULLIVAN: THE CHICKENS COME HOME TO ROOST

The controversy over the relation of subsidies to freedom heated to a boiling point in the 1991 Supreme Court decision in the case of *Rust v. Sullivan.* The issue in this case was whether it was unconstitutional for the federal government to prohibit family-planning programs that received federal subsidies from offering any counseling on abortion as a "method of family planning." (The regulations did not prohibit doctors from discussing abortions in cases of medical emergencies.) The Supreme Court upheld the federal restriction; Chief Justice William Rehnquist announced, "Within far broader limits than petitioners are willing to concede, when the Government appropriates public funds to establish a program it is entitled to define the limits of that program."[278] Rehnquist further asserted, "The Government has not discriminated on the basis of viewpoint; it has merely chosen to fund one activity to the exclusion of the other."[279]

The court's decision sparked outrage. Justice Harry Blackmun huffed, "The Court, for the first time, upholds viewpoint-based suppression of speech solely because it is imposed on those dependent upon the Government for economic support."[280] Rep. Ron Wyden declared, "The United States Supreme Court has . . . thrown the First Amendment in the trash can."[281] Rep. Rosa Delauro bewailed, "The regulation is really the most offensive kind of paternalism that government can practice."[282] Harvard Law School professor Kathleen Sullivan added, "This says he who takes the king's shilling becomes the king's mouthpiece. That really is a step backwards toward a day when the government could use its leverage to bribe people to say . . . things that it couldn't bludgeon them into saying."[283] Duke University professor Walter Dellinger observed that the decision "is especially alarming in light of the growing role of government as subsidizer, landlord, employer and patron of the arts."[284]

The *Rust* decision betrayed liberals' idealistic concept of government. The reaction to the decision exemplifies the triumph of the neutered concept of political power among much of the intellectual elite. The federal government has imposed thousands of restrictions on federal grant recipients in recent decades, yet little controversy has followed as long as the restrictions generally sought to force recipients to behave according to politically liberal fashions.

CONCLUSION

The impact of subsidies on personal freedom will loom far greater in the future if President Clinton's plan for government national health care is approved. Under Clinton's September 1993 proposal, citizens would lose the right to choose their own physicians and to choose their own specific insurance package. Under Clinton's proposal, the amount of money that a person could spend on health care could be politically controlled, with federal officials imposing limits on the amount that hospitals or doctors could charge—thereby indirectly limiting the service that they could provide. The Clinton proposal also envisions driving hundreds of insurance companies out of business.

The more subsidies the government forces each citizen to bankroll for others, the less the citizen is able to provide for himself and for his family. Subsidies, by eroding self-reliance, guarantee a spiral of growing demands for more subsidies. The average worker is forced to bankroll Section 8 housing certificates so that other people can live in fancier apartments than he can afford and then is forced to apply for a government-subsidized mortgage to buy his own home. He is forced to help pay the college tuition for other families' youths and then cannot afford to pay his own son's or daughter's college tuition.

Subsidies mix everyone's paychecks into a common pot and then allow politicians and bureaucrats to decide who will be allowed to help themselves and on what terms. The more things are financed by subsidies, the more activities become dependent on bureaucratic approval and political manipulation. To depend on government subsidies means either to be currently restricted—or to be only one *Federal Register* notice away from being restricted. To tax oneself in order to subsidize oneself is to transfer one's fate from one's own hands to the hands of the bureaucracy. The one certainty with cross-subsidies is that politicians will be more powerful than they otherwise would be. Cross-subsidies effectively give politicians and bureaucrats an excuse to meddle with almost everyone's life. Few people favor directly taxing themselves in order to directly subsidize themselves; the charade depends on politicians making people think they will get something for nothing. The federal government can change the terms on a subsidy program with the citizenry at any time. Congress exists to bind citizens, not itself.

The growth of subsidies is a Chinese water torture on individual liberty. The proliferation of subsidies means the proliferation of restrictions on how resources can be used. More and more people are treated as if they are effectively using other people's property, with a host of conditions and restrictions. Subsidies mean trying to be free with somebody else's money. With subsidies, a person can only be as free as the prevailing political winds allow.

Government subsidies allow the government to progressively dominate each activity that it sets out to aid. Politicians first assert their sacred duty to help those in need by creating a subsidy program—and then assert their sacred duty to taxpayers to regulate the subsidized in order to protect taxpayers' "investment." With every subsidy it is a question of which strings are attached and when they will be pulled. Government starts out acting generous and soon ends up dictating terms and conditions. Subsidies mean political behavior modification. The more rewards and penalties the government possesses, the more the individual will be influenced in his daily decisions by the preferences and values of the bureaucratic-political rulers.

Subsidies inherently represent a transfer of sovereignty from private citizens to politicians and bureaucrats. The citizen whose taxes "subsidize" the government has no effective right to control that government, while the government that subsidizes the citizen has a de facto right to control him. Thus, the more subsidies, the greater the subjugation. The expansion of subsidies guarantees the expansion of political power.

Every subsidy creates a power vacuum—a vacuum that will eventually be filled by bureaucratic or political ambition. To assume that subsidies do not subvert liberty is to believe that politicians do not like power. It is only a question of time until some politician or some bureaucrat finds it in their interest to exercise the power latent in the subsidy. As soon as a tax dollar enters the Treasury, it becomes political-bureaucratic property, to be used as politicians and bureaucrats please. Subsidies mean politicians taking the citizen's paycheck and then using it to buy his submission.

-6-

The Opportunity Police

Insofar as the coercive powers of government are to be used to insure that particular people get particular things, it requires a kind of discrimination between, and an unequal treatment of, different people which is irreconcilable with a free society.

—Friedrich Hayek (1960)[1]

Seeking the best person for the job has gone from being part of the American heritage to being a federal crime. Currently, it is practically illegal for many businesses not to be biased against the wrong people. The Equal Employment Opportunity Commission (EEOC) represents the epitome of the Paternalist State's contempt for rendering justice to individuals. The EEOC exists largely to compel employers to treat job applicants and employees unequally. Hundreds of thousands of companies have been forced to change their daily operations in order to comply with federal agencies' undefined, constantly changing, and basically dishonest concept of social justice.

The Equal Protection Clause of the Fourteenth Amendment declares that "no state shall make or enforce any law which shall . . . deny to any person within its jurisdiction the equal protection of the laws." The Fourteenth Amendment was enacted in response to a wave of legislation in Southern states that decimated the rights of freed slaves. Unfortunately, Southern states scorned the Fourteenth Amendment and imposed pervasive restrictions on the ability of freed slaves to vote, to contract, and to own property. In 1896 the Supreme Court sanctified government-imposed racial discrimination in the *Plessy v. Ferguson* decision. State and local governments shackled blacks with pervasive restrictions, thereby preventing them from raising themselves or achieving any semblance of legal equality with whites. The pervasive legal repression of blacks was a travesty of the U.S. Constitution and a long-term national embarrassment.

Beginning in the 1940s, the Supreme Court began striking down state and local racial restrictions in housing, education, and other areas. Congress enacted the Civil Rights Act of 1964 in response to a wave of violence and repression in Southern states against blacks. Though the act had good intentions, the employment section (Title VII) was an inversion of an American ideal. Equal opportunity had long been a popular American ideal, so Congress decided to make it a legally enforceable right. But government cannot claim a right to punish businessmen for allegedly providing unequal opportunity without implicitly asserting the right to control the distribution of all opportunity. Once government made equal opportunity a legal right, government officials began intervening to measure and judge who received which opportunities—and to punish those who government officials decreed did not give the right opportunities to the right people or right groups.

MASS GUILT BY THE NUMBERS

The 1964 Civil Rights Act created the Equal Employment Opportunity Commission (EEOC). The EEOC soon began seeking to effectively contradict the law that had created the agency. The 1964 act explicitly banned racial quotas, declaring:

> It shall be an unlawful employment practice for an employer (1) to fail or refuse to hire or to discharge any individual, or otherwise to discriminate against any individual with respect to his compensation, terms, conditions, or privileges of employment, because of such individual's race, color, religion, sex, or national origin; or (2) to limit, segregate, or classify his employees or applicants for employment in any way which would deprive or tend to deprive any individual of employment opportunities or otherwise adversely affect his status as an employee, because of such individual's race, color, religion, sex, or national origin."

The 1964 act also specifically required that an employer have shown an intent to discriminate in order to be found guilty. Sen. Hubert Humphrey, the majority leader in the U.S. Senate, declared, "The express requirement of intent is designed to make it wholly clear that inadvertent or accidental discriminations will not violate the title or result in entry or court orders. It means simply that the respondent must have intended to discriminate."[2]

However, by the late 1960s, the EEOC had intentionally subverted the law by establishing a definition of discrimination far wider than Congress authorized. EEOC chairman Clifford Alexander announced in 1968: "We . . . here at EEOC believe in numbers . . . our most valid standard is in numbers . . . The only accomplishment is when we look at all those numbers and see a vast improvement in the picture."[3] Hugh Davis Graham, in his history *The Civil Rights Era*, noted of the EEOC's early top staff:

> As the infant EEOC's brains trust, they began the process of maximizing agency power by subverting the congressional restrictions [on agency power]. . . . The EEOC's own first Administrative History clearly stated, "Under the traditional meaning" which was the "common definition of Title VII"—an act of discrimination "must be one of intent in the state of mind of the actor." . . . By the end of the

> Johnson Administration the EEOC, by its own self-description, was disregarding Title VII's intent requirement.[4]

The EEOC created tests that would allow it to convict almost any employer that EEOC officials felt did not have sufficient blacks on the payroll.

In 1970 the EEOC issued regulations to severely restrict the use of testing for hiring and promotion. The agency had no authority to issue such restrictive regulations, which clearly contradicted the actual wording of the 1964 Civil Rights Act. Herman Belz, author of *Equality Transformed,* noted, "Achievement of identical rejection rates for minority and non-minority job applicants was expressly stated as a policy objective. . . . Yet the guidelines did not stipulate a concern with *qualified* minority applicants."[5] In 1971 the Supreme Court sanctioned the EEOC's restrictions on private testing in a decision on *Griggs v. Duke Power Co.* Duke Power Company had a policy of not promoting employees unless they were high school graduates or could pass a written test. A group of black workers sued, claiming the promotion requirements illegally discriminated. The Supreme Court ruled against Duke Power Company, stating that "practices . . . neutral on their face, and even neutral in terms of intent, cannot be maintained if they operate to 'freeze' the status quo of prior discriminatory employment practices."[6] Chief Justice Warren Burger declared that Title VII "proscribes not only overt discrimination but also practices that are fair in form, but discriminatory in operation." Thus, if an employment practice that operates to exclude blacks "cannot be shown to be related to job performance, the practice is prohibited." Even though Duke Power Company had a special program to pay the costs for undereducated employees to receive high school training, the Court disregarded the company's effort. Burger ruled that "good intent . . . does not redeem employment procedures or testing mechanisms that operate as 'built-in headwinds' for minority groups and are unrelated to measuring job capability." Burger's disregard of an employer's intent effectively meant that the Supreme Court nullified the 1964 Civil Rights Act and instead imposed a law to accord with the EEOC's regulations. The *Griggs* decision unleashed a flood of EEOC activism; Herman Belz notes, "*Griggs* was used to attack a wide range of recruitment, hiring, assignment, testing, seniority, promotion, discharge, and supervisory selection practices."[7]

The EEOC strove to further slant employment law in favor of plaintiffs by creating new definitions of discrimination. In 1978 the EEOC revealed that a private company could be presumed guilty of discrimination if its employees represent less than 80 percent of the racial groups in its surrounding area.[8] In its Uniform Guidelines on Employee Selection Procedures, the EEOC officially defined "adverse impact" as "a substantially different rate of selection in hiring, promotion, or other employment decisions which works to the disadvantage of members of a race, sex, or ethnic group."[9] EEOC then defined "unfairness of selection procedure" as "a condition in which members of one race, sex, or ethnic group characteristically obtain lower scores on a selection procedure than members of another group, and the differences are not reflected in differences in measures of job performance."[10] EEOC revealed: "*Disparate treatment* occurs where members of a race, sex, or ethnic group have been denied the same employment, promotion, membership, or other employment opportunities as have been available to other employees or applicants."[11] Thus, almost any instance where EEOC officials felt that an employer should have more blacks, women, or Hispanics on the payroll could allow a lawsuit on disparate treatment. The EEOC declared regarding affirmative action plans: "Goals and timetables should be reasonably related to . . . the availability of basically qualified or *qualifiable* applicants."[12]

The history of the EEOC exemplifies how government agencies can achieve near-absolute power simply by issuing incomprehensible regulations. When the EEOC issued the Uniform Guidelines in 1978, the regulations were widely denounced for their vagueness and complexity. The General Accounting Office noted that one study of the regulations concluded that "their reading difficulty level is at about grade 23—that is, beyond the Doctor of Philosophy education level."[13] GAO noted: "An EEOC official told us that the Guidelines were not meant for use by laymen but, rather, by lawyers and psychologists. However . . . the reading difficulty of the Guidelines . . . was probably beyond that of most personnel managers, lawyers and psychologists."[14] The EEOC official's comment captures the arrogance of the Equalizers: The rules for pursuing or imposing equality are so complex that commoners need not understand them. The EEOC's official statement reveals the EEOC's disdain for the organizations that it regulates: the regulated businesses do not need to understand the law, as long as they comply with EEOC's wishes. The purpose of the guidelines was not to enable employers to make a good-faith effort to comply with federal regulations but to provide a slew of pretexts for individuals to sue or threaten to sue companies. The vagueness of EEOC regulations provides a huge advantage to plaintiffs in court cases since it is unclear what is legal or illegal. The only sure way employers can comply is by imposing affirmative action programs and hiring by the numbers.

A long string of Supreme Court decisions helped convert the Civil Rights Act of 1964 into a blank check to compel businesses to hire by the numbers. Justice Antonin Scalia noted in dissent in a 1987 case:

> The Court today completes the process of converting this from a guarantee that race or sex will not be the basis for employment determinations, to a guarantee that it often will. Ever so subtly . . . we effectively replace the goal of a discrimination-free society with the quite incompatible goal of proportionate representation by race and by sex in the workplace. . . . It is impossible not to be aware that the practical effect of our holding is to accomplish de facto what the law . . . forbids anyone from accomplishing de jure: in many contexts it effectively requires employers, public as well as private, to engage in intentional discrimination on the basis of race or sex.[15]

When the Supreme Court in the late 1980s enacted a series of decisions slightly rolling back the Civil Rights Act closer to its original meaning, Congress passed a new civil rights act effectively nullifying the Supreme Court decisions. A survey of chief executive officers revealed that 72 percent of Fortune 500 companies relied on some form of quota hiring system.[16] Lawrence Ashe, an Atlanta labor lawyer, confirmed the survey's findings: "A substantial majority of Fortune 500 companies have very clear affirmative-action goals for minority hiring, and they treat those goals as quotas."[17] Journalist Stuart Taylor recently wrote in *Legal Times*, "An increasingly serious cost is the inherent dishonesty and unfairness in branding as discriminators employers whose only sin is hiring the best employees they can find."[18] EEOC chairman Evan Kemp observed in 1992, "During the private debates over the Civil Rights Act of 1991, so-called civil rights leaders went so far as to plead with the White House for one more generation of quotas for blacks, and yet publicly they proclaimed this is not a quota bill."[19]

DAY-TO-DAY EQUAL OPPORTUNITY

It is difficult to exaggerate the creativity of some interpretations of "equal employment opportunity." In a 1992 case, the EEOC sued an Oklahoma company for firing a Hispanic employee who punched another employee, causing the truck the second employee was driving to crash into a ditch. (The EEOC claimed the firing was based on discrimination against a member of a "protected class"; a federal appeals court rejected the EEOC's claim.)[20] A Denver teacher sued for racial discrimination after she was dismissed from her job after school officials caught her helping a student involved in a fight to hide a knife, and after she pled guilty to Medicaid fraud.[21] Kemper Life Insurance was sued for racial discrimination after it discharged a black employee who committed expense account fraud and missed scheduled appointments with clients.[22] An ex-employee sued Buckeye Cellulose Corporation of Georgia, claiming that the company's policy of terminating employees for "absence and tardiness" was racially biased because it had a disparate impact on blacks.[23] Mobil Oil Corporation was sued for racial discrimination after it fired a black employee who had misappropriated company property, violated conflict-of-interest policies, and falsified expense reports.[24] Piedmont Aviation Company was sued for racial discrimination after it fired a black flight attendant after she refused to accept a flight assignment, forcing Piedmont to cancel the flight.[25] The U.S. Postal Service was sued in 1990 by a job applicant whose driver's license had been suspended four times and who claimed that the agency's policy of not hiring individuals as mail carriers whose licenses had been suspended unfairly discriminated against blacks—even though carriers must drive government vehicles to deliver the mail.[26] The city of Houston was sued for racial discrimination by a white employee who, as a federal judge noted, was "repeatedly out of the office for long stretches of time without explanation, slept frequently at his desk, and shirked direct requests from his supervisors."[27]

The EEOC has long been one of felons' best friends. In the 1970s the EEOC began suing companies that refused to hire people with criminal records. Some minority groups tend to have higher rates of criminal convictions than whites. A *New York Times* article noted in 1992 that "a disproportionate percentage of homicides are committed by blacks, with murders by blacks about seven times greater per capita than murders by whites";[28] a *New York Times* editorial noted that "national surveys estimate that blacks commit robbery at a rate 10 times that of whites."[29] The EEOC often argues that "discrimination" against ex-convicts is simply an illegal pretext for discriminating against minorities.

In 1989 the EEOC sued Carolina Freight Carrier of Hollywood, Florida, for refusing to hire as truck drivers people who had been convicted of felonies (especially larceny) and who had served prison time. Carolina Freight truckers carried "high risk" freight such as computers, munitions, and drugs. The company's average loss from a theft exceeded $100,000 and the company attributed 85 percent of the thefts to employee misconduct. Since drivers were largely unsupervised, the company believed the drivers to be the primary sources of theft losses.[30] The EEOC sued on behalf of a Hispanic man who had twice been arrested and who had served eighteen months in prison for larceny. The EEOC asserted that since Hispanics have a higher rate of felony convictions than do whites, the company's policy violated Title VII because of its disparate impact on Hispanics. The EEOC argued that the only legitimate qualification for the job was the ability to operate a tractor trailer.

The EEOC had bad luck in the federal judge who was selected for the case. The judge—Jose Gonzalez, Jr.—was outraged at the EEOC's condescending attitude toward Hispanics:

> EEOC's position that minorities should be held to lower standards is an insult to millions of honest Hispanics. Obviously a rule refusing honest employment to convicted applicants is going to have a disparate impact upon thieves. . . . That apparently a higher percentage of Hispanics are convicted of crimes than that of the "white" population may prove a number of things such as: (1) Hispanics are not very good at stealing, (2) whites are better thieves than Hispanics, (3) none of the above, (4) all of the above. . . . Regardless, the honesty of a prospective employee is certainly a vital consideration in the hiring decision. If Hispanics do not wish to be discriminated against because they have been convicted of theft then they should stop stealing.[31]

The judge fumed that "to say that an applicant's honest character is irrelevant to an employer's hiring decision is ludicrous. In fact, it is doubtful that any one personality trait is more important to an employer than the honesty of the prospective employee. . . . To hold otherwise is to stigmatize minorities by saying, in effect, your group is not as honest as other groups."

According to Kathleen Courtney of the EEOC's Office of General Counsel, the *Carolina Freight* decision has had no influence on EEOC's national litigation policy.[32] In June 1992, EEOC sued Continental Air Transport, claiming that its policy of not hiring people with arrest records violated federal civil rights law. EEOC attorney Elaine Chaney explained that the law was discriminatory because "blacks and Hispanics are far more likely than whites to have arrest records."[33]

It is ironic that the government penalizes a private company for relying on a person's criminal record, since both the federal and state governments suspend many of a person's civil and constitutional rights once he is convicted of a felony. Convicted felons are prohibited, for example, from owning guns or voting in most states. The government declares that a convicted felon cannot be trusted to pull a lever in a voting booth yet seeks to penalize private companies who feel the person cannot be trusted with $100,000 in private property.

In 1991 EEOC chairman Evan Kemp warned of a "crime wave of discrimination."[34] What type of crime wave was the EEOC battling at that time? The EEOC sued the Daniel Lamp Company in 1991 for allegedly discriminating against blacks. The company was in a Hispanic neighborhood in Chicago and relied on Hispanic organizations to refer job-seekers. All of the company's twenty-six employees were either black or Hispanic. The EEOC ran a computer test, compared Daniel Lamp to much larger employers within a three-mile radius, and informed the company that it was guilty of breaking federal law because it did not have 8.45 black employees. The EEOC also based its lawsuit on the complaint of one black woman who applied but was not hired. The EEOC "demanded that Daniel Lamp not only pay her back wages of some $340, but also that it spend $10,000 in advertisements to detect other blacks who might have answered want ads, and to pay them another $123,000 in back pay."[35] Morley Safer of CBS's "60 Minutes" noted: "Daniel Lamp Company is in an old building on the southwest side, broken into so many times that [the owner] has had to bar every window in the place."[36] Though the city of Chicago was largely unable to provide basic police protection to the company, the federal government had sufficient resources to punish the company for hiring too many of the wrong minorities. EEOC officials publicly asserted that Daniel Lamp had refused to hire any blacks; but "60 Minutes" investigated and found that during the time that the EEOC said Daniel Lamp was discriminating, the company had actually hired eleven black employees. Safer interviewed Jim Lafferty, the EEOC's director of legislative affairs, and asked him if an employer "has three black employees and doesn't hire a fourth for whatever reason, and that fourth accuses him of discrimination, do you prosecute?" Lafferty replied, "Yes we do."[37] Such a standard gives almost any frustrated minority job applicant a legal bomb to throw at potential employers. Lafferty also commented on the 8.45 number: "All too often when confronted with such numbers, employers have assumed that they represent quotas. Consequently, many employers have come to believe the law requires quotas and have *surreptitiously* hired by numbers to avoid challenges."[38] When the EEOC filed its lawsuit, it announced: "This is an action under Title VII of the Civil Rights Act of 1964 . . . to correct unlawful employment practices on the basis of race (Black) and to make whole Lucille Johnson, and all other Black applicants and Black *potential* applicants for employment aggrieved by the unlawful employment practices."[39]

Mike Welbel, the owner and manager of Daniel Lamp Company, observed, "The government went through our records of job applicants, and called up people and asked, 'Are you white, Hispanic, or black? Did you know you may have been discriminated against and that you may have money coming to you?' What really burnt me and hurt me is that the government said that other people came forward [and alleged discrimination]. Other people did not know about the case—the government solicited other people."[40] Welbel was shocked at the government's overreaching; but, his lawyer explained to him, "They are the government—they can do anything." Welbel eventually settled the EEOC's lawsuit by agreeing to pay $8,000 a year for three years into a settlement fund. Welbel observed, "My whole life was fighting this thing. And I could not do it any more. My family and I could not function." Welbel agreed to the settlement partly because he just wanted to be "left alone." Welbel noted that he and his black and Hispanic employees "got along just fine—until Big Brother came in. We never had a racial incident—we never had anything—the church and civic and community leaders backed us up." Welbel concludes of the EEOC's methods: "I am sure that these kinds of things are going on everyday."[41]

The heavy-handed arguments used by the EEOC in the Daniel Lamp case were not unique. Thomas Maggiore, the owner of two Phoenix restaurants, complained:

> In 1987 EEOC's local field office wrote me a letter saying they had reason to believe I didn't have enough women "food servers" and "busers." No woman had complained against me. So the EEOC advertised in the local paper to tell women whose job applications we had rejected—or even women who had just thought of applying—that they could be entitled to damages. Twenty-seven women became plaintiffs in a lawsuit against me. The EEOC interviewed me for hours to find out what kind of person I was. I told them in Sicily where I came from I learned to respect women. I supplied them with hundreds of pounds of paper. I had to hire someone full time for a year just to respond to EEOC demands. Six months ago I finally settled. I agreed to pay $150,000 damages, and as jobs open up, to hire the women on the EEOC's list. Even if they don't know what spaghetti looks like! I have to advertise twice a year even if I have no openings, just to add possible female employees to my files. I also had to hire an EEOC-approved person to teach my staff how not to discriminate. I employ 12 food servers in these two restaurants. Gross sales, around $2 million. How much did it all cost me? Cash outlay, about $400,000.[42]

The EEOC will sue a company over almost any procedure that results in an "inappropriate" number of minority employees. It spent seven years pursuing Consolidated Services Company, a Chicago janitorial service owned by Koreans. Federal judge Richard Posner noted in a March 1993 decision,

> There is no direct evidence of discrimination. The question is whether the circumstantial evidence compels an inference of discrimination—intentional discrimination. . . . Mr. Hwang relies on word of mouth to obtain employees rather than reaching out to a broader community less heavily Korean. It is the cheapest method of recruitment. . . . Persons approach Hwang or his employees—most of whom are Korean too—at work or at social events, and once or twice Hwang has asked employees whether they know anyone who wants a job. . . . Hwang did buy newspaper advertisements on three occasions—once in a Korean-language newspaper and twice in the Chicago Tribune—but these ads resulted in zero hires. . . . Although the respective percentages of Korean and of non-Korean applicants hired were clearly favorable to Koreans (33 percent to 20 percent), the EEOC was unable . . . to find a single person out of the 99 rejected non-Koreans who could show that he or she was interested in a job that Mr. Hwang ever hired for. Many, perhaps most, of these were persons who responded to the ad he placed in the Chicago Tribune for a contract that he never got, hence never hired for.

At the federal trial of Consolidated Services, the EEOC provided only four witnesses: a secretary who Posner believed did not honestly want a janitorial job, a second whose testimony was judged "incredible" and who openly contradicted himself, a third whose testimony was also dismissed as unbelievable, and a fourth who had been fired from his last job for stealing and who insisted that he saw Hwang's ad in the *Chicago Sun Times*, where Hwang had never advertised. Posner concluded, "This was a sorry parade of witnesses, especially when we recall that the [EEOC] culled it from a list of 99." Posner concluded, "It would be a bitter irony if the federal agency dedicated to enforcing the antidiscrimination laws succeeded in using those laws to kick [immigrants] off the ladder by compelling them to institute costly systems of hiring. . . . Consolidated has been dragged through seven years of federal litigation at outrageous expense for a firm of its size."[43] (In a similar case, the EEOC compelled a $2 million settlement out of World's Finest Chocolate, a Chicago candy maker; EEOC's Allison Nichol explained, "Their method of recruitment was primarily by word-of-mouth through their existing work force, which at the time, was primarily white, thereby excluding blacks from knowing about the jobs.")[44]

Discrimination cases have expanded far beyond what a reasonable person would define as racial prejudice. Employment lawyer Gregory Hammond described a new area of employment discrimination cases in *The EEO Review:*

> More and more age- and race-related lawsuits, especially those involving termination, include a new claim: failure to train. An eastern manufacturer hired a black quality control inspector who seemed very well qualified. He had worked for a household-name manufacturer, had excellent experience, and was exceptionally bright. His job was to document every defect in flawed machine parts, the stage of production at which it occurred, which inspector had discovered the flaw, and

> whether the problem was in the production process or the original supplies. When the company discovered after his first month on the job that he had not input any of this information into the computer system, and that much of it could not be retrieved, he was fired. Although his race charge to a local [Fair Employment Practices] agency was rejected, he sued for racial discrimination. Win, lose, or settle, the suit will be very costly to his former employer.[45]

A CONSPIRACY AGAINST COMPETENCE

Affirmative action is so complex in part because its enforcers and promulgators are dishonest. The government has created numerous administrative tests to give it power to cajole, intimidate, leverage, and pressure private companies to do what government officials want.

The EEOC strives to enforce a "know-nothing egalitarianism" on companies' hiring policies. It routinely presumes that businessmen who seek to hire workers with more than minimal qualifications are acting unfairly toward less qualified workers. Much of the EEOC's routine work consists of punishing corporations because their standards are too high. The Civil Rights Act of 1964 specified that a company can discriminate among job applications based on "business necessity" or Bona Fide Occupational Qualifications (BFOQ). But with its interpretation of BFOQ, EEOC officials effectively appoint themselves czars over how competent American workers need to be. *The EEOC almost always intervenes against competence*—in support of the notion that workers do not need to be as intelligent, as literate, or as capable as an employer demands.

In 1973 the EEOC compelled AT & T to sign a consent decree to increase its hiring of minorities and women. As Belz notes, "There was a pioneering wrinkle in the decree: the 'affirmative action override.' To meet its goals, the company could promote a 'basically qualified' person rather than the 'best qualified' or 'most senior.'"[46] This was a radical change in the meaning of the law. Equal opportunity went from requiring that the best man or the best woman be given the job to a demand that jobs be distributed to minimally qualified applicants, or even to applicants who could be made qualified at sufficient expense to the company. The CEO of AT & T publicly accused the EEOC of trying to force the company to lower its hiring standards and denounced the agency's policy as "a misguided form of paternalism."[47]

The EEOC routinely effectively punishes employers if minority job applicants give the wrong answers to test questions. As Robert Holland of the *Richmond Times-Dispatch* noted, "The EEOC's chief psychologist has promoted a definition of 'test fairness' that condemns any test, no matter how job-related or unbiased, as 'unfair' when racial groups differ in their score averages."[48] This means that because different groups of people score differently on tests, the people who give the tests must be punished. A primary activity of the EEOC over the last decades has been to punish businesses for not hiring individuals who, according to job application tests, appeared to be less intelligent or less capable than other applicants. Herman Belz observed, "Since 1966, the underlying purpose of the EEOC test guidelines was to place enough obstacles in the way of employee selection so that employees would choose to hire by race rather than objective criteria of merit."[49] The EEOC regulations made race the critical consideration in employment practices and attempted to discourage professional ability testing. William Gorman, a Civil Service Commission staff psychologist, noted: "Based upon an untested hypothesis, tests were presumed guilty of being anti-equal employment opportunity until proven innocent."[50] David Rose, the Justice Department representative to the Equal Employment Opportunity Coordinating Council, concluded in 1976 that "the thrust of the present [EEOC regulations] is to place almost all test users in a posture of noncompliance; to give great discretion to enforcement personnel to determine who should be prosecuted; and to set aside objective selection procedures in favor of numerical hiring."[51] The EEOC assumed that a fair test would automatically provide equal scores among all racial groups of test-takers although it had no evidence for that assumption—only a surfeit of moral self-righteousness and legal authority. University of Delaware professor Linda Gottfredson noted:

> The National Assessment of Educational Progress . . . has documented large gaps on specific skills and knowledge among high-school students. Throughout the 1980s, black 17-year-olds (excluding dropouts) had proficiency levels in math, reading, science and other subjects that were more comparable to white 13-year-olds than white 17-year-olds. A 1987 NAEP report found similarly large gaps in the functional literacy of young adults age 21 to 25. The average black college graduate could comprehend and use everyday reading materials, such as news articles, menus, forms, labels, street maps and bus schedules, only about as well as the average white high-school graduate with no college. In turn, black high school graduates function, on the average, only about as well as whites with no more than eight years of schooling. The pervasiveness of such huge gaps in current skills and knowledge explains why employment tests typically have disparate impact, especially in mid-to-high level jobs.[52]

Race norming was a result of the EEOC's attack on private tests. Race norming is the covert manipulation of people's test scores to produce an equal number of winners in each race. With race norming, each citizen has an equal opportunity to have his job test scores secretly raised or lowered in response to government manipulation or intimidation. The most frequently race-normed test was the General Aptitude Test Battery, a test that the National Academy of Science twice concluded accurately predicted job performance for all racial groups that took it. But since blacks tended to score much lower than whites, the U.S. Department of Labor compelled state employment agencies to "fix" the test scores to make it appear that different racial groups had equal scores. Race norming subjected over "16 million test-takers to a quota system they knew nothing about."[53] University of Delaware professors Jan Blits and Linda Gottfredson noted:

> Race-norming frequently doubles or triples scores for blacks, especially for higher skilled jobs. For example, if a black, a Hispanic and a white or Asian all received raw scores of 300 on a test for machinist, cabinet maker and similarly skilled work, the black would be referred to an employer with a converted score of 79, the Hispanic with a converted score of 62, and the white or Asian with a converted score of 39—and the employer would not be told the race of any of the applicants.[54]

Gottfredson noted, "By this formula, the worse the black (and Hispanic) applicants perform as a group, the *more* bonus points they all individually receive."[55] Test scores were race-normed on the pretext that the tests were culturally biased, yet the government severely discriminated against Asian-Americans (as well as whites) simply because of their test-taking ability. The EEOC threatened to sue major companies that refused to race-norm tests taken by job applicants.[56] In a prosecution of Atlas Paper Box Company, a Tennessee corporation, EEOC officials argued that the fact that the company did not race-norm job applicants' test scores was evidence of bias against black applicants.[57]

Race norming is based on the principle that the government has a right to deceive and defraud the citizenry in order to advance equality. The EEOC's threat of lawsuits against corporations that did not race-norm sought to make it a federal crime for a private corporation to refuse to lie about test results. An Asian immigrant had his test scores reduced by up to 40 percent, while a Hispanic immigrant had his test scores raised by 25 percent—simply because that is what the government believed to be "fair." Race norming is the perfect example of the EEOC's concept of "fairness"—lying about people's ability so that it can secretly pick the winners and losers among job applicants.

Many police and fire departments have adopted a variation of race norming in response to lawsuits or threats of lawsuits from private citizens or from the U.S. Department of Justice. The Los Angeles Police Department has instituted a racial hiring policy that has made it almost impossible for white applicants to get jobs as policemen. As the *Los Angeles Times* noted in August 1993, "Testing requirements for white male officer candidates have become so steep that in some recent classes, only scores higher than 100—on a 100-point test—qualify a candidate for a job. That limits eligible white males to those who served in Operation Desert Storm because the City Charter gave those candidates a 5-point bonus."[58] Latino applicants can be hired with a score of 96, black applicants can be hired with a score of 95, and female candidates can be hired with a score of 94. The city several years earlier shifted from relying on written exams to oral exams in order to reduce the disparity in test scores between whites and minorities. Yet the city still feels compelled to race-norm the test scores from the oral exam.

The EEOC's war on standards could be a major factor in the lower rate of productivity growth of American workers since the 1960s. Peter Brimelow and Leslie Spencer reported in *Forbes:* "The civil rights revolution has also virtually aborted the use of tests devised by industrial psychologists, which in the 1950s promised to make employee selection a science. . . . Today, industrial psychologist John Hunter estimates that total U.S. output would be about $150 billion higher if every employer in the country were free to use tests and select on merit. That's about 2.5% of GNP."[59]

The push for equal racial results in hiring and promotions is leading to growing attacks on the idea of competence itself. As Heather MacDonald noted in the *New Republic,* "The concept of 'valuing differences' is the cornerstone of the managing diversity movement. It translates questions of competence into questions of culture. Proponents argue that 'non-traditional' workers who fail to advance are not underqualified, just 'differently qualified.'"[60] Ann Morrison, a leading diversity booster and director of the Center for Creative Leadership, said, "The weight placed on math, science and engineering credentials may be considerably biased."[61] MacDonald notes, "Diversity consultants argue that expectations of literacy should be challenged as well."[62]

The EEOC has sued private companies for almost any conceivable practice that had an adverse impact on black job applicants. Yet at the same time, U.S. Department of Labor training programs have long had a disparate negative impact on young blacks. While the EEOC forces businesses to bear any burden to promote employment of blacks, the DOL actively undermines black work skills. The liberal Urban Institute concluded that CETA (the Comprehensive Employment and Training Act) training and public service employment programs, which consumed over $53 billion between 1974 and 1983, produced "significant earnings losses for young men of all races and no significant effects for young women."[63] GAO reported in 1991 that many federally-funded training programs provide blacks with less training, or training for lower-paying jobs, than whites receive.[64] In 1993, a damning six-year DOL-financed study revealed that young black males enrolled in federal Job Training Partnership Act programs had 10.7 percent *lower* earnings than a control group who did not participate in JTPA; the report bluntly concluded that federal training "actually reduced the earnings of male out-of-school youths."[65] Similarly, federal summer job programs for teenagers, which disproportionately enroll minorities, have long been recognized as corroding young people's work ethics. The General Accounting Office noted as early as 1969 that some people hired in the government summer programs "regressed in their conception of what should reasonably be required in return for wages paid."[66] Robert Woodson of the National Center for Neighborhood Enterprise observes, "The programs instill a false sense of work in kids and make it more difficult for them when they go out and try to get a real job."[67]

RESCUING SKIMPILY CLAD WOMEN

The EEOC also polices and punishes practices that it claims discriminate against women. On July 21, 1992, the EEOC announced that it was filing a sex discrimination complaint against Sands Hotel and Casino in Atlantic City, New Jersey, for "maintaining a dress code that is enforced unequally against cocktail servers based on gender. In addition, the dress policy of Sands Hotel places a disparate standard on the female cocktail servers based on their sex in violation of Title VII, by requiring them to wear a sexually provocative and revealing costume, and high heels, while males wear tuxedo-type uniforms and comfortable dress shoes. The Philadelphia District office of the EEOC . . . suing on behalf of female cocktail servers, alleges that they have been *adversely affected by Defendant's discriminatory dress code standards and application.*"[68] It is strange to characterize requiring high heels as a civil rights violation since millions of women voluntarily wear such shoes. This case might have merit if Sands Casino had the power to conscript women at random and force them into wearing skimpy outfits. There are hundreds of thousands of jobs in New Jersey for women who do not want to flaunt their anatomy—but instead of simply telling the potential plaintiffs to change their line of work, the EEOC instead tries to force Sands hotel to change its corporate style. (Perhaps it is only a matter of time until the EEOC files a lawsuit on behalf of the prostitutes at Mustang Ranch in Nevada, alleging that they are discriminated against by job requirements that limit their ascent into managerial positions.)

The EEOC has brought several lawsuits against women's health clubs for their refusal to hire male employees. Women usually choose to join an exclusively female health club in order to get away from male oglers and sexual innuendos while doing squats and bench presses. But the EEOC considers health clubs that serve only females and hire only females to be unfairly discriminating against men. In a major case in Chicago, EEOC sued the Women's Workout World chain of health clubs for sex discrimination. A federal judge initially awarded the EEOC summary judgement but then reversed her decision in 1993 after Women's Workout World (WWW) provided more evidence and petitions signed by over 10,000 members "who vowed not to patronize the clubs if males were hired." *Daily Labor Report* summarized: "WWW claims that because of the intimate physical contact with members, and exposure to nudity and partial nudity in showers, locker rooms, and exercise rooms, the employment of men would violate legitimate privacy interests of the club members. It argued that the female-only requirement for these jobs is a bona fide occupational qualification." Federal judge Ann Claire Williams found that the health club has "articulated a legitimate privacy interest with regard to nudity." *Daily Labor Report* noted, "The court said it also will assume at this point that members of the club have a privacy interest in preventing the opposite sex from touching their breasts and buttocks."[69] Yet at the same time the EEOC is prosecuting WWW, it is creating expansive doctrines of sexual harassment to prosecute other companies.

USING TITLE VII FOR EXTORTION

The EEOC's policy of routinely investigating and/or prosecuting companies who fail to hire a black complainant effectively ignores the realities of modern job searches. The average job seeker files five job applications before finding a job.[70] Discrimination lawsuits cost businesses an average of $80,000 in legal expenses alone[71]—more than six times the amount the average bank robber collects.[72] The threat of a discrimination lawsuit frequently compels businesses to pay off complainants regardless of the merits of their case.

The EEOC measures its good deeds in part by the size of the cash settlements it finagles for blacks, Hispanics, and other "protected classes." The EEOC often forces employers to pay off complainants even when the EEOC lacks clear evidence that the employer was guilty of discrimination. The commission's concept of "conciliation" is basically to let one party threaten to sue another party, and then to see how much the second party will give the first party to cease threatening. Unless EEOC conciliators get some type of benefit for the complainant, then their conciliation cannot be considered successful. A 1981 General Accounting Office report concluded, "EEOC has obtained negotiated settlements for some charges on which GAO believes there was no reasonable cause to believe that the charge were true. . . . The three district offices we reviewed strongly emphasized obtaining negotiated settlements on all charges" regardless of the evidence of employer guilt.[73]

Furthermore, EEOC investigative procedures are often shoddy. A 1988 GAO report noted deficiencies in investigations by EEOC investigators in up to 87 percent of cases in one office. The EEOC found that of the 60,000 complaints it received in 1987, there was cause to believe discrimination had occurred in fewer than 3 percent of the complaints. Yet, as GAO noted, "In an additional 12.5 percent of closed charges, EEOC obtained settlement from the employer in which some relief was provided for the charging party without determining whether there was cause to believe discrimination had occurred."[74] GAO further noted, "In the past, EEOC imposed quantitative production goals on its investigators. EEOC headquarters officials maintain that such goals are no longer imposed. However, investigative staff in four of the six district offices we reviewed said they were still required to meet headquarters-established production goals, or face some adverse action such as low performance rating. In one EEOC district office, some supervisors commented that they frequently placed more emphasis on meeting their quantitative goals than adhering to the *Compliance Manual* requirements for investigators."[75] When a federal agency confronts a small company accused of discrimination, there is almost always the danger of an abuse of power—a Goliath versus David situation where David is prohibited from having a slingshot. As one former high-ranking EEOC official observed, "The official line is that we do not take sides. We just want to find out the truth about how bad the employer is. But obviously, we are out to suspect the employer."[76]

EEOC settlements sometimes maximize EEOC officials' power to extort money from the alleged corporate wrongdoers. In 1986 the EEOC sued C. W. Transport Inc., a Wisconsin trucking firm, for not hiring enough blacks and Hispanics and for not keeping paperwork in order from the mid-1970s. The EEOC initially demanded $8.6 million, but settled for $1 million in 1987. After the $1 million bounty was rendered to the EEOC, EEOC lawyer John Milton was placed in charge of finding 200 blacks and Hispanics who were illegally denied jobs by the company up to fifteen years before. Finding the rightful recipients of the windfall was especially tricky since the company's files of old job applications had been destroyed by a flood. Milton proved that government employees also have entrepreneurial talents. He cut a deal to allow personal acquaintances, his brother, three former Yale Divinity School students, and others to file false claims of having been denied employment by C. W. Transport. After the claimants cashed their $6,000 compensation checks, Milton then allowed them to keep $1,000 to $1,700 of the money, while pocketing the balance."[77] Milton and his brother were convicted of conspiracy, theft, and making false statements to the EEOC.[78] Erma Fields, an EEOC paralegal, was also convicted in this case after four members of her family received settlement checks.[79]

OTHER RACIAL, SEXUAL, AND "DIVERSITY" QUOTAS

Even starker racial quotas are imposed by the Labor Department's Office of Federal Contract Compliance Programs (OFCCP), which regulates the personnel and hiring policies of 400,000 corporations and companies that do business with the government and employ 42 percent of the U.S. workforce. The federal government is by far the largest buyer of goods and services in the country and for many products, it is a monopoly buyer—private companies that produce these products have a choice of meeting the government's conditions or of perishing. The OFCCP has over 500 compliance officers and conducts over 5,000 compliance reviews a year. In 1991 the OFCCP reached almost 3,000 "conciliation agreements" with government contractors.[80] According to a former high-ranking OFCCP official, the conciliation agreements routinely explicitly require the contractor to hire specific numbers of blacks and other protected classes.[81]

President Lyndon Johnson issued Executive Order 11246 in 1965, which imposed severe pressure on federal contractors to increase their hiring of minorities. President Richard Nixon imposed mandatory racial hiring goals on federal contractors in 1969; the OFCCP officially defined underutilization of minorities as "having fewer minorities in a particular job category than would reasonably be expected by their availability."[82] The presidential order implicitly made racial underrepresentation in a government contractor's workforce a federal crime. But the OFCCP neglected to explain how a company could measure "availability" or "underrepresentation" or other key terms. The OFCCP policy is based on the presumption that any company that sells a bolt or hammer to a federal agency has received such an overwhelming benefit from the government that political appointees and bureaucrats should be granted near-absolute control over the company's personnel policies.

The OFCCP bans companies from receiving any federal contract unless they implement an active affirmative action program. Many companies have been barred from applying for federal contracts because government officials ruled that they did not have enough blacks on their payrolls, or did not have enough blacks in the right positions. On October 22, 1992, the OFCCP announced that the Milwaukee Fence Company would henceforth be banned from bidding on any federal contracts or subcontracts.[83] Among the reasons: "Defendant failed to encourage present minority employees to recruit other minorities and women" and "Defendant failed to invite applicants and employees to identify themselves as individuals with handicaps." Perhaps the OFCCP's most damning charge was that Milwaukee Fence "*failed to inventory its minority employees* for promotional opportunities as required by 41 CFR 60-4.3(a)71" (emphasis added). To require a firm to "inventory its minority employees" makes it sound as if the company is supposed to count black employees like widgets, to be put in higher pegs on a strict timetable. This phrase vivifies the dehumanization inherent in affirmative action.

OFCCP regulations have given federal bureaucrats broad power over the day-to-day operations of American universities. The OFCCP ordered Marshall University of West Virginia to get more blacks on its faculty even though the representation of minorities at the university was already equal to the state's minority population (roughly 3.5 percent). Marshall's president, Dale Nitzschke, complained that the university had difficulty attracting black faculty because it could not pay top salary and because West Virginia was apparently not a preferred location for black professors.[84] In May 1992, the OFCCP began an investigation of the City University of New York based on allegations that the university had discriminated against Italian-Americans. The OFCCP was investigating charges that the university was biased against the director of the university's Italian-American Institute, since it did not allow him to teach courses, while heads of other ethnic-studies institutes were permitted to teach.[85] In order to avoid being accused of bias in hiring, many federal contractors have ceased requesting high school diplomas from job applicants.[86]

Harsh penalties are ladled out for violating OFCCP regulations. Harris Trust and Savings Bank of Chicago paid $14 million in 1989 to settle OFCCP allegations of discrimination. Kenneth West, chairman of the bank, denied the bank was guilty but noted that "from a corporate point of view, it's a pure business decision."[87] Whitney National Bank of New Orleans was forced to pay $1.9 million in back pay to settle a federal lawsuit that the company had violated OFCCP regulations by not hiring or promoting sufficient numbers of blacks and women.[88] No evidence of discrimination is necessary for conviction under OFCCP rules; instead, simply an insufficient number of the right races and gender of employees proves guilt.

While politicians loudly declare their opposition to quotas, the federal government itself imposes strict quotas on hiring by federal agencies. In 1989 the Environmental Protection Agency notified the EEOC that it was setting an affirmative action goal of 14.1 percent for black males at administrative levels and a 2.3 percent goal for Asian-American/Pacific Islander females in clerical positions.[89] A U.S. Forest Service Task Force on Work Force Diversity announced in 1991 that the agency was setting a 5.9 percent quota for disabled employees to be achieved within five years.[90] The federal government has bent over backward in order to try to achieve racial hiring goals, even abolishing typing tests for secretarial job applicants.[91]

While some federal agencies apply severe pressure to private companies to hire by the numbers, federal law enforcement agencies flunk the same tests. A 1992 GAO report observed that minorities and women are underrepresented in the workforce and upper management of the FBI, the DEA, and the Immigration and Naturalization Service. Bernard Ungar of the GAO testified: "There were no white women or minority women among these 342 senior executives at the FBI or the other Justice Department agencies, and none at the four Treasury Department agencies."[92] GAO deduced that "the FBI needed 206 additional black female agents, 45 more Hispanic male agents, 36 additional Hispanic female agents, four additional Asian women agents, 34 more American Indian male agents, and six additional American Indian female agents."[93]

AFFIRMATIVE ACTION AS A SCARLET "A"

It would be naive to assume that government racial preferences are an unmixed blessing to blacks and other favored groups. Shelby Steele, a black professor at San Jose State University in California, argues that affirmative action has had adverse psychological impact on blacks:

> [O]ne of the most troubling effects of racial preferences for blacks is a kind of demoralization. Under affirmative action, the quality that earns us preferential treatment is an implied inferiority. . . . The effect of preferential treatment—the lowering of normal standards to increase black representation—puts blacks at war with an expanded realm of debilitating doubt, so that the doubt itself becomes an unrecognized preoccupation that undermines their ability to perform, especially in integrated situations. . . . [M]uch of the "subtle" discrimination that blacks talk

> about is often (not always) discrimination against the stigma of questionable competence that affirmative action marks blacks with. In this sense, preferences make scapegoats of the very people they seek to help.[94]

The stigmatizing effect of affirmative action was made clear in a 1989 dispute over hiring of classical musicians. In 1989, the Michigan legislature withheld half of the Detroit Symphony Orchestra's annual subsidy to punish the orchestra for not having enough black musicians. State senator David Holmes argued that the orchestra had no excuse for not hiring more blacks: "Music is music. Do-re-mi-fa-so-la-ti-do. I learned that in school. Music has been one of the major contributions of African Americans."[95] The *New York Times* noted, "At the root of the problem is the critical shortage of black classical musicians, a scarcity that has made it difficult for some orchestras to find blacks even to audition for opening. Blacks make up only 1 percent of the 4000 classical musicians playing in the country's major orchestras. Furthermore, for more than a decade most orchestra managers have used blind auditions, in which applicants perform behind a screen, to prevent discrimination and favoritism. Use of a screen makes affirmative action nearly impossible, they say."[96] The *New Republic* quipped: "What Michigan legislators seem to have in mind are auditions that are not blind but deaf—taking place without a screen but with earplugs."[97] The orchestra groveled beyond the legislators' demands, hiring a black bassist without an audition and issuing a press release declaring, "The orchestra has implemented a policy of holding auditions only when at least one black musician is present. At least one minority participant is on every audition committee, and black musicians assist in the technical procedures of auditions. . . . Minority representation on the administrative staff and on the DSO board has increased as well. With the hiring in October 1988 of William Terry as its first black vice president, DSO has exceeded its minority hiring goals for professionals. . . . The music of black composers is receiving greater exposure by the DSO."[98] The state legislature's dictate hurt the orchestra's prestige and credibility. When the orchestra sought to hire James DePreist, who is black, as music director from his job as music director of the Oregon Symphony, DePreist refused the offer: "It's impossible for me to go to Detroit because of the atmosphere. People mean well, but you fight for years to make race irrelevant, and now they are making race an issue."[99]

DISABLING INDIVIDUAL RIGHTS

American society has made great progress in recent decades in attitudes toward the handicapped. Most Americans have outgrown the medieval notion that a disability, handicap, or retardation is some type of embarrassing stigma or a special scourge from God. The changed public attitude toward the handicapped is proven by a proliferation of government programs to aid the handicapped in recent decades. Many of the newer government programs are examples of government helping those who cannot help themselves—a legitimate intervention by government often supported even by those cold-hearted conservatives who favor starving the poor. It is virtuous and commendable to voluntarily help the handicapped.

But because many Americans were voluntarily treating the handicapped with far more respect and concern, Congress decided it would be a good idea to force American businesses to give special treatment to the handicapped. The great progress in social opinions and voluntary conduct toward the handicapped became a pretext for one of the worst written, most morally pretentious laws of the modern era.

Congress enacted the Americans with Disabilities Act (ADA) in 1990, asserting that "the Nation's proper goals regarding individuals with disabilities are to assure equality of opportunity . . . for such individuals."[100] Congress sought to use the moral rhetoric of the civil rights movement to camouflage a vast expansion of an entitlement program—a program to be financed not by the government but by any business with sufficient assets to be compelled to provide special services to handicapped job applicants or employees. But there is no way to equalize job opportunities for a normal, healthy individual and someone who is blind, deaf, and semiparalyzed.

The 1990 act defined disability as "(A) a physical or mental impairment that substantially limits one or more of the major life activities of such individual; (B) a record of such an impairment; or (C) being regarded as having such an impairment."[101] This is a definition that means both everything and nothing. As American Enterprise Institute economist Carolyn Weaver noted: "At the moment, there are 43 definitions of disability in use by the federal government, and hundreds more in use by state and local governments."[102] Lawyer Julie C. Janofsky notes that "the definition of 'disability' casts so wide a net that it includes even allergies and learning problems. And because disabilities are self-identified by the employee under the ADA, that means that the accommodations required of the employer are also defined by the employee. Once an employee identifies himself or herself as having a 'disability,' there are virtually no limits to what accommodations can be demanded."[103] The EEOC, in its regulations implementing the ADA, decreed: "An individual with hearing loss would be considered to have an impairment even if the condition were correctable through the use of a hearing aid."[104] But there is no more reason to classify people with hearing aids as deaf than there is to classify people with thick glasses as blind. The main effect of such a judgment is to sharply increase the number of people who are classified as disabled—even though many people wearing hearing aids would probably consider such a label to be "fighting words."

In the ADA's "findings and purposes," Congress declared that "individuals with disabilities" have been "subjected to a history of purposeful unequal treatment, and relegated to a position of political powerlessness in our society."

The ADA thus made history—the first law enacted to provide sweeping benefits and superior legal rights to a "politically weak" group. It passed the House of Representatives by a margin of 377 to 28 and the Senate by a vote of 91 to 6. Congress's complaint that society had previously done so little for the disabled is puzzling. In 1986 the federal government provided almost $170 billion in support to disabled people.[105] Besides, if not enough was being done by the federal government to help the disabled, Congress bears much of the responsibility. Yet the preface to the ADA sounds as if the members of Congress themselves had just arrived in America a few weeks earlier and bore no responsibility for society's previous treatment of the disabled.

Congress declared, "It is the purpose of this Act . . . to provide clear, strong, consistent, enforceable standards addressing discrimination against individuals with disabilities." This is one of the core frauds of the ADA: that asserting numerous times in the act that the new law was "clear" was a sufficient substitute for actually writing a comprehensible law. The phrase "enforceable standards" is the heart of the ADA—federal standards that can be enforced by government officials. But the ADA can hardly be characterized as a "law" in the sense that the word law is traditionally understood. Rather, the ADA is simply a congressional invitation for scores of thousands of Americans to sue other Americans based on the sweeping yet vague standards of the law. The lawmakers' inability or refusal to clearly define illegal behavior under the ADA created a much larger contingent liability for American businesses. Congress did not have the courage to specify what it meant, so instead it simply announced that the courts and regulatory agencies could fill in the blanks however they saw fit.

The EEOC, in its official regulations, declared: "The ADA is intended to enable disabled persons to compete in the workplace based on the same performance standards and requirements that employers expect of persons who are not disabled." And how is this laudable goal to be achieved? In many cases, by forcing the employer to make extremely expensive "accommodations" for the disabled worker and by changing the performance standards and requirements. The EEOC revealed that "the obligation to make reasonable accommodation is a form of non-discrimination. It applies to all employment decisions and to the job application process." Accommodation was defined as "any change in the work environment or in the way things are customarily done that enables an individual with a disability to *enjoy equal employment opportunities*" (emphasis added). Thus, the employer must restructure a person's job and other activities in order to create a facade of equal opportunity. The EEOC also noted, "Providing personal assistants, such as a page turner for an employee with no hands . . . may also be a reasonable accommodation." Chris Bell, EEOC's assistant legal counsel, observed, "If a person with the disability had a job coach, it would be a reasonable accommodation for the employer to permit that person to bring it. It might also be an accommodation for the employer to pay for that job coach."[106] How can the hiring of a page turner or job coach for one worker but not for the next worker be a form of nondiscrimination? This illustrates the fundamental dishonesty of the ADA's lexicon. The EEOC decreed, "An individual's need for an accommodation cannot enter into the employer's or other covered entity's decisions regarding hiring, discharge, promotion, or other similar employment decisions, unless the accommodation would impose an undue hardship on the employer."[107] This makes a farce of the concept of equal opportunity: requiring an employer to spend an extra $25,000 per year to provide "equal opportunity" to one employee—$25,000 that could have gone instead to the salaries of other employees.

The ADA increases the power of federal bureaucrats and lawyers over normal, law-abiding American businesses. As lawyer Julie Janofsky notes, "These [business] people have not suddenly chosen to become outlaws. Their problem is that the law is so complicated and unclear that the only way they can know exactly what it requires of them is to be told by a judge."[108] When the initial ADA regulations were promulgated, the National Federation of Independent Business complained, "The Justice Department has sadly neglected its duty to define the law. Instead of making firm decisions, the government appears to prefer seeing small businesses dragged into court."[109]

President George Bush characterized the ADA, which he championed: "The ADA works because it calls upon the best in the American people, and then Americans respond. . . . The passage of the ADA, the world's first declaration of equality for people with disabilities, made this country the international leader on this human rights issue."[110] But that is not quite how the law is working in practice. In the first thirteen months of the law's operation, the EEOC received over 13,000 allegations of illegal discrimination against the disabled.

Stephen Shamy sought to transfer into the University of Illinois and asked the university to disregard his previous bad grades and allow him far more time than other students to complete examinations because he claimed he had a learning disability. As *Forbes* noted, "When Illinois rejected his application, Shamy sued, demanding $500,000 for pain and suffering. His grounds? That the university violated his rights as a disabled person."[111]

A California group known as Citizens for a Toxic-Free Marin sought to invoke the Americans with Disabilities Act in 1992 to demand that Marin County ban the use of perfume, cologne, after shave, and hairspray in county buildings. Julia Kendall, cochair of the group, announced: "We expect the public to stop wearing toxic chemicals." (The group's members shared a "debilitating sensitivity to fragrances.")[112]

Diane Emery, a nonsmoker with cystic fibrosis, sued a Fort Worth, Texas, nightclub, claiming it discriminated against her because it did not ban all smoking on its premises. (The ADA requires that "public accommodations" make "reasonable accommodations" for the disabled.) Emery explained: "The problem with smoking is that it poisons everyone in the vicinity. And for people like me who have pulmonary disability, it severely reduces my lung function to where I can't breathe properly and start coughing."[113] Emery's solution—armed with the federal law—was to try to force potentially everyone who patronized the nightclub to change their behavior to meet her special needs. (People with respiratory ailments and sensitivity to smoke can sue for up to $100,000 in damages if they are not given what they consider to be "reasonable accommodations" by restaurants and others.)[114]

According to the EEOC, the larger a person's waistline becomes, the more legal rights he acquires. The EEOC announced in August 1993 that obesity should be regarded as a "protected" disability under the Americans with Disabilities Act. The agency declared: "There is neither a basis for nor a need to craft special rules or an analytic approach just for obesity cases. Rather, the standard approach to determining whether a condition is a disability . . . as reflected in case law and administrative guidance, should simply be applied to obesity. Doing so yields the conclusion that obesity may, in appropriate circumstances, constitute a disability. Obesity may be a disability . . . if it constitutes an impairment and if it is of such duration that it substantially limits a major life activity or is regarded as so doing."[115] Critics of the EEOC position argued that a person's weight is usually a factor of a person's voluntary behavior, but EEOC was not persuaded. This ruling potentially adds millions of people to the classes "protected" by the ADA.

The Justice Department sued Becker CPA Review, a California-based firm that offers classes for individuals preparing for accountancy exams, for violating the ADA. Becker offered scripts of its class presentations to hearing-impaired students at no extra charge, but the Justice Department charged that the company broke the law because it did not also provide a sign interpreter in the classes. While the sign-language interpreter cost $5,000 to $9,000, the course tuition was only $1,200.[116] The Justice Department sued the company even after its owner caved in to federal lawyers' demands to hire a translator.[117]

Some people have sought to turn the ADA into a Criminals Relief Act. Florida district appeals judge Eugene Garrett was nabbed shoplifting a VCR remote control; when the Florida Supreme Court ordered Garrett removed from the bench, Garrett claimed that his removal would violate the Americans with Disabilities Act. Garrett claimed he was disabled because he was "depressed" because his daughter failed to get into law school and his son was getting poor grades in school. (Garrett's appeal was rejected.)[118] Nationwide, many ADA lawsuits have been filed seeking special treatment or dismissal of charges for criminal conduct.

The ADA requires that in some cases, businesses must hire people to work as readers, interpreters, or travel attendants to accommodate the needs of disabled employees. When the EEOC first announced its regulations on this in July 1991, disabled groups were outraged that the federal government had not also required businesses to provide toilet assistants to the handicapped as a "reasonable accommodation" to achieve equal opportunity with other workers. As the *New York Times* reported:

> Advocates for disabled people expressed anger that Federal rules issued today do not require employees to provide attendants to help severely handicapped workers with personal needs at work. . . . The advocates said that unless employers provided personal assistance to severely disabled employees, like helping them go to the bathroom, the workers would not be able to remain on the job. . . . Judy Heumann, Vice President of the World Council of Disability, a public policy research and advocacy group in Oakland, California, said, "I would argue that if a person cannot go to the bathroom during the day, then the accommodation is job-related. . . . Evan Kemp, chairman of the EEOC . . . said the rules were left vague on the subject of personal attendants on the job to allow for the expansion of interpretations in the future.[119]

Mary Johnson, a disability activist, denounced the initial regulations' refusal to require companies to provide toilet assistance to disabled workers as the equivalent of "sweatshop conditions."[120] Chris Bell, EEOC assistant legal counsel, observed in 1991, "Whether or not a personal assistant would be required for toileting and eating is going to have to be determined on a case by case basis. We didn't rule it out. . . . It may be in some circumstances that will be required."[121]

The ADA is leading to absurd decisions in other areas. In March 1993, a federal judge ruled that the District of Columbia's practice of excluding blind people from jury service violates the ADA.[122] This decision on blind people's right to serve on juries is especially harebrained considering that juries in criminal cases require a unanimous verdict. Thus, one blind person who did not see incriminating evidence—or the darting eyes of a shifty witness—could have veto power over eleven people who did see the evidence. This ruling could lead criminal defense attorneys to strive to get blind people put on juries. Catering to blind people's egos is apparently more important than rendering justice.

One provision of the ADA might be caricatured as "The Typhoid Mary Full Employment Act." The EEOC announced: "Determining whether an individual [with an infectious disease] poses a significant risk of substantial harm to others must be made on a *case by case* basis."[123] "Significant risk" was defined in congressional reports authorizing the law as a high probability of substantial harm.[124] Simply announcing that decisions "must be made on a case by case basis" creates a presumption that a person with an infectious disease has a right to a job handling food unless the employer has clear and convincing evidence that the person should not be hired or maintained in his current position. The EEOC announced that it would henceforth be a federal crime for a private company to refuse to violate a local or state law regarding hiring the disabled: "An employer allegedly in violation of this part cannot successfully defend its actions by relying on the obligation to comply with the requirements of any state or local law that imposes prohibitions or limitations on the eligibility of qualified individuals with disabilities to practice any occupation or profession."[125] Thus Congress effectively ordered restaurant owners to give a potentially fatal benefit of the doubt to people with contagious diseases. (James Coleman, an attorney for the National Council of Chain Restaurants, observes, "What we were told in no uncertain terms was—'We [Congress] are going to use the restaurant industry as a vehicle for forcing a change in public attitude with respect to AIDS. If it costs you money, too bad.'")[126] In the past, a person with a contagious disease bore the burden of proof to show that he was not a public health threat to work in a restaurant; now, the employer must prove that the contagious individual would pose a direct and substantial threat. EEOC declared:

> The HHS is to prepare a list of infectious and communicable diseases that are transmitted through the handling of food. If an individual with a disability has one of the listed diseases and works in or applies for a position in food handling, the employer must determine whether there is a reasonable accommodation that will eliminate the risk of transmitting the disease through the handling of food. If there is an accommodation that will not pose an undue hardship, and that will prevent the transmission of the diseases through the handling of food, the employer must provide the accommodation to the individual. The employer, under these circumstances, would not be permitted to discriminate against the individual because of the need to provide the reasonable accommodation and would be required to maintain the individual in the food handling job.[127]

Civil rights law has gone from letting black people sit at luncheon counters to entitling people with infectious diseases to prepare and serve them lunch. This exemplifies how civil rights have degenerated from seeking equal legal rights for all to seeking special privileges for some—in this case, the privilege to potentially infect healthy Americans.

At the 1991 press conference announcing the EEOC's initial ADA regulations, EEOC Legal Counsel Thomasina Rogers observed: "The determination of whether someone poses a direct threat must be based on individualized assessment on the present ability to safely perform essential functions. We also added the imminence of potential harm to the list of factors to be considered when determining whether an individual would pose a direct threat."[128] Chris Bell, the EEOC's assistant counsel, elaborated: "The commission has stated that the employer may not exclude a person from a job that he or she is qualified to perform without accommodation based on the elevated risk of injury to the employee or others. Rather, we have said that the employer may only make such an exclusion if the employer can meet the *very stringent direct threat* standard, which means that the employer must show that the person's disability impairs their present ability to safely perform the job and imposes a direct threat, in other words, *a significant risk of substantial harm* to that individual or to others that cannot be eliminated or reduced by reasonable accommodation."[129]

The federal Department of Health and Human Services penalized a Westchester County, New York, hospital in 1992—prohibiting it from receiving Medicare and Medicaid payments—because it prevented an HIV-positive pharmacist from preparing intravenous solutions, even though the hospital did offer the pharmacist another position with the same pay rate where there was far less danger of directly transferring the disease. *Hospital,* the journal of the American Hospital Association, noted that the hospital "has justified its stance by noting its large number of very ill patients and that pharmacists often stick themselves accidentally and must break glass vials in order to prepare IV solutions. In a worst-case scenario . . . pharmacists could stick themselves with a fine-gauge needle and be unaware of it. That needle would then be inserted in a bag with solutions, contaminate the solution, and then infect a patient."[130] But federal officials ruled that the hospital violated the rights of the infectious pharmacist. The hospital was required to pay the infected pharmacist $330,000 for, among other things, the "emotional damage" it had inflicted on him. In 1993, an HIV-infected employee sued the M. D. Anderson Cancer Center in Houston for transferring him out of the operating room and into the purchasing department.[131]

In 1992 a federal court ruled that the District of Columbia must hire a firefighter who was HIV-positive because there was "no measurable risk" that he could transmit the disease in the line of duty—despite the fact that he might be required to perform mouth-to-mouth resuscitation to fire victims. The D.C. government was ordered to pay the firefighter applicant $25,000 in damages for "emotional pain and suffering . . . as a result of the District's intentional discrimination" as well as back pay.[132] In June 1993, AIDS Project Los Angeles and the American Civil Liberties Union filed a suit accusing the Associated Technical College of Los Angeles of violating the ADA for refusing to allow an HIV-positive student to finish his Emergency Medical Technician training course. The lawsuit stressed that there are no federal, state, or local laws prohibiting HIV-carriers from being emergency medical technicians.[133]

Federal regulations are resulting in a cloak of secrecy being imposed on what may be life-or-death information to patients. *The ADA Compliance Guide* newsletter reported in June 1993, "One modification made to Kaiser Permanente (which employs 8,600 physicians nationwide) . . . is that questions about physical limitations and illnesses have been struck from physician's application forms in accordance with the ADA."[134] The *New York Law Journal* noted, "The fact that an employee suffers from epilepsy or is HIV-positive, even if job-related, may not be disclosed to an employee's supervisor or manager. A supervisor or manager, under these circumstances, may only be told about 'necessary restrictions on the work or duties of the employee and necessary accommodations' but the nature of the disability must remain confidential."[135]

In August 1993, the EEOC ruled that the Harborview Medical Center in Seattle had violated the civil rights of a nursing assistant who was fired after refusing to cover up a large "HIV POSITIVE" tattoo on his arm. John

Baldetta worked bathing and feeding the residents of the medical center; the hospital merely requested that Baldetta cover up the tattoo while on the job. EEOC District Director Jeannette Leino said the medical center, in its decision to fire Baldetta, "relied solely upon speculation about the perceived prejudice and ignorance of its patients."[136] Baldetta hailed the decision: "I want this to be a good teaching experience for Harborview and other employers that ignorance and hate . . . won't be tolerated any longer."[137] Yet while hospitals and nursing homes are prohibited from firing workers with AIDS, they are still liable for lawsuits from patients who claim to have contracted AIDS from their medical personnel.

The ADA's mandates will have a major impact on the roughly 7,000 physicians with HIV in the United States.[138] There have been cases of medical professionals transmitting AIDS to their patients. The most famous case involved a Florida dentist who transmitted AIDS to six of his patients. The federal Centers for Disease Control estimated, based on a theoretical statistical analysis, that medical practitioners may have transmitted AIDS to up to 128 patients as of 1991.[139] While this is not a great number of victims in a nation with a population of 250 million, it still raises questions about the federal government's policies regarding AIDS and medical practitioners. The federal restrictions on limiting exposure to infectious health care workers could become far more damaging to public health in the coming years as HIV-positive individuals have a high rate of developing tuberculosis—which, unlike AIDS, is highly contagious.

The ADA also gave health care workers the right to continue operating on people without disclosing to their patients that there is a risk that the patient could contract AIDS from the health care provider. Federal judge Richard Posner, in a dissenting 1993 opinion on OSHA regulations on occupational exposure to blood-borne pathogens, noted,

> I am well aware that many individuals in the medical community oppose disclosure of a health care professional's HIV status. I disagree with their point of view for I believe the consumer-patient's interest is paramount for he or she is entitled to be made aware of this information in order that they might make an informed health care decision before undergoing any medical or dental procedure (if indeed there is a risk of HIV infection as OSHA contends). . . . Certainly it cannot be labeled discrimination when enacting rules and/or regulations that prevent one with a communicable virus from spreading that infectious virus to an uninformed, trusting consumer. . . . Does not the consumer have at least equal rights to protection against infection as the health care provider has? . . . The root of much of this dispute is a vocal minority's emphasis on the rights of the individual at the expense of the common good of all. . . . It is incumbent upon Congress to address and take an in-depth look at the AIDS problem and achieve a balance that reflects the paramount interest of all mankind and not let the overriding concern be with the individual's right of privacy.[140]

One indication of the possible future rulings on "significant risk" comes from a 1988 New Jersey Supreme Court decision made under the federal

Rehabilitation Act of 1973, which uses similar standards to the ADA. Food Circus Supermarkets fired a epileptic meat cutter after he suffered an epileptic seizure on the job while cutting meat with a large steak knife. As the *New York Law Journal* noted, "The court ruled that the employer had failed to establish that the employee presented a safety risk to himself and others because the employer's medical expert failed to distinguish between the risk of a future seizure and the risk of future injuries."[141] There is nothing to prevent visionary judges from applying the same standard to surgeons in the future that the New Jersey Supreme Court has already applied to meat cutters.

The ADA appears premised on the notion that mental anguish is the worst type of suffering that any American could possibly undergo—and thus it is better to compel hospitals to expose patients to HIV-positive health care workers than to cause anguish to HIV-infected health care workers. Congress and the EEOC apparently concluded that it is more important to seek to minimize public prejudice against people with infectious diseases than it is to minimize the spread of the disease itself.

The disabled-rights provisions in the ADA are a stark example of Congress dictating a hierarchy among the citizenry—dictating that some citizen's needs are superior to others and that those others should be forced to pay almost any price to serve the group with superior rights. The greater the physical or mental inequalities between people, the more coercion will be necessary in order to create the illusion of equality of opportunity between disabled and normal workers.

The ADA states that the "accommodations" a business is required to provide can be limited by the need not to provide an "undue hardship" on a company based on "business necessity." But this presumes the government's right to impose hardship per se on businesses for social work. The concept of "business necessity" presumes that politicians have a right to commandeer as much of a corporation's income or assets that the corporation itself does not absolutely need for survival. The EEOC regulations note: "The term 'undue hardship' means significantly difficult or expense in, or resulting from the provision of the accommodation. The 'undue hardship' provision takes into account the financial realities of the particular employer or other covered entity."[142] There is no justice to the EEOC's concept of "undue hardship"—a small business might be forced to spend $500 for a disabled employee, while a large corporation could conceivably be forced to spend $50,000 to accommodate the same disabled employee. The concept of "business necessity" in the ADA allows politicians to practically expropriate a business's property and income to the brink of bankruptcy.

Medical and rehabilitation professionals seek to minimize the number of Americans who are truly disabled and to make the handicaps as minimally disabling as possible. But Congress, with the ADA, has acted as if disabilities should be a pork barrel, distributed to as many people as possible. Congress has turned disabilities into prized legal assets to be cultivated and to be flourished in courtrooms to receive financial windfalls. The ADA creates a powerful incentive to maximize the number of Americans who claim to be disabled, since the claim of disability amounts to *instant empowerment* in the eyes of the law, converting disabilities from a physical liability into a political asset. University of Rochester Professor Walter Y. Oi (who himself is blind) observes, "The ADA will result in an inflated population of disabled persons whose welfare will become increasingly dependent upon an ever growing federal bureaucracy."[143]

Society can and should help those who cannot help themselves. If people want to provide more help to the handicapped, it would be far more effective to provide additional subsidies to employers who hire the disabled—as is currently being done under numerous federal and state programs. But it is politically corrupt for the government to endow some people with the legal power to make potentially unlimited demands from others and claim that the result is simply "equal opportunity."

CONCLUSION

The government launched a noble-sounding crusade to equalize opportunities between blacks and whites, and soon began suing private companies to force them to provide equal opportunities to ex-convicts and law-abiding citizens, to more literate and less literate people, and to highly qualified and minimally qualifiable applicants. Equal opportunity policy has degenerated to pursuing almost everything except equality.

For most of the last twenty-five years, federal courts have done a contemptible job of standing up for American citizens' constitutional rights in employment policy. In a 1982 case, Supreme Court Justice John Paul Stevens ruled that while a hiring plan did severely discriminate against white teachers, the teachers' injury was "not based on any lack of respect for their race."[144] A federal appeals court sanctioned one local government's quota-hiring program in 1984: "The self-esteem of whites as a group is not generally endangered by attempting to remedy past acts militating in their favor. . . . In such instances the white majority is simply not being subjected to what amounts to a constitutionally invidious stigma."[145] This is a contemptible judicial sleight of hand: judging "equal rights" not by whether a government-enforced policy preserved neutrality but by whether the victims of discrimination felt stigmatized by their race. It is absurd to define coercion according to the supposed self-esteem of the victim, rather than the nature of the government action. This is like judging a government prohibition on a newspaper's publication by whether a judge believes that the editors of the newspaper will feel that the censorship insults their intelligence, rather than by whether censorship occurs. In 1986, the Supreme Court upheld a racially discriminatory hiring policy because the policy did not "unnecessarily trammel the interests of white employees."[146] In a 1987 decision written by Justice William Brennan, the Supreme Court upheld a discriminatory hiring program because it did not "unnecessarily trammel the *rights* of white employees" (emphasis added). The Supreme Court has used the same phrase in other cases, implying that it is legitimate to trammel the rights of certain groups—as long as they are not "unnecessarily" trammeled. Naturally, the Supreme Court has never stooped to define how much trammeling is necessary and how much is too much. The sanctioning of the trammeling of the rights of some Americans makes a mockery of any pretension to equal opportunity.

The premise of modern civil rights law is that federal coercion produces a fairer result than the voluntary agreements of private citizens. Pervasive mendacity has been the trademark of American civil rights policy for almost thirty years. Politicians for decades have refused to admit what government officials were actually demanding of private firms. The EEOC plays a major role in this contemporary political-moral thinking as a symbol of the government's willingness to coerce some people and to trammel some groups for the benefit of others. The EEOC epitomizes the sweeping expansion of government in recent decades to coercively impose moral values.

If the government sought to impose the same type of coercion on job-seekers as it does on employers, federally imposed affirmative action programs would not survive a week. If the government sent each job-seeker a certified letter prohibiting him from applying for work at an enclosed list of companies simply because those companies already had sufficient workers of his race, the public outcry would be deafening. Instead, the government simply effectively compels private companies not to hire people of certain races and ethnicities under threat of lawsuit or cancellation of contracts. The system is tolerated only because it is not understood, and it is not understood largely because it is cloaked in secrecy and deception.

Federal civil rights policy is based on "the end justifies the means"—on the righteousness of the goal, not the fairness of the process. Federal civil rights law is based on the "justice" of using force, threats, and intimidation to compel businesses to hire more blacks and other minorities. The *New York Times*, in a July 12, 1992, article entitled, "Threats Used to Push Jobs for Minorities," reported that

> a growing number of groups demanding jobs for black and Hispanic workers have been disrupting construction sites in New York City, beating workers and extorting money for labor peace. . . . The proliferation of these groups, called minority coalitions, has bred sometimes-violent competition, with members waging intramural gun battles in the fight over turf. . . . Last month a 20-count Federal indictment in Manhattan charged four men with using violence and threats to extort jobs for minority workers and more than $20,000 from contractors in Harlem between last October and April."[147]

In June 1993, the *New York Times* reported the indictments of thirty-one officials in groups with such names as United Hispanic Construction Workers, Black and Latin Economic Survival, and Hispanic and Black Coalition. The *Times* noted, "New York and federal officials said the leaders of the so-called minority coalitions purported to provide workers to help contractors meet Federal and local laws that required them to hire minimum percentages of minority workers. Instead, the officials said, the gangs extorted protecting money, sometimes by beating owners and foremen, disrupting work or preventing workers from entering job sites."[148]

The goals of the New York extortionate groups on the surface are similar to the goals of the EEOC and OFCCP: immediate hiring of more blacks and Hispanics. The extortionate groups apparently pay little or no attention to the fairness of a company's hiring policy or to how it treats minority workers; the OFCCP judges private companies largely by their preferential treatment of minorities and by whether the company "inventories its minority employees for promotional opportunities." While the extortionate groups threaten violence if a company does not hire more minorities, the OFCCP can financially destroy a construction company with a single regulatory notice, simply by banning it from working on government contracts. The methods of the extortionate groups are more brutal, but the OFCCP can impose far heavier financial penalties. The minority scam groups, like the federal government, have no right to dictate that people of a certain color or ethnicity be placed on payrolls; but, like the federal government, the use and threat of force are often sufficient to achieve their goals. (The criticisms of the minority groups' extortion efforts should not excuse the racist hiring practices of those labor unions that continue to discriminate against black and Hispanic job-seekers.)

The Civil Rights Act of 1964, as it is now applied, is based on coercive redistribution of opportunity. The vast majority of efforts by both the EEOC and OFCCP has not been concerned with preventing and punishing private discrimination, but with compelling private companies to discriminate in favor of some groups and against other groups. Federal civil rights policy tacitly presumes that the only way to achieve a level playing field in private hiring is to allow government officials to pick the winners and losers.

Currently, racial discrimination in hiring is immoral and illegal except when it is dictated by government coercion. The EEOC issues press releases denouncing private companies that make notations on job applications specifying the applicant's race in cases where blacks may be discriminated against. Yet the OFCCP explicitly requires hiring by race and preferential treatment for "protected classes"—everyone except for white males, while race norming compelled private companies to cut some applicants' test scores and raise others' scores. Racial discrimination is apparently evil except when government officials decide who will be discriminated against. Only government officials have the right to set the job-values of different colors of skin, different national backgrounds, and different genders—as if federal civil rights officials were some type of moral priesthood exempt from the rules governing all other Americans.

Equal opportunity may be an excellent abstract ideal, but in day-to-day life, who is going to judge whether each person has received his rightful opportunities? It is an almost impossible task for government officials who are less than omniscient to determine whether two individuals of different abilities were given correct quantities of opportunity. Equal opportunity policy is enforced by government bureaucrats who have neither the time nor the ability to determine whether individuals were given equal opportunity in each case and is driven by a "numbers mentality" that measures success not by the decrease in unequal opportunities but in the increase of hiring of protected classes.

The same defects that characterize current civil rights policy also permeate the Americans with Disabilities Act. The essence of the ADA is more government coercion against private citizens and companies to serve the preferences of congressional and bureaucratic policymakers. It exemplifies the "liberation" concept of freedom—whereby government uses its coercive powers to present one group with its "liberty" on a silver platter. The goal of the ADA is not so much to create a new entitlement for the so-called disabled, but rather to create potentially unlimited (and undefinable) duties for the other Americans who come in contact with them. This is a concept of individual rights that is diametrically opposed to the concept of equal rights. The ADA presumes that freedom is something that the government creates for some people by inflicting specific, new, potentially unlimited duties on other people—that government creates freedom by coercively subjugating some people to other people.

The Civil Rights Act of 1866 declared that all citizens of the United States "shall have the same right, in every State and Territory, to make and enforce contracts, to sue, to be parties, to give evidence, to inherit, purchase, lease, sell, hold and convey real and personal property, and to the full and equal benefit of all laws and proceedings for the security of person and property, as is enjoyed by white citizens."[149] Unfortunately, courts, state legislatures, and the federal government often ignored the law. But the Civil Rights Act of 1866 is a higher moral ideal than the Civil Rights Act of 1964. The Civil Rights Act of 1866 was based on maximizing individual rights and individual liberty; the Civil Rights Act of 1964 and subsequent bastardized interpretations are instead maximizing government power. The Civil Rights Act of 1866 summoned the government to defend the rights of the citizen; the Civil Rights Act of 1964 empowered government agencies to redistribute, trammel, and stigmatize. The 1964 Act, enacted to protect the rights of individual Americans, has degenerated into a group rights system under which government officials have almost unlimited power to decree which groups will be benefited and which will be penalized.

Affirmative action has had a devastating cost, both to the American economy and to the American political system. Peter Brimelow and Leslie Spencer of *Forbes* estimated that the various effects of federal civil rights legislation may have imposed a cost equal to 4 percent of the gross national product—roughly $225 billion.[150]

In a 1986 editorial, the *New York Times* declared, "Discrimination, cumulatively, can be as poisonous as mugging or burglary. Both kinds of pain diminish the civility of modern life."[151] Racial discrimination is contemptible, but it is absurd to morally equate not giving someone the benefit of a doubt with brutally assaulting and robbing that same person on the street. The government has a duty to prevent muggings, but it has no duty to punish people for underestimating other Americans' abilities.

Affirmative action and racial-preference policies have often been justified as a cure for racism in America. In essence, this assumes that a massive increase in government power is the best way to change some people's bad attitudes—that pervasive government coercion in favor of one specific race will reduce the overall level of racial animosity within society—that the way to cure racism is for the federal government to forcibly intervene in favor of specific races, and against other races. But affirmative action is almost certainly sparking more racial animosity than it is alleviating.

According to Attorney General Janet Reno, "Ultimately a failure to vigorously protect civil rights is an intolerable breach of faith with the people who have entrusted tremendous power to their government. If we can keep that faith, and bring justice to those seeking the opportunities in this country, then all Americans will benefit."[152] It is not so much that people "have entrusted tremendous power to their government"—but that government policymakers have seized far more power over private employers than most Americans realize. "Opportunities" are not some government-owned commodity that politicians have a right to control and distribute. Rather than creating equal opportunity, this process simply led to a general political confiscation and redistribution of opportunity.

Government officials cannot be given the power to equalize without also having the power to discriminate against politically disfavored groups. John Phillip Reid, author of *The Concept of Liberty in the Age of the American Revolution,* observed, "Eighteenth-century constitutional theory could not contemplate the use of government to work for equality in the form of social or economic justice, because it could not trust government."[153] Economist Milton Friedman aptly captured the futility of government efforts to level the citizenry: "A society that puts equality—in the sense of equality of outcome—ahead of freedom will end up with neither equality nor freedom. The use of force to achieve equality will destroy freedom, and the force, introduced for good purposes, will end up in the hands of people who use it to promote their own interests."[154]

There is far greater difference between individuals than there is between the average persons of different races. To classify people by their race is to ignore the talents and characters of individuals of all races. As federal judge Alex Kozinski observes, "No one has yet proposed a satisfactory rule that distinguishes proper racial classifications—permissible exercises of the government's power to classify people for the common good—from those based on hatred, prejudice or a desire to help one's own at the expense of others."[155]

-7-

Guns, Drugs, Searches, and Snares

Each year, more and more actions are being criminalized. The proliferation of new crimes has coincided with the erosion of due process. What was considered "outrageous government conduct" by judges twenty-five years ago is widely tolerated and accepted by the judiciary today. The criminal justice system is increasingly like a socialist factory, designed solely to maximize output (the number of convictions) without regard to the fairness of the case.

THE WAR ON DRUG USERS, THEIR NEIGHBORS, AND THEIR CITIES

H. L. Mencken observed in 1918, "A politician normally prospers under democracy in proportion . . . as he excels in the invention of imaginary perils and imaginary defenses against them."[1] In recent years, politicians have found few better ways to frighten voters than with the specter of drugs. The government's war on drug users is subverting public health, ruining the neighborhoods of millions of Americans, and setting precedents for expanded government power in other areas. Most of the drugs outlawed are indeed harmful, but political grandstanding and endless crackdowns on users have failed to end widespread illicit drug use. Federal drug policy has been vastly more effective in punishing people—over one million Americans are arrested for drug crimes each year[2]—than in reforming their habits.

The United States has had numerous "drug crises" throughout its history. The late 1800s saw a national panic over opium, orchestrated in part by U.S. labor unions fearful of low-wage Chinese competition.[3] Cocaine was widely used and abused in the early 1900s, thanks in part to Sigmund Freud's ecstatic recommendations; cocaine was sold in cigarettes, cordials, and other forms, and even Coca-Cola originally contained cocaine.[4] A backlash against cocaine arose partly because of the drug's popularity with blacks. A 1910 presidential commission report warned that cocaine "has been a potent incentive in driving the humbler negroes all over the country to abnormal crimes."[5]

In 1914, Congress passed the Harrison Act, which severely restricted the availability of many drugs and signaled the beginning of the first major war on drugs.[6] Supreme Court decisions in the first years after the Harrison Act effectively made it a crime for doctors to prescribe controlled drugs in most cases and made possession of controlled drugs without a prescription a federal crime. The Harrison Act was denounced by medical authorities. The *New York Medical Journal* commented in May 1915: "The really serious results of this legislation . . . will only appear gradually and will not always be recognized as such. These will be the failures of promising careers, the disrupting of happy families, the commission of crimes which will never be traced to their real cause, and the influx of many who would otherwise live socially competent lives into hospitals for the mentally disoriented."[7] *American Medicine* criticized the new law, claiming that as one of its effects, drug users "would be driven into an unsanitary and criminal underworld . . . afflicted individuals [would be] under the control of the worst elements of society."[8] Drug-related corruption surged after the federal ban was imposed. Robert Schess wrote in the *American Mercury* in 1925, "The Harrison Act made the drug peddler, and the drug peddler makes drug addicts."[9]

During the 1920s, the U.S. Department of Agriculture encouraged farmers to grow cannabis to boost their sagging incomes (hemp was used for such things as paper and rope).[10] Marijuana also grew in popularity during the 1920s as a result of Prohibition, which inflated the price and curtailed the availability of alcohol. During the Great Depression, Mexican immigrants surged into the United States searching for work and brought marijuana with them. Hostility toward the immigrants led to the Marijuana Tax Act of 1937, which effectively criminalized the possession of marijuana and, according to Yale professor David Musto, "mostly put a lot of jazz bands in jail."[11] Most states also passed laws against marijuana use in the 1930s, inspired partly by the lobbying of alcohol producers who were trying to suppress competition from a "cheap popular intoxicant," as Harvard professor Lester Grinspoon observed in 1971.[12] The American Medical Association staunchly opposed the ban on marijuana: over 100 medical journal articles between 1840 and 1900 discussed uses and benefits of marijuana. But Congress effectively prohibited any use of marijuana for ailing Americans, although it did create a special exemption for birdseed manufacturers who warned that "canaries would not sing as well . . . if marijuana seeds were eliminated from their diet."[13] The Federal Bureau of Narcotics used marijuana as a launching pad to build its power. Marijuana was labeled by federal antidrug agents as "the weed with roots in hell" and denounced as "the Killer Drug 'Marihuana'—a powerful narcotic in which lurks Murder! Insanity! Death!"[14]

In the 1970s, attitudes toward marijuana softened. In 1972 the Presidential Commission on Marihuana and Drug Abuse recommended the decriminalization of marijuana, and the Carter administration endorsed legalizing possession of up to an ounce of marijuana.[15] But in 1981 First Lady Nancy Reagan had severe problems with her public image, in part due to her collecting $1 million in contributions for new White House china and furnishings.[16] One of her advisers suggested finding a more positive social issue to redeem her image—and thus Nancy Reagan became the avenging angel of the drug war. President Ronald Reagan used his bully pulpit to whip up a new frenzy on the war on drugs, and President George Bush took up the cause with even greater fervor. Federal spending for fighting drugs rose from under $1 billion in 1980 to $13 billion in 1993.[17] Since 1980, over ten million people have been arrested for violating narcotics laws.

Government officials have responded to the failure of their attempts to suppress drug use with demands for ever-increasing violence against drug users and suspected drug users. In 1989, Los Angeles police chief Daryl Gates recommended that drug users "be taken out and shot."[18] (Gates's recommendation could have meant executing up to two million people in Los Angeles County alone.) In March 1989, federal drug czar William Bennett suggested abolishing habeas corpus to aid the fight against drugs and later said he would not be opposed to public beheadings of drug dealers.[19] The U-2 planes that once spied on the Soviet Union have targeted Americans' homes and fields, searching for any evidence of illicit drug production.[20] In September 1991, federal officials in Florida conducted a test of radar-guided rockets to be potentially used against the planes of suspected drug traffickers.[21] The headquarters of NORAD (the North American Aerospace Defense Command), in a mountain outside of Colorado Springs, Colorado, is now devoting much of its expertise to searching for signs of incoming planes that might be carrying narcotics.[22]

The National Guard is now actively campaigning against private citizens in drug eradication sweeps. In 1992, National Guard members assisted in making almost 20,000 arrests, searching over 120,000 cars, entering (without a warrant) over 1,200 privately owned buildings, and trespassing onto private property over 6,500 times.[23] Col. Richard R. Browning III, chief of the Drug Demand Reduction Section of the National Guard Bureau, declared in 1992: "The rapid growth of this drug scourge has shown that military force must be used to change the attitudes and activities of Americans who are dealing and using drugs. The National Guard is American's legally feasible attitude-change agent."[24] Assistant Secretary of Defense Stephen Duncan declared at a 1991 Conference of the Association of the U.S. Army: "We can look forward to the day when our Congress . . . allows the Army to lend its full strength toward making America drug-free."[25]

The war on drugs is providing a license to terrorize American citizens. In 1986, 100 state and federal narcotics agents swept into Jerome, Arizona, a small old mining town with 460 residents. The *New York Times* noted, "To law-enforcement officials, Jerome had become a 'hippie' redoubt in the wilderness highlands, where dropouts and outcasts form the counterculture of the 1960s had taken over the local government, established their own rules and officially tolerated the production of marijuana in the nearby hills."[26] One resident complained: "To bring 100 policemen into a small town at 5 o'clock in the morning, dragging women and children out of bed, scaring them half to death, to get 9 or 10 pounds of marijuana, is asinine."[27] In 1991, 200 Drug Enforcement Agency, Federal Bureau of Investigation, and National Guard officials descended on the town of Punta de Agua, New Mexico, in armored personnel carriers and surveillance helicopters but failed to find any drugs.[28]

In a 1989 California marijuana-suppression operation, military convoy trucks crashed through environmentally sensitive areas that had previously been banned to any heavy trucks.[29] Garberville, California, residents were threatened with $1,000 fines and a year in prison for hiking on their own property in violation of a government order cordoning off large areas of land being searched for drugs by the military.[30] Army infantrymen with no warrant trampled private property in sweep searches to try to find the illegal plants. Federal judge Fern Smith blocked the federal enforcement effort declaring, "These operations deliberately employed methods that reach or exceed the boundaries of constitutionally valid law enforcement conduct."[31]

Each year since 1990, Kentucky residents have witnessed numerous sweeps by the National Guard through the poorest areas of the state: military helicopters buzz low over people's homes and terrify children and farm animals. *High Times*, a magazine devoted to cannabis production, noted, "Indignation reached a peak in October [1990] when growers, fed up with helicopter raids and the Guard's occupation army, blew up a Kentucky State Police radio tower near Mozelle in Leslie County. The explosion disrupted communications in the area for about a week."[32] The 1991 marijuana eradication effort in Kentucky involved twenty-five aircraft and 300 federal, state, and local officials.[33] In McCurtain County, Oklahoma, in 1992, "Helicopters suddenly appeared over the hills and hundreds of men in fatigues began sliding down ropes into the fields below" as part of a DEA slash-and-burn campaign.[34] Oklahoma narcotics agents reported that they were told to exaggerate the amount of marijuana they eradicated in order to boost federal funding for the state drug war.[35]

The federal crackdown on outdoor marijuana growers has helped drive up the price of marijuana, thereby making it even more profitable to grow cannabis in closets, in basements, and even under waterbeds.[36] Federal officials estimate that hundreds of thousands of people are now cultivating marijuana indoors—but DEA raids hit fewer than 4,000 indoor marijuana operations.[37] The war on drugs vivifies how the day-to-day discretionary power of government officials has vastly increased in recent decades. The Supreme Court long upheld strict controls over government agents' abilities to conduct sweep searches of businesses. In 1924, the Supreme Court struck down a Federal Trade Commission demand that the American Tobacco Company provide all its letters and telegrams sent out to its jobber customers: "Anyone who respects the spirit as well as the letter of the Fourth Amendment would be loath to believe that Congress intended to authorize one of its subordinate agencies to sweep all our traditions into the fire . . . and to direct fishing expeditions into private papers on the possibility that they may disclose evidence of crime. . . . It is contrary to the first principles of justice to allow a search through all the respondents' records, relevant or irrelevent, in the hope that something will turn up."[38] Twelve years later, the Supreme Court again yanked in the reins on government agencies: "A general, roving . . . investigation, conducted by a commission without any allegations . . . is unknown to our constitution and laws; and such an inquisition would be destructive of the rights of the citizen, and an intolerable tyranny."[39]

Luckily, federal judges nowadays have a much more tolerant view of "intolerable tyranny" and permit government agencies far more latitude. One example is DEA's Operation Green Merchant, which crippled many indoor-gardening businesses as a means to dissuade people from cultivating the wrong types of plants in their closets. Beginning in 1987, DEA sent agents to "81 stores and mail order houses specializing in indoor-gardening supplies, asking for information regarding the growing of marijuana."[40] Two years later, DEA agents toting automatic weapons raided seventy-one gardening stores in forty-six states, commandeering business records, customer lists, and merchandise; eight stores were seized by the government even though no charges were filed against the store owners, and over $9 million in assets were confiscated.[41] Several gardening stores were driven out of business as a result of DEA's action.[42] DEA assumed that practically any store that offered lighting or watering equipment for sale could be treated as a potential accomplice or as a coconspirator to a drug dealer. The Associated Press reported in 1991 that DEA agents "working on Operation Green Merchant have told dozens of garden-supply houses to hand over the names of anyone who has bought so much as a fluorescent lamp or a box of plant food."[43] As a result of DEA's seizures of the sales and customer lists of gardening stores, over 100,000 Americans came under federal investigation.[44] Journalist Peter Gorman reported that "one couple had their parental rights terminated for growing pot at home; several school teachers and at least one nurse lost their state licenses: others simply got caught up in the legal system, and found that trying to extricate themselves nearly ruined them."[45] DEA is continuing its crackdown on indoor-gardening stores; the *Chicago Tribune* published a series of articles in 1993 on DEA's harassment of the owner and customers of the Chicago Indoor Garden Supply store. Government agents sat in a car outside the entrance to the door, obviously watching the business; agents even installed a spy camera (poorly disguised as a transformer) on a pole outside the store. After Brian Kuehling, a thirty-five-year-old salesman from Cary, Illinois, shopped at the store, federal agents showed up at his front door and asked to search his house; other customers of the store stated that they had permitted searches of their houses.[46]

The motto of the drug war seems to be "The only good drug user is a dead drug user." Current drug policy implicitly decrees that anyone using any illegal drug deserves to be poisoned. DEA banned the export of ether to Colombia, where it was used to process cocaine. As a result, over half of the cocaine coming through Miami in 1986 was made with benzene. Benzene is a deadly carcinogen, causing leukemia even at very low doses.[47] DEA, which thus made a bad drug far more dangerous, estimated in 1986 that four to five million Americans may be "systematically exposing themselves to benzene."[48]

DEA is spraying paraquat and other herbicides on marijuana plants in foreign countries and in U.S. national parks. A 1983 report by the federal Centers for Disease Control estimated that from 1975 to 1979, over 9,000 Americans a year were exposed to potentially toxic concentrations of paraquat as a result of U.S. government drug-spraying operations.[49] A National Academy of Sciences study concluded that ingestion of even small amounts of paraquat can cause irreversible lung damage. In 1989, as the *Washington Post* reported, "10 percent of marijuana street samples tested by the DEA in five cities were found to be laced with paraquat and glyphosate, two toxic herbicides used in U.S. funded drug eradication programs overseas. . . . Joan Zolak, a research specialist in DEA's Office of Strategic Intelligence, said the agency never tested for concentration levels because it was not investigating potential health dangers: 'I would think that the health concern would be more from smoking the marijuana itself . . . as opposed to what chemicals might be in there.'"[50] (In contrast to the effect of government herbicides, no one has ever died from the physiological effects of smoking marijuana itself.)[51] DEA, under court order, issued an Environmental Impact Statement in 1986 that estimated that under a "worst case accidental scenario, the maximum cancer risk from spraying of herbicides is eight chances in a million for the general public . . . and four chances in 100,000 for smokers of contaminated marijuana."[52] Considering that the federal government estimated that over fourteen million Americans used marijuana each month in 1986, DEA herbicide spraying could potentially have caused hundreds of cancer cases, along with many fatalities.

Foolish drug regulations are the leading cause for the spread of AIDS among heterosexuals. Drug laws spread AIDS through government regulations that prohibit users from buying clean needles for heroin injections. (Purchase or possession of hypodermic needles without a doctor's prescription is outlawed in most states.) As a result, the same needles are shared by dozens of heroin users, spreading AIDS like wildfire. Roughly half of New York City's 250,000 heroin users are thought to carry the AIDS virus.[53] One third of all AIDS cases are now tied directly to the injection of drugs; in Baltimore, Maryland, 42 percent of AIDS cases are drug related.[54] In Hartford, Connecticut, an estimated 70 percent of AIDS cases are related to intravenous drug use.[55] The vast majority of heterosexuals with AIDS are hard-core drug users, and most young children who have AIDS contracted it as a result of a mother or father who was a drug user or who had intercourse with a drug user. Daniel Lazare observed in the *Village Voice*, "The state could not have designed a more effective policy for spreading the AIDS virus if it had tried."[56] The federal government reported that heroin use killed fewer than 3,000 Americans in 1991.[57] Assuming that almost all of the infected New York heroin users will eventually die of AIDS, regulations designed to make heroin use less safe could easily kill more than thirty times as many people as the heroin itself.

A 1991 *Journal of the American Medical Association* report found that intravenous drug users who were also diabetic had an AIDS rate much less than half of that of nondiabetic intravenous drug users because the diabetics had access to an ample supply of clean needles.[58] A Yale University study found that needle exchange programs reduced new HIV infections by 33 percent among participants.[59] Yet in March 1991, eight people were arrested for illicit possession of hypodermic needles after they sought to offer clean needles to heroin addicts. (A judge refused to convict the eight people.)[60] President George Bush in December 1991 opposed needle exchange programs because they would "harm traditional values"[61]—as if spreading AIDS somehow promotes traditional values. Modern drug warriors are treading the moral high road paved in the 1920s, when some prohibition agents were happy that moonshiners sold wood alcohol that blinded and killed people since that discouraged any alcohol consumption.

Drug laws result in a huge variance in drug doses—the equivalent of a person not knowing whether an aspirin tablet contains the dose of one or twenty aspirins. Since drugs such as cocaine and heroin are routinely mixed with fillers, and different dealers cut the drugs they sell differently, a person has almost no way to determine the purity of the illicit drugs he purchases. In the early 1980s, $10 heroin bags in New York contained only 3 or 4 percent heroin; now, the average purity is 64 percent.[62] Heroin sold in San Francisco is up to 80 percent pure.[63] The stronger heroin has led to skyrocketing fatality rates among heroin users.[64]

Though the federal government has failed to ban the use of narcotics, more widely used drugs have been added to the prohibition list in recent years. Steroids are often prescribed by physicians to help individuals rebuild damaged muscle tissue but have also become very popular with athletes as strength-enhancers in recent decades. A 1989 federal study estimated that 262,000 teenagers use steroids to improve athletic performance and even to "enhance sexual capacity or enjoyment."[65] In 1990, Congress, at DEA's behest, decreed that steroids were illegal, putting twenty-seven different steroids and steroid derivatives in the same legal category as opium and morphine. Possession of steroids without a prescription is now a felony, punishable by up to one year in prison. Once Congress criminalized steroids, federal officials wasted little time demonizing steroids and steroid users: Assistant Attorney General Stuart Gerson declared that steroids "are in reality poisons that are destroying the health and the integrity of athletes . . . and the public in general."[66] People who were previously law-abiding weightlifters overnight became renegades, fodder for prison uniforms. DEA administrator Robert C. Bonner estimated in 1992 that over a million Americans were using steroids and that over half of these users were adolescents.[67] Bonner declared that DEA intended to pursue individual steroid users as part of the government's overall "user accountability" approach. An FBI press release issued August 10, 1992, lectured Americans: "Weight gain and enhancing athletic performance are not legitimate uses of steroids, even if authorized by a physician."[68] But should it be a federal crime if someone tries to artificially boost their bench press total? The *San Antonio Express News* reported that the federal ban resulted in an explosion of steroid smuggling across the Mexican border by high-school kids.[69] Rudy Santos, chief Customs Service inspector in Laredo, Texas, observed: "Everybody knows about steroids, and everybody is into them." Many young people were buying steroids intended for veterinary use in Mexico and using the drugs themselves, a practice that one veterinarian called "pharmaceutical roulette." After Congress banned steroids, athletes began using much more dangerous bodybuilding drugs; the Food and Drug Administration announced in early 1991 that GHB (gamma-hydroxy-butyrate), a substitute drug, was a "dangerous and powerful hypnotic" that could cause coma, seizures, and cessation of breathing.[70] (Sports organizations and leagues can rightfully fine and ban competitors who test positive for steroid use. The private policing of steroid use to prevent unfair athletic competition is far preferable to government's heavy-handed attempts to enforce a steroid ban.)

Politicians are outlawing more and more types of nonviolent behavior to strike at drug use. Alexandria, Virginia, enacted a law imposing up to a two-year prison sentence for people who loiter on streets for fifteen minutes and "have at least two face-to-face contacts with others that last less than two minutes, and involve motions 'consistent with an exchange of money or other small objects.'"[71] The ACLU argued that the law could justify arresting a lawyer for handing out business cards. In 1991 the Maryland House of Delegates voted to crack down on oregano profiteering, mandating a $500 fine and/or a one-year jail sentence for the sale of oregano or parsley if it was packaged to look like illegal drugs.[72] Rep. Kweisi Mfume of Maryland proposed the Beeper Abuse Prevention Act in 1991 to ban teenagers from owning electronic beepers and to require a seven-day waiting period and a criminal check for beeper purchasers with violators subject to up to three years in prison.[73] In 1992, Tifton, Georgia, outlawed the sales of books, magazines, and pamphlets advocating usage of illegal narcotics.[74] City officials invoked the law in 1993 to prevent stores from selling hats bearing marijuana leaves and slogans.

Antidrug hysteria is increasingly victimizing those who use legal drugs. In Fairfax County, Virginia, a thirteen-year-old girl was suspended from eighth grade for a week and forced to attend a drug abuse prevention program because a teacher saw she had allergy medication in her purse. The

Washington Post reported, "Under Fairfax schools policy, any prescription drugs, or other medication a student must take, must be stored in the school clinic. . . . The [school] policy . . . defines substance abuse as having or distributing an 'imitation controlled substance' with appearance, color or size that would lead 'a reasonable person to believe that the substance is a controlled substance.' Fairfax schools spokeswoman Dolores Bohen said even students taking allergy drugs or flu medication "are not supposed to carry it around. . . . The parent is supposed to make the school aware. The nurse should know and the administrators should know."[75] In Washington, D.C., a ten-year-old girl was prohibited from taking aspirin for her frequent migraine headaches; instead, the school system repeatedly called her mother away from work to come and take the girl home. School officials insisted that only nurses could administer medication to students; unfortunately, most of the schools did not have nurses.[76] In Hamilton, Ohio, a school suspended two students after a girl gave her classmate two Tylenol tablets for a headache.[77] Shortly after the drug conspirators were apprehended, the school system discovered that the first-aid kit that one of its elementary schools was selling as a fundraiser included two Tylenol tablets. Superintendent Jeffrey Sittson declared, "Luckily, the kids had only been taking orders one day and none had been delivered, so we canceled the project immediately."[78] It is almost as if school officials are so frightened of being accused of being soft on drugs that they are attempting to turn back the clock a hundred years and deny the wonders of modern pharmacology.

In the 1930s, the Soviet regime rewarded young children who betrayed to the authorities words of criticism their parents had spoken about the great Stalin. As Robert Conquest noted in his classic history, *The Great Terror: Stalin's Purge of the Thirties*, "Stalin's idea of a good young Communist demanded . . . the qualities of an enthusiastic young nark."[79] Some critics allege that public schools are now adopting some of Stalin's methods. Drug Abuse Resistance Education (DARE) is currently being taught by police officers to more than five million children in more than 200,000 classrooms each year. The DARE program sometimes resembles a religious crusade; as a Minneapolis *Star Tribune* article noted, "Schools in Minnesota fly the DARE flag. Students can buy DARE frisbees, wear a DARE wristwatch or sing the official DARE song."[80] Policemen seek to win the children's trust, and children sometimes confide to police the names of people the children suspect are illegally using drugs. Drug education programs have split some families apart. A mother and father in Caroline County, Maryland, were jailed for thirty days after their daughter informed a policeman providing a school antidrug program that her parents had marijuana plants in their home. The girl's action was hailed by Caroline County state's attorney Christian Jensen: "The child set the example by standing up for her rights. This is the most extreme example of when parents fail their children and family."[81] A ten-year-old boy in Englewood, Colorado, phoned 911, announced,

"I'm a DARE kid," and summoned police to his house to discover a couple of ounces of marijuana hidden in a bookshelf.[82] The policeman assigned to the boy's school praised the boy's action. A thirteen-year-old boy in Wisconsin reported his parents to the police for possession of marijuana in 1991; Menomonee Falls police captain Jack Pitroff praised the boy and declared, "Our officers assigned to schools say they are seeing more kids coming forward and saying they've seen various things their parents are doing with drugs."[83] Nine-year-old Darrin Davis of Douglasville, Georgia, called 911 after he found a small amount of speed hidden in his parent's bedroom because, as he told a reporter, "At school, they told us that if we ever see drugs, call 911 because people who use drugs need help. . . . I thought the police would come get the drugs and tell them that drugs are wrong. They never said they would arrest them. It didn't say that in the video. The police officer held me by the shoulder and made me watch them put handcuffs on my mom and dad and put them in the police car. I always thought police were honest and told the truth. But in court, I heard them tell the judge that I wanted my mom and dad arrested. That is a lie. I did not tell them that."[84] The arrest wrecked his parents' lives; both parents lost their jobs, a bank threatened to foreclose on their homes, and his father was kept in jail for three months.[85] Gary Peterson of Fort Collins, Colorado, leader of a group called Parents Against DARE, said "What has happened is the confidant of the child is the police officer, not the parent."[86] Neal Sonnett, chairman of the ABA's Criminal Justice Committee, observed: "It is terribly disturbing when police knowingly abuse that respect to intimidate young children to turn state's witness against their parents."[87] In Nicholasville, Kentucky, a DARE school demonstration went awry when a police dog named Bruiser savagely attacked a ten-year-old girl, who required fifty stitches on the back of her head and elsewhere.[88]

Thousands of schools across the nation proudly post "Drug-Free School Zone" signs outside their buildings. Yet while schools attempt to indoctrinate children with an almost unlimited fear of illicit drugs, schools routinely arrange to have kids drugged for the teachers' benefit. Schools pressure parents to administer Ritalin to hyperactive and allegedly hyperactive kids in order that the children are more docile in the classroom. Ritalin can have extremely harsh side effects, including "stunted growth, facial ticks, agitation and aggression, insomnia, appetite loss, headaches, stomach pain and seizures."[89] Patrick Welsh, an Alexandria, Virginia, teacher, noted in the *Washington Post:* "A former Fairfax teacher told me, only half joking, that most little boys in her elementary school were 'either labeled gifted and talented, or on Ritalin.'"[90] Federal judge Martin Loughlin ruled that a New Hampshire school district had violated federal education law by prohibiting an eight-year-old from attending school unless his parents agreed to drug him with Ritalin. (The parents complained that Ritalin made their son act like a "zombie.")[91] Loughlin declared that the child's "right to a free appropriate education could not be premised on the condition that he be medicated without his parents' consent."[92] The *Atlanta Journal and Constitution* noted in 1992, "In Gwinnett [County, Georgia], lawsuits have been filed by parents against school officials and doctors alleging malpractice and fraud when they advised the use of Ritalin without telling parents about severe side effects."[93] Teachers in Georgia even routinely insist on seeing a child's prescription, so they could know exactly how many milligrams of Ritalin a child was receiving each day.[94] Since 1990, the number of schoolchildren in Massachusetts being administered Ritalin has doubled. The *Boston Globe* noted that "some specialists say that schoolchildren are being diagnosed and medicated for the disorder in too cavalier a fashion" in part because of "increased pressure on financially troubled schools to provide a quick fix for disruptive children."[95] Apparently drugs are bad—except when they are administered for the benefit of the State. School officials often effectively presume that if a seven-year-old boy will not sit still for six hours a day while an often weary teacher drones at him, the boy must be mentally ill.

Federal drug crackdowns have many unrecognized casualties, including millions of Americans undergoing surgery who are denied adequate pain relief. *Scientific American* stated in 1990: "Society's failure to distinguish between the emotionally impaired addict and the psychologically healthy pain sufferer has affected every segment of the population. Perhaps the most distressing example is unnecessary pain in children."[96] Up to 70 percent of terminal cancer patients do not get enough pain relief medication.[97] According to Dr. Richard Blonsky, president of the American Academy of Pain Medicine, "For a person experiencing pain, narcotics are the best painkillers we know. A lot of doctors fear that if they write too many prescriptions, Big Brother will get after them."[98] Dr. Russell Portnoy, director of analgesic studies at Sloan-Kettering Memorial Hospital in New York, declared in 1987: "The undertreatment of pain in hospitals is absolutely medieval."[99] Morphine is often the only medicine that can adequately control cancer pain, but doctors have sharply reduced their prescriptions of morphine for people in severe pain in response to a crackdown by federal and state drug enforcement agencies. Federal and state drug officials have effectively pressured physicians to underprescribe pain killers because of a paranoia about the creation of drug addicts, but a 1980 study published in the *New England Journal of Medicine* found that of 11,882 hospital patients treated with painkillers, only 4 became addicted.[100] A 1982 survey of 10,000 burn patients who received narcotics as part of their treatment found that none became addicted, and of 2,000 headache patients who were treated with narcotics, less than 1 percent became addicted.[101] Frank Adams, an Arlington, Texas, pain specialist, has had his office searched eighteen times by DEA agents and local police checking his patient files. Adams observed, "Drug agents have been turned loose and are totally out of control and they do not know how to discriminate between the legitimate and illegitimate use of these drugs. This is police-state medicine."[102]

With today's drug laws, the government routinely destroys people's lives for having even trace amounts of politically incorrect chemicals in their pocket. Possession of less than a teaspoonful of crack results in five years in federal prison.[103] In Oklahoma, two people who had earlier convictions were sentenced to fifty years in prison for the sale of less than one gram of cocaine.[104] In Michigan, a grandmother who picked up her grandson from the Lansing airport was sentenced to life in prison without parole after police stopped her car and found that her grandson (unbeknownst to her) had a large amount of cocaine in his suitcase.[105] Ricky Isom of Cobb County, Georgia, was sentenced to life in prison in 1990 for selling a quarter of a gram of cocaine for $20 (his second conviction in two years.)[106] Columnist Doug Bandow observes, "It is perverse to punish someone satisfying another's desire for a dangerous substance, however unfortunate, more severely than someone assaulting, raping, robbing, or murdering another person."

Congress and several states have enacted "mandatory minimum" sentences, which, combined with the constantly expanding scope of drug laws, pose a growing threat to average Americans. As Eric Sterling, director of the Criminal Justice Policy Foundation, notes,

> If, after surgery, you use your wife's Valium or your husband's pain medication, and the prescription was not issued to you, you are an unlawful user of drugs. If you also happen to be exercising your Second Amendment rights and possess a firearm in your closet or gun cabinet, your continuing possession of the firearm makes you a Federal felon subject to a ten year sentence and a quarter million dollar fine. This also applies to the millions of American gun owners who use marijuana.[107]

Julie Stewart, director of an organization called Families Against Mandatory Minimums, confirms that many people have had five years tacked to their prison sentences simply because a pistol or rifle was in the same house as marijuana plants.[108]

Mandatory minimum drug sentences have created fierce controversy among judges, lawyers, and others. Moderners ridicule medieval scholastics for debating topics such as how many angels could dance on the head of a pin. But federal mandatory sentencing guidelines for drug violations are sometimes equally absurd. Federal law focuses on the weight of the drug as the key to how many years a person should be locked away. In one case, three judges on the federal appeals court in Boston wrestled over whether the weight of a fiberglass suitcase, with or without metal frames, should be considered as part of the cocaine seized in a drug raid, and therefore as a factor in the resulting prison sentences.[109] Dissenting in one case where the medium was included in the weight of the illicit drug, Judge Richard Posner called such judgments "loony," concluding: "To base punishments on the weight of the carrier medium makes about as much sense as basing punishment on the weight of the defendant."[110]

This quirk in the mandatory minimum requirements has allowed the DEA to launch a crackdown on Deadheads, fans of the Grateful Dead, who frequently sell or consume trace amounts of LSD at concerts. Because the LSD may be in a sugar cube or on blotter paper, sellers routinely get ten- or twenty-year mandatory prison sentences. Deadheads receive longer prison sentences for selling $1,500 worth of LSD than they would receive for selling $100,000 worth of heroin.[111] Stanley Marshall of El Paso, Texas, was arrested in 1988 for possessing less than a gram of LSD, but since the drug was on 113 grams of paper, Marshall got a twenty-year federal prison sentence.[112] Five hundred Grateful Dead fans are serving terms for LSD violations in federal prisons, and between 1,000 and 4,000 are serving terms in state prisons.[113] Gene Haislip, DEA's chief of LSD enforcement, said: "We've opened a vein here. We're going to mine it until this whole thing turns around."[114] Although federal agents are working round-the-clock to effectively wreck hundreds of people's lives with long prison sentences for selling speckles of LSD, LSD itself killed only three people in 1991, according to the federal National Institute of Drug Abuse.[115]

Federal efforts to prevent narcotics imports are a dismal failure. Attorney General Janet Reno conceded in 1993 that federal experts estimate that "to have any impact on drugs in America you would have to interdict 75 percent of the stuff and that would be economically prohibitive."[116] Yet DEA estimates that only about 10 percent of illicit drugs entering the United States are seized by law enforcement officials,[117] while an August 1993 confidential National Security Council review of military efforts to detect and prevent drug smuggling found virtually no impact on the price or supply of cocaine imports.[118] The FBI recently discovered that Colombian cocaine exporters are building plastic and fiberglass products out of cocaine paste and exporting dog kennels made of cocaine. The *Los Angeles Times* noted, "Once inside the U.S., the kennels were stripped apart and ground into dust. . . . The dust was treated with acids, ammonia and other chemicals to remove the fiberglass and other substances. What was left was pure crack cocaine."[119] FBI special agent Charlie J. Parsons said: "This investigation demonstrates that cocaine can be molded into any imaginable shape or form and shipped into any port in the United States." Heroin prices have plummeted in recent years partly because Nigerians have organized an army of "swallowers" who fly into the United States with as many as 125 condoms containing heroin in their stomachs. Nigeria's per capita income is $250 a year, and swallowers earn up to $15,000 per trip to the United States.[120]

Drug prohibition has resulted in millions of casualties (people who used drugs tainted with benzene or paraquat, people sentenced to prison for possessing drugs, innocent bystanders shot or terrorized by drug battles in their neighborhoods or housing complexes), yet has failed to prevent pervasive use of illicit drugs. Despite a vast expansion of interdiction efforts, the real price per gram of pure heroin in New York City fell over 95 percent since 1982,[121] and the number of heroin addicts has reportedly increased from 500,000 to 700,000 since the mid-1980s.[122] Cocaine prices have fallen by up to

90 percent over the last ten years.[123] The only drug that federal enforcers have succeeded in sharply inflating the price of is marijuana, widely perceived to be the least harmful of any major illicit drug. And even driving up marijuana's price has not ended its availability; in a 1989 survey, 84 percent of high-school students said that marijuana was either "fairly easy" or "very easy" to get.[124] According to the National Institute on Drug Abuse, 20 percent of the nation's teenagers have used items such as whipped cream aerosol cans, typewriter correction fluid, and butane as inhalants to get a quick "legal" high. The federal Drug Abuse Warning Network reported seventy-six deaths from the use of inhalants in 1991.[125]

Attorney General William Barr proclaimed in 1992 that the federal war on drugs had been a success—"a decade of achievement"—in part because 6,176 drug leaders, managers, and other key drug violators were serving more than ten years each in prison.[126] American University professor Arnold Trebach has referred to "the American drug gulag" to describe prisons full of drug offenders."[127] The United States now has the highest incarceration rate in the world. The average length of prison sentences for drug offenses almost tripled between 1986 and 1991 (from twenty-seven months to seventy-eight months).[128] In New York City, prisoners have been kept on barges.[129] The federal Bureau of Prisons is acquiring college campuses and religious seminaries and converting them into minimum-security facilities.[130] The number of people incarcerated in federal and state prisons in 1992 was 883,593—almost triple the number of people who were incarcerated in such prisons in 1980. The number of people in federal and state prisons on drug charges has increased tenfold since 1980; since 1987, drug defendants have accounted for three-quarters of all new federal prisoners.[131] Despite politicians' efforts to portray drug users and dealers as dangerous social agents, almost 80 percent of the people sentenced to state prisons on drug charges had no history of criminal violence.[132]

Being sent to jail for drug possession, especially in places like New York City, gives a person an excellent chance to acquire tuberculosis or AIDS. The *Annals of Internal Medicine* reported in July 1992 that "three medical groups warn that massively overcrowded conditions in jails and prisons are creating a public health emergency. That is true in other states, said Kim M. Thorburn, president of the American Correctional Health Services Association and an author of the report. Prison overcrowding has serious public health consequences. . . . In virtually every prison and big city jail, two and in some cases three inmates are routinely confined to cells built to accommodate one person. That makes prisons ideal breeding grounds for potentially lethal diseases such as AIDS, hepatitis B and especially tuberculosis."[133] John Raba, M.D., director of ambulatory services at Cook County Hospital in Chicago, said: "By cramming more people who are [infected with tuberculosis and HIV] into tremendously overcrowded facilities that were not built to provide the ventilation needed for preventing the spread of respiratory diseases, we have set the table for a terrible dinner of tuberculosis to serve the public."[134]

In 1990, for the first time, the number of people sentenced to prison for drug crimes exceeded the number of people sentenced for violent crimes.[135] Almost 19,000 state and local law enforcement officials are assigned to the drug war on a full-time basis[136]—at a time when most big cities have record numbers of unsolved murders on the books. Focusing law enforcement resources on drug violations means fewer police to protect Americans against other crimes. Florida State University economists Bruce Benson and David Rasmussen, in a study published in *Contemporary Policy Issues,* concluded that "cracking down on drugs unintentionally fosters theft, burglary and other property crimes because law enforcement resources are diverted. . . . Between 1982 and 1987, when Florida police focused on drug law enforcement, drug arrests rose 90%, while total arrests rose only 32%. Property crimes escalated, with robbery rates rising 34% and auto thefts by 65%. As more resources are allowed to fight drug crime, the chance of arrest for property crime falls."[137] The *Washington Post* reported in late 1990, "Florida released 130,000 felons early to make room in state prisons—largely for new drug offenders."[138] Forty thousand of the early releases went on to commit new crimes: "Florida has been plagued by repeated 'horror stories' about early-release inmates who committed sensational crimes. In July 1988, Bryan Keith Smith went on a headline-producing crime spree—murdering a restaurant dishwasher, a motel clerk, and a convenience store clerk in three armed robberies that started 12 days after he was released under the program."[139] Florida cleared room for drug offenders by giving early release to Walter Ross Lewis, who had been convicted for raping a sixty-three-year-old woman and pistol-whipping a bus driver; Lewis capitalized on parole to stab to death a pregnant woman.[140] In 1992, Florida granted early release to 140 former prisoners convicted of murder, attempted murder, and child abuse.[141] Drug expert James Ostrowski observed, "In a world of scarce prison resources, sending a drug offender to prison for one year is equivalent to freeing a violent criminal to commit 40 robberies, 7 assaults, 110 burglaries, and 25 auto thefts."[142] Forty-two states are currently under court orders to reduce prison overcrowding.[143] The American Bar Association, in a special report, concluded: "While drug use is decreasing and violent crime is increasing, the criminal justice system is directing more of its resources to drug offenses and less to violent crime—resulting in an increasing proportion of persons imprisoned for drug offenses and a decreasing proportion imprisoned for violent crimes."[144]

President George Bush, in a June 29, 1992, speech dedicating a new Drug Enforcement Agency office building, declared, "I am delighted to be here to salute the greatest freedom fighters any nation could have, people who provide freedom from violence and freedom from drugs and freedom from fear."[145] But people are killing each other over drugs not because of the drugs themselves but because of the illegal nature of the drug business. Drug laws epitomize how government punishment of a victimless crime makes life less safe for almost all Americans. Nobel laureate Milton Friedman observed that the homicide rate soared in the late 1960s after President Richard M. Nixon launched the war on drugs and estimated that the war on drugs could be causing an extra 5,000 homicides per year.[146] A 1984 study by the New York State Division of Substance Abuse Services estimated that the average urban heroin user commits 160 nondrug crimes a year, including 6 robberies, 18 burglaries, 51 shopliftings, 16 other larcenies, 35 con games, 27 prostitution events, and 13 other crimes.[147] Dallas police chief Bill Rathburn observed that boosting the price of illegal drugs can backfire: "With those who are committing crime to support their drug habit, you force them to commit more crime."[148] In New York City, drug addicts have begun tearing up and stealing copper cables from the subway lines to sell to scrap dealers for quick cash, causing subway breakdowns that delays thousands of riders.[149]

The war on drugs is essentially a civil war to uphold the principle that politicians should have absolute power over what citizens put into their own bodies. The key to the drug laws is the concept of *controlled substances*. The drug war gives certain government officials absolute power to draw the line between permitted and forbidden substances. The war on drugs means that comfortable politicians and political appointees sitting in their cushioned chairs should have absolute power to decree what people on their death beds with cancer are permitted to take to kill their pain.

Drug czar William Bennett declared in 1990, "I find no merit in the [drug] legalizers' case. The simple fact is that drug use is wrong. And the moral argument, in the end, is the most compelling argument."[150] (Some law enforcement officers find peculiar ways to enforce goodness: a Dayton, Ohio, police officer confessed that he scorched a young drug suspect on the stomach and chest with a hot iron to force the man to divulge information.)[151] The only reason that using certain drugs is wrong is, ultimately, because politicians say it is wrong. Does it make sense to say that a person who takes regular Tylenol without a prescription is a law-abiding citizen—but that a person who takes Tylenol-3 (with codeine) without a prescription deserves to be locked away? Bennett's position means allowing the question of good or evil of any plant or chemical combination to be up to an uninformed group of timid legislators who have little or no expertise in pharmacology.[152] Carlton Turner, special assistant to the president on drug abuse, declared in 1984: "You cannot let one drug come in and say, 'Well, this drug is all right.' We've drawn the line, and the American public is responding. . . . There's no such thing as a soft drug."[153] But there is no clear, self-evident line between which drugs are legal and which are illegal. Far more people die from legal drugs each year than die from illegal drugs. As Paul Scriven noted in a Drug Policy

Foundation study, "In 1988, approximately 400,000 deaths were associated with tobacco usage, 100,000 deaths with alcohol usage, 5,000 deaths with prescription drug usage (primarily sedative/hypnotic or 'sleeping pills' abuse) and 6,756 deaths combined from all illegal drug usage."[154] Professor Thomas Szasz observed, "In the modern Western therapeutic societies, the political and medical decision makers control the definition of drugs as therapeutic or toxic, and hence also their legitimacy and availability in the marketplace. The question is: Who is an addict? That's like saying, 'Who is a witch?' Does the priest decide?"[155] And the more drugs federal officials outlaw, the more power they have over other Americans.

If drugs were legal, then the drug business would likely be no more violent than the beer or whiskey business. Advocates of drug prohibition warn that legalization would sharply increase usage and thereby lead to more fatalities. The Netherlands legalized marijuana in 1970; as of 1985, American high school seniors were more than ten times more likely than Dutch high school seniors to be heavy marijuana users.[156] Alaska decriminalized marijuana in 1975; as of 1982, daily use of marijuana was one-third lower among Alaska high school seniors compared to other Americans (6.3 percent vs. 4 percent).[157] As for fatalities, it is almost impossible to conceive of legalized drugs killing as many people as the number of heroin addicts who will die of AIDS because of their use of infected needles.

The black market prices of heroin and cocaine are as much as a hundred times higher than the cost of producing and marketing the drugs. Economist Sam Staley, author of *Drug Policy and the Decline of American Cities*, observed, "The cost of supplying heroin legally would run less than 25 cents per day."[158] According to the Drug Enforcement Agency, growers in Colombia receive only $2 a pound for their marijuana—which then sells for $725 a pound wholesale in the United States.[159] Do we really need a massive network of spies and informants, helicopter gunships, and spy satellites in order to make marijuana vastly more expensive than tobacco? How much public safety and individual privacy should we sacrifice in order to inflate the price of a handful of drugs?

Use of marijuana, quaaludes, and cocaine declined once the public became convinced of the drug's adverse impacts. Public understanding is a far more effective deterrent than government punishments. Even if there was a slight increase in the number of people using drugs after legalization, they would be using much safer drugs than are currently being used. It would be better to have six million people using clean cocaine than five million people using cocaine laced with benzene.

As Sen. Daniel Patrick Moynihan observed, "It is essential that we understand that by choosing [drug] prohibition we are choosing to have an intense crime problem concentrated among minorities. . . . Clearly federal drug policy is responsible for a degree of social regression for which there does not appear to be any equivalent in our history."[160] How much social chaos should

America endure in politicians' quixotic effort to achieve absolute control over how individuals use their own bodies? According to the federal Substance Abuse and Mental Health Services Administration, sixty-seven million Americans have used marijuana at least once in their lifetime, and over twenty-two million Americans have used cocaine at least once in their lifetime. Thirty-six percent of the U.S. population over the age of twelve has used illicit drugs at least once in their lifetime. Given the pervasive use of illicit drugs, it is time both to stop demonizing drug use and to admit that government punishments cannot end drug abuse.[161]

The ultimate question is: Who should pay the cost of drug abuse—society or the drug abuser? If drugs were legal, we would still see deaths from overdoses, but there would be far fewer deaths from gun battles among drug dealers, far fewer neighborhoods destroyed by drug dealers, and far fewer deaths from contaminated drugs. The question is not whether drugs are bad for the individual but whether society has a right to punish people for how they treat their own bodies. It is naive to view most drug users as innocent victims of pushers. But it is ludicrous to view casual drug users as dangerous social enemies that deserve a dose of Ayatollah-justice. Most drug addicts' worst failing is garden-variety stupidity or weakness of will.

GRABBING GUNS

Gun control has a long and sordid history in the United States. The British army's attempt to seize privately owned weapons in Lexington and Concord led to the first battles of the American Revolution. Some of the earliest gun control laws were bans on slaves and free blacks owning any type of weapon. In 1870, the Tennessee legislature banned possession of any handgun except the Colt .45, which ex-slaves could not afford.[162] Roy Innis of the National Association for the Advancement of Colored People observed, "Gun-control legislation of the late 19th and early 20th centuries, enacted at the state and local levels, were implicitly racist in conception. And in operation, those laws invidiously targeted blacks."[163] One Florida judge declared in 1941 that that state's nineteenth-century gun control laws were "passed for the purpose of disarming the negro laborers . . . and never intended to be applied to the white population."[164] Two black scholars, writing in the *Georgetown Law Journal*, examined the history of gun control and concluded, "Overall, these [gun] laws reflect the desire to maintain white supremacy and control."[165]

The Second Amendment states, "A well-regulated militia, being necessary to the security of a free State, the right of the people to keep and bear arms, shall not be infringed." Even liberal law professors have recently begun to concede—with embarrassment—that the Second Amendment actually does guarantee the people's right to own guns.[166] Rep. Major Owens of New York responded to the growing recognition of the Bill of Rights' true meaning by

proposing a bill in 1993 to repeal the Second Amendment.[167] In 1992, Sen. John H. Chafee proposed a bill to require government confiscation of almost all of the over sixty million privately owned handguns in the nation.[168]

Bans on gun ownership are never total prohibitions; instead, they represent political judgments on who will be permitted to legally own or carry a gun. In 1982 Chicago banned any resident from acquiring a handgun and prohibited almost everyone in the city from carrying a handgun—but city aldermen are exempted from the restriction. At a 1991 meeting in South Side Chicago to discuss political redistricting, Chicago alderman Dorothy Tillman got into a fist fight with residents who criticized her, reached into her purse, whipped out a revolver, and began waving it in the air.[169] Not only can Chicago politicians ban private citizens from owning a gun, but they can whip out their own weapon in a heated political discussion to intimidate their critics.

Five Chicago area municipalities banned all handguns. State representative Grace Mary Stern of Highland Park proudly declared, "The northern suburbs are ready to put handguns where they belong—in policemen's holsters."[170] Unfortunately, the criminals in nearby Chicago who often visit the suburbs do not share the same moral ideals. The local government of Oak Park, Illinois, prosecuted Donald Bennett in 1986 after he shot back at two people who robbed his gas station late at night. Oak Park Village president Clifford Osborn pompously declared that instead of depending on guns, Bennett should rely on burglar alarms or guard dogs.[171]

Maryland governor Donald Schaefer campaigned vigorously in 1988 in favor of a referendum to ban the sale of certain handguns. On the eve of the election, police officers forcibly entered a progun owners' rights organization and, despite the lack of a warrant, conducted a vigorous search, disrupted the organization's telephone bank and the get-out-the-vote effort, and shoved workers around.[172] The *Baltimore Sun* editorialized on the pre-election raid: "The police knock on the door in the dark of night, followed by rummaging through personal effects of any sort—but particularly those related to a political matter—is the hallmark of totalitarian societies. . . . Police with political assignments are more dangerous than Saturday Night specials."[173] The day after the referendum passed by a narrow margin, Schaefer publicly admitted that he himself carried a revolver—even though he had twenty-four-hour police protection.[174] If Schaefer had admitted carrying heat before the vote, Maryland voters likely would have denied the state government additional power to ban guns. (Handgun Control, Inc., an antigun group, still gave Schaefer an award a few years later; apparently as long as the Maryland governor was in favor of restricting other people's right to own guns, it was okay that he carried one.)[175] On March 15, 1993, Schaefer called a press conference to urge support for a proposal to ban fifteen types of semiautomatic pistols. After a reporter smiled at one of the governor's foreboding comments, Schaefer pointed a nine-millimeter pistol at the reporter and declared: "Some

of you have never had it in your face. I bet you wouldn't be laughing. I bet you wouldn't be smiling. I don't know what would happen to your pants, but I can imagine."[176] Police routinely arrest people who point guns at people (even unloaded guns) on charges of criminal assault. The governor's press secretary, Page Boinest, later explained: "Because he did not mean it in a threatening way, I don't see that it was a problem, from his perspective."[177]

Twelve states now have waiting periods for gun purchases. While it is reasonable to have some type of instant background check of who buys a gun (as Virginia currently has) to keep guns out of the hands of felons and lunatics, laws requiring police approval for gun ownership have long been abused. As David Kopel, author of *The Samurai, the Mountie, and the Cowboy,* wrote:

> In St. Louis, gun ownership permits have routinely been denied to homosexuals, nonvoters, and wives who lack their husbands' permission . . . Although New Jersey law requires that the authorities act on gun license applications within 30 days, delays of 90 days are routine; some applications are delayed for years, for no valid reason. Licensing fees may be raised so high as to keep guns out of the hands of the poor. Until recently, Dade County, Florida, charged $500 for a license; nearby Monroe County charged $2,000. Or licensing may simply turn into prohibition. Mayor Richard Hatcher of Gary, Indiana, ordered his police department never to give anyone license application forms. The police department in New York City has refused to issue legally required licenses, even when commanded by courts to do so. The department has also refused to even hand out blank application forms.[178]

California requires a fifteen-day waiting period for purchasing guns. But there are no penalties for police who dally long past the fifteen-day waiting period to approve or disapprove an application.[179] Bonnie Elmasri, a Wisconsin woman, and her two children were murdered on March 6, 1991, by her estranged husband—a day after she had tried to buy a gun for self-defense, but was informed that Wisconsin had a forty-eight-hour waiting period.[180] As Stephen Halbrook notes, "In some cases, it has taken years of protracted litigation to require [police] to issue firearms permits to which citizens are entitled. In some states the courts have upheld police denials of firearms permits under the dogmas that handguns can never be effectively used by private citizens for self-defense. Physicians who carried narcotics in their bags in high crime areas at night were not entitled to permits because the New Jersey Supreme Court alleged, 'their possession of handguns in the streets would . . . furnish hardly any measure of self-protection.'"[181]

In recent years, several states and many cities have banned or severely restricted the ownership of "assault weapons" or "assault rifles"—a term that the Pentagon considers to mean a rifle that is capable of both automatic (machine-gun) fire and semiautomatic (one shot per trigger pull) fire, but that most of the media implicitly defines as "politically incorrect rifle."[182] Some of the bans define "assault weapon" as almost any semiautomatic rifle. As a study by Denver's Independence Institute noted, "American civilians have owned semiautomatics since the 1890s, and currently an estimated

twenty to thirty million own the firearms covered by the broader definitions of 'assault weapon.' Americans own approximately 3.3 million so-called 'assault weapons.'"[183] In 1989, Sen. Howard Metzenbaum proposed a bill that would have subjected law-abiding citizens to fifty years in prison for ownership of numerous types of semiautomatic rifles.[184]

New Jersey in 1990 banned ownership of so-called assault rifles. The ban was so extensive that even some models of BB guns were outlawed.[185] Owners of the restricted guns were required to surrender them to the police, sell them to a licensed dealer, or render the guns inoperable.[186] The ban was justified as a crime-fighting measure, but between 1984 and 1988, shotguns and rifles were used for only 30 murders in New Jersey, while blunt objects such as baseball bats were used in 197 murders.[187] Ira Marlowe of the Coalition for New Jersey Sportsmen reported that "there was not one murder . . . with a semiautomatic assault weapon" in New Jersey in 1989, the year before the ban took effect.[188] Joseph Constance, deputy chief of the Trenton, New Jersey, Police Department, told the Senate Judiciary Committee in August 1993: "Since police started keeping statistics, we now know that assault weapons were used in an underwhelming .026 of 1 percent of crimes in New Jersey. This means that my officers are more likely to confront an escaped tiger from the local zoo than to confront an assault rifle in the hands of a drug-crazed killer on the streets."[189] Constance denounced the gun ban: "At best, the State's assault weapons ban is a fig leaf behind which frightened politicians hide their impotence in the face of rising crime."[190] New Jersey had an estimated 300,000 owners of so-called assault weapons, each potentially facing up to five years in prison for violating the state law.[191] Under the new law, the New Jersey attorney general can add almost any rifle he chooses to the list of banned guns.

California in 1989 banned the sale of assault weapons and required all existing owners to register their guns. The California law was extremely poorly drafted; California attorney general Dan Lungren later admitted that some of the gun models specifically banned by the California legislature did not exist. San Francisco lawyer Don Kates, Jr., suggested that legislators, in compiling the list of prohibited guns, appeared to have selected from "some picture book . . . of mislabeled firearms they thought looked evil."[192] The *Los Angeles Times* noted, "Asked what action a police officer should take in dealing with an apparently illegal but misidentified gun, Lungren's press secretary, Dave Puglia, said local authorities 'are going to have to use their discretion.'"[193] Thus, since the state legislature made a mess of the statute, local officials should have the arbitrary power to pick and choose which guns to ban and which gun owners to arrest and imprison. According to Michael McNulty, chairman of the California Organization for Public Safety, "Hundreds of citizens have been arrested and prosecuted for firearms not on the regulated list."[194] The vast majority of Californians did not register their guns; thus, the law may have created as many as 300,000 new criminals in the state.

The assault weapon ban had been passed after politicians and prosecutors painted vivid pictures of the damage the weapons were wreaking on the streets. But Torrey Johnson of the California Bureau of Forensic Services concluded in a confidential report, "It is obvious to those of us in the state crime lab system that the presumption that the [assault weapons] constitute a major threat in California is absolutely wrong."[195]

In 1967, New York City mayor John Lindsay led a campaign to require citizens to register all rifles with the city government. Many gun owners fiercely opposed Lindsay's proposal, warning that registration would be a prelude to a general confiscation of weapons (as happened in Nazi Germany prior to the Holocaust). The city council passed a law requiring roughly one million owners of rifles and shotguns to register with the police and seek to obtain a license to retain ownership of their guns.[196] The *New York Times* editorialized on September 26, 1967: "No sportsman should object to a city law that makes it mandatory to obtain a license from the Police Department and to register rifles. . . . In contrast . . . [c]arefully drawn local legislation would protect the constitutional rights of owners and buyers. The purpose of registration would be not to prohibit but to control dangerous weapons."[197] But in 1992, New York banned the ownership of almost all semiautomatic and many other rifles.[198] New York mayor David Dinkins demagogued the issue: "There is no legitimate role for these weapons of war in our society. Nobody hunts ducks and deer with machine guns."[199] Yet the legal ownership of machine guns has been severely restricted nationwide since 1934, and there is no overlap between the weapons listed in the New York City ban and federally restricted machine guns. The ban was largely due to the police commissioner's claim that policemen were in grave danger because of assault rifles; yet, no policemen had been killed by a so-called assault rifle in New York in the previous ten years.[200] The New York ban included semiautomatic rifles with bayonets—even though it makes little sense to ban bayonets without also banning all knives. (Perhaps the city council feared that crazed gun owners might launch a bayonet charge on city hall.) Police used the registration lists to crack down on gun owners; police sent out threatening letters, and then policemen in many cases went door-to-door demanding that people surrender their guns. Stephen Halbrook, a lawyer and author of two books on gun control, notes that the New York ban "prohibits so many guns that they don't even know how many are prohibited" and that the law is so vague that the city police "arbitrarily apply it to almost any gun owner."[201]

The bans on assault weapons are products of political hysteria rather than a public safety campaign. A 1990 Florida state commission estimated that "only one-tenth of one percent of the guns used in crimes were so-called 'assault weapons.'"[202] The FBI Uniform Crime Reports indicated that rifles of all kinds account for only 4 percent of the nation's homicides.[203] A 1990 FBI report noted that despite media concern over Uzis and AK-47s, no law enforcement officers had been killed by those weapons in the previous ten years.[204] Furthermore, government prohibitions will not cut off the gun supply. David Kopel observed, "A competent backyard mechanic can build even a fully automatic rifle. Indeed Afghan peasants, using tools considerably inferior to those in the Sears catalogue, have built fully automatic rifles capable of firing the Soviet AK-47 cartridge. Illegal home production of handguns is already common; a BATF study found that one-fifth of the guns seized by the police in Washington, DC were homemade."[205] Teachers in a school shop class in Detroit manufactured machine guns and illegally sold them for $500.[206] In the summer of 1993, California was afflicted by an epidemic of homemade potato guns—long plastic pipes and apparatuses fueled by lighter fluid—that could shoot potatoes at speeds of up to 1,000 feet per second.[207] (Some people feared that the proliferation of the new type of "guns" might result in government licensing of potato sales, or restrictions on how many potatoes a person could buy.)

Many states have enacted mandatory jail sentences for simple possession of guns. As Don Kates, Jr., notes, "A first-offense mugger generally will receive less actual jail time than New York makes 'mandatory' for the subway rider who carries a gun—unless the rider has a gun permit." But in New York City and many other places, it is almost impossible for the average citizen to get the necessary permit. In Brooklyn, a transit toll collector was jailed for shooting one member of a gang of hoodlums who attacked him and tried to rob him. In Massachusetts, a man was sentenced to a year in prison for shooting a coworker who was busy knifing him—for the second time—even though the Massachusetts Supreme Court admitted that "it is possible that the defendant is alive today only because he carried the gun that day for protection."[208]

The federal government has long acted as if the Constitution does not apply when government seizes people's guns. In 1983, Rep. John Dingell, liberal chairman of the House Energy and Commerce Committee, called the federal Bureau of Alcohol, Tobacco and Firearms "a jack-booted group of fascists who are perhaps as large a danger to American society as I could pick today."[209] The Senate Subcommittee on the Constitution investigated the BATF and concluded, "Enforcement tactics made possible by current firearms laws are constitutionally, legally, and practically reprehensible. . . . Approximately 75% of BATF gun prosecutions were aimed at ordinary citizens who had neither criminal intent nor knowledge, but were enticed by agents into unknowing technical violations."[210] John Lewis of the Second Amendment Foundation noted in 1980 that the BATF routinely refuses to return seized weapons: "Not only does BATF seize weapons without making any arrest; it also continues to withhold collections even after acquittal of the defendant. As a tax agency, BATF argues, it is entitled to retain seized weapons (and the vehicles from which they were confiscated, if applicable) to compensate the government for lost revenue."[211] David Kopel notes, "BATF's zeal to inflate its seizure count turns its agents into Keystone Kops.

One year in Iowa, the BATF hauled away an unregistered cannon from a public war memorial; in California it pried inoperable machine guns out of a museum's display."[212]

The Los Angeles riots in 1992 illustrated why people cannot rely on police to protect their lives or their livelihoods. When mobs began looting, burning, and savagely assaulting defenseless individuals, the Los Angeles police turned tail and ran, leaving hundreds of business owners to see their life savings plundered. When asked on the first day of the riots about the lack of police protection for people being beaten by mobs, Los Angeles police chief Daryl Gates replied, "There are going to be situations where people are going to go without assistance. That's just the facts of life. There are not enough of us to be everywhere."[213] Gates later admitted that "a little panic and paralysis settled in" among police officers.[214] (Armand Arabian, a California Supreme Court justice, noted that if the Los Angeles Police Department had responded any slower to the riots, "we would have seen photos of policemen pasted on milk containers and listed as missing.")[215] While the police effectively ran away from the violent rioters, they did return later to seize the guns and handcuff some of the Korean store owners who fought to defend their property. The city government even banned law-abiding citizens from buying bullets or picking up previously purchased weapons after the riots began.[216]

Guns are far more effective defensive weapons than many politicians admit. Florida State University criminologist Gary Kleck reported "that in 83% of cases in which a victim has a handgun, the criminal surrenders or flees."[217] According to Kleck, citizens successfully defend themselves with guns more than 700,000 times each year.[218] The National Center for Policy Analysis (NCPA), a Dallas think tank, reported, "Each year, gun-wielding citizens kill an estimated 2000 to 3000 criminals in self-defense, three times the number killed by police."[219] Nor are private citizens less accurate with their defensive fire; in fact, police are more than five times as likely to shoot innocent people in a conflict situation than are private gun owners.[220] The NCPA further noted: "At a maximum, criminals take a gun away from armed victims only 1% of the time, while 10% of police who are shot are shot with their own guns."[221] In New York City, almost half of the thirty-nine police officers wounded in 1991 were shot by other cops or with their own guns; in the first five months of 1992, ten of fourteen New York police shot were hit by "friendly fire."[222]

Gun control has become a moral and emotional substitute for the vigorous prosection of violent criminals. Massachusetts governor Michael Dukakis, the Democratic party's 1988 presidential nominee, declared on June 16, 1986: "I do not believe in people owning guns, only police and military. I am going to do everything I can to disarm this state."[223] Yet Dukakis was renowned for his lenient policy toward criminals, such as the weekend furlough program for convicted murderers. Similarly, Washington, D.C., mayor Marion Barry in 1985 proposed abolishing jail sentences for burglars; his government issued a report that announced to an incredulous local populace that "there is nothing inherently dangerous or violent about the offense (of burglary). . . . It is a property offense."[224] (At the time Barry endorsed the report, he was living in a house that enjoyed special round-the-clock police protection.) U.S. attorney Joseph diGenova denounced Barry's proposal, stating that "three-fifths of rapes in the home, three-fifths of home robberies and one-third of aggravated and simple assaults are committed by burglars."[225] But Barry apparently believed in giving burglars every benefit of the doubt, unlike gun owners. (Washington, D.C., effectively banned private ownership of handguns in 1976.)

Some politicians claim an unlimited right to seize private weapons of self-defense yet accept no concrete obligation to provide safe neighborhoods. A 1984 national survey found that 94 percent of respondents believed that police did not respond quickly enough to their phone calls for help. (One hundred percent of blacks and Hispanic respondents stated that police should have responded faster.)[226] As Stephen Halbrook testified in 1991, "Public officials have been held not liable for negligent failure to issue firearms permits even where the person disarmed thereby is murdered. It is well established that 'official police personnel and the government employing them are not generally liable to victims of criminal acts for failure to provide adequate police protection.'"[227] A federal appeals court declared in 1982, "There is no constitutional right to be protected by the state against being murdered by criminals or madmen."[228] Some of the Jewish victims of the 1991 Crown Heights riot in New York City later sued New York mayor David Dinkins for the city's failure to defend them; in its official reply, the Dinkins administration asserted that "the plaintiffs simply had no constitutional or Federal right to have the police respond to their calls for assistance or to receive police protection against potential harm caused by private parties."[229] Government has no obligation to defend the individual citizen, and, with gun bans, the individual has no right to defend himself.

The more successful gun control is in disarming citizens, the more dependent people become on government officials for protection. But crippling citizens' right to defend themselves has far more impact on poor people than on rich people, since low-income inner-city neighborhoods have far higher crime rates. In inner-city Miami, crime is so rampant that police are often afraid to respond to calls for help. As David Kopel notes, "In Brooklyn, New York, 911 callers have allegedly been asked if they are black or white."[230] Almost five million Americans were violently attacked last year, victims of murder, rape, robbery, or a life-threatening assault.[231] Even Chief Justice William Rehnquist publicly complained: "We are rapidly approaching the state of savagery. . . . In the Nation's Capital, law enforcement authorities cannot protect the lives of employees of this very Court who live four blocks from the building in which we sit."[232]

Gun bans don't ban guns; rather, they only ban citizens from legally defending themselves with guns. There are already an estimated 200 million guns in private hands in the United States. The more difficult government makes it for law-abiding citizens to get guns, the more power criminals who do have guns will have. Gun bans destroy the possibility of a balance of firepower between law-abiding citizens and violent criminals. The question is not whether America would be a better country if fewer people owned guns but whether government seizures of some private guns will make people more safe. Given the fact that the government can neither successfully ban guns nor defend American citizens, does the government have the moral right to attempt to selectively seize guns from law-abiding citizens?

Gun bans are an attempt to confiscate the right of self-defense. Politicians perennially react to the police's total failure to control crime by trying to disarm law-abiding citizens. In a nutshell, gun bans mean that because criminals abuse guns, law-abiding citizens have no right to defend themselves.

Gun bans in response to high crime rates mean closing the barn door after the horse has escaped. The higher the crime rate, the less right the government has to restrict or impede people's ability to defend themselves. According to gun ban advocates, government has a specific, concrete obligation to disarm each citizen, but only an abstract obligation to defend the citizen.

The creeping political repeal of the right to self-defense is a huge decrease in the modern American's liberty because the government has completely failed to fill the void. The government has stripped millions of people of their right to own weapons—yet generally left them free to be robbed, raped, and murdered. Gun bans are one of the best cases of laws that corner private citizens—forcing them either to put themselves into danger or to be a lawbreaker.

Ruby Ridge: Murder in the Name of Gun Control?

Randy Weaver lived with his wife and four children in an isolated cabin and twenty acres on Ruby Ridge in the Idaho mountains forty miles south of the Canadian border. Weaver was a white separatist—he did not favor violence against blacks or any other race, but merely believed that the races should live separately. Because of his odd beliefs, Weaver was targeted for a government undercover sting. In 1989, a BATF undercover agent approached Weaver and sought to get him to sell the agent sawed-off shotguns. Weaver refused, but the agent was persistent and even showed Weaver exactly where to saw off a shotgun barrel. Weaver eventually relented to the undercover agent's pressure and sold him two sawed-off shotguns for $300. Because the guns' barrels were a quarter-inch less than sixteen inches, Weaver was guilty of violating federal firearms laws. As Alan Bock noted in an article for *Reason* magazine, "In December 1990, Randy Weaver was indicted for manufacturing, possessing, and selling illegal firearms. . . . The trial was originally set for February 19, 1991, then changed to February 20 for the convenience of the BATF. But Probation Officer Karl Richins sent Weaver a letter, dated February 7, instructing him to appear on March 20. Although Assistant U.S. Attorney Ron Howen, who later acted as a prosecutor, knew Weaver had been sent an erroneous notification, he appeared before the grand jury on March 14 (six days before the date Richins gave Weaver) and got an indictment for failure to appear on February 20."[233] The judge granted a warrant for Weaver's arrest, and a bizarre federal crusade against one isolated mountain man and his family shifted into full gear.

Federal agents launched an elaborate eighteen-month surveillance of Weaver's cabin and land. David Nevin, a lawyer involved in the subsequent court case, noted later in a *Washington Post* article: "The marshals called in military aerial reconnaissance and had photos studied by the Defense Mapping Agency. . . . They had psychological profiles performed and installed $130,000 worth of solar-powered long-range spy cameras. They intercepted the Weavers' mail. They even knew the menstrual cycle of Weaver's teenage daughter, and planned an arrest scenario around it."[234] Two covert video cameras were installed to record the family's activities and any visitors to their cabin.

On August 21, 1992, six U.S. marshals trespassed onto Weaver's property, outfitted in full camouflage and ski masks and carrying machine guns. Three agents circled close to the cabin and threw rocks at the cabin in order to get the attention of Weaver's dogs. As Weaver's fourteen-year-old son, Sammy, and Kevin Harris, a twenty-five-year-old family friend who was living in the cabin, ran to see what the dogs were barking at, U.S. marshals shot and killed one of the dogs. Sammy Weaver shouted, "You son of a bitch—you killed my dog!" and fired in the direction from where the shots had come.[235] Randy Weaver came out from his cabin and hollered for his son to come back to the cabin. Sammy yelled, "I'm coming, Dad," and was running back to the cabin when a federal marshal shot him in the back and killed him. Kevin Harris responded to Sammy's shooting by fatally shooting a federal marshal. Federal agents testified in court that the U.S. marshal had been killed by the first shot of the exchange, but evidence later showed that the marshal had fired seven shots from his gun during the exchange before he was shot.

The death of the U.S. marshal sent the U.S. government into a frenzy. The commander of the FBI's Hostage Rescue Team was called in from Washington, D.C., and ordered federal agents to "shoot to kill" any armed adult outside the Weaver cabin, regardless of whether that person was doing anything to threaten or menace federal agents. (Thanks to the surveillance, the FBI knew that members of the Weaver family always carried guns when outside their cabin.) With the massive firepower that the federal agents had in the area surrounding the cabin—the automatic weapons, the deadly accurate sniper rifles, the night vision scopes—this was practically an order to assassinate. Four hundred government agents quickly swarmed in the mountains around the cabin.

The next day, August 22, Randy Weaver walked from his cabin to the little shack where his son's body lay to say one last good-bye to his boy. As Weaver was lifting the latch on the shack's door, he was shot from behind by a federal sniper. As he struggled back to the cabin, his wife, Vicki, stood in the doorway, holding a ten-month-old baby in her arms and calling for her husband to hurry. An FBI sniper took the opportunity to shoot Vicki Weaver in the face, killing her instantly. (The FBI is very proud of its talented sharpshooters; the agent who killed Weaver's wife testified in court that he could hit within a quarter-inch of a target at a distance of 200 yards.) As Bock noted, "Bo Gritz, the former Green Beret commander who eventually negotiated Randy Weaver's surrender, said that after he became a negotiator the FBI showed him a psychological profile of the family prepared for the Marshals Service before the siege that described Vicki as the 'dominant member' of the family. 'Vicki was the maternal head of the family,' Gritz told the *Spokane Spokesman-Review*. 'I believe Vicki was shot purposely by the sniper as a priority target. . . . The profile said, if you get a chance, take Vicki Weaver out.'"[236] Weaver and others inside the cabin did not fire a single shot at the federal agents that day or in the following days.[237]

Federal agents used loudspeakers to bombard the cabin in the following days. Though federal agents would later claim that the killing of Weaver's wife had been a regrettable accident, the FBI capitalized on her death to try to psychologically torture the survivors during the siege. As Jerry Seper noted in the *Washington Times*, "Court records show that while the woman's body lay in the cabin for eight days, the FBI used the microphones to taunt the family. 'Good morning Mrs. Weaver. We had pancakes for breakfast. What did you have?' asked the agents in at least one exchange. Weaver's daughter, Sara, 16, said the baby, Elisheba, often was crying for its mother's milk when the FBI's messages were heard."[238]

After eleven days, Weaver surrendered and was jailed and charged, along with Harris, for the murder of the U.S. marshal and other charges. At the trial, the government sought to prove that Weaver had conspired for nine years to have an armed confrontation with the government. But this argument collapsed after it became obvious that Weaver's confrontation with the government began only after being entrapped by an undercover federal agent and that the subsequent conflict was initiated by heavily armed federal agents who trespassed on his land and opened fire. The government tried to prove that Harris had fired first in the initial confrontation, but this claim was contradicted by other government witnesses. Nor was the government's case helped by revelations that the FBI fabricated evidence that it submitted to the court.[239]

Weaver's lawyer, Gerry Spence, did not call a single witness in Weaver's defense, instead relying on all the contradictions provided by the government's witnesses. A jury found Weaver and Harris not guilty—effectively deciding that the shooting of the marshal was an act of self-defense, though Weaver was found guilty for failing to appear at the 1991 trial and violating conditions of his release before that trial. Gerry Spence commented on the final verdict: "A jury today has said that you can't kill somebody just because you wear badges, and then cover up those homicides by prosecuting the innocent. What are we now going to do about the deaths of Vicki Weaver, a mother who was killed with a baby in her arms, and Sammy Weaver, a boy who was shot in the back? Somebody has to answer for those deaths."[240] Unfortunately, thus far, no one has had to answer for the killings by government agents.

Weaver was sentenced for the two charges he was convicted for in October 1993. Though Weaver could have been hit with a fifteen-year prison sentence, the judge infuriated prosecutors by sentencing him to only eighteen months and giving Weaver credit for the time he had already been jailed—thus allowing him to go free shortly after the sentencing. At the sentencing, federal judge Edward Lodge told Weaver: "You've suffered probably far beyond what the court could do. I think you're a good person."[241] Judge Lodge also issued a seven-page list detailing the Justice Department's delays, misconduct, and refusal to obey court orders.[242] Sen. Larry Craig of Idaho observed: "Frankly, I have never before seen the level of anger, fear and distrust being displayed today by Idahoans toward the federal government as a result of these events. The case is widely regarded as an example of powerful, corrupt government persecuting vulnerable citizens and trying to cover up its misdeeds."[243]

TURNING POLICEMEN INTO DICTATORS

The Founding Fathers were keenly aware of the oppressive nature of random government searches. In colonial days, King George issued "writs of assistance" that let British soldiers search settlers' belongings at random to find out who was evading import taxes by smuggling whiskey or tea.[244] These writs empowered "a civil officer [to] search any house, shop, warehouse, etc.; break open doors, chests, packages . . . and remove any prohibited or uncustomed goods or merchandise." James Otis, a lawyer arguing against the writs in a Boston court in 1761, denounced them as "the worst instrument of arbitrary power, the most destructive of English liberty, and the fundamental principles of law, that ever was found in an English law book" and declared the writs conferred "a power that places the liberty of every man in the hands of every petty officer."[245] In 1772, the Massachusetts Committee of Correspondence described the writs' effects: "Thus our houses and even our bedchambers are exposed to be ransacked . . . and plundered by wretches, whom no prudent man would venture to employ even as menial servants. . . . By this we are cut off from the domestic security which renders the lives of the most unhappy in some measure agreeable."[246] Colonial opposition to writs, according to John Adams, ignited the flame that led to American independence.[247]

The Fourth Amendment states, "The right of the people to be secure in their persons, houses, papers, and effects, against unreasonable searches and seizures, shall not be violated, and no Warrants shall issue, but upon probable cause, supported by Oath or affirmation, and particularly describing the place to be searched, and the persons or things to be seized." The purpose of the Fourth Amendment was to prevent government officials from having "dictatorial power over the streets"[248] and elsewhere—to restrain the arbitrary power of officials clothed with the coercive power of the State.

Limiting government officials' power to stop, search, and seize private citizens was long a guiding principle of American jurisprudence. The Supreme Court decreed in 1891, "No right is held more sacred, or is more carefully guarded, by the common law, than the right of every individual to the possession and control of his own person, free from all restraint or interference of others, unless by clear and unquestionable authority of law."[249] Federal judge Rudkin decreed in 1931: "Personal liberty, which is guaranteed to every citizen under our constitution and laws, consists of the right . . . to go where one pleases, and when, and to do that which may lead to one's business or pleasure, only so far restrained as the rights of others may make it necessary for the welfare of all other citizens."[250] Supreme Court Justice Robert Jackson wrote in 1949 that "uncontrolled search and seizure is one of the first and more effective weapons in the arsenal of every arbitrary government."[251] The Supreme Court declared in 1967, "Wherever a man may be, he is entitled to know that he will remain free from unreasonable searches and seizures."[252] Law professor Yale Kamisar observes that the Fourth Amendment "is the one procedural safeguard that . . . 'polices' the police."[253] But in recent years, the Supreme Court has emaciated the Fourth Amendment.

Policemen ask for permission to search a person because in most cases they have no right to conduct a search. A request by a policeman to search a car, home, or suitcase is effectively a request for an individual to voluntarily waive his constitutional rights to privacy. Whether a person voluntarily gave permission for a search thus becomes a key determinant in the constitutionality of a government official's action. Lawyers Nancy Hollander and Gary Nelson observed, "It is remarkable how many people who are carrying large quantities of drugs assist the police officers in finding them in their cars. According to the police, the defendants freely offer to unlock trunks, pull back hidden compartments and open suitcases. Oddly enough, the defendants usually deny that they were so cheerfully helpful. In speaking with large numbers of defendants of these cases, we have discovered that the officers frequently have their hands on their guns, frequently demand rather than ask for consent, and frequently make veiled threats about what will happen if consent is not given."[254] Myron Orfield, a Minnesota state representative and University of Minnesota law professor, conducted a confidential survey of Chicago judges, prosecutors, narcotics agents, and public defenders on Fourth Amendment issues.[255] One Chicago prosecuting attorney observed: "In fifty percent of small drug cases [police] don't accurately state what happens." Twenty-two percent of Chicago judges surveyed reported that they believed that police are lying in court more than half of the time they testify in relation to Fourth Amendment issues; 92 percent of the judges said they believed that police lie at least "some of the time." Thirty-eight percent of the Chicago judges said they believed that police superiors encourage policemen to lie in court.

To safeguard the American citizen's liberty from arbitrary search and seizure, the Fourth Amendment requires government officials to have a search warrant before carrying out a search, except in cases of exigent circumstances. As law professor Lyle Larson observed, "The use of a search warrant particularly describing the places that may be searched, coupled with the exigent circumstances exception, allows searching officials to seize anything and everything they have probable cause to seize, while at the same time protecting citizens against general searches."[256] But as police are now allowed to conduct far more searches without a warrant, one of the most important protections the citizen has against arbitrary police treatment has been nullified.

Guilty, Guilty Everywhere

Federal, state, and local police have invented various methods in recent years to exempt themselves from the Fourth Amendment. Drug courier profiles—"an informally compiled abstract of characteristics thought typical of persons carrying illicit drugs"[257]—have proven the "philosopher's stone" that allow police to stop and search anyone they please—or anyone who displeases them. Once the police create a drug profile, police claim "reasonable suspicion" to stop and demand information from people and to pressure or force a citizen to submit to a search. Drug courier profiles in many states include drivers who exceed the speed limit, even though a 1991 Federal Highway Administration survey found that over half of drivers on surveyed roads exceeded posted speed limits.[258] And for those cars that are not speeding, New Mexico state police invented a drug courier profile to justify stopping drivers who showed "scrupulous obedience to traffic laws."[259] The Georgia state police profile instructed state troopers to be wary of "cars carrying a box of tissues, which signals cocaine use, and cars carrying empty McDonald's cartons or pillows and blankets in the back seat, which may signal drug runners in a hurry."[260]

One Florida trial judge observed of the Florida police's courier profile: "When you boil the profile down to its essentials, it covers just about every rental automobile or private automobile with out of state license plates traveling north on the turnpike or I-95."[261] One University of New Hampshire policeman created his own drug courier profile—targeting and stopping cars with Grateful Dead bumper stickers.[262]

Numerous drug courier profiles have been devised for airplane passengers. Some profiles reveal that the first person off the plane is a likely drug suspect, other profiles insist that the last person off is the likely drug dealer, and some profiles assert that people who try to blend into the middle are the ones to suspect.[263] In federal court cases, drug courier profiles have justified government agents' accosting plane passengers who had nonstop flights—and those who changed planes; persons traveling alone—and persons traveling with a companion; people who appeared nervous—and people who appeared too calm.[264] Among the telltale characteristics in a widely used DEA courier profile are "the almost exclusive use of public transportation, particularly, taxicabs, in departing from the airport" and "immediately making a telephone call after deplaning."[265] People are also routinely stopped if they are flying to or from cities considered narcotics source cities by the DEA, including Detroit and Miami.[266] When the Founding Fathers created the Fourth Amendment, they were not thinking of "going to Detroit" as a "reasonable suspicion" to justify a policeman in accosting a private citizen. During a 1990 federal court trial, federal prosecutors went even further, conceding that a "source city" for drug traffic is "virtually any city with a major airport."[267]

In one federal court case, U.S. government prosecutors sought to justify a drug courier profile by claiming that "the combination of facts in this case will rarely, if ever, describe an innocent traveler."[268] One DEA spokesman declared that government agents "can spot a drug dealer the way a woman can spot a deal at the supermarket."[269] But at the Buffalo airport in 1989, federal agents detained 600 individuals as suspected drug couriers—and 590 were innocent.[270] Even though federal agencies have provided almost no statistical evidence on profiles' success rate, the Supreme Court has repeatedly endorsed their use.

Some police forces use legal technicalities to selectively stop and search cars. The Tinicum, Pennsylvania, police department from 1989 to 1992 routinely stopped blacks and Hispanics driving through or near the town on the pretext of a motor vehicle code provision that prohibits cars from having rabbit's feet, dice, or air fresheners hanging on the rearview mirror and even stopped cars for having tinted windows. They then searched the automobiles for drugs and contraband. In a six-month period, according to the *Philadelphia Inquirer,* 96 percent of the cars stopped by one Tinicum police officer were driven by blacks. The Delaware County, Pennsylvania, district attorney justified the racial targeting: "Everybody knows that the drug trade in Chester, Philadelphia and Wilmington is controlled by blacks. It's a truism."[271]

An individual's constitutional rights can also be nullified by the sniff of a dog.[272] Nowadays, when a canine graduates from a drug-sniffing training program, government officials act as if the dog has actually been awarded a Juris Doctor degree with the ability to instantly declare "probable cause" and justify a search. If a private dog owner announced that he automatically had a right to temporarily control whatever item his dog pawed or urinated on, he would be denounced as a megalomaniac. But this is effectively the right asserted by police whose dogs sniff at someone's property or person. No traveler has a right to avoid having his bags or his auto being sniffed by a government dog. An *Orlando Sentinel* 1992 exposé on search and seizure tactics of local police noted that if the police dog "barked or wagged his tail, deputies would have had 'probable cause' to believe that drugs or drug money were inside, and they could search without a driver's consent."[273] The Federal Fifth Circuit of Appeals declared in a 1990 ruling that police dogs can be "trained to alert . . . only when they detect" narcotics.[274] But drug dogs routinely get a significant number of false positive-alerts when sniffing the clothing of women having their menstrual periods. As a result, women's constitutional rights apparently vary according to the time of the month. As two lawyers quipped, "We might as well allow dogs to sit as jurors too."[275]

Working the Buses

Each year, thousands of people traveling Greyhound or other intercity buses are searched as they pass through locales with police itching to boost their arrest numbers. On August 27, 1985, Broward County, Florida, police searched a bus and arrested Terrence Bostick after they found cocaine in his traveling bag. Bostick denied that he had consented to a search.[276] In late 1989, the Florida Supreme Court, in a 4 to 3 vote, denounced and banned the practice of mass bus searches, declaring: "Roving patrols, random sweeps and arbitrary searches would go far to eliminate [drug courier] crime in this state. Nazi Germany, Soviet Russia and Communist Cuba have demonstrated all too tellingly the effectiveness of such methods. Yet we are not a state that subscribes to the notion that ends justify means."[277]

The state of Florida appealed the decision to the U.S. Supreme Court, where U.S. solicitor general Kenneth Starr argued, "Because law enforcement officers in this country must respect an individual's right to be left alone, the 'police state' images invoked by the Florida Supreme Court miss the mark."[278] Apparently, because the Fourth Amendment was written on a piece of paper in 1789, it magically became impossible that government officials in United States could ever subsequently use "police state" tactics. Solicitor General Starr argued that Bostick "was not confronted by the threatening presence of several officers speaking in commanding tones and blocking his exit or requiring him to move to an interview room. Instead, respondent was approached by two officers who spoke in conversational tones, who did not force him to move, and who stood in a manner that did not block his access to the aisle."[279] However, the U.S. government conceded in its brief that one of the officers partially blocked the aisle in front of Bostick, and the aisle was only about fourteen inches wide. The bus driver had closed the bus door and left the bus after the officers arrived, thereby making it appear that the bus was sealed off for the duration of the search. Starr further noted, "Moreover, it is clear that law enforcement officers may draw no inference justifying a search or seizure from a refusal to cooperate. That is, officers lacking legal justification to detain a person may not bootstrap noncompliance into justification for a detention, because in that event a citizen would in effect have no way of declining to participate in a 'consensual' encounter with the police." Yet, as the Justice Department must have known, that is exactly what some police forces are doing. Charles Sullivan, a DEA spokesman in Louisiana, observed, "I think 99 percent of people would be cooperative. As for people who are uncooperative, you cast all your suspicions toward them."[280] Thus, a citizen's refusal to allow himself to be searched creates grounds to get a search warrant—a Catch-22 that gives police officers the de facto right to search anyone. As the ACLU noted in their brief in this case, "In at least two reported cases officers testified that a refusal to cooperate 'might be [deemed] suspicious' and might cause police to notify authorities at the next stop of their suspicions."[281]

In 1991, the Supreme Court overturned the Florida decision. Justice Sandra D. O'Connor, writing for the majority, declared, "The state court erred . . . in focusing on whether Bostick was 'free to leave' rather than on the principle that those words were intended to capture. . . . [W]hen the person is seated on a bus and has no desire to leave, the degree to which a reasonable person would feel that he or she could leave is not an accurate measure of the coercive effect of the encounter. . . . So long as a reasonable person would feel free to disregard the police and go about his business, the encounter is consensual and no reasonable suspicion is required."[282] O'Connor wrote, "The mere fact that Bostick did not feel free to leave the bus does not mean that the police seized him," and asserted that Bostick's predicament—"his sense of confinement . . . was the natural result of his decision to take the bus; it says nothing about whether or not the police conduct at issue was coercive."[283] Supreme Court justices are not exactly experts on the disadvantages of traveling with the masses; the justices often rely on government-paid chauffeurs. One law professor quipped of Justice O'Connor: "The only bus she's ever been on was a tour bus at Disneyland."[284]

Justice Thurgood Marshall dissented: "Because the bus is only temporarily stationed at a point short of its destination, the passengers are in no position to leave as a means of evading the officers' questioning. . . . This burdens the experience of traveling by bus with a degree of governmental interference to which, until now, our society has been proudly unaccustomed. . . . The Fourth Amendment clearly condemns the suspicionless, dragnet-style sweep of intrastate or interstate buses."[285]

The Supreme Court's decision sent a green light to police to sharply increase their dragnet searches on buses. Orange County, California, began using police dogs to stop and check the belongings of children on school buses. Children as young as eleven years old were ordered off buses and forced to leave all their possessions behind for sniffing by police dogs.[286] Police Chief John Robertson explained, "In all the bus searches, a school administrator was present, and the search was conducted by a juvenile investigator who talked to the kids, explained what was going on, and made it an educational experience."[287] The bus searches turned up no drugs.

Search and Destroy Missions

A search of a home is often not a question of some gentlemanly government officials walking through the rooms of one's domicile to see if there are any elephants on the premises. Instead, a search can mean rapacious agents wantonly destroying property and leaving a family's life in shambles. Few burglars ransack a home the way that some police officials do when exercising a search warrant. For some policemen, permission to search is taken as de facto permission to destroy, especially since the average citizen has little hope of successfully suing the police for compensation for property damage. Describing a search of Harry Davis's apartment in Fort Washington, Maryland, the *Washington Post* noted:

> Fifteen police officers, carrying assault weapons and dressed in black garb that looked like some kind of ninja outfits, stormed in, knocked Davis to the floor and held him there with a shotgun to his head. Davis said: "They run through the house and pull my girlfriend out of bed with no clothes on, and then they spread her legs out like she was hiding up in her. I'm wearing pants and no shirt and she's naked, and they open the windows. It's winter. We're freezing. Then they proceed to destroy the place." During the raid on Davis's apartment, police tore out the walls and crushed family photographs in their frames.[288]

One raid on a St. Louis home was ended, as a 1992 federal appeals court decision laconically noted, after a detective of the St. Louis Police Department "in an effort to search the ceiling for drugs, accidentally stepped on the head of a baby while attempting to climb onto a couch."[289] If a private citizen stepped on the head of a baby, he could be jailed for assault or reckless endangerment. But there was no penalty imposed on the policeman.

In 1988, a Los Angeles Police Department captain apparently instructed police to use a search to "level" and make "uninhabitable" four apartment units in south-central Los Angeles that were suspected of harboring drug dealers.[290] The search ended with the seizure of less than six ounces of marijuana and less than an ounce of crack, but the Los Angles Police Department had to pay out $3 million in civil claims for damage. Policeman smashed dozens of holes in the wall, destroyed furniture and kitchen cabinets, and even threw a dining room table out the window. The *Los Angeles Times* noted that LAPD officer Todd Parrick "swung the red ax so wildly as he tore from room to room in the apartments . . . that his fellow LAPD officers believed he was going to hurt himself or the other policemen in his path."[291] A police Internal Affairs evaluation concluded, "Of 37 suspects detained, only seven were arrested. But dozens were injured, and the reports level allegations that police officers kicked, slapped and beat apartment residents while they were handcuffed outside. Charlotte Waters told investigators that an officer dropped a flashlight on her head, then nonchalantly uttered, 'Oops.'"[292] The policemen even smashed toilets in the apartments, although an Internal Affairs investigation noted that "it was not uncommon to break a toilet during a search warrant service."[293]

Several individuals and businessmen in Bridgeport, Connecticut, made formal complaints that the Bridgeport Tactical Narcotics Team routinely devastated homes or businesses they "searched." In a 1992 raid, a Jamaican grocer and restaurant owner was surprised as heavily armed plainclothes policemen smashed into his store and shouted, "Stick up, niggers! Don't move!" The *Hartford Courant* reported:

> The police tore open boxes of detergent and potato chips. They searched shelves and behind a stack of paper bags stored under the cash register. They dumped garbage onto the floor, digging through it for evidence.
>
> The officers kept asking Gordon, "Where'd you hide it?" Shawn Gordon saw an officer try to open the cash register. Gordon watched the officer take the money out. He didn't put it back, Gordon said. Within moments, officers ushered him out of the store. After searching for an hour, the police seized one item: David Gordon's registered gun. A judge later ordered them to return it.
>
> Officers swept off entire shelves of merchandise. Boxes of cigarettes were opened, and cigars were broken in half, Gordon said. Bags of beans, rice, flour and sugar were ripped and the contents spilled onto the floor. Pots filled with oxtail, rice, beans and curry were dumped. Even the Jamaican tourist posters on the walls were torn. Empty beer bottles and potato chips littered the floor.
>
> The men never identified themselves as police, the Gordons say. David Gordon learned they were police when they threw him into a cruiser, took him to headquarters and booked him. Charges against the Gordons—interfering with a search warrant and possession of a handgun without a permit—were dismissed.[294]

The Fourth Amendment also influences how police may conduct searches. As early as 1603, English courts recognized that law officers were obliged to knock and announce their purpose before entering a private citizen's home. Early American courts, such as the New York Supreme Court in 1813, adopted a similar requirement.[295] Justice Brennan declared in 1963, "The protection of individual freedom carried into the Fourth Amendment . . . undoubtedly included this firmly established requirement of announcement by police officers of purpose and authority before breaking into an individual's home. . . . Rigid restrictions upon unannounced entries are essential if the Fourth Amendment's prohibition against invasion of the security and privacy of the home is to have any meaning."[296] Brennan wrote for four dissenting judges, and his position, though often quoted by judges, has never been formally adopted by the Supreme Court.

Unfortunately, contemporary law enforcement practices have turned back the clock to an era prior to the landing of the *Mayflower*. Police now routinely use battering rams to conduct surprise raids. In Atlanta, in November 1991, local police battered down a suspected drug dealer's apartment door and shot and killed an eight-year-old boy (Xavier Bennett, Jr.) in the resulting cross fire.[297] An Atlanta police official showed a compassionate side after the shooting, telling a local newspaper that the detective who killed the boy is "going to have to live with that. In a way, you can call him a victim as well."[298] When the case against the suspected drug dealer went to trial, as the *Atlanta Constitution* noted, "Assistant District Attorney Fran Shoenthal told jurors they should disregard discussion of the youngster's death, noting that the child 'very unfortunately and tragically was killed during the cross-fire. [But] that is not the issue in this case.'"[299] In 1991 Garland, Texas, police dressed in black and wearing black ski masks burst into a trailer, waved guns in the air, and kicked down the bedroom door where Kenneth Baulch had been sleeping next to his seventeen-month-old son. A policeman claimed that Baulch posed a deadly threat because he held an ashtray in his left hand, which explained why he shot Baulch in the back and killed him.[300] (A police internal investigation found no wrongdoing by the officer.) In March 1992 a police SWAT team killed Robin Pratt, an Everett, Washington, mother in a no-knock raid carrying out an arrest warrant for her husband. (Her husband was later released after the allegations upon which the arrest warrant were based turned out to be false.) The *Seattle Times* summarized the police raid:

> Instead of using an apartment key given to them, SWAT members threw a 50-pound battering ram through a sliding-glass door that landed near the heads of Pratt's 6-year-old daughter and 5-year-old niece. As [policeman] Aston rounded the corner to the Pratts' bedroom, he encountered Robin Pratt. SWAT members were yelling, "Get down," and she started to crouch onto her knees. She looked up at Aston and said, "Please don't hurt my children." . . . Aston had his gun pointed at her and fired, shooting her in the neck. According to Muenster, she was alive another one to two minutes but could not speak because her throat had been destroyed by the bullet. She was handcuffed, lying face down.[301]

Citizens are prosecuted for defending themselves or their homes against plainclothes policemen conducting no-knock raids. In 1986 William Grass of Kentucky was sentenced to two years in prison for firing a bullet through a door and wounding a SWAT team officer who was forcibly entering his residence late at night without knocking in order to search his house.[302] A Boston narcotics agent was shot and killed by a citizen as he and other policemen tried to batter down Albert Lewin's door in a no-knock raid in 1989. The government sought to prosecute Lewin for murder but a judge threw the case out after a policemen admitted he lied in order to get the search warrant to conduct the raid.[303]

At 2:00 A.M. on January 25, 1993, police smashed down the door and rushed into the home of Manuel Ramirez of Stockton, California. Ramirez awoke, grabbed a pistol, and shot and killed one policeman by his bedroom door before other police killed him. The police were raiding the house based on a tip that drugs were on the premises, but they found no drugs.[304] Sacramento County sheriff's lieutenant Dan Lewis later sought to justify the raid's methods: "Our problem is that a lot of times you're dealing with drug dealers, and their thought process is not always right from the start. That's when things get real dangerous for us."[305]

In 1989 Titusville, Florida, policemen conducted a nighttime no-knock drug raid on the home of fifty-eight-year-old painter Charles DiGristine. The raid began as the police set off a concussion grenade and then smashed through DiGristine's front door. DiGristine's wife screamed; he hurried to his bedroom to get a pistol; a man dressed in dark clothing and a black mask crashed into his bedroom; gunfire was exchanged; and the policeman was fatally wounded. The local government prosecuted DiGristine for first-degree murder, but a jury acquitted him. (The police believed—based on bogus information from a single anonymous informant—that the DiGristine home was a center for heavily armed drug dealers; the only drug they found in the raid was a small amount of marijuana owned by DiGristine's sixteen-year-old son.)[306]

Police planning no-knock raids are often as incompetent and inaccurate as the Postal Service is in delivering letters. DEA agents used an ax to break down the door of an innocent Guthrie, Oklahoma, man in 1991 and then handcuffed and kicked the man in front of his wife and daughters before they realized they were at the wrong address; the agents left without apologizing.[307] The *San Diego Tribune* noted in 1992, "In July, an informant's bum tip led San Diego police to storm a Logan Heights home. The residents say their daughters were subjected to genital searches while a gun was held to the head of their 6 year old son. No drugs were found."[308]

On August 25, 1992, Customs Service officials and local police raided the San Diego home of businessman Donald Carlson, setting off a bomb in his backyard, smashing through his front door, and shooting him three times after he tried to defend himself with a gun. Police even shot Carlson in the back after he had given up his gun and was lying wounded on his bedroom floor. The Customs Service believed that there were four machine guns and a massive cache of illegal narcotics in Carlson's home. Carlson related in congressional testimony in 1993 that even after agents failed to find any drugs, "No one offered me medical assistance while I lay on the floor of my bedroom. . . . Eventually, paramedics arrived, and took me to the hospital. I was kept in custody under armed guard and shackled for several days at the hospital. During that time, I was aware of hospital personnel referring to me as a criminal, of police officers and agents coming into my room, and the like."[309] The raid was launched based on a tip from a paid informant named Ron, who later told the *Los Angeles Times* that he had never formally identified any specific house to be searched. (The DEA had previously dealt with Ron and considered him unreliable.[310]) Customs officials had the home under surveillance for many hours before they launched their raid; even though they got a search warrant based on their assertion that the house was a vacant drug storehouse, the raid was carried out even after it became obvious that Carlson was living a normal life there. The agents could easily have arrested Carlson when he arrived home at 10:00 P.M. but instead watched and waited to attack until after midnight, when Carlson was asleep, in order to maximize the surprise. Carlson observed that he and his lawyer "have been forced to conduct an expensive investigation of the underlying facts of this nightmare. The government has refused to share their knowledge of the events with us. We fear that this can cause loss of evidence or aid in a cover-up. In addition, my house was riddled with bullet holes. . . . Walls were destroyed, apparently as part of the government's investigation. . . . My medical bills exceed $350,000 and I will have lifetime medical expenses related to this horrible shooting. But to date, the government has made no offer whatsoever to compensate me for these damages. We had administrative claims on file with the federal government since the beginning of December [1992], and have received no response. . . . At this point I have given up ever expecting the federal government to apologize for their conduct."[311] Carlson surmised that his house was raided in part because federal agents hoped to seize it under asset forfeiture provisions: "That kind of financial incentive may well have played a real role in the conduct of federal agents in raiding my home and in ignoring every sign that day that they were in the wrong place."[312] A *San Diego Union-Tribune* analysis of the raid concluded that it occurred partly as a result of "heavy pressure from Customs managers—who stand to gain professionally by generating arrests and big caseloads—on street agents to produce headline-grabbing cases."[313]

Florida police came up with a profound rationale to justify no-knock raids. In the 1991 case of *State v. Bamber*, Florida prosecutors argued that the existence of flush toilets effectively repeals any Fourth Amendment requirement for the police to knock on people's doors before they set off bombs and smash in the door. As a Florida court described the case:

> The deputy executed the [search] warrant with the assistance of the Hillsborough County Sheriff's Emergency Response Team. The group of officers went to the Bambers' home at approximately 4:30 P.M. on Friday, August 18, 1989. They were dressed in police fatigues with orange vests. They set off a "diversionary bomb" and entered the home without knocking or announcing. Mr. and Mrs. Bamber, their son, and two repairmen were in the home at the time. One of the repairmen testified that an officer put a gun to his head and slammed him to the ground.[314]

Florida prosecutors argued that the no-knock raid was necessary because the suspect might flush drug contraband away. According to this argument, the more advanced a nation's plumbing becomes, the less protection individual rights should receive. The Florida court ruled:

> We are not convinced that the existence of normal plumbing in one's home dispenses with the need to knock and announce during the execution of a warrant to search for small quantities of cocaine. Plumbing is required in virtually any home that complies with applicable building codes.[315]

The victory for the sanctity of Florida homes was short-lived. In 1992, the Florida Fifth District Court of Appeals in September 1992 ruled that "the presence of normal plumbing inside a house to be searched for small quantities of cocaine will justify dispensing with the state's knock-and-announce rule." The court ruled, "Certainly if the officers viewed the destruction of evidence from outside, or heard the suspects planning or carrying out the destruction, the *Bamber* test might be met. That is of little comfort, of course, if the small quantities of contraband have been destroyed during this delay. The practical effect of *Bamber* will render the execution of search warrants where only a small amount of contraband is involved totally ineffective."[316] The Florida Supreme Court is expected to issue a decision in late 1993 or early 1994 resolving the conflict between the Florida courts.

Unfortunately, Florida is not alone in granting sweeping power to police to batter down doors without warning. As Charles Patrick Garcia noted in a 1993 *Columbia Law Review* article, "Seven states, favoring strong law enforcement, have chosen a 'blanket approach,' which holds that once police have probable cause to search a home for drugs, they are not required to follow the constitutional 'knock and announce' requirement."[317] And even in states where search warrants require a knock on the door before entering, police routinely disregard such a formality. In a 1991 corruption trial, a former Los Angeles policeman testified that the accused officers falsely reported that they complied with the "knock and announce" rule—when in reality they violated the rule in 97 percent of the search warrants they executed.[318] (The trial also revealed that Los Angeles police "planted" drugs on citizens and then arrested them.)

There will always be some cases where no-knock raids are justified, such as when a person inside a house is holding a hostage or when a person is a fleeing felon and is known to be armed. But the vast majority of no-knock raids are now being carried out as part of attempts to seize narcotics. The proliferation of no-knock raids is a redefinition of American liberty. So that politicians can go through the motions of controlling what substances Americans are allowed to consume, an American citizen no longer has the right not to have his front door smashed down and to be placed at gunpoint—one finger twitch from death. No-knock raids in response to alleged narcotics violations presume that government should have practically unlimited power to endanger some people's lives in order to control what other people ingest. The right to batter down the front door necessarily includes the right to kill any private citizen who tries to stop the police from forcibly entering his home.

Stripped for the Glory of the State

Strip searches have become far more common in recent years, especially in public schools. In a 1980 case, a federal appeals court "determined that high school officials in Highland, Ind., violated the rights of four students who were forced to completely undress in a search for drugs. That kind of strip search, the court said, 'was an invasion of constitutional rights of some magnitude. More than that, it is a violation of any known principle of human decency.'"[319] But in recent years, government officials have revolutionized the principles of human decency. At Independence High School in Kansas City, Missouri, school officials on September 20, 1989, strip-searched twenty students for drugs and suspended two students who refused to strip.[320] In late 1992, the Ben Franklin Junior High School in New Castle, Pennsylvania, carried out a strip search of six junior high school students suspected of possessing marijuana; no drugs were found.[321]

Schools' aggressive search policies appear to be especially victimizing certain teenage males. In Chicago's Sandburg High School, on March 8, 1991, two teachers decided that sixteen-year-old Brian Cornfield, who was wearing sweatpants, "appeared to be 'too well-endowed'"; federal judge John Nordberg noted gravely that a schoolteacher "observed for himself what appeared to be an unusually generous bulge in the crotch area of the plaintiff's pocketless sweatpants."[322] The student was taken to a locker room and forced to strip for inspection by school officials. No drugs were found. The student sued the school and two teachers for violation of his constitutional rights. Judge Nordberg declared that the search did not violate the boy's rights because teachers "did all they could to ensure that the plaintiff's privacy was not eroded" (except that they forced him to remove his clothes). Nordberg said the search was justified partly by the boy's allegedly suspicious behavior, citing a teacher's report that Cornfield "avoided direct eye contact with [two teachers]; he looked from side to side as he walked down the hall; he appeared nervous; and he was generally withdrawn and noncommunicative."[323] But this is practically the definition of being an adolescent. Nordberg concluded his decision: "School administrators must be given the latitude to combat the problem of drug use and sales among students—so long as they stay within the dictates of the Fourth Amendment."[324] If stripping an American citizen based on his anatomy is the judge's concept of a reasonable search, what would the judge consider to be an unreasonable search—having the police pull off the person's skin to check his blood vessels for evidence of dilation? Nordberg's decision is practically a grant of absolute power to school officials.

In a 1985 decision, the Supreme Court announced that there is a "special" relationship between school officials and students, thereby waiving some of the student's normal constitutional rights.[325] The court ruled that school administrators do not have to have "probable cause" that the student has broken the law before searching the student, his locker, or his other possessions. This decision has resulted in a proliferation of sweep searches in schools. In Tazewell County, Illinois, in 1990, police teams with dogs raided all eight county high schools. As columnist Nat Hentoff reported, students were held captive in their classrooms for up to two hours; "There had been no prior indications of any specific drug dealing or drug possession in the high schools. So, the officers and their excitable companions were engaged in a mass random search. . . . Tazewell County sheriff James Donahue explained that the invasions were 'to find out if there was a problem. You never know until you go in to take a look.'"[326]

The Exclusionary Rule

The Fourth Amendment often becomes a centerpiece in criminal trials because of the exclusionary rule. In 1914, the Supreme Court ruled that evidence seized by federal agents in violation of the Fourth Amendment must be excluded from use in court; the court extended the rule to state and local law enforcement in 1961. A 1979 study by the U.S. General Accounting Office concluded that the exclusionary rule has resulted in the suppression of evidence in only 1.3 percent of 2,804 cases examined.[327] A *Chicago Tribune* investigation concluded that "fewer than 1% of Chicago defendants accused of violent crimes have their cases thrown out because the evidence was illegally obtained. . . . [T]he exclusionary rule plays a significant role only in drug cases where violence is not involved. In 13% of such cases, evidence is excluded."[328]

Since it is effectively hopeless to rely on suits by wronged civilians to control police conduct (courts rarely vindicate such suits),[329] the only effective restraint that can be imposed is for policemen to know that if they violate people's constitutional rights, the unlawfully seized evidence will be thrown out of court. To repeal the exclusionary rule would effectively give policemen a blank check to violate other people's rights. Myron Orfield, who surveyed Chicago judges, prosecutors, and public defenders, notes, "When asked, 'Does the exclusionary rule deter unlawful police behavior?' all of the judges and public defenders and all but one prosecutor (40 of 41 respondents) answered 'yes.'"[330] As Orfield noted, in major criminal cases, the exclusionary rule is almost never a bar to a conviction.

Why the Police Never Trespass

In recent years the Supreme Court has exempted the vast majority of private land in the United States from the Fourth Amendment. On July 18, 1980, Kentucky state police, acting in response to an anonymous tip, ignored four NO TRESPASSING signs on the road entering Ray Oliver's two thousand-acre farm, ignored a locked gate, entered his field through a hole in a fence, hiked a mile onto Oliver's property—and found marijuana plants. Oliver's lawyer claimed that the government officials needed a search warrant to trespass on his land and that evidence acquired without a valid warrant could not be admitted in court. A federal district court suppressed the evidence gathered in violation of the Fourth Amendment, but a federal appeals court overturned the decision. Oliver appealed to the Supreme Court.

U.S. solicitor general Rex Lee, arguing the government's position on the case, declared:

> The posting of "No Trespassing" signs, as a practical matter, gives a landowner little assurance that outsiders will not enter his property . . . Nor does the existence of a fence surrounding an open field necessarily increase the expectation of privacy in that field. Fences around large areas of rural property are usually designed to mark a boundary or to keep animals in rather than to keep people out, and they pose little impediment to entry by a person. Like posting, the existence of such a fence does not give a landowner a reasonable assurance that outsiders will not enter onto his land. . . . Moreover, it is undisputed that the gate blocked only vehicular passage, and there was no physical impediment to entry by foot. . . . [A]n individual may lack a legitimate expectation of privacy in an area like a field, where private activities do not ordinarily take place, even if the field is private property.[331]

In other words, because Oliver's land was not surrounded by an impregnable twenty-foot concrete wall, government officials did not violate his expectation of privacy by trespassing. The solicitor general effectively argued that government agents have an unlimited right to trespass on private land in order to seek evidence of lawbreaking and that only the immediate area around a person's house and the house itself is exempt from government officials searching without a warrant. The fact that government agents could enter a person's property thereby somehow proved that they had a right to enter that property. Criminal trespass is a misdemeanor in most states, carrying fines of up to $500; yet the solicitor general effectively argued that government agents, unlike other Americans, should be exempted from any fines for trespassing on other people's property. A majority of the Supreme Court decreed that "open fields do not provide the setting for those intimate activities that the [Fourth] Amendment is intended to shelter from government interference or surveillance."[332] (The Founding Fathers apparently forgot to include a parenthesis in the original Fourth Amendment specifying that it applied only to "intimate activities.") And the court made it clear that it was not referring only to open fields, decreeing: "A thickly wooded area nonetheless may be an open field as that term is used in construing the Fourth Amendment."[333]

Justice Marshall dissented: "Many landowners like to take solitary walks on their property, confident that they will not be confronted in their rambles by strangers or policemen."[334] Law professor Stephen Saltzburg observed, "Under *Oliver*, law enforcement officials may break down fences without violating the Fourth Amendment."[335] Saltzburg concluded, "That people should receive more protection in a taxi than on land they own, care for, and seek to keep private for themselves is a proposition difficult to defend."[336]

Drunken Checkpoints

In 1925, the Supreme Court declared, "It would be intolerable and unreasonable if a prohibition agent were authorized to stop every automobile on the chance of finding liquor, and thus subject all persons lawfully using the highways to the inconvenience and indignity of such a search."[337] But as the twentieth century progressed, judges and prosecutors gained a more rarefied understanding of the Bill of Rights. In the early 1980s, police departments began setting up checkpoints to stop and search all cars traveling along a road to see if the driver was intoxicated. Law professor Nadine Strossen wrote that checkpoint "searches are intensely personal in nature, involving a police officer's close-range examination of the driver's face, breath, voice, clothing, hands, and movements."[338] The checkpoints were extremely controversial; in 1984 the Oklahoma Supreme Court banned the practice in that state, declaring that drunk-driving roadblocks "draw dangerously close to what may be referred to as a police state."[339] In 1988 the Michigan Court of Appeals, in a case involving driver Rick Sitz, also concluded that the practice was unconstitutional. The Michigan Department of State Police appealed the case to the Supreme Court. As Strossen observed, "The *Sitz* plaintiffs argued that mass, suspicionless searches and seizures at drunk driving roadblocks violate the Fourth Amendment because they are not based on any individualized suspicion."[340] But the Supreme Court disregarded the privacy concerns and approved the checkpoints. Justice Stevens dissented: "On the degree to which the sobriety checkpoint seizures advance the public interest . . . the Court's position is wholly indefensible. . . . The evidence in this case indicates that sobriety checkpoints result in the arrest of a fraction of one percent of the drivers who are stopped, but there is absolutely no evidence that this figure represents an increase over the number of arrests that would have been made by using the same law enforcement resources in conventional patrols."[341] He continued: "A Michigan officer who questions a motorist [seized] at a sobriety checkpoint has virtually unlimited discretion to [prolong the detention of] the driver on the basis of the slightest suspicion. . . . [T]he Court's decision . . . appears to give no weight to the citizen's interest in freedom from suspicionless unannounced investigatory seizures."[342]

In the *Sitz* decision, the Supreme Court assumed that since checkpoint searches were equally intrusive on all drivers, no individual had a right to complain about an intrusive search. But this stands the Bill of Rights on its head—reading the Fourth Amendment to require the government to equally violate the rights of all citizens, rather than restrict government violations of any citizen's rights.[343] Strossen noted, "It is ironic that Chief Justice Rehnquist essentially supports the view that searches and seizures become more constitutional as more people are subjected to them."[344]

Naturally, once the Supreme Court sanctioned drunk-driving checkpoints, police expanded their use. One California police chief set up a checkpoint purportedly for the purpose of checking licenses and vehicle registrations. But in reality, the roadblock was a pretext for drug searches, since drug-sniffing dogs would circle all the stopped cars. The local police chief admitted in court that he set up the license-and-registration roadblock because he knew he could not lawfully establish a roadblock that was only "looking for drugs."[345] (A judge squelched the chief's program.) Nebraska police in 1992 set up a checkpoint consisting of a sign announcing a narcotics checkpoint; police then watched to see which drivers passing the sign showed "furtive movements," thereby supposedly justifying the police to pursue, stop, and search the auto.[346] (A state court struck down the procedure as unconstitutional.) Police in New Braunfels, Texas, set up a checkpoint in late 1992, pulling over and searching for drugs every twentieth car heading north on Interstate 35. Lt. Sumner Bowen, commander of the Alamo Area Narcotics Task Force, told a reporter: "It's amazing what you'll find in every 20th car. Based on the success of this one, we will be doing others at random times at random places."[347]

Drunk-driving checkpoints respond to the incompetence of the police in controlling previously convicted drunken drivers by greatly increasing the police's power to harass everyone. Many localities have been criminally negligent in not revoking the licenses of habitual drunk drivers. Adam Gelb reported in the *Atlanta Journal and Constitution*, "Nationally, drunk drivers involved in fatal crashes are about five times more likely to be repeat offenders than first offenses."[348] The state of Georgia allowed chronic drunks to continue driving even after they had killed people while driving drunk. The forty-three worst drivers still on the road had each amassed at least fifteen drunk-driving convictions over the last twenty-five years.[349] The reliance on intrusive dragnet checkpoints is especially unjustified considering that there are new test methods that could far better test a potential drunk's reflex ability, such as computer game–like devices attached to car ignitions.

The Fourth Amendment was enacted in part to dictate what kind of government the United States would have—one where politicians were prevented from trying to absolutely control what everyone had in their pockets, in their homes, in their basements, and on their land. The Fourth Amendment was meant to be not only a leash on how government enforces laws—but also a principle as to what types of laws should be decreed. Modern legislators reason backward, thinking first of the behavior they want to control and then assuming that their goal gives them the right to use any means to achieve it. Thus, the Fourth Amendment is seen by some people as an impediment to good government, rather than as a standard by which to judge any government policy.

ENTRAPPING FOR FUN AND PROFIT

Entrapment is "the act of officers or agents of the government in inducing a person to commit a crime not contemplated by him, for the purpose of instituting a criminal prosecution against him."[350] In 1894, a person who illegally mailed contraceptive information successfully claimed entrapment after proving that the mailing was in response to a request for information from an undercover government agent.[351] Prohibition provided a golden opportunity for entrapment—until the Supreme Court in 1931 overturned the conviction of a man who had been befriended and repeatedly entreated by a federal agent to sell him moonshine. The Court ruled: "The act for which defendant was prosecuted was instigated by the prohibition agent . . . and that defendant had no previous disposition to commit it."[352] In a 1958 case of a person entrapped into selling narcotics, the Supreme Court announced: "Congress could not have intended that its statutes were to be enforced by tempting innocent people into violations."[353]

Up until the mid-1970s, defendants often successfully challenged entrapment schemes as a violation of due process. Professor Paul Marcus observed, "Some of the most strongly worded condemnations of police conduct are found in cases involving so-called 'take-back' sales. These cases involve clear evidence showing that one police agent provided illicit drugs to the defendant, who then illegally dispensed the drugs to a second agent." But in 1973, the Supreme Court, in an opinion written by William Rehnquist, gutted most defenses against government entrapment. Rehnquist's opinion focused almost solely on the "subjective disposition" of the entrapped person. If prosecutors could find any inkling of a defendant's disposition to the crime, then the person would be guilty, no matter how outrageous or manipulative the government agents' behavior. Rehnquist sneered that "the defense of entrapment is not intended to give the federal judiciary a 'chancellor's foot' veto over law enforcement practices of which it did not approve."[354] Justice William Brennan dissented, warning that the decision could empower law enforcement agents to "round up and jail all 'predisposed' individuals."[355] Thanks to the prevailing judicial sentiments, it is a federal crime to be unable to resist repeated government temptation or to resist deadly threats from undercover federal agents intent on making a case. A 1982 Senate report on undercover operations condemned government agents for "the use of threats by police to induce targets to commit criminal acts" and "the manipulation by police of a target's personal or vocational situation to increase the likelihood of the target's engaging in criminal conduct."[356]

Numerous schemes have been created to try to ensnare money launderers. In 1988, the Customs Service launched Operation Flying Kite. As Greg Rushford reported in *Legal Times,* federal agents relied on childishly forged documents to entrap a Chicago-based consul general for the Yugoslav government and the chairman of a Yugoslav bank in New York City.[357] Customs alleged that the Yugoslav counsel general was involved in a scheme to carry $500,000 out of the United States in suitcases without notifying the U.S. government. Customs set up and relied upon an informant who had been previously been indicted for forgery and theft and confined to a state hospital for paranoid personality disorders. Customs claimed that the Yugoslav official was guilty because it got hold of a suitcase with the money that it provided the informant, and the suitcase was supposedly sealed with a Yugoslav diplomatic seal. But it turned out that the so-called diplomatic seal was actually a forgery—a gold notary public seal that the informant bought in a Chicago stationery store. (The actual Yugoslav seal had Cyrillic lettering.) The State Department warned Customs that the seal was a blatant forgery, but Customs went ahead and prosecuted the Yugoslavs anyhow. The scam resulted in a major diplomatic row between the United States and Yugoslavia. The case was thrown out of court, and the judge reprimanded Customs for "egregious and shocking violations of due process."[358]

In Los Angeles, police officers have gone undercover to pose as high school students in order to implore other students to buy drugs for them, after which the students are arrested, expelled, and permanently denied federal college loans for their education. In one case, an attractive female undercover police officer had a long romance with a high school football player whom she constantly begged to buy drugs for her. As UPI reported, "Akili Calhoun, 17, Kennedy High School's football team's star defensive tackle, was in love for the first time. Because he cared so much, he overlooked Sharon's persistent interest in drugs. He even tried to get her to talk to a narcotics counselor he knew. Connie Calhoun, Akili's mother, told the newspaper that she had been concerned about her son's romance after finding sexually explicit letters written to her son by his new girlfriend."[359] When the football player finally bought drugs for the policewoman, she promptly arrested him. The American Civil Liberties Union complained, "When other adults try to get young people involved with drugs, we call it contributing to the delinquency of a minor. When the LAPD does it, we call it the school-buy program."[360] (Police decided not to prosecute Calhoun because of the undercover officer's questionable behavior.) The previous year, the ACLU sued the San Diego police to end similar undercover operations; the ACLU's Gregory Marshall commented,

"Anybody would be outraged if they learned that the co-worker at the next desk or the shortstop on the softball team turned out to be a secret police spy. Obviously, the schools, especially, are no place for secret police."[361] In late 1992 and 1993, New Jersey school systems were compelled by the state attorney general's office to sign agreements authorizing police undercover operations (called "School Zone Narcotics Enforcement Working Groups") in their schools despite the strong objections of some school officials.[362]

In Mount Clemens, Michigan, policemen dressed in street clothes, loitered in areas known for drug activity, and then arrested people who came up and asked to buy drugs; police also seized the cars, cash, and jewelry of those they arrested.[363] Entrapment efforts in Michigan suffered a setback when the Michigan Supreme Court ruled in 1992 that Michigan police have no statutory authority to "sell" controlled drugs to private citizens, thus invalidating many convictions achieved as the result of policemen masquerading as drug dealers.[364] In another 1992 Michigan case, a defendant alleged that undercover FBI agents lured his daughter out of a drug rehabilitation program, gave her cash to buy narcotics, and resulted in getting her re-addicted to drugs.[365] Federal drug officials have enticed individuals to accept government money and a government-supplied airplane to fly to Colombia to pick up cocaine; when the person returns, he is busted.[366]

Pudenda are increasingly being used to inflate arrest statistics. FBI agents recruited Helen Miller, a prostitute and heroin addict, to work as an undercover agent to avoid being imprisoned on drug abuse charges. Miller was supplied with heroin by FBI agents while on assignment and was permitted to keep a $10,000 profit from a heroin deal done with the FBI's knowledge.[367] Following orders, she initiated a sexual liaison with a suspected heroin dealer, eventually persuading him to sell heroin to undercover FBI agents. Federal judge Terry Hatter condemned the government's action: "Government cannot be permitted to stoop to these depths to investigate suspected criminal offenders." Hatter declared that the government must be "den[ied] the fruits of its heinous acts." Naturally, a higher panel of federal judges overturned Hatter's decision and convicted the dealer. The judges declared: "The deceptive creation and/or exploitation of an intimate relationship does not exceed the boundary of permissible law enforcement tactics."[368]

In Michigan, a man's wife and an undercover officer posing as her cousin hectored a man for two months to buy them cocaine; when the harried husband finally relented, he was busted for cocaine possession. A Michigan judge, reversing a lower court's conviction, threw the case out in 1991, ruling, "the [police] officer engaged in reprehensible behavior. Not only did the undercover officer initiate the crime, he exploited and manipulated a marital relationship and created a fictitious family relationship to carry out the crime."[369] In 1991, federal agents recruited a former lover of Washington, D.C., mayor Marion Barry to fly to Washington, lure the mayor to her hotel room, and successfully urge him to use crack cocaine.

involving five different government entities to ensnare a Nebraska farmer who had never been convicted or accused of any crime in his life (except for a drunk-driving conviction thirty years earlier). Kenneth Starr, the U.S. solicitor general, declared, "The government is not required to have a reasonable basis to believe a person is engaged in criminal activity before it may approach that person as part of an undercover investigation. . . . A reasonable suspicion requirement would severely hinder, if not altogether preclude, some commonly used undercover investigations premised on random contact with members of the general public. . . . Prohibiting such valuable law enforcement tools is far too high a price for society to pay for protections that are neither constitutionally nor congressionally mandated. That is particularly true in light of the fact that the entrapment defense is available to any person who believes that he was an innocent, law-abiding citizen whom the government caused to break the law."[388] This last touch is especially ironic as the government's brief effectively argues that entrapment is almost never a valid defense and urges the court to almost never recognize it. The Supreme Court rejected the government's argument, condemning government agents for going too far in their quest for convictions.[389]

The proliferation of entrapment schemes represents the triumph of an authoritarian concept of justice—as if government should be allowed anything it chooses in order to catch anyone who any government official thinks might be a criminal. As Gail Greaney wrote in 1992 in the *Notre Dame Law Review*, "The due process defense is basically a nullity. . . . With each case, it appears that the line of intolerable police conduct is being pushed further toward the outlandish."[390] Entrapment epitomizes the triumph of a "body count" approach to law enforcement. Entrapment schemes have proliferated partly because it is easier to manufacture crime than to protect private citizens. Entrapment schemes wreck individuals' lives in order to boost arrest statistics. Some politicians have sought to justify entrapment schemes as a necessary response to the crime wave of recent years. Thus, the worse the government fails to prevent crime, the more power government should have to violate people's constitutional rights—the worse police fail, the more power they must have.

WACO: HOW FEDERAL AGENTS SHOW "REMARKABLE RESTRAINT"

The trends of increased power and aggressiveness in law enforcement were exemplified in the 1993 Waco disaster. The Branch Davidians lived in a compound outside of Waco, Texas. The Davidians, led by David Koresh, helc beliefs and indulged in personal practices that are considered either fring like or immoral by most Americans, but were generally peaceful members society, and many members of the group held jobs outside of their compou Several of the Davidians were licensed gun dealers, and group members

In July 1992, a federal appeals court in California threw out an entrapment conviction achieved via death threats. Jennifer Skarie, a forty-one-year-old mother of three, let one of her ex-husband's relatives, John Byrd (nicknamed "Bear") move in on her ranch in Valley Center, California, in late 1988. The relative turned out to be an undercover government drug agent who frequently used methamphetamine in her house and endlessly pressured Skarie to put him in touch with people who would sell him drugs. As the federal appeals court decision noted, "After Bear moved in with Skarie, he began to make sexual advances towards her and towards the women living with her. Bear was a violent person who threatened people regularly and was usually armed, even in the house."[370] Skarie finally evicted Bear; the court noted, "Bear reacted violently to being thrown out, and made a variety of threats against Jennifer Skarie. In February 1989, Bear asked Skarie to put him in touch with some people who could sell him drugs. Skarie demurred. Bear continued to pressure her to introduce him to people she knew who sold drugs; he would call as often as ten times a day and would often come by Skarie's house uninvited. Bear also made a variety of threats to Skarie and other members of the household. He impaled one of her chickens on a stick and left it outside her back door; he later stated that what had happened to the chicken could happen to people as well. He told Skarie that it would be easy to slit the throats of her horses, and threatened to kidnap her six-year-old son 'so that you will never see him again.'"[371] Skarie finally relented and arranged for him to buy methamphetamine from a person she knew. As soon as the sale was completed, she was arrested for possession of narcotics with intent to distribute (because of the drugs in her acquaintance's car). After a vigorous federal prosecution, she was sentenced to ten years in prison without parole. The appeals court decision noted, "Skarie refused to participate for over two months in the face of repeated requests by the government, and relented only after the government's agent made a number of graphic and violent threats against her and her family. Skarie's testimony that she was induced in part by Bear's threats was not contested at trial."[372] The U.S. Justice Department apparently believes that putting a person in contact with another person to purchase an illegal substance is a worse crime than maiming animals and threatening to kill young children.

Prostitution entrapment schemes are a dime a dozen among the nation's police forces. Arlington, Virginia, police crossed the state line into Washington, D.C., picked up prostitutes, drove them back into Virginia, let them begin undressing, and then arrested them for offering sex for money.[373] In Albuquerque, New Mexico, police placed a classified ad in a local paper advertising for men to work as paid escorts and then arrested fifty men who answered the ad for violating laws against prostitution.[374] In Honolulu, police paid private citizens to pick up prostitutes in their cars, poke, pay, and then drive the prostitutes to nearby police cars for arrest. (One convicted prostitute's lawyer complained: "You can now serve your community by fornicating. . . . Once the word

In July 1992, a federal appeals court in California threw out an entrapment conviction achieved via death threats. Jennifer Skarie, a forty-one-year-old mother of three, let one of her ex-husband's relatives, John Byrd (nicknamed "Bear") move in on her ranch in Valley Center, California, in late 1988. The relative turned out to be an undercover government drug agent who frequently used methamphetamine in her house and endlessly pressured Skarie to put him in touch with people who would sell him drugs. As the federal appeals court decision noted, "After Bear moved in with Skarie, he began to make sexual advances towards her and towards the women living with her. Bear was a violent person who threatened people regularly and was usually armed, even in the house."[370] Skarie finally evicted Bear; the court noted, "Bear reacted violently to being thrown out, and made a variety of threats against Jennifer Skarie. In February 1989, Bear asked Skarie to put him in touch with some people who could sell him drugs. Skarie demurred. Bear continued to pressure her to introduce him to people she knew who sold drugs; he would call as often as ten times a day and would often come by Skarie's house uninvited. Bear also made a variety of threats to Skarie and other members of the household. He impaled one of her chickens on a stick and left it outside her back door; he later stated that what had happened to the chicken could happen to people as well. He told Skarie that it would be easy to slit the throats of her horses, and threatened to kidnap her six-year-old son 'so that you will never see him again.'"[371] Skarie finally relented and arranged for him to buy methamphetamine from a person she knew. As soon as the sale was completed, she was arrested for possession of narcotics with intent to distribute (because of the drugs in her acquaintance's car). After a vigorous federal prosecution, she was sentenced to ten years in prison without parole. The appeals court decision noted, "Skarie refused to participate for over two months in the face of repeated requests by the government, and relented only after the government's agent made a number of graphic and violent threats against her and her family. Skarie's testimony that she was induced in part by Bear's threats was not contested at trial."[372] The U.S. Justice Department apparently believes that putting a person in contact with another person to purchase an illegal substance is a worse crime than maiming animals and threatening to kill young children.

Prostitution entrapment schemes are a dime a dozen among the nation's police forces. Arlington, Virginia, police crossed the state line into Washington, D.C., picked up prostitutes, drove them back into Virginia, let them begin undressing, and then arrested them for offering sex for money.[373] In Albuquerque, New Mexico, police placed a classified ad in a local paper advertising for men to work as paid escorts and then arrested fifty men who answered the ad for violating laws against prostitution.[374] In Honolulu, police paid private citizens to pick up prostitutes in their cars, poke, pay, and then drive the prostitutes to nearby police cars for arrest. (One convicted prostitute's lawyer complained: "You can now serve your community by fornicating. . . . Once the word gets out there will be no shortage of volunteers.")[375] In San Francisco, the police planted hidden cameras in the city's leading hotels to make videotapes of prostitutes satisfying their customers.[376] But given the minimal control over the videotaping operation, there was little to stop local police from also observing normal married couples engaging in coitus solely for the purpose of procreation. In Houston, a thirty-eight-year-old salesman was sitting by himself in a hotel bar when an undercover policewoman wearing a red wig sat down at a nearby bar stool and struck up a conversation. The policewoman informed him that she was in the entertainment business, said she had a paid room in the hotel, announced that she took credit cards, and inquired about his sex fantasies. The *Houston Chronicle* noted that the businessman testified in court: "She wanted me to relate some of my fantasies to her. She asked again and again." He said he dodged her by saying he'd had a bad day. After the woman had hassled him for an hour, the businessman finally told her that he would meet her upstairs and pay $100. After the woman left by herself to go to the hotel room, the businessman ordered and drank another drink and was leaving the hotel when he was arrested by vice cops for allegedly agreeing to pay for sex. Houston judge Bill Ragan denounced the police department for entrapment and threw the case out of court.[377]

Police sting operations are routinely carried out even where there is no problem simply to boost arrest statistics. Glendale, California, police arrested two dozen men in one week for soliciting sex from provocatively clad undercover female officers on busy city streets. Glendale police sergeant Lief Nicolaisen told the *Los Angeles Times:* "We don't have a major streetwalking problem. But if you don't do these, you run the risk of prostitution getting out of control."[378] In Des Moines, Washington (a Seattle suburb), police hired a convicted rapist to have sex with masseuses. The local police explained that they hired the felon after plainclothes policemen could not persuade women at the local Body Care Center to have intercourse. Local police chief Martin Pratt claimed that the ex-rapist was uniquely qualified for the job and, when asked why the police instructed the felon to consummate the act with the alleged prostitutes, Pratt explained that stopping short "wouldn't have been appropriate."[379] Shortly after the Washington, D.C., police began their program in 1992 to seize the cars of would-be johns, one driver sped off after a plainclothes policeman tried to force his way into his car. A policeman's foot was slightly injured, and policemen fired six shots into the rear of the car.[380] The police volley could have killed several people—a high price for temporarily decreasing the rate of prostitution in one neighborhood.

Even the Interior Department's Fish and Wildlife Service is entrapping. In a 1986 Montana case, a federal judge ruled that it was permissible for an undercover federal agent to illegally kill protected wildlife as part of a scheme to entrap other individuals into violating federal wildlife laws.[381] On March 6, 1989, 275 heavily armed federal and state wildlife officers, supported by planes and helicopters, assaulted San Luis Valley, Colorado (the most impoverished region in the state, with an extremely high unemployment rate), in a predawn raid to arrest people who had sold game to an undercover federal agent. A Fish and Wildlife Service agent had set up a shop and advertised for people to sell him elk and deer hides and carcasses, antlers, eagles, and bears. In the two and a half years of the operation, the agent purchased at least 500 elk, 2,000 deer and 95 eagles. As the *Los Angeles Times* reported, "Many of those arrested . . . say they would not have violated the game laws if the government had not set up the market. Some said that [the FWS agent] openly encouraged them to kill game."[382] After the raid, the local sheriff received "about 30 complaints from people who said wildlife agents kicked in doors, dragged people outside in their underwear at gunpoint and improperly stopped and searched people," according to the Associated Press. United States attorney Mike Norton declared after the raid: "We will not tolerate the theft of the public's wildlife resources. We will use every available legal means to stop this activity."[383] But considering that the U.S. government owns up to 80 percent of the land in some western states, and considering the poverty of many Americans living in those areas, the U.S. government's massive persecution resembles English monarchs' vendettas against peasants for hunting in the king's forests.

The U.S. Postal Service is currently the nation's largest distributor of child pornography, thanks to its entrapment operations. As lawyer Lawrence A. Stanley notes, "Anyone looking for the child-porn underground will find only a vast network of postal inspectors and police agents."[384] In 1985, the Postal Inspection Service got the name of Keith Jacobson, a fifty-seven-year-old Nebraska farmer and veteran of the Korean and Vietnam wars, from a bookstore that had sold him a legal nudie magazine in early 1984. Over the next two and a half years, five different government-created entities sent Jacobson twelve different solicitations to buy pictures. A Postal Inspector "prohibited mail specialist," masquerading as a "pen pal," wrote a letter to the defendant describing his "male-male" interest.[385] Jacobson explicitly wrote to his government contact that he was opposed to pedophilia. One of the government-created companies, Far Eastern Trading Company, supposedly located in Hong Kong, required Jacobsen to affirm that he was "not an undercover law enforcement agent trying to entrap Far Eastern."[386] (Solicitations from Far Eastern sometimes included a brochure stating: "THERE ARE NO VISUAL DEPICTIONS OF ANY PERSON UNDER THE AGE OF EIGHTEEN (18).")[387] Eventually, Jacobson placed an order for one child-porn magazine; the Postal Service delivered it, and a few minutes later, the Postal Inspection Service swooped down to arrest Jacobson and search his house for other evidence of his deviancy. They found only the material that the government had sent him.

A major issue in the Supreme Court's review of the case was whether the federal government had a reasonable basis to launch the major effort involving five different government entities to ensnare a Nebraska farmer who had never been convicted or accused of any crime in his life (except for a drunk-driving conviction thirty years earlier). Kenneth Starr, the U.S. solicitor general, declared, "The government is not required to have a reasonable basis to believe a person is engaged in criminal activity before it may approach that person as part of an undercover investigation. . . . A reasonable suspicion requirement would severely hinder, if not altogether preclude, some commonly used undercover investigations premised on random contact with members of the general public. . . . Prohibiting such valuable law enforcement tools is far too high a price for society to pay for protections that are neither constitutionally nor congressionally mandated. That is particularly true in light of the fact that the entrapment defense is available to any person who believes that he was an innocent, law-abiding citizen whom the government caused to break the law."[388] This last touch is especially ironic as the government's brief effectively argues that entrapment is almost never a valid defense and urges the court to almost never recognize it. The Supreme Court rejected the government's argument, condemning government agents for going too far in their quest for convictions.[389]

The proliferation of entrapment schemes represents the triumph of an authoritarian concept of justice—as if government should be allowed anything it chooses in order to catch anyone who any government official thinks might be a criminal. As Gail Greaney wrote in 1992 in the *Notre Dame Law Review*, "The due process defense is basically a nullity. . . . With each case, it appears that the line of intolerable police conduct is being pushed further toward the outlandish."[390] Entrapment epitomizes the triumph of a "body count" approach to law enforcement. Entrapment schemes have proliferated partly because it is easier to manufacture crime than to protect private citizens. Entrapment schemes wreck individuals' lives in order to boost arrest statistics. Some politicians have sought to justify entrapment schemes as a necessary response to the crime wave of recent years. Thus, the worse the government fails to prevent crime, the more power government should have to violate people's constitutional rights—the worse police fail, the more power they must have.

WACO: HOW FEDERAL AGENTS SHOW "REMARKABLE RESTRAINT"

The trends of increased power and aggressiveness in law enforcement were exemplified in the 1993 Waco disaster. The Branch Davidians lived in a compound outside of Waco, Texas. The Davidians, led by David Koresh, held beliefs and indulged in personal practices that are considered either fringe-like or immoral by most Americans, but were generally peaceful members of society, and many members of the group held jobs outside of their compound. Several of the Davidians were licensed gun dealers, and group members had

have invoked the fact that a small minority of Americans use illegal drugs to greatly increase their power over all Americans—to stop and search their cars, to accost them in airports and in train stations, and to force them to urinate on command. The future for self-government bodes ill when the government claims vast power over citizens in order to force them to live as government officials think they should.

-8-

Taxing and Tyrannizing

The Internal Revenue Service is the authoritarian means to paternalist ends. A government that is anxious to give alms to as many people as possible is even more anxious to commandeer their earnings. Increasingly, the average American's guilt or innocence is left to the eye of the tax auditor, not to the citizen's actual behavior. Federal tax policy is now largely oppression in the name of revenue maximization.

The U.S. Treasury Department defines a tax as "a compulsory payment for which no specific benefit is received in return."[1] No matter how many taxes a person pays, or what politicians promise, the taxpayer is not irrevocably entitled to a single benefit from government. The level of taxation is thus a stark measure of government compulsion of the citizenry. The tax level measures government's financial power over the individual—a precise gauge of the subjugation of the citizen to the financial demands of the State. The citizen's obligations to the IRS are vastly greater than the IRS's obligation to the citizen. As a result, the more power the IRS acquires, the more subjugated the citizen becomes. In American politics, "tax fairness" usually refers almost solely to whether government is seizing the right amount of money from different economic classes—not to how the tax collectors are treating the individual citizen.

THE WAR ON THE SELF-EMPLOYED

The IRS is carrying out a campaign to slash the number of Americans permitted to be self-employed and to severely punish the companies that pay them. Since 1988, the IRS's attack has devastated thousands of small businesses and is undermining high-tech industries, the health care industry, and even freedom of religion. The IRS is enforcing with a vengeance legal standards that even the U.S. Treasury Department admits are vague and unpredictable. The IRS's attack on the self-employed is an effort to fundamentally change millions of Americans' way of life—simply to make people more subjugated to tax collectors.

This controversy originates in arcane federal regulations on the proper classification of workers. If a person is an employee, the employer must withhold payroll taxes and remit them to the IRS and pay half of the employee's Social Security taxes and all of the unemployment insurance tax. But if an individual is an independent contractor, a business need only send a Form 1099 to the IRS reporting how much it paid that person, and the contractor pays his taxes directly to the IRS.

The IRS has long striven to minimize the number of self-employed. The General Accounting Office reported in 1977 that the IRS "tends to classify as many persons as possible as employees, thereby subjecting their earnings to (tax) withholding."[2] GAO stated that the IRS's heavy penalties on companies relying on independent contractors imposed "many hardships and inequities on unsuspecting businesses"[3] and subtly noted that "Congress has given no indication that it believes the distinction between self-employed workers and employees should be eliminated."[4] In 1978 Congress enacted a provision to prevent the IRS from penalizing companies that had a "reasonable basis" (such as "standard industry practice") for classifying people as independent contractors. In 1988 the IRS launched a new campaign, targeting small businesses with less than $3 million in assets—in most cases, businesses without in-house counsel that cannot afford a lengthy court fight against the agency.

The IRS makes its classification decisions primarily based on a list of twenty questions on the relation between the employer and the contractor/employee derived from common law precedents dating back to the Magna Carta era. Assistant U.S. Treasury secretary Donald Lubick admitted in 1981 that the common law employment test was "developed centuries before the income tax to determine the rules of the doctrine that the master is liable for the torts of his servant."[5] An official Internal Revenue Commissioner advisory group report concluded in 1990 that "the process of classifying workers is confusing, complex, antiquated and unfair."[6] A 1991 Treasury Department report conceded that "the common law tests . . . lack precision and predictability" and "in many cases . . . [do] not yield clear, consistent, or satisfactory answers, and reasonable persons may differ as to the correct classification."[7] The House Government Operations Committee concluded in a 1992 report that "IRS' enforcement activities [on independent contractors] present small business taxpayers with a veritable nightmare of problems and policies that defy common sense."[8]

IRS agents ask a businessman the twenty questions, after which they sometimes destroy his business.[9] Once an IRS agent announces that the company misclassified its employees (as happens in nine out of ten audits), the company often faces a staggering tax bill, largely because the IRS intentionally forces businesses to double-pay taxes already paid by independent contractors. The House Government Operations Committee noted, "The assessments are based on the use of preset mandatory formulas which even the IRS admits result in double tax collections. These back tax assessments have been responsible for putting a number of those businesses out of business."[10] IRS agents have assessed over $500 million in penalties and back taxes since 1988 (averaging $68,000 per company) and forced businesses to reclassify over 400,000 independent contractors as employees. The IRS is now "converting" almost 2,000 independent contractors as employees each week.[11]

The IRS's crackdown has sparked widespread fear. Bob Rasmussen, a spokesman for the National Association of the Remodeling Industry, observed, "The lack of clear language has left the general contractor and the independent contractor vulnerable to possible destruction. Contractors are left to rely on a case by case interpretation of who is or is not a legitimate independent contractor even if the practice is long standing and common within the industry."[12]

The IRS crackdown is disrupting the health care industry. Marc Catalano, president of the Private Care Association, an association of health care agencies, accused the IRS of following a "search and destroy posture with respect to businesses that use independent contractors."[13] Comprehensive Care Corporation, a St. Louis–based company, was hit in 1991 with an IRS demand for $19.4 million in back taxes and penalties for treating psychologists and physicians as independent contractors.[14] The IRS also tried to penalize several Pennsylvania corporations for paying dentists as independent contractors instead of as employees. But the Pennsylvania Dental Board warned the corporations that it would be illegal under state law for the corporation to hire dentists as employees since the corporations were not licensed to practice dentistry. The IRS argued in federal court that the corporations' "reliance on the alleged advice of counsel for the Dental Board does not rise to a reasonable basis for relief of the tax liabilities under the act."[15] The IRS apparently believed it was unreasonable for the corporations to refuse to violate Pennsylvania law in order to boost the IRS's payroll-tax collections; federal judge William Caldwell threw the case out of court in 1991.

The IRS is forcing health-care agencies to reclassify physical therapists from contractors to employees. Physical therapists overwhelmingly prefer to remain contractors, partly because they automatically lose their certification to practice independently under the Medicare program if they become employees.[16] John Bailey, a psychologist at the Family Therapy Center of Madison, Wisconsin, complained to a congressional committee in 1992 that his clinic "has come under attack. . . . The IRS methods have been too subjective, applied with ferocity and arbitrariness, and have caused untold grief for us and other well-meaning small businesses."[17] Bailey reported that the IRS "attack has threatened the very survival" of several Wisconsin clinics. As part of its crackdown, IRS agents seized $2,000 out of the Center's bank account, and then, after being forced to concede that its case was baseless, claimed that it could not return the money because of difficulties with its computer system. The IRS's persecution of the Center ended after a Justice

Department attorney reviewed the case and concluded that the IRS's charges were so weak that they would be thrown out of court.[18]

The IRS is launching a high-profile assault on the use of independent contractors in the film industry. Pamela Christensen, an IRS chief field examiner in Los Angeles, told a meeting of Hollywood attorneys and accountants in 1992: "The entertainment industry is on the hit list."[19] The IRS launched a similar crackdown on the Minnesota film industry. Patti Fuller, owner of Fuller Productions, a Minnesota film company, complained that IRS agents "want me to classify a lighting tech who works for two hours and who I never see again as a part-time [employee]. That's absurd."[20]

IRS officials in some areas have ordained that all United Methodist ministers must be reclassified as employees. Reverend Robert McKibben of Alabama informed the House Ways and Means Committee that he was told by an IRS examiner that "all ministers" are "statutory employees." McKibben told the IRS agent about a U.S. Tax Court decision upholding the self-employment status of United Methodist ministers, but the IRS official claimed that he was not bound by the court's ruling. McKibben observed, "The systematic misclassification of United Methodist ministers also results in a violation of First Amendment rights . . . [with] the IRS dictating to the church the type of relationship they must have."[21] Craig Hoskins, counsel for the United Methodist Church, estimated that over a thousand Methodist clergymen have faced IRS audits over their employment status.[22] Hoskins complained, "The IRS . . . procedurally wishes to treat the tax filing status of United Methodist clergy as a *tax shelter matter.* We find it incredible that a system of clergy selection and placement in place in this country for over two hundred years is to be procedurally comparable to concerns about tax avoidance schemes."[23] (The IRS has not yet attempted to impose penalties on God for not withholding taxes from the ministers' pay.)

High-tech industries have probably been hit hardest by the IRS's crackdown. In the Tax Reform Act of 1986, Sen. Patrick Moynihan slipped in an amendment—known as Section 1706—that revoked the 1978 "reasonable basis" protection for specific professions including engineers, computer programmers, and other technical-service professionals.[24] Moynihan's amendment wreaked havoc. A 1987 Data Processing Managers Association survey found that 74 percent of firms decreased contracts made directly with independent technical-service consultants as a result of Section 1706.[25] Rep. Judd Gregg complained in 1987 that Section 1706 was "strangling small businesses in the computer and engineering fields."[26] An article in *PC Week* observed, "One has to wonder what is going on in the minds of government officials who lately seem to be going out of their way to set up roadblocks in the path to increasing America's productivity and creativity through the use of computers."[27] The Treasury Department, in a March 1991 study, concluded that Section 1706 "may have an adverse effect on the efficiency of the labor markets" for technical-service workers.[28] Rep. Major Owens of New York reported that "many African-American computer programmers and analysts have had the door to self-employment slammed in their faces because of Section 1706."[29]

IRS agents are often heavy-handed in how they carry out employment tax audits. Harvey Shulman, counsel for the National Association of Computer Consultant Businesses, observed that "in many cases, the IRS agents are acting like the Gestapo."[30] Shulman told the Senate Finance Committee:

> In almost every employment tax matter of which we are aware the IRS employee has simply visited the technical service offices without any prior appointment. Instead, the official has advised a receptionist or other employee that he or she is from the IRS and wants to see the firm's owners. The official has then demanded to see various documents right then and there, including 1099s, W-2s, and sometimes even corporate documents, in many cases from as much as three or four years back . . . Taxpayers have been told that if they cooperated in providing this information then the IRS official could close the matter and drop the "lead." When the taxpayers have asked that the IRS officials put these requests for information in writing the officials have often responded that the taxpayer's refusal to cooperate then and there with an oral request is "suspicious" or otherwise unwarranted and that such refusal itself will require the IRS to open a formal audit.[31]

IRS officials have encouraged private companies to secretly betray their competitors. At a 1990 meeting in California, an IRS agent distributed "snitch sheets" to businessmen and asked them to make allegations of illegal independent contractor use by their competitors. The IRS agent told the attendees to mail the completed "snitch sheets" to him in unmarked plain envelopes and promised to follow up on all leads.[32] When asked by the House Small Business Committee if such practices were still occurring, IRS Commissioner Shirley Peterson replied in 1992: "The IRS does not refuse to accept information bearing on a tax liability from any legitimate source."[33]

It is difficult to understand why the IRS would launch such a heavy-handed campaign against businesses that, in most cases, have not broken any clear law or shown any intent to dodge taxes. Shulman observed, "I have had grown men and women—40 or 50 years old—cry on the phone to me telling me that their marriage is threatened—they are seeking counseling—all because the business that they built up on the last fifteen years of their lives—the house and other things they've earned from the fruits of their labor—is all threatened by this IRS employment classification audit. They ask me, 'What did I do wrong? Why am I being persecuted?' "[34]

The IRS has lost a number of federal court decisions on this issue but has generally refused to abide by court decisions. (Until a decision is affirmed by the Supreme Court, the IRS can ignore the precedent outside the district where the court ruled for the taxpayer.) The IRS effectively has a bottomless war chest with which to attack businesses, and only businesses that can afford $50,000 or more in legal costs can have their rights upheld in federal court. The IRS prosecuted REAG, Inc., an Oklahoma organization that used real estate appraisers as independent contractors. When the case went before a federal judge, the U.S. government's trial brief asserted that "the evidence will show that at the time of the creation of REAG, the overwhelming majority of entities using appraisers in the manner the Corporation was using the Workers treated them as employees and not independent contractors." But federal attorneys could produce no evidence to support that assertion at trial. Federal judge Robin Cauthron scorned the IRS in 1993 for "boasting" about evidence it did not have, and concluded, "The United States obviously overplayed its hand in a transparent attempt to force settlement prior to trial."[35]

Many IRS agents threaten exorbitant penalties to coerce businesses to sign agreements swearing never to use independent contractors again in return for a reduction or waiver of the penalties. Such perpetual cease-and-desist orders may be appropriate when the government is dealing with wife beaters or child molesters, but they are bizarre when the federal government is seeking a pretext to permanently control the day-to-day operations of small businesses. The IRS is capitalizing on the vagueness and inconsistencies in the current law in order to greatly increase its own power over small businesses. GAO concluded in 1977 that the IRS "opposes clarifying the law for fear of increasing" the number of self-employed.[36]

The IRS estimates that there are 3.4 million Americans now working as independent contractors who should be reclassified as employees.[37] The Small Business Administration estimates that there are roughly 5 million independent contractors nationwide. Thus, if the IRS achieves "total compliance," over half of all the current independent contractors in the United States could be forced to abandon their own businesses.

Some observers believe that the IRS is attempting to singlehandedly abolish Americans' right to work for themselves. David McFadden, president of a New York referral agency for architects, declared last year: "I believe that the IRS wants to make every working person in America someone's employee."[38] Rep. Richard Schulze declared in 1989, "The mind-set of the IRS is to eliminate any . . . independent relationship to ensure that all American workers are easily tracked through corporate payroll accounting."[39] A 1992 House Government Operations Committee report observed, "The IRS has a long-standing preference for employee designations rather than independent contractor designations. The IRS preference is due to the administrative convenience it produces for them (e.g., collection of taxes through withholding), the large back tax assessments that are calculated by using mandatory formulas when workers are reclassified, and a general assumption that employees are more compliant with the tax laws than independent contractors."[40]

The IRS justifies its crackdown because some self-employed individuals dodge taxes. But, as the Treasury Department concluded in a 1991 report on technical service workers, "Misclassification of employees as independent contractors *increases tax revenues*, however, and tends to offset the revenue loss from undercompliance by such individuals, because direct compensation to independent contractors is substituted for tax-favored employee fringe benefits."[41] Yet the IRS is continuing to press its campaign to get a prior lien on almost everyone's paycheck through payroll withholding.

Being self-employed and starting one's own business has long been part of the American dream. But the IRS has apparently decided that it can no longer afford to permit people to pursue their dreams.

CARPET BOMBING CITIZENS WITH TAX PENALTIES

The IRS champions the idea that people pay taxes voluntarily. The IRS's 1992 Annual Report declared, "Our system of taxation is based on the willingness of citizens to assess and pay their taxes voluntarily."[42] Unfortunately, this is a doctrine that exists largely in the minds of the IRS public relations staff. The IRS's 1987 Annual Report noted: "Voluntary compliance with the tax laws in the United States self-assessment system of taxation relies heavily on the deterrent effect of successful criminal prosecutions."[43] Rep. Charles Rangel, a senior member of the House Ways and Means Committee, stated: "It is clear to me . . . that what makes a voluntary system work is the fear of sanctions and penalties."[44] Senator Harry Reid echoed that theme in 1990: "The IRS uses scare tactics to keep the American taxpayer honest."[45] Senator John Heinz complained in 1987 of an IRS agent using "loan shark tactics"—showing up at a person's home in Philadelphia without warning on a Saturday morning and announcing, "You owe the Government money, and if you don't pay, something very unpleasant is going to happen to you." Heinz observed, "We do not want . . . government employees from the IRS to go out and act like mob employed enforcers."[46] The IRS, in its 1992 annual report, even characterized its program of compelling businesses to convert independent contractors into employees subject to tax withholding as a "way to improve voluntary compliance."[47]

Tax codes have become minefields for the average citizen. Thomas Field, director of Tax Analysts and Advocates, wrote in 1974, "From the perspective of the IRS, the more ambiguous the law, the more powerful the enforcing agency."[48] An instructor at an IRS training school declared that agents could find errors in 99.9 percent of all tax returns.[49] *Money* magazine noted, "Although the Internal Revenue Manual runs to 260 densely printed volumes, tax collectors enjoy tremendous latitude, partly because courts have ruled over the years that the manual is not the law. As a result, the IRS can flaunt its own rules with impunity."[50] David Burnham, author of *A Law Unto Itself: The IRS and the Abuse of Power*, notes, "The reality that so many are somehow in violation of a supremely murky law gives the agency and the individual agent an astonishingly free hand to pick and choose their targets."[51]

Since 1954, the number of different penalties that the IRS can impose on taxpayers has increased over tenfold—from 13 to over 150.[52] In 1992 the IRS imposed over thirty-three million penalties on taxpayers.[53] The amount of penalties the IRS assesses has soared from a total of $1.3 billion in 1978 to $12.5 billion in 1992.[54] The over one hundred new penalties created in recent decades amount to decks of trump cards the government can play against the citizen. Sen. David Pryor complained that the IRS used penalties "as a weapon, as a whip over the innocent and the guilty taxpayer's head, and as a point of leverage."[55]

Citizens who receive IRS penalty letters may be perplexed by the agency's statements about a voluntary tax system. These letters threaten to drop the entire weight of the federal government on the citizen's head—often for meager violations or late payments of tiny amounts of taxes that would not even pay for a congressman's subsidized massage. Stephen Krieder Yoder, a *Wall Street Journal* reporter, related how, after he and his wife hired a nanny to care for their young child, they would occasionally misunderstand some IRS form or mail in the nanny's Social Security tax payments slightly late. One IRS notice, sent a month after the IRS demanded $39.98, warned in capital letters: "WE HAVE PREVIOUSLY BILLED YOU FOR THE OVERDUE TAX AND MUST NOW CONSIDER FILING A NOTICE OF FEDERAL TAX LIEN AND SEIZING YOUR PROPERTY, WAGES, OR OTHER ASSETS TO SATISFY YOUR UNPAID TAX."[56] Yoder received another notice, regarding a slightly overdue $27.11 payment, warning that he and his wife faced "CRIMINAL PROSECUTION THAT INCLUDES A FINE, IMPRISONMENT, OR BOTH."

The IRS sometimes stacks its penalties in order to bludgeon taxpayers for picayune alleged errors. In 1983, Rohm & Haas, a chemical manufacturer, sent the IRS a check for $4,448,112.88 for payroll taxes; the IRS claimed the check was ten cents short and penalized the company $46,806.37. The company assigned a team of accountants to the dispute and, after five months, the IRS dropped the penalty—but without explaining or apologizing for its action.[57] Former congressman Henson Moore testified to the Senate Finance Committee in 1987 that one small businessman who wished to remain anonymous "was assessed $400 for paying the IRS 2 cents less than he owed."[58] Mary Frances Stinson of Dorchester, Massachusetts, underpaid her taxes by ten cents in 1987—for which she was hit with $54.84 in penalties and interest fines in 1990.[59] In August 1993, the IRS notified a Santa Rosa, California, barber that he owed $4 billion in back taxes to the agency. (A glitch in a computer program resulted in the IRS sending 3,000 people nationwide identical demands for payments of $4 billion in taxes—perhaps part of a secret Clinton administration plan to pay off the national debt.)[60]

The IRS occasionally commandeers bank accounts as a penalty for failing to file tax returns exactly as the IRS demands. In 1983 Congress required that all credit unions filing more than fifty Form 1099 reports (showing interest paid to individuals) submit computer diskettes or tapes to the IRS listing the payments.[61] Two old ladies who ran a credit union for a Catholic church in Coopersville, Michigan, sent a letter to the IRS in 1985 requesting a waiver because they did not have a computer and had only fifty-nine form slips to file. The IRS never responded, and the credit union filed its tax return on paper. A year later, the IRS slapped a $2,950 penalty plus interest on the two women; when they refused to pay the bill, the IRS imposed a lien on their checking account.[62] Sen. David Pryor described a similar case in 1987:

> A small businessman in El Dorado, Arkansas, filed over two hundred forms with the IRS. He then received a letter from the IRS informing him that he was subject to a $50 a form fine for not filling out the forms using a ten pitch typewriter. He called the IRS to let them know that his business only owned one typewriter and it was a 12 pitch. The agent told him to buy a new typewriter and pay the fines. The result of the IRS action: $10,000 in fines and $150 for a new typewriter.[63]

The IRS also inflicts $500 penalties on citizens who allegedly file a "frivolous" tax return. The penalty in practice often amounts to simply a "talking back to the government" penalty. Among the things that the IRS has defined as frivolous is adding a few words of complaint to one's tax form. In 1983, Donna Todd of Billings, Montana, typed the statement "Signed involuntarily under penalty of statutory punishment" above her signature on an otherwise accurate return. An IRS agent slapped a $500 fine on Todd for her comment. When Todd refused to pay the $500, IRS agents imposed a lien on her bank account and on her property. Todd countered by suing the IRS and the IRS agent for violation of her constitutional rights. In a (temporarily) pathbreaking 1985 decision, federal judge James F. Battin observed that the IRS officials "contend that because they were not sure whether the return was frivolous they were justified in invoking the penalty and putting the burden on the plaintiff to prove them wrong and to get her money back. Such a cavalier attitude towards the citizens of this country by a government agency will not be tolerated."[64] The judge concluded that the IRS violated Todd's freedom of speech and, "by attaching her bank account and putting a lien on her property without first having a hearing . . . violated plaintiff's Fifth Amendment right to due process."

The Internal Revenue Service appealed the decision to the federal Ninth Circuit Court of Appeals. Commenting on the appeal, Justice Department attorney Elaine Ferris warned, "This case is an excellent example of where a government employee makes an error and a person uses that error to harass that employee. In the tax area we have legislation allowing for redress of errors. But you can't try to provide one-to-one justice because it will open a real Pandora's box that will drive the IRS crazy."[65] This is a peculiar interpretation of the relation between the State and the citizen: an IRS agent is not harassing a private citizen when he wrongfully seizes her bank account and "freezes" the land she owns, but the citizen is harassing the IRS agent when she sues him for violating her constitutional rights. The court came to the IRS's rescue, ruling that "Todd has no clearly established First Amendment right to express her dissatisfaction with the government on her tax return."[66] The judges announced that federal tax law "promotes effective collection of revenue, yet seeks to protect taxpayers from overzealous and occasionally unscrupulous tax collectors."[67] But if placing a legal claim on someone's land to pay for a fine for writing seven words on a tax return is not "overzealous," it is difficult to know what behavior is. Stephen Piver, the ACLU attorney who represented Todd, summarized the judgment: "It appears that what the court is saying is, if an agent punishes you improperly and also violates your constitutional rights, what you're expected to do is have that punishment or the penalty rescinded and forget your constitutional rights."[68]

For the IRS, rendering justice to the individual taxpayer is the lowest priority. *Money* magazine estimated in 1990 that almost half of the over thirty million penalty notices the IRS mails each year are erroneous.[69] The proliferation of tax penalties enables the IRS to threaten the average taxpayer with "massive retaliation" for the slightest error—yet IRS agents themselves are almost never punished for their errors. A 1989 internal survey found that IRS employees at toll-free numbers gave erroneous tax advice to citizens over 30 percent of the time.[70] In the 1992 tax filing season, fewer than one-third of the calls to special IRS tax assistance phone numbers were answered—the rest were blocked by busy signals or the caller gave up after waiting too long for a live person to answer the phone.[71] If a private bill-collection agency sent out millions of unjustified demands for payment, it would almost certainly be prosecuted for attempted extortion. *Money* estimated that the IRS wrongfully collected up to $7 billion in penalties it assessed in 1989 but were not owed by taxpayers.[72] The millions of inaccurate penalties could be part of an exercise in mass intimidation—an effort to achieve "presence" in far more people's personal lives.

IRS agents make over 10,000 direct seizures of homes, cars, or pieces of property each year.[73] The IRS has long rewarded its agents based on the amount of taxpayers' property they confiscate. In 1980, IRS collection officers in Detroit publicly protested that, for IRS managers, a seizure of a taxpayer's property "is no longer a means to an end; the seizure statistic is an end in itself."[74] IRS revenue officer Shirley Garcia told the Senate Finance Committee in 1987 that IRS managers pressure employees to make more seizures partly so that the managers can win "merit pay" bonuses; the IRS personnel system used tax dollars to provide incentive bonuses for seizing taxpayers' property.[75] One IRS memo exhorted IRS agents: "Our goal should continue to be to make every seizure in every inventory every month. . . . Now is the time for seizure action." In a San Francisco IRS office, a notice was posted on the bulletin board: "Seizure fever. Catch it."[76] (Congress passed legislation in 1988 formally prohibiting IRS quota systems for seizures, but it remains to be seen whether IRS officials choose to obey the law. IRS revenue officer John Connor told the Senate Finance Committee in 1990: "In its attempt to cleanse itself with an emphasis on quality, the IRS is reverting to an emphasis upon statistical measurements and production that is worse than ever before.[77])

IRS seizure actions sometimes resemble hostage taking. On November 28, 1984, IRS agents raided the Engleworld Learning Center in the Detroit suburb of Allen Park, Michigan, because of overdue taxes. The IRS agents then set up a creative scheme to force parents to pay the center's taxes when they came to pick up their children. As the *Washington Times* reported,

> Inside [the Learning Center] were a handful of bewildered parents, unable even to see their children until they paid money for taxes they did not owe to two IRS agents sitting near the entrance. Allegedly, the children—as many as 30 of them—could not run to greet their parents . . . as ordinarily was their custom. IRS agents kept them closely guarded in Room C of the day-care center. At least one agent was posted in another room where pre-schoolers, some still in diapers, were detained.[78]

Sue Stoia, a parent of one of the children, observed, "It was like something out of a police state. They indicated you could not take your child out of the building until you had settled your debt with the school, and you did that by signing a form to pay the IRS. What we were facing was a hostage-type situation. They were using the children as collateral."[79] Engleworld director Marilyn Derby said, "Parents were not allowed to see their children until they had signed an agreement with the IRS. It was a very scary situation, like the Gestapo was here. Children were crying, parents were trembling. I told one woman whose hands were shaking that she shouldn't sign anything she didn't want to. She signed anyway."[80]

The IRS imposes almost no controls over its own agents' property seizures. GAO reported in September 1992 that each agent was practically on the "honor system" to officially report and account for property he seized from taxpayers. Many IRS officials make little or no effort to safeguard seized property after they take control of it; yet if the property "disappears" after an IRS seizure, the agency refuses to credit the taxpayer whose property was looted. This effectively makes the taxpayer liable for the IRS's incompetence or knavery. GAO found that among the items seized by IRS agents which were later stolen were "televisions, VCRs, telephones, and scuba equipment in Atlanta; $10,000 in groceries from a seized market in Miami; and a 1980 gold Krugerrand in Phoenix."[81] GAO's Jennie Stathis reported, "Each revenue officer independently decides when to sell [seized] property, how to advertise it, and the time and place of the sale. Neither we nor IRS managers know the total amount, value, or types of property in IRS' possession; where it is located; how long it has been there. . . . Without records and physical inventories, thefts can go unnoticed. Thus, IRS relies heavily on the integrity of its staff to protect this property. . . . In 80 percent of collection cases . . . no receipts were obtained showing who had the property."[82] Rep. Clay Shaw of Florida concluded that there is "certainly ample opportunity for the seized property never to show up at all, and simply to be taken by an official of the federal government, without any accountability at all."[83] Rep. J. J. Pickle declared, "It is a sorry state of affairs when IRS management does not have a clue about what it has seized, where many of these assets are located, and whether seized property has disappeared. The current program is an open invitation for disaster and there is no excuse for it."[84]

The IRS has multiplied its use of force against American citizens in the last fifteen years. Since 1980, the number of levies—IRS seizures of bank accounts and paychecks—has increased fourfold, reaching 3,253,000 in 1992.[85] GAO estimated in 1990 that the IRS imposes over 50,000 incorrect or unjustified levies on citizens and businesses per year.[86] GAO estimated that almost 6 percent of IRS levies on businesses were incorrect.[87] (Almost 13 percent of the levy-seizures by the IRS's Memphis Service Center were incorrect.) The most frequent reason for the wrongful levies was the IRS's failure to accurately record citizens' and businesses' tax payments; GAO found one levy occurred because the IRS delayed posting tax payments to the correct taxpayers' account for three years.[88] GAO noted, "IRS procedures require that levy notices be reviewed for completeness and readability prior to mailing. This process, however, is normally limited to a check of the name and address appearing on the levy." This is a pathetic standard of review for seizing private citizens' savings. GAO concluded that as many as two-thirds of the erroneous levies could have been avoided if the IRS had thoroughly checked to see if the victim had made recent tax payments. Levies are routinely financial ambushes; a report by the House Small Business Committee noted, "Levies on checking accounts require no notice to the taxpayer, so that a taxpayer's first word of such a levy comes when its checks to creditors are returned as a result of the levy."[89]

The IRS also imposes almost one and a half million liens each year, an increase of over 200 percent since 1980.[90] *Money* magazine conducted a survey in 1990 of 156 taxpayers who had IRS liens imposed on their property and found that 35 percent of the taxpayers had never received a thirty-day warning notice from the IRS of an intent to impose a lien and that some first learned of the liens when the magazine contacted them. *Money* noted, "The IRS has never done a study on the accuracy of its liens. . . . By law, the IRS is supposed to levy paychecks and bank accounts only after a taxpayer fails to respond to five tax-due notices sent at five- to six-week intervals. The final notice, which warns of the IRS' power to levy and file liens, is supposed to be sent by certified mail."[91]

An IRS lien can torpedo a person's or company's credit rating. Larry Coble of the National Association of Private Enterprise observed, "It is critically important for small business to maintain flawless credit ratings. If there is a single cloud hanging over that record, banks will not make loans, vendors will demand payment on delivery, and lenders will call lines of credit. In short, they will be out of business. The worst credit stain a small business person can receive is an IRS lien. Creditors . . . are very much aware of the IRS's unlimited ability to freeze bank accounts and seize essential equipment."[92] Sen. David Pryor proposed in 1993 to require the IRS to formally notify credit agencies after it concludes that it has wrongfully attached a lien on a taxpayer's property. Yet the IRS strongly resisted the requirement, claiming that it would unduly burden IRS employees.

PRESUMED CORRECT: THE IMPERIAL PREROGATIVE OF THE IRS

In 1979 Alex and Kay Council invested a $300,000 bonus he received in a tax shelter that their accountant advised them was legitimate. After the three-year statute of limitations for their tax liability expired, the IRS sent them a statement in October 1983 demanding $183,021 in taxes, penalties, and interest for their 1979 return. The Councils' accountant quickly wrote back to the IRS requesting a copy of the official assessment and an explanation of the alleged tax deficiency and also informed the IRS that the statute of limitations had already expired for 1979. The IRS did not furnish an explanation of the deficiency notice until February 1985, when they claimed they had mailed a certified letter stating the tax deficiency to the Councils in early 1983 before the statute of limitations expired. But the agency refused to provide the Councils with a copy of the certified mailing list it used until 1987. The mailing list showed that the IRS sent the notice of tax deficiency to the wrong address, yet IRS lawyers insisted in federal court that the Councils had to prove that they had not received the letter.[93] In 1987 the IRS imposed a $284,718 lien on the Councils' property for the alleged 1979 tax liability. Alex Council had borrowed money to finance his construction business, but the IRS lien destroyed his credit rating. After Council's construction business collapsed, he committed suicide and left a note to his wife: "My dearest Kay, I have taken my life in order to provide capital for you. The IRS and its liens which have been taken against our property illegally by a runaway agency of our government, have dried up all sources of credit for us. So I have made the only decision I can. It's purely a business decision. I hope you can understand that."[94] (Alex Council had an insurance policy that paid benefits to survivors even in the event of suicide.) When the case finally went to trial, the judge threw the IRS's case out of court, ordering the agency to revoke its deficiency assessment and remove the liens on Kay Council's property.[95] Judge Frank Bullock noted that "despite the Councils' notifying the IRS as early as October of 1983 that they had received no notice of deficiency and their continued request for information from the IRS, the IRS never consulted the one piece of information which might well have settled this dispute and avoided litigation, i.e., the Postal Service records regarding the delivery of the Councils' notice of deficiency."[96]

Despite the judge's order, the IRS dallied several more months before removing the lien. Kay Council came to Washington to testify before the Senate Finance Committee on how IRS abuses helped to ruin her life. IRS officials responded to her testimony by seeking to sabotage her credibility with a whispering campaign to the media, alleging that Alex and Kay Council had other tax violations that they had not admitted in public. David Keating, vice president of the National Taxpayers Union, observed, "The IRS's officials' conduct was reprehensible. There is every reason to believe they complied with the tax law. Worse, it is a violation of federal law for an IRS official to publicly discuss information from confidential personal tax returns."[97]

In another IRS "wrong address" case, Clayton and Darlene Powell moved from Adelphi, Maryland, to Mitchellville, Maryland, in late 1987 and filed a tax return with their new address in early 1988. A few weeks after the IRS received the Powells' new address, the agency sent a notice of deficiency for their 1984 tax return to their old address. (The IRS previously audited the Powells' 1984 return and the Powells' signed a final settlement with the IRS and paid an additional $472.69 in taxes in July 1986.) The local post office—even though it had the Powells' forwarding address—returned the notice to the IRS. Though the statute of limitations had expired on the Powells' 1984 return, on December 28, 1988, the IRS mailed a notice to the Powells' new address—warning them that they must pay $6,864 in back taxes, interest, and penalties within ten days or the IRS would seize their property. The Powells paid the $6,864 and then sued the IRS in federal court to get a refund. The Federal Court of Appeals for the Fourth Circuit ruled that "the Powells are entirely innocent" and ordered a refund. The federal government appealed the decision to the Supreme Court. The government contended that as long as the IRS mailed a deficiency notice to a taxpayer's "last known address"—even if the IRS had information on the correct address—the taxpayer must be presumed to have received the notice—even when it is indisputable that he did not receive it. The Justice Department, in its brief on this case, asserted that the IRS "is not equipped to track down current addresses for millions of delinquent taxpayers each year. . . . The (IRS) advises us that it issues more than 2 million notices of deficiency each year and that approximately 240,000 of those notices were returned undelivered during the past year."[98] The Justice Department whined that requiring the IRS to actually notify citizens of tax assessments before final seizure notices would impose "*unmanageable detective burdens*" on the IRS.[99] (The Powells, in their brief to the Supreme Court, noted, "Common sense dictates that the IRS at least dial information for a taxpayer's telephone number and current address.")[100] The Justice Department characterized allowing the IRS to issue final notices threatening seizure of property within ten days as a "practical balancing of interests" between the taxpayer and the IRS and noted that the taxpayer "may still contest his liability by paying the tax and bringing a refund suit in federal district court or the Claims Court."[101] (Many taxpayers would be devastated by the government's seizure of their property and would not be able to afford the thousands or tens of thousands of dollars in legal fees necessary for a federal court case.) The Justice Department fretted that "this case threatens to create a *'window of time' during which the Internal Revenue Service may be helpless to protect its rights in pursuing delinquent taxpayers.*"[102] The notion of the IRS being "helpless to protect its rights" is something that could only occur to a federal employee. Apparently, the IRS will be "helpless" if it is obliged to actually notify people whose property it intends to seize before it issues a final seizure notice. The Supreme Court denied the government's request to hear the Powell case.

The "last known address" doctrine is a license for the IRS to send threats and seizure notices to the wrong address, and then issue ultimatums to people at their correct address. The Powell case epitomizes the IRS perspective that the citizen has an unlimited obligation to comply with the IRS demands—even when the IRS fails to notify the citizen of its demands. Unfortunately, the IRS is only obeying the federal appeals court decision limiting its absolute power in states of the Federal Fourth Circuit Court of Appeals jurisdiction (Maryland, North Carolina, South Carolina, West Virginia, and Virginia). Citizens in all other states are subject to receiving final notices demanding immediate payment of any alleged tax deficiency within ten days—or having their property seized. Though this may seem like an arcane issue, roughly 200,000 people are victimized each year by IRS threats to seize their property within ten days unless they almost instantly meet IRS demands.[103]

With a simple form letter, the IRS can give itself an overwhelming presumption to seize a citizen's property or bank account and put the citizen at an overwhelming disadvantage in trying to defend his right to retain what he earned. An IRS form letter can force the citizen to either surrender his property or to spend tens of thousands of dollars trying to prove his innocence. Author James Payne estimates that the average cost of representation and taxpayer involvement for a U.S. Tax Court case is $37,265, and the average cost for the citizen in a federal court criminal tax case is $74,530.[104]

Similar problems occur as a result of unjustified IRS deficiency letters. In 1982 the IRS sent a tax deficiency notice to Howard and Ethel Scar, announcing that they owed $96,000 for the 1978 tax year because of their use of an illegal Nevada mining project tax deduction scheme. The IRS deficiency notice conceded that the agency had not even examined the Scars' 1978 tax return before issuing the deficiency. The Scars had never been involved with the Nevada scheme and filed a petition with the Tax Court to force the IRS to revoke its determination. IRS officials conceded that their original allegation was incorrect, but insisted that the fact that the IRS sent the Scars a deficiency notice automatically invalidated the statute of limitations on the

Scars' tax return. The Tax Court upheld the IRS's position, declaring that the "requirements [of a formal IRS demand for more tax payments] are met if the notice of deficiency sets forth the amount of the deficiency and the taxable year involved."[105] Yet this essentially meant that no matter how unjustified or invalid the IRS's assertion, the citizen must be presumed guilty, even after IRS officials admit that their original assessment was totally unfounded. The Scars appealed to federal court; judge Betty Fletcher noted that "the Commissioner [of the IRS] argues that, because the notice contained the Taxpayers' names, social security number, the tax year in question, and 'the' amount of deficiency, it was 'clearly sufficient.'"[106] Judge Fletcher threw the IRS's case out of court.

IRS officials can penalize citizens and drag them through years of legal hell. In 1983 the Internal Revenue Service decided to investigate Melvin Powers for his 1978 and 1979 tax returns. Powers was a Houston builder and owner of five office buildings who had only an eighth-grade education.[107] The IRS had made no effort to examine Powers's tax returns during the three years of the statute of limitations. Six weeks before the limitation expired, an IRS agent asked Powers to sign a waiver of his statute of limitations, allowing the IRS additional time to investigate Powers. Powers willingly agreed. On March 31, 1986, Powers notified the IRS of his intention to end the extension of the period of investigation for his 1978 and 1979 returns, since the IRS had made no effort to examine his records in the years since 1983. On July 1, 1986, The IRS responded by disallowing almost all of Powers's business deductions for 1978 and 1979 and demanding $7,145,266.71 in back taxes, interest, and penalties. Shortly after the IRS's assessment, a bankruptcy court trustee "seized all of [Powers's] operations, caused [Powers] to vacate his office premises, and took possession of his books and records for all years."[108] In early 1991 the IRS conceded that Powers actually had large losses both in 1978 and 1979 and thus owed no taxes for those years. After IRS officials dropped the $7 million tax bill, Powers sued the IRS to cover his legal costs for the case. U.S. Tax Court judge John Colvin noted in 1993 that the IRS "contends that there is a basis in law for the notice of deficiency because the notice of deficiency is presumed correct" and that the IRS "made no attempt to obtain information about the case before" demanding a $7 million payment.

IRS agents sometimes vigorously pursue people for additional taxes even though agency officials may not believe they underpaid their taxes. Ramon Portillo, an elderly Mexican immigrant living in El Paso, Texas, worked as a self-employed house painter. The IRS audited him in 1987; a general contractor sent the IRS a Form 1099 claiming to have paid Portillo $35,000 in 1984, but Portillo stated that he received only $13,925. Sen. David Pryor summarized the case: "The contractor could only document $13,925 worth of work. He said he paid the rest in cash, which Portillo denied. The IRS decreed that Portillo had to prove he did not receive the cash and billed him for $17,000, including penalties and interest. Portillo's volunteer attorney investigated and found that the IRS's own files showed that the agency did not believe the contractor. Indeed, an IRS auditor could find no evidence to support the contractor's allegation. The IRS insisted, nonetheless, that Portillo was fully liable for taxes on the income, unless he could prove that he didn't receive the money."[109] Portillo appealed to the U.S. Tax Court. Tax Court judge James Fay ruled, "All that is required for a statutory notice of deficiency to be valid is that it advise the person who is to pay the deficiency that the Commissioner means to assess him; anything that does this unequivocally is good enough."[110] Portillo appealed the decision to federal court. The IRS sent in a team of lawyers and ultimately spent more money trying to win the case than the total amount Portillo owed. Mike Leeper, Portillo's lawyer, noted that the IRS "relies on its presumption of correctness on a broad spectrum of cases. Many times it will introduce no evidence at all. And because of the legal fiction that it is presumed correct, they can win their cases."[111] A federal appeals court ruled for Portillo, declaring that the IRS's "deficiency determination is clearly arbitrary and erroneous" and "lacked any ligaments of fact."[112]

COMPLEX, MORE COMPLEX, AND ETERNALLY DAMNED

Since 1914 the number of pages in the U.S. Statutes at Large devoted to income tax regulations has increased more than 500-fold—from 14 pages to over 9,000 pages.[113] *Money* magazine annually has a contest to test whether tax professionals can correctly ascertain a family's tax obligation in a relatively complex case; in 1993, over 95% of tax experts gave the wrong answer.[114] If the experts cannot even correctly compute a person's tax obligation, then government officials end up with far more discretion to penalize people for giving wrong answers—even though the government officials themselves may not understand the law. Tax laws are so complex that IRS staffers provide congressmen and their staffs with the equivalent of up to $100,000 in free help each year in filling out their own returns.[115] (Congressmen are provided with far more assistance than the IRS will render to the average taxpayer who seeks help.)

The complexity of the tax code has become like an unlimited contingent liability for the average citizen—a blank check that government agents may fill in with his name. The more complex the tax law becomes, the more difficult it is for the average citizen to defend himself against the IRS. An IRS official can routinely cite some unwritten or unpublished revenue ruling, or some decision from a stacked U.S. Tax Court, or some new provision in a law that Congress just enacted. Robert LeBaube, IRS director of taxpayer services, complained in 1989: "Since 1976 there have been 138 public laws modifying the Internal Revenue Code. Since the Tax Reform Act of 1986 there have been 13 public laws changing the code, and in 1988 alone there were seven public laws affecting the code."[116] "Tax law" is simply the latest creative interpretation by government officials of the mire of tax legislation Congress has enacted. IRS officials can take five, seven, or more years to write the regulations to implement a new tax law—yet Congress routinely changes the law before new regulations are promulgated. Almost all tax law is provisional—either waiting to be revised according to the last tax bill passed, or already proposed for change in the next tax bill.

In 1989, the IRS reversed its rules for the taxation of extended service contracts sold by auto dealers. *Automotive News* noted: "The interpretation by the IRS turns on whether the dealer is primarily obligated to customers or whether the obligation is between the manufacturer and the customer or the insurer and the customer."[117] The IRS's reversal had devastating results. An editorial in *Automotive News* lamented:

> When the National Automobile Dealers Association asked the IRS to rule on the type of contract in which the dealer is a party to the contract as obligor, the service put the whammy on the industry. The IRS said those dealers are not agents and must amortize expenses over the life of the contract but must declare income immediately and apply the ruling retroactively. The IRS also has threatened wide-scale audits—including every dealer in at least one state. Dealers are being socked for back taxes and assessed interest and penalties of as much as $500,000 at a time when many dealerships are struggling to keep the lights on and the doors open. According to one estimate, the ruling could wipe out 10 percent of the nation's new-car dealerships—some 2,300 outlets with 100,000 employees. It is horrifying that one IRS ruling could accelerate the mortality rate of a whole entrepreneurial class. . . . Because the IRS imposed this ruling retroactively, it violated a basic American tenet by holding dealers responsible for taxes prior to the ruling. The irony is that the ruling doesn't mean additional revenue, it only collects it sooner—although the arbitrary, unfair assessments of interest and penalties do generate new revenue and imperil viable businesses.[118]

At one point in 1992, the IRS was auditing over 1,000 auto dealers for selling extended service contracts and not accounting for them according to the IRS's revised guidelines.[119] The IRS policy was especially surprising because many auto dealers had been audited in years prior to the new rule, and IRS officials raised no objections to the accounting process. National Automobile Dealers Association counsel Peter Kitzmiller noted that under the revised rules, the paperwork and recordkeeping burdens on auto dealers have increased tenfold.[120] The arcane rules put independent warranty companies at a severe competitive disadvantage to warranty programs offered by the Big Three auto makers, and, according to Kitzmiller, a lot of the warranty companies "probably have gone out of business as a result of this." The IRS eventually offered auto dealers a compromise settlement whereby it promised to impose its new rules retroactively for only three years back.[121]

Another example of the chaos that can result from an alteration of an obscure tax provision occurred in 1987. Just after the Civil War, the United States imposed a Special Occupancy Tax (SOT) for any business manufacturing, distributing, or selling alcohol. This tax, which produced scant revenue, was administered by the Internal Revenue Service, which has made minimal efforts to collect it during this century. In 1976, GAO concluded that the SOT was inefficient and inequitable and recommended its repeal. In 1987 Congress—without issuing any warning or holding any hearings to alert the public—increased the tax by up to 1,000 percent and transferred authority for collection to the Bureau of Alcohol, Tobacco and Firearms (BATF). Though BATF admitted in congressional testimony that thousands of the 600,000 bars, taverns, restaurants, and grocery stores that sold alcohol had never been informed by the government of their obligation to pay the SOT, it proceeded to collect back taxes with a vengeance.[122] The Elks Club of Wilkes-Barre, Pennsylvania, got hit with a $9,776 tax bill for failure to pay the SOT every year since 1940, the year it got its first liquor license. A California pizza shop owner received a $2,911 tax notice. Neither establishment had ever heard of the SOT prior to receiving a demand for payment.[123] Since nonpayment of the SOT was considered to be tax fraud, the BATF ruled that no statute of limitations applied to any potential penalties. Rep. Paul Kanjorski complained: "The BATF took this position even though the statute of limitations for most tax violations is 3 years, and even though the statute of limitation for violent crimes like kidnapping, arson, and robbery is rarely more than 5 years. Yet in this case the BATF said they were required to collect back taxes, interest, and penalties as far back as 1866."[124] Apparently, every citizen has a duty to read the small print in the *Federal Register* each day to make sure that he has not overlooked any of his debts to Washington.

Many citizens are finding themselves ambushed by demands for retroactive sales tax payments even though they did the shopping in a foreign country. The *Wall Street Journal* reported in early 1990:

> Last month, relying on travelers' reports to U.S. Customs, California sent use-tax returns to 4000 residents for items brought in from abroad. That provoked outcries that Californians hadn't been warned about the 55 year old tax. Now the tax board has voted 4 to 1 to suspend enforcement and return 1,286 checks totalling $182,651. A spokesman says the board wants time to publicize the new program and to be sure of approval for the program's $735,000 budget; estimated revenue is $9.4 million a year. . . . Other states also seek leads from Customs. New York recently received $300,000 from a stamp collector for tax and interest on years of foreign purchases. Since May, Illinois has collected $160,000 using Customs leads.[125]

Probably not one Illinois tourist in a thousand understands that if he buys a shirt in Karachi, Pakistan, he will be obliged to pay a sales tax to a government in Springfield, Illinois. Yet there are heavy penalties for failure to comply with such sales tax payments—even though few state governments have made the effort to educate their citizens about their international duties. New York residents are liable for a $50 penalty each time they fail to pay a sales tax on an out-of-state purchase within twenty days; a state tax official assured financial writer Andrew Tobias that a crackdown on scofflaws was coming.[126] New York residents are liable for taxes, penalties, and interest on all out-of-state purchases they have made since 1965—thus making tax cheats out of most of the state's residents.

The more complex the tax code becomes, the more power prosecutors have over citizens. The Justice Department combined the vagueness of the tax laws and the breadth of the RICO law to destroy Princeton/Newport, a New Jersey investment partnership with over $3 billion in assets and investors including Harvard University. Just before Christmas 1987, forty federal agents with automatic weapons and bulletproof vests raided Princeton/Newport's office, rummaged for ten hours, and carted off 275 boxes of documents. Justice Department officials alleged that Princeton/Newport officials violated some arcane provisions in the tax code. Nine months later, federal prosecutors filed a thirty-five-part indictment for so-called tax parking (manipulating securities to illegally avoid tax obligations) and demanded the forfeiture of over $30 million of the company's assets and the homes of the company's officers. The forfeiture order, by destroying the company's access to credit, destroyed the company. As the *Wall Street Journal*'s Gordon Crovitz reported, "Princeton/Newport was forced into liquidation—before being able to defend itself in court. The result was not only sentence before verdict, but the death penalty."[127]

The Princeton/Newport prosecution was essentially an extremely complex tax case based on fifty-nine securities transactions between 1984 and 1986. Because Princeton/Newport officials had used the phone and the mail to help arrange the transactions, prosecutors insisted they were guilty of mail and wire fraud—and thus turned garden-variety tax violations into a RICO case. The case went to trial in 1989; *Manhattan Lawyer* reported:

> The lead defendant, James Regan, took the stand July 10 and testified to the exceedingly complex tax landscape in which he and his firm operated, discussing the changing laws, regulations and rulings governing the tax treatment of convertible hedged positions held by noncorporate traders like Princeton/Newport during the relevant time period. He explained why he thought the trades had economic substance within the meaning of the tax laws and why, if one properly construed something called the five-day recognition rule and something else known as the wash-sale rule, the trades were lawful. . . .
>
> The government maintained that the case was simpler than that. Prosecutors argued that the sales and repurchases were prearranged and therefore "rigged" and "sham" trades intended to create "fraudulent, false, fictitious and bogus" tax deductions. To keep the case as simple as they claimed it was, the prosecutors asked U.S. District Judge Robert Carter to keep out of evidence the federal tax statutes, regulations, bulletins and rulings Regan claimed he had relied upon.[128]

The government prosecutor summed up his case to the jury: "You don't need a fancy tax law expert because common sense tells you it's fraudulent, its phony . . . doesn't it feel wrong? Doesn't it sound sleazy? If it sounds sleazy it's because it is sleazy. Your common sense tells you that."[129] U.S. attorneys were so intent on keeping jurors ignorant of the intricacies of tax law that they persuaded the judge to prohibit two of the nation's leading tax experts —Yale Law School professor Boris Bittker and former IRS commissioner Donald Alexander—from appearing as witnesses. (Both intended to testify that Princeton/Newport's complex dealings were legal.) First the government creates a tax code whose comprehensibility defies human reason (President Carter justly called the Internal Revenue Code a "disgrace to the human race") and then prohibits defendants from having reputable experts explain their tax-related actions to a jury. The jury convicted the Princeton/Newport defendants on sixty-three of sixty-four counts, sentencing three of the firm's officers to prison, but a federal appeals court overturned almost all of the convictions. The IRS later conceded that Princeton/Newport had actually overpaid their taxes.[130] One commentator observed, "Whatever happens, the price of the investigation and trial has been steep. A company was ruined; lives were interrupted for two years; and the emotional strain on families was visible in the courtroom every day during the trial. The legal defense alone cost more than $5 million."[131]

While the IRS imposes almost impossible record-keeping and compliance burdens on taxpayers, it neglects to obey its own laws. GAO announced in June 1993, after examining the IRS's own financial records, "We were unable to express an opinion on the reliability of IRS' 1992 Principal Financial Statements because critical supporting information was not available. Where information was available, we found that it was generally unreliable. We found that IRS' internal controls did not effectively safeguard assets, [or] provide a reasonable basis for determining material compliance with relevant laws and regulations."[132] GAO also noted, "Our work identified some instances of noncompliance with certain provisions of the Internal Revenue Code relating to distribution of excise taxes."[133] The Internal Revenue Code—like many other federal laws and regulations—is apparently only something to be inflicted on private citizens, not something for the government itself to obey.

PICK A TARGET, ANY TARGET

In 1985 the IRS launched a major investigation of Jordache Inc., a blue jeans manufacturer. The Jordache probe was instigated by Ronald Saranow, chief of the Los Angeles office of the IRS's Criminal Investigation Division, and an extremely influential figure in the agency.[134] Saranow had close social ties with the Marciano brothers, owners of Guess Jeans Co., and had negotiated and accepted a job offer from the Marcianos at the time he was involved in the bureaucratic persecution of Jordache. Saranow even described himself in sworn testimony as a "front man" for the Marcianos.[135] A report by the House Government Operations Committee noted, "The investigations of Jordache . . . were initiated based solely on the information brought to the Government by the Marcianos and championed by Ronald Saranow while Mr. Saranow was in a conflict-of-interest situation."[136] The information that the Marcianos provided on their competitors led to a massive government raid on Jordache facilities in New York and New Jersey and the confiscation of 3 million documents and over 100 computer tapes in early 1986, severely disrupting Jordache's operations.[137] In November 1989, the investigation of Jordache ended and all charges were dropped. The congressional report concluded that the IRS may have engaged in a massive cover-up and destruction of documentation to whitewash its attack on Jordache.[138]

IRS employees have ample opportunity to abuse their power. Roughly half of the IRS's 115,000 employees have access to computer systems containing the confidential personal tax information of other Americans. In August 1993, the IRS revealed that 369 employees in a single region had been investigated and/or punished for using government computers to browse through friends', relatives', celebrities', and other people's tax returns. Some IRS employees created fraudulent tax returns and altered their neighbor's computer tax files. For many of the IRS wrongdoers, the only penalty they received was "counseling." Sen. Byron Dorgan of North Dakota was outraged at a hearing discussing the abuses: "What on earth kind of counseling would be advisable for an employee that violates confidentiality of taxpayers' returns? . . . If people misuse financial information of taxpayers and then work for the IRS, we don't need counseling. They just need to be relieved of their job quickly."[139] IRS commissioner Margaret Milner Richardson responded to the scandal by declaiming to a Senate committee: "I feel very strongly about protecting the integrity of the tax system, and . . . we will not tolerate anything that will impinge on that integrity or the credibility of the American people." When one senator urged the IRS to at least notify the private citizens whose tax files had been perused and/or abused by IRS employees, Richardson rejected the idea, declaring: "I'm not sure there would be a serious value to that in terms of tax administration or in connection with what I see as protecting the taxpayers' rights."[140] (The IRS has generally neglected protecting the confidentiality of taxpayer's financial information. An August 1993 report by the National Research Council concluded that the IRS, in an ongoing multi-billion dollar overhaul of its computers,"has shown little progress" in safeguarding taxpayer confidentiality and that its program could "lead to a wide range of potentially disastrous privacy and security problems for the IRS unless the IRS develops effective, integrated privacy and security policies.")[141]

Rep. Douglas Barnard led a courageous investigation of IRS wrongdoing in the late 1980s and early 1990s. (Acting IRS commissioner Michael Murphy lobbied congressmen in 1989 to prevent Barnard's committee from being permitted to hold public hearings on IRS corruption and abuses.)[142] Barnard's House Government Operations subcommittee concluded that IRS officials "guilty of wrongdoing frequently escaped punishment because the Office of Inspection was either unwilling or unable to thoroughly investigate the allegations against them."[143] The congressional investigators compiled a lengthy report detailing cases of abuses by IRS senior managers but noted, "In the specific cases of senior manager wrongdoing examined by the subcommittee, only 1 of the approximately 25 individuals involved was administratively punished . . . and none have been criminally prosecuted."[144] The IRS's response to all the scandals was, among other things, to announce a "Servicewide Ethics Plan" that identified ethics as "one of the five major strategies that will shape tax administration in the years to come."[145]

IRS officials have shown open disdain about congressmen's efforts to monitor their activity. A 1991 survey of IRS executives and managers revealed that three out of four IRS managers feel entitled to deceive or lie when testifying before a congressional committee. *Roll Call* reported, "Only 47 percent of the managers feel the need to be 'completely honest' when testifying before a Congressional committee—and the number drops to 24% when appearing before a committee chaired by 'a critical or headline-seeking chairman.'"[146] (Private citizens convicted of perjuring themselves in sworn congressional testimony face several years in prison.) IRS managers apparently feel that when congressmen criticize the IRS, IRS officials are somehow absolved of their duty to be honest with the American public. Sen. David Pryor observed, "We probably know more about the KGB in the Soviet Union than we do about our own Internal Revenue Service."[147] Pryor, who sponsored legislation to curb IRS abuses in 1987 and 1988, commented on getting support among fellow members of Congress: "I saw real fear of the possible IRS retaliation among many members of the Senate and the House of Representatives."[148] David Burnham notes that the IRS's independent power is protected by "the congressional imperative that *nothing* must stop the collection of taxes. . . . The historical failure of Congress tax committees to show any real interest in examining the performance of the IRS except when it is totally awash in scandal is a shocking and important failure that further enhances the authority of the agency."[149] In congressional deliberations on taxpayers' rights, the big question is often whether violating fewer rights might mean less revenue for congressmen to spend.

AGENTS, AGENTS EVERYWHERE

The Internal Revenue Service has conducted hundreds of undercover operations in recent years[150] in which IRS agents are officially permitted to masquerade as professionals. A 1984 IRS internal document proposed authorizing undercover IRS agents to "give sworn testimony in a proceeding while still retaining the use of the false identity, remain undercover despite 'a significant risk of violence or physical injury to individuals or a significant risk of financial loss to an innocent individual,' and lie about the activities or involvement of an innocent person."[151] The proposal evoked sharp protest; Baltimore accountant Marvin Garbins observed, "If you go to a priest or lawyer or physician, you should not have to worry whether he is an IRS agent."[152] IRS officials, responding to the outcry, promised to impose some limits on its undercover activities.[153]

The IRS recruited St. Louis accountant James Checksfield in 1979 as "controlled informant No. 43111."[154] Checksfield was enticed to become an IRS informant in part because he was facing a criminal investigation for failing to pay his own taxes for three years; the IRS dropped its investigation after Checksfield went on the IRS payroll. Checksfield provided the IRS with information on how a client, Steve Noles, was allegedly skimming money from his pizza business and not reporting it on his tax returns. Noles was indicted by a federal grand jury and faced up to twenty-four years in prison and $900,000 in fines. The *Wall Street Journal* reported, "The appearance of entrapment taints the government's case against Mr. Noles, some tax lawyers say. . . . Internal IRS memos on file in court show that Mr. Checksfield had helped Mr. Noles create an 'officers' account' for his pizza restaurant—a key element in his alleged scheme to hide income. . . . Mr. Noles might never have become entangled with the IRS had Checksfield done his job properly. In an affidavit . . . Mr. Checksfield said that 'any omission of income on Steve Noles's . . . income-tax returns could have been prevented through further inquiry and accounting work on my part.'"[155] IRS assistant regional commissioner Michael Orth defended the IRS's role in the sting: "We don't recruit informants. They generally come to us on their own initiative because they're upset someone else is avoiding their share of taxes. Why should we discourage this sort of patriotism?"[156] Edward Fererico of the IRS criminal investigation asserted that an "accountant has a moral and legal obligation to turn over information" to the IRS.[157] Fererico apparently believes that every American citizen has an obligation to inform against every other citizen to the IRS; perhaps it is only a question of time until the IRS, following drug warriors' lead, begins to make heroes out of children who turn in their parents for tax evasion. Federal magistrate William Bahn observed that the "tawdry facts" of the case left a "bitter taste" in the mouth and observed that the case "strongly suggests a lack of honesty and integrity on the part" of the IRS agents supervising Checksfield.[158] The IRS dropped charges against Noles just before the case was to go trial. But as Keith Stroup of the National Association of Criminal Defense Lawyers observed, "I'm sure they did it because they knew the judge was going to slam them."[159] The IRS admitted in 1989 that it was using 900 controlled informants (double agents) and that 40 of those informants were accountants. The IRS has refused to provide any information in response to

Freedom of Information Act requests filed by this author to determine the current number of IRS double agents, but there is no reason to believe that the agency has reduced its covert activities since 1989.

One of the most controversial undercover operations was Project Layoff, in which the IRS squandered over half a million dollars in Las Vegas in a botched attempt to ensnare the nation's top illegal gamblers. Sen. Harry Reid of Nevada observed that the IRS officials involved in Project Layoff were "so incompetent that they couldn't even agree on who was going to pay the monthly phone bill."[160] The General Accounting Office noted that the IRS operation lost money partly "because the IRS could not use the normal methods bookmakers use to collect unpaid debts, such as threats, bodily harm or loan-sharking."[161] The IRS destroyed many of the key documents from the investigation, thus preventing federal investigators from determining whether IRS agents themselves may have robbed the till. (An IRS internal audit report subtly noted, "As this type of operation was new to the Service, there was some uncertainty as to proper recordkeeping.")[162] Sen. Richard Bryan of Nevada observed: "Any businessman in Las Vegas would be thrown in jail if his books looked like Project Layoff's. It amazes me that the IRS can, on the one hand produce such careless records, and, on the other hand, demand accurate records from every adult in America."[163] The lackadaisical attitude toward safeguarding tax dollars in Project Layoff was par for the agency; a GAO review found that the IRS failed to do closeout financial audits of almost half of all undercover operations in which tax dollars had been spent.[164]

MAKE A NAME, ANY NAME

Any citizen who places a false name on a tax return is guilty of a felony and entitled to up to three years in a federal prison.[165] But in 1992 IRS revenue officers were explicitly granted the official right to lie to the public when a taxpayer asks the revenue officer's name. The *Washington Post* described a ruling by a government employees arbitration panel:

> All fake names . . . would be registered so that a taxpayer would know how to reach that IRS official again. . . . And no obviously fake names, such as Mickey Mouse, Mr. X or 007, would be allowed. . . . Phillip Proffit of the National Coalition of IRS Whistleblowers predicted that the new policy will make it more difficult for a taxpayer to locate a revenue officer and that there would be no way to prevent an officer from using a fake name and not registering it with a supervisor as required.[166]

Larry Wright, an IRS spokesman in San Francisco, justified this deception of taxpayers: "We deal with the dregs of society. Drug dealers. Gamblers. Prostitutes. Anarchists. We deal with some extremely fringe individuals."[167] Apparently, because some people that the IRS audits are anarchists, IRS agents are entitled to act like dictators toward any taxpayer. Among the reasons a federal arbitrator gave for allowing IRS employees to lie to the public was that IRS officials have "had false liens filed against them and their property" by angry taxpayers.[168] But IRS agents themselves file thousands of unjustified liens against citizens' property every year. Why should government employees be exempt from the same threat of unjustified action they inflict on private citizens?

ROUGH JUSTICE AND TAXPAYERS' HEARTS

IRS commissioner Fred Goldberg, in a May 1992 memo, declared that IRS regulations "should make do with 'rough justice.' . . . All too often, detailed rules result in the worst of both worlds—they suffocate the many taxpayers who try to do what's right, while providing a road map for the few with larceny in their hearts."[169] Writing regulations more vaguely than necessary increases the discretionary power of IRS agents. Goldberg implied that the IRS needs to keep a certain vagueness in its regulations so that IRS agents will have the power to decree which taxpayers have "larceny in their hearts" and to punish them accordingly. Since when are IRS agents supposed to be able to gaze into people's hearts and make determinations of a person's motives or worthiness before deciding whether or not they have complied with federal tax law?

While IRS regulation-writers intentionally leave the law vague, federal prosecutors often portray tax dodging as a question of good versus evil. Current tax law effectively gives the IRS the legal authority to send millions of Americans to prison. Though the IRS exercises this power in only a tiny percentage of cases, the potential power creates a severe imbalance between the agency and individual taxpayers. The United States has an expansive concept of criminal tax evasion. The Supreme Court ruled in 1943 that criminal tax evasion included "conduct such as keeping a double set of books, making false entries or alterations, or false invoices or documents . . . concealment of assets or covering up sources of income, handling of one's affairs to avoid making the records usual in transactions of the kind, and any conduct the likely effect of which would be to mislead or to conceal."[170] Because of this expansive concept, the IRS has the power to try to send someone to prison for three years for knowingly failing to report on his tax return $100 in cash income he received. This concept of tax fraud has allowed the U.S. government to engage in high-profile prosecutions of prominent individuals, often based on relatively small amounts of disputed taxes.

DUE PROCESS, IRS-STYLE

Suing the IRS for violation of one's constitutional or legal rights is about as effective as barking at the moon. David Keating of the National Taxpayers

Union observes, "IRS employees are often allowed to violate IRS rules, regulations, policies, procedures, and guidelines at will and without fear of recourse. The law is so overwhelming and sweeping in its power conferred upon the tax collecting authority that there are almost no checks and balances on the exercise of that authority."[171] The IRS imposes negligence penalties on citizens in cases of "any careless, reckless, or intentional disregard of rules or regulations, as well as any failure to make a reasonable attempt to comply with the provisions of the Code."[172] Yet no such standard is applied to the IRS itself or to IRS agents who abuse private citizens.

The Internal Revenue Manual has over 2,000 of pages that specify how IRS agents must act, among other things. Yet if an IRS agent violates the official manual, there is nothing a citizen can do. The courts have ruled that IRS employee regulations do not have the force of law, and provide no enforceable legal protection for taxpayers—except to go whining to a federal judge, who will then almost inevitably inform the citizen that the IRS agent is immune to suits for violations of the citizen's rights. In the 1988 Taxpayer Bill of Rights, Congress added Section 7432 to allow taxpayers to sue IRS employees who "recklessly" or "intentionally" disregard any provision of the Internal Revenue Code when collecting a tax. But Justice Department tax lawyer Edward Robbins scorned such suits in 1992, asserting that lawsuits for violating official IRS regulations are "not relevant to anything" except maybe "throwing dirt at the revenue agent."[173] *Tax Notes Today* reported that Robbins "stressed that the Justice Department knows that violations of the Internal Revenue Manual will not go anywhere in a court case."[174]

THE POLITICIAN'S FRIEND . . . AND ENEMY

The power to tax has long been the power to destroy one's political opponents. Karl Hess, a former speechwriter for presidential candidate Barry Goldwater, observed, "One of the rights of the victors in a presidential election is to audit the losers."[175] David Burnham notes that "in almost every administration since the IRS's inception the information and power of the tax agency have been mobilized for explicitly political purposes. . . . Eleanor Roosevelt prompted Treasury Secretary Morgenthau to order a tax investigation of a conservative newspaper publisher who had become one of the Roosevelt administration's leading critics."[176] President John F. Kennedy in 1962 ordered special audits of steel company executives who resisted his demand to lower the price of steel. Nixon administration officials gave the IRS a list of official enemies to, in the words of presidential assistant John Dean, "use the available federal machinery to screw our political enemies."[177] On September 11, 1972, Dean gave the IRS commissioner a list of 579 McGovern contributors and staff members and asked for investigation of their taxes.

Congress responded to the political abuse of the IRS during the Nixon era by banning in 1974 any contact between the White House and the IRS. But this prohibition apparently did not restrain the Clinton administration. In May 1993, seven employees of the White House Travel Office, an organization that primarily arranged trips for press corps members who followed the president's gallivanting, were fired by Clinton administration officials. The *Washington Post* noted, "White House officials hinted broadly of corruption among the seven when they were fired, and told reporters tales of lavish lifestyles, minimal work, kickbacks and missing money."[178] The employees of the travel office were fired in order to allow a cousin of Clinton to take over the office and redirect business to Clinton campaign contributors. But to create a public relations cover for the firing (some of the employees had worked at the White House for over fifteen years), White House officials called in and pressured FBI officials to issue a press release announcing that the travel office personnel were being investigated for serious criminal violations. White House associate counsel William Kennedy told a high-ranking FBI official that the Clinton administration was considering contacting the IRS to investigate UltrAir, the private company that had received most of the travel office's business. A few days later, three IRS agents appeared at the company's Smyrna, Tennessee, headquarters with an administrative subpoena, demanding to see all the company's records. Yet the company—which was less than a year old—had never filed a tax return. Thus the IRS effectively had nothing to audit. *Tax Notes Today,* a tax newsletter, noted that the IRS audit of UltrAir had extreme irregularities, and asked: "Do IRS agents read the newspaper and then just hop in the car, summons and Slurpee in hand, to visit a taxpayer who may be doing something wrong? If there is no criminal investigation of UltrAir, why was the IRS treating the company like criminals?"[179] Sen. Bob Dole of Kansas concluded, "It appears that agents from the IRS were used as political foot soldiers in a White House damage control operation."[180]

The IRS also does freelance political work and has a long history of trying to ruin the political careers of its critics. In 1924, Sen. James Couzens of Michigan launched a probe into what was then known as the Bureau of Internal Revenue; a year later, Internal Revenue commissioner David Blair confronted Couzens as he left the Senate floor and handed him a letter demanding $10,860,131.50 in back taxes.[181] Couzens fought the case and eventually proved that he had actually overpaid his taxes by roughly $1 million. David Burnham notes, "Treasury Secretary Andrew Mellon and Commissioner Blair were engaged in a blatant retaliatory act that they hoped would bully the senator into abandoning his investigation of the agency and the corrupt deals it was cutting."[182] In the 1960s, Sen. Edward V. Long of Missouri held congressional hearings investigating IRS abuses. The IRS responded by leaking information to a *Life* magazine reporter purportedly linking Long to Teamster president Jimmy Hoffa; the accusations in

Life played a key role in Long's defeat in an election the following year.[183] In 1972, Sen. Joe Montoya of New Mexico announced plans to hold hearings evaluating IRS behavior; the IRS quickly launched a tax investigation of Montoya and later leaked information on the case to the *Washington Post.* Partly as a result of the IRS leak, Montoya was defeated in a primary the following year.[184] The IRS has also abused its discretionary power to punish federal judges who did not ratify the agency's power grabs. Tax lawyer Charles Adams observed: "Justice Abe Fortas's career was destroyed after his nomination as Chief Justice in 1968 when an IRS agent gave information from his records to a *Life* magazine reporter."[185]

WELFARE RIGHTS VS. TAXPAYER DUTIES

The federal government follows diametrically opposed practices depending on whether it is taking or giving. Welfare recipients today often have a stronger legal right to their welfare benefits than workers have to their bank accounts. Welfare recipients are entitled to a fair hearing before the government can terminate their benefits;[186] on the other hand, the IRS can impose a levy on an individual's bank account with no evidence of his wrongdoing. In a welfare termination hearing, the welfare recipient is presumed deserving of continued government aid unless the government shows convincing evidence that the person should not be on the dole; in the U.S. Tax Court, a worker is presumed guilty of receiving any unreported income the IRS alleges he received.

In 1989 Congress enacted the Computer Matching and Privacy Protection Act to require states to verify independently all computer-generated information before acting to suspend, reduce, or revoke federal benefit payments.[187] But no such restriction limits the IRS, which mails out millions of incorrect or unjustified tax penalties each year.

It is inconceivable that a federal social program would promulgate retroactive regulations and then force welfare recipients to pay back a portion of the benefits they had received during the previous years. Yet the IRS routinely issues retroactive regulations each year that compel taxpayers to render portions of previous years' earnings or profits to the government. As part of the 1993 tax hike legislation, the Clinton administration imposed almost $9 billion in retroactive taxes—even raising the estate taxes on people who had already died.[188]

Tax forms have become far more complex in recent years, forcing the average American family to spend more hours than ever before struggling to calculate their debt to the government. In contrast, Congress in 1989 prohibited school systems from requiring both parents to submit their Social Security numbers when requesting free school lunches for their children.[189] Congress lightened the paperwork burden on parents even though the

USDA Inspector General estimated up to 30 percent of the recipients of free school lunches were ineligible under federal income guidelines.

In 1975 Congress created the Earned Income Credit—a program to send handouts to lower-income families based on their level of income. The program was greatly expanded in 1990. In 1992, under congressional pressure to give money to any taxpayer eligible for the handout, the Internal Revenue Service mailed checks to over 175,000 families who were not legally entitled to such checks under the Earned Income Credit Act. Even families who had not requested the handout were sent checks, regardless of whether they deserved the payment. IRS commissioner Fred Goldberg declared in March 1993: "The measure of our success is if every family entitled to this credit claims it and gets every dollar they are due." Yet at the same time, the IRS was fighting tooth and nail to prevent many other taxpayers from taking legitimate deductions (such as home office expenses).

TAX-MADE PAUPERS

Taxation has a far greater effect on people's lives than most Americans realize. Taxation epitomizes the modern political preemption of the individual's life. In recent decades, federal, state, and local tax codes have destroyed the possibility of millions of Americans of achieving financial independence and self-reliance. Nowadays, the politicians' *need* for more revenue almost always trumps the citizens's *right* to his paycheck.

Tax rates measure the nation's most important and costly entitlement program—how much of a person's income politicians are entitled to take. According to the Tax Foundation, the average citizen had to work 123 days in 1992 to pay his taxes—from January 1 through May 3.[190] In high-tax states, the citizen's "tax sentence" was even higher: in New York, the average citizen had to work until May 22 to pay his taxes, and in Connecticut, until May 14. If the government announced a program of forced labor, and conscripted every taxpayer for over a third of a year without compensation, there would likely be a national revolt. But as long as taxes are seized through payroll tax withholding, most citizens have little opportunity for resistance.

Most Americans pay far more taxes than they realize. Self-employed people must pay 15.3 percent of their income (up to $60,600) to bankroll Social Security payments for other Americans. Employed workers pay 7.65 percent of their wages directly into Social Security, which is matched by their employer (money that would have gone to their wages instead, according to most economists). Financial writer Andrew Tobias observed that a freelance employee in New York City making $29,000 a year faces an income tax rate of 58.3 percent.[191] This is not including sales, property, and other taxes that a person pays in New York. Richard Gullotta, a California CPA, notes that a single self-employed person working in California enters the 50 percent tax bracket at an income level of $22,816.[192] The average state income tax now is 6%, and cities and counties in many areas impose additional income taxes. On top of this, the average sales tax rate for states, counties, and cities reached 7.87% in 1991.[193] The Tax Foundation reported that total taxes collected by government at all levels in 1992 were 85 percent higher than total taxes collected in 1982. Between 1982 and 1992, combined state and federal taxes increased twice as fast as personal income and more than 50 percent faster than inflation.[194]

While the direct burden of taxes are stark, the indirect costs are often difficult to perceive. The indirect costs of taxes include the things that taxation has prevented from coming into being—preempting the economy from growing, preventing people from saving enough to buy their own homes or to open their own business, or preventing companies from hiring more workers. The *Wall Street Journal* noted that "some accountants . . . are charging as much as 2% of a small firm's revenue simply to prepare a tax return."[195] The Arthur D. Little accounting firm estimated in 1985 that Americans spend 5.427 billion hours each year complying with federal taxes. As James Payne notes, this was the equivalent of 2.9 million Americans "working full time on federal tax compliance activities in 1985."[196] This is almost equal to the total number of federal civilian employees.

The average American family head will be forced to do 20 years' labor to pay taxes in his or her lifetime. The federal tax system has turned individuals into *sharecroppers of their own lives*. At current tax rates, workers are effectively forced to produce two bales of cotton for their political rulers for each three bales of cotton they are allowed to retain for themselves. In an age of unmatched prosperity, government tax and regulatory policies have turned the average citizen's life into a financial struggle and insured that he will almost certainly become a ward of the state for his last decades.

The more of a person's paycheck the government takes, the more of the citizen's life the government controls, directly or indirectly. Historian W. H. Chamberlin observed in 1958:

> One of the most insidious consequences of the present burden of personal income tax is that it strips many middle-class families of financial reserves and seems to lend support to campaigns for socialized medicine, socialized housing, socialized food, socialized everything. The personal income tax has made the individual vastly more dependent on the State and more avid for state handouts. It has shifted the balance in America from an individual-centered to a State-centered economic and social system.[197]

If the government routinely sent U.S. marshals into people's homes and seized almost half of all their belongings, many people would denounce the government for its brutal oppression and for stripping people of the means of their existence. Yet the government currently imposes a withholding system that takes almost half of many citizens' income before citizens ever see it. The payroll tax-withholding system (imposed in 1942 as a temporary "victory tax" program) has immortalized the principle that politicians have "first dibs" on the workers' paycheck. Politicians have given hundreds of different groups, industries, and special interests a preemptive lien to the paycheck of the individual citizen.

Commandeering the fruits of twenty years of labor radically changes a person's life, effectively insuring that he will be subjugated to the government schools in his youth, reliant on government handouts in his old age, and looking over his shoulder at the tax collector for all the years in between.

UNLIMITED TAXATION MEANS UNLIMITED POWER

Some local governments do not go through the "voluntary" song-and-dance charade that the IRS performs. The Fairfax County, Virginia, government launched a ten-minute cable television show in 1993 called "Tax Evaders!" Half of the TV screen showed in large print the names and addresses of delinquent local taxpayers; the other half of the TV screen showed pictures of deputy sheriffs seizing automobiles and auctioning off houses. An announcer ominously warned viewers: "Rest assured. If you owe taxes, we will collect them."[198] Fairfax County officials told the *Washington Post* that they expected to seize 150 vehicles and "slap 100,000 liens on wages or bank accounts in this fiscal year."[199] Fairfax Board of Supervisors chairman Thomas M. Davis said: "The fear factor is an important motivator for people to pay taxes."[200] The show appeals to the basest instincts of viewers: "The 10-minute show . . . has inspired dozens of county residents to call a hot line to turn in neighbors whose cars don't show that they've paid their taxes."[201] Fairfax officials have received calls from many other local governments across the nation who are interested in copying the Fairfax model. Fairfax residents are forced to pay $1.6 million in surcharges on their cable bills for the county government to provide "public service" cable programming each year.[202] The government forces people to pay for a TV channel for the county government that is then used to browbeat the county residents.

The constant dishonest recitation of the word "voluntary" in relation to taxes is an attempt to delude people about how they are being coerced. Taxation is the most forceful contact most people have with the government: every paycheck time, the government takes the lion's share. The dogma of a "voluntary tax system" is much more important psychologically than just another politically opportunistic slogan. People pay taxes in order to avoid being put in prison and having their property seized by heavily armed government agents.

Alexander Hamilton, who later became the first secretary of the treasury, wrote in 1782: "The genius of liberty reprobates everything arbitrary or discretionary in taxation. . . . Whatever liberty we may boast in theory, it cannot exist in fact while [arbitrary tax] assessments continue."[203] Unfortunately, as Gale Ann Norton, now Colorado's attorney general, noted in 1985, "The constitutional principles governing taxation generally reflect the law school adage, 'If Congress will pass it, it's constitutional.'"[204] This creates an almost invincible presumption in favor of the legislator's prerogative to seize people's paychecks.

The most important development in modern political thinking may be the shift in presumption as to who has the right to a dollar: the person who earned it or the politicians who control the machinery of state. The Sixteenth Amendment to the Constitution gave Congress unlimited power to tax. In 1943 the Supreme Court declared that "an income tax deduction is a matter of legislative grace."[205] This statement, quoted hundreds of times in subsequent federal court decisions, confirms that Congress has acquired an unlimited right to any citizen's income simply by legislative decree. "Grace" means "favor," and thus the Supreme Court effectively means that allowing citizens to retain some of their income is simply a favor that politicians choose to give (at least until further notice).

The more of people's income the government seizes, the more control politicians have over private citizens' lives. Current tax policy is based on the unwritten premise that the citizen has an unlimited obligation to the government—and to the politicians who control that government. Taxes are a debt to the State—a debt that politicians can unilaterally increase at any time, for any pretext, for any corporation or group or class. At what point does taxation become a form of political slavery? The city of Boston resolved in May 1772: "It's evident to the meanest Understanding that Great Britain can have no Right to take our Moneys from us without our consents unless we are her Slaves, unless our bodies and our Persons are her property she surely cannot have the least claim to dispose of our earnings."[206] It is absurd to assume that, simply because a citizen lives in the geographical territory of a government, that the citizen automatically consents to have that government seize all or almost all of his earnings.

Tax rates are a moral magic wand by which politicians magically transform the nature of property. Politicians can change the "distribution" of property between themselves and all other citizens simply by adding a few lines to a thousand-page obscure bill that not a single congressman has read, and few congressmen understand. Congressmen can add a single sentence to a revenue bill—and ensure that the individual citizen becomes a criminal if he does not promptly deliver another portion of his income to the government.

There is a fundamental dichotomy in politicians' right to seize workers' paychecks and their duty to spend the workers' money wisely. President Grover Cleveland declared in 1886, "When more of the people's sustenance is exacted through the form of taxation than is necessary to meet the just obligations of government and expenses of its economical administration, such exaction becomes ruthless extortion and a violation of the principles of a free government." Yet according to the 1993 Clinton administration report *Reinventing Government*, "The average American believes we waste 48 cents of every tax dollar."[207] Government has a right to imprison people for not paying their taxes but no duty to spend their tax dollars wisely. The justice of taxation is especially doubtful when so many government programs simply transfer money from one person to another person, or from one business to another business. On what basis can politicians rightfully seize one man's earnings and give them to another man? The Supreme Court, in the 1875 case of *Savings and Loan Association v. Topeka*, declared, "To lay with one hand the power of the government on the property of the citizen and with the other to bestow it upon favored individuals to aid private enterprises and build up private fortunes is none the less a robbery because it is done under the forms of law and is called taxation."[208]

-9-

Spiking Speech, Bankrupting Newspapers, and Jamming Broadcasts

The First Amendment states that "Congress shall make no law . . . abridging the freedom of speech, or of the press." Despite the apparent lucidity of this restriction on government power, the meaning of the First Amendment has been hotly debated for almost 200 years. In recent years, zealous bureaucrats and ambitious politicians have discovered a flock of new exemptions to the First Amendment. Though Americans in some ways have more freedom of speech than their ancestors, the growth of government power is generating new threats and restrictions our forefathers never experienced. We will survey some of the current controversies over government censorship.

COMBATING ILLICIT PORTRAYALS OF NIPPLES ET AL.

Thanks to recent government crackdowns, millions of Americans have been prevented from poisoning their minds by watching such video movies as *Bimbo Bowlers from Buffalo*.[1] Technology is now allowing people to enjoy more diverse entertainment in their own homes, thereby ending the problem of adult movie theaters tainting decent neighborhoods. But some politicians have responded by declaring that some books, magazines, and videos are so immoral that the government must achieve absolute control over what people are allowed to view in private. The war on pornography has become a political crusade—combining vague concepts of crimes and a total lack of scruples by prosecutors.

In the early years of the American republic, few states had laws banning sexually obscene material, and prosecutions were a rarity in the decades before the Civil War.[2] But with the onset of the Victorian era, the suppression of vice became the path to fame for many postal inspectors.

The Supreme Court has struggled for decades to get a clear, coherent rule on the relationship of adult erotica to the First Amendment. The Supreme

Court, in the 1957 decision on *Roth v. U.S.*, declared that the proper test of obscenity is "whether to the average person, applying contemporary community standards, the dominant theme of the material taken as a whole appeals to prurient interest."[3] The Court explained that "appeal to prurient interest is defined as material having a tendency to excite lustful thoughts."[4] The Court did not explain, however, why sparking lustful thoughts should be considered criminal conduct. In 1963 the Supreme Court noted that constitutionally protected expression is "often separated from obscenity only by a dim and uncertain line."[5] In 1969 the Supreme Court declared in the case of *Stanley v. Georgia:*

> If the First Amendment means anything, it means that a State has no business telling a man, sitting alone in his own house, what books he may read or what films he may watch. . . . Whatever may be the justifications for other statutes regulating obscenity, we do not think they reach into the privacy of one's own home. . . . Our whole constitutional heritage rebels at the thought of giving government the power to control men's minds.[6]

This was a high-water mark in the history of Supreme Court decisions concerning sexually oriented material. In 1973 the Supreme Court deduced a new test to measure the limits of First Amendment protections, declaring that obscenity would be judged by:

> (a) whether the average person, applying contemporary community standards would find that the work, taken as a whole, appeals to the prurient interest . . . (b) whether the work depicts or describes, in a patently offensive way, sexual conduct specifically defined by the applicable state law; and (c) whether the work, taken as a whole, lacks serious literary, artistic, political, or scientific value.[7]

But it is often impossible to know what the "community standards" are until after alleged pornographers have been prosecuted—and the "standards" can differ greatly depending on which twelve people are least able to dodge jury duty. The government does not simply ask a dozen people at random whether they personally have seen anything recently in their community that they have considered obscene. Instead, prosecutors go out and commandeer the most revolting material, put twelve people in a government courtroom, show it to them while declaiming how terrible it is, and then seek to use that small group to restrict what everyone else in the community can see. The Justice Department has repeatedly refused to provide any formal definition of what it considers obscene. (Justice Department spokesman Doug Tillett did reveal in 1991 that "all we have to do is hear the titles and we know" whether a video or magazine is legally obscene.)[8]

In 1985 Attorney General Ed Meese appointed members to a federal commission to examine pornography and its social effects. Meese announced that his appointments "reflected the concern a healthy society must have regarding the ways in which its people *publicly* entertain themselves."[9] But from the start, the Meese Commission devoted itself largely to the ways that people *privately* entertain themselves. (Even the Meese Commission conceded in its final report that the "predominant" use of "standard pornography . . . is as a masturbatory aid.")[10] The Meese Commission began by using a far broader definition of pornography than the Supreme Court justified, labeling as "pornography" all material that is "predominantly sexually explicit and intended primarily for the purpose of sexual arousal."[11] An official from the commission sent a letter to two dozen convenience and drug store chains informing them that they had been identified as distributors of pornography for selling various popular men's magazines. Over 8,000 drug and convenience stores quickly ceased selling *Playboy* and *Penthouse.* A federal judge ruled a few months later that the commission had violated the First Amendment because of its "implied threat" to publicly identify the stores as porn distributors.[12] After tours of numerous adult bookstores, the commission issued a 2,000-page report in July 1986. (The long report had a lot of padding; as columnist Michael Kinsley noted, 108 pages were devoted to an alphabetized list of suspect magazines, including "Big Boobs, Big Boobs #1 and #2, Big Boobs Bonanza, Big Boys and Their Buddies, Big Bust Bondage" et al.)[13] The Meese Commission concluded that more government restrictions were needed because "we live in a society unquestionably pervaded by sexual explicitness."[14]

Inspired by the commission's recommendations, Meese created the National Obscenity Enforcement Unit within the Justice Department. The number of federal obscenity indictments quickly jumped by over 800 percent.[15] The first director of the unit, Rob Showers, declared that "any kind of nudity, particularly frontal nudity, male or female, and any sex act [is] immoral and obscene." Showers even reportedly believed that a woman's bare breasts are "offensive and repugnant."[16]

Federal porn warriors inverted the 1973 Supreme Court "community standards" rule to try to destroy the adult entertainment industry. Federal judge Barefoot Sandres observed in 1991, "What the government seeks to do, is to prosecute obscenity cases in what they perceive to be the most conservative communities in the nation and then to impose such standards on the rest of the nation by means of seeking the forfeiture of all assets of any company convicted for the sale of even two videos based upon those local standards."[17] The Justice Department also carried out a war of attrition against their targets, suing each company in multiple jurisdictions. Federal judge Thomas Penfield Jackson condemned the Justice Department's strategy, declaring that "simultaneous criminal prosecutions of the same individual for the same offense in four separate federal judicial districts . . . cannot possibly be consistent with Due Process,"[18] and called the government's tactics "annihilation by attrition."[19] In a 1990 case, federal judge Joyce Green declared: "The enormous disparity between plaintiffs' resources and the resources of the government means, as a practical matter, that plaintiffs could be swiftly driven out of business before they ever set foot inside a courtroom."[20] A federal appeals court denounced the government's conduct in 1992 as "a persistent and widespread campaign to coerce" individuals "into surrendering their First Amendment rights."[21]

The Justice Department combined the inverted "community standards" test with the Racketeering Influence and Corrupt Organizations Act (RICO). RICO was passed in the early 1970s to provide federal agents with a nuclear bomb to drop on suspected drug kingpins and Mafia types. RICO allows the government to seize almost all of a suspected criminal's assets—thereby crippling his ability to hire defense attorneys. Obscenity violations are offenses under RICO; anyone who sells more than one obscene item officially becomes a racketeer.

Virginians Dennis and Barbara Pryba were imprisoned and required to forfeit $1 million to the federal government in 1988 for selling six obscene magazines and four videotapes, valued at $105.[22] The Dallas police set up Good Vibrations, Inc., a video store in Texas, ordered two adult video tapes costing $9.90 each from California Publisher Liquidating Corp., and then filed suit along with the U.S. Justice Department to seize millions of dollars in assets from the California producers for violating Texas standards of decency.[23] The Justice Department also sought to confiscate a $7.5 million California printing plant because the company had printed one video box (for which it received 60 cents) for a movie later judged obscene in Dallas.[24] (Judge Sandres blocked the government's seizure attempt.) On June 30, 1992, a federal judge levied a forfeiture penalty of $500,000 on a New York videotape distributor for the crime of sending a single obscene video (titled "Caught in the Middle") from New York to northern Virginia in 1986.[25] In September 1992, the Justice Department seized $3.5 million in assets from a California firm as a penalty for mailing videotapes to Tallahassee, Florida.[26]

The Justice Department has vigorously encouraged U.S. attorneys to file local obscenity cases. Minneapolis's city government had previously indicated that it would initiate obscenity prosecutions only against purveyors of smut depicting child porn or bestiality. (The animal rights movement is very strong in Minnesota.) But, disregarding the local government's standard, one assistant U.S. attorney launched a major effort against the owner of thirteen local erotica shops.[27] After a fourteen-month grand jury investigation and a four-month trial, Ferris Alexander was convicted of the sale of four obscene magazines and three obscene videos (none of which featured children or animals)—a minuscule percentage of the material sold at his wholesale and retail adult-entertainment outlets.

U.S. marshals quickly seized over 100,000 books, magazines, and videotapes from Alexander's stores, as well as the stores themselves, ten plots of land, bank accounts, two vans, and a trailer. While Alexander appealed his conviction, the government burned his books and crushed his videotapes. The massive destruction of the three tons of materials overwhelmed a Minnesota garbage processing plant, resulting in a minor explosion.[28] The vast majority of the items destroyed by the feds had never been declared to be obscene; some of the books and magazines were not even related to sex.

Alexander estimated the value of the seized businesses and other assets at roughly $25 million. (The government claimed it had to destroy the confiscated goods because it could not afford the $5,000 monthly storage fee.)[29] Thus, for each obscene magazine and video Alexander was convicted of selling, the Justice Department effectively imposed a penalty of over $3 million. In July 1992, after the Supreme Court accepted the case for review, federal attorneys awarded the title on a $145,000 plot of Alexander's land to the Minneapolis city government for only $1.[30] (This is typical of the political racketeering that occurs under RICO, with federal and local governments divvying up the plunder they seize from private citizens.) The Supreme Court on June 28, 1993, upheld the judgment against Alexander, but did remand the decision to an appeals court to determine whether the forfeiture penalty was excessive. Justice Anthony Kennedy issued a sharp dissent to the ruling:

> The admitted design and the overt purpose of the forfeiture in this case are to destroy an entire speech business and all its protected titles, thus depriving the public of access to lawful expression. . . . It is censorship all too real . . . Here the inventory forfeited consisted of hundreds of original titles and thousands of copies, all of which are presumed to be protected speech. In fact, some of the materials seized were the very ones the jury here determined not to be obscene. Even so, all of the inventory was seized and destroyed. . . . The Court embraces a rule that would find no affront to the First Amendment in the Government's destruction of a book and film business and its entire inventory of legitimate expression as punishment for a single past speech offense.[31]

The Justice Department's RICO-obscenity double whammy poses a growing threat to the nation's cultural institutions. If a Cincinnati jury had found the Cincinnati Museum of Art guilty of obscenity for displaying the photographs of Robert Mapplethorpe, federal officials could potentially have seized the entire museum and all its other paintings.[32] If a local jury found that certain rap records sold by Tower Records were obscene, the Justice Department could file to seize all Tower Records stores in the nation. If a major Hollywood film studio makes two movies later declared obscene in one locale, the Justice Department could conceivably confiscate the entire studio and burn its film archives. The Justice Department could also start using the obscenity offenses in the same way it uses offenses for possession of small amounts of drugs—as a license to throw people out of their own homes. If someone sold two dog-eared sex magazines to his next-door neighbor in Forkville, Mississippi, prosecutors could try to label the person a racketeer and seize the person's house.

At least one local official has used the "community standards" definition of obscenity to destroy a national corporation. In March 1990, Montgomery County, Alabama, district attorney Jimmy Evans sought to boost his campaign for state attorney general by cracking down on a satellite television transmission service. Home Dish Satellite Corp. was a New York–based company that beamed hard- and soft-core sex films to over a million homes nationwide, including roughly fifty homes in Montgomery County.[33] Evans proclaimed at a press conference: "There is more human degradation and exploitation of the female [in the companies' programming] than the human spirit can abide," and denounced Home Dish Satellite for transmitting "the most extreme examples of the diabolical craft of hard-core pornography."[34] Evans indicted Home Dish Satellite for violating local obscenity laws and asked New York to extradite the company's four officers. When New York governor Mario Cuomo refused to extradite the company's directors to Alabama for trial, Evans denounced Cuomo and declared, "By his action, Cuomo has invited the smut peddlers to come to New York to peddle their filthy wares across the nation with the promise he will protect them from prosecution."[35] The resulting legal costs and threats of imprisonment quickly drove the satellite company out of business. Thus, one county's obscenity laws were used to prevent people in the other 3,044 counties in the United States from paying to receive the programming of their choice.[36]

The vague "community standards" definition also makes it easy for law enforcement officials to harass and intimidate local businesses. On June 26, 1992, Hendricks County, Indiana, prosecutor Kevin Hinkle sent a letter to local video store owners giving them seven days to remove all X-rated videos from their stores and warned them that he would begin prosecuting all store owners who retained any material deemed obscene under Indiana law. The Indiana Civil Liberties Union quickly struck back, informing Hinkle in a letter that "you clearly have no authority either by virtue of your office or under obscenity law to 'pronounce' what constitutes a community standard." The prosecutor backed down, but warned that he would find other ways to restrain the stores.[37] An ACLU study noted, "Law enforcement authorities in Georgia, Iowa, Ohio, Pennsylvania, Nebraska and other states have threatened to bring obscenity prosecutions against distributors who rent or sell X-rated, NC-17 rated, and even unrated videos."[38]

The war on porn necessarily diverts scarce law enforcement resources from fighting more dangerous crimes. In Miramar, Florida, police were staking out a convenience store to prevent armed robberies. While the police were awaiting bandits, they witnessed store clerk Elaine Ott sell a copy of *Playboy* to two sixteen-year-old boys. The police quickly arrested, strip-searched, and jailed the fifty-two-year-old woman, who faced five years in prison and a $5,000 fine for the felony of selling obscene material to a minor. Ott complained that she could not understand why she could sell condoms to minors, but not magazines.[39] The following night, after the police were no longer there, Mrs. Ott's husband was robbed at gunpoint.

Congress has effectively made every photo development company a spy for the local police and FBI. Federal law now requires photo development companies to examine all photos that they process and to send suspicious-looking photographs (for example, photographs with nudity) to local police for possible prosecution. As a result, photo labs routinely copy and secretly deliver to the police thousands of rolls of film each year. Photo labs that fail to turn in their customers to the police face heavy fines and loss of business licenses. Lawyer Lawrence Stanley noted in the *Cardozo Arts and Entertainment Law Journal,* "At least dozens of parents have been arrested after innocently photographing their children naked and then attempting to have those pictures developed at local film processing stores."[40]

Alice Sims was a forty-one-year-old commercial photographer in Alexandria, Virginia, and mother of two in 1988 when she did a photo session of a nude four-year-old daughter of a friend; the pictures were intended to be models for a series of paintings of naked children and water lilies entitled "Water Babies."[41] (The child's mother was in attendance at the photo session.) Sims took the roll of film to a Dart Drug store to be developed. A Dart Drug employee looked at the photographs and called the Postal Inspection Service, who alerted the Alexandria police. Police and postal inspectors then swarmed upon Sims's house. As *Legal Times* reported, "Armed with a search warrant, the police proceeded to rip through her house, removing three bags of cameras, undeveloped film, slides of an adult who had posed nude for a portrait, several commercial adult videos, and address books that might reveal the names of others in a possible kiddy-porn network."[42] Later that day, state social workers seized custody of Sims's children and handed her a form letter declaring, "This is to inform you that it is necessary to remove your child(ren) from your custody and place them temporarily until a more permanent solution can be found. . . . There will be a court hearing in the near future . . . to explore the evidence of alleged abuse or neglect of your child(ren)." Her children were held at a foster home overnight. At a subsequent hearing, the police and the Department of Social Services (DSS) produced no evidence of child abuse except for the photographs. The judge harshly criticized the DSS and ordered the children to be returned to Sims, and the prosecution for child porn was dropped.

One of the most famous child porn prosecutions was the FBI's April 1990 raid on the San Francisco studio of Jock Sturges, an internationally known photographer whose pictures have been displayed in the Metropolitan Museum of Art. Sturges sent some pictures he took on a nude beach to a local film developer, who forwarded the film to the FBI. Six FBI agents raided Sturges's home and office. The *Los Angeles Times* reported that the agents "turned his apartment upside down, stuffed most everything he owned into a van and drove off."[43] An ACLU report noted, "The agents . . . seized hundreds of thousands of his photo negatives and thousands of photographic prints (most not even nudes), as well as his personal papers, address books, business records, computer and photographic equipment, and passport."[44] Federal prosecutors asserted in December 1990 that Sturges's pictures were undoubtedly child pornography and included one picture of Sturges having sex with an underage female.[45] As the ACLU report noted, "After a massive international investigation—including interrogation of art gallery owners and demands for their customer lists—and a lengthy presentation to a federal grand jury in the spring of 1991, the grand jury refused to indict Sturges. But the damage to Sturges's career had been done. His ability to function as a commercial photographer was seriously impaired by the seizure of his equipment and records and by the government's continuing accusations that he was a child pornographer. When the government finally returned Sturges's equipment, some of it was badly damaged. About 80 percent of his commercial negatives were returned smudged or ruined. Police wrote 'no porn scene' in heavy black marker across the bindings in which the negatives were kept."[46] Sturges estimates that the government spent over $1 million prosecuting him.[47]

Some state laws on pornography and obscenity are potentially all-encompassing. In November 1991, the Florida Supreme Court struck down in part the Florida child-porn statute because the law defined illegal "sexual conduct" with children to include "actual physical contact with a person's clothed or unclothed genitals, pubic area, buttocks, or if such a person is a female, breast." As the court noted,

> A comparison of [the child pornography] statute with Florida's civil child-abuse statute reveals a puzzling inconsistency. . . . On the face of the former statute, anyone who owns a photograph of a parent changing a baby's diaper technically has committed the crime of unlawfully possessing a depiction of "sexual conduct by a child," at least as that term is defined in subsection 827.071(1)(g). This crime is a third degree felony punishable by up to five years in prison. Yet the actual act of changing the diaper is expressly declared not to be a form of child abuse under chapter 415 and thus would not even prompt a state investigation of the matter.[48]

The decision noted that "virtually any photograph of close physical contact with a minor violates the statute." (The Florida legislature subsequently revised the statute.)

Child pornography laws have also stoked the creativity of federal judges. In 1991 a federal judge convicted Stephen Knox, a graduate student at Penn State University, of violating the child pornography statutes because he had in his possession three videotapes that showed girls aged ten to seventeen wearing swimsuits, leotards, shorts, or underwear. The girls' genital areas were covered in all of the videotapes. But—revealing that anatomy experts have been mistaken for hundreds of years—the judge announced that the uppermost portion of the inner thigh is part of the "pubic area"—and thus Knox was guilty because of the girls' bare thighs. Knox was sentenced to five years in prison, but the judge permitted him to remain free on bail while appealing the decision because there was "absolutely no evidence of any inclination by the defendant of untoward conduct toward anyone else."[49] The

Third Circuit of Federal Appeals rejected the "thigh as pubic area" discovery of the lower federal judge but condemned Knox on new grounds. Even though the girls' pubic areas were covered in all pictures, the covered areas were still a pornographic "lascivious exhibition of the genitals or pubic area" because the "video tapes clearly were designed to pander to pedophiles." The court declared whether an item is "lascivious" depends on a "subjective inquiry into whether or not the material is intended to elicit a sexual response from the viewer."[50] With this definition, almost anything that a federal judge suspects could incite an erection could be criminalized. Knox's brief appealing the decision to the Supreme Court noted, "Depictions of minors in bathing suits, leotards, shorts, underwear, and other similar clothing are created every day and may be found everywhere throughout society. . . . Anyone who has photographed a minor at a dance recital, swim or gymnastics meet, at the beach, or at home, will understand the danger of photographing a minor in a pose which could ultimately be deemed to be pornographic under federal law."[51] The Supreme Court was also urged to overturn the expansive new definition of pornography by the American Booksellers Foundation and the Magazine Publishers of America, which feared that publishers would be prosecuted as pornographers for selling common, everyday magazines.

Of course, prosecuting people for child sexual abuse is completely different from prosecuting people for bearskin rug photos. The government should vigorously prosecute and harshly punish people guilty of abusing children; too many child abusers have gotten off with light sentences and have repeated their ravages. But the child porn prosecutions of recent years have done a poor job of finding cases of actual child abuse; federal sting operations resulted in 225 individuals being indicted for possessing child pornography, but the vast majority of those indicted had not committed any other indictable offenses involving children.[52] (The indictments did produce four suicides.)[53] The government would be better off devoting its prosecutorial resources against people who actually abuse children, rather than people guilty of taking pictures of babies in bathtubs.

The Federal Communications Commission regulates indecency and imposes many more restrictions on broadcasts than the government imposes on print media. In 1987 the FCC issued new guidelines to crack down on indecent programming. But the guidelines were extremely vague, defining "indecent programming" as programming "that describes in terms patently offensive as measured by contemporary community standards for the broadcast medium, sexual or excretory activities or organs."[54] FCC commissioners warned at that time that they would begin cracking down on innuendos. The FCC also officially decreed that it considers "talk of the penis" to be indecent;[55] yet public school sex education teachers have children from kindergarten onward repeat the word like a mantra.

In 1987 Pacifica Radio sent a transcript of a planned broadcast to FCC commissioner James Quello for a ruling on whether the broadcast would be illegal. Quello initially denounced the material but retracted his criticism after he discovered it was an excerpt from James Joyce's *Ulysses*. Quello then complained that Pacifica Radio had "entrapped" the commission by asking for a ruling on the material without initially revealing that it came from a famous novel.[56]

FCC commissioners have struggled valiantly in recent years to protect Americans against double entendres. In a 1987 ruling, the FCC declared that "in certain circumstances, innuendo or double-entendre may be rendered explicit or capable of only one meaning when intermingled with explicit references that make the meaning of the entire discussion clear and thus may give rise to actionable indecency."[57] After an intensive textual analysis by government experts, the FCC decreed in a case regarding Houston's radio station KLOL that "references to 'pee pee enlargement' leaves no doubt that the descriptions of length and shape refer to sexual organs. Accordingly, the surrounding context of these broadcasts points to only one possible interpretation, a sexual one. Under these circumstances, a finding of indecency is clearly supported."[58] In a 1988 case, the FCC commissioners, perhaps succumbing to the general depravity of contemporary American culture, ruled that the song "I Want to Kiss Her, But . . ." was not indecent, despite the double entendre: "The lyrics at issue here are not such that they are capable of only one, sexual meaning. Rather, the lyrics are capable of two meanings—one innocent, one sexual."[59]

In 1992 the FCC fined Infinity Broadcasting $600,000 because nationally syndicated broadcaster Howard Stern allegedly violated community standards. The FCC also threatened to revoke Infinity Broadcasting's federal license, thereby effectively destroying the company.[60] At the time, Stern had the top-rated morning radio show in both New York and Los Angeles. As an *Orange County Register* editorial noted, "It's just silly to contend that a personality who becomes No. 1 in radio's most important sector, morning drive time, has done so by flagrantly violating a community's standards. . . . Popular radio personalities generally get to be popular by reflecting prevailing standards, rather than by violating them."[61] The FCC printed a transcript of comments that the commissioners considered indecent, including Stern's assertion that if he were actress Michelle Pfeiffer's lover, "her rump would be more black and blue than a Harlem Cub Scout" and his confession that "the closest I came to making love to a black woman was [when] I masturbated to a picture of Aunt Jemima on a pancake box."[62]

While the FCC is increasingly cracking down on private broadcasters, the FCC is more lenient on public broadcasting. In 1989 a Tennessee man complained about language used on a National Public Radio report about mobster John Gotti. The FCC commissioners voted 4 to 1 in 1991 that NPR had not violated the FCC's decency guidelines and that the Gotti segment was "an integral part of a bona fide news story concerning organized crime."[63] But dissenting commissioner Ervin Duggan complained that the FCC should not ignore the language simply because it was contained in a newscast that repeated ten times, in Duggan's words, "the one expletive that has traditionally been considered the most objectionable, the most forbidden, and the most patently offensive to civilized and cultivated people: the F-word."[64] The FCC justifies broadcast restrictions in part because of a fear that young children may be corrupted by what they hear. Thus the FCC's position on the Gotti broadcast is peculiar. Should mothers explain to young children that using the word *fuck* is perfectly acceptable as long as someone is discussing the Mafia—i.e., "If you want to disregard my fucking phone calls I'll blow you and the fucking house up"?[65]

Most government restrictions on adult erotica have been based on the assumption that pornography directly causes violence and sexual assault against women and children. But as federal judge Jerry Buchmeyer observed in 1986, "There is . . . judicial recognition that the tenuous link between pornography and crime is not sufficiently established to form the basis of any sound public policy."[66] A 1988 Justice Department report on porn complained, "Pornography is now available in virtually every neighborhood in America through video cassette rental outlets, cable and pay television access, and 'dial-a-porn' telephonic communications."[67] The Adult Video Association asserted that fifty-two million Americans rented about 400 million X-rated videos from neighborhood video shops in 1990.[68] If people in almost every community choose to rent certain videos, then how can it be that such movies violate community standards? With the proliferation of video movies, cable channels, and satellite broadcasting, the Supreme Court's definition of obscenity—"the average person, applying contemporary community standards"—is more irrelevant than ever before. The "community standards" definition may be appropriate for judging billboards or other direct public displays, but it makes no sense to allow the majority to decide what people will be allowed to see in the privacy of their own homes. The best "community standard" is simply that if individuals in a certain community don't want certain types of smut, they won't buy it. People should have unlimited freedom to denounce the evils of pornography, but the right to denounce should not be extended to the right to control one's neighbor.

POLICE STATE SHENANIGANS

The First Amendment was intended to create a haven from politicians' power lust. Yet police and local officials sometimes blatantly disregard constitutional restrictions on their power to censor private citizens. In 1988 the Chicago School of Art Institute held its annual student art competition. One student entered a work entitled *Mirth and Girth*, a portrait of the late Mayor Harold Washington in bra and panties, holding a pencil.[69] Within hours of hearing of the painting's existence, the city council passed resolutions demanding that the picture be taken down immediately and threatening to cut off all public funds if the Art Institute did not apologize for displaying the work.[70] Three city aldermen marched into the Institute's art gallery, grabbed *Mirth and Girth,* and sought to leave the Institute. (Alderman Dorothy Tillman, a federal court decision noted, "stated that she intended to tear, burn and destroy the painting and that she did not care that it was private property.")[71] The Institute's security guard prevented them from leaving with the painting, so they marched to the office of the Institute's president, loudly denouncing the painting all the way. Chicago police took possession of the painting a few hours later; by then, the painting had a foot-long gash in it. Before the aldermen would relinquish the painting to the police, they forced the Institute's director, Anthony Jones, to sign a formal statement declaring, "The work, if returned by any person to this school, will not be displayed or shown in any way without a meeting and resolution of the Board of Trustees and members of the City Council."[72] The painter, David Nelson, sued the aldermen and the city of Chicago for damages and for violations of his constitutional rights.

The aldermen later claimed in a court deposition that the painting, which was by a white student, "increased tensions in the African-American community to the point where violence on the scale of the 1960s West Side riots was imminent."[73] But federal judge Elaine E. Bucklo ruled, "The aldermanic defendants cannot assert a threat of violence that they themselves caused to justify an infringement of Mr. Nelson's First Amendment rights." The three aldermen claimed that they had not infringed upon the painter's First Amendment rights because their seizure of his painting made him temporarily famous. The judge rejected this claim, noting that "Mr. Nelson, not the City or other government actors, was entitled to choose before whom to display his painting." Federal judge George Lindberg ruled in August 1992 that the aldermen violated the painter's First, Fourth, and Fourteenth Amendment rights.[74]

In San Francisco in May 1992, police confiscated thousands of copies of the *San Francisco Bay Times* newspaper after it ridiculed Police Chief Richard Hongisto by putting a picture of him on the cover with a police baton extending from his groin with the headline, "Dick's Cool New Tool: Martial Law."[75] (The cover was a jab at Hongisto for alleged police overreaction to a public disturbance the previous week.) San Francisco Police Commission president Harry Low told the press: "We believe that the chief initiated a conversation and suggested to a subordinate . . . that large quantities of newspapers should be collected."[76] Hongisto was fired as a result of the newspaper seizure, but the FBI and Justice Department chose not to file charges against him for violating the newspaper's constitutional rights.

Some federal agents act as if high-tech communications are effectively exempt from the First Amendment. On March 1, 1990, Secret Service agents raided the premises of an Austin, Texas, computer game manufacturer and seized a book manuscript, three computers, a computer bulletin board and all the private messages on it, and over 300 computer discs primarily because they suspected that a computer game the company was about to release would be a "handbook for computer crime." Their action effectively imposed "prior restraint" on the company to prevent it from publishing—even though the Secret Service had no evidence that the game could actually be used by anyone to commit a computer crime and even though the federal agents were informed at the time of the raid that their action was a blatant violation of the federal Privacy Protection Act. The Secret Service refused to return the "Gurps Cyberpunk" material for four months, and Steve Jackson, the company's owner, was forced by the seizure to layoff half of his seventeen employees.[77] Jackson complained, "It's as if the Secret Service targeted Parker Brothers for marketing Clue because it's a handbook for murder."[78] Jackson sued the Secret Service; in an April 1993 decision, federal judge Sam Sparks ruled, "Prior to March 1, 1990, and at all other times, there has never been any basis for suspicion that [Steve Jackson] engaged in any criminal activity, violated any law, or attempted to communicate, publish, or store any illegally obtained information or otherwise provide access to any illegally obtained information or to solicit any information which was to be used illegally."[79] The judge concluded that "Secret Service personnel or its delegates did read all electronic communications seized and did delete certain information and communications" without Jackson's permission.

SUING PEOPLE INTO SILENCE

Libel laws are the bulwark of the First Amendment. Speech about public figures is constitutionally protected unless it is inaccurate, defamatory, and malicious. But increasingly in America, we have free speech for public officials but not for private citizens. Federal officials, congressmen, and many state and local officials are immune to libel charges for almost anything they say about private citizens. Yet these same officials are suing and financially destroying private citizens for criticizing them.

In June 1993, a citizens committee in Orange, Ohio, launched a recall petition demanding new elections for mayor and city council; Mayor Joseph Dubyak and Council President Marc Silberman responded by threatening to file $6 million lawsuits for slander and libel against each member of the committee.[80] The threat spiked a protest movement; Carmen Centanni, a leader of the citizens committee, complained: "This is another case of winning through intimidation."[81] The city of Worcester, Massachusetts, filed a $500,000 lawsuit against twenty-three citizens who requested a state environmental agency to review plans for expansion of the city's airport.[82] Colleen Densic and Lavena Leese requested public records from Garden City, Michigan; a city manager illegally denied their request. When the women put out a civic newsletter detailing request denials and raising questions about city government spending, Garden City councilwoman Mary Jane Schildberg and former councilman Paul Majka sued them for defamation.[83]

Sociologists have coined a new word—SLAPPs (Strategic Lawsuits Against Public Participation)—to capture the recent proliferation of a new type of lawsuit. SLAPPs are "civil lawsuits . . . that are aimed at preventing citizens from exercising their political rights or punishing those who have done so."[84] As *Newsweek* noted,

> The most harmful SLAPPs involve politicians attacking their constituents. An Agoura Hills, Calif., neighborhood association that tried to recall several city council members—for alleged violations of the state's open-meetings law—found itself facing a $1 million defamation suit from one of the officials. . . . Two Hudson Falls, N.Y., citizen groups who went to court last February to stop construction of a $74 million trash incinerator were countersued by Washington and Warren counties for $1.5 million. Officials contend that the opposition drove off prospective buyers of bonds to finance the project, hiking costs. Warren County Attorney Thomas Lawson added an intimidating touch by announcing that the defendants risked losing their homes. The suit was dismissed by a state appellate court in January.[85]

One study found that the average SLAPP case remains in court for three years.[86] SLAPP suits have become so common that activist Ralph Nader organized a coalition of lawyers to provide free counsel to people attacked by SLAPPs.[87]

Libel suits and threats of libel suits are now routinely used to muzzle the press and media. In 1992 the Democratic National Committee launched a series of radio ads attacking the congressional Republican leadership in their home districts. When the Republicans retaliated by sending out radio ads hammering leading Democrats, lawyers for Democratic congressman Dick Gephardt flooded the radio stations in his district with letters warning of libel suits if they aired the ads.[88] Former Massachusetts governor Edward King sued the *Boston Globe* over, among other things, three editorial cartoons that portrayed him unfavorably.[89] In May 1992, Rep. Mary Rose Oakar of Ohio sued the *Cleveland Plain Dealer* for $18 million for reporting that she had been forced to resign from a House task force because of allegations that she had placed two ghost employees on the task force's payroll.[90] (In 1987 Oakar admitted paying a personal assistant a congressional office salary even though the woman lived and worked in New York.)[91] In 1990 a Pennsylvania jury awarded $6 million to a state Supreme Court justice because the *Philadelphia Inquirer* allegedly defamed him by reprinting a 1983 series of articles. The jury concluded that the original series on the state Supreme Court was not actionable, but that the reprint of the series was malicious because the *Inquirer* included an editorial and a cartoon in the reprint.[92] (A judge subsequently overturned the jury's verdict.) In 1991 a Philadelphia assistant district attorney sued a Philadelphia newspaper for defamation because, during a name-the-gorilla contest conducted for the Philadelphia

Zoo, the paper published a suggestion from a convict to use the attorney's name.[93] In 1992 a real estate salesman and would-be politician sued the *Orlando Sentinel* for an editorial that asserted that he was practicing negative political campaigning. A Florida circuit court rejected the complaint, noting that "the Plaintiff does not stand accused of any conduct incompatible with his profession as a real estate broker."[94] Donald Gillmor, author of *Power, Publicity, and the Abuse of Libel Law,* noted, "Two South Carolina legislators didn't bother with a civil suit against the publisher of a small weekly in 1988 for criticizing their handling of state funds. They had him arrested, charged with criminal libel and jailed. On sober second thoughts, the lawmakers withdrew their complaints, and a grand jury indictment was voided. . . . The South Carolina statute remains in place, as do criminal libel statutes in at least 24 other jurisdictions, waiting to be used to inflict provisional pain on editors who express disrespect for their elected officials."[95]

Some libel suits almost defy belief. A Philadelphia-area television station aired a story criticizing a local judge's handling of a violation-of-probation hearing that resulted in a convicted criminal remaining at large; the convict subsequently murdered a little girl. The judge sued the television station, seeking damages of "not less than $5 million for defamation, not less than $5 million for invasion of privacy, not less than $6 million for intentional infliction of emotional distress, not less than $1 million for injury to his wife's reputation, and not less than $1 million for his wife's loss of consortium."[96] The case was dismissed on summary judgement in December 1986 by a federal judge who concluded that the television report was "substantially true and based upon court records."[97] The family of a murdered girl has no legal rights against the judge whose action may have contributed to their daughter's death, yet the judge can sue a private corporation that criticized his handling of the case.

When the *New York Times* sneezes from the cost of defending itself against a libel suit, a hundred smaller papers die of pneumonia. In 1985, the average libel suit cost $150,000 in legal fees for the accused.[98] Some small newspapers have stopped covering controversial stories for fear of the crushing legal fees required to defend even an accurate story. As Gene Roberts, former editor of the *Philadelphia Inquirer,* notes, "We have turned a precious right—freedom of speech—over to lawyers who, with their qualifying, quibbling and quarreling, are pricing it out of existence." Irvin Lieberman, publisher of several Pennsylvania papers, declared in 1985 that his papers had stopped doing "any investigative work. Now we are concerned only with births, weddings, deaths and stuff like that."[99] Libel is also becoming a greater threat because of juries' tendencies to award stratospheric amounts to plaintiffs. The average jury award for compensatory and punitive damages in libel cases in 1990 and 1991 was almost $9 million, according to the Libel Defense Resource Center.[100]

The modern standards for libel concerning public officials were established in the 1964 case of *New York Times v. Sullivan.* In 1959, the National

Association for the Advancement of Colored People paid for an advertisement in the *New York Times* asserting that the police and other white officials in Alabama were repressing the civil rights movement. Anthony Lewis, author of *Make No Law,* noted, "The ad spoke of brutal tactics by the police and other white officials to put down the civil rights movement. It named no names; but L. B. Sullivan, a city commissioner of Montgomery, Ala., sued for libel, claiming that brutality would be attributed to him because he was in charge of the Montgomery police. An all-white jury awarded him all he had demanded in damages: $500,000, the largest libel verdict in Alabama history. Other Alabama officials sued over the advertisement, and across the South officials seized on libel suits as a new way to keep the national press from covering the civil rights struggle—by intimidation."[101] The Supreme Court overturned the decision; Justice Brennan, writing for the majority, declared, "Erroneous statement is inevitable in free debate and . . . must be protected if the freedoms of expression are to have the 'breathing space' that they need . . . to survive." The Supreme Court decision established a new test for libel, requiring that a statement about public figures must be malicious as well as inaccurate and defamatory.

Justices Goldberg and Black concurred with Brennan's opinion but argued that citizens and the press should be completely immune from libel actions for their criticism of government officials' conduct, even where deliberate falsehood was alleged. Black observed: "'Malice,' even as defined by the Court, is an elusive, abstract concept, hard to prove and hard to disprove. In my opinion, the Federal Constitution has dealt with this deadly danger to the press in the only way possible without leaving the free press open to destruction—by granting the press an absolute immunity for criticism of the way public officials do their public duty. . . . An unconditional right to say what one pleases about public affairs is what I consider the minimum guarantee of the First Amendment."[102]

Professor Thomas Emerson critiqued the malice test: "Super-refined attempts to separate statements of fact from opinion, to winnow truth out of a mass of conflicting evidence . . . to probe into intents, motives and purposes . . . all these do not fit into the dynamics of a system of freedom of expression. The health and vitality of the system depends more upon untrammeled freedom of discussion, in which all citizens contend vigorously, than in judicial attempts to establish the motives of participants."[103] Ronald Cass, dean of the Boston University School of Law, observed: "The actual malice rule . . . discourages litigation least by the very group with which it was directly concerned"—public officials.[104] Martin Garbus wrote in *The Nation,* "In the absence of a clear definition, malicious conduct is whatever a jury or an appellate court says it is."[105]

The First Amendment does not, however, provide a license for unlimited fabrication by the press. In November 1992, the NBC show "Dateline" aired a segment showing a General Motors truck exploding into flames as it was hit by a car. NBC forgot to mention that a small bomb had been installed on the truck and was exploded by remote control just as the car impacted. GM investigated, found proof of the bomb, and sued for defamation. NBC caved in the following day and agreed to make a formal public apology and to pay all the expenses GM incurred in investigating NBC's novel methods.[106] GM's counterattack devastated the credibility of NBC News and made the network (at least temporarily) a laughingstock in the eyes of the American public.

Government officials routinely make false accusations against private citizens. If government officials were not exempt from libel, then every prosecuting attorney could be potentially sued for each case that he failed to win—since he publicly accused a person of committing a crime, yet did not persuade a judge or a jury of his charge. Every citizen has the right to be a prosecuting attorney against the government for which he is paying. Current libel laws can empower government officials to determine when, where, and how they will be criticized. The harsher the libel penalties, the more political wrongdoing will likely escape public notice.

Even if all journalists were swine, freedom of the press would still be invaluable. Governments rarely admit their mistakes until some outsider exposes their failures. If we wish to know how America's major institutions are really operating, libel law must not be turned into a full-employment program for lawyers. Journalists who do concrete economic damage to private citizens for writing starkly false, knowingly inaccurate reports and malicious statements should be held responsible for their actions. But simply because journalists sometimes make mistakes does not mean that politicians should be allowed to hide their misdeeds.

WHY COMMERCIAL SPEECH IS NOT SPEECH

In 1942 the Supreme Court decreed: "We are . . . clear that the Constitution imposes no . . . restraint on government as respects purely commercial advertising."[107] Federal judge Alex Kozinski explained in 1990, "The Supreme Court plucked the commercial speech doctrine out of thin air. The most remarkable aspect of Justice Roberts' opinion, delivered for a unanimous Court, is that it cites no authority. None. And so was born the commercial speech doctrine."[108] The Supreme Court's decision sharply narrowed the First Amendment and fueled federal agencies' efforts to restrict the statements that private citizens and corporations could make. The decision also begat endless quibbles over what is commercial speech, since the extent of commercial speech delineates the government's power to censor.

In 1976 the Supreme Court modified its stance and extended some constitutional protections to commercial speech. In the case of *Virginia State Board of Pharmacy v. Virginia Citizens Consumer Council*, the Court ruled that a state had no right to restrict price advertising by pharmacists, despite the state's claim that open competition could debase pharmacists' ethics. The Court declared, "It is precisely this kind of choice, between the dangers of suppressing information, and the dangers of its misuse if it is freely available, that the First Amendment makes for us."[109] The Court further noted, "As to the particular consumer's interest in the free flow of commercial information, that interest may be as keen, if not keener by far, than his interest in the day's most urgent political debate." The Supreme Court parenthetically defined commercial speech as speech that "does no more than propose a commercial transaction."

After several subsequent muddled decisions (including a 1980 decision that invented an arcane four-prong test for restrictions on commercial speech),[110] the Supreme Court had a paternalistic relapse in 1986 regarding Puerto Rico's restrictions on local casinos' advertising. The Court declared,

> The Puerto Rico Legislature surely could have prohibited casino gambling by the residents of Puerto Rico altogether. In our view, the greater power to completely ban casino gambling necessarily includes the lesser power to ban advertising of casino gambling. . . . It would just as surely be a strange constitutional doctrine which would concede to the legislature the authority to totally ban a product or activity, but deny to the legislature the authority to forbid the stimulation of demand for the product or activity through advertising on behalf of those who would profit from such increased demand.[111]

This may sound reasonable; but at last report, there was little or nothing that some congressman or regulatory agency did not claim a right to regulate or restrict. According to this doctrine, once some government agency asserts a right to regulate some activity, then people involved in that activity practically automatically forfeit their constitutional rights.

Federal agencies often have the power to muzzle corporations or individuals that they regulate. The Food and Drug Administration has vast discretionary power to ban any drug used in the United States as well as the power to severely restrict what corporations are allowed to say about food and drug products.

Manufacturers must get formal FDA approval for each specific recommended use of their drug. For example, a pharmaceutical company will receive formal FDA approval for a drug to be used to treat a specific type of cancer. Doctors, hospitals, and researchers often later discover that the drug is also effective at treating other types of cancers. Pharmaceutical companies routinely publicize the results of further research on their drugs after the drugs have been approved by the FDA, thereby alerting physicians of other possible ways to save lives.

But in 1991, FDA commissioner David Kessler prohibited pharmaceutical companies from informing doctors of new uses for approved drugs. As an official FDA magazine announced, "FDA Commissioner David A. Kessler, M.D., has warned that the agency will not tolerate the practice of promoting drugs and medical devices for unapproved uses. While physicians may prescribe products for off-label uses, promotion of such uses is illegal, Kessler said . . . [the] FDA is prepared to enforce the law through legal steps such as seizure, injunction and prosecution."[112] Kessler warned, "We will subject not only the manufacturers, but all those involved in the manufacturer's promotion, to the full force of the law. We also intend to identify promotional activities that are disguised as education or public relations and hold these activities to the same standards as traditional promotional techniques."[113]

But the FDA can't keep up with modern medicine. The *New York Times* noted, "In the fast-changing world of cancer treatment, the uses on an F.D.A. label often lag years behind standard treatment. Today, cancer specialists estimate that 60 percent of legitimate chemotherapy falls outside of the uses recognized by the [F.D.A.]."[114] Dr. Cary Presant, chairman of the Los Angeles Oncologic Institute, said, "The oncology community knows how to apply new drugs very rapidly. Results of recent clinical trials come out at national meetings and through oncology organizations, so we know the results of research six months before it gets into medical literature, two years before it is accepted by the three compendia and five years before it is on [an] F.D.A. label. . . . I've had patients die waiting for drugs."[115] FDA officials insisted that it was the responsibility of the companies to apply for official FDA approval for new uses for their drug even though approval costs millions of dollars.

Over one million Americans are diagnosed with cancer each year.[116] The FDA's restrictive policies almost certainly result in more Americans dying from cancer. As former FTC official and Boston University professor John Calfee noted,

> Since the summer of 1991, the FDA has conducted a wide ranging attack on the promotion of off-label uses. This will greatly reduce the speed with which practicing physicians learn of the newest and best ways to treat such illnesses as heart disease and cancer. In the past six months or so, the FDA has largely dismantled this system by cracking down on the promotion of off-label uses. Cancer newsletters have been shut down. Symposiums have nearly been brought to a halt. . . . Press conferences announcing new applications (usually from controlled clinical trials) are for the most part eliminated.
>
> The FDA position is that mentioning any unapproved use, no matter how well established, is inherently misleading to physicians. Worst of all are the effects on information. A leading support group for cancer patients has strongly objected that the new policy will keep patients from receiving the best therapies. Oncologists have declared that patients will die because physicians will not learn of efficacious treatments. The director of the National Cancer Institute's Division of Cancer Treatment has objected specifically to the shutting down of newsletters from pharmaceutical firms, saying "what really matters is the content of the report" on new research results.
>
> Drug firms put up with these absurdities because the FDA staff has so much discretion in the approval process that only a foolhardy pharmaceutical executive would do anything to offend that staff. Over and over again, individual firms and the

> entire industry have agreed without a fight to the most onerous of staff demands, even forsaking their First Amendment right to tell practicing physicians about the results of clinical trials or about the therapeutic recommendations of the National Cancer Institute.[117]

Columnist Steve Chapman noted that the FDA "sometimes finds itself in the ludicrous position of urging insurance companies to pay for therapies that it forbids pharmaceutical manufacturers to publicize."[118]

FDA's censorial policies have probably also resulted in more Americans having heart attacks and more heart attack victims dying. Calfee noted that the FDA for many years prohibited food manufacturers from alerting Americans to the benefit of low-fat diets:

> In 1957, the American Heart Association pointed out that according to recent epidemiological studies, people who consumed less cholesterol and saturated fat had less heart disease. Sellers of food with lesser amounts of these ingredients immediately began to advertise their advantages—and the FDA quickly stopped them, arguing that the connection between heart disease and dietary fat and cholesterol had not been proved. Sellers were put on notice that if their advertisements suggested that their foods could help prevent an illness such as heart disease, the FDA would reclassify the food as a drug, and the food/drug would be subject to immediate seizure for lack of clinical trials, dosage instructions, and the like. . . . It was not until the 1970s . . . that the FDA finally gave up on its campaign to keep manufacturers from telling consumers the extent to which the foods they ate met the recommendations of their doctor and nutritionists.[119]

Similarly, regarding aspirin and heart attacks, economist Paul Rubin observes:

> A 1988 study indicated the beneficial effects of aspirin in preventing heart attacks. This study found that the risk for male physicians over fifty was reduced by almost 50 percent. Some manufacturers of aspirin understandably began advertising the results of the research. One producer even began selling aspirin in a "one-a-day" package, presumably for this use. But the FDA in July 1989 told manufacturers that they must not advertise the benefits of aspirin in reducing the chances of a heart attack.
>
> The FDA had the power to do this in part because aspirin is not labeled as a preventative for heart attacks, so any advertising of this property would be contrary to the previously approved label. . . . Manufacturers of aspirin were unwilling to contest the issue with the FDA because of the agency's general power. This decision was an administrative ruling by the FDA: there were no hearings and no litigation. The FDA simply used its informal powers, and the threat of further actions was enough to block the efforts of firms to publicize the aspirin study's findings.[120]

In 1991 researchers at the National Heart, Lung and Blood Institute reported that Vasotec, a hypertension drug made by Merck & Co., sharply cut the number of cardiovascular deaths in people suffering from chronic congestive heart failure and that the drug also curbed heart failure among people with damaged hearts. But, as *Business Week* noted, Merck's "sales force couldn't give doctors copies of published studies about the new research or similar earlier studies. In fact, doctors can call the Food and Drug Administration toll-free to inform on companies giving out such information."[121] Research at the National Heart, Lung and Blood Institute is federally funded; thus, in this case, one federal agency is prohibiting the dissemination of another government agency's research results.

Despite a barrage of criticism from medical professionals, the FDA in 1993 issued new proposed rules to further muzzle pharmaceutical companies. As a *New Jersey Law Journal* article observed, "The FDA's proposal in most instances would prevent discussion of any medical uses for a product that have not already been approved by the FDA. . . . Under the FDA advertising regulations, any discussion of non-label uses during an industry-sponsored activity would render the product in question misbranded."[122] Once a drug is officially certified as "misbranded" by the FDA, federal agents can confiscate all available supplies of the drug without a court order.

The FDA presumes that its right to ban unsafe drugs includes a right to control all information about drugs. FDA officials are acting like high priests, angry that someone is trying to infringe on their monopoly on truth. The FDA test prohibition on mentioning new uses of approved drugs effectively turns back the clock five years on the advancement of medical science and imposes a "cost of truth" test that requires spending millions of dollars and the loss of countless lives. How many people will die in order for the FDA to continue its absurd assertions that its officials have a monopoly on truth? And for how much longer will companies that report findings of valuable uses for drugs not approved by the FDA be, by definition, liars and treated as public enemies? Though there are no newspaper photos of lines of body-bagged victims of FDA censorship, the FDA's decrees are having a stark effect on the lives of many American families. Unfortunately, the FDA appears to have far more concern for its own prerogatives and power than it does for the lives of American citizens.

Many congressmen and bureaucrats have discovered a "tobacco exemption" hidden somewhere between the lines in the First Amendment. Though citizens can still see old films portraying famous actresses puffing on a Chesterfield, Congress banned cigarette ads from television in 1971. The Federal Trade Commission has sought to suppress other speech by tobacco companies. In 1986, R. J. Reynolds Corporation ran an editorial advertisement criticizing federal officials' statements on a $115 million study on cigarette smoking and fatality rates. (The ten-year study did not find as clear a link between cigarette smoking and fatality rates as most previous studies.) FTC commissioners voted 4 to 1 to prosecute the complaint; FTC chairman Daniel Oliver dissented, noting that Reynolds's message "engages an issue that is a subject of public concern, and expresses a point of view that is unlikely to be articulated elsewhere. . . . It is valuable for the public to hear all sides of an issue, and I am concerned about taking any action that may inhibit free expression of views that may not be popular to Government regulators."[123] FTC administrative law judge Montgomery Hyun heard the agency's false advertising case against Reynolds and ruled on August 4, 1986, that Reynolds's ad "does not name any brand name or list prices or discuss desirable attributes of a product or show where the product may be purchased" and concluded that the ad "will be easily understood by any reasonable reader as an op-ed type piece, not a cigarette ad." The judge explained that noncommercial speech, such as Reynolds's ad, "does not lose the full protection of the First Amendment simply because it has inaccurate or incomplete information, or some language which may arguably be construed or misconstrued to imply a promotional message, or some other message regarded by complaint counsel to be contrary to the public interest or otherwise objectionable."[124] The FTC commissioners disregarded the agency's own judge's ruling and voted 4 to 1 to revive the charge against Reynolds in 1988.[125] R. J. Reynolds ended the FTC investigation by consenting in 1990 to a ban on making any "false and misleading advertising claims regarding the health effects of smoking."[126] (Reynolds denied that any of its previous statements were false or misleading.) FTC commissioner Andrew J. Strenio, Jr., hailed the settlement, declaring that the agency's action "means that an advertiser who blows this kind of smoke is going to get burned. . . . This is the format where advertising wolves attempt to dress up in the sheep's clothing of editorials."[127] But, as Reynolds's counsel Floyd Abrams earlier observed, the government's action was "in flat violation of the First Amendment. One would not ask the writer of an Op-Ed piece why he wrote it."[128] In August 1993, the FTC staff renewed the attack on tobacco companies by voting to recommend banning Camel cigarette advertisements featuring the "Old Joe" cartoon emblem. (The staff claimed that the ads were an "unfair" business practice because many children recognize "Old Joe"—thereby supposedly proving that the cigarette maker was illegally appealing to minors to buy cigarettes.)[129]

Newspapers, developers, and realtors are increasingly being hammered by the Fair Housing Act Amendments of 1988. The act declares that it is "unlawful to make, print, or publish, or cause to be made, printed, or published, any notice, statement, or advertisement, with respect to the sale or rental of a dwelling, that indicates any preference, limitation, or discrimination because of race, color, religion, sex, handicap, familial status, or national origin."[130] Though this may sound reasonable, the federal Department of Housing and Urban Development (HUD) has an extremely expansive interpretation of what constitutes fair housing ad violations: "References to a synagogue, congregation or parish may . . . indicate [an illegal] religious preference. Names of facilities which cater to a particular racial, national origin or religious group such as country club or private school designations . . . may indicate [an illegal] preference."[131] HUD even warns of lawsuits against housing developers who do not patronize foreign-language newspapers:

"The use of English language media alone or the exclusive use of media catering to the majority population in an area, when, in such area, there are also available non-English language or other minority media, may have discriminatory impact."

HUD is increasingly punishing companies that fail to use racial quotas in their use of models in real estate ads. HUD states that it is illegal to use "photographs, drawings, or other graphic techniques . . . to indicate exclusiveness because of . . . handicap," among other factors. HUD requires that "models should be clearly definable as reasonably representing majority and minority groups in the metropolitan area, both sexes, and when appropriate, families with children" and that models "should portray persons in an equal social setting."[132]

A federal jury awarded $850,000 in damages to a black Georgetown professor and two housing groups in a lawsuit they filed against an Arlington, Virginia, real estate developer that had used only white models in *Washington Post* advertisements.[133] (The *Washington Post* succumbed to lawsuit threats and imposed upon advertisers a requirement that one in four models be a minority.) The *New York Times* was found guilty for publishing a disproportionate number of real estate ads with white models. A panel of federal appeals court judges ruled on the *Times* case in 1991 that "we read the word 'preference' to describe any ad that would discourage an ordinary reader of a particular race from answering it."[134] In an August 1993 settlement of a lawsuit, the *Times* announced that it would judge each real estate ad on a case-by-case basis, and that ads with a "substantial number" of people but fewer than 20 percent black people would be rejected.[135] The Supreme Court ruled in 1992 that hate speech—such as burning a cross on someone's lawn—is protected by the First Amendment; yet speech such as a real estate ad that does not portray the right quotas of minorities can be penalized as if it were more harmful than cross burning.

In January 1990, Richard Jacobson placed a tiny classified ad in an Oconomowoc, Wisconsin, newspaper stating: "Fully Winterized Cottage, 2 bedrooms, ideal for couple. Not suitable for pets or children. Available February 1 or 15. Security deposit required." The Metropolitan Milwaukee Fair Housing Council saw the ad and promptly filed a complaint with the Wisconsin Equal Rights Division accusing Jacobson of illegally stating "a preference or limitation based on marital status in violation of the Wisconsin Open Housing Law" because Jacobson's ad mentioned "ideal for couple"—thus supposedly discriminating against single individuals. (Jacobson rented the cottage to a single individual shortly after the ad appeared.) The Equal Rights Division found Jacobson guilty, but he appealed to the Wisconsin Labor and Industry Review Commission, which acquitted Jacobson and ruled that "an ordinary reader would not have understood the advertisement to state or indicate discrimination." The Fair Housing Council, utilizing generous federal grants it receives to fuel its litigation, appealed the decision to Waukesha County Circuit Court, which also found Jacobson innocent. The Council then appealed to the Wisconsin Court of Appeals, which also found Jacobson innocent and stated that the Fair Housing Council's interpretation of the ad "lacks an objective perspective and, as a result, is the product of the suspicious—not the ordinary—reader." Appeals Judge Daniel Anderson observed: "Such trifling complaints may well reduce available rental housing by having a chilling effect on potential landlords who would rather hold property off the market than risk the expense of defending against a complaint over an innocuous and inoffensive advertisement."[136]

A suit stemming from a Fair Housing advertisement complaint destroyed twenty newspapers in California. The California Fair Housing Council sued the Southern California Community Newspapers chain because one of its newspapers printed an apartment rental classified ad that stated "adults preferred."[137] This phrase violated the 1988 Fair Housing Act Amendments, which prohibit "discrimination" against renters with children. The publisher, Ric Trent, offered the Fair Housing Council $50,000 in free advertising to promote the need for fair housing, but the council refused. Fair Housing Council attorney Christopher Brancart observed, "We refused to settle this case because we felt the newspaper had an obligation to make things right in the community."[138] Trent estimated that trial expenses for the ad violation would have cost him $500,000, so he filed for Chapter 11 bankruptcy protection, and a bank foreclosed on the papers shortly thereafter.[139] The January 1993 shutdown destroyed over a hundred jobs.

PROTECTING PEOPLE FROM BEER BOTTLE LABELS

The Twenty-first Amendment's passage in 1933 prohibited the federal government from outlawing all consumption of alcoholic beverages. However, many federal officials over the years have sought to decrease alcohol consumption by restricting the advertising and marketing of alcohol and, in more recent times, by fanning hysteria regarding alcohol consumption. Though federal officials cannot yet ban adults from drinking, there is a growing effort to treat them as village idiots that cannot be trusted to read a bottle label. At a time when the abuse of alcohol by Americans is decreasing (Americans now rank twenty-fourth in the world in average consumption of alcohol),[140] the abuse of the alcohol industry by politicians appears to be skyrocketing.

Health and Human Services secretary Louis Sullivan declared in March 1992, "The numbers of Americans who consume alcohol is staggering. Two-thirds of all adults drink alcoholic beverages, and of those, approximately half are moderate to heavy drinkers."[141] It is peculiar for a public health official to speak as if the fact that a person has had one drink in the past month (the official definition of "drinks alcoholic beverages") is "staggering." Defining any alcohol consumption as a national problem makes it easier for federal bureaucrats to demand more funding from Congress to fight this menace and to justify new controls on the alcohol industry and private citizens. Surgeon General Antonia Novello was even shriller, declaiming in November 1991: "I called for the industry voluntary elimination of alcohol advertising that appeals to use on the basis of lifestyle, on the basis of sexual appeal, on the basis of sports figures, and on the basis of risky activities, as well as the advertising with the more blatant use of appeals of cartoon characters and those ones that have used slang, absolutely so."[142] Novello sought to marshal public opinion to ban the Anheuser-Busch cartoon character Bud Man.

Alcohol may not be sold in the United States without a label approved by the federal Bureau of Alcohol, Tobacco and Firearms. BATF has been extremely paternalistic in its label rulings. In 1991 Heileman Brewing Company began marketing a new malt liquor known as PowerMaster. Surgeon General Novello, revealing her genius for linguistic analysis, denounced the new product: "When you look at PowerMaster, it is almost as if you are giving people an empty and deceitful promise. It offers power to no one and makes no one a master of anything."[143] Novello condemned the marketing of PowerMaster to blacks as "socially irresponsible . . . It's true this is a legal product, but the problem is that they are targeting some populations that are already very prone [to health risks]. . . . In a subconscious way, I think they think these people are expendable."[144] Novello implied that the U.S. government should impose different standards for alcohol sold to minorities than for that sold to other groups. Though BATF had already approved the label and name of the new drink, the agency became intimidated by the controversy and revoked permission, claiming that PowerMaster's name was an illegal allusion to its high alcohol content.[145] At the time that BATF banned PowerMaster, Heileman had spent over $2 million on developing and marketing for the brand.

In July 1989, BATF approved a bottle label showing a smiling skull and crossbones for Black Death Vodka, imported from Belgium. Black Death Vodka is marketed in over forty countries and won three gold medals at London's prestigious International Wine and Spirits Competition.[146] But Surgeon General Novello protested after she heard the new vodka's name. On June 12, 1992, BATF official Candice Moberly canceled BATF label approval for Black Death.[147] At the time, the company had over 10,000 cases of Black Death on order or in shipment and had already invested millions in the product. BATF spokesman Tom Hill explained the revocation: "We have said that Black Death, according to the dictionary, involves people with bubonic plague. They are sort of mocking it. It gives a false impression to the consumer that it is OK to consume it."[148] Hill did not explain why BATF concluded that the image of death on the bottle gives a false impression that it is "OK to consume," or, if this was true, why other vodka makers had not previously proposed labels celebrating famines. BATF's Jack Killorin added: "If you take it seriously, 'black death' and a skull would inform you, 'This is poison, this is death.' But this is not true."[149] Since high-ranking federal health officials at that time seemed to be trying to persuade people that drinking alcohol is inherently suicidal, it is difficult to understand why BATF was unhappy with the label. Perhaps BATF believed that the government should have a monopoly in trying to frighten people about alcohol.

Cabo Distribution Company, Black Death's importer, sued BATF in federal court; as Cabo's attorney George Wyckart observed, "There is no easier way to put you out of business than to cancel your label approval. If you can't use the label, you can't fill orders, you're out of business."[150] Cabo, in its petition to the federal court, stated that Terry Cates, BATF's chief of industry compliance, "fancies himself to be the 'Chief of the Thought Police' of the United States."[151] On July 10, 1992, federal judge Lowell Jensen issued a preliminary injunction against BATF's ban; in October 1992, Jensen ruled that BATF's action was "arbitrary and capricious" and a violation of the company's constitutional rights.[152]

In March 1992, the Hornell brewery introduced Crazy Horse Malt Liquor. Hornell brought out Crazy Horse as part of a new series of Wild West–type drinks scheduled to include Jim Bowie Mountain Spring Pilsner, Wild Bill Hickock's Porter, and Annie Oakley Lite. BATF formally approved the name and label for forty-ounce bottles of the new malt liquor. The resulting political feeding frenzy brought on perhaps the first crucifixion of an American corporation for the sin of "commercial blasphemy."

Surgeon General Novello went on the warpath when she heard about Crazy Horse Malt Liquor. She flew to Rapid City, South Dakota—near the largest Sioux Indian reservation—held a press conference, and denounced Hornell for "insensitive and malicious marketing."[153] Novello claimed that the new drink "may appeal to drinkers who want to go 'crazy,'" and concluded: "I look to the leaders of the Indian Nations to help me mount a campaign to stop this exploitation, to use public outrage to force 'Crazy Horse' off the market." A few weeks later, Novello hyperventilated before a congressional committee: "Let them know that proud Indian Nations will not be brought to their knees," and appealed for more public denunciations of the brewers.[154]

Many congressmen jumped on Novello's antibeer bandwagon. Rep. David Obey of Wisconsin declared that the companies that brew and market Crazy Horse should be driven out of business.[155] Rep. Joseph Kennedy of Massachusetts, whose inherited wealth stemmed largely from his grandfather's bootleg racket, loudly bewailed that brewers "don't care what the effect is on the American Indian people, on the black people of this country, on the young people of this country . . . as long as they can make money."[156] On June 5, 1992, Rep. Frank Wolf of Virginia proposed an amendment to prohibit any company from naming any alcoholic beverage after any renowned dead person. (Wolf's amendment mortified the Boston Beer Company, since it would have outlawed Samuel Adams beer.) Congress eventually enacted an amendment in September 1992 that forced Hornell to cease and desist sales of Crazy Horse within six months. Banning Crazy Horse meant the likely bankruptcy of the company and loss of scores of jobs at brewers, marketers, and wholesalers.

This brouhaha was peculiar because there are already dozens of alcoholic beverages named after Indians and Indian tribes, such as Thunderbird wine, Black Hawk Stout, and Chief OshKosh Red Lager. Crazy Horse's name has been previously held in reverence through its use for tobacco products, strip joints, and saloons.[157] Hornell spokesman Mark Rodman estimated that the company had invested over $1 million in packaging, labeling, and trademark efforts, and that the label dispute cost the company over $100,000.

The surgeon general used her attacks on Crazy Horse to spearhead new controls on alcoholic beverages, declaring: "The Indians are only the beginning of the [minority] populations" to be helped by more restrictive alcohol labeling.[158] When asked whether her proposed ban would violate brewers' freedom of speech, Novello replied: "If this goes to any high court, it would be very contended whose rights are more violated."[159] Shortly after Congress revoked Hornell's license, Novello declared, "I probably feel better about this victory for all of us than almost anything else that has happened while I've been Surgeon General."[160] In April 1993, federal judge Carol Bagley Amon struck down the congressional ban, ruling, "The Crazy Horse label, as commercial free speech, is entitled to First Amendment protection because it concerns lawful activity and is not misleading. It bears repeating that the desire to protect society, or certain members of society, from the purported offensiveness of particular speech is not a substantial interest which justifies its prohibition."[161]

It is especially hypocritical for congressmen to denounce beer labels for corrupting the public since Congress itself, thanks to a 1935 law, censored all beer labels by prohibiting breweries from listing their alcohol content. (In contrast, wine and liquor bottles are required by federal law to have the alcohol content on their labels.) In 1987 the counsel for the House of Representatives filed a court brief that declared that Uncle Sam must continue suppressing beer's alcohol content to "shield the public . . . from unhealthy blandishments to select beers on the basis of their efficacy as intoxicants."[162] The House of Representatives' position is demeaning to average citizens. If people are drinking only to get drunk, they can drink wine, or whiskey, or any other liquor far more potent than beer. It makes no sense to pick out the beverage with the lowest alcohol content and assume that people will go on drinking binges unless Congress blindfolds them. Federal judge Zita Weinshienk ruled in October 1992 that the government's prohibition of brewers' listing alcohol content on labels violated the First Amendment.[163]

THE NATTERING NATIONAL BROADCAST NANNY

Radio and television stations have often been treated like feudal tenants of the airwaves by the federal government, hit with as many fetters as Congress and the Federal Communications Commission (FCC) consider politically profitable. Broadcast regulations have been long permeated by a dishonest paternalism—politicians claiming to intervene to protect people and instead rigging the rules to flatter and protect themselves. While FCC regulations were rolled back during the Reagan administration, the Clinton administration is reviving FCC paternalism. As Rep. Edward Markey, chairman of the House Subcommittee on Telecommunications, announced at a March 1993 hearing: "Broadcasters beware. The new era has begun."[164] Markey stated, "I think the F.C.C. has the . . . daily regulatory clout to insist upon higher standards."[165]

Broadcast law is based on the notion that the airwaves are public property; thus, politicians and political appointees must control who is permitted to use them. Radio and television stations do not own the frequencies upon which they broadcast; instead, they borrow them from the government—and the government can revoke the license on a number of different pretexts. Television and radio licenses expire every five years and must be renewed each time. As one broadcaster observed, "We live or die . . . by the FCC gun."[166] FCC commissioner Ervin S. Duggan told broadcasters in early 1993, "If your voluntary concern for the public interest is present and visible, you have little to fear from government."[167]

Government officials claim that the FCC must have control over who is permitted to broadcast because of the natural shortage of broadcast spectrums. The Supreme Court ruled in 1943: "Unlike other modes of expression, radio inherently is not available to all. . . . That is its unique characteristic, and that is why, unlike other modes of expression, it is subject to governmental regulation."[168] But the notion of a scarcity of available spectrum for radio and television stations is largely a myth designed to justify political control of the broadcast industry. University of Texas law professor Lucas Powe noted in his 1987 book *American Broadcasting and the First Amendment*, "Outside the legal literature, the belief in scarcity exists—or at least the assertion of scarcity exists—because those who wish to continue broadcast regulation believe that it must exist; otherwise, broadcasters could not be controlled by the government."[169] In 1985 the FCC had over 500 vacant television channels available throughout the nation, and over 1,266 radio allotments were vacant in 1987.[170] The alleged shortage provides a pretext for political allocation of broadcast licenses.

The FCC has long practiced censorship through intimidation. Jonathan Emord, author of *Freedom, Technology, and the First Amendment*, notes that FCC commissioners "stretched mightily to suggest that they had plenary authority to review a licensee's programming and determine whether it ought to be deemed 'in the public interest.'... The FCC's elaborate system of administrative second-guessing became known by the pundits as regulation by 'raised eyebrow.'"[171] The FCC used its administrative discretion to cancel the licenses of New York and Chicago radio stations that exclusively promoted socialist doctrines.[172] In the 1970s, Pennsylvania governor Milton Shapp asked the FCC to revoke the licenses for two Pennsylvania radio stations and three television stations owned by Walter Annenberg. (Annenberg was a harsh critic of Shapp.)[173] The Nixon administration succeeded in using its licensing leverage to browbeat CBS into killing "The Smothers Brothers Comedy Hour."[174]

From 1949 through 1987, the FCC imposed the "Fairness Doctrine" on radio and television stations. The FCC abolished the Fairness Doctrine in 1987 because it concluded that it violated the First Amendment. Under the Fairness Doctrine, radio and television stations are liable for FCC investigation and license revocations if federal officials decide that their news coverage or editorials or commentary were not sufficiently balanced. The Fairness Doctrine rested on unlimited faith in the fairness of political appointees. The Fairness Doctrine effectively gave politicians and political appointees the power to dictate what is fair to say about politicians and public issues.

The Fairness Doctrine provided a license for censorship in the name of fairness. The FCC has often concluded that stations were "unfair" if they were too critical of politicians—or did not give incumbent congressmen free air time to respond to criticism. In the 1960s the Democratic National Committee used the Fairness Doctrine to attack radio stations sharply critical of the Kennedy and Johnson administrations. Bill Ruder, Kennedy's assistant secretary of commerce, declared, "Our massive strategy was to use the Fairness Doctrine to challenge and harass right-wing broadcasters and hope that the challenges would be so costly to them that they would be inhibited and decide it was too expensive to continue."[175] Stations were also forced to give free air time to people who supported the Kennedy and Johnson administrations. A 1969 confidential White House memorandum revealed that President Nixon ordered his staff to take "specific action relating to what could be considered unfair news coverage" twenty-one times in one thirty-day period.[176]

Interest groups besieged the FCC with allegations that radio and television stations were unfair; the FCC received 6,787 inquiries and complaints regarding the Fairness Doctrine in 1984 alone.[177] Stations were often required to present elaborate defenses in formal FCC hearings; NBC spent four years and over $100,000 defending itself against charges that one television broadcast was overly critical of often fraudulent private pensions. Because of fear of complaints of Fairness Doctrine violations, many TV stations refused to sell air time relating to ballot propositions, thereby depriving voters of information on major issues on which they were required to decide.[178]

The FCC, under the leadership of Chairman Mark Fowler, concluded in 1985 that

> The fairness doctrine, in operation, actually inhibits the presentation of controversial issues of public importance to the detriment of the public and in degradation of the editorial prerogative of broadcast journalists. . . . Journalists who have worked in both the broadcast and print media have testified that the very existence of the fairness doctrine creates a climate of timidity and fear, unexperienced by print journalists, that is antithetical to journalistic freedom. . . . CBS news anchor Dan Rather observed, "Once a newsperson has to stop and consider what a Government agency will think of something he or she wants to put on the air, an invaluable element of freedom has been lost."[179]

Reviving the Fairness Doctrine is especially inappropriate because, as *Investor's Business Daily* noted, "In 1949, the typical household was lucky if it could receive more than three or four radio stations. Today, residents of mid- to large-sized cities may receive 2 dozen local radio stations, up to 10 broadcast television stations, and 20 or more cable television channels."[180]

The FCC has numerous other regulations inhibiting the criticism of politicians. In 1992 a local cable operator in Wichita, Kansas, launched a blitz of ads criticizing Rep. Dan Glickman and urging his defeat in the coming election. Glickman complained to the station and demanded equal time. The station offered to allow Glickman to run thirty free ads a day touting his candidacy, but Glickman complained that that was not as many ads as the station was running criticizing him. Glickman quickly ran to the FCC with a complaint against the station.[181]

In 1952 Congress held hearings so that congressmen could protest excessive violence on television. In the spring of 1993 members of Congress launched another in a long series of highly publicized attacks on television violence. Sen. Paul Simon of Illinois announced: "We face a choice of censorship or responsible voluntary conduct."[182] Sen. Howard Metzenbaum of Ohio promised that Congress would "come down heavily on the television industry if you don't do that which is necessary."[183] Metzenbaum bluntly asserted: "Maybe we need to find a way to take back some of those television franchises."[184] He singled out NBC's reenactment of the Branch Davidian standoff in Waco, Texas, as an example of the networks' venal attempts to lure viewers with violence. While Metzenbaum was outraged at NBC's reenactment of the attack, he made no criticism of BATF's original attack on a compound full of women and children, or of the FBI's later use of armored vehicles to smash in the walls of the compound.[185] Apparently, the private television network's commercial exploitation of the shootout was worse than the government's attack on its own citizens.

Congress and the FCC have been especially paternalistic regarding children's television. The FCC first issued regulations requiring broadcasters to present special programs for children in 1962,[186] even though educators at that time were already criticizing television as the great stupefier of young minds. In 1968 Congress created public broadcasting networks in part to provide educational programming to children and teenagers. In 1990

Congress decided that commercial television stations and networks did not provide enough healthy fare for youngsters and enacted the Children's Television Act to force them to do more. Sen. Frank Lautenberg of New Jersey declared: "Under the new law, a broadcaster who ignores children risks his license, because service to children will be part of any review of a license renewal. That's the way it should be. In return for the privilege of using the public's airwaves, as public trustees broadcasters should use the medium to serve our children."[187]

Though the act threatened license revocations for violators, the law did not define "educational and informational programming." The *New York Times* noted that the Children's Television Act is "notoriously vague."[188] Congress and the FCC told television stations to jump through the hoops—but did not tell broadcasters where the hoops are, how high they are, or in which direction they must jump. FCC commissioner Sherrie Marshall said the rules "strike the right balance between the goal of providing television programming responsive to the needs of children and [the FCC's] duty to avoid intruding on the First Amendment rights of broadcasters."[189] But the First Amendment does not require federal officials to balance free speech with other concerns but to avoid censoring free speech. As a brief from the Reporters Committee for Freedom of the Press, the Media Institute, and the Society of Professional Journalists, observed: "If children's educational and informational programming can be lawfully coerced, why not coerce the same special attention by television for the benefit of other societal groups (e.g., the elderly) that are viewed to be too weak economically to have their special program needs met?"[190] If Congress dictated that every book publisher must begin printing and distributing a certain percentage of books for children, this would have been widely denounced as oppressive. But little outcry occurred over the Children's Television Act. In May 1993 the FCC began considering a proposal to require television stations to air an hour of educational programs for children each day.[191]

The Children's Television Act also decreed that television programs for kids could not have more than twelve minutes of commercials per hour on weekdays or more than ten and a half minutes of commercials per hour on weekends. The restrictions on ad times may have been enacted partly in order to protect the dignity of elected representatives; Sen. James Exon of Nebraska complained to his colleagues, "On more than one occasion, my grandchildren, under 4 years of age, have stood up and asked for silence in the room when [the station] went to a commercial."[192] WTTA of St. Petersburg, Florida, was fined $10,000 for exceeding the official limits for advertisements by two and a half minutes in one hour and by one and a half minutes in another.[193] In early 1993 the FCC delayed renewing the licenses of six television stations because the stations had not proved they were providing sufficient broadcast nutrients for children.[194]

The threatening language of Children's TV Act violation notices from Edythe Wise, chief of the Complaints and Investigations Branch of the

FCC's Mass Media Bureau's Enforcement Division, contrasts with the names of the television programs involved in the offense. In January 1993 chief enforcer Wise informed WTBS (the Turner Broadcasting System Superstation) that it was guilty of fifteen seconds too many commercials on a January 14, 1992, broadcast of "Tom and Jerry's Funhouse."[195] Wise also pronounced KWGN-TV of Denver guilty of one minute's worth of excessive commercials during broadcasts of "Dennis the Menace" and "Merrie Melodies" between 7:00 and 8:00 A.M. on Tuesday, January 14, 1992.[196] KITV-TV in Honolulu, Hawaii, was found guilty of excessive commercials on a January 11, 1992, broadcast of the "Bugs & Tweety" show.[197] The conclusion of most such notices warn, "We hereby ADMONISH you for said violation of our commercial limits. . . . This matter will be made a part of our permanent records." With the somber air of the FCC notices, one would think that the "Bugs & Tweety" show was some type of religious revelation that broadcasters had a sacred duty to show uncut.

There are no compulsory attendance laws requiring people to watch television. The basic premise of the law is that children's television is so bad that Congress must intervene, but the restrictions on commercials implies that the problem is not the dismal quality of the shows but the fact that children do not see enough of the shows. If government really wants educational television, then perhaps it should simply require every television station to run a flashing test pattern one hour each day declaring "Go read a book!" Since parents will not control the television watching of their kids, Congress and the FCC are supposedly entitled to exert more control over television stations. Television has numerous adverse physiological effects on children; studies have shown that excessive television watching by children sharply increases their risk of obesity and high cholesterol.[198] Insofar as federal regulation seeks to make television more attractive to children (by fewer commercials, for instance), federal intervention can harm children's health. The mute button on television remote controls—and extensive competition between channels—is a much better regulator of excessive ads than is the FCC.

Arcane FCC regulations occasionally give politicians a chance to strike a death blow at their critics. The FCC in 1975 restricted cross-ownership of television stations and newspapers in the same market by the same corporation in order to prevent domination of local news coverage. However, the FCC routinely granted waivers and extensions of waivers to broadcast-newspaper owners. In October 1987 Congress approved a 1194-page appropriations bill that few congressmen had read. A few days after the bill was signed by the president, an amendment was discovered that had been inserted into the bill late at night prohibiting the FCC from extending any existing waivers to the cross-ownership ban. The FCC had granted a temporary exemption in 1986 when Rupert Murdoch, who owned television stations in Boston and New York, bought the *Boston Herald* and the *New York Post*. Only Murdoch's corporation had a waiver from the ban at the time the congressional amendment was passed; thus, only one corporation was affected by the ban on extensions. The *Herald* had been extremely critical of Sen. Ted Kennedy, and Kennedy retaliated by knifing Murdoch with an act of Congress—a federal decree that effectively forced Murdoch to sell his Boston television station and the *New York Post.* Sen. Ernest Hollings, who inserted the amendment into the appropriations bill on behalf of Senator Kennedy, denounced Murdoch on the Senate floor as "sneaky," a "prevaricator," and a "manipulator."[199] Sen. Kennedy openly bragged about his hit job, claiming the bill was in "the best interest of Boston and the best interest of the First Amendment." New York mayor Ed Koch disagreed: "What Senator Kennedy and Senator Hollings have done rivals the worst in a totalitarian country that still professes to have a parliamentary structure. . . . The Senators did it in the dead of night without alerting their colleagues, who became unwilling accomplices."[200] Murdoch sued, and a federal court ruled that the "Hollings Amendment struck at Murdoch with the precision of a laser beam," forbidding waiver extensions only to him, and not to any other prospective applicants.[201] But by the time the judge struck down the congressional provision as unconstitutional, Murdoch had already sold the *New York Post.*

Cable Cut-Ups

While no local government would likely even attempt to grant a monopoly to a local newspaper, cable television systems routinely receive such preference. Over 99 percent of the cable markets in the United States are served by only one cable company.[202] An FCC survey found that cable systems with monopolies charged an average of sixty-five cents a channel per month, while those that faced competition charged only forty-eight cents per channel.[203] William Squadrun, New York City's commissioner of telecommunications, said, "There have been a number of analyses that have found essentially you've got a 30 to 40 percent monopoly rent markup."[204] Former FCC official Sol Schildhause wrote in *Texas Lawyer* that "local governments almost universally refuse to license second systems. The reason: Local politicians have cut deals, written and unwritten, with their chosen cable operator to keep out competition."[205] As lawyer David Saylor notes, "Cable operators have even given city councils absolute programming control over certain cable channels. Such operators have been forced to finance the construction of municipally controlled television studios, to deliver free production equipment to city officials and institutions, and to provide free installation and program service to schools and other city designees."[206] Schildhause notes, "With the exception of C-SPAN at the national level, local cable systems are noticeably chary about reporting on political wrongdoing. Why? Because cable operators are licensed members of the press, and licensees are usually nice to the local dispensers of licenses." Economist Thomas Hazlett noted that "the Florida Cable TV Association open[ed] a space-age studio just across from the state legislature. The 'Sunshine Channel' will not only air such snappy shows as 'The Governor Meets the Press' and 'The Florida League of Cities'; it will give state legislators full editorial control of their own program. Don't expect them to feature a segment on their 1987 passage of a law protecting cable operators from upstart competitors."[207]

Monopoly cable franchises were heavily criticized in the early 1980s, and the Supreme Court ruled in 1986 that such monopolies may violate the First Amendment.[208] But in 1984 Congress explicitly sanctioned the granting of local cable monopolies. Between 1987 and 1990, nine states granted existing local franchises de facto monopoly rights in their markets.[209] The 1984 cable act also banned telephone companies from offering cable television service, thereby protecting thousands of local cable monopolies from a natural competitor.

Largely as a result of the local monopolies, cable bills rose twice as fast as inflation in the late 1980s and early 1990s. (In the sixty-five cities that permitted two or more cable companies to compete, prices fell 20 to 25 percent.)[210] Congress responded in 1992 by enacting the Cable Television Consumer Protection and Competition Act. The act's Statement of Policy declared Congress's intent to "promote the availability to the public of a diversity of views and information through cable television . . . and ensure that cable television operators do not have undue market power vis-à-vis video programmers and consumers."[211] While the 1992 act liberally praised competition, the act "eliminated damage awards against cities that refuse to issue competitive franchises";[212] thus, local governments have nothing to lose from granting monopolies to favored cable companies. Congress perpetuated an earlier prohibition on telephone companies offering cable service, thereby preventing the provision of a greater "diversity of views." The 1992 cable act responded to cable monopolies not by removing the barriers to competition, but by increasing politicians' and bureaucrats' power to dictate how monopolists must behave. The act required the FCC to regulate local cable companies' monthly fees; the FCC responded in May 1993 by issuing 475 pages of arcane provisions to regulate cable pricing and promised to issue additional regulations to further clarify permitted pricing policies. Once the politicians gave cable operators monopoly control over their cable customers, the politicians naturally felt entitled to exercise control over the cable companies. First the government creates unnecessary monopolies, and then it issues hundreds of pages of unnecessary rules to try to make the monopolies serve the public interest—as perceived by politicians and political appointees.

The 1992 act forced cable systems both to transmit local broadcast television stations' signals (a "must-carry" provision) and to pay them for the honor. Congress inserted the "must-carry" provision in the law even though federal courts had twice previously struck down the provision as an unconstitutional violation of the cable companies' rights. Cable companies sued in federal court, challenging the new law. A federal appeals court upheld the "must-carry" provision, but judge Steven Williams sharply dissented: "If findings as scantily connected to the conclusion as these can justify must-carry, then the door is open—even in the area of First Amendment rights—to exercise of the most naked interest-group preferences."[213] If Congress dictated that all newspapers had to publish certain politically favored syndicated columnists on their editorial or op-ed pages, almost everyone would recognize this as a violation of freedom of the press. Yet when Congress dictates that cable companies must carry certain politically favored television networks or broadcast stations on their limited cable lines, then the courts shrug it off.

As a result of "must-carry," thirteen cable systems slashed their airing of C-SPAN, the public affairs network.[214] Brian Lamb, chief executive of C-SPAN, complained: "We've been made a second-class citizen under this legislation. We no longer have the same chance of succeeding as any broadcast channel."[215] Thus, fewer people are able to watch the House and Senate in action—which probably suits many politicians just fine. New York Mets fans were jilted when the cable system in Dover, New Jersey, dropped the company carrying their games in order to make room for two tiny local broadcast television stations.[216]

The "must-carry" provisions of the 1992 act require the FCC to rule which stations are in the public interest—and to implicitly knock other stations off the air. In July 1993 the FCC ruled that over 100 home-shopping channels were programming in the public interest and thus that cable systems could be forced to carry them free of charge. Though the Home Shopping Network generates roughly $1 billion a year,[217] the FCC effectively labeled the company as deserving preferred treatment. The FCC certified the Home Shopping Network as a public interest venture at the same time that, as the *Washington Post* reported, a federal grand jury was "investigating a laundry list of allegations against the company and its chairman, including bribery, ties to organized crime and secret ownership of vendors that supplied products sold on the network."[218] Critics denounced the FCC decision on the shopping networks as "force feeding [the public] schlock."

Bell Atlantic Corporation filed a lawsuit challenging the ban on phone companies providing cable service, and federal judge T. S. Ellis struck down the law in August 1993 as unconstitutional "on its face."[219] (Bell sought permission to build a system to provide local viewers with 384 channels of television.) Though cable companies appealed the ruling, the court decision could sound the death knell for efforts by Congress to manipulate the cable industry for its own political advantage.

Rather than granting television and radio licenses by political and bureaucratic fiat, it would be far more profitable for the government to auction off the licenses. Congress in 1993 permitted the FCC to auction off unused radio airwaves; the agency expects to collect $7 billion from the sales.[220] Far more could be collected from selling off other broadcast frequencies. If the government auctioned off airwaves the same way that it auctions the right to drill for oil on federal land, there would be no shortage of airwaves. If the price was set at a market-clearing price, demand would not exceed supply. The notion that the airwaves are a "public good" to be distributed as government thinks best means, in reality, that airwaves become political property.

A NOTE ON SO-CALLED HATE SPEECH CRIMES

In the last ten years, state and local governments, public schools, and colleges have sought to ban and punish many types of politically incorrect speech. (For instance, the University of Connecticut in 1990 banned "inappropriately directed laughter" and "inconsiderate jokes.")[221] No punishments based on speech alone should be imposed by the government. As Supreme Court Justice Antonin Scalia wrote in 1992, "The point of the First Amendment is that majority preferences must be expressed in some fashion other than silencing speech on the basis of its content."[222] In cases where the so-called hate speech is connected to specific illegal actions (such as the 1992 Supreme Court case involving white skinheads that burned a cross on a black family's lawn, or the 1993 Supreme Court case involving black youth who attacked a white teenager after watching the movie "Mississippi Burning"), the government should punish the action and give the perpetrators the opportunity to reflect on their speech in the solitude of a jail cell.

CONCLUSION

Three hundred and fifty years ago, poet John Milton pointed out the futility of government censorship to preserve public manners:

> If we think to regulate printing, thereby to rectify manners, we must regulate all recreations and pastimes, all that is delightful to man. No music must be heard, no song be set or sung, but what is grave and Doric. There must be licensing dancers, that no gesture, motion or deportment be taught our youth, but what by their allowance shall be thought honest. It will ask more than the work of 20 licensers to examine all the lutes, the violins, and the guitars in every house; they must not be suffered to prattle as they do, but must be licensed what they may say.[223]

Regrettably, politicians are confirming Milton's fears with one new proposal after another to censor. Yet the more controls the government imposes, the louder the complaints become that public morality is going to hell.

There is growing political manipulation of the information that the average American is allowed to receive. But do politicians, bureaucrats, and county prosecutors have an automatic right to control what other American citizens read, write, view, and photograph? Where does the government acquire a right to dictate what other Americans are allowed to know?

Because someone gets a government job, does that confer the right to blindfold other Americans?

Restrictions on free speech are routinely a self-serving effort to make people more submissive to politicians' power grabs. Censorship is almost always the handservant of statism—trying to delude the public as to the competence and the character of their rulers. How can we trust politicians to censor for our own good when they are widely perceived to lie for their own purposes? The more control the government has over what information people can receive, the more control politicians and bureaucrats will have over how people live—from a cancer sufferer finding out about a drug that may save her life, to a social drinker knowing whether he has consumed too much alcohol, to a person that wants more variety from his television. The principle of government control over information is inseparable from the principle of government control over people's lives.

There is no objective censorship; censorship almost always is done in the government's own interest. Government prosecutors talk of abstract "community standards"—and then seize thirteen bookstores and crush and burn a hundred thousand magazines, books, and videos. Government officials warn of the dangers of fraudulent advertising—and then forcibly muzzle a corporation from voicing criticism of studies that its tax dollars helped finance. Censorship is coercion—sending people to prison for saying or showing or photographing things that other people don't believe should be said, shown, or photographed. What right do politicians and bureaucrats have to jail people for offending the taste or sensibility of the government elite?

For government agencies, the power to define truth routinely includes the right to punish error. But the more government censors, the less capable people will be of forming their own judgments. Paternalism is most dangerous in the realm of information. As Justice Harry Blackmun observed, restrictions on speech often involve "a covert attempt by the State to manipulate the choices of its citizens, not by persuasion or direct regulation, but by depriving the public of the information needed to make a free choice. . . . The State's policy choices are insulated from visibility and scrutiny . . . and the conduct of citizens is molded by the information that government chooses to give them."[224] Pervasive restrictions on speech and information undermine the intellectual principle of democracy. If people cannot even judge beer labels for themselves, how can they be competent to choose the great leaders who decide what may be printed on beer labels?

-10-

CONCLUSION

I have no reason to suppose, that he, who would take away my Liberty, would not when he had me in his Power, take away every thing else.

—JOHN LOCKE (1690)[1]

Thomas Paine, in his writings to stir Americans to support the Revolution, noted the widespread belief "that government is some wonderful mysterious thing."[2] Paine rightfully concluded that this naive perspective—by granting government far more unexamined, unrestrained power—led to tyranny. The Founding Fathers succeeded in creating a government where individual rights and liberties were respected because they were cynical about political power: they realized that, as George Washington wrote, government is like "fire . . . a dangerous servant and a terrible master."[3] Today, most Americans base their concept of government not on how government actually performs but on what they feel the government needs to do. Most American political philosophies are based on a list of social and economic imperatives rather than on political reality. Yet without a realistic concept of government, political philosophy is only an exercise in moral aesthetics.

Nineteenth-century reformers built their utopias on the expectation of an imminent change in human nature. Twentieth-century reformers have built leviathans and then awaited a change in the nature of politicians. Faith in changing the masses has been replaced by faith in changing their rulers. Almost every expansion of government power is premised on the triumph of hope over experience. Each new program is justified only by denying the character of the people who will be controlling the program's levers. Albert Einstein warned in 1945 that with the invention of the atomic bomb, mankind had far more destructive power than people were capable of controlling responsibly. The same is true of government power: Governments have now amassed far more power than politicians are capable of responsibly and intelligently wielding. If politicians were angels, we would not need so many jails and prisons for their edification.

"Fairness" has been the driving engine in the expansion of government control over citizens' lives, property, and opportunities. But as the old German proverb says, "The more laws, the less justice." In area after area in American society, basic justice and fundamental fairness are being subverted and ridiculed by legislative and regulatory decrees. Few people would consider it just that zoning officials can revoke permits they had already granted and force people to tear down part or all of their homes—but it is happening. Few people would consider it just that trucking companies can force their customers to pay massive surcharges for service rendered years ago, solely because the trucker failed to file his rates with a federal bureau—but it is happening. Few people would think it just that the Equal Employment Opportunity Commission can attack small businesses for hiring too many Hispanics and not enough blacks—but it has happened. Few people think it just that law enforcement officials can achieve their quotas for arrests by browbeating other Americans into committing crimes—but it is happening. Few people would think it just that IRS auditors can impose draconian penalties on small businesses for the "crime" of dealing with independent contractors—but it is happening. The larger and more interventionist the government, the more unfair daily life becomes. Over 1,500 years ago, St. Augustine asked: "What are States without Justice but robber-bands enlarged?"[4]

Politicians have sought to maximize social progress by maximizing the number of people labeled as criminals. The federal ban on steroid use or possession created hundreds of thousands of new criminals overnight. The New Jersey and California bans on so-called assault rifles created hundreds of thousands of lawbreakers. Over twelve million Americans regularly violate prohibitions against possession of marijuana and other illicit substances. And depending on the shifting definitions of local prosecutors, millions of other Americans could be in violation of local bans on the possession of allegedly pornographic material. These new criminal classes were not created through changes in people's behavior but by politicians moving the line between legal and illegal behavior. Though this creates more opportunity for politicians and prosecutors to make the evening news, it profoundly distracts law enforcement from concentrating on real crimes of violence and fraud against private citizens. The more new crimes politicians have invented, the less government has protected citizens against the old crimes.

Faith in government is faith in prohibitions, fines, injunctions, and jails. The limits of coercion are the limits of government. Government is a far more effective tool for preventing harm than for achieving good. Those who see the state as the engine of progress see progress as originating from some men having the power to force other men to obey them, not from the voluntary association of free individuals. Too many Americans hold a blind faith in the talismanic power of legislators—their ability to proclaim a new law and thereby make society a better place.

In the antebellum South, slaves were put on the auction block, their fate decided by the bidders' fancy. Today, Americans' liberties are put on the election block, and their rights are sold and bartered according to the latest political deal making. In the same way that white people had no right to buy and sell black people, politicians have no right to auction off the liberties of the American people. While slave auctions were premised on the idea that there was no rightful limit to some people's power over other people, modern elections are often based on an implicit assumption that there is no rightful limit to politicians' power over other Americans. In the same way that blacks had absolute rights that slavery grossly violated, American citizens' have rights that are routinely trampled by politicians who are hungering for votes or campaign contributions.

Is there any rightful limit to the power of some men over other men? If there is no rightful limit, then any amount of government coercion is presumably legitimate. And if there is a rightful limit, then all action outside that limit becomes the political equivalent of slavery. The Supreme Court declared in 1943: "One's right to life, liberty and property . . . and other fundamental rights may not be submitted to a vote; they depend on the outcome of no elections."[5] Yet while the Supreme Court has done a fine job of generating flowery rhetoric, its justices and most other federal judges have been lackadaisical about protecting citizens from abuses of government power.

Is the facade of majority rule more valuable than the reality of individual choice? The glorification of democratic processes cannot disguise the fact that government tends to be an oligopoly of special interests—the noisiest or richest or pushiest faction on any issue. Majority rule is an excellent principle for those functions that government must perform, but the further government power is stretched beyond its rightful bounds, the more fragile democratic processes become. Democracy has routinely collapsed in Third World nations because electoral victors sought to exercise dictatorial power—as if their poll victories gave them the right to absolutely control everything in the nation's geographical domain. We would be wise to harken to this lesson. Democracy must be something more than two wolves and a sheep voting on what to have for dinner.

The Bill of Rights recognized the rights of American citizens—it did not bestow those rights on a conquered populace. The United States owes its existence to the Bill of Rights. Were it not for the Bill of Rights' explicit promise to limit government power over the citizenry, the U.S. Constitution would never have been ratified. Americans of the Revolutionary Era would only permit a national government to come into existence if the leaders of that government would solemnly pledge to limit their power in perpetuity. But this sacred compact is now violated by thousands of officials at all levels of government. If the government will not keep its pact with the people, what do the people owe the government?

Liberty by itself will not create an ideal society. As Friedrich Hayek observed, "The results of freedom must depend on the values which free individuals pursue." Unfortunately, the more powerful government has become, the more likely the people's values are to be debased. Current tax and welfare policy maximizes the rewards for dependency and the penalties for self-reliance. There is a great deal that people can do to help themselves and to help their neighbors and those in need. But the more powerful government has become, the more people devote their attention to Washington rather than to their own efforts. John Stuart Mill wrote in 1859:

> the most cogent reason for restricting the interference of government is the great evil of adding unnecessarily to its power. Every function superadded to those already exercised by the government causes its influence over hopes and fears to be more widely diffused, and converts, more and more, the active and ambitious part of the public into hangers-on of the government, or of some party which aims at becoming the government.[6]

We have paid dearly for idealizing the state. There is no virtue in denying the law of gravity, and there should be no virtue in denying the limitations of government. Good intentions are no excuse for perpetual failure and growing oppression. The more we glorify government, the more liberties we will lose. Freedom is largely a choice between allowing people to follow their own interests or forcing them to follow the interests of bureaucrats, politicians, and campaign contributors. This is the soul of the debate between liberty and pseudopaternalism, between letting people build their own lives and forcing them to build their lives as politicians dictate.

We must depoliticize American life—to roll back the tide of government control over the individual's life. Politicians are expropriating a larger share of people's lives each decade. The expansion of government power is increasingly like the invasion of a foreign army in the territory of one's own life. For politicians, the duty to protect always includes the right to control.

America needs fewer laws, not more prisons. Rather than trying to dictate wages, or hiring, or the size of nectarines, or the use of private land, government should confine itself to protecting people against overt violence and fraud. Thomas Babington Macaulay, the British historian, wisely observed in 1839 that "government should be organized solely with a view to its main end; and no part of its efficiency for that end should be sacrificed in order to promote any other end however excellent."[7] Government can make great contributions to social progress by upholding law and order, by maintaining a legal code that recognizes individual rights and the sanctity of contract, and by preserving national security. The important thing is not what government attempts, but what it achieves. We have abandoned the tasks that government can and should perform to pursue goals that government has no ability to achieve.

The time has come for a repeal session of Congress—time to recognize the failure of hundreds of existing government policies. Rather than further decimating people's rights and liberties, we should decimate the federal statute book and sharply reduce the domain of people's lives subject to political whim and bureaucratic fiat.

Henry David Thoreau wrote, "If you see a man approaching you with the obvious intent of doing you good, run for your life."[8] Unfortunately, the entire American society cannot pick up and run from the government. The time has come to face up to the pervasive failures and to radically reduce government officials' power to coerce, expropriate, and subjugate other Americans. The American public placed its faith in the State, and the State failed. We need a new faith in individual liberty.

Acknowledgments

I would like to thank Sam Kazman for suggesting the book title. I would like to thank Jim Moody, David Keating, Leonard Liggio, Jim Powell, Stanley Greer, Tom Jackson, and numerous sources who wish to remain anonymous for help in understanding some of the issues in this book. I would like to thank my editors at the *Wall Street Journal*—Amity Shlaes, Melanie Kirkpatrick, Tim Ferguson, and Barbara Phillips—for helping me to flesh out and sharpen my ideas on some of the subjects in this book. Finally, I would like to thank my editor at St. Martin's Press, Simon Winder.

Numerous topics were not covered in this book because of space and time limitations. Among the more important subjects not analyzed were the Endangered Species Act, the Community Reinvestment Act, the Securities and Exchange Commission's creative definitions of insider trading, antitrust policy, sovereign immunity, federalism, and Social Security. Silence on any of these subjects should not be interpreted as condoning current government policy.

Notes

Chapter 1

1. Quoted in H. L. Mencken, *Prejudices,* 2nd ser. (New York: Knopf, 1924), p. 221.
2. John Phillip Reid, *The Concept of Liberty in the Age of the American Revolution* (Chicago: University of Chicago Press, 1988), p. 65.
3. Nancy Hollander, "'The More Corrupt the Republic, the More the Laws,'" *Champion,* November 1992, p. 3.
4. A. V. Dicey, *Law of the Constitution* (Indianapolis, IN: Liberty Classics, 1982), p. 184.
5. Steven Wisotsky, "Crackdown: The Emerging 'Drug Exception' to the Bill of Rights," *Hastings Law Journal,* vol. 38, July 1987, p. 889.
6. Dan Baum, "The Drug War on Civil Liberties," *Nation,* June 29, 1992.
7. Sharon LaFraniere, "FBI Asks Wiretap Access to Digital Phone Systems," *Washington Post,* March 7, 1992.
8. Lawrence A. Stanley, "The Child Porn Myth," *Cardozo Arts and Entertainment Law Journal,* vol. 7, 1989, p. 322.
9. David Johnston, "Clinton Calls for Expansion of Child Pornography Laws," *New York Times,* November 12, 1993.
10. For the 1960 number, see William E. Simon, *A Time for Truth* (New York: Berkeley Books, 1978), p. 101. For the current number of federal subsidy programs, see U.S. Office of Management and Budget, *Catalog of Federal Domestic Assistance Programs* (Washington, D.C.: Government Printing Office, 1992), p. iii.
11. Milton Friedman, "The Real Free Lunch: Markets and Private Property," Cato Policy Report, July/August 1993.
12. Report of the National Performance Review—Vice President Al Gore, *Creating a Government That Works Better and Costs Less,* p. 32.
13. Milton Friedman, "The Real Free Lunch."
14. Alexander Hamilton, James Madison, and John Jay, *The Federalist Papers* (New York: New American Library, 1961), p. 321.
15. Report of the National Performance Review, Vice President Al Gore, *Creating a Government That Works Better and Costs Less* (Washington, D.C.: Government Printing Office, 1993), p. 20.
16. Jerry Seper, "'92 prison population in U.S. hits new high," *Washington Times,* May 10, 1993.
17. Cary Copeland, "National Code of Professional Conduct for Asset Forfeiture," *The Police Chief,* October 1993, p. 87.
18. Don Oldenburg, "In Self-Defense," *Washington Post,* November 9, 1993.
19. Thomas Sowell, *Inside American Education* (New York: Free Press, 1993), p. 277.
20. For a good analysis of the intellectual controversies that helped pave the way to the Revolution, see Reid, *The Concept of Liberty in the Age of the American Revolution.*
21. John Locke, *Two Treatises of Government* (New York: New American Library, 1965), p. 297.
22. Silks Downer, "A Discourse at the Dedication of the Tree of Liberty," in *American Political Writing during the Founding Era, 1760-1805,* ed. Charles S. Honeymoon and Donald S. Lutz (Indianapolis, IN: Liberty Press, 1983), p. 1071.

Chapter 2

1. James Ely, *The Guardian of Every Other Right: A Constitutional History of Property Rights* (New York: Oxford University Press, 1992), p. 14.
2. L. Gordon Crovitz, "Justices Should Defend a Revolutionary Idea—the Contract," *Wall Street Journal,* December 4, 1991.

3. Robert Greenhalgh Albion, *Forests and Sea Power* (Cambridge, MA: Harvard University Press, 1926), p. 262.
4. Joseph Malone, *Pine Trees and Politics* (Seattle, WA: University of Washington Press, 1964), p. 140.
5. Albion, *Forests and Sea Power,* p. 255.
6. Jonathan Sewall, *Ancient Dominions of Maine* (Boston: Crosby and Nichols, 1859), p. 328.
7. Buchanan v. Warley, 245 U.S. 60, 74 (1917).
8. The federal government had possessed seizure powers since 1789, but these were limited to areas such as smuggling and customs evasion.
9. Cary Copeland, "Civil Forfeiture for the Non-Lawyer," U.S. Department of Justice, Bureau of Justice Assistance Forfeiture Project, Spring 1992.
10. Brief of the Institute for Justice, U.S. v. James Daniel Good Real Property, et al., No. 92-1180, U.S. Supreme Court, June 7, 1993, p. 11.
11. In California alone, more than $180 million worth of property has been forfeited since 1989 under a state forfeiture law. Gary Webb, "Police Lobbying to Save State Asset Forfeiture Law," *San Jose Mercury News,* September 7, 1993.
12. Interview with Steven Kessler, September 21, 1993. Kessler's study on forfeiture is titled *Civil and Criminal Forfeiture: Federal and State Practice* (New York: Clark, Boardman, and Callaghan, 1993).
13. Lynne Marek, "Hyde Seeks to Curb Property Seizures by U.S.," *Chicago Tribune,* June 16, 1993.
14. Paul Kirby, "S.C. Woman: Criminal Asset Forfeiture Program Needs Reforms," States News Service, June 22, 1993.
15. Paul Finkelman, "The Latest Front in the War on Drugs: The First Amendment," *Drug Law Report,* March-April 1991.
16. Willie Jones v. U.S. Drug Enforcement Administration, 1993 U.S. Dist. LEXIS 5409 (April 23, 1993).
17. Andrew Schneider and Mary Pat Flaherty, "Police Profit by Seizing Homes of Innocent," *Pittsburgh Press,* August 12, 1991.
18. Gary Fields, "'Robbery with a Badge' in the Nation's Capital," *USA Today,* May 18, 1992.
19. Ibid.
20. Jeff Brazil and Steve Berry, "Tainted Cash or Easy Money?" *Orlando Sentinel,* various dates, 1992. The series of articles won the 1993 Pulitzer Prize.
21. "Weeks After Seizing Pickups, Feds Still Mum About Charges," *Livestock Weekly,* May 21, 1992.
22. Interview with Anthony Nicholas, counsel for the Smiths, July 31, 1993.
23. Written statement of W. B. Smith, December 1992.
24. U.S. Congress, House Government Operations Committee, *Asset Forfeiture,* June 22, 1993. Written statement submitted by Nancy Hollander, p. 9.
25. Andrew Schneider and Mary Pat Flaherty, "Government Seizures Victimize Innocent," *Pittsburgh Press,* August 11, 1991.
26. Phil Reeves, "Gun Law Claims a Rich Recluse," *The Independent,* October 18, 1992.
27. Editorial, "Thieves with Badges," *Sacramento Bee,* April 2, 1993.
28. Carol Bidwell, "Motives for Raid Questioned," *Houston Chronicle,* April 4, 1993.
29. Michael Fessier, "Trail's End," *Los Angeles Times Magazine,* August 1, 1993.
30. Daryl Kelley, "Block Challenges Critical Report on Malibu Ranch Raid," *Los Angeles Times,* April 9, 1993.
31. Editorial, "Thieves with Badges."
32. U.S. Department of Justice, *Annual Report of the Department of Justice Asset Forfeiture Program 1991* (Washington, D.C.: Government Printing Office, 1992), p. 7.
33. As lawyer Terrance G. Reed noted, "This probable cause standard for seizure allows the government to dispossess property owners based only upon hearsay or innuendo—'evidence' of insufficient reliability to be admissible in a court of law." Terrance G. Reed, "American Forfeiture Law: Property Owners Meet the Prosecutors," Cato Institute Policy Analysis No. 179, September 29, 1992.
34. Andrew Schneider and Mary Pat Flaherty, "With Sketchy Data, Government Seizes House From Man's Heirs," *Pittsburgh Press,* August 14, 1991.

35. Mary Pemberton, "Baltimore Public-Housing Tenants Begin a Rent Strike," Associated Press, February 24, 1993.
36. "In War on Narcotics, Tough New Statutes Target Owners of Drug-Ridden Properties," *Wall Street Journal,* March 29, 1989.
37. Schneider and Flaherty, "Police Profit by Seizing Homes of Innocent."
38. "Landlords Upset with Board-ups," United Press International, July 29, 1992.
39. Written Statement by Forfeiture Endangers American Rights, of Franklin, NJ, September 30, 1992.
40. U.S. Department of Justice, *Annual Report* (1991), p. 29.
41. Brazil and Berry, "Tainted Cash or Easy Money?"
42. Jeff Brazil, "Attacks on Property Seizure Laws Spread," *Orlando Sentinel,* June 20, 1993.
43. Jay Romano, "Protests Mount Over Police Confiscations," *New York Times,* September 13, 1992.
44. David Kaplan, Bob Cohn, and Karen Springen, "Where the Innocent Lose," *Newsweek,* January 4, 1993, p. 42.
45. Terrance G. Reed, "American Forfeiture Law: Property Owners Meet the Prosecutors," Cato Institute Policy Analysis No. 179, September 29, 1992, p. 12.
46. Ibid., p. 1.
47. Rick Brand and Katti Gray, "DWI? They Might Take Your Car," *Newsday,* May 12, 1993.
48. "New Bill Would Penalize Polluters," *Massachusetts Lawyers Weekly,* February 15, 1993, p. 21.
49. U.S. v. Twelve Thousand, Three Hundred Ninety Dollars, 956 F. 2d 801, 808 (1992).
50. "Sheriff's Own Pay Raise Leads to Indictment," Associated Press, August 19, 1993.
51. U.S. Department of Justice, "Message from the Director: 'Do the Right Thing,'" *Asset Forfeiture News,* September-October 1992, p. 2.
52. U.S. Department of Justice, Executive Office for Asset Forfeiture, "Departmental Policy Regarding Seizure of Occupied Real Property," Directive No. 90-10, October 9, 1990.
53. Claudio Riedi, "To Shift or to Shaft: Attorney Fees for Prevailing Claimants in Civil Forfeiture Suits," *University of Miami Law Review,* vol. 47, September 1992, p. 147.
54. Brazil and Berry, "Tainted Cash or Easy Money?"
55. U.S. v. All Assets of Statewide Auto Parts, Inc., 971 F. 2d 905 (1992).
56. Statement of Cary H. Copeland before the Subcommittee on Legislation and National Security, Government Operations Committee, U.S. House of Representatives, June 22, 1993, p. 4.
57. U.S. Department of Justice, *Annual Report,* p. 27.
58. Interview with Mark Sakaley, August 3, 1993.
59. Dianna Hunt, "Forfeiture Law Leads to Bad Deals for Feds," *Houston Chronicle,* July 27, 1992.
60. U.S. v. One Parcel of Property Located at 508 Depot Street, Docket No. 91-2382SD, May 20, 1992.
61. Brief of American Library Assoc. et al., in Ferris J. Alexander v. U.S., U.S. Supreme Court, No. 91-1526, September 2, 1992, p. 6. "Criminal forfeiture *in personam* arose in medieval England, where, following a felony conviction, the entire estate of the felon was confiscated and any inheritance from the felon was prohibited. In the Magna Carta, forfeiture on the ground of commission of a felony was sharply curtailed, but survived to an extent in the English common law."
62. Brief for the United States, Ferris J. Alexander v. U.S., No. 91-1526, October 29, 1992, p. 43.
63. Marcia Coyle, "Property Revival; Economic Rights Gurus Look to High Court," *National Law Journal,* January 27, 1992, p. 1.
64. Yale Rabin, "Expulsive Zoning: The Inequitable Legacy of *Euclid,*" in *Zoning and the American Dream,* ed. Charles M. Haar and Jerold S. Kayden (Chicago: Planners Press, American Planning Association, 1989), p. 101.
65. Ibid., p. 108.
66. Charles Oliver, "Brickbats," *Reason,* March 1990, p. 18.
67. Mark Edward Crane, "Brickbats," *Reason,* December 1988, p. 12.
68. Mark Edward Crane, "Brickbats," *Reason,* July 1986, p. 16.
69. Louis S. Richman, "Housing Policy Needs a Rehab," *Fortune,* March 27, 1989, p. 84.
70. Matthew Nickerson, "Signs of Times: Smaller but Tasteful," *Chicago Tribune,* May 21, 1993.
71. Erick Damian Kelly, "Enforcing Zoning and Land-Use Controls," American Planning Association Planning Advisory Service Report No. 409, 1988, p. 4.
72. G. Jeannette Avent, "Landowners Sue Over Interim Zoning Law," *Los Angeles Times,* April 11, 1993.

73. John Williams, "Officials Downplay Zoning Threat to Business; City Finds Only 128 Bars, Liquor Stores That Would Close Under New Law," *Houston Chronicle*, February 16, 1993.
74. Peter Baker, "Zoning Office Gets Tough in Fairfax," *Washington Post*, April 25, 1993.
75. Barbara Marsh, "Tolerance Rises for Businesses Run in Homes," *Wall Street Journal*, July 8, 1991.
76. Ibid.
77. "Rabbi Criticized for Using Home as Office," United Press International, November 16, 1986.
78. Julie Fanselow, "Zoning Laws vs. Home Businesses," *Nation's Business*, August 1992, p. 35.
79. "When Home is Where the Business Is," *Zoning News* (American Planning Association), December 1991.
80. Ibid.
81. Peter G. Chronis, "Small Gun Dealerships Up in Arms," *Denver Post*, April 12, 1992.
82. JoAnn Butler and Judith Getzels, "Home Occupation Ordinances," American Planning Association Planning Advisory Service Report No. 391, 1985, p. 12. Funded by a grant from the U.S. Department of Health and Human Services.
83. Frank Messina, "Judge Allows Lawsuit Over House Color," *Los Angeles Times*, May 8, 1992.
84. Leslie Earnest, "Homeowner Feels Fenced In; City Design Panel Says White Picket Enclosure is Too High," *Los Angeles Times*, July 16, 1991.
85. Daryl Kelley, "Making the Neighbors Toe the Line," *Los Angeles Times*, December 15, 1991.
86. Wendelyn A. Martz and Marya Morris, "Preparing a Landscaping Ordinance," American Planning Association Planning Advisory Service Report No. 431, December 1990, p. 13.
87. Vicki Torres, "Property Ordinance Gets Mixed Reviews," *Los Angeles Times*, September 27, 1990.
88. Vicki Torres, "Front-Yard Faux Pas," *Los Angeles Times*, September 16, 1990.
89. Leslie Berkman, "Was Jailed Laguna Beach Santa Naughty or Nice?" *Los Angeles Times*, March 23, 1992.
90. Jackie Majerus, "A Man's Home Is His Castle. Well, Maybe Not," *National Law Journal*, January 13, 1992, p. 43.
91. Peter Pae, "'Big Brother' Says Paint," *Washington Post*, August 19, 1993.
92. Rick Hampson, "Too-Tall Tower: The Incredible Shrinking High Rise," Associated Press, April 19, 1993.
93. Shelby Grad, "Home's Dome Must Go, Council Rules," *Los Angeles Times*, August 25, 1993.
94. Editorial, "Hitting the Roof," *Orange County Register*, May 14, 1993.
95. John Penner, "House Is Too High, City Says; Home Had Council's OK, Now Must Shrink," *Los Angeles Times*, January 23, 1992.
96. Editorial, "Policing the Design Board," *Orange County Register*, May 15, 1992.
97. Annette Welch, "Government Watch: Coming Up Babylon Zoning Board of Appeals," *Newsday*, January 19, 1992.
98. William Murphy, "Greenbacks Help City 'Expediters' Battle Red Tape," *Newsday*, April 29, 1991.
99. Dean Baquet and William Gaines, "Zoning Makes the Alderman a King," *Chicago Tribune*, October 11, 1987.
100. Kelly, "Enforcing Zoning and Land-Use Controls," p. 15.
101. City of Galena v. Dunn, Appellate Court of Illinois, 583 N.E. 2d 616 (1991).
102. Joseph Hudachek v. Zoning Hearing Board of Newtown Borough, 147 Pa. Commw. 566; 608 A.2d 652, April 29, 1992.
103. Tom Gagliardo, "E-Day In Takoma Park; There's No Good Reason for the Evictions," *Washington Post*, February 28, 1988.
104. Reuben McCornack, "Tenant Turmoil in Takoma," *Washington Post*, March 17, 1988.
105. States News Service, "Eviction of Renters Begins in Maryland Town," May 1, 1988.
106. Joseph Calve, "Worst Five Cases of 1991," *Connecticut Law Tribune*, February 17, 1992, p. 7a.
107. Craig M. Collins, "Twice Burned," *Reason*, August/September 1992, p. 42.
108. Jube Shiver, Jr., "Red Tape, Weak Economy Cast Pall Over Rebuilding," *Los Angeles Times*, August 29, 1992.
109. Kenneth Regan, "You Can't Build That Here: The Constitutionality of Aesthetic Zoning and Architectural Review," *Fordham Law Review*, vol. 58, April 1990, p. 1013.
110. Ibid.
111. Thomas J. Hall, "Is 'Land Use Law' Becoming an Oxymoron?" *New Jersey Law Journal*, October 24, 1991, p. 6.

112. Elsa Brenner, "And Now, Is It Politically Aesthetic?" *New York Times,* September 13, 1992.
113. Interview with Bill Moshofsky, November 7, 1992.
114. Gary Eisler, "Dear Government: No Trespassing," *Wall Street Journal,* August 27, 1993.
115. "Camping Restraints in Hood River," *Looking Forward* (published by Oregonians in Action Education Center), July/August 1992, p. 6.
116. "Litigation Update," *Looking Forward,* September/October 1992, p. 6.
117. For an analysis of some of the peculiarities of USDA's system of defining farmers, see James Bovard, *The Farm Fiasco* (San Francisco: ICS Press, 1989), pp. 44-48.
118. Forster v. Polk County, 115 Ore. App. 475, October 14, 1992.
119. Jim Kadera, "A Mirror Image?: As Vermont Looks at Its Future, Should It Look at Oregon's Past?" *Vermont Business Magazine,* November, 1987, p. 12.
120. Interview with Bill Moshofsky, November 17, 1992.
121. Robert Gray, "How Good Intentions Ruined Howard County Agriculture," *Washington Post,* June 23, 1991.
122. James E. Peters, "Saving Farmland: How Well Have We Done?" *Planning,* September 1990, p. 12.
123. Arthur C. Nelson, "Preserving Prime Farmland in the Face of Urbanization—Lessons From Oregon," *APA Journal,* Autumn 1992, pp. 467-484.
124. Digest of Recent Opinions, "Regulation Limiting Use To Farm and Related Uses Is Not a Taking," *New Jersey Law Journal,* September 5, 1991, p. 37.
125. Richard Babcock and Charles Siemon, *The Zoning Game Revisited* (Cambridge, MA: Lincoln Institute for Land Policy, 1985), p. 52.
126. Lewis Goldshore and Marsha Wolf, "Takings Cases Shed New Light On Wetlands, Owners' Rights," *National Law Journal,* October 14, 1991, p. 18.
127. Digest of Recent Opinions, "Regulation Limiting Use To Farm and Related Uses Is Not a Taking," p. 37.
128. Paul W. Valentine, "Growth: Md.'s Developing Problem; Agency's Report Says Pace of Land Consumption Across State Poses Ecological Risks," *Washington Post,* February 20, 1992.
129. Charles Babington, "Crowded Schools in Montgomery May Bring Housing Moratorium," *Washington Post,* June 13, 1992.
130. Michael Abramowitz, "Drawing the Line on Developers' Dollars," *Washington Post,* April 30, 1991.
131. Ibid.
132. Fred Strasser, "Just Whose Land Is It—Anyway? New Ground for Suits," *National Law Journal,* December 22, 1986, p. 1.
133. Advisory Commission on Regulatory Barriers to Affordable Housing, *"Not in My Back Yard"—Removing Barriers to Affordable Housing* (Washington, D.C.: Department of Housing and Urban Development, 1991), p. 6.
134. According to the National Association of Home Builders, 130,000 apartment units were built in 1992. Interview with Dean Crist of the National Association of Home Builders, September 14, 1993.
135. Patrick H. Hare, "Speaking Out: Accessory Units Can Ease House Shortage," *Los Angeles Times,* November 17, 1991.
136. Ann Mariano, "District May Allow Home Apartments," *Washington Post,* July 3, 1993.
137. Gayle Young, "Prince William Board Rejects Proposal to Allow 'Granny Flats,'" *Washington Post,* February 4, 1984.
138. Kirstin Downey, "Ruling May Encourage Multifamily Housing," *Washington Post,* August 24, 1991.
139. Advisory Commission on Regulatory Barriers to Affordable Housing, *"Not in My Back Yard"—Removing Barriers to Affordable Housing,* p. 6.
140. "Under Siege: What Regulations Cost Builders," *Builder,* August 1993, p. 46.
141. Denise Hamilton, "Affluent Cities Creative with Housing Quotas," *Los Angeles Times,* April 23, 1993.
142. Sylvia Lewis, "Land-Use Law: Today's Rules," *Planning,* November 1991, p. 22.
143. Friedrich Hayek, *The Constitution of Liberty* (Chicago: Regnery Gateway, 1972), p. 240. First published in 1960 by the University of Chicago Press.
144. Kelly, "Enforcing Zoning and Land-Use Controls," p. 18.
145. Dick Cowden, "The Search for Affordable Housing," *Regulation,* Fall 1991, p. 6.

146. William Tucker, *The Excluded Americans* (Washington, D.C.: Regnery, 1989), p. 113.
147. Terence Moran, "Taking On the Tories of Local Zoning," *Legal Times,* March 16, 1992.
148. Richard Epstein, *Forbidden Grounds* (Cambridge, MA: Harvard University Press, 1992), p. 115.
149. Interview with Paul Edmonson, National Trust for Historic Preservation, November 19, 1992.
150. Jim Herron Zamora, "Landmark Big Boy Case Ignites Rights Debate in Burbank," *Los Angeles Times,* November 12, 1992.
151. *The Preservationist,* Montgomery County [Maryland] Historic Preservation Commission, January-February-March 1993.
152. Ann Mariano, "20th-Century Sites Said to Be Historic," *Washington Post,* December 3, 1988.
153. Jonathan Gaw, "What's Historic? Escondido Reviews Its Law in Wake of Shack Owner's Protest," *Los Angeles Times,* March 24, 1991.
154. H. Jane Lehman, "Property-Rights Advocates Fight Against Restrictions; Growing Movement Targets Land-Use Laws," *Washington Post,* January 11, 1992.
155. "Kingman (President Monroe) Apartment Building," Case No. 90-14, Historic Preservation Review Board of the District of Columbia.
156. James Bovard, "This Is No Way to Preserve History," *Wall Street Journal,* May 13, 1993.
157. Caryle Murphy, "HUD Raps Parker-Gray Decision; Report Finds Bias in Alexandria Action," *Washington Post,* January 15, 1988.
158. Bobby Kaplow, "Neighbors Clash Over Maywood Historic Designation," *Washington Post,* July 18, 1991.
159. Interview with cynic land-use expert who wished to remain anonymous, November 18, 1992.
160. David W. Dunlap, "Church's Landmark Status Is Upheld," *New York Times,* September 13, 1990.
161. Angela C. Carmella, "Houses of Worship and Religious Liberty: Constitutional Limits to Landmark Preservation and Architectural Review," *Villanova Law Review,* vol. 36, no. 2, 1991, p. 443.
162. Ibid., pp. 451, 478, 506.
163. Statement by Andrea C. Ferster, Assistant General Counsel, National Trust for Historic Preservation, in *Forum,* Summer 1990, p. 23.
164. Anice Read, "Demolition Spurs Landmarks Legislation in Texas," *Preservation Newsletter,* January-February 1992, p. 5.
165. Pamela Plumb, "Planning for Preservation: Managing Growth in Urban Areas," *Forum,* Summer 1990, p. 13.
166. Linda Wheeler, "Scofflaws Imperiling Historic Districts, Activists Warn," *Washington Post,* March 5, 1992.
167. Dunlap, "Church's Landmark Status Is Upheld."
168. S. R. Carroll, "At Home in the History Books—Getting National Register Status Isn't Always a Monumental Chore," *Chicago Tribune,* November 3, 1991.
169. Wheeler, "Scofflaws Imperiling Historic Districts, Activists Warn."
170. Benjamin Forgey, "Where Historic and Modern Meet: The Debate Over Preservation of The Christian Science Complex," *Washington Post,* January 11, 1992.
171. Interview with Mel Garbow, September 30, 1993.
172. Telephone interview with U.S. Census Bureau official, November 18, 1992.
173. Tom DeLay, "Why I Proposed to Strike Federal Funding for the National Trust for Historic Preservation," *Land Rights Letter,* September 1993, p. 7.
174. Arnold Berke, "Property Rights and Wrongs," *Historic Preservation News,* May 1992, p. 6.
175. Brief of Defenders of Property Rights, Supreme Court of Pennsylvania, No. 48—E.D., Appeal Docket 1990. United Artists Theatre Circuit, Inc., Appellant., v. City of Philadelphia, Philadelphia Historical Commission, Appellees. On Reargument of the Decision and Order Entered by the Supreme Court on July 10, 1991. Dated October 10, 1991.
176. "Ohio Trial Court Finds Dayton's Historic Preservation Ordinance to be Unconstitutional," *Preservation Law Reporter,* January 1992, p. 1001.
177. Leovy v. U.S., 177 U.S. 621, 686 (1900).
178. "News Conference with EPA Administrator William Reilly," Federal News Service, November 25, 1991.
179. Rick Henderson, "Is California 40 Percent Wetlands?" *New York Times,* April 3, 1991.
180. Maura Dolan, "Wetlands Law Swamped by Rising Tide of Criticism," *Los Angeles Times,* July 5, 1991.

181. Statement of the National Association of State Departments of Agriculture, U.S. Congress, Senate Environment and Public Works Committee, Hearing on Federal Wetlands Regulatory Policy, September 15, 1993.
182. U.S. Congress, House Committee on Merchant Marine and Fisheries, *Takings, Compensation, and Pending Wetlands Legislation,* May 21, 1992 (Washington, D.C.: Government Printing Office, 1992), p. 74.
183. Robert J. Pierce, "Redefining Our Regulatory Goals," *National Wetlands Newsletter,* November/December 1991, p. 12.
184. Carrie Dowling, "Dumping on Wetlands in Yard Gets Man 2-Month Sentence," *Detroit News,* December 10, 1991.
185. Editorial, "Public Enemies," *National Review,* February 1, 1993, p. 16.
186. *Congressional Record,* March 8, 1991, p. E 843.
187. Paul D. Kamenar, "The Federal Government Flunks Test for Regulating Wetlands on Oregon School District Property," Washington Legal Foundation, October 23, 1992.
188. U.S. Congress, Senate Committee on Environment and Public Works, *Implementation of Section 404 of the Clean Water Act,* June 10, 1991 (Washington, D.C.: Government Printing Office, 1992), p. 69.
189. U.S. Congress, *Takings, Compensation, and Pending Wetlands Legislation,* p. 6.
190. U.S. Congress, *Implementation of Section 404 of the Clean Water Act,* p. 70.
191. U.S. Congress, *Takings, Compensation, and Pending Wetlands Legislation,* p. 19.
192. William Laffer, "Drowning in EPA's Rules on Wetlands," *Orange County Register,* July 28, 1991.
193. Editorial, "Bill Reilly's Family Values," *Washington Times,* September 28, 1992.
194. Editorial, "EPA's Most Wanted," *Wall Street Journal,* November 18, 1992.
195. Editorial, "Bill Reilly's Family Values."
196. Hoffman Homes, Inc. v. Administrator, United States Environmental Protection Agency, 1992 U.S. App. LEXIS 7329, April 20, 1992.
197. Robert Wilhelm, "Bureaucratic Ingenuity Has Made a Mess of Wetlands Policy," *Houston Chronicle,* November 24, 1991.
198. Interview with Tom Jackson, counsel for Hoffman Homes, October 7, 1993.
199. Ibid.
200. Hoffman Homes, Inc. v. Administration, Civ. Action No. 90-3810 (7th Cir. July 19, 1993).
201. Virginia Albrecht and David Isaacs, "Wetlands Jurisdiction and Judicial Review," *Natural Resources and Environment,* Summer 1992, p. 29.
202. Bernard Goode, "Section 404 Permit Delays," National Association of Home Builders, 1991.
203. Warren Brookes, "Swamping the Economy?" *Washington Times,* April 11, 1991.
204. Ibid.
205. Editorial, "EPA's Most Wanted."
206. Jerry Gray, "Judge Reduces Tax Bill on Tract of Wetlands," *New York Times,* May 1, 1992.
207. American Farm Bureau Federation, "Wetlands Statement," September 27, 1990.
208. Jonathan Tolman, "The Dry Facts About 'Wetlands,'" *Wall Street Journal,* August 25, 1993.
209. U.S. General Accounting Office, "Clean Water Act—Private Property Takings Claims as a Result of the Section 404 Program," August 1993, p. 2.
210. White House Office on Environmental Policy, "Protecting America's Wetlands: A Fair, Flexible, and Effective Approach," August 24, 1993, p. 23.
211. "Administration Unveils 'Fair' Wetlands Policy," United Press International, August 24, 1993. Emphasis added.
212. White House Office on Environmental Policy, "Protecting America's Wetlands," p. 24.
213. "Analysis of Army Corps of Engineers Permit Decisions under the Section 404 Program," Beveridge and Diamond law firm, October 15, 1993.
214. White House Office on Environmental Policy, "Protecting America's Wetlands," p. 25.
215. Michael Mansur and Jeff Taylor, "'Blatant' Favoritism for Dakota Farmers Alleged," *Kansas City Star,* December 9, 1991.
216. The phrase, "beautify or else!" is from an editorial in the *Orange Counter Register,* May 29, 1965.
217. U.S. Congress, Senate Committee on Public Works, *Highway Beautification and Scenic Road Program* (Washington, D.C.: Government Printing Office, 1965), p. 95.

218. Ibid., p. 314. The quote is from a March 15, 1965, editorial in the *Rocky Mountain News.*
219. U.S. Congress, Senate Committee on Environment and Public Works, *Federal Highway Beautification Assistance Act of 1979,* July 17, 1979 (Washington, D.C.: Government Printing Office, 1979), p. 215.
220. Ibid.
221. Ibid., p. 353.
222. Mary Ann Gwinn, "Wild Rivers—How Do You Save Something That Knows No Boundaries?" *Seattle Times,* May 20, 1990.
223. *Congressional Record,* May 14, 1991, p. H 3014.
224. Ibid., p. H 3016.
225. Zach Willey, "Freer Markets Would Protect Northwest Salmon," *Wall Street Journal,* March 9, 1992.
226. Bill Dietrich, "Gorge Panel Taking a Lot of Heat," *Seattle Times,* February 14, 1991.
227. Ibid.
228. Bill Dietrich, "Scenic Area: Discontent in Columbia River Gorge," *Seattle Times,* April 1, 1993.
229. Don Smith, "Senator Asks Looser River Rules; Bill: Peconic Wild and Urban," *Newsday,* June 26, 1991.
230. Jeanne Dugan Cooper, "This Owner Is No Paper Tiger; Frustrated Businessman Takes Company South, Vowing to Leave State's Reputation Among Trash," *Newsday,* December 9, 1991.
231. Jeanne Dugan Cooper, "River of No Return; The Battle Over the Peconic River Comes Down to Economics vs. the Environment," *Newsday,* October 13, 1990.
232. Thompson v. Consolidated Gas Corp., 300 U.S. 55, 80 (1937).
233. Martin Anderson, *The Federal Bulldozer* (Cambridge, MA: MIT Press, 1964), p. 188.
234. John Weicher, *Urban Renewal* (Washington, D.C.: American Enterprise Institute, 1973), p. 5.
235. Anderson, *The Federal Bulldozer,* p. 54.
236. Ibid., pp. 189-190.
237. Berman v. Parker, 348 U.S. 26 (1954).
238. Anderson, *The Federal Bulldozer,* p. 4.
239. Sonya Bekoff Molho and Gideon Kanner, "Urban Renewal: Laissez-Faire for the Poor, Welfare for the Rich," *Pacific Law Journal,* vol. 8, July 1977, p. 674.
240. Interview with Gideon Kanner, September 16, 1993.
241. U.S. Congress, House Committee on Banking, Finance and Urban Affairs, *CDBG and UDAG Displacement,* September 29, 1988 (Washington, D.C.: Government Printing Office, 1989), p. 59.
242. Ibid., p. 64.
243. Larry Bivins, "'Upscale' Urban Renewal Housing Hit," *Newsday,* November 23, 1988.
244. Michael Rezendes, "City Wins Suit Against Rappaport," *Boston Globe,* November 2, 1990.
245. John Fredrickson, "City Announces New Plans for Lower East Side," *Newsday,* June 18, 1988.
246. James C. McKinley, "Metrotech Waits Approval Amid Protests," *New York Times,* June 28, 1987.
247. Weicher, *Urban Renewal,* p. 87.
248. Gonzales v. City of Santa Ana, 1993 Cal. App. LEXIS 83, January 29, 1993.
249. Malcolm Gladwell, "Rooms with a View to Housing the Poor," *Washington Post,* March 28, 1993.
250. David G. Savage, "Supreme Court Rules New York Cannot Compel Landlords to Rent Units to Poor," *Los Angeles Times,* November 28, 1989.
251. "SRO Laws Are Found to Be Unconstitutional and Compensable; 245-259 Realty Co. v. City of New York, Supreme Court, IA Part 25, Justice DeGrasse," *New York Law Journal,* June 19, 1991, p. 21.
252. Adam Sparks, letter to the editor, *The Recorder* (San Francisco), July 1, 1991.
253. Lisa Greim, "Pacific Bay Inn Still Sparks Row," *San Francisco Business Times,* July 5, 1991, p. 1.
254. Ibid.
255. Jonathan Marshall, "New Business Digest Vows to Be Different by Speaking Out," *San Francisco Chronicle,* April 6, 1992.
256. Dave Lesher, "Debate Is Raging on Housing Funds, Redevelopment," *Los Angeles Times,* February 10, 1991.
257. Robert Guskind, "Games Cities Play," *National Journal,* March 18, 1989, p. 634.
258. Editorial, "Blight Fight," *Orange County Register,* March 11, 1992.

259. Dan Walters, "Blight Infests California's Urban-Redevelopment Laws," *Orange County Register,* May 7, 1991.
260. City of Wheaton v. Sandberg, Appellate Court of Illinois, 574 N.E. 2d 697 (1991).
261. AAAA Enterprises v. River Place Community Urban Redevelopment Corporation, 74 Ohio App. 3d 170, May 16, 1991.
262. Interview with Gideon Kanner, September 16, 1993.
263. Cass Plumbing & Heating Co. v. PPG Industries, 52 Commw. 600, 416 A.2d 1142, 1149 (1980).
264. "Poletown Plant Employs Few Workers from Area," United Press International, November 29, 1989.
265. Sheldon Richman, "The Rape of Poletown," *Inquiry,* August 3, 1981.
266. U.S. General Accounting Office, "Urban Action Grants: Information on Resident and Business Relocation from Poletown Project," November 1989.
267. "Detroit Levels Neighborhood," *Engineering News-Record,* March 5, 1987, p. 13.
268. Nancy Costello, "Detroit Official Proposes Turning Blighted Neighborhoods into Pastures," Associated Press, May 5, 1993.
269. Linda Greenhouse, "Justices Uphold Hawaii's Statue on Land Reform," *New York Times,* May 31, 1984.
270. Midkiff v. Tom, 702 F.2d 788, 790 (1983).
271. Richard Epstein, *Takings: Private Property and the Power of Eminent Domain* (Cambridge, MA: Harvard University Press, 1985), p. 333.
272. Wendy Swallow, "Limited Benefit Seen in Hawaii Land Law," *Washington Post,* November 24, 1984.
273. Susan Faludi, "How Everyone Got Hawaiians' Homelands Except the Hawaiians," *Wall Street Journal,* September 9, 1991.
274. Bovard, *The Farm Fiasco,* pp. 62-66.
275. David L. Callies, "Property Rights: Are There Any Left?" *Urban Lawyer,* vol. 20, Summer 1988, p. 597. Emphasis added.
276. *Congressional Record,* June 12, 1991, p. S 7556.
277. Iver Peterson, "Builders Battle 'Takings' of Property," *New York Times,* February 28, 1988.
278. *Congressional Record,* June 12, 1991, p. S 7553.
279. Quoted in Doug Bandow, *The Politics of Plunder* (New Brunswick, NJ: Transaction Books, 1991), p. 329.
280. Nasierowski Brothers Investment Co. v. City of Sterling Heights, 949 F.2d 890 (1991).
281. Edward J. Sullivan, "The Plan as Law," *Urban Lawyer,* vol. 24, Fall 1992, p. 877.

Chapter 3

1. Yick Wo v. Hopkins, 118 U.S. 356, 369 (1886).
2. City of St. Paul v. Robert Morris, 258 Minn. 467, 104 N.W.2d 902, July 22, 1960. (Supreme Court of Minnesota).
3. Quoted in Marvin G. Pickholz and Paul N. Murphy, "Corporate Officers and Employees after *Braswell*: Is No Document Sacred?," *Securities Regulation Law Journal,* vol. 18, 1991, p. 1.
4. Kenneth Davis, *Administrative Law Treatise* (San Diego, CA: K.C. Davis, 1982), p. 114.
5. Thomas Paine, *Common Sense and The Crisis* (Garden City, NY: Doubleday, 1973), p. 41.
6. Friedrich Hayek, *The Road to Serfdom* (Chicago: University of Chicago Press, 1944), p. 72.
7. Friedrich Hayek, *The Constitution of Liberty* (Chicago: Regnery Gateway, 1972), p. 205.
8. John Phillip Reid, *The Concept of Liberty in the Age of the American Revolution* (Chicago: University of Chicago Press, 1988), p. 55.
9. American Banana Co. v. United Fruit Co, 213 U.S. 347, 356 (1908).
10. "Roosevelt Is Urged to Ask Wide Power as 'Farm Dictator,'" *New York Times,* March 12, 1993, p. 1.
11. Michael Fumento, "Some Dare Call Them Robber Barons," *National Review,* March 13, 1987, p. 38.
12. Ibid.
13. Comments submitted to the Agricultural Marketing Service, U.S. Department of Agriculture, in response to a request for comments on the navel orange marketing order, 1990.
14. *Federal Register,* November 18, 1991, p. 58175.
15. *Federal Register,* November 3, 1991, p. 47738.
16. Comments submitted to the Agricultural Marketing Service, U.S. Department of Agriculture, in response to a request for comments on the navel orange marketing order, 1990.

17. Riverbend Farms Inc. v. Edward Madigan, Petition for Rehearing and Suggestion for Rehearing En Banc Nos. 15505 & 15781, U.S. Court of Appeals for the Ninth Circuit. Submitted by attorney James Moody, April 10, 1992.
18. *Federal Register,* October 22, 1990, p. 42552.
19. Thomas M. Lenard and Michael P. Mazur, "Harvest of Waste," *Regulation,* May/June 1985, p. 25.
20. Brief for Cal-Almond, et al., v. U.S., No. 91-1048C, U.S. Claims Court, September 1991, p. 5. (Brief written by attorneys Brian Leighton and James Moody.)
21. Ibid., p. 6.
22. Press Release, "USDA Sets Record Penalty on Federal Marketing Order Violation," U.S. Department of Agriculture, Agricultural Marketing Service, October 25, 1991.
23. Brief for Cal-Almond, et al., v. U.S., p. 31.
24. Ibid., p. 57.
25. *Federal Register,* October 26, 1992, p. 48446.
26. *Federal Register,* November 6, 1992, p. 53017. Emphasis added.
27. *Federal Register,* June 19, 1992, p. 27348.
28. Interview with John Field, July 27, 1992.
29. James Bovard, "A Fruitless Massacre in California," *Wall Street Journal,* August 11, 1992. Also, interview with Dan Gerawan, August 7, 1992.
30. Interview with Dan Gerawan, August 7, 1992.
31. Interview with lawyer James Moody, November 11, 1993. McMillan made this statement during testimony in federal court in 1985. See also U.S. Congress, House Committee on Small Business, *The Regulatory Flexibility Act,* April 16, 1986 (Washington, D.C.: Government Printing Office, 1986).
32. Wileman Bros. et al. v. Giannini et al., No. CV-F-88-251 OWW Memorandum Opinion and Order Re: Defendants' Motion to Dismiss or For Summary Judgment. 1992. Slip Op. at 9.
33. U.S. Congress, House Agriculture Committee, *Review of the Egg Products Inspection Act,* November 21, 1985 (Washington, D.C.: Government Printing Office, 1986), p. 55.
34. Ibid.
35. Doug Bandow, *The Politics of Plunder* (New Brunswick, NJ: Transaction Books, 1991), p. 333.
36. David Reyes, "Unfair Practices Claimed; Maker of Egg Separator Sues Producers Group," *Los Angeles Times,* March 11, 1986.
37. James Taranto, "Breaking Mr. Maynard," *Reason,* June 1988.
38. John Taylor, *Tyranny Unmasked* (Washington, D.C.: Davis and Force, 1822), p. 38.
39. Paul Blustein, "Unfair Traders: Does the U.S. Have Room to Talk?," *Washington Post,* May 24, 1989.
40. *Federal Register,* September 5, 1989, p. 36851.
41. Office of the U.S. Trade Representative, "Arrangement Concerning trade in certain steel products between the Government of the Polish People's Republic and the Government of the United States of America," 1985, p. 3.
42. Presidential Proclamation No. 4026, December 31, 1970, *Weekly Compilation of Presidential Documents,* vol. 7, no. 1, p. 8.
43. *Code of Federal Regulations,* 6.44 Subtitle A, January 1, 1989 edition (Washington, D.C.: Government Printing Office, 1989), p. 222.
44. For a list of thousands of textile and apparel products restricted by import quotas, see U.S. Department of Commerce, *Correlation: Textile and Apparel Categories with the Harmonized Tariff Schedule of the United States* (Washington, D.C.: Commerce Department, 1993).
45. *International Trade Reporter,* January 3, 1990, p. 10.
46. Interview with textile trade expert who wished to remain anonymous, February, 24, 1990.
47. U.S. Customs Service, Ruling Letter HQ 086022, February 15, 1990.
48. U.S. Congress, House Ways and Means Committee, *Review of U.S. Customs Service Operations,* June 9, 1988 (Washington, D.C.: Government Printing Office, 1989), p. 122.
49. Editorial, "Civic Shame," *Wall Street Journal,* February 19, 1992.
50. U.S. Congress, House Committee on Ways and Means, *Abuses and Mismanagement in U.S. Customs Service Commercial Operations,* February 8, 1990 (Washington, D.C.: Government Printing Office, 1990), p. 39.
51. U.S. Congress, House Committee on Ways and Means, *Review of U.S. Customs Service Operations,* June 9, 1988 (Washington, D.C.: Government Printing Office, 1989), p. 571.

52. U.S. Congress, House Committee on Ways and Means, *Abuses and Mismanagement in U.S. Customs Service Commercial Operations,* p. 7.
53. James Bovard, "The Custom Service's Chainsaw Massacre," *Wall Street Journal,* March 27, 1992.
54. Ibid.
55. For more information on the dumping law, see James Bovard, *The Fair Trade Fraud* (New York: St. Martin's Press, 1991), pp. 107-168.
56. *Federal Register,* May 26, 1992, p. 21937. Also, interviews with various attorneys involved in the case, June 3, 4, 5, 1992. For further details, see James Bovard, "Miniban," *New Republic,* June 22, 1992, p. 19.
57. *Federal Register,* April 15, 1988, p. 12568.
58. *Federal Register,* March 25, 1987, p. 9518. Also, interviews with attorneys involved in the case.
59. *Federal Register,* July 27, 1990, p. 30744.
60. The U.S. International Trade Commission reported that average "profits before income taxes for all U.S. corporations in 1986 were 6% of sales." U.S. International Trade Commission, "Foreign Protection of Intellectual Property Rights and the Effect on U.S. Industry and Trade," ITC Publication No. 2065, February 1988, p. ix.
61. *Federal Register,* August 23, 1990, pp. 34585-34602.
62. Interview with Washington trade lawyer who wished to remain anonymous, December 9, 1989.
63. *Federal Register,* July 16, 1991, p. 32376.
64. "Dumping Ruling Forces Firm's Output Abroad," *San Jose Mercury News,* August 17, 1991.
65. Andrew Pollack, "Duties on Japanese Screens for Laptops Cleared by U.S.," *New York Times,* August 16, 1991.
66. James Bovard, "America's Biggest Trade Secret," *Los Angeles Times Magazine,* April 12, 1992.
67. Valerie Rice, "U.S. Probe of Japanese Screen Sales Splits Industry," *Journal of Commerce,* July 5, 1991.
68. Zenith Radio Corp. v. Matsushita Elec. Indus. Co., 513 F. Supp. 1100, 1333 (1981).
69. Speech by Anne Brunsdale, U.S. International Trade Commissioner, July 15, 1992, Heritage Foundation, Washington, D.C.
70. Ibid.
71. Interview with David Palmeter, January 7, 1990.
72. Marjorie A. Chorlins, Speech to the American Wire Producers Association Annual Meeting, Scottsdale, Arizona, January 31, 1991.
73. Julie Kosterlitz, "High-Wire Act," *National Journal,* May 30, 1992, p. 1289.
74. Malcolm Gladwell, "FDA Chief Relishes Label of Lawmen," *Washington Post,* October 24, 1991.
75. Editorial, "Tough Guys at FDA," *Washington Times,* September 12, 1991.
76. Sam Kazman, "Deadly Overcaution: FDA's Drug Approval Process," *Journal of Regulation and Social Costs,* September 1990.
77. Ibid.
78. Letter to the Editor, William F. Von Valtier, M.D., Rochester, MI, "When the FDA First Went Power Mad," *Wall Street Journal,* October 15, 1992.
79. Charles Strother, "Will the FDA Let Me Treat My Patients?" *Washington Post,* April 17, 1992.
80. Kazman, "Deadly Overcaution: FDA's Drug Approval Process."
81. Editorial, "The FDA's Long March," *Wall Street Journal,* December 15, 1991.
82. Malcolm Gladwell, "Congress Approves Measure to Speed FDA Drug Approval," *Washington Post,* October 8, 1992.
83. Paul Abrahams, "When Time Can Cost a Fortune," *Financial Times,* April 22, 1993.
84. Quoted in Lawrence M. Fisher, "Frustration for Medical Innovators," *New York Times,* June 30, 1993.
85. Editorial, "The FDA Meets a Patient," *Wall Street Journal,* April 22, 1992.
86. Ibid.
87. Press Release, "Sporicidin and FTC Staff Reach Mutual Agreement on Claims," PR Newswire, May 27, 1992.
88. Associated Press, "Sporicidin Settles with Government," *Washington Post,* May 16, 1992.
89. Rudolph A. Pyatt, Jr., "Federal Agencies Prosecute Rockville Firm, Despite a Lack of Proof," *Washington Post,* January 9, 1992.

90. Associated Press, "Sporicidin Settles with Government."
91. Rudolph A. Pyatt, Jr, "Sporicidin Faces Agencies More Forceful Than Fair," *Washington Post*, December 24, 1992.
92. Ibid.
93. Steve Sakson, "Company Agrees to Reformulate Sterilizing Solution Banned by Government," Associated Press, May 15, 1992.
94. Peter Samuel, "Who Will Regulate the Regulators?" *National Review*, November 2, 1992, p. 38.
95. Daniel Southerland, "Sporicidin, FTC Settle Fight Over Sterilizing Solution," *Washington Post*, February 5, 1993.
96. Ibid.
97. "Sporicidin, Two Federal Agencies Settle Disputes," *ADA News* (published by the American Dental Association), March 8, 1993, p. 40.
98. Samuel, "Who Will Regulate the Regulators?"
99. Kazman, "Deadly Overcaution: FDA's Drug Approval Process."
100. U.S. Postal Service, *History of the U.S. Postal Service, 1775-1982* (Washington, D.C.: U.S. Postal Service, 1983), p. 3. Congress granted the Post Office a monopoly shortly after its creation in 1789, but the monopoly lacked teeth until the 1840s.
101. U.S. Congress, Joint Economic Committee, *The Future of Mail Delivery*, June 18, 1982 (Washington, D.C.: Government Printing Office, 1982), p. 12.
102. Associated Third Class Mail Users v. U.S., 600 F.2d 824, March 9, 1979.
103. James Bovard, "Governors Can't Hold Post Office in Check," *Wall Street Journal*, June 20, 1985.
104. Associated Press, "Threat of Fine Ends Scouts' Good Deed," *New York Times*, December 20, 1980.
105. Sonja Isger, "Postal Service Gives Boy's Lawn-Job Fliers Stamp of Approval," *Palm Beach Post* (West Palm Beach, FL), June 19, 1991.
106. *Business Mailers Review*, July 26, 1993.
107. Interview with Postal Service spokesman Lou Eberhardt, September 29, 1993; "Businesses Fined by Postal Service for Using Couriers," *Atlanta Constitution*, September 22, 1993.
108. Elinor Burkett, "Door to Door No More," *Miami Herald*, July 25, 1988.
109. Ibid.
110. U.S. Congress, House Government Operations Committee, *Postal Service Moves Toward Centralized Delivery*, March 15, 1983 (Washington, D.C.: Government Printing Office, 1983), p. 48.
111. *Business Mailers Review*, January 27, 1986.
112. Thomas Dibacco, "Slow Mail Has Roots in American History," *Washington Times*, October 20, 1989.
113. U.S. Congress, House Post Office and Civil Service Committee, *Implementation of New First-Class Mail Delivery Standards*, September 27, 1990 (Washington, D.C.: Government Printing Office, 1990), p. 1.
114. U.S. Congress, House Government Operations Committee, *Slower Delivery Standards*, September 6, 1990 (Washington, D.C.: Government Printing Office, 1991).
115. *Business Mailers Review*, August 6, 1990.
116. U.S. Postal Service, Rates and Classification Department, *Origin-Destination Information System Quarterly Statistics Report*, 1969 and 1993. The average time for delivery of a first-class letter increased from 1.5 days to 1.78 days.
117. U.S. General Accounting Office, "Priority Mail: Advertised 2-Day Service Is Not Guaranteed," July 1993, p. 2.
118. *Direct Mail News*, March 1, 1988.
119. J. P. Mackley, "Inspectors Find Little to Boast About in Philadelphia Division," *Federal Times*, September 19, 1988.
120. Mark Kodama, "Inspection Service Chalks Up 5,800 Arrests in Six Months," *Federal Times*, June 25, 1990.
121. *Business Mailers Review*, November 9, 1987.
122. *Third Class Mail Association Bulletin*, February 29, 1988.
123. The Postal Service is paying for expensive private surveys that reveal how many letters it loses each year but claims that it must keep the survey results confidential. The Postal Service is now delivering over 40 billion third-class letters each year; since numerous private surveys

have shown that the Postal Service loses 10 percent or more of third-class "junk mail," one billion letters is a very conservative estimate for how many letters the Service loses each year.

124. Marina Milligan, "A Falling Out Briefly Cancels Mail Delivery," *Pasadena Star-News,* November 10, 1990. The post office decided to resume delivery after postal managers discovered that a reporter was writing a story about the incident.
125. "Postal Service Cutoff, Lynn, Massachusetts," United Press International, July 3, 1989.
126. Bill McAllister, "Tuesday, Thursday: No Mail?" *Washington Post,* October 15, 1992.
127. James Bovard, "Prepare for Talks by Parceling Out the Mail," *Wall Street Journal,* January 9, 1987.
128. Quoted in Dirk Johnson, "Critics Say 'Privatizing' the Post Office Is Long Overdue," *New York Times,* January 31, 1988.
129. John Haldi, *Postal Monopoly: An Assessment of the Private Express Statutes* (Washington, D.C.: American Enterprise Institute, 1974), p. 5.
130. Press Release, "Justice Department Announces Third Straight Record Year for Environmental Enforcement," U.S. Newswire, May 8, 1992.
131. Press Release, "Justice Department Announces Record $2 Billion Year for Environmental Enforcement," U.S. Newswire, October 29, 1992.
132. Tom Diemer, "Superfund has Little to Show for 13 Years," *Plain Dealer* (Cleveland), May 9, 1993.
133. J. Kent Holland, Jr., "Superfund Liability Law Prevents Cleanups," American Bar Association Conference: "Superfund: Is It 'Super'? Does It 'Fund'?" August 5, 1990.
134. U.S. Congress, House Committee on Public Works, *Reauthorization of Superfund,* July 24, 1985 (Washington, D.C.: Government Printing Office, 1985), p. 566.
135. *Federal Register,* February 5, 1985, p. 5034.
136. U.S. v. Rohm & Haas, 721 F. Supp., 666, 686 (1989).
137. Max Gates, "Dealers Face EPA Bills," *Automotive News,* October 21, 1991, p. 3.
138. Mary Anne Shreve, "Superfund Sign-Off?" *Automotive Executive,* June 1992, p. 21.
139. Editorial, "Time to Reform Superfund," *Washington Post,* September 2, 1993.
140. "An Overview of Five Federal Superfund Sites in New York," National Strategies, Inc., July 15, 1993, p. 14.
141. Ibid., p. 2.
142. "Compass Industries Superfund Site Study, Tulsa, Oklahoma," National Strategies, Inc., February 1, 1992, p. 7.
143. "An Overview of Seven Federal Superfund Sites in Minnesota," National Strategies, Inc., February 1, 1993, p. 20.
144. "An Overview of Five Federal Superfund Sites in New York." Emphasis added.
145. "McKin Company Superfund Site Study, Gray, Maine," National Strategies, Inc., July 1, 1991.
146. U.S. Congress, Senate Judiciary Committee, *Superfund Improvement Act of 1985,* June 7, 1985 (Washington, D.C.: Government Printing Office, 1985) p. 255.
147. "Lowry Landfill Superfund Site Study, Arapahoe County, Colorado," National Strategies, Inc., July 1, 1991, p. 6.
148. "No Cleanup at Lowry—Landfill Scorecard: $5 Million for Cleanup, $80 Million for Motions," *Denver Business Journal,* August 21, 1992, p. 1.
149. Stephen L. Kass and Michael B. Gerrard, "The Taming of the EPA," *New York Law Journal,* April 23, 1993, p. 3.
150. Tex Tin Corp. v. EPA, 935 F.2d 1321 (1991).
151. Kass and Gerrard, "The Taming of the EPA."
152. Anne Arundel County v. EPA, 963 F2d 412 (1992).
153. "Compass Industries Superfund Site Study, Tulsa, Oklahoma."
154. Peter Passell, "Experts Question Staggering Costs of Toxic Cleanups," *New York Times,* September 1, 1991.
155. "Superfund Risk, Liability Rules Under More Fire from Industry," *Chemical Marketing Reporter,* December 2, 1991, p. 4.
156. Jonathan Adler, "Hazardous Waste Regulation in South Carolina," South Carolina Policy Council, 1993. Adler's source was *Environmental Investments: The Cost of a Clean Environment,* U.S. Environmental Protection Agency, December 1990, p. 2-2.
157. John D. Fognani, "Environmental Laws Complex, But Compliance Is Crucial," *Oil & Gas Journal,* October 19, 1992, p. 67.

158. Richard Stoll, Introduction to *RCRA Policy Documents*, ed. Theodore L. Garrett and Joshua D. Sarnoff (Section of Natural Resources, Energy and Environmental Law, American Bar Association, 1993).
159. Interview with Frank Blake, January 17, 1989.
160. Matthew Kibbe, "Regulatory Nightmares Range from Costly to Deadly to Stupid," *San Diego Union-Tribune*, May 3, 1992.
161. James Bovard, "Some Waste Cleanup Rules Are a Waste of Resources," *Wall Street Journal*, February 15, 1989.
162. Ripley Hotch, "A Criminal Trap for Businesses," *Nation's Business*, September 1991, p. 56.
163. "Arkansas Landmark Environmental Case Sends Message to the EPA to Stop Government Goliath Environmental Enforcement Tactics," Southwest Newswire, November 16, 1992.
164. Leslie Spencer, "'Designated Inmates,'" *Forbes*, October 26, 1992, p. 100.
165. Keith A. Onsdorff and James M. Mesnard, "The Responsible Corporate Officer Doctrine in RCRA Criminal Enforcement: What You Don't Know Can Hurt You," *Environmental Law Reporter*, February, 1992.
166. Spencer, "'Designated Inmates.'"
167. Kent Jeffreys, "Whale of an Oil-Slick Deal," *Washington Times*, November 4, 1991.
168. "Alaska Judge Rejects Exxon's Criminal Plea Bargain," *Oil Spill U.S. Law Report*, May 1991.
169. *Congressional Record*, May 11, 1993, p. S 5630.
170. Ibid.
171. Mary Jordan, "Alaskans Pepper EPA with Complaints After Decree on Bear Spray," *Washington Post*, August 29, 1993.
172. Bryan Tabler and Mark Shere, "The EPA's Practice of Regulation by Memorandum," in *The Environmental Law Manual*, ed. Theodore L. Garrett (Chicago: American Bar Association, 1992), p. 32.
173. William Niskanen, "Heads I Win, Tails You Lose," *National Review*, August 31, 1992, p. 45.
174. Robert E. Litan, "Deposit Insurance, Gas on S & L Fire," *Wall Street Journal*, July 29, 1993.
175. Niskanen, "Heads I Win, Tails You Lose."
176. Glenn Yago, "The Regulatory Reign of Terror," *Wall Street Journal*, March 4, 1992.
177. Ibid.
178. L. Gordon Crovitz, "Even a Junk Lawsuit Can Separate Villains from Phantoms," *Wall Street Journal*, May 29, 1991.
179. Editorial, "Credit Crunching Lawsuits," *Wall Street Journal*, October 1, 1991.
180. Paul Craig Roberts, "Who Could Forget 'Junk Bonds'?" *Washington Times*, July 10, 1992.
181. Winstar v. United States, 25 Cl. Ct. 541, April 21, 1992.
182. Mark Sell, "Critics Charge That Thrift Agency Oversteps Bounds; OTS: A Law Unto Itself," *Legal Times*, November 25, 1991, p. 1.
183. Patrick Crawford, "Inefficiency and Abuse of Process in Banking Regulations," *Virginia Law Review*, vol. 79, February 1993, p. 207.
184. Stephanie B. Goldberg, "Kaye, Scholer: The Tremors Continue—Part I: Welcome to the New Uncertainty," *ABA Journal*, July 1992, p. 50.
185. Marvin E. Frankel, "Lawyers Can't Be Stool Pigeons," *New York Times*, March 14, 1992.
186. James Podgers, "Kaye, Scholer: The Tremors Continue—Part II: Changing the Rules," *ABA Journal*, July 1992, p. 53.
187. In re Murchison, 349 U.S. 133, 136 (1955).
188. Kenneth Culp Davis, *Administrative Law Treatise*, vol. 3 (San Diego, CA: K.C. Davis, 1980), p. 223.
189. Martin Shapiro, "On Predicting the Future of Administrative Law," *Regulation*, May/June 1992, p. 19.
190. "What Constitution Says on Freeze Orders," *National Law Journal*, June 8, 1992, p. 18.
191. U.S. General Accounting Office, "Administrative Law Judges: Allegations of Interference by the Department of the Interior," October 1992, p. 10.
192. Debra Cassens Moss, "Judges Under Fire: ALJ Independence at Issue," *ABA Journal*, November 1991, p. 56.
193. Ibid.
194. David Gram, "Critics Say Disability System Puts Holes in 'Social Safety Net,'" Associated Press, July 3, 1990.

195. Quoted in U.S. Congress, House Committee on Ways and Means, *Judicial Independence of Administrative Law Judges at the Social Security Administration,* June 13, 1990, (Washington, D.C.: Government Printing Office, 1990), p. 30.
196. Robert F. McFadden, "U.S. Wrongly Denied Aid For Impaired, Judge Rules," *New York Times,* May 9, 1992.
197. *Congressional Record,* March 4, 1992, p. S 2800. Statement of Sen. David Pryor.
198. Utica Packing Co. v. John R. Block, 781 F.2d 71 (1986).
199. Saulsbury Orchards and Almond Processing, Cal-Almond, U.S. Department of Agriculture Docket No. 85-4297, March 14, 1987.
200. Sequoia Orange Co., Inc., U.S. Department of Agriculture Docket No. CV-F-88-98, January 29, 1988.
201. Ibid.
202. Ibid.
203. Interview with James Moody, April 29, 1988.
204. Richard Barbieri, "Administrative Judges Seen Biased Toward Agencies," *Manhattan Lawyer,* November 17, 1987, p. 3.
205. Joseph Lentol, "About Justice: But Are They Impartial?" *Newsday,* January 22, 1988. Lentol is an assemblyman from Brooklyn.
206. Ibid.
207. Gary Spencer, "Cuomo Seeks to Insulate Hearing Officers," *New York Law Journal,* May 20, 1993, p. 1.

Chapter 4

1. John Taylor, *Tyranny Unmasked* (Washington, D.C.: Davis and Force, 1822), p. 114.
2. Slaughter-House Cases, 83 U.S. 36 (1873).
3. Coppage v. Kansas, 236 U.S. 1, 10, 14 (1915).
4. Ives v. South Buffalo Ry. Co., 94 N.E. 431, 439 (1911).
5. Greene v. McElroy, 360 U.S. 474, 491 (1959).
6. S. David Young, *The Rule of Experts* (Washington, D.C.: Cato Institute, 1987), p. 1.
7. Kim McKinnon, "Interior Designers Must Now Register," *Austin Business Journal,* September 2, 1991, p. 11.
8. Tex. Rev. Civ. Stat. art. 249e (1993) Regulation of practice of interior design.
9. Reginald G. Damerell, "Teachers Colleges Foster an Educational Underclass," *Wall Street Journal,* November 24, 1985. Damerell attributed the "intellectual slums" statement to Thomas Sowell.
10. James Bovard, "How Teachers Teach Selfishness," *Washington Monthly,* June 1981.
11. Rita Kramer, *Ed School Follies: The Miseducation of America's Teachers* (New York: Free Press, 1991), p. 209.
12. Susan Chira, "Would-Be Teachers Who Are Being Turned Away," *New York Times,* September 9, 1992.
13. Lawrence Shepard, "Licensing Restrictions and the Cost of Dental Care," *Journal of Law and Economics,* April 1978, p. 62.
14. U.S. Federal Trade Commission, Bureau of Economics Staff Report, "Restrictions on Dental Auxiliaries," May 1987, p. 2.
15. Federal Trade Commission v. Indiana Federation of Dentists, 476 U.S. 447 (1986).
16. Paul Schnitt, "Dental Association Accused of Restricting Competition," *Sacramento Bee,* March 8, 1991.
17. Editorial, "The Teething Ring," *Orange County Register,* December 7, 1989.
18. Carolyn Cox and Susan Foster, *The Costs and Benefits of Occupational Regulation* (Washington, D.C.: U.S. Federal Trade Commission, 1990), p. 3.
19. James Bovard, "Shutting Mouths to Aliens," *Baltimore Sun,* August 12, 1988.
20. Keith Blair, "The FTC Persists," *Journal of the American College of Dentists,* Fall 1987, p. 3.
21. Doug Bandow, "The Legal Monopoly," *Christian Science Monitor,* October 9, 1990.
22. Doug Campbell, "Bar Files Complaint on Cheap Legal Advice," *Nashville Business Journal,* November 4, 1991, p. 1.

23. Alan Abrahamson, "The Case of the Lawyers vs. the Paralegals," *Los Angeles Times,* January 16, 1990.
24. Ibid.
25. "Complaints About Lawyers Made Public," *News Media and the Law,* Spring 1990, p. 27.
26. Ibid.
27. Mary Collins, "The Wrong Side of the Lawyers; Clients Are Often Kept in the Dark About Attorney Wrongdoing," *Washington Post,* January 26, 1992.
28. Robert Enstad, "Masseur's Plea to Cut Fee Turned Down Cold," *Chicago Tribune,* May 11, 1993.
29. Kay Torrance, "Duluth Sees 'Knead,' Changes Massage Law," *Atlanta Journal and Constitution,* March 9, 1993.
30. Cy Ryan, "Nevada Supreme Court Rules on Massage Parlors," United Press International, June 5, 1989.
31. Teresa Wiltz, "Spa Regains License After Sex Dispute," *Chicago Tribune,* September 23, 1992.
32. Erin Marcus, "List of 'Questionable Doctors' Compiled; From Dentists to Podiatrists, Research Group Names," *Washington Post,* June 29, 1990.
33. Andrew Stein, "Picking a Doctor in an Information Vacuum," *New York Times,* August 17, 1986.
34. Susan Schmidt, "Md. Moves To Punish Bad Doctors; Bill Would Toughen Physician Discipline," *Washington Post,* April 7, 1988.
35. Ibid.
36. Susan Schmidt, "Bad Medicine: Doctor Discipline in Maryland," *Washington Post,* January 10, 1988.
37. Richard Perez-Pena, "Doctor Held in a Sex Case Had a Record," *New York Times,* May 6, 1993.
38. Cox and Foster, *The Costs and Benefits of Occupational Regulation,* p. 40.
39. Ibid., p. vii.
40. Milton Friedman, *Capitalism and Freedom* (Chicago: University of Chicago Press, 1962), p. 157.
41. Cox and Foster, *The Costs and Benefits of Occupational Regulation,* p. 23.
42. Clifford F. Thies, "The First Minimum Wage Laws," *Cato Journal,* Winter 1991, p. 727.
43. Finis Welch, "The Cruelty of the Minimum Wage," *Jobs and Capital,* Summer 1993.
44. Benjamin M. Anderson, *Economics and the Public Welfare: A Financial and Economic History of the United States, 1914-1946* (Indianapolis, IN: Liberty Press, 1979), p. 458.
45. "Kennedy, Hawkins Call for $1.30 Hike in Minimum Wage," *Daily Labor Report,* March 26, 1987.
46. U.S. General Accounting Office, "Minimum Wage Policy Questions Persist," 1983. Cited in Matthew B. Kibbe, "The Minimum Wage: Washington's Perennial Myth," Cato Institute Policy Analysis No. 106, May 23, 1988.
47. Michael S. Bernstam, "Minimum Wage: Bulwark of the Privileged," *Wall Street Journal,* June 15, 1987.
48. Finis Welch, *The Minimum Wage: Issues and Evidence* (Washington, D.C.: American Enterprise Institute, 1978), p. 1.
49. Editorial, "The Minimally Useful Minimum Wage," *New York Times,* March 21, 1977.
50. Michael E. Hurst, president and chairman, National Restaurant Association, Letter to the Editor, *New York Times,* January 15, 1991.
51. Welch, "The Cruelty of the Minimum Wage."
52. Robert B. Reich, Secretary of Labor, "Memo to the President: Reconciliation, the EITC, and the Minimum Wage: How Much Progress Towards the Make Work Pay Goal?" July 20, 1993.
53. Letter from Peter Sajevic, National Association of Private Residential Resources, to Lynn Martin, Secretary of Labor, April 3, 1992.
54. U.S. Department of Labor, Wage and Hour Memorandum 88.48, Paula V. Smith, Administrator, June 30, 1988.
55. Interview with Hyman Richman, September 10, 1993.
56. Ibid.
57. Bouchard, et al. v. Regional Governing Board of Region V Mental Retardation Services, July 25, 1991 (U.S. Ct. of Appeals, 8th Circ.). Reported in *Labor Relations Reporter, 1991.*
58. Robert F. Howe, "U.S. Does Turnabout on Salvation Army; Secretary Dole Will Ask Congress to Exempt Group From Wage Law," *Washington Post,* September 27, 1990.
59. Nancy Hill-Holtzman, "Salvation Army Pay; 'Beneficiaries' Must Get Minimum Wage, U.S. Rules," *Los Angeles Times,* September 20, 1990.

60. Nell Henderson and Linda Wheeler, "District's Wage Battle Focuses Critical Eye on Little-Known Board; City, Labor Officials See Need for Change," *Washington Post*, December 8, 1991.
61. Linda Wheeler, "D.C. Raising Wages—and Fears," *Washington Post*, November 25, 1991.
62. Jonetta Rose Barras, "Minimum Wage, Maximum Chaos," *Washington Times*, January 29, 1992.
63. James A. Prozzi, "Docking the Pay of Managerial Employees: The Wage and Hour Law's Potential Trap for the Employer," *Labor Law Journal*, July 1992, p. 444.
64. Kirk Victor, "Clock-Watching," *National Journal*, August 14, 1993, p. 2055.
65. Linda Froehlich, "The Labor Department is Anti-Family," *Wall Street Journal*, August 7, 1992.
66. Secretary of Labor Lynn Martin v. Malcolm Pirnie, Inc., 949 F.2d 611 (1991).
67. L. M. Sixel, "New Law Redefines Overtime," *Houston Chronicle*, August 9, 1993.
68. Statement of John Foster, submitted to U.S. Congress, House Education and Labor Committee, Hearing on Flexible Leave, July 1, 1993.
69. Statement of William J. Kilberg, submitted to U.S. Congress, House Education and Labor Committee, Hearing on Flexible Leave, July 1, 1993.
70. Ibid.
71. Jerry Moskal, "Congress Considers Move to Ban Salaried Workers' Overtime," Gannett News Service, July 20, 1992.
72. Alexander v. Chicago, CA 7, No. 92-1441, May 12, 1993.
73. Burnison v. Memorial Hospital, DC Kan, No. 91-1072-MLB, April 15, 1993.
74. Jim Doyle, "Some Inmates Entitled to the Minimum Wage," *San Francisco Chronicle*, June 25, 1992.
75. "U.S. Set to Probe Accounting Profession for Abuses in Overtime Pay," Business Wire, April 2, 1992.
76. Ralph Schusler, "Pending Bills May Force Cruise Lines Offshore," *South Florida Business Journal*, April 2, 1993, p. 9.
77. Liz Spayd, "Child Labor Violations Widespread, U.S. Says," *Washington Post*, April 20, 1992.
78. Janet Battaile, "Retail Chain Faces Child-Labor Case," *New York Times*, November 8, 1992.
79. Spayd, "Child Labor Violations Widespread, U.S. Says."
80. Associated Press, "Burger King Faces Charges It Violated Child Labor Laws," *New York Times*, March 10, 1990.
81. Barbara Vobejda, "Home Alone, Glued to the TV," *Washington Post*, December 10, 1992.
82. Tim W. Ferguson, "A Worse Child-Labor Scandal May Be the Number Not Working," *Wall Street Journal*, March 27, 1990.
83. Editorial, "Raiding the Young," *Wall Street Journal*, April 14, 1992.
84. "Criminal Sanctions for Child Labor Violations Proposed by Rep. Lantos," *BNA Washington Insider*, March 19, 1993.
85. Frank Swoboda, "Burger King Tried to Hide Records, U.S. Says," *Washington Post*, April 23, 1992.
86. Peter T. Kilborn, "A First Job Fades as the Paper Route Grows Up," *New York Times*, August 16, 1992.
87. Richard R. Nelson, "State Labor Legislation Enacted in 1990," *Monthly Labor Review*, January 1991, p. 41.
88. Richard R. Nelson, "State Labor Legislation Enacted in 1992," *Monthly Labor Review*, January 1993, p. 35.
89. "Move to Lift Ban on Young Bat Boys, Girls Runs Counter to Child Labor Panel's Advice," *Daily Labor Report*, June 1, 1993, p. d7.
90. Doug Bandow, *The Politics of Plunder* (New Brunswick, NJ: Transaction Books, 1991), p. 297.
91. United Press International, "North Carolina Woman Fighting the System," May 19, 1986.
92. "2 N.Y. Firms Pay Largest Fine for Homework; Teammate Fashion Inc., Reflex Accessories Inc., Home Labor Violations," *Women's Wear Daily*, October 15, 1991.
93. Jason B. Johnson, "Garment Workers Fear Labor Law Crackdown," *Dallas Morning News*, May 21, 1992.
94. Steve Smith, "Sewing is Target of Labor Case," *Fort Worth Star Telegram*, April 25, 1992.
95. "Legal Curb on Sewing Draws Ire," *New York Times*, June 15, 1989.
96. "Employment Rights Issues Led 1991 Agendas of State Lawmakers," *Daily Labor Report*, March 10, 1992.

97. "New Jersey Law Prohibits Homework in Manufacture of Men, Women's Apparel," *Daily Labor Report,* March 13, 1991.
98. U.S. Congress, House Committee on Education and Labor, *Oversight Hearings on the Department of Labor's Proposal to Lift the Ban on Industrial Homework,* September 16, 1986 (Washington, D.C.: Government Printing Office, 1987), p. 182.
99. H. J. Cummins, "Garment Workers Face a Crisis in Child Care," *Newsday,* November 13, 1991.
100. U.S. Congress, House Committee on Education and Labor, *Oversight Hearings on the Department of Labor's Proposal to Lift the Ban on Industrial Homework,* p. 185.
101. Henry Weinstein, "Continued U.S. Ban on At-Home Garment Work Draws Support," *Los Angeles Times,* March 23, 1989.
102. Laura Romei, "Telecommuting: A Workstyle Revolution," *Modern Office Technology,* May 1992, p. 38.
103. "Interview with CWA President Morton Bahr," *Telecommuting Review,* April 1, 1992.
104. Bill Keller, "Unions Battle Against Jobs in the Home," *New York Times,* May 20, 1984.
105. "Interview with CWA President Morton Bahr," p. 4.
106. Carla Rivera, "Costa Mesa Dayworker Exclusions Thrown Out," *Los Angeles Times,* June 23, 1990.
107. Ibid.
108. David Reyes and Carla Rivera, "Critics Say Entrapment Possible, Costa Mesa Sting Snares 12 Alleged Job Seekers," *Los Angeles Times,* September 21, 1989.
109. Carla Rivera, "Costa Mesa: Worker Ordinance Has Cost City $89,000," *Los Angeles Times,* April 10, 1990.
110. Editorial, "Anti-Dayworker Law is Flawed, Ill-Advised," *Los Angeles Times,* September 24, 1989.
111. Editorial, "The Right to Work," *Orange County Register,* March 14, 1989.
112. Seth Mydans, "In Costa Mesa, a Ban on Job Soliciting," *New York Times,* October 29, 1989.
113. Sebastian Rotella, "Suit Says Laws Against Day Laborers Incite Tension," *Los Angeles Times,* September 19, 1991.
114. Cathy Cleland-Pero, "Day Laborers Dodge Law to Seek Jobs," *Atlanta Constitution,* November 5, 1992.
115. Hanson v. Innis, 211 Mass. 301, 305 97 N.E. 756, 756 (1912). Quoted in Edwin Vieira, Jr., "Communication Workers of America v. Beck: A Victory of Non Union Employees Already Under Attack," *Government Union Review,* vol. 11, Spring 1990, p. 1.
116. J.I. Case v. NLRB, 321 U.S. 332, 337 (1944).
117. Medo Photo Supply Corp, 321 U.S. 678, 697 (1944).
118. Editorial, "Labor's Day, 1935," *Washington Times,* September 7, 1992.
119. Jim Puzzanghera, "Damage Cited During Strike," *Newsday,* February 1, 1991.
120. "Strikers Turn to Violence on Picket Line," United Press International, September 4, 1990.
121. Michael J. O'Neill, "36,000 Hours of Overtime," *New York Times,* November 8, 1990.
122. Kevin Cullen, "Violence Grows on Picket Lines," *Boston Globe,* November 4, 1990.
123. David Gonzalez and James McKinley, "Violence and the News Strike: Anger, Blame and Distrust," *New York Times,* March 2, 1991.
124. David E. Pitt, "At Rally, Cuomo Supports Unions in News Strikes," *New York Times,* December 11, 1990.
125. Howard Kurtz, "N.Y. News Publisher Faults Rivals in Strike," *Washington Post,* February 3, 1991.
126. Michael Gartner, "Nation Shrugs as Thugs Firebomb Freedom," *Wall Street Journal,* November 29, 1990.
127. Pat Widder, "Pittsburgh Struggles Along Without Papers Strike Is Choking Off Information," *Chicago Tribune,* July 26, 1992.
128. Jeffrey Bair, "Company Quits Printing Papers, Cites Violence; Talks Resume," Associated Press, July 28, 1992.
129. John Wagner, "No Daily Papers Means Bad News for Pittsburgh; Strike's Economic, Social Effects Felt Throughout City," *Washington Post,* August 9, 1992.
130. Michael deCourcy Hinds, "Pittsburgh Journal: 'Mouse' that Inherited Pittsburgh," *New York Times,* January 19, 1993.
131. "Federal Agents Charge Nine in Bombing UMW-Struck Mine," United Press International, October 19, 1989.

132. "New Beckley Closes, Sues UMWA; Cites Strike Violence for Both," *Coal Week*, January 8, 1990, p. 3.
133. "RICO Suit Against UMW Thrown Out," *Coal Outlook*, November 30, 1992.
134. Gonzalez and McKinley, "Violence and the News Strike: Anger, Blame and Distrust."
135. "Construction Labor Racketeering Rampant in New York City, Panel Finds," *Daily Labor Report*, January 23, 1991.
136. Ibid.
137. Editorial, "The Railway Labor Act Dinosaur," *Washington Times*, June 25, 1992.
138. Selwyn Raab, "Unions Relax Rules At Javits Center Shows," *New York Times*, June 2, 1992.
139. "Union Members Arrested by Local Authorities for Alleged Shakedowns at New York Exhibit Hall," *Daily Labor Report*, February 7, 1992.
140. Peter F. Drucker, "Workers' Hands Bound by Tradition," *Wall Street Journal*, August 2, 1988.
141. Nestle Dairy Systems, Inc. (31-RC-6878; 311 NLRB No. 100), *NLRB Weekly Summary*, July 16, 1993.
142. Steven Antosh, "Workers' Rights in Labor Law," in *Agenda '83*, ed. Richard N. Holwill (Washington, D.C.: Heritage Foundation, 1983), p. 233.
143. "Divided NLRB Orders Reinstatement of Worker Who Threatened to Kill Boss," *Daily Labor Report*, August 16, 1991, p. A-14.
144. "Threat to Kill Supervisor Forfeits Labor Law Protections, Court Holds," *Daily Labor Report*, May 14, 1992, p. A-10.
145. Luxuray v. NLRB, 447 F2d 112 (1971).
146. Behring International, Inc. v. NLRB, 675 F2d 83 (1982).
147. Soule Glass & Glazing Co. v. NLRB, 652 F2d 1055 (1981).
148. S. Bernstein, "Increase, or Promise of Increase, Of Wages as Unfair Labor Practice Under National Labor Relations Act," 17 L. Ed. 2d 1067.
149. NLRB v. John Zink Co., 551 F2d 799 (1977).
150. Armand J. Thieblot, Jr., and Thomas R. Haggard, *Union Violence: The Record and the Response by Courts, Legislatures, and the NLRB* (Philadelphia: University of Pennsylvania Press, 1983), p. 334.
151. Boilermakers, Iron Ship Builders, Blacksmiths, Forgers and Helpers, Local Union No. 85, AFL-CIO, (International Tank Service, Inc.), National Labor Relations Board, Office of General Counsel, Case No. 8-CP-329, January 19, 1990.
152. Ibid.
153. Ibid.
154. Ibid.
155. "Greyhound Charges Striking Union with Violating Federal Rico Statute," *Daily Labor Report*, April 10, 1990, p. A-13.
156. Gonzalez and McKinley, "Violence and the News Strike: Anger, Blame and Distrust."
157. "Greyhound Breaks Off Talks with Striking Transit Workers," *Daily Labor Report*, March 20, 1990, p. A-14.
158. "NLRB Threatening to Tell Greyhound to Call Back Strikers," *Los Angeles Times*, May 31, 1990.
159. Karen Ball, "Drivers Agree to NLRB Anti-Violence Order," Associated Press, June 20, 1990.
160. Interview with Rosemary Collier, counsel for Greyhound, September 28, 1993.
161. James Cox, "Greyhound's Last Stop? Strike-forced Chapter 11 Is a Bitter Pill," *USA Today*, June 6, 1990.
162. Amalgamated Council of Greyhound Local Unions, AFL-CIO (Greyhound Lines, Inc.), Case No. 30-CB-3099, Labor Relations Board, Office of General Counsel, July 11, 1990.
163. Jodie DeJonge, "Bus Line Begins Defense Against Unfair Labor Charges," Associated Press, September 10, 1991.
164. Ibid.
165. Interview with Rosemary Collier, September 28, 1993.
166. Ibid.
167. Armand J. Thieblot, Jr., and Thomas R. Haggard, *Union Violence: The Record and the Response by Courts, Legislatures, and the NLRB* (Philadelphia: University of Pennsylvania), 1983, p. 442.
168. Decision of the National Labor Relations Board in the case of Electromation, Inc. v. International Brotherhood of Teamsters, Local Union No. 1049, AFL-CIO. 309 NLRB No. 163. December 14, 1992.

169. Ibid.
170. Ibid.
171. "NLRB Official's Memo Warns of Traps in Setting Up Involvement Committees," *Government Employee Relations Report,* May 3, 1993, p. 588.
172. "Mandated Safety and Health Committees Come Under Fire at House Panel Hearing," *Daily Labor Report,* July 15, 1993, p. d8.
173. Editorial, "Quality Circle Busters," *Wall Street Journal,* June 9, 1993.
174. Reed Larson, "Harry Beck's Earthquake," *Policy Review,* Summer 1989, p. 74.
175. Jonathan Groner, "Unionized Lawyers Clash with Board Member," *Legal Times,* September 21, 1992.
176. Ibid.
177. "NLRB Staff Lawyers Press Charges Against Board Member Raudabaugh," *Government Employees Relations Report,* October 5, 1992.
178. Jonathan Groner, "NLRB Official Settles Charges in Union Dispute," *Legal Times,* November 16, 1992.
179. Bill Keller, "Unions Battle Against Jobs in the Home," *New York Times,* May 20, 1984.
180. Steve Finlay, "Telecommuting on the Agenda at Work Options Meeting," *Telecommuting Review,* June 1, 1992, p. 12.
181. Sylvester Petro, *The Labor Policy of The Free Society* (New York: Ronald Press Co., 1957), p. 113.
182. Stephen C. Fehr, "Metro Proposes Cuts in 40 Percent of Its Bus Routes," *Washington Post,* April 10, 1991.
183. Dick Netzer, "Congestion by Default," *The City Journal,* Spring 1992, p. 71.
184. Bethany Kandel, Tanya Jones, Kevin Johnson, Mary-Ann Bendel, and Sandra Sanchez, "Commuter Woes: Ride Isn't Getting Any Easier," *USA Today,* July 31, 1992.
185. Caryn Eve Wiener, "Gypsy Van Operators Left Waiting at Curb," *Newsday,* November 12, 1989.
186. Seth Faison, "Bus-Fare Cuts Fail to Lure Queens Riders," *New York Times,* November 29, 1992.
187. Ibid.
188. Daniel Machalaba, "Opportunistic Vans Are Running Circles Around City Buses," *Wall Street Journal,* July 24, 1991.
189. Robert Zimmerman, "New York's War Against the Vans," *The Freeman,* April 1992, p. 150.
190. Ibid.
191. Ibid.
192. "Pulse: Subway Crime," *New York Times,* September 22, 1992, p. B1.
193. "Challenging Denver's Taxicab Monopoly," Institute for Justice Litigation Backgrounder, 1993.
194. Allen Randolph, "New York Taxi Policy Is a Lemon," *Wall Street Journal,* March 17, 1992.
195. Alan Finder, "Dinkins to Offer Plan for Improving Taxi Service," *New York Times,* October 13, 1992.
196. Calvin Sims, "Inspectors Held in Bribe Scheme To Hide Cab Defects in New York," *New York Times,* July 23, 1992.
197. Randolph, "New York Taxi Policy Is a Lemon."
198. James Bovard, "Torpedo Shipping Protectionism," *Wall Street Journal,* November 26, 1991.
199. Interview with Mark Sullivan, November 11, 1991.
200. Louisville & Nashville, R.R. Co. v. Maxwell, 237 U.S. 94, 97 (1915).
201. Steve Chapman, "Busting the Trucking Cartel," *New Republic,* September 30, 1978, p. 21.
202. "Deregulation Proposal Gets Cool Reception by Senate Subcommittee, *Daily Report For Executives,* September 30, 1985, p. A-4. See also, William E. Simon, *A Time for Truth* (New York: Berkeley Books, 1978), p. 101. (Simon stated that the ICC had 40 trillion rates on file.)
203. U.S. Interstate Commerce Commission, "The U.S. Motor Carrier Industry Long After Deregulation," March 1992, p. 6.
204. Ibid., p. 72.
205. William Tucker, "Back From the Grave," *Forbes,* May 13, 1991.
206. Maislin Industries, U.S., Inc., et al., v. Primary Steel, 497 U.S. 116 (1990) (J. Stevens, dissenting).
207. Ibid.
208. Kirk Victor, "Buyer Beware," *National Journal,* July 3, 1993, p. 1730.
209. Don Phillips, "Law Lets Trucking Firms Raise Rates Retroactively," *Washington Post,* June 16, 1992.

210. Kevin G. Hall and Stephanie Kneel, "Shippers Win Another Big Victory in Los Angeles Undercharge Case," *Journal of Commerce,* December 14, 1992.
211. Janie Baird, "Disqualified Discounts: Bankrupt Firms Leave Shippers with Load of Bills," *Houston Chronicle,* July 27, 1992.
212. Ibid.
213. "Alleged Undercharge Victim Rips Gephardt for Helping Kill Relief Bill," *Kansas City Business Journal,* December 11, 1992, p. 9.
214. Stephanie Kneel, "Charity Is Latest Undercharge Target," *Journal of Commerce,* January 19, 1993.
215. Editorial, "The Truck Rate Scam," *Journal of Commerce,* March 29, 1993.
216. U.S. Congress, House Committee on Public Works and Transportation, *Regulatory Issues,* March 24, 1992 (Washington, D.C.: Government Printing Office, 1992), pp. 769, 775.
217. Tom Locke, "Edson Express Trustee Files 86 Suits," *Denver Business Journal,* February 12, 1993, p. 1.
218. U.S. Congress, House Committee on Public Works and Transportation, *Regulatory Issues,* p. 150.
219. Press Release (untitled), U.S. Attorney, Eastern District of Pennsylvania, U.S. Department of Justice, September 28, 1993. Also, James Bovard, "The Great Truck Robbery," *Wall Street Journal,* November 3, 1993.
220. U.S. Congress, House Committee on Public Works and Transportation, *Regulatory Issues,* p. 156.
221. Kenneth R. DeJarnette, "The Truckline Undercharge Problem," Congressional Research Service, June 19, 1993, p. 18.
222. Interview with Census Bureau analyst Marilyn Monahan, October 18, 1993. The Census Bureau estimated that the total nationwide loss to burglars was $4.1 billion in 1991 and the total lost to theft was $3.5 billion.
223. Interview with Federal Elections Commission spokesman Fred Eiland, September 7, 1993.
224. Thies, "The First Minimum Wage Laws," p. 734.
225. Alexander Hamilton, James Madison, and John Jay, *The Federalist Papers* (New York: New American Library, 1961), p. 472.

Chapter 5

1. Wickard v. Filburn, 317 U.S. 111 (1942).
2. Lemon v. Kurtzman, 403 U.S. 602, 621 (1970).
3. U.S. Office of Management and Budget, *Catalog of Federal Domestic Assistance Programs* (Washington, D.C.: Government Printing Office, 1992), p. iii.
4. Wayne King, "Report Says Richer States Are Stingier with Schools," *New York Times,* August 15, 1992.
5. Lina A. Graglia, *Disaster by Decree: The Supreme Court Decisions on Race and the Schools* (Ithaca, NY: Cornell University Press, 1976), p. 194.
6. For 1950 statistic, see Paul Copperman, *The Literacy Hoax* (New York: William Morrow, 1978), p. 56. For 1993, see C. Emily Feistritzer, "Report Card on American Education 1993," American Legislative Exchange Council and the National Center for Education Information, September 1993.
7. Feistritzer, "Report Card on American Education 1993."
8. Benno C. Schmidt, "Educational Innovation for Profit," *Wall Street Journal,* June 5, 1992.
9. Regina Lee Wood, "That's Right—They're Wrong," *National Review,* September 14, 1992, p. 49.
10. Carol Innerst, "College: No Kick for the Bucks," *Washington Times,* April 2, 1990.
11. William Celis, "Study Says Half of Adults in U.S. Can't Read or Handle Arithmetic," *New York Times,* September 9, 1993.
12. "Press Conference with Secretary of Education Richard Riley; Subject: Release of National Adult Literacy Survey," Federal News Service, September 8, 1993.
13. Mark Sacerdote, "The Board of Education Fails a Math Test," *New York Times,* April 17, 1993.
14. Lawrence A. Uzzell, "Education Reform Fails the Test," *Wall Street Journal,* May 10, 1989.
15. Sari Horowitz, "34 D.C. Schools Make Learning Failproof in Early Grades," *Washington Post,* November 9, 1993.
16. Office of Educational Research and Improvement, "National Excellence: A Case for Developing America's Talent," U.S. Department of Education, November 1993, p. 19.

17. "Baby-Boomers Books Faulted in S.A.T. Drop," *New York Times*, November 3, 1993.
18. Michael Meyers, "Black Racism at Taxpayer Expense," *Wall Street Journal*, July 30, 1991.
19. Dana Mack, "War on Drugs? War on Parents," *Wall Street Journal*, June 17, 1993.
20. Priscilla Van Tassel, "Debate on Sex Education Flares Anew in Trenton," *New York Times*, May 16, 1993.
21. Carol Innerst, "Cultural Battle Lines Drawn in NYC School Board Elections," *Washington Times*, May 3, 1993.
22. Mary Jordan, "Guidance on Gays Divides Parents," *Washington Post*, December 8, 1992.
23. William Tucker, "Revolt in Queens," *American Spectator*, February 1993, p. 33.
24. Innerst, "Cultural Battle Lines Drawn in NYC School Board Elections."
25. Editorial, "The Parents Rebel—II," *Wall Street Journal*, October 6, 1992.
26. Editorial, "Brother, Can You Spare a Condom?" *Washington Times*, May 26, 1993.
27. Catherine Woodard, "Buyer Beware: Condom Quality Varies," *Newsday*, November 26, 1991.
28. Clifford J. Levy, "Fifth Graders Get Condoms In New Haven," *New York Times*, July 28, 1993.
29. Joseph Berger, "Key to Condom Vote: Dinkins Power Grasp," *New York Times*, September 13, 1991.
30. Joseph Berger, "Parents vs. Condom Plan," *New York Times*, October 1, 1991.
31. Sari Horwitz, "Parents Skirted On Condoms In High School; District Nurses Are Ordered To Ignore Notes From Home," *Washington Post*, September 4, 1992.
32. Stephanie Gutmann, "The Bilingual Ghetto," *City Journal*, Winter 1992, p. 29.
33. Ibid.
34. Joseph Berger, "School Programs Assailed as Bilingual Bureaucracy," *New York Times*, January 4, 1993.
35. John McCaslin, "Inside the Beltway," *Washington Times*, February 12, 1993.
36. Thomas Sowell, *Inside American Education* (New York: Free Press, 1993), p. 76.
37. "Texas Orders School to Stop Practice of Brick Punishment," Associated Press, May 18, 1988.
38. Editorial, "Next They'll Be Fluoridating the Water," *Washington Times*, November 13, 1990.
39. "School Reprimands Youth Over Batman Enemy on T-Shirt," Associated Press, November 11, 1992.
40. "Too Much Academic Work Is Found in High Schools," *New York Times*, November 8, 1976, p. 18.
41. Jay Mathews, "States Remodel Education in Shop Class," *Washington Post*, October 26, 1991.
42. Jackson Toby, "Violence in Schools," National Institute of Justice, U.S. Department of Justice, 1983, p. 1.
43. Interview with Richard E. Whalen, Statistician, U.S. Department of Education, September 27, 1993.
44. Home School Legal Defense Association, *Court Report*, July/August 1992, p. 12.
45. Shaun Sutner, "1st Truancy Policy Hailed, Enforcement Questioned," *Washington Post*, November 28, 1991.
46. Sandra Evans, "Protesting Students Walk Out at Reston High School," *Washington Post*, May 30, 1992.
47. Ibid.
48. DeNeen L. Brown, "New School Attendance Policy Fuels Reston Protest," *Washington Post*, April 18, 1992.
49. John Taylor Gatto, "I May be a Teacher, but I'm Not an Educator," *Wall Street Journal*, July 25, 1991.
50. Ronald Brownstein, "Tough Love Comes to Politics; Laws Are Setting Standards for Personal Behavior," *Los Angeles Times*, November 19, 1991.
51. Laura Wisniewski, "Maryland Adopts City Schools' Plan," *Atlanta Journal and Constitution*, August 7, 1992. Also, Editorial, "Requirements and Rewards of Service," *Chicago Tribune*, August 5, 1992.
52. Woody West, "Pomp and Compulsion," *Washington Times*, August 5, 1992.
53. "Community Service Rule Stirs Debate," *Atlanta Journal and Constitution*, July 29, 1992.
54. David Goodman, "Michigan Mom Jailed in Home School Dispute," Associated Press, March 12, 1993.
55. Donald D. Dorman, "Michigan's Teacher Certification Requirement as Applied to Religiously Motivated Home Schools," *University of Michigan Law Review*, Summer 1990, p. 733.
56. Christopher J. Klicka, *The Right Choice—Home Schooling* (Gresham, OR: Noble Publishing Associates, 1992), p. 232.

57. Donald P. Baker, "More Parents Choose to Be Their Children's Teachers," *Washington Post*, May 23, 1993.
58. Dorman, "Michigan's Teacher Certification Requirement as Applied to Religiously Motivated Home Schools," p. 733.
59. William Celis 3d, "Schooling at Home Draws Lawsuits to Doorsteps," *New York Times*, May 6, 1992.
60. Graglia, *Disaster By Decree: The Supreme Court Decisions on Race and the Schools*, p. 14.
61. Interview with Nathaniel Douglas, November 8, 1993. Many other school districts have adopted racially oriented busing plans "voluntarily" in order to avoid federal or private civil rights lawsuits. Many of the nation's largest school systems are currently under busing orders.
62. Keyes v. School Dist. No. One, Denver, Col., 413 U.S. 189, 247-48 (1973).
63. George V. Higgins, "Boston's Busing Disaster," *New Republic*, February 28, 1983.
64. Diego Ribadeneira and Larry Tye, "Racial Gap Widens in Boston Schools," *Boston Globe*, January 8, 1992.
65. Sowell, *Inside American Education*, p. 96.
66. David J. Armor, "Families Spur Black Students' Gains," *Wall Street Journal*, June 30, 1992.
67. Graglia, *Disaster By Decree: The Supreme Court Decisions on Race and the Schools*, p. 277.
68. Robert Lindsey, "School Integration Looks More Than Ever Like a Lost Horizon," *New York Times*, August 24, 1980.
69. Edward Walsh, "Des Moines Cites 'White Flight' in Curbing School Choice," *Washington Post*, December 12, 1992.
70. Ibid.
71. C. Sheldon Smith, "A Bureaucracy Scorned; Iowa's Open-Enrollment Law for Public School Children," *National Review*, March 29, 1993, p. 25.
72. Isabel Wilkerson, "Des Moines Acts to Halt White Flight After State Allows Choice of Schools," *New York Times*, December 16, 1992.
73. Eric Harrison, "Plan for Busing By Income Splits Wisconsin City," *Los Angeles Times*, March 23, 1992.
74. Michael Abramowitz, "'The School Board Just Lost Touch,'" *Washington Post*, July 19, 1992.
75. Carol Innerst, "School Busing Plan to Mix Rich, Poor," *Washington Times*, November 1, 1991.
76. Michael C. Buelow, "School Plan Mixes Needy, Affluent Kids," Associated Press, January 16, 1992.
77. National Public Radio, August 11, 1992.
78. Innerst, "School Busing Plan to Mix Rich, Poor."
79. Rob Hotakainen, "School Busing Plan Fizzles; La Crosse Votes Out Four Who Wanted to Integrate According to Family Income," *Star Tribune* (Minneapolis), July 16, 1992.
80. Sheldon and Kathleen Richman, "Help! Our Daughter is Being Held Captive by Bossy Boneheads!" *City Paper*, July 19, 1991.
81. Patrick Welsh, "Staying on Tracks; Can We Teach Honors Kids and Hard Cases Together?" *Washington Post*, March 7, 1993.
82. Peter Y. Hong, "Un-Grouping Students; Educator's Case for Mixing Pupils of Varying Abilities," *Washington Post*, March 25, 1993.
83. Steve Bates, "School Policy Riles Alexandria Parents," *Washington Post*, March 28, 1993.
84. Steve Bates, "More Parents Are Challenging School Quality," *Washington Post*, April 20, 1993.
85. Welsh, "Staying on Tracks; Can We Teach Honors Kids and Hard Cases Together?"
86. Patrick Welsh, "Board Silly," *Washington Post*, June 20, 1993.
87. Welsh, "Staying on Tracks; Can We Teach Honors Kids and Hard Cases Together?"
88. Jonathan Rabinovitz, "In Suburbs, a Stealthy War Against Infiltrating Students," *New York Times*, November 6, 1992.
89. Sam Dillon, "Schools Seek Laws Deterring Illegal Students," *New York Times*, January 29, 1993.
90. Ralph Blumenthal, "Choosing Schools Through Fakery; New York Parents Use Many Schemes for False Enrollment," *New York Times*, September 21, 1992.
91. Dwight Roper, "Parents as the Natural Enemy of the School System," *Phi Delta Kappan*, December 1977, p. 239.
92. Neal Pierce, "Save Our Public Schools from Their School Board," *Baltimore Sun*, April 27, 1992.
93. Rene Sanchez, "D.C. School Enrollment Decline Starts to Slow," *Washington Post*, December 11, 1990.

94. Sari Horwitz, "Smith Defends School Budget Against Critics," *Washington Post*, December 18, 1992.
95. Jonetta Rose Barras, "Auditor Hammers Schools' Spending," *Washington Times*, February 13, 1993.
96. Peter Brimelow and Leslie Spencer, "The National Extortion Association?" *Forbes*, June 7, 1993.
97. Jo Seker, "The Union Label," *Orange County Register*, June 2, 1991.
98. For instance, teacher unions are especially strong in Washington, D.C., Los Angeles, Chicago, and New York.
99. Rachel Flick, "How Unions Stole the Big Apple," *Reader's Digest*, January 1992.
100. James Bovard, "How Teachers Teach Selfishness," *Washington Monthly*, June 1981, p. 45.
101. Staff of the *Chicago Tribune, Chicago Schools: "Worst in America?"* (Chicago: Chicago Tribune, 1988), p. 77.
102. Ibid., p. 78.
103. Editorial, "Montgomery's Unlettered Teachers," *Washington Post*, November 12, 1991.
104. Thomas Sowell, "Against Choice, the Empire Strikes Back," *Orange County Register*, April 22, 1992.
105. Sari Horowitz, "Teachers Draft Parents in D.C. Furlough Battle," *Washington Post*, October 1, 1992.
106. Staff of the *Chicago Tribune, Chicago Schools: "Worst in America?"* p. 61.
107. Quoted in Klicka, *The Right Choice—Home Schooling*, p. 60. Cite is from "Shielding Bad Teachers, A Special Three Part Report," *Detroit Free Press*, March 15, 1992, p. 1.
108. Sari Horwitz, "Panel Assails D.C. Method of Grading Teachers," *Washington Post*, December 16, 1992.
109. David Boaz, "The Public School Monopoly: America's Berlin Wall," in *Liberating Schools*, ed. David Boaz (Washington, D.C.: Cato Institute, 1991), p. 9.
110. Bonita Brodt, "Inside Chicago's Schools," in Boaz, ed., *Liberating Schools*, p. 69.
111. George Will, "When the State Fails Its Citizens," *Washington Post*, March 7, 1993.
112. Brimelow and Spencer, "The National Extortion Association?"
113. John E. Coons, "*Perestroika* and the Private Provider," in *Liberating Schools*, ed. Boaz, pp. 183, 193.
114. Suzanne Fields, "Bill and Hillary, Meet Luis and Maria," *Orange County Register*, January 8, 1993.
115. See, for instance, James S. Coleman and Thomas Hoffer, *Public and Private High Schools* (New York: Basic Books, 1987).
116. Brief of the Institute for Justice, Susan Marie Arviso, et al., v. Bill Honig, et al. Superior Court of the State of California for the County of Los Angeles. No. BC 057,321, January 29, 1993, p. 38.
117. In Great Britain, the Newcastle Commission of 1861 reported, "It is a subject of wonder how people so destitute of education as laboring parents commonly are, can be such just judges as they commonly are on the effective qualifications of a teacher." E. G. West, *Education and the State* (London: Institute of Economic Affairs, 1970), p. 164.
118. Editorial, "Choice Facts," *Wall Street Journal*, February 6, 1992.
119. Carol Innerst, "Parents Prefer Private Schools," *Washington Times*, July 24, 1991.
120. John Collis, *Educational Malpractice* (Charlottesville, VA: Michie Co. Law Publishers, 1990), p. xvii.
121. Collis, *Educational Malpractice*, p. 82. The case was Peter Doe v. San Francisco Unified School District, 60 Cal. App. 3d 814, 131 Cal. Rptr. 854 (1976).
122. Collis, *Educational Malpractice*, p. 87. Cite is 60 Cal. App. 3d 814, 825, 131 Cal. Rptr 854, 861 (1976).
123. Collis, *Educational Malpractice*, p. 98. Cite is 47 N.Y.2d 440, 445, 418 N.Y.S.2d 375, 378 (1979).
124. Collis, *Educational Malpractice*, p. 106. Cite is 47 Md. App. 709. 715-16, 425 A.2d 681, 684-85 (1981).
125. Collis, *Educational Malpractice*, p. 127.
126. Ibid., p. 131. Case was Denson v. Ohio Board of Education, in the Court of Appeals of Ohio, Seventh District, Jefferson County, Case No. 85-J-31 (1985).
127. Collis, *Educational Malpractice*, p. 455.
128. C. Emily Feistritzer, "Report Card on American Education 1993," American Legislative Exchange Council and the National Center for Education Information, September 1993.
129. Edward B. Fiske, "Commission on Education Warns 'Tide of Mediocrity' Imperils U.S.," *New York Times*, April 27, 1983.
130. Bill Turque, "SLAPPing the Opposition," *Newsweek*, March 5, 1990, p. 22.

131. Sam Dillon, "In District 21, Schools Plus Politics Equal Gain," *New York Times*, April 26, 1993.
132. Collis, *Educational Malpractice*, p. 466.
133. Fred Hechinger, "Instilling the Desire to Read," *New York Times*, September 28, 1992.
134. Alexis de Tocqueville, *Democracy in America* (New York: Doubleday, 1969), p. 55.
135. Klicka, *The Right Choice—Home Schooling*, p. 75.
136. John Taylor Gatto, *Dumbing Us Down* (Philadelphia, PA: New Society Publishers, 1992), p. 94.
137. Jack D. Douglas, "Resolving the Crisis in Higher Education," *Cato Policy Report*, May/June 1991.
138. Barbara Vobeda, "Carnegie Report Calls Colleges 'Troubled,'" *Washington Post*, November 2, 1986.
139. Douglas, "Resolving the Crisis in Higher Education."
140. National Center for Education Statistics, *Digest of Educational Statistics* (Washington, D.C.: U.S. Department of Education, 1993), table 350.
141. Jim Sleeper, "The Policemen of Diversity: How the Middle States Accreditors Threaten Academic Freedom," *Washington Post*, June 30, 1991.
142. John Bunzel, "Inequitable Equality on Campus," *Wall Street Journal*, July 25, 1990.
143. Editorial, "The Accreditation Wars," *Wall Street Journal*, April 23, 1991.
144. Howard L. Simmons, "Equity Doesn't Require Quotas," *Newsday*, June 5, 1991.
145. Carol Innerst, "Accrediting Body Disputes Alexander," *Washington Times*, August 2, 1991.
146. Carol Innerst, "Alexander Takes Aim at Diversity Standards," *Washington Times*, April 15, 1992.
147. Bunzel, "Inequitable Equality on Campus."
148. Carol Innerst, "Minority Graduation 'Equity' Sought," *Washington Times*, December 7, 1990.
149. Bunzel, "Inequitable Equality on Campus."
150. Speech, First Washington Conference on Public Housing, January 27, 1934, Washington D.C. Sponsored by the National Public Housing Conference.
151. United States Housing Act of 1937, P.L. 75-412, September 1, 1937.
152. Irving Welfeld, "Policies or Programs; Legislative Origins of PHA Problems," *Journal of Housing*, July/August 1985, p. 140.
153. Michael Norman, "Newark Ponders Plight of Its Housing Projects," *New York Times*, September 22, 1982.
154. John McCormick, "Chicago Housecleaning," *Newsweek*, August 19, 1991, p. 58.
155. U.S. Department of Housing and Urban Development, *Crime in Public Housing: A Review of Major Issues and Selected Crime Reduction Strategies, Volume I* (Washington, D.C.: Government Printing Office, 1979) p. i.
156. Ibid.
157. George Papajohn and William Recktenwald, "Living in a War Zone Called Taylor Homes, Residents Trapped in Battles Over Drug Turf," *Chicago Tribune*, March 10, 1993.
158. U.S. Department of Housing and Urban Development, *Crime in Public Housing*, p. 3.
159. Mark Plotkin, "Cracking the D.C. Crime Nut," *Legal Times*, January 13, 1992.
160. U.S. Department of Housing and Urban Development, *Crime in Public Housing*, p. 4.
161. Lyle V. Harris, "Some Question If It's Smart to Spend $51,000 a Unit to Rebuild East Lake," *Atlanta Journal*, November 5, 1992. The quote is from Louis Brown, who manages apartments for Greenway Properties in Atlanta.
162. "Public Housing Tenants Organizing for Self-Help," *New York Times*, June 2, 1991.
163. Diane Geraghty, "CHA's Sweep Searches Went Too Far," *Chicago Tribune*, January 4, 1989.
164. Sharman Stein and William Recktenwald, "65 Seized in Sweep at CHA Homes," *Chicago Tribune*, April 7, 1992.
165. Mike Royko, "A Modest Proposal For a Clean Sweep," *Chicago Tribune*, August 24, 1993.
166. Matt O'Connor, "Gun Sweeps at CHA Defended," *Chicago Tribune*, September 1, 1993.
167. Steven Yarosh, "Operation Clean Sweep: Is the Chicago Housing Authority 'Sweeping' Away the Fourth Amendment?" *Northwestern University Law Review*, vol. 86, Summer 1992, p. 1103.
168. John McCarron, "Votes Give CHA Slums a Reason for Life," *Chicago Tribune*, August 30, 1988.
169. William Tucker, *The Excluded Americans: Homelessness and Housing Policies in Washington, D.C.* (Washington, D.C.: Regnery Gateway Inc., 1989), p. 186
170. Institute for Community Design Analysis (New York), Review and Analysis of the Chicago Housing Authority and Implementation of Recommended Changes, Final Report of Phase I, March 31, 1982. HUD Contract No.: HC-5524, p. 5.

171. Michael deCourcy Hinds, "With Help of Federal Rescue Effort, Philadelphia Housing Agency Falters," *New York Times,* June 9, 1993.
172. Nell Henderson, "D.C. Agency Owes U.S., Audit Says," *Washington Post,* August 13, 1993.
173. Editorial, "Subsidized Scandal," *Wall Street Journal,* November 14, 1991.
174. "The Silent Scandal: Management Abuses in Public Housing," National Center for Neighborhood Enterprise, Washington, D.C., 1991, p. 4.
175. Shaun Sutner, "Fate of City-Owned NW Houses Debated," *Washington Post,* April 9, 1992.
176. Tucker, *The Excluded Americans,* p. 181.
177. *Congressional Record,* January 19, 1972, p. 372. Reprint of article by William Lilley III and Timothy B. Clark, "Federal Programs Spur Abandonment of Housing In Major Cities," *National Journal,* January 1, 1972.
178. John C. Weicher, *Housing: Federal Policies and Programs* (Washington, D.C.: American Enterprise Institute, 1980), p. 45.
179. *Congressional Record,* January 19, 1972, p. 372.
180. Charles A. Krause, "HUD Blamed as Detroit Homes Rot," *Washington Post,* March 15, 1976.
181. *Congressional Record,* June 22, 1975, p. 20267.
182. *Congressional Record,* July 10, 1975, p. 22039.
183. *Congressional Record,* April 29, 1975, p. 12267.
184. *Congressional Record,* June 22, 1975, p. 20267.
185. U.S. General Accounting Office, "Section 8 Subsidized Housing—Some Observations on its High Rents, Costs, and Inequities," June 6, 1980, p. 10.
186. Interview with U.S. Department of Housing and Urban Development spokeswoman Vivian Potter, November 8, 1993. The subsidies vary according to prevailing local rents; the $1,657 a month is authorized for Stamford, Connecticut.
187. U.S. General Accounting Office, "Section 8 Subsidized Housing," p. 64.
188. Ibid., p. 66.
189. Ibid., p. 68.
190. Ibid., p. 70.
191. Advertising brochure, "Alexander House—Affordable Luxury in the Heart of Silver Spring," distributed in 1993 by the Housing Opportunities Commission, Montgomery County, Maryland.
192. U.S. General Accounting Office, "Section 8 Subsidized Housing," p. 77.
193. Editorial, "Subsidy Clusters Burden Suburbs," *Chicago Tribune,* September 10, 1992.
194. "Subsidized Housing, Destabilized Suburbs; Officials Confront the Shortcomings of Section 8," *Central Penn Business Journal,* September 1992, p. 18.
195. Jerry Thomas, "Hunt for a Home; Many Doors in Suburbs Closed to Section 8 Clients," *Chicago Tribune,* May 19, 1993.
196. "Subsidized Housing, Destabilized Suburbs; Officials Confront the Shortcomings of Section 8," p. 18.
197. Editorial, "Subsidy Clusters Burden Suburbs."
198. Kirstin Downey, "HUD Report Renews Debate on Rent Rates," *Washington Post,* June 1, 1991.
199. Ibid.
200. Irving Welfeld, *HUD Scandals* (New Brunswick, NJ: Transaction Books, 1992), p. 161.
201. William Hathaway and Mary Otto, "Value of Integration Questioned as Poor Gain New Mobility," *Hartford Courant,* March 22, 1992.
202. Labarbara Bowman, "$1 Homes Will Lift 10 Families from Projects," *Washington Post,* April 17, 1981.
203. Margaret Rankin, "Some Poor Home Buyers Hit Jackpot," *Washington Times,* February 6, 1993.
204. Nicholas Goldberg, "The Island Park Way; 25 Years of Evicting Blacks, Favoring Village Insiders in Housing," *Newsday,* March 18, 1990.
205. Nicholas Goldberg, "God's Chosen: the Fonz and His Buddies; Sen. Alfonse D'Amato and the HUD Scandal," *New Republic,* May 14, 1990, p. 13.
206. William Tucker, "A Model for Destroying a City," *Wall Street Journal,* March 12, 1993.
207. Penny Loeb, "City Tops Slumlord Business," *Newsday,* January 3, 1993.
208. Mark Riebling, "Who's Warehousing Now?" *NY: The City Journal,* Autumn 1991, p. 24.
209. Ibid.
210. Charles Babington, "Montgomery Votes to Tax Residential Construction," *Washington Post,* December 4, 1991.

211. Retha Hill, "Potter Calls for Housing Incentives," *Washington Post,* January 15, 1992.
212. Ibid.
213. Peter Salins, "Correcting New York's Housing Mistakes," *City Journal,* Spring 1992, p. 59.
214. Jonetta Rose Barras, "Half of Residents Who Rent from City Found Delinquent," *Washington Times,* January 14, 1992.
215. Jason DeParle and Stephen Engelberg, "Billions in Losses Seen in Mortgages Insured by H.U.D.," *New York Times,* June 20, 1993.
216. Steven Engelberg, "Leader of H.U.D. Assesses It Harshly," *New York Times,* June 23, 1993.
217. U.S. Congress, Congressional Budget Office, "The Cost-Effectiveness of the Low-Income Housing Tax Credit Compared with Housing Vouchers," April 1992.
218. U.S. Congress, Joint Committee on Taxation, "Description and Analysis of Tax Provisions Expiring in 1992," January 27, 1992 (Washington, D.C.: Government Printing Office, 1992). Cited in Carl Horowitz, "Time to Let Low-Income Housing Tax Credit Program Expire," Heritage Foundation Issue Bulletin No. 175, June 25, 1992.
219. Mitchell Pacelle, "Affordability of Home Buying Is Rising, But Low-Cost Rentals Wane, Study Says," *Wall Street Journal,* October 1, 1992.
220. See James Bovard, *The Farm Fiasco* (San Francisco, CA: ICS Press, 1989).
221. U.S. General Accounting Office, "Transition Series—Food and Agriculture Issues," December 1992, p. 6.
222. For details on the calculation of these figures, see Bovard, *The Farm Fiasco.* For more recent information on the costs of farm programs, see James Bovard, "Clinton's Agriculture Budget Cut Mirage," *New Republic,* March 21, 1993.
223. U.S. Congress, House Agriculture Committee, *Wheat Price Guaranteed by Congress,* February 3, 1919 (Washington, D.C.: Government Printing Office, 1919), p. 166.
224. Cited in Cassius M. Clay, *Mainstay of American Individualism* (New York: Macmillan, 1934), p. 110.
225. Editorial, *New York Times,* July 21, 1930.
226. Theodore W. Schultz, *Vanishing Farm Markets and Our World Trade* (Boston: World Peace Foundation, 1935), p. 5.
227. Franklin D. Roosevelt, "Address on the Accomplishments of and Future Aims for Agriculture," speech, September 28, 1935, in *Public Papers and Addresses of Franklin D. Roosevelt* (New York: Random House, 1938).
228. United States v. Butler et al., 297 U.S. 1 (1936).
229. Wickard v. Filburn, 317 U.S. 111 (1942).
230. Ibid.
231. Paul Findley, *Federal Farm Fable* (New Rochelle, NY: Arlington House, 1968), p. 106.
232. Ibid., p. 71.
233. James Bovard, "Fiasco on the Farm," *Reader's Digest,* April 1984.
234. Donald Ratajckack, "Monthly Projections," Georgia State University study, April 18, 1983.
235. *Federal Register,* March 4, 1993, p. 12332.
236. *Federal Register,* January 14, 1993, p. 4303.
237. *Federal Register,* March 23, 1993, p. 15416.
238. Written testimony of Dennis Avery, submitted for hearing on "The Export Competitiveness of U.S. Agriculture," U.S. Congress, Joint Economic Committee, March 4, 1992.
239. A GAO study noted, "CRP is an expensive way to reduce the environmental problems linked to agricultural production. . . . Furthermore, CRP postpones rather than resolves environmental problems associated with agriculture." U.S. General Accounting Office, "Conservation Reserve Program—Cost-Effectiveness Is Uncertain," March 1992, p. 1.
240. Isabel Wilkerson, "With Rural Towns Vanishing, States Choose Which to Save," *New York Times,* January 3, 1990.
241. "The Conservation Reserve," *The Cargill Bulletin,* January 1993.
242. Ibid.
243. Ibid.
244. Dan Dvoskin, *Excess Capacity in U.S. Agriculture: An Economic Approach to Measurement,* U.S. Department of Agriculture, Agricultural Economic Report No. 580, 1988, p. 22.
245. Ibid., p. 23.

246. James Bovard, "The Ag Bill Turns Farmer Against Farmer," *Wall Street Journal,* March 6, 1986.
247. U.S. Congress, House Agriculture Committee, *Establishing Farm Program Payment Yields; Dry Edible Beans Amendment of 1986; and Nonprogram Crop Amendments of 1986,* February 19, 1986 (Washington, D.C.: Government Printing Office, 1986).
248. U.S. Department of Agriculture, "Tobacco—Background for 1990 Farm Legislation," October 1989, p. 34.
249. Verner Grise, "The Tobacco Program and Its Effects," *National Food Review* (published by USDA), January 1990, p. 66.
250. U.S. General Accounting Office, "Peanut Program—Changes Are Needed to Make the Program Responsive to Market Forces," February 1993, p. 3.
251. The U.S. International Trade Commission reported that average "profits before income taxes for all U.S. corporations in 1986 were 6% of sales." U.S. International Trade Commission, "Foreign Protection of Intellectual Property Rights and the Effect on U.S. Industry and Trade," ITC Publication No. 2065, February 1988, p. ix.
252. Sharon LaFraniere, "'Windfall' Subsidies for Just Peanuts," *Washington Post,* June 14, 1993.
253. U.S. General Accounting Office, "Sugar Program—Changing Domestic and International Conditions Require Program Changes," April 1993, p. 32.
254. Bruce Ingersoll, "Inequities in Farm Program Anger Minnesota Farmers," *Wall Street Journal,* June 26, 1990.
255. U.S. Department of Commerce, *United States Sugar Policy—An Analysis* (Washington, D.C.: Government Printing Office, 1988), p. v.
256. Editorial, "Protect Consumers, Not Dairy Farmers," *New York Times,* July 25, 1991.
257. James Vicini, "Dairy Surplus Keeps Growing," Reuters News Service, December 21, 1982.
258. For more details, see Bovard, *The Farm Fiasco,* pp. 110-113.
259. Barbara Bradley, "Texans Bridle at U.S. Dairy Herd Buyouts," *Christian Science Monitor,* May 2, 1986.
260. Iver Peterson, "U.S. Plan for Dairy Market Puts Beef Industry in a Vise," *New York Times,* April 10, 1986.
261. Don Kendall, "Cattlemen Claim More than $200 Million Damages from Dairy Buyout Program," Associated Press, September 11, 1986.
262. U.S. General Accounting Office, "Dairy Programs—Effects of the Dairy Termination Program and Support Price Reductions," June 1993, p. 7.
263. U.S. Congress, House Committee on Banking, Finance, and Urban Affairs, *Farm Debt,* March 20, 1985 (Washington, D.C.: Government Printing Office, 1985), p. 80.
264. Interview with Vance Clark, February 24, 1988.
265. U.S. General Accounting Office, "Farmers Home Administration: Problems and Issues Facing the Emergency Loan Program," November 1987, p. 42.
266. U.S. General Accounting Office, "Farmers Home Administration: Billions of Dollars in Farm Loans Are at Risk," April 1992.
267. Quoted in Mark Rohner and Dennis Camire, "The Golden Yoke: The Farmers Home Administration in Mississippi," Gannett News Service reprint, 1984.
268. U.S. Congress, Senate Agriculture Committee, *Proposed Changes in Farmers Home Administration Credit Regulations,* March 11, 1987 (Washington, D.C.: Government Printing Office, 1987), p. 22.
269. Kim Masters, "Politics of Arts Grants Questioned," *Washington Post,* September 18, 1991.
270. "National Press Club Luncheon Speaker John Frohnmayer, Chairman, National Endowment for the Arts," Federal News Service, March 23, 1992.
271. *Congressional Record,* October 11, 1990, p. H 9406.
272. Robert Brustein, "The First Amendment and the NEA," *New Republic,* September 11, 1989, p. 27.
273. Mark Lasswell, "How the NEA Really Works," *Spy,* November 1990, p. 58.
274. Roger Kimball, "Diversity Quotas at NEA Skewer Magazine," *Wall Street Journal,* June 24, 1993.
275. Ibid.
276. John Chodes, "The S.E.C.'s War on the Theater," *New York Times,* January 11, 1992 (adapted from an article in the November 1991 issue of *The Freeman* magazine).
277. John Lancaster, "Payback Time for Parks' Poke at 'Perks,'" *Washington Post,* November 20, 1990.

278. "Excerpts From Court Ruling Curbing Family Planning Clinics," *New York Times*, May 24, 1991.
279. Ibid.
280. Ibid.
281. "Press Conference with Representative Henry Waxman (D-CA), Representative Ron Wyden (D-OR), Representative John Portner (R-IL) and Representative Vic Fazio (D-CA). Topic: Supreme Court Decision on Abortion," Federal News Service, May 23, 1991.
282. "Press Conference with Congressional Caucus on Women's Issues. Topic: Supreme Court Decision in Rust v. Sullivan and the Introduction of the Wyden-Porter Bill," Federal News Service, May 23, 1991.
283. Ibid.
284. Ruth Marcus, "Ruling Could Limit Speech; Restrictions May Expand Beyond Abortion," *Washington Post*, May 25, 1991.

Chapter 6

1. Friedrich Hayek, *The Constitution of Liberty* (Chicago: University of Chicago Press, 1960), p. 258.
2. Hugh Davis Graham, *The Civil Rights Era* (New York: Oxford University Press, 1990), p. 191.
3. Herman Belz, *Equality Transformed* (New Brunswick, NJ: Transaction Books, 1991), p. 28.
4. Graham, *The Civil Rights Era*, p. 243.
5. Belz, *Equality Transformed*, p. 119.
6. Griggs v. Duke Power Co., 401 U.S. 424 (1971).
7. Belz, *Equality Transformed*, p. 54.
8. Richard Epstein, *Forbidden Grounds*, (Cambridge, MA: Harvard University Press, 1991), p. 212.
9. 29 Code of Federal Regulations (C.F.R.) Section 1607.16 Definitions (Uniform Guidelines on Employee Selection Procedures, first issued in 1978).
10. Ibid.
11. Ibid., Section 1607.11 (Disparate Treatment).
12. Ibid., Section 1608.3 (Circumstances under which voluntary affirmative action is appropriate).
13. U.S. General Accounting Office, "Uniform Guidelines on Employee Selection Procedures Should Be Reviewed and Revised," July 30, 1982, p. 9.
14. Ibid., p. 10.
15. Johnson v. Transportation Agency, Santa Clara County, 480 U.S. 616 (1987).
16. *Congressional Record*, January 21, 1993, p. S 143.
17. Bob Cohn and Tom Morganthau, "The Q-Word Charade," *Newsweek*, June 3, 1991, p. 16.
18. Stuart Taylor, "Clinton and the Quota Game," *Legal Times*, December 28, 1992, p. 23.
19. "National Press Club Luncheon with Evan Kemp, Chairman, Equal Employment Opportunity Commission," Federal News Service, November 24, 1992.
20. EEOC v. Flasher Company, No. 91-6279 (U.S. Ct. Appl. 10th Circ.) December 29, 1992.
21. Allen v. Denver Public School Board, 928 F.2d 978 (1991).
22. McCarthy v. Kemper Life Insurance, 924 F.2d 683 (1991).
23. Ross v. Buckeye Cellulose Corp. (51 FEP Cases 1157). *Fair Employment Practices Cumulative Digest and Index* (Washington, D.C.: Bureau of National Affairs, 1990), p. 310.
24. York v. Mobil Oil Corp., 1991 U.S. Dist. LEXIS 20081, January 18, 1991.
25. Donohue v. Piedmont Aviation, 723 F.2d 921 (October 12, 1983).
26. Ray v. Frank, 1990 U.S. Dist. LEXIS 9878, July 25, 1990.
27. Young v. City of Houston, 906 F.2d 177, July 20, 1990.
28. Fox Butterfield, "Dispute Threatens U.S. Plan on Violence," *New York Times*, October 23, 1992.
29. Editorial, "Fear of Blacks, Fear of Crime," *New York Times*, December 28, 1986.
30. "Court Finds No Discrimination in Hiring Bar of Convicted Felons," *BNA Washington Insider*, November 27, 1989.
31. "Decision of U.S. District Court for Southern Florida in EEOC v. Carolina Freight Carriers Corp.," *Daily Labor Report*, November 27, 1989, p. D-1.
32. Interview with Kathleen Courtney of the EEOC, November 8, 1993.
33. "EEOC Sues Continental Air Transport," United Press International, June 2, 1992.
34. W. John Moore, "On the Case," *National Journal*, March 2, 1991, p. 501.
35. Epstein, *Forbidden Grounds*, p. 70.

36. *Congressional Record,* October 11, 1991, p. S 12755.
37. Ibid.
38. *Congressional Record,* June 26, 1991, p. S 8682.
39. Ibid. Emphasis added.
40. Interview with Mike Welbel, September 10, 1993.
41. Ibid.
42. Peter Brimelow and Leslie Spencer, "When Quotas Replace Merit, Everybody Suffers," *Forbes,* February 15, 1993, p. 80.
43. EEOC v. Consolidated Service Systems, 989 F.2d 233 (1993).
44. "EEOC Settles Discrimination Suit with Chocolate Maker for $2 Million," *BNA Washington Insider,* November 27, 1991.
45. Gregory L. Hammond, "Supervisors Are Finding That Failure to Train Can Turn into Legal Action Months or Years Later," *The EEO Review,* May 1993, p. 3.
46. Belz, *Equality Transformed,* p. 80.
47. Ibid., p. 82.
48. Robert G. Holland, "Preferential Policies Will Be Hot Issue in 1991 and 1992," *Richmond Times-Dispatch,* January 2, 1991.
49. Belz, *Equality Transformed,* p. 132.
50. Ibid., p. 121.
51. Ibid., p. 127.
52. Linda Gottfredson, "Clinton's New Form of Race-Norming," *Wall Street Journal,* June 3, 1993.
53. Brimelow and Spencer, "When Quotas Replace Merit, Everybody Suffers," p. 80.
54. Letter to the Editor from Jan H. Blits and Linda S. Gottfredson, "Civil Rights Bill Alters Fairness of '64 Law; Test Profits Blacks," *New York Times,* June 11, 1991.
55. Linda Gottfredson, "When Job Testing 'Fairness' Is Nothing But a Quota," *Wall Street Journal,* December 6, 1990.
56. Peter A. Brown, "Normin' Stormin'," *New Republic,* April 29, 1991, p. 12.
57. EEOC v. Atlas Paper Box Company, 680 F. Supp. 1184 (1987).
58. Jim Newton, "White Male Applicants Struggle for LAPD Jobs," *Los Angeles Times,* August 25, 1993.
59. Brimelow and Spencer, "When Quotas Replace Merit, Everybody Suffers," p. 80.
60. Heather MacDonald, "The Diversity Industry," *New Republic,* July 5, 1993, p. 22.
61. Ibid.
62. Ibid.
63. National Research Council, *Youth Employment and Training Programs* (Washington, D.C.: National Academy Press, 1985), p. 177.
64. U.S. General Accounting Office, "JTPA—Racial and Gender Disparities in Services," September 1991, p. 4.
65. Howard S. Bloom et al., "The National JTPA Study: Title II-A Impacts on Earnings and Employment at 18 Months," Abt Associates (under contract to the U.S. Department of Labor), 1993, p. 4.
66. James Bovard, "Clinton's Summer Jobs Sham," *Wall Street Journal,* March 7, 1993.
67. Interview with Robert Woodson, November 4, 1989.
68. Press Release, "EEOC Files Lawsuit Against Sands Hotel, Casino and Country Club Alleging Unlawful Employment Practices on the Basis of Sex," Equal Employment Opportunity Commission (Philadelphia District office), July 21, 1992. Emphasis added.
69. "Court Clears Way for Trial in EEOC Suit Challenging Hiring in All-Female Health Clubs," *Daily Labor Report,* April 23, 1993, p. d7.
70. John J. Donohue and Peter Siegelman, "The Changing Nature of Employment Discrimination Litigation," *Stanford Law Review,* vol. 43, 1991, p. 1027.
71. Transcript, "Afternoon Session of the Senate Judiciary Committee Hearing on Supreme Court Justice-Nominee Ruth Bader Ginsberg," Federal News Service, July 20, 1993.
72. Interview with press spokesman for the American Bankers Association, September 5, 1993.
73. U.S. General Accounting Office, "Further Improvements Needed in EEOC Enforcement Activities," April 9, 1981, p. 13.
74. U.S. General Accounting Office, "Equal Employment Opportunity: EEOC and State Agencies Did Not Fully Investigate Discrimination Charges," October 1988, p. 2.

75. Ibid., p. 31.
76. Interview with former EEOC official who wished to remain anonymous, June 7, 1993.
77. Michelle E. Klass, "Deals and Suits: United States v. Milton, et al.," *Legal Times*, August 19, 1991, p. 21.
78. Ibid.
79. Jerry Seper, "Ex-Counsel Indicted in EEOC Theft," *Washington Times*, January 9, 1991.
80. "OFCCP Report Shows Overall Decline in Agency's Enforcement Activities," *Daily Labor Report*, October 13, 1992.
81. Interview with former high-ranking OFCCP official who wished to remain anonymous, June 10, 1993.
82. Belz, *Equality Transformed*, 92.
83. *Federal Register*, October 22, 1992, p. 48240.
84. "Marshall Told to Hire Minorities," United Press International, July 29, 1988.
85. Dennis Hevesi, "Federal Inquiry into Bias Charges Against CUNY," *New York Times*, May 6, 1992.
86. C. Boyden Gray and Evan J. Kemp, "Flunking Testing: Is Too Much Fairness Unfair to School Kids?" *Washington Post*, September 19, 1993.
87. Carol Kleiman, "Harris Bank Settles $14 Million Bias Case," *Chicago Tribune*, January 11, 1989.
88. "Equal Opportunity," *Federal Contracts Report*, September 14, 1987, p. 339.
89. Michael Kinsley, "Quotas: The President Blinks," *Washington Post*, November 27, 1991.
90. John Leo, "Racial Arithmetic, California Style," *Washington Times*, June 19, 1991.
91. Gray and Kemp, "Flunking Testing: Is Too Much Fairness Unfair to School Kids?"
92. "Minorities, Women Do Not Get Top Jobs in Law Enforcement Agencies, GAO Says," *Government Employee Relations Report*, October 5, 1992, p. 1336.
93. Ibid.
94. Shelby Steele, "A Negative Vote on Affirmative Action," *New York Times*, May 13, 1990.
95. Isabel Wilkerson, "Discordant Notes in Detroit: Music and Affirmative Action," *New York Times*, March 5, 1989.
96. Ibid.
97. Editorial, "False Note; Withholding of Detroit Symphony State Funding Due to Affirmative Action," *New Republic*, March 27, 1989, p. 9.
98. "Bassist Robinson Appointed to Detroit Symphony Orchestra," PR Newswire, February 21, 1989.
99. Tom Hundley, "Bias Charge Causes Symphonic Discord," *Chicago Tribune*, February 12, 1989.
100. Americans with Disabilities Act, 101 P.L. 336, July 26, 1990.
101. Ibid.
102. Carolyn Weaver, "Disabilities Act Cripples Through Ambiguity," *Wall Street Journal*, January 31, 1991.
103. Julie C. Janofsky, "Whoever Wrote ADA Regs Never Ran a Business," *Wall Street Journal*, March 15, 1993.
104. 29 C.F.R. Section 1630 (Regulations to Implement the Equal Employment Provisions of the Americans with Disabilities Act).
105. "National Press Club Luncheon with Evan Kemp."
106. "Press Conference with Equal Employment Opportunity Commission on Americans with Disabilities Act Employment Regulations," Federal News Service, July 25, 1991.
107. 29 C.F.R. Section 1630.9(b) (Not Making Reasonable Accommodation).
108. Janofsky, "Whoever Wrote ADA Regs Never Ran a Business."
109. Press Release, "Disability Rules Too Vague, Small-Business Group Charges," National Federation of Business, February 28, 1991.
110. "Remarks Commemorating the First Anniversary of the Signing of the Americans with Disabilities Act of 1990," *Public Papers of the Presidents*, vol. 27, July 26, 1991, p. 1042.
111. David Frum and Jody Brennan, "Oh My Aching . . . You Name It," *Forbes*, April 26, 1993, p. 52.
112. Ingrid Becker, "Coalition Claims Protection from Fragrances under ADA," Gannett News Service, January 27, 1992.
113. United Press International, "CF Sufferer Fights to Make Nightclub Smoke-free," May 1, 1993.
114. Teresa Moore, "Asthmatics to Use Disability Law to Battle Smoking," *San Francisco Chronicle*, May 26, 1993.

115. "EEOC Weighs In: Obesity Is Protected Disability Under ADA, Rehabilitation Act," *Daily Labor Report,* August 6, 1993, p. d3.
116. Editorial, "ADA Signs In," *Wall Street Journal,* January 4, 1993.
117. Bradford McKee, "The Disabilities Labyrinth," *Nation's Business,* April 1993, p. 18.
118. Randall Lane, "There Goes the Judge," *Forbes,* May 10, 1993, p. 19.
119. Steven A. Holmes, "Advocates of Disabled Workers Say New Rules Don't Do Enough," *New York Times,* July 26, 1991. Emphasis added.
120. Mary Johnson, "When It Comes to Helping the Disabled, the Administration Is All PR Hype," *Los Angeles Times,* August 25, 1991.
121. "Press Conference with Equal Employment Opportunity Commission on Americans with Disabilities Act Employment Regulations."
122. Michael York, "Excluding Blind People from Juries Unlawful," *Washington Post,* March 17, 1993.
123. 29 C.F.R. Section 1630.2(r) (Direct Threat). Emphasis added.
124. Richard Corenthal, "Balancing Interests Under the ADA," *New York Law Journal,* July 2, 1993, p. 1.
125. 29 C.F.R. Section 1630 (Regulations to Implement the Equal Employment Provisions of the Americans with Disabilities Act).
126. Joan Oleck, "AIDS in the Kitchen," *Restaurant Business,* July 20, 1992, p. 51.
127. 29 C.F.R. Section 1630.16(3) (Infections and Communicable Diseases; Food Handling Jobs). Emphasis added.
128. "Press Conference with Equal Employment Opportunity Commission on Americans with Disabilities Act Employment Regulations."
129. Ibid. Emphasis added.
130. Therese Hudson, "HIV-Positive Health Care Workers Pose Legal, Safety Challenges for Hospital," *Hospitals,* September 20, 1992, p. 24.
131. Ruth Piller, "AIDS-related Litigation Jamming Court Dockets," *Houston Chronicle,* February 14, 1993.
132. Michael York, "D.C. Must Hire HIV-Infected Firefighter; Judge Says Public Will Not Be at Risk," *Washington Post,* July 2, 1992.
133. "HIV-Positive EMT Student Sues School," United Press International, June 3, 1993.
134. "The ADA, HIV and Physicians," *ADA Compliance Guide,* June 1993, p. 5.
135. Richard Corenthal, "Balancing Interests Under the ADA," *New York Law Journal,* July 2, 1993, p. 1.
136. "Seattle Journal—A Tattoo Tale," *Seattle Times,* September 24, 1993.
137. Peggy Andersen, "Newsbriefs," Associated Press, September 24, 1993.
138. "The ADA, HIV and Physicians," p. 5.
139. Patrick Boyle, "Ex-Patient Demands AIDS Test from GWU," *Washington Times,* June 27, 1991.
140. American Dental Assn. v. Martin, Nos. 91-3865, 92-1482, January 28, 1993. Reported in the *Daily Labor Report,* February 3, 1993, p. F-1.
141. Corenthal, "Balancing Interests Under the ADA," p. 1.
142. 29 C.F.R. Section 1630.2(p) (Undue hardship).
143. Walter Y. Oi, "Disability and a Workfare-Welfare Dilemma," in *Disability and Work,* ed. Carolyn A. Weaver (Washington, D.C.: American Enterprise Institute, 1991), p. 45.
144. Belz, *Equality Transformed,* p. 218.
145. Ibid., p. 263.
146. Local 28, Sheet Metal Workers v. EEOC, 106 S. Ct. 3019, 3052 (1986).
147. Donatella Lorch, "Threats Used to Push Jobs for Minorities," *New York Times,* July 12, 1992.
148. Richard D. Lyons, "U.S. Indicts 31 for Extortion Plots in Minority Hiring in Construction," *New York Times,* June 30, 1993.
149. Epstein, *Forbidden Grounds,* p. 134.
150. Brimelow and Spencer, "When Quotas Replace Merit, Everybody Suffers," p. 80.
151. Editorial, "Fear of Blacks, Fear of Crime."
152. "Remarks of Attorney General Janet Reno before the American Bar Association," Federal News Service, April 30, 1993.
153. John Phillip Reid, *The Concept of Liberty in the Age of the American Revolution* (Chicago: University of Chicago, 1988), p. 114.

154. Milton Friedman and Rose Friedman, *Free to Choose* (New York: Harcourt Brace Jovanovich, 1980), p. 139.
155. Alex Kozinski, "The Color-Blind Constitution," *New Republic*, February 1, 1993, p. 72.

Chapter 7

1. H. L. Mencken, *In Defense of Women* (New York: Time Inc., 1963), p. 115. First published by Knopf in 1918.
2. Dan Baum, "Study Refutes Link Between Drug Use, Crime," *Chicago Tribune*, May 4, 1993.
3. Glenn Garvin, Charles Wheeler, Earl Byrd, and John Holmes, "Heroin: The Unwinnable War," *Washington Times*, September 27, 1984.
4. Hilary Appelman, "America's Love-Hate Affair with Drugs Has Deep Roots," Associated Press, May 28, 1993.
5. Henry Allen, "Up in Smoke: Marijuana in America," *Washington Post*, November 7, 1987.
6. Alfred Lindesmith, *The Addict and the Law* (Bloomington, IN: Indiana University Press, 1971), p. 5.
7. Roy Childs, "Crime in the Cities," *Libertarian Review*, August 1981.
8. Ibid.
9. Robert Schess, "The Drug Addict," *American Mercury*, June 1925, p. 197.
10. Garvin et al., "Heroin: The Unwinnable War."
11. Meg Cox, "Abuse of Narcotics in U.S. Is by No Means a Recent Phenomenon," *Wall Street Journal*, November 28, 1984.
12. Lester Grinspoon, *Marijuana Reconsidered* (Cambridge, MA: Harvard University Press, 1971), p. 16.
13. Sam Staley, *Drug Policy and the Decline of American Cities* (New Brunswick, NJ: Transaction Books, 1992), p. 187.
14. Grinspoon, *Marijuana Reconsidered*, p. 19.
15. David F. Musto, "Opium, Cocaine, and Marijuana in American History," *Scientific American*, July 1991, p. 40.
16. Arnold S. Trebach, *The Great Drug War* (New York: Macmillan, 1987), p. 134.
17. For antidrug spending in 1980, see T. R. Reid, "A New Assault Planned Against Formidable Foe," *Washington Post*, August 10, 1986. For 1993 spending levels, see Peter Reuter, "Truce in Needle Park," *Washington Post*, February 28, 1993.
18. Robert Scheer, "The Mother of All Street Crimes," *Playboy*, July 1991, p. 37.
19. Editorial, "Crackmire," *New Republic*, September 11, 1989, p. 7.
20. National Organization for the Reform of Marijuana Laws v. Francis M. Mullen, 608 F. Supp. 945, 950 (1985). The judge stated that he was "troubled by such domestic use of spy planes."
21. "U.S. Army Unit to Test Rockets for Use Against Drug Smugglers," *Vancouver Sun*, September 11, 1991.
22. Eric Schmitt, "Colorado Bunker Built for Cold War Shifts Focus to Drug Battle," *New York Times*, July 18, 1993.
23. Ed Vaughn, "National Guard Involvement in the Drug War," *Justicia* (the newsletter of the Judicial Process Commission), December 1992.
24. Ibid.
25. Ed Vaughn, "National Guard Involvement in the Drug War," *NORML Reports*, 1993.
26. Robert Lindsey, "Ghost Town That Was Restored to Life is Now in Uproar Over Raid for Drugs," *New York Times*, January 21, 1986.
27. Ibid.
28. "Bad Bust," *Insight*, December 8, 1991, p. 20.
29. Saundra Torry, "Civil Liberties Caught in Antidrug Cross Fire," *Washington Post*, March 20, 1989.
30. Rick DelVecchio, "Pot War Has Humboldt up in Arms," *San Francisco Chronicle*, August 1, 1990.
31. Katherine Bishop, "Military Takes Part in Drug Sweep and Reaps Criticism and a Lawsuit," *New York Times*, August 10, 1990.
32. John Asbury, "The Grass Blues States," *High Times*, April 1991, p. 22.
33. Joe Davidson, "Appalachian Kentucky Relies on Marijuana to Buttress Economy," *Wall Street Journal*, December 24, 1992.
34. Kevin Johnson, "Across the USA, Drug Enforcers Uproot a Bumper Marijuana Crop," *USA Today*, October 8, 1992.

35. Paul English, "Agents Say Drug Reports Exaggerated," *Saturday Oklahoman,* December 7, 1991.
36. Rochelle Carter, "State Battles 'Growing' Problem," *The Tennessean* (Nashville), December 3, 1992.
37. "Indoor Marijuana Farming Takes Root, Thrives Across America," Agence France Presse, April 28, 1993.
38. FTC v. American Tobacco Co., 264 U.S. 305-306 (1924).
39. Jones v. SEC, 298 US 1, 27 (1936).
40. Peter Gorman, "Green Merchant: The First 18 Months," *High Times,* May 1991.
41. Ibid.
42. Katherine Bishop, "Business Data Is Sought in Marijuana Crackdown," *New York Times,* May 24, 1991.
43. "DEA Seeks Garden Centers' Customer Records," Associated Press, October 22, 1991.
44. Gorman, "Green Merchant: The First 18 Months."
45. Ibid.
46. Michael A. Lev, "Garden-supply Store Probe Angers Owner," *Chicago Tribune,* March 24, 1993.
47. Mary Thornton, "Cocaine on Street Contains Potent Carcinogen, DEA Says," *Washington Post,* March 2, 1986.
48. Ibid.
49. William Kronholm, "Study Attacked for Saying Paraquat a Safe Tool Against Marijuana," Associated Press, May 22, 1986.
50. Michael Isikoff, "DEA Finds Herbicides in Marijuana Samples," *Washington Post,* July 26, 1989.
51. Daniel Lazarre, "How the Drug War Created Crack," *Village Voice,* January 23, 1990.
52. Larry Margasak, "DEA Wants to Extend Herbicides to Private, State Lands in Marijuana War," Associated Press, January 16, 1986.
53. Joseph B. Treaster, "To Avoid AIDS, Users of Heroin Shift from Injecting to Inhaling It," *New York Times,* November 17, 1991.
54. Editorial, "Needles and AIDS," *Washington Post,* April 15, 1993.
55. Eric Lipton, "City Police Interfere with Needle Program," *Hartford Courant,* April 14, 1993.
56. Lazarre, "How the Drug War Created Crack."
57. National Institute on Drug Abuse, *Annual Medical Examiner Data 1991—Data from the Drug Abuse Warning Network* (Washington, D.C.: U.S. Department of Health and Human Services, 1992), p. 16.
58. Kenrad E. Nelson et al., "Human Immunodeficiency Virus Infection in Diabetic Intravenous Drug Users," *JAMA (Journal of the American Medical Association),* October 23/30, 1991, p. 2259.
59. Mireya Navarro, "Yale Study Reports Clean Needle Project Reduces AIDS Cases," *New York Times,* August 1, 1991.
60. Ronald Sullivan, "Needle-Exchanger Had Right to Break Law, Judge Rules," *New York Times,* June 26, 1991
61. John Mashek, "White House Acknowledges Recession's Grip," *Boston Globe,* December 18, 1991.
62. Joseph Treaster, "With Supply and Purity Up, Heroin Use Expands," *New York Times,* August 1, 1993.
63. Paul Avery, "Heroin Use Making a Comeback in the City," *San Francisco Examiner,* September 28, 1992.
64. Nancy Lewis, "Heroin Overdose Deaths Rise as Drug's Purity Triples Here," *Washington Post,* June 10, 1990.
65. Michael Isikoff, "DEA Launching Steroid Crackdown," *Washington Post,* February 22, 1991.
66. Michael Isikoff, "FDA Calls Bodybuilding Drug 'Dangerous,'" *Washington Post,* March 13, 1991.
67. Peter G. Chronis, "Steroid Use Spreading, Top U.S. Drug Cop Says," *Denver Post,* June 26, 1992.
68. "FBI Conducts Crackdown on Illegal Anabolic Steroid Distribution," U.S. Newswire, August 10, 1992.
69. Shellee Bratton, "Steroid-Smuggling Now Booming Along Border," *San Antonio Express-News,* August 2, 1992.
70. Isikoff, "FDA Calls Bodybuilding Drug 'Dangerous.'"
71. "Anti-Loitering Ordinance Faces Friday Legal Challenge," United Press International, September 5, 1990.

72. Howard Schneider and Richard Tapscott, "Reports from Annapolis," *Washington Post,* March 18, 1991.
73. Mildred Charley, "Mfume Again Tries to Stop Beeper Sales to Minors," *Washington Times,* March 4, 1991.
74. Joe Earle, "Columbus Targets Drug-use Apparel," *Atlanta Journal,* August 3, 1993.
75. DeNeen L. Brown, "Teen Punished For Carrying Allergy Pills; Va. School Prescribes Drug Abuse Program," *Washington Post,* December 16, 1991.
76. Melanie Howard, "Proposed Rule Lets School Staff Dispense Pills," *Washington Times,* April 17, 1992.
77. March 1, 1992.
78. *School Board News,* March 31, 1992.
79. Robert Conquest, *The Great Terror: Stalin's Purge of the Thirties* (New York: Collier, 1973), p. 379.
80. Mike Kaszuba, "Critics Question Antidrug Program," *Star Tribune* (Minneapolis), June 7, 1992.
81. "Parents Turned in by Teen Are Jailed in Marijuana Case," *Washington Post,* January 6, 1993.
82. John C. Enssling, "Boy, 10, Spots Marijuana in House, Turns in His Parents," *Rocky Mountain News,* September 24, 1991.
83. Associated Press, "Boy Turns in Parents for Suspected Drug Use," December 4, 1991.
84. Mark Curriden, "Casualty of the War on Drugs?" *Dallas Morning News,* November 10, 1992.
85. Ibid.
86. Joan Abrams, "War on Drugs D.A.R.E.," *Lewiston Morning Tribune* (Idaho), July 5, 1992.
87. Curriden, "Casualty of the War on Drugs?"
88. "Drug-Sniffing Dog Attacks Fifth-Grader," Associated Press, December 19, 1990.
89. Rebecca Perl, "Use of Drug to Calm Kids Drops in U.S.," *Atlanta Constitution,* August 26, 1992.
90. Patrick Welsh, "The Bored of Education: An Apology From a Teacher," *Washington Post,* July 21, 1992.
91. Associated Press, "Court Criticizes School's Ordering Drugs for Boy," *New York Times,* August 8, 1991.
92. Ibid.
93. Rebecca Perl, "Overdosing on Ritalin?" *Atlanta Journal and Constitution,* November 8, 1992.
94. Linda Jacobson, "Ritalin: Mother Resists Pressure, 'Testimonials' From Teachers," *Atlanta Journal and Constitution,* November 8, 1992.
95. Alison Bass, "More Mass. Pupils Get Ritalin, and Doubts Rise," *Boston Globe,* July 26, 1993.
96. Ronald Melzack, "The Tragedy of Needless Pain; Morphine for Pain Relief Is Not Addictive and Should Be Prescribed More Often," *Scientific American,* February, 1990, p. 27.
97. Daniel Q. Haney, "Doctors Treating Cancer Begin to Take Pain Seriously," Associated Press, February 9, 1992.
98. Ibid.
99. Daniel Goleman, "Patient Care; Physicians Said to Persist in Undertreating Pain and Ignoring the Evidence," *New York Times,* December 31, 1987.
100. Ibid.
101. Elisabeth Rosenthal, "Patients in Pain Find Relief, Not Addiction, in Narcotics," *New York Times,* March 28, 1993.
102. Diana Hunt, "Living with Pain; Doctors' Insensitivity, Legal Fear Cause Needless Suffering," *Houston Chronicle,* December 15, 1991.
103. Garry Sturgess, "Mandatory Minimum Sentences Under Attack," *New Jersey Law Journal,* June 13, 1991, p. 11.
104. "Judicial Review Sought for 3 in Drug Case," *Tulsa World,* March 6, 1992.
105. Jeff Holyfield, "Michigan Supreme Court: Drug Lifer Law is Unconstitutionally Harsh," Associated Press, June 17, 1992.
106. Eric Postpischil, "Attacks on the Bill of Rights," *Whole Earth Review,* March 22, 1991, p. 28.
107. Eric Sterling, "The Bill of Rights," *Vital Speeches,* November 1, 1991.
108. Interview with Julie Stewart, October 1, 1993.
109. David Margolick, "Chorus of Judicial Critics Assail Sentencing Guides," *New York Times,* April 13, 1992.
110. Ibid.

111. Dennis Cauchon, "Attack on Deadheads Is No Hallucination," *USA Today,* December 17, 1992.
112. Jim Newton, "Long LSD Prison Terms—It's All in the Packaging," *Los Angeles Times,* July 27, 1992.
113. Dennis Cauchon, "The Scales of Justice Weigh LSD Convictions," *USA Today,* April 6, 1993.
114. Cauchon, "Attack on Deadheads Is No Hallucination."
115. National Institute on Drug Abuse, *Annual Medical Examiner Data 1991,* p. 36.
116. "Attorney General Janet Reno and Office of National Drug Control Policy Director-Designate Lee Brown Address to the 1993 National Summit on U.S. Drug Policy," Reuter Transcript Report, May 7, 1993.
117. Matt Lait, "O.C. Task Force is at Center of Drug Legalization Debate," *Los Angeles Times,* October 11, 1992.
118. Michael Isikoff, "U.S. Considers Shift in Drug War," *Washington Post,* September 16, 1993.
119. Jim Newton, "Smugglers Make Kennels with Cocaine," *Los Angeles Times,* October 28, 1992.
120. George Gedda, "Nigerians Take Lead Role in U.S. Heroin Market," *Dallas Morning News,* December 5, 1992.
121. U.S. General Accounting Office, "War on Drugs: Heroin Price, Purity, and Quantities Seized Over the Past 10 Years," May 1992.
122. Scott Ladd, "Heroin's Comeback," *Newsday,* October 25, 1992.
123. Daniel Benjamin, "Federal Policy Pushes Heroin," *San Francisco Examiner,* December 4, 1992.
124. Staley, *Drug Policy and the Decline of American Cities,* p. 92.
125. Shari Roan, "Cheap Thrill Can Become a Deadly High," *Los Angeles Times,* April 27, 1993.
126. U.S. Department of Justice, "Barr Praises OCDETF in War on Drugs," U.S. Newswire, September 3, 1992.
127. William Dunn, "Drug-Tested Officials," *USA Today,* February 7, 1990.
128. Michael Isikoff, "Number of Imprisoned Drug Offenders Up Sharply," *Washington Post,* April 25, 1991.
129. Lazarre, "How the Drug War Created Crack."
130. Stuart Taylor, Jr., "Ten Years for Two Ounces," *American Lawyer,* March 1990, p. 65.
131. Stuart Taylor, Jr., "How a Racist Drug War Swells Crime," *Legal Times,* February 22, 1993.
132. Ibid.
133. Sandra G. Boodman, "Prison Medical Crisis; Overcrowding Created by the War on Drugs Poses a Public Health Emergency," *Washington Post,* July 7, 1992.
134. Andrew A. Skolnick, "Some Experts Suggest the Nation's 'War on Drugs' Is Helping Tuberculosis Stage a Deadly Comeback," *JAMA (Journal of the American Medical Association),* December 9, 1992, p. 3177.
135. Jerry Seper, "'92 Prison Population in U.S. Hits New High," *Washington Times,* May 10, 1993.
136. U.S. Department of Justice, "Almost 19,000 State, Local Law Officers Fight Drugs Full Time," U.S. Newswire, May 7, 1992.
137. Quoted in "Notes on a Failed War," *Business Week,* December 12, 1991, p. 22.
138. Michael Isikoff, "Florida's Crime Crackdown is Freeing Felons Early," *Washington Post,* December 28, 1990.
139. Ibid.
140. Jack Anderson and Michael Binstein, "Drug Laws Let Violent Criminals Loose," *Washington Post,* April 22, 1993.
141. Susan Vesey, "When Should the Violent Go Free?" *Atlanta Journal and Constitution,* January 24, 1993.
142. James Ostrowski, "Thinking About Drug Legalization," Cato Institute Policy Analysis No. 121, May 25, 1989.
143. Stephanie Mencimer, "Righting Sentences," *Washington Monthly,* April 1993, p. 26.
144. Anderson and Binstein, "Drug Laws Let Violent Criminals Loose."
145. "Remarks by President Bush at the Dedication of the DEA New York Headquarters," Federal News Service, June 29, 1992.
146. Milton Friedman, "A War We're Losing," *Wall Street Journal,* March 7, 1991.
147. *Science News,* December 1, 1984.
148. "Basic Flaws Seen in U.S. Strategy," *Orange County Register,* December 20, 1992.
149. Seth Faison, "Thefts of Copper Cable Threaten to Cripple New York's Subways," *New York Times,* May 1, 1993.

150. William Bennett, "Should Drugs Be Legalized?" *Reader's Digest,* March 1990.
151. "Brutality Victim Files Suit," United Press International, August 9, 1990.
152. Interview with Eric Sterling, September 9, 1992. Sterling, former counsel to the House Judiciary Committee, commented that many members of Congress greatly fear being accused of being soft on drugs.
153. Garvin et al., "Heroin: The Unwinnable War."
154. Paul Scriven, "Drugs, Sex and Pufferfish," in *New Frontiers in Drug Policy,* ed. Arnold Trebach and Kevin Zeese (Washington, D.C.: Drug Policy Foundation, 1991), p. 169.
155. Garvin et al., "Heroin: The Unwinnable War." For further elaboration, see Thomas Szasz, *Ceremonial Chemistry: The Ritual Persecution of Drugs, Addicts, and Pushers* (London: Routledge & Kegan Paul, 1974).
156. Ostrowski, "Thinking About Drug Legalization."
157. Ibid.
158. Staley, *Drug Policy and the Decline of American Cities,* p. 110. Staley notes, "In England, heroin can be prescribed for terminally ill patients. Twenty 10 milligram tablets of heroin cost approximately one dollar" (p. 117).
159. Ibid., p. 167. Staley's source is Drug Enforcement Agency, "From the Source to the Street," *Intelligence Trends,* vol. 14, no. 3, 1987, pp. 2-5.
160. Daniel Patrick Moynihan, "Iatrogenic Government," *American Scholar,* Summer 1993, p. 362.
161. Substance Abuse and Mental Health Services Administration, "Preliminary Estimates from the 1992 National Household Survey on Drug Abuse," U.S. Department of Health and Human Services, June 1993.
162. Terence Moran, "Recalling a Disturbing Past," *Recorder,* June 13, 1991, p. 6.
163. Roy Innis, "Gun Control Sprouts from Racist Soil," *Wall Street Journal,* November 21, 1991.
164. Watson v. Stone, 4 So. 2d 700, 703 (Fla. 1941).
165. Robert J. Cottrol and Raymond T. Diamond, "The Second Amendment: Toward an Afro-Americanist Reconsideration," *Georgetown Law Journal,* vol. 80, December 1991, p. 309.
166. Sanford Levinson, "The Embarrassing Second Amendment," *Yale Law Journal,* vol. 99, 1989, p. 637.
167. *Congressional Record,* February 4, 1993, p. H 536.
168. Helen Dewar, "Chafee Pushes Handgun Confiscation," *Washington Post,* June 2, 1992.
169. John Kass, "It's Hats Off to Chaos in Ward Remap Fight," *Chicago Tribune,* November 15, 1991.
170. John Lucadamo, "North Shore Towns Take the Lead in Handgun Fight," *Chicago Tribune,* April 9, 1989.
171. Susan Kuczka, "Handgun Owner Switches to Shotgun," Associated Press, October 26, 1986.
172. Gary Amo, "A Political Mugging," *American Rifleman,* January 1989.
173. Ibid.
174. Page Boinest, "Supporters of Historic Gun Law Bask in Victory," United Press International, November 9, 1988.
175. "Gov. Schaefer to be Honored by National, Local Gun Control Groups," U.S. Newswire, July 9, 1991.
176. Richard Tapscott, "Schaefer Takes Aim to Make Point," *Washington Post,* March 16, 1993.
177. Ibid.
178. David Kopel, "Trust the People: The Case Against Gun Control," Cato Institute, Policy Analysis No. 109, July 11, 1988, p. 26.
179. Editorial, "Self-Defense Delayed," *Orange County Register,* May 11, 1992.
180. David B. Kopel, "Hold Your Fire," *Policy Review,* Winter 1993, p. 58.
181. U.S. Congress, House Committee on the Judiciary, *Brady Handgun Violence Prevention Act,* March 21, 1991 (Washington, D.C.: Government Printing Office, 1991), p. 293.
182. Eric Morgan and David Kopel, "The Assault Weapon Panic: 'Political Correctness' Takes Aim at the Constitution," Independence Institute (Denver), October 10, 1991, p. 9.
183. Ibid.
184. Stephen Halbrook, "Guns and Prohibition," *Wall Street Journal,* April 11, 1989.
185. Kopel, "Hold Your Fire," p. 58.
186. Peter Kerr, "Florio Defiantly Vetoes Softer Assault-Rifle Ban," *New York Times,* July 9, 1991.
187. Kevin Gonzalez, "Gun Collectors Take Aim at N.J. Weapon Ban," Gannett News Service, July 22, 1991.

188. Randy Diamond, "Gun Proponents Take Their Fight to the Courts," *Christian Science Monitor,* August 14, 1990.
189. Testimony submitted by Joseph Constance, Deputy Chief, Trenton New Jersey Police Department, U.S. Congress, Senate Judiciary Committee, "Assault Weapons: A View from the Front Lines," August 3, 1993.
190. Ibid.
191. Associated Press, "Toughest Ban on Assault Rifles in U.S. Takes Effect in N.J. Today," *Los Angeles Times,* May 31, 1991.
192. Carl Ingram, "Assault Weapons Ban Called Unenforceable," *Los Angeles Times,* June 25, 1991.
193. Ibid.
194. Michael McNulty, "The Holes in the State's Assault Weapons Law," *Orange County Register,* August 16, 1993.
195. David Morris, "Documents Show Trouble with California Gun Law," Associated Press, March 17, 1993.
196. Ronald Maiorana, "City Council Unity Backs Gun Curbs," *New York Times,* October 19, 1967.
197. Editorial, "Taking Aim at Rifles," *New York Times,* September 26, 1967.
198. James Dao, "Owners of Assault Guns Slow to Obey Law," *New York Times,* April 17, 1992.
199. John Shanahan, "Dinkins Wants Legal Owners of Assault Rifles to Get Rid of Them," Associated Press, January 3, 1991.
200. James Dao, "On Eve of Ban on Assault Weapons, Most Gun Owners Have Not Complied with Law," *New York Times,* April 17, 1992.
201. Interview with Stephen Halbrook, September 26, 1993.
202. Kopel, "Hold Your Fire."
203. James Jay Baker, "Should U.S. Ban Assault Weapons?" Gannett News Service, July 18, 1990.
204. National Rifle Association, "FBI Crime Report Debunks Gun Control Myth, Says NRA," U.S. Newswire, August 6, 1990.
205. *Congressional Record,* May 15, 1989, p. E 1676.
206. Carrige Dowling and Rosalva Hernandez, "Police Say Teachers May Have Made Guns," *USA Today,* February 21, 1992.
207. Dan Reed, "Potato Guns Are No Joke," *San Francisco Chronicle,* July 24, 1993.
208. Commonwealth v. Lindsay, 396 Mas. 840, 489 N.E. 2d 666, 669 (1986).
209. Stephen Halbrook, "Afraid to Trust People with Arms," in *The Free Market Reader,* ed. Llewellyn H. Rockwell, Jr. (Burlingame, CA: Ludwig Von Mises Institute, 1988), p. 153.
210. Kopel, "Trust the People: The Case Against Gun Control," p. 12.
211. John D. Lewis, Jr., "American Gestapo," *Reason,* April 1980, p. 24.
212. Kopel, "Trust the People: The Case Against Gun Control," p. 12.
213. Robert Reinhold, "As Rioting Mounted, Gates Remained at Political Event," *New York Times,* May 5, 1992.
214. Timothy Egan, "Los Angeles' Police Realize They Are No Longer Heroes," *New York Times,* May 11, 1992.
215. Ibid.
216. Robert Dvorchak, "Merchants Enforced Their Own L.A. Law—With Guns," Associated Press, May 6, 1992.
217. Don Kates, Jr., "Defensive Gun Ownership as a Response to Crime," in *The Gun Control Debate,* ed. Lee Nisbet (Buffalo, NY: Prometheus, 1991), p. 259.
218. Gary Kleck, "Guns in the Home," *Chicago Tribune,* June 8, 1992.
219. Morgan O. Reynolds and W. W. Caruth III, "Myths About Gun Control," National Center for Policy Analysis Report No. 176, December 1992, p. 10.
220. Ibid., p. 12.
221. Ibid., p. 11.
222. David Kocieniewski, "Firepower Fear; Cop's Concern: 9-mm. Deaths," *Newsday,* June 12, 1992.
223. Quoted in Edward Walsh, "Dukakis Looks at Gun, Water Issues in West," *Washington Post,* August 7, 1988. The quote was from a 1986 interview; Dukakis later denied he made the statement, though the interviewer and two others present contradicted him.
224. "Some Dizzy 'Thinking' About Crime," *Chicago Tribune,* February 17, 1985.

225. "Law Enforcement Officials Blast Prison Report," United Press International, February 13, 1985.
226. Julie Pearl, "The Highest Paying Customers: America's Cities and the Costs of Prostitution Control," *Hastings Law Journal*, vol. 38, April 1987, p. 769.
227. U.S. Congress, House Committee on the Judiciary, *Brady Handgun Violence Prevention Act*, p. 293.
228. Bowers v. DeVito, 686 F.2d 616, 618 (1982).
229. Sam Roberts, "Quotations That Win or Lose Elections," *New York Times*, June 28, 1993.
230. Kopel, "Trust the People: The Case Against Gun Control," p. 16.
231. Reynolds and Caruth, "Myths About Gun Control," p. 25.
232. David B. Kopel, *The Samurai, the Mountie, and the Cowboy* (Buffalo, NY: Prometheus, 1992), p. 375.
233. Alan Bock, "Ambush at Ruby Ridge," *Reason*, October 1993, p. 24.
234. David Z. Nevin, "It Could Happen to Anyone," *Washington Post*, July 18, 1993.
235. Jerry Seper, "The Shootout on Ruby Ridge," *Washington Times*, September 22, 1993.
236. Bock, "Ambush at Ruby Ridge."
237. Editorial, "Another Federal Fiasco," *New York Times*, July 12, 1993.
238. Jerry Seper, "FBI Agents Waged War on Minds," *Washington Times*, September 22, 1993.
239. Associated Press, "FBI Admits Photos of Idaho Shootout Scene Were Staged," *Los Angeles Times*, May 28, 1993.
240. Timothy Egan, "Rebuking the U.S., Jury Acquits 2 in Marshal's Killing in Idaho Siege," *New York Times*, July 9, 1993.
241. Associated Press, "18 Months in Jail for Supremacist," *New York Times*, October 20, 1993.
242. Jim Fisher, "Weaver Case: More Comeuppance for the FBI," *Lewiston Morning Tribune* (Idaho), November 1, 1993.
243. Letter to Treasury Secretary Lloyd Bentsen from U.S. Senator Larry Craig, July 23, 1993.
244. Tracy Thompson, "Fourth Amendment Is Trampled in Drug Offensive, Critics Say," *Washington Post*, May 7, 1990.
245. Nadine Strossen, "*Michigan Department of State Police v. Sitz:* A Roadblock to Meaningful Judicial Enforcement of Constitutional Rights," *Hastings Law Journal*, vol. 42, January 1991.
246. Nat Hentoff, "The State of Freedom: Looking for Vital Signs in the Bill of Rights," *Playboy*, September 1991, p. 49.
247. Adams's opinion was cited in an 1886 Supreme Court decision: Boyd v. U.S., 116 U.S. 616, 624 (1886).
248. Tracey Maclin, "The Decline of the Right of Locomotion: The Fourth Amendment on the Streets," *Cornell Law Review*, vol. 75, September 1990, p. 1258.
249. Union Pacific Railway Company v. Botsford, 141 U.S. 250, 251 (1891).
250. Hawaii v. Anduha, 48 F.2d 171, 172 (1931).
251. Brinegar v. United States, 338 U.S. 160, 180-181 (1949).
252. Katz v. United States, 389 U.S. 347, 359 (1967).
253. Yale Kamisar, "The Fourth Amendment and Its Exclusionary Rule," *Champion*, September/October 1991, p. 20.
254. Nancy Hollander and Gary Nelson, "Highway Stops and Searches for Drugs Based on Drug Courier Profiles," *Drug Law Report*, vol. 2, May-June 1989.
255. Myron W. Orfield, Jr., "The Exclusionary Rule in Chicago," *Search and Seizure Law Report*, vol. 19, December 1992.
256. Lyle D. Larson, "An End-Run Around the Fourth Amendment: Why Roving Surveillance Is Unconstitutional," *American Criminal Law Review*, vol. 28, 1990, p. 156.
257. U.S. v. Mendenhall, 446 U.S. 544, 547 n. 1 (1980).
258. "Surprise, Surprise: Traffic Engineers Conduct a Scientific Study of Speed Limits," *Car and Driver*, May 1991, p. 87.
259. Steven Wisotsky, "Crackdown: The Emerging 'Drug Exception' to the Bill of Rights," *Hastings Law Journal*, vol. 38, July 1987, p. 889.
260. Edwin W. Lempinen, "The Guilty Look," *Student Lawyer*, December 1988, p. 5.
261. Morgan Cloud, "Search and Seizure by the Numbers: The Drug Courier Profile and Judicial Review of Investigative Formulas," *Boston University Law Review*, vol. 65, November 1985, p. 855.
262. Cauchon, "Attack on Deadheads Is No Hallucination."

263. Maclin, "The Decline of the Right of Locomotion: The Fourth Amendment on the Streets," p. 1258.
264. United States v. Sokolow, 109 S. Ct. 1581, 1588 (1989).
265. Cloud, "Search and Seizure by the Numbers," p. 871.
266. Lisa Belkin, "Airport Anti-Drug Nets Snare Many People Fitting Profiles," *New York Times*, March 20, 1990.
267. Michael R. Cogan, "The Drug Enforcement Agency's Use of Drug Courier Profiles: One Size Fits All," *Catholic University Law Review*, vol. 41, Summer 1992, p. 943.
268. U.S. v. Sokolow, 831 F.2d, 1413, 1420 (1987) ("The government assures us that '[t]he combination of facts in this case will rarely, if ever, describe an innocent traveler.' The obvious lack of substantiation for this claim betrays its lack of merit."). From Maclin, "The Decline of the Right of Locomotion," pp. 1258ff.
269. Belkin, "Airport Anti-Drug Nets Snare Many People Fitting Profiles."
270. Michael R. Cogan, "The Drug Enforcement Agency's Use of Drug Courier Profiles: One Size Fits All," p. 943. The cite for the case is United States v. Hooper, 935 F.2d 484, 500 (1990).
271. "Foglietta Asks for Justice Department Inquiry into Tinicum Highway Stops," PR Newswire, September 1, 1992.
272. Wisotsky, "Crackdown: The Emerging 'Drug Exception' to the Bill of Rights," p. 889.
273. Jeff Brazil and Steve Berry, "Tainted Cash or Easy Money?" *Orlando Sentinel*, various 1992 dates.
274. Quoted in Greg Gladden and Don Gladden, "Challenges to Dog Sniff Searches," *Drug Law Report*, vol. 2, November-December 1990, p. 205.
275. Ibid.
276. Ruth Marcus, "Court to Scrutinize Random Questioning of Bus, Train Passengers," *Washington Post*, February 26, 1991.
277. Mike Clary, "Bus Busts Are End of Line for Florida Drug Couriers," *Los Angeles Times*, July 7, 1992.
278. Brief for the United States as Amicus Curiae, Kenneth W. Starr Solicitor General, Florida v. Terrance Bostick, No. 89-1717, November 23, 1990.
279. Ibid.
280. Tracy Thompson, "Fourth Amendment Is Trampled in Drug Offensive, Critics Say," *Washington Post*, May 7, 1990.
281. Brief Amicus Curiae of the American Civil Liberties Union et al., Florida v. Terrance Bostick, No. 89-1717, December 19, 1990.
282. Florida v. Bostick, 111 S.Ct. 2382 (1991).
283. Ibid.
284. Gerald F. Uelmen, "2001: A Bus Trip—A Guided Tour of the Fourth Amendment Jurisprudence," *Champion*, July 1992.
285. Melissa Goodman, "A Long Journey: One Case Travels From a Bus in Florida to the U.S. Supreme Court," *Life*, Fall 1991, p. 76.
286. Helaine Olen, "Orange County Focus: Schools to Review Bus Drug Searches," *Los Angeles Times*, January 14, 1993.
287. Bill Billiter, "Orange County Focus: Chief Defends Use of Drug-Sniffing Dogs," *Los Angeles Times*, April 1, 1993.
288. Courtland Milloy, "For Ex-Defendant, P Street Case Still a Nightmare," *Washington Post*, February 7, 1993.
289. U.S. v. Twelve Thousand, Three Hundred Ninety Dollars, 956 F. 2d 801 (1992).
290. David Ferrell, "Dalton Raid Prosecutor Hammers on Destruction," *Los Angeles Times*, May 23, 1991.
291. Richard A. Serrano, "Reports Tell of Frenzy and Zeal in Police Raid," *Los Angeles Times*, November 26, 1990.
292. Ibid.
293. Ibid.
294. Kathryn Kranhold, "Grand Jury Probe May Be Sought Against Team of Bridgeport Police," *Hartford Courant*, April 24, 1992.
295. Kemal Alexander Mericli, "The Apprehension of Peril Exception to the Knock and Announce Rule—Part I," *Search and Seizure Law Report*, vol. 16, July 1989, p. 131.

296. Ker v. California, 374 U.S. 23, 53 (1963).
297. Editorial, "Drug Raids May Risk Lives Needlessly," *Atlanta Journal*, November 17, 1991.
298. Kathy Scruggs, "Office: Police Bullet Killed Boy," *Atlanta Constitution*, November 14, 1991.
299. Debra Warlick, "Boy's Death Not the Issue, D.A. Says; East Lake Assault, Drug Trial Opens," *Atlanta Journal and Constitution*, March 18, 1992.
300. Tracey Everbach, "Family Sues Garland Officer Over '91 Fatal Shooting," *Dallas Morning News*, January 28, 1993.
301. Jolayne Houtz, "Suit Filed Against City, County in SWAT Death—Officers Also Named in Everett Shooting," *Seattle Times*, October 16, 1992.
302. "Supreme Court Reverses Appellate Ruling," United Press International, October 6, 1988.
303. Diego Ribadeneira, "Flynn Forms Panel to Study Police Drug Unit's Methods," *Boston Globe*, April 14, 1989.
304. Sam Stanton, "Stockton Man, Cop Die; Family Blames Mistake," *Sacramento Bee*, January 26, 1993.
305. Sam Stanton, "Drug Raid Tactics Put Heat on Police," *Sacramento Bee*, January 29, 1993.
306. "Man Innocent of Police Murder During Drug Raid," United Press International, August 17, 1989.
307. Ed Godfrey, "Federal Agents Raid Wrong Guthrie Home; Resident Tells of Forced Entry, Claims Abuse," *Oklahoman*, December 21, 1991.
308. Philip J. LaVelle, "Excesses Blamed in 'Bad' Raids," *San Diego Union-Tribune*, December 13, 1992.
309. Written testimony of Donald Carlson, U.S. Congress, House Government Operations Committee, Hearing on Asset Forfeiture, June 22, 1993.
310. H. G. Reza and Mark Platte, "Agents in Raid Forged Papers, Sources Say," *Los Angeles Times*, September 18, 1992.
311. Written testimony of Donald Carlson, U.S. Congress, House Government Operations Committee, Hearing on Asset Forfeiture, June 22, 1993.
312. Ibid.
313. LaVelle, "Excesses Blamed in 'Bad' Raids."
314. State of Florida v. Earl R. Bamber, Court of Appeal of Florida, Second District, 592 So. 2d 1129, December 20, 1991.
315. Ibid.
316. State v. Thomas, Fla. Ct. App., 5th Dist, No. 91-1756, September 11, 1992. Reported in *Criminal Law Reporter*, October 7, 1992. p. 1022.
317. Charles Patrick Garcia, "The Knock and Announce Rule: A New Approach to the Destruction-of-Evidence Exception," *Columbia Law Review*, vol. 93, 1993, p. 685.
318. Ibid.
319. Ronald Koziol and Jerry Shay, "Students Criticize Strip Search of Girls," *Chicago Tribune*, January 31, 1992.
320. "ACLU Takes High School Strip-Search Case to Court," United Press International, July 21, 1989.
321. "ACLU, New Castle School District Reach Accord on Strip-search Policy," United Press International, August 25, 1993.
322. Brian Cornfield and Janet Lewis v. Consolidated High School District 230 et al., 1992 U.S. Dist. Lexis 2913, March 12, 1992.
323. Ibid.
324. Ibid.
325. New Jersey v. T.L.D., 469 U.S. 325 (1985).
326. Nat Hentoff, "The Day All the County's Kids Were in Custody," *Washington Post*, August 18, 1990.
327. George Kannas, "Liberals and Crime: The Reclaiming of an Issue," *New Republic*, December 19 1988, p. 19.
328. Joseph Tybor and Mark Eissman, "Illegal Evidence Destroys Few Cases: Justice in Chicag *Chicago Tribune*, January 5, 1986.
329. Ibid.
330. Myron W. Orfield, Jr., "The Exclusionary Rule in Chicago," *Search and Seizure Law Report*, no. 11, December 1992.
331. Brief for the United States, Rex E. Lee, Solicitor General, Ray E. Oliver v. United S 82-15, May 20, 1983.
332. Oliver v. U.S., 466 U.S. 170, 179 (1984).

333. Oliver v. U.S., 466 U.S. 170, 180 ftn. 11 (1984).
334. Oliver v. U.S., 466 U.S. 170, 192.
335. Stephen A. Saltzburg, "Another Victim of Illegal Narcotics: The Fourth Amendment (As Illustrated by the Open Fields Doctrine)," *University of Pittsburgh Law Review*, vol. 48, 1986.
336. Ibid.
337. Carroll v. United States, 267 U.S. 132 (1925).
338. Nadine Strossen, "*Michigan Department of State Police v. Sitz:* A Roadblock to Meaningful Judicial Enforcement of Constitutional Rights," *Hastings Law Journal*, vol. 42, January 1991, p. 287.
339. Ibid., p. 360.
340. Ibid., p. 300.
341. Michigan Dept. of State Police v. Sitz, 496 U.S. 444, 465 (1990).
342. Ibid.
343. Strossen, "*Michigan Department of State Police v. Sitz*," p. 389.
344. Ibid., p. 371.
345. "Vehicle Stops—Pretext Stops—Roadblock to Check License and Vehicle Registration," *Criminal Law Reporter*, September 30, 1992, p. 1563.
346. "Summary of Cases Recently Filed," *United States Law Week*, February 16, 1993, Section 3.
347. "Officers Call Texas Drug Checkpoint a Success, Plan More," *Dallas Morning News*, December 10, 1992.
348. Adam Gelb, "Georgia's DUI Scandal: The State Can't Get Drunks off the Road," *Atlanta Journal and Constitution*, November 13, 1991.
349. Ibid.
350. Emily K. Smith, "Sex, Lies, and Entrapment: *U.S. v. Jacobsen*," *Creighton Law Review*, vol. 24, 1991, p. 1082.
351. Paul Marcus, *The Entrapment Defense* (Charlottesville, VA: Michie Company, 1989), p. 99.
352. Paul Marcus, "The Development of Entrapment Law," *Wayne Law Review*, vol. 33, Fall 1986, p. 16.
353. Sherman v. United States, 356 U.S. 369 (1958).
354. Marcus, *Entrapment Defense*, p. 99.
355. Ibid., p. 100.
356. Ibid., p. 702.
357. Greg Rushford, "'Flying Kite' Gets Caught in a Storm," *Legal Times*, May 1, 1989.
358. Greg Rushford, "Botched Customs Sting May Spark Hill Inquiry," *Legal Times*, September 18, 1989.
359. Alice Crane, "Cop-Student Romance Leaves Police Embarrassed," United Press International, December 22, 1986.
360. Letter to the Editor from Joan W. Howarth and Catherine Leslie of the ACLU, "LAPD Drug Buys in the Schools," *Los Angeles Times*, February 27, 1987.
361. Jim Schachter, "Police Chief Calls ACLU Extremely Ignorant," *Los Angeles Times*, August 14, 1985.
362. Russ Bleemer, "Is Big Brother in the Schoolyard?" *New Jersey Law Journal*, January 25, 1993, p. 1.
363. "Police Pose as Drug Dealers to Catch Buyers," United Press International, December 7, 1989.
364. Marcia M. McBrien, "No Legal Authority For Police Drug 'Sales' To Suspects?" *Michigan Lawyers Weekly*, August 24, 1992, p. 1.
365. Allan Lengel, "FBI Sting Defendant Tells Court He Played Along," *Detroit News*, December 8, 1992.
366. Bob Sablatura, "Customs Air Team Credited for Seizure of 'Government Dope,'" *Houston Chronicle*, August 16, 1992.
367. Jim McGree, "War on Crime Expands U.S. Prosecutors' Powers," *Washington Post*, January 10, 1993.
368. Kim Murphy, "Court OKs Government Use of Sex to Seize Suspect," *Los Angeles Times*, April 9, 1987.
"Entrapment—Reprehensible Conduct," *Michigan Lawyers Weekly*, October 14, 1991, p. 17A.
J.S. v. Jennifer Skarie, No. 91-50007, 1992 U.S. App. LEXIS 16884, July 28, 1992.
[illegible]d.

[illegible]tine Bohlen, "A Tougher Line on Prostitution; Arlington Methods Criticized," Washington [illegible]ay 4, 1982.
[illegible]" United Press International, December 23, 1983.

375. "Prostitutes," Reuters, April 15, 1983.
376. "Police Allowed to Wire Rooms to Document Prostitution, Paper Says," Associated Press, July 11, 1987.
377. John Makeig, "Entrapment Ruled in Man's Arrest; Bar Patron Enticed by Policewoman," *Houston Chronicle*, December 29, 1992.
378. "Police Net 24 Men in Prostitution Sting," *Los Angeles Times*, February 6, 1992.
379. "Police Paid Rapist to Have Sex with Prostitutes in 'Sting,'" *The Gazette* (Montreal), April 9, 1992.
380. Brian Mooar and Avis Thomas-Lester, "D.C. Police Open Fire on Fleeing Suspect; Motorist was Stopped on Sex Solicitation," *Washington Post*, August 2, 1992.
381. United States v. Stenberg, 803 F2d 422 (1986).
382. Ward Marchant, "Excessive Force, Entrapment Charges After Arrest of 110," *Los Angeles Times*, April 16, 1989.
383. Julia Rubin, "Wildlife Officials Defend Tactics in Huge Poaching Raids," Associated Press, March 7, 1989.
384. Lawrence A. Stanley, "The Child-Pornography Myth," *Playboy*, September 1988.
385. Gregory J. Wallance, "The Entrapment Defense After 'Jacobson,'" *New York Law Journal*, June 24, 1992, p. 1.
386. Brief of the United States, Kenneth Starr, Solicitor General, Keith Jacobson, Petitioner, v. United States, No. 90-1124, August 5, 1991.
387. Charles R. Clauson and Lawrence A. Stanley, "The Postmaster Rings Twice," *Playboy*, February 1989, p. 45.
388. Brief of the United States, Kenneth Starr, Solicitor General, Keith Jacobson, Petitioner, v. United States, No. 90-1124, August 5, 1991.
389. Jacobson v. U.S., 112 S. Ct. 1535 (1992).
390. Gail Greaney, "Crossing the Constitutional Line. Due Process and the Law Enforcement Justification," *Notre Dame Law Review*, vol. 67, 1992, pp. 746, 764.
391. Daniel Wattenberg, "Gunning for Koresh," *American Spectator*, August 1993.
392. Larry McMurty, "Return to Waco," *New Republic*, July 12, 1993.
393. Pierre Thomas, "ATF's 60-Second Raid Now a 27-Day Standoff," *Washington Post*, March 27, 1993.
394. U.S. Department of Justice, "Recommendations of Experts for Improvements in Federal Law Enforcement After Waco," October 8, 1993, p. 3.
395. Sam Howe Verhovek, "Criticism of Raid Heartens Cult Members," *New York Times*, October 1, 1993.
396. Larry Pratt, "Fear the Government that Fears Your Gun," *The Gun Owners*, September 1993.
397. U.S. Department of the Treasury, *Report of the Department of the Treasury on the Bureau of Alcohol, Tobacco, and Firearms Investigation of Vernon Wayne Howell, also known as David Koresh* (Washington, D.C.: Government Printing Office, 1993), p. 175.
398. Jerry Seper, "FBI Used Chemical Banned for War," *Washington Times*, April 22, 1993.
399. Michael Isikoff, "FBI Clashed Over Waco, Report Says," *Washington Post*, October 9, 1993.
400. Wesley Pruden, "A Fatigued Excuse for a Holocaust," *Washington Times*, April 20, 1993.
401. Paul Craig Roberts, "Unsettling Questions in Probe of Waco," *Washington Times*, June 1, 1993.
402. Michael Isikoff, "Reno Strongly Defends Raid on Cult; Attorney General Shows Anger When Challenged by Rep. Conyers," *Washington Post*, April 29, 1993.
403. Ibid.
404. Stephen Labaton, "Report on Initial Raid on Cult Finds Officials Erred and Lied," *New York Times*, October 1, 1993.
405. Stephen Labaton, "Reno Contradicted in New Report on Decision to Attack Waco Cult," *New York Times*, October 9, 1993.
406. Stephen Labaton, "Inquiry Won't Look at Final Waco Raid," *New York Times*, May 16, 1993.
407. Ibid.
408. Ibid.
409. Isikoff, "FBI Clashed Over Waco, Report Says."
410. Jerry Seper, "Tragedy Blamed on Cult," *Washington Times*, October 9, 1993.
411. Ibid.
412. David Johnston and Stephen Labaton, "Doubts on Reno's Competence Rise in Justice Department," *New York Times*, October 26, 1993.

413. Edward S. G. Dennis, Jr., "Evaluation of the Handling of the Branch Davidian Stand-off in Waco, Texas, February 28 to April 19, 1993," U.S. Department of Justice, October 8, 1993, p. 35.
414. U.S. Department of Justice, "Report to the Deputy Attorney General on the Events at Waco, Texas, February 28 to April 19, 1993," October 8, 1993, p. 289. The phrase "remarkable restraint" is used twice on this page.
415. Ibid., p. 58.
416. Ibid., p. 237.
417. Ibid., p. 277.
418. Edward S. G. Dennis, Jr., "Evaluation of the Handling of the Branch Davidian Stand-off in Waco, Texas, February 28 to April 29, 1993," p. 59. Emphasis added.
419. Press Release, "An Apparent Deviation: The Federally-Caused Fire at Waco," California Organization for Public Safety, November 11, 1993.
420. Fred Bruning, "The FBI and Other Washington Wackos," *Maclean's,* May 10, 1993, p. 9.
421. Editorial, "The War in Waco, Texas," *Nation,* May 10, 1993, p. 615.
422. Bob Herbert, "Blacks Killing Blacks," *New York Times,* October 20, 1993.
423. "Agents Set $45 Million Marijuana Fire," *McCurtain Daily Gazette* (Idabel, Oklahoma), August 20, 1992.
424. David Kopel, "Extreme Drug Law Tramples Bill of Rights," The Independence Issue Paper No. 2/92, January 22, 1992.
425. Luiz Simmons, "Drug User Laws Overstep Justice," *Christian Science Monitor,* January 24, 1990.

Chapter 8

1. Cited in Tax Notes Column, *Wall Street Journal,* September 19, 1979, p. 1.
2. U.S. General Accounting Office, "Tax Treatment of Employees and Self-Employed Persons by the Internal Revenue Service: Problems and Solutions," November 21, 1977, p. 4.
3. Ibid., p. 44.
4. Ibid., p. 26.
5. U.S. Congress, Senate Finance Committee, *IRS Implementation of the Taxpayers' Bill of Rights,* April 6, 1990 (Washington, D.C.: Government Printing Office, 1990), p. 138.
6. U.S. Internal Revenue Service, Report of 1990 Commissioner's Advisory Group Report on Compliance—Subgroup on Compliance and Small Business, December 13, 1990; reprinted in *Tax Notes Today,* TNT 257-21, December 19, 1990.
7. U.S. Treasury Department, "Taxation of Technical Services Personnel: Section 1706 of the Tax Reform Act of 1986," March 15, 1991. Reprinted in *Tax Notes Today,* March 20, 1991.
8. U.S. Congress, House Committee on Government Operations, *Improving the Administration and Enforcement of Employment Taxes* (Washington, D.C.: Government Printing Office, 1992), p. 1.
9. The House Government Operations Committee reported in 1992: "ETEP's emphasis on worker classifications results in relatively innocent businesses that are not trying to hide anything from IRS being subjected to a mandatory back tax formula that can literally bankrupt them if they mistakenly classify a worker as an independent contractor instead of as an employee." U.S. Congress, House Committee on Government Operations, *Improving the Administration and Enforcement of Employment Taxes,* p. 1.
10. Ibid, p. 3.
11. Internal Revenue Service, *1992 Annual Report* (Washington, D.C.: Government Printing Office, 1993), p. 8.
12. U.S. Congress, House Committee on Ways and Means, *Misclassification of Employees and Independent Contractors for Federal Income Tax Purposes,* July 23, 1992 (Washington, D.C.: Government Printing Office, 1992), p. 600.
13. U.S. Congress, Senate Finance Committee, *Taxpayer Bill of Rights 2,* December 10, 1991, and February 21, 1992 (Washington, D.C.: Government Printing Office, 1992), p. 272.
14. Patricia Miller, "CompCare to Fight Over $19.4 Million Tax Bite," *St. Louis Business Journal,* May 13, 1991, p. 3A.
15. Queensgate Dental Family Practice v. U.S., 1991 U.S. Dist. LEXIS 13333, September 5, 1991.
16. Interview with Bob Asztalos of the American Physical Therapy Association, March 30, 1993.
17. U.S. Congress, House Committee on Ways and Means, *Misclassification of Employees and Independent Contractors for Federal Income Tax Purposes,* p. 457.

18. Interview with John Bailey, August 21, 1993.
19. Neal Koch, "IRS Agents Stalk the Hollywood Hills," *New York Times,* December 27, 1992.
20. "Film Studios Form Group to Battle Fines from IRS," *Minneapolis-St. Paul City Business,* July 17, 1992, p. 10.
21. U.S. Congress, House Committee on Ways and Means, *Misclassification of Employees and Independent Contractors for Federal Income Tax Purposes,* p. 673.
22. Interview with Craig Hoskins, March 31, 1993.
23. U.S. Congress, House Committee on Ways and Means, *Misclassification of Employees and Independent Contractors for Federal Income Tax Purposes,* p. 677.
24. Willie Schatz, "Putting Their Heads on the Tax Block," *Datamation,* March 15, 1987, p. 32.
25. U.S. Congress, House Committee on Small Business, *Impact of Independent Contractor Reclassification on Small Business,* July 30, 1991 (Washington, D.C.: Government Printing Office, 1992), p. 73.
26. Willie Schatz, "Murky IRS Ruling Won't Stop Opponents of Section 1706," *Datamation,* August 1, 1987, p. 24.
27. Joseph Scordato, "Tax Law's Squeeze on Consultants Will Severely Pinch Productivity Flow," *PC Week,* August 4, 1987, p. 51.
28. U.S. Treasury Department, "Taxation of Technical Services Personnel: Section 1706 of the Tax Reform Act of 1986," March 15, 1991. Reprinted in *Tax Notes Today,* March 20, 1991.
29. Major R. Owens, "One More Aid to Discrimination," *Computerworld,* September 28, 1992, p. 33.
30. Interview with Harvey Shulman, March 26, 1993.
31. U.S. Congress, Senate Finance Committee, *IRS Implementation of the Taxpayers' Bill of Rights,* p. 131.
32. Ibid., p. 133.
33. U.S. Congress, House Committee on Small Business, *Impact of Independent Contractor Reclassification on Small Business,* p. 144. Peterson's statement was made in an April 24, 1992, reply to questions from Committee members; Peterson's reply was printed along with the 1991 hearing.
34. Interview with Harvey Shulman, April 3, 1993.
35. "Government Pays for 'Boasting' About Its Position That Real Estate Appraisers Are Employees," *Tax Notes Today,* April 15, 1993.
36. U.S. General Accounting Office, "Tax Treatment of Employees and Self-Employed Persons by the Internal Revenue Service: Problems and Solutions," November 21, 1977, p. 37.
37. "Today's Tax Highlights," *Tax Notes Today,* May 19, 1992. Statement of David R. Fuller, senior attorney with the IRS Office of Chief Counsel. See also U.S. Congress, House Government Operations Committee, *Tax Revenue Losses and Tax Administration Problems Involving Independent Contractors,* May 16, 1989 (Washington, D.C.: Government Printing Office, 1989), p. 76 (testimony of Acting Commissioner of the Internal Revenue Service Michael Murphy).
38. U.S. Congress, House Committee on Ways and Means, *Misclassification of Employees and Independent Contractors for Federal Income Tax Purposes,* p. 442.
39. *Congressional Record,* November 19, 1989, p. E 3961.
40. U.S. Congress, House Committee on Government Operations, *Improving the Administration and Enforcement of Employment Taxes,* p. 1.
41. U.S. Treasury Department, "Taxation of Technical Services Personnel: Section 1706 of the Tax Reform Act of 1986," March 15, 1991. Reprinted in *Tax Notes Today,* March 20, 1991. Emphasis added.
42. Internal Revenue Service, *1992 Annual Report,* p. 7.
43. James L. Payne, *Costly Returns: The Burdens of the U.S. Tax System* (San Francisco, CA: ICS Press, 1993), p. 35.
44. Ibid.
45. "Statement by U.S. Senator Harry Reid Before the Subcommittee on Commerce, Consumer and Monetary Affairs on 'Project Layoff,'" *Tax Notes Today,* May 10, 1990.
46. U.S. Congress, Senate Finance Committee, *Taxpayer's Bill of Rights,* June 22, 1987 (Washington, D.C.: Government Printing Office, 1987), p. 24.
47. Internal Revenue Service, *1992 Annual Report,* p. 9.
48. David Burnham, *A Law Unto Itself: The IRS and the Abuse of Power* (New York: Random House, 1989), p. 20.

49. James Dale Davidson, *The Squeeze* (New York: Simon and Schuster, 1980), p. 36.
50. Denise M. Topolnicki, "Presumed Guilty by the IRS," *Money*, October 1990, p. 80.
51. Burnham, *A Law Unto Itself*, p. 21.
52. "Full Text: Ways and Means Subcommittee on Oversight Report on Legislation to Reform Civil Penalty System," *Tax Notes Today*, June 20, 1989.
53. Internal Revenue Service, *1992 Annual Report*, p. 42.
54. "Full Text: Ways and Means Subcommittee on Oversight Report on Legislation to Reform Civil Penalty System." See also Internal Revenue Service, *1992 Annual Report*, p. 42.
55. Greg Anrig, Jr., and Elizabeth M. MacDonald, "Tax Penalty Ambush," *Money*, June 1992, p. 156.
56. Stephen Kreider Yoder, "IRS—the Hand That Taxes the Cradle," *Wall Street Journal*, March 25, 1992.
57. Associated Press, "IRS Tries to Penalize Chemical Company $46,000 for Being a Dime Short," March 22, 1985.
58. Oswald Johnston, "Working to Correct Excessive Penalties, IRS Chief Says," *Los Angeles Times*, March 15, 1988.
59. "IRS, Owed a Dime, Bills for $54.94 in Penalties and Interest," Associated Press, March 8, 1990.
60. Ron Sonenshine, "IRS Tells Haircutter He Owes $4 Billion," *San Francisco Chronicle*, August 11, 1993.
61. Jonathan Clements, "Why Whitman Paid Up," *Forbes*, April 18, 1988.
62. Ibid.
63. *Congressional Record*, February 26, 1987, p. S 2562.
64. Todd v. United States, 613 F. Supp. 552, July 22, 1985.
65. Terrence M. Finan, "'Frivolous' tax return case considered," United Press International, August 6, 1986.
66. Donna L. Todd v. United States, 849 F.2d 365, June 10, 1988. This was the officially revised version of a decision originally handed down October 20, 1986, at 802 F.2d 1152.
67. Associated Press, "Court Bars Suits Against Agents," October 21, 1986.
68. Ibid.
69. Anrig and MacDonald, "Tax Penalty Ambush."
70. Jim Luther, "IRS Helpers Giving More Wrong Answers to Taxpayer Questions This Year," Associated Press, March 10, 1989.
71. U.S. General Accounting Office, "Tax Administration—Examples of Waste and Inefficiency in IRS," April 1993, p. 23.
72. Lawrence J. Haas, "Troubled Tax Man," *National Journal*, June 30, 1990, p. 1601.
73. Topolnicki, "Presumed Guilty by the IRS."
74. Payne, *Costly Returns: The Burdens of the U.S. Tax System*, p. 71.
75. U.S. Congress, Senate Finance Committee, *Taxpayer's Bill of Rights*, p. 24.
76. "Oversight Subcommittee Hears More Cases of Abuse of Taxpayers in Collections Process by Current IRS Revenue Officers," *Tax Notes Today*, June 23, 1987.
77. U.S. Congress, Senate Finance Committee, *IRS Implementation of the Taxpayers' Bill of Rights*, April 6, 1990 (Washington, D.C.: Government Printing Office, 1990), p. 24.
78. William F. Willoughby, "IRS Accused of Intimidating Families at Day Care Center," *Washington Times*, March 11, 1985.
79. "IRS Denies Misconduct in Tax Raid at Day Care Center," Associated Press, January 19, 1985.
80. Ibid.
81. Rita L. Zeidner, "Auditors Slam IRS for Keeping Poor Tabs on Seized Property," *Tax Notes Today*, September 25, 1992.
82. "Full Text: Unofficial Transcript of Oversight Subcommittee Hearing on IRS's Handling of Seized Property," *Tax Notes Today*, September 29, 1992.
83. Ibid.
84. Ibid.
85. Internal Revenue Service, *1992 Annual Report*, p. 43. In 1980, the IRS imposed 611,000 levies. Interview with IRS spokeswoman Johnelle Hunter, September 27, 1993.
86. U.S. General Accounting Office, "Tax Administration: Extent and Causes of Erroneous Levies," December 21, 1990.

87. Ibid.
88. Ibid.
89. Quoted in Creighton R. Meland, Jr., "Omnibus Taxpayers' Bill of Rights Act: Taxpayers' Remedy or Political Placebo?" *Michigan Law Review,* vol. 86, June 1988, p. 1806.
90. Internal Revenue Service, *1992 Annual Report,* p. 43. In 1980, the IRS imposed 445,000 liens. Interview with IRS spokeswoman Johnelle Hunter, September 27, 1993.
91. Topolnicki, "Presumed Guilty by the IRS."
92. U.S. Congress, Senate Finance Committee, *Taxpayer Bill of Rights 2,* p. 96.
93. Kay Council v. IRS, 713 F. Supp. 181, December 16, 1988.
94. Megan Rosenfeld, "The Audit, the Suicide, and the Widow's Battle," *Washington Post,* April 16, 1990.
95. Ibid.
96. Kay M. Council v. John E. Burke, District Director of Internal Revenue, et al., 1989 U.S. Dist. LEXIS 10746, August 29, 1989.
97. Interview with David Keating, March 17, 1993.
98. U.S. Solicitor General, Petition for a Writ of Certiorari, Commissioner of Internal Revenue v. Clayton J. Powell and Darlene W. Powell, (No. 92-452), September 1992, p. 16.
99. Ibid. Emphasis added.
100. Clayton Powell, Brief in Opposition to Certiorari, Commissioner of Internal Revenue v. Clayton J. Powell and Darlene W. Powell, (No. 92-452), September 1992, p. 14.
101. U.S. Solicitor General, Petition for a Writ of Certiorari, Commissioner of Internal Revenue v. Clayton J. Powell and Darlene W. Powell, (No. 92-452), September 1992, p. 12.
102. Ibid., p. 17. Emphasis added.
103. The 200,000 estimate is derived from adjusting the IRS's estimate of 240,000 people nationwide who receive final notices of intent to levy for tax assessments and subtracting such notices issued in the Fourth Federal Circuit. (There are twelve federal circuits.)
104. Payne, *Costly Returns: The Burdens of the U.S. Tax System,* pp. 58, 62.
105. Scar v. Commissioner, 81 T.C. 855, 860-61 (1983).
106. Scar v. Commissioner of Internal Revenue, 814 F. 2d 1363 (April 14, 1987).
107. Powers v. Commissioner, No. 38805-86, 100 T.C. No. 30, May 25, 1993.
108. Ibid.
109. David Pryor, "American Taxpayers Need a New 'Bill of Rights,'" *Houston Chronicle,* March 30, 1992.
110. Ramon Portillo and Dolores Portillo v. Commissioner of Internal Revenue, U.S. Tax Court Docket No. 6011-68, T.C. Memo 1990-68.
111. U.S. Congress, Senate Finance Committee, *Taxpayer Bill of Rights 2,* p. 7.
112. Ramon Portillo v. Commissioner of Internal Revenue, 932 F.2d 1128, 1133 (June 11, 1991). Emphasis added.
113. Thomas DiBacco, "Simpler in the Beginning," *Washington Times,* April 15, 1992.
114. Harriet Hanlon, "Only Two Preparers Come Within $500 of Target Tax in *Money* Magazine Survey," *Tax Notes Today,* March 11, 1993.
115. Elizabeth MacDonald, "How Congress Does Its Taxes," *Money,* April 1993, p. 96.
116. Luther, "IRS Helpers Giving More Wrong Answers to Taxpayer Questions This Year."
117. Charles M. Thomas, "Toyota Dealers Feel IRS Bite; Mazda Stores also Periled by Service Contract Ruling," *Automotive News,* March 16, 1992, p. 1.
118. Editorial, "Bush Must Halt IRS Grab on Service Contracts," *Automotive News,* March 16, 1992, p. 12.
119. Charles M. Thomas, "Service Contract Tax Deal Set," *Automotive News,* September 7, 1992, p. 1.
120. Interview with Peter Kitzmiller, June 16, 1993.
121. Charles M. Thomas, "IRS Ruling Benefits Dealer Cash Flow," *Automotive News,* November 30, 1992, p. 3.
122. Thomas K. Zaucha, Testimony of the National Grocers Association on the Special Occupational Tax, *Tax Notes Today,* April 10, 1991.
123. Jeff Barker, "Administration Willing to Compromise on Obscure Liquor Tax," Associated Press, October 27, 1989.
124. "House Postpones Proceedings on Alcohol-Related Taxes Bill," *Tax Notes Today,* August 14, 1992.
125. Tax Report, *Wall Street Journal,* February 21, 1990, p. 1.

126. Andrew Tobias, "My Troubles with the Taxman," *New York Times,* January 18, 1987.
127. L. Gordon Crovitz, et. al.,"Symposium: Perspectives on Rico: Debate and Discussion," *Notre Dame Law Review,* vol. 65, 1990, p. 1073.
128. Roger Parloff, "Princeton Prosecutor Asks Wrong Question; Query Allows Defense to Cite Opinions of Barred Tax Experts," *Manhattan Lawyer,* August 1, 1989, p. 1.
129. L. Gordon Crovitz, "RICO and the Man," *Reason,* March 1990.
130. L. Gordon Crovitz, "The RICO Monster Turns Against Its Master," *Wall Street Journal,* January 15, 1992.
131. George M. Taber, "The Bizarre End to the Bizarre Princeton/Newport Trial," *Business for Central New Jersey,* November 27, 1989, p. 3.
132. U.S. General Accounting Office, "Examination of IRS's Fiscal Year 1992 Financial Statements," June 1993, p. 1.
133. Ibid., p. 7.
134. U.S. Congress, House Committee on Government Operations, *Misconduct by Senior Managers in the Internal Revenue Service* (Washington, D.C.: Government Printing Office, 1990), p. 34.
135. Ibid., p. 26.
136. Ibid., p. 7.
137. Ibid., p. 40.
138. Ibid., p. 22.
139. "Hearing of the Senate Governmental Affairs Committee; Subject: Waste and Abuse at IRS and U.S. Customs Service," Federal News Service, August 4, 1993.
140. Stephen Barr, "Accused of Failing to Protect Data, IRS Says It Will Buttress Safeguards," *Washington Post,* August 5, 1993.
141. Stephen Barr, "IRS Computer Revamp Faulted by Study Panel," *Washington Post,* August 20, 1993.
142. Richard Behar, "Delinquent Taxmen," *Time,* May 29, 1989, p. 66.
143. "Full Text: Government Operations Committee on IRS Misconduct—IRS' Program to Combat Senior-Level Misconduct: Getting Stronger But Still a Long Way to Go," *Tax Notes Today,* November 30, 1992.
144. U.S. Congress, House Committee on Government Operations, *Misconduct by Senior Managers in the Internal Revenue Service,* p. 6.
145. Ibid.
146. Craig Winneker, "Heard on the Hill," *Roll Call,* March 28, 1991.
147. *Congressional Record,* October 21, 1988, p. S 17193.
148. Burnham, *A Law Unto Itself,* p. 303.
149. Burnham, *A Law Unto Itself,* p. 21.
150. "Full Text: GAO Official's Testimony at House Panel Hearings on IRS Officials' Misconduct," *Tax Notes Today,* July 24, 1992.
151. W. John Moore, "Bar Aghast at Guises Allowed Under New IRS Regs for Agents," *Legal Times,* May 28, 1984, p. 1.
152. Ibid.
153. "Undercover Guidelines to be Changed, Says Egger," *Legal Times,* August 20, 1984, p. 7.
154. Larry Fruhling, "Pizza Magnate Cries Foul: His Accountant Informed to IRS," Gannett News Service, October 4, 1990.
155. Lee Berton, "Tax Nightmare: Accountant's Sideline as an IRS Informant Brings Grief to Client," *Wall Street Journal,* February 22, 1990.
156. Ibid.
157. "Taxpayer Sues CPA Over Disclosures to IRS," *Tax Notes Today,* July 25, 1989.
158. Fruhling, "Pizza Magnate Cries Foul."
159. Milo Geyelin and Ellen Joan Pollock, "U.S. Drops Accountant-Informant Case," *Wall Street Journal,* November 25, 1991.
160. "Senator Harry Reid—Opening Statement—May 9 Hearing on IRS Integrity Issues—House Government Operations Committee," *Tax Notes Today,* May 10, 1990.
161. James E. Roper, "Uncle Sam a Failure as Las Vegas Bookie," *Houston Chronicle,* May 17, 1992.
162. Ibid.
163. "Senator Richard Bryan—Opening Statement—May 9 Hearing on IRS Integrity Issues—House Government Operations Committee," *Tax Notes Today,* May 10, 1990.

164. "Full Text: GAO Official's Testimony at House Panel Hearings on IRS Officials' Misconduct," *Tax Notes Today*, July 24, 1992.
165. "Any person who . . . willfully makes and subscribes any return, statement, or other document, which contains or is verified by a written declaration that it is made under the penalties of perjury, and which he does not believe to be true and correct as to every material matter . . . is guilty of filing a false return." Quoted in John J. Tigue, Jr, and Bryan C. Skarlatos, "Federal Prosecutions," *New York Law Journal*, March 30, 1993, p. 3.
166. Jane Seaberry and Patricia Davis, "That IRS Revenue Officer May Be Using a Fake Name," *Washington Post*, June 1, 1992.
167. Steve Rubenstein, "IRS Does Some Evading of Its Own," *San Francisco Chronicle*, June 3, 1992.
168. Federal Service Impasses Panel, "Department of the Treasury—Internal Revenue Service and National Treasury Employees Union," F.S.I.P. No. 326, March 10, 1992.
169. "Full Text: Treasury-IRS 1992 Business Plan," *Tax Notes Today*, May 18, 1992. Memo was dated May 1, 1992, and officially from Fred Goldberg, Shirley Peterson, Hap Shashy, and Alan Wilensky. David Keating of the National Taxpayers Union has a more charitable interpretation of the memo language, reading it instead as part of a plan by the IRS to decrease the delays in issuing regulations.
170. Spies v. U.S., 317 U.S. 492, 498 (1943).
171. U.S. Congress, Senate Finance Committee, *IRS Implementation of the Taxpayers' Bill of Rights*, p. 22.
172. "Full Text: Ways and Means Subcommittee on Oversight Report on Legislation to Reform Civil Penalty System," *Tax Notes Today*, June 20, 1989.
173. "Violations of IRS Manual Are Not Relevant in Civil Damages Action, Says Justice Official," *Tax Notes Today*, September 15, 1992.
174. Ibid.
175. Charles Adams, *For Good and Evil—The Impact of Taxes on the Course of Civilization* (New York: Madison Books, 1993), p. 466
176. Burnham, *A Law Unto Itself*, p. 162.
177. Jeff Schnepper, *Inside IRS* (New York: Stein and Day, 1978), p. 147.
178. Ann Devroy, "Review of 7 Firings Raps Clinton Aides," *Washington Post*, July 2, 1993.
179. Lee Sheppard, "What the IRS Travelgate Report Does and Does Not Say," *Tax Notes Today*, June 30, 1993.
180. Michael Isikoff and Ann Devroy, "FBI Says White House Invoked IRS," *Washington Post*, June 11, 1993.
181. Burnham, *A Law Unto Itself*, p. 294.
182. Ibid.
183. Ibid., p. 296.
184. Ibid., pp. 300-302.
185. Charles Adams, "More Reasons to Dislike the I.R.S.," *New York Times*, April 10, 1993.
186. Goldberg v. Kelly, 397 U.S. 254 (1970).
187. Computer Matching and Privacy Protection Act Amendments of 1989, 101 P.L. 56, July 19, 1989.
188. Editorial, "Petty Retroactivity," *Wall Street Journal*, August 19, 1993.
189. Child Nutrition and WIC Reauthorization Act of 1989, 101 P.L. 147, November 10, 1989.
190. "Tax Foundation's 1993 Tax Freedom Day Release," *Tax Notes Today*, April 16, 1993.
191. Andrew Tobias, "New York's Tax Burdens May Drive People Out," *New York Times*, January 30, 1987.
192. U.S. Congress, House Committee on Ways and Means, *Misclassification of Employees and Independent Contractors for Federal Income Tax Purposes*.
193. Tax Report, *Wall Street Journal*, January 15, 1992.
194. "Corporate and State Taxes Show Biggest Gains in Decade," *Tax Notes Today*, August 28, 1992.
195. Hilary Stout, "Tax Law Is Growing Ever More Complex, Outcry Ever Louder," *Wall Street Journal*, April 12, 1990.
196. Payne, *Costly Returns: The Burdens of the U.S. Tax System*, p. 54.
197. William Chamberlin, "The Power to Destroy," in *Essays on Liberty*, vol. 4 (Irvington-on-Hudson, NY: Foundation for Economic Education, 1958).
198. Peter Baker, "As Seen on TV: Fairfax Tax Evaders Make Debut on Cable," *Washington Post*, April 14, 1993.

199. Ibid.
200. Peter Baker, "Putting Scofflaws on Cable TV Yields Tax Bonanza for Fairfax," *Washington Post,* August 23, 1993.
201. Ibid.
202. Michael D. Shear, "Learning to Channel Cable's Potential," *Washington Post,* April 8, 1993.
203. Quoted in Charles Adams, *For Good and Evil,* p. 283. Adams's source is Harold Syrett, ed., *The Papers of Alexander Hamilton,* vol. 3 (New York, 1962), p. 104.
204. Gale Ann Norton, "The Limitless Federal Taxing Power," *Harvard Journal of Law and Public Policy,* vol. 8, Summer 1985, p. 591.
205. Interstate Transit Lines v. Commissioner, 319 U.S. 590, 593 (1943).
206. John Phillip Reid, *The Concept of Liberty in the Age of the American Revolution* (Chicago: University of Chicago Press, 1988), p. 92.
207. Report of the National Performance Review and Vice President Al Gore, *Creating a Government That Works Better and Costs Less* (Washington, D.C.: Government Printing Office, 1993), p. 1.
208. Savings and Loan Association v. Topeka, 20 Wall. 655, (1875).

Chapter 9

1. Bob Cohn, "The Trials of Adam and Eve," *Newsweek,* January 7, 1991, p. 48.
2. Karl A. Groskaufmanis, "What Films We May Watch: Videotape Distribution and the First Amendment," *University of Pennsylvania Law Review,* vol. 136, April 1988, p. 1263.
3. Roth v. U.S., 354 U.S. 476 (1957).
4. Roth v. U.S., 354 U.S. 476, 487 (fn. 20) (1957).
5. Bantam Books, Inc. v. Sullivan 372 U.S. 58, 66 (1963).
6. Stanley v. Georgia, 394 U.S. 557, 565 (1969).
7. Miller v. California, 413 U.S. 15, 24 (1973).
8. Charles S. Clark, "Obscenity Unit Raids Smut with New Gusto," *Houston Chronicle,* December 28, 1991.
9. Barry Lynn, "Polluting the Censorship Debate: A Summary and Critique of the Final Report of the Attorney General's Commission on Pornography," American Civil Liberties Union, July 1986, p. 5.
10. U.S. Department of Justice, Attorney General's Commission on Pornography, Final Report (Washington, D.C.: Government Printing Office, 1986), p. 266. Emphasis added.
11. U.S. Department of Justice, Final Report, p. 229.
12. Pete Yost, "Meese Says Porn Report Won't Lead to Unconstitutional Censorship," Associated Press, July 9, 1989.
13. Michael Kinsley, "Yucks in the Yuckiness of the Porn Report," *Wall Street Journal,* July 17, 1986.
14. U.S. Department of Justice, Final Report, p. 277.
15. U.S. Department of Justice, *Beyond the Pornography Commission: The Federal Response* (Washington, D.C.: Government Printing Office, 1988), p. 45.
16. Stephen Rae, "X-Rated Raids: National Obscenity Enforcement Unit," *Playboy,* June 1992, p. 44.
17. Arthur S. Hyes, "U.S. Obscenity Law Is Rejected in Texas," *Wall Street Journal,* November 26, 1991.
18. Robert F. Howe, "U.S. Accused of 'Censorship by Intimidation' in Pornography Cases," *Washington Post,* March 26, 1990.
19. Jim McGree, "U.S. Crusade Against Pornography Tests the Limits of Fairness," *Washington Post,* January 11, 1993.
20. Tom Watson, "DOJ Campaign Against Porn Loses Key Tactic," *Legal Times,* July 30, 1990, p. 7.
21. McGree, "U.S. Crusade Against Pornography Tests the Limits of Fairness."
22. Doug Bandow, *The Politics of Plunder* (New Brunswick, NJ: Transaction Books), p. 376.
23. Hyes, "U.S. Obscenity Law Is Rejected in Texas."
24. Barry Tarlow, "RICO Report," *Champion,* March 1992, p. 24.
25. Robert F. Howe, "Videotape Costs New York Dealer $500,000," *Washington Post,* July 1, 1992.
26. John Johnson, "Major Sex Tape Distributor Is Sentenced to 4 Months Home Detention," *Los Angeles Times,* September 22, 1992.
27. Brief of Petitioner, Ferris J. Alexander v. U.S., Supreme Court, October 1992 term, No. 91-1526, September 4, 1992.

28. Steve Brandt, "Confiscated Stimulant Is a Blast in the Trash," *Minneapolis Star Tribune*, October 19, 1991.
29. Brief Amicus Curiae of the American Civil Liberties Union and Minnesota Civil Liberties Union, Ferris J. Alexander v. U.S., Supreme Court, October 1992 term, No. 91-1526, August 1992, p. 26.
30. Brief of Petitioner, Ferris J. Alexander v. U.S., Supreme Court, October 1992 term, No. 91-1526, September 4, 1992.
31. Supreme Court of the United States, Alexander v. United States, June 28, 1993, Slip Opinion.
32. Brief of Amici Curiae American Library Assoc. et al., Ferris J. Alexander v. U.S., No. 91-1526, September 2, 1992, p. 6.
33. Neil Lewis, "Obscenity Law Used in Alabama Breaks New York Company," *New York Times*, May 2, 1990.
34. Laura Malt, "Obscenity Indictment Hits GTE," *Electronic Media*, February 26, 1990, p. 4.
35. "Alabama Prosecutor Says New York's Cuomo Coddling Criminals," Associated Press, June 21, 1990.
36. Denise Barricklow, "Porn Channel Exec Decries 'Bully Effect' of Alabama Obscenity Law," United Press International, May 4, 1990.
37. "Prosecutor Still Vows to Fight X-rated Videos," United Press International, July 17, 1992.
38. American Civil Liberties Union, "Above the Law: The Justice Department's War Against the First Amendment," December 1991.
39. Daniel Seligman, "Great Moments in Police Protection," *Fortune*, March 11, 1991, p. 124.
40. Lawrence A. Stanley, "The Child Porn Myth," *Cardozo Arts and Entertainment Law Journal*, vol. 7, 1989, p. 322.
41. Kent Jenkins, "Va. Artist Wins Custody of Children; Pornography Investigation Revealed No Evidence of Abuse," *Washington Post*, August 25, 1988.
42. Skip Kaltenheuser, "'They Don't Understand My Art'; Accused of Kiddy Porn, Artist Had to Fight to Keep Her Children," *Legal Times*, September 26, 1988.
43. Chuck Phillips, "A War on Many Fronts; Censorship," *Los Angeles Times*, December 26, 1990.
44. American Civil Liberties Union, "Above the Law: The Justice Department's War Against the First Amendment," December 1991, p. 17.
45. Ibid, p. 15.
46. Ibid.
47. Rick Vanderknyff, "A Blurred Line Over Art vs. Pornography," *Los Angeles Times*, October 11, 1991.
48. Kenneth D. Schmitt v. State of Florida, Supreme Court of Florida (1991), 590 So. 2d 404.
49. Petition for a Writ of Certiorari, Stephen A. Knox v. U.S., No. 92-1183, U.S. Supreme Court, January 12, 1993, p. 45.
50. Brief of American Booksellers Foundation for Free Expression et al., Stephen A. Knox v. U.S., No. 92-1183, U.S. Supreme Court, August 4, 1993, p. 22.
51. Petition for a Writ of Certiorari, Stephen A. Knox v. U.S., No. 92-1183, U.S. Supreme Court, January 12, 1993, pp. 9, 27.
52. Frank Kuznik, "Operation Borderline; Sting Operations," *Playboy*, September 1988, p. 45.
53. Stanley, "The Child Porn Myth," p. 334.
54. Infinity Broadcasting Corp., 3 FCC Rcd 930 (1987).
55. Infinity Broadcasting Corp., 2 FCC Rcd. 2705 (1987).
56. "'Indecency' Policy Clear as Mud," *News Media and the Law*, Summer 1987, p. 3.
57. Kim I. Mills, "Stern Will Tone Down Sexual Innuendos, Lawyer Says," Associated Press, May 1, 1987.
58. The Rusk Corporation, Licensee, Radio Station KLOL (FM), 1993 FCC LEXIS 2277, No. FCC 93-229, May 6, 1993.
59. Deborah Mesce, "FCC Dismisses Five Indecency Complaints Against Broadcasters," Associated Press, April 7, 1988.
60. Paul Fahri, "Stern Gets Some Shock Treatment," *Washington Post*, August 13, 1993.
61. Editorial, "Air Heads," *Orange County Register*, December 21, 1992.
62. Infinity Broadcasting Corp., 8 FCC Rcd 2688 (1992).
63. Peter Branton, Report No. 44-9, FCC 1991 FCC Lexis 3141, Release No. FCC 91-27 (38103), January 25, 1991.

64. "FCC Refuses to Find News Broadcasts Indecent," *News Media and the Law,* Spring 1991, p. 29.
65. Peter Branton, Report No. 44-9, FCC 1991 FCC Lexis 3141, Release No. FCC 91-27 (38103), January 25, 1991.
66. Dumas v. City of Dallas, 648 F. Supp. 1061, 1065 (1986).
67. U.S. Department of Justice, *Beyond the Pornography Commission: The Federal Response,* p. 6.
68. Kathryn Kahler, "Federal Prosecutors Hot on Obscenity's Trial," *Newark Star-Ledger,* October 23, 1991.
69. Jeff Lyon, "Point Man: Being on the Front Lines in 'Art Wars' Is Not a Pretty Picture, but Tony Jones Wouldn't Have It Any Other Way," *Chicago Tribune,* January 27, 1991.
70. David K. Nelson, Jr. v. Alderman Allan Streeter et al., Case No. 88 C 5434., U.S. Dist. Ct. for No. Ill, Eastern Div., 1992 U.S. Dist. LEXIS 5443, March 31, 1992.
71. David K. Nelson, Jr. v. Alderman Allan Streeter, et. al., 1992 U.S. Dist. LEXIS 5443, 5448.
72. Ibid.
73. "Artist Whose Painting of Lingerie-Clad Mayor Was Removed Wins Court Ruling," Associated Press, August 11, 1992.
74. David K. Nelson, Jr. v. Alderman Allan Streeter et al., No. 88 C 5434, 1992 U.S. Dist. LEXIS 11936, August 10, 1992.
75. "Chief Fired over Removal of Paper with Critical Article," *News Media and the Law,* Summer 1992, p. 7.
76. Richard C. Paddock, "S.F. Police Chief Dismissed for Abuse of His Authority," *Los Angeles Times,* May 16, 1992.
77. Craig Bromberg, "In Defense of Hackers," *New York Times Magazine,* April 21, 1991, p. 45.
78. Matthew Childs, "Computer Cops versus the First Amendment," *Playboy,* May 1992, p. 46.
79. Steve Jackson Games, Inc., v. U.S. Secret Service, 816 F. Supp. 432, March 12, 1993.
80. Timothy Heider, "Dubyak Uses Threat to Derail Recall Drive," *Cleveland Plain Dealer,* June 30, 1993.
81. Ibid.
82. Ross Gelbspan, "Worcester Sues Group Questioning Airport Plan," *Boston Globe,* January 7, 1992.
83. Said Deep, "Public Officials Try to Silence Critics with a Slapp," Gannett News Service, June 8, 1992.
84. Thomas A. Waldman, "SLAPP Suits: Weaknesses in First Amendment Law and in the Courts' Responses to Frivolous Litigation," *UCLA Law Review,* April 1992, p. 979.
85. Bill Turque, "SLAPPing the Opposition," *Newsweek,* March 5, 1990, p. 22.
86. "SLAPP Lawsuits Proliferate in New York Courts," Cable News Network, July 8, 1992, Transcript #95-4.
87. Stephanie Simon, "Nader Suits Up to Strike Back Against 'Slapps,'" *Wall Street Journal,* July 9, 1991.
88. John Elvin, "Inside the Beltway," *Washington Times,* April 23, 1992.
89. "Suits Over Cartoons Chill Commentary," *News Media and the Law,* Summer 1986, pp. 14-15.
90. "Oakar Sues PD, Contends Post Office Reports Untrue," *Cleveland Plain Dealer,* May 23, 1992.
91. Charles H. Wilbanks, "Congressional Ethics Committee Reports the Latest," States News Service, October 20, 1989.
92. Associated Press, "Jury Finds Reprint Libelous, Awards State Judge $6 Million," *Washington Post,* December 8, 1990.
93. Loren Feldman, "War of Words," *American Lawyer,* October 1991, p. 62.
94. Binford v. Sentinel Communications Co., Florida Circuit Court, Eighteenth Judicial Circuit, Seminole County, 20 Med. L. Reprt 1934, October 22, 1992.
95. Donald Gillmor, *Power, Publicity, and the Abuse of Libel Law* (New York: Oxford University Press, 1992), p. 25.
96. Feldman, "War of Words," p. 62.
97. Ibid.
98. Floyd Abrams, "Why We Should Change the Libel Law," *New York Times Magazine,* September 29, 1985, p. 34.
99. Ibid.
100. Associated Press, "Libel Case Awards Found Increasing," *New York Times,* September 20, 1992.
101. Anthony Lewis, "Staving Off the Silencers," *New York Times Magazine,* December 1, 1991.

102. Anthony Lewis, *Make No Law: The Sullivan Case and the First Amendment* (New York: Random House, 1991), p. 254.
103. Gillmor, *Power, Publicity, and the Abuse of Libel Law,* p. 70.
104. Ibid., p. 34.
105. Martin Garbus, "Abolish Libel—The Only Answer," *Nation,* October 8, 1983.
106. Elizabeth Kolbert, "NBC Settles Truck Crash Lawsuit," *New York Times,* February 10, 1993.
107. Valentine v. Chrestensen, 316 U.S. 52, 54 (1942).
108. Alex Kozinski and Stuart Banner, "Who's Afraid of Commercial Speech?" *Virginia Law Review,* vol. 76, May 1990, p. 627.
109. Virginia State Board of Pharmacy v. Virginia Citizens Consumer Council, 425 U.S. 748, 770 (1976).
110. Central Hudson Gas & Electric Corp. v. Public Service Commission, 447 U.S. 557 (1980).
111. Posadas De Puerto Rico Associates v. Tourism Company of Puerto Rico et al., 478 U.S. 328. Emphasis added.
112. "Kessler Warns about Drug, Device Promotion," *FDA Consumer* (Washington, D.C.: Government Printing Office, September 1991), p. 3.
113. Ibid.
114. Elisabeth Rosenthal, "Rules on Approved Uses of Drugs Could Bar Help for Some Patients," *New York Times,* August 11, 1991.
115. Ibid.
116. Carole Sugarman, "A Diet to Fight the Risk of Cancer," *Washington Post,* July 2, 1992.
117. John E. Calfee, "The FDA vs. the First Amendment," *Wall Street Journal,* February 13, 1992.
118. Stephen Chapman, "FDA Censorship Is a Real Danger to Your Health," *Chicago Tribune,* April 15, 1993.
119. John Calfee, "FDA Underestimates Food Shoppers," *Wall Street Journal,* May 29, 1991.
120. Paul Rubin, "Regulatory Relief or Power Grab: Should Congress Expand FDA's Enforcement Authority?" Heritage Foundation Backgrounder No. 900, June 11, 1992.
121. Commentary, "An FDA Rule That's Poor Science and Poor Policy," *Business Week,* December 9, 1991, p. 36.
122. Charles Walsh and Alissa Pyrich, "Drug Companies Gag on Proposed FDA Order," *New Jersey Law Journal,* August 9, 1993, p. 6.
123. Floyd Abrams, "R. J. Reynolds vs. The Government: A Chilling Effect on Corporate Speech," *New York Times,* July 6, 1986.
124. "Reynolds' Ad on Smoking, Health Held Immune from FTC's Challenge by First Amendment," *Daily Report for Executives,* August 7, 1986.
125. Associated Press, "FTC Reviving RJR Ad Complaint; Ruling on '85 Smoking Study Campaign to be Reviewed," *Los Angeles Times,* April 12, 1988.
126. Carlos Brezina, "R. J. Reynolds Agrees Not to Misrepresent Tobacco Studies," United Press International, June 20, 1990.
127. Ibid.
128. Associated Press, "FTC Reviving RJR Ad Complaint; Ruling on '85 Smoking Study Campaign to be Reviewed."
129. Jonathan Adler, "Camel Hunting with the FTC," *Washington Times,* September 3, 1993.
130. *Federal Register,* January 23, 1989, p. 3308.
131. Ibid.
132. Ibid., p. 3310.
133. William F. Powers, "$850,000 Award in Ad Bias Case," *Washington Post,* May 15, 1992.
134. Luther M. Ragin, Jr., et al. and Open Housing Center, Inc., v. New York Times, 923 F.2d 995, January 23, 1991.
135. Harry Berkowitz, "Changing Times; Real Estate Ads Can't Be All-White," *Newsday,* August 14, 1993.
136. "Court Finds Housing Agency Overzealous," *Star Tribune* (Minneapolis), January 9, 1993.
137. Bob Pool, "Bad News: Chain's 20 Community Papers Disappear at Auction," *Los Angeles Times,* March 25, 1993.
138. "Newspaper Chain Seeking Shelter from Ad Lawsuit," *Los Angeles Business Journal,* October 4, 1992, p. 5.

139. Pool, "Bad News: Chain's 20 Community Papers Disappear at Auction."
140. Greg W. Prince, "Middle of the Road," *Beverage World,* September 1992, p. 41.
141. "Remarks by Secretary Louis Sullivan, Health and Human Services, and Dr. Antonia Novello, U.S. Surgeon General, Conference on Alcohol Related Injuries," Federal News Service, March 23, 1992.
142. "News Conference with U.S. Surgeon General Antonia Novello, Re: Youth and Alcohol," Federal News Service, November 4, 1991.
143. "U.S. Surgeon General Seeks Malt Liquor Name Change," Reuters, June 26, 1991.
144. Paul Farhi, "Surgeon General Hits New Malt Liquor's Name, Ads," *Washington Post,* June 26, 1991.
145. Alix Freedman, "Heileman Will Be Asked to Change Potent Brew's Name," *Wall Street Journal,* June 20, 1991.
146. "Black Death Beats the U.S. Government," Business Wire, October 30, 1992.
147. Complaint of Cabo Distributing Inc. and Black Death USA for Injunction and Damages. United States District Court, Northern District of California, Cabo v. Nicholas Brady, etc. July 6, 1992.
148. Associated Press, "Feds Tell Importer of Black Death That Marketing Illegal," April 6, 1992.
149. Jonathan Glater, "Federal Crackdown on Alcohol," *San Francisco Chronicle,* July 24, 1992.
150. "Black Death Hauls Feds into Court," Business Wire, July 7, 1992.
151. Complaint of Cabo Distributing Inc. and Black Death USA for Injunction and Damages.
152. "Black Death Beats the U.S. Government."
153. "Surgeon General Speaks Out Against Crazy Horse Malt Liquor," Associated Press, April 25, 1992.
154. *Congressional Record,* May 19, 1992, p. S 6886.
155. Adrien Seybert, "House Lawmakers Want New Name for Crazy Horse Malt Liquor," States News Service, June 25, 1992.
156. Chet Lunner, "Panel Wants to Stop Sale of Crazy Horse Malt Liquor," Gannett News Service, May 19, 1992.
157. PR Newswire, "Statement of the Marketers of the Original Crazy Horse Malt Liquor," June 20, 1992.
158. Interview with Antonia Novello, September 13, 1992. First quoted in James Bovard, "The Second Murder of Crazy Horse," *Wall Street Journal,* September 15, 1992.
159. Interview with Antonia Novello, September 13, 1992.
160. Kim I. Mills, "'Crazy Horse' Beer Label Ban Unconstitutional, Company Says," Associated Press, November 7, 1992.
161. Chet Lunner, "Court: Crazy Horse Ban Unconstitutional," Gannett News Service, April 13, 1993.
162. Ann Pelham, "Beer Battle Brewing; Labeling Rules Cause Rifts Within Industry, Government," *Legal Times,* August 21, 1989, p. 1.
163. Eben Shapiro, "Advertising: Ruling Allows Brewers to Print Alcohol Content on Labels," *New York Times,* October 30, 1992.
164. Christy Fisher, "Broadcast Regulators Turn Up the Heat; Congress, FCC Start by Looking at Kids TV," *Advertising Age,* March 15, 1993, p. 52.
165. Edmund L. Andrews, "'Flintstones' and Programs Like It Aren't Educational, F.C.C. Says," *New York Times,* March 4, 1993.
166. *Federal Register,* August 30, 1985, p. 35418.
167. Joe Flint, "Washington to INTV: We Will Be Watching," *Broadcasting,* February 1, 1993, p. 23.
168. National Broadcasting Co. v. United States, 319 U.S. 190, 226 (1943).
169. Groskaufmanis, "What Films We May Watch: Videotape Distribution and the First Amendment."
170. Ibid., fn. 109.
171. Jonathan W. Emord, *Freedom, Technology, and the First Amendment* (San Francisco: Pacific Research Institute, 1991), p. 186.
172. Editorial, "Congress' Attempt to Prevent Freedom on the Airwaves," *Chicago Tribune,* June 14, 1987.
173. Jack Shafer, "News Bites: Walter Annenberg's Billion-Dollar Reputation," *Washington City Paper,* June 25, 1993, p. 14.
174. Thomas W. Hazlett, "The Fairness Doctrine Was Never Quite Fair," *Los Angeles Times,* October 4, 1987.

175. Ibid.
176. *Federal Register,* August 30, 1985, p. 35418.
177. Ibid.
178. Ibid.
179. Ibid.
180. Charles Oliver, "Can FCC Muzzle Rush Limbaugh?" *Investor's Business Daily,* August 16, 1993.
181. Mary Lu Carnevale, "Congressman Seeks Regulators' Ruling Following Cable System's 'Editorials,'" *Wall Street Journal,* October 22, 1992.
182. Robert Green, "TV Networks Promise to Tone Down Violent Programs," Reuters, May 21, 1993.
183. Howard Rosenberg, "Execs Vow Change While Programming Violence," *Los Angeles Times,* May 24, 1993.
184. Robert L. Jackson, "TV Execs Vow Stronger Effort to Reduce Violence," *Los Angeles Times,* May 22, 1993.
185. Interview with Nancy Coffee, spokeswoman for Sen. Metzenbaum, Sept. 13, 1993.
186. Emord, *Freedom, Technology, and the First Amendment,* p. 191.
187. *Congressional Record,* October 23, 1990, p. S 16844.
188. Andrews, "'Flintstones' and Programs Like It Aren't Educational, F.C.C. Says."
189. Patrick J. Sheridan, "FCC Endorses Children's TV Act," *Broadcasting,* April 15, 1991, p. 90.
190. Harry A. Jessell and Kim McAvoy, "FCC Comments Call for Constitutional Challenge to Children's Act," *Broadcasting,* January 28, 1991, p. 48.
191. Brian Donlon, "Airtime for Educational Shows," *USA Today,* April 27, 1993.
192. Daniel Seligman, "More Kidvid Capers," *Fortune,* November 5, 1990, p. 188.
193. Harry A. Jessell, "Six TV's Hit for Violating Kids TV Rules," *Broadcasting,* January 18, 1993, p. 95.
194. Editorial, "The Educational TV Police," *Washington Times,* March 9, 1993.
195. SuperStation, Inc., Licensee, Television Station WTBS, 8 FCC Rcd 490, DA 93-47, January 22, 1993.
196. WGN of Colorado, Inc., Licensee, KWGN-TV, 8 FCC Rcd 489, DA 93-46, January 22, 1993.
197. Tak Communications, Inc., D.I.P., Licensee, KITV (TV), 8 FCC Rcd 488, DA 93-45, January 22, 1993.
198. Shari Roan, "Tuned In and At Risk; Too Much Time in Front of the Tube Is Not Only Bad for Kids' Minds, Experts Say, But Is Ruining Their Health," *Los Angeles Times,* March 10, 1993.
199. News America Publishing, Inc., v. F.C.C., 844 F.2d 800 (1988).
200. Editorial, "Kennedy's Boast," *Wall Street Journal,* January 6, 1988.
201. News America Publishing Inc. v. FCC, 844 F. 2d at 810 (1988).
202. Mark Robichaux, "Cable Firms Say They Welcome Competition But Behave Otherwise," *Wall Street Journal,* September 24, 1992.
203. Edmund L. Andrews, "F.C.C. Tilts Toward Lower Cable TV Rates," *New York Times,* March 15, 1993.
204. Ibid.
205. Sol Schildhause, "Municipalities Short-Circuit Cable TV's Signal," *Texas Lawyer,* May 4, 1992.
206. David J. Saylor, "Municipal Ripoff: The Unconstitutionality of Cable Television Franchise Fees and Access Support Payments," *Catholic University Law Review,* vol. 35, Spring 1986, p. 671.
207. Thomas W. Hazlett, "Wired: The Loaded Politics of Cable TV," *New Republic,* May 29, 1989.
208. David Savage, "L.A. Must Justify Cable TV Policy, Justices Decide," *Los Angeles Times,* June 3, 1986.
209. Thomas Hazlett, "For Cable TV, Rerun of a Horror Show," *New York Times,* August 8, 1990.
210. Editorial, "The Great Cable TV Battle," *Wall Street Journal,* October 2, 1992.
211. The Cable Television Consumer Protection and Competition Act of 1992, 102 P.L. 385, October 5, 1992.
212. Thomas Hazlett, "In Cable War, Consumers Get Snagged," *Wall Street Journal,* October 2, 1992.
213. Dennis Wharton, "June D-Day for Cablers," *Daily Variety,* April 12, 1993, p. 5.
214. Paul Fahri, "Battle Looms Over What Cable Will Carry," *Washington Post,* June 17, 1993.
215. Paul Fahri, "Dimming Cable's Eye on Congress," *Washington Post,* September 7, 1993.
216. Elizabeth Jensen and Mark Robichaux, "Cable-TV Systems, Broadcasters to Play High-Stakes Game That Public May Lose," *Wall Street Journal,* June 15, 1993.
217. Edmund L. Andrews, "F.C.C. Lets TV-Shopping Stations Demand Access to Slots on Cable," *New York Times,* July 3, 1993.

218. Paul Fahri, "FCC Set to Give a Boost to Home-Shopping Channels," *Washington Post,* June 22, 1993.
219. Edmund L. Andrews, "Ruling Frees Phone Concerns to Enter Cable TV Business," *New York Times,* August 25, 1993.
220. Jube Shiver, "Panel OKs Plan to Auction Unused Airwaves," *Los Angeles Times,* May 12, 1993.
221. Thomas L. Jipping, "What Washington Can Do to Protect Campus Free Speech," Heritage Foundation, June 12, 1991.
222. Nat Hentoff, "Scalia Outdoes the ACLU," *Washington Post,* June 30, 1992.
223. John Milton, "Areopagitica, or A Speech for the Liberty of Unlicensed Printing, to the Parliament of England" (November 1644), *The Portable Milton* (New York: Viking Press, 1949), p. 172.
224. Central Hudson Gas & Electric Corp., 447 U.S. at 574-575 (1980).

Chapter 10

1. John Locke, *Two Treatises of Government* (New York: New American Library, 1965), p. 320.
2. Quoted in Charles Adams, *For Good and Evil—The Impact of Taxes on the Course of Civilization* (New York: Madison Books, 1993), p. 533.
3. David Z. Nevin, "It Could Happen to Anyone; Law Enforcement Out of Control," *Washington Post,* July 18, 1993.
4. Paul Johnson, *The Recovery of Freedom* (Oxford: Basil Blackwell, 1980), p. 135.
5. West Virginia State Board of Education v. Barnette, 319 U.S. 624, 639 (1943).
6. John Stuart Mill, *Utilitarianism, Liberty, and Representative Government* (New York: Dutton and Co., 1951), pp. 222-223.
7. Thomas Babington Macaulay, *Critical and Miscellaneous Essays,* vol. 3 (Philadelphia: Carey and Hart, 1842), p. 310.
8. Henry David Thoreau, *Walden and Other Writings* (New York: Penguin, 1974).

Index

C

d

e

f

i

j

k

l

q

r

S

t

y

z